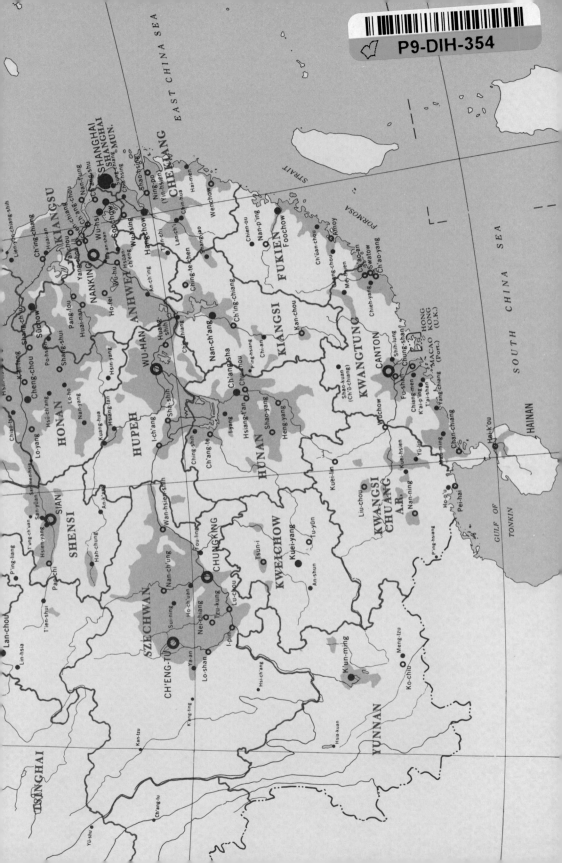

# THE CITY
# IN COMMUNIST CHINA

*Contributors*

Jerome Alan Cohen

John Philip Emerson

John Gardner

Paul F. Harper

Christopher Howe

Ying-mao Kau

John Wilson Lewis

Victor H. Li

Janet Weitzner Salaff

Ezra F. Vogel

Lynn T. White III

# THE CITY
# IN COMMUNIST CHINA

*Edited by* JOHN WILSON LEWIS

*Stanford University Press, Stanford, California* 1971

STUDIES IN CHINESE SOCIETY

Sponsored by the Subcommittee on Research on Chinese Society
of the Joint Committee on Contemporary China of the Social
Science Research Council and the American Council of
Learned Societies, 1970–71

*Previously published in this series*
Maurice Freedman, ed., *Family and Kinship in Chinese Society*

Stanford University Press, Stanford, California
© 1971 by the Board of Trustees of the Leland Stanford Junior University
Printed in the United States of America
ISBN 0-8047-0748-0   LC 78-130828

# Preface

This book represents a cooperative venture by social scientists whose interests have become focused on the Chinese city. During the 1960's a number of publications and theses on China's urban development signaled the maturing of these interests, and Professor G. William Skinner and others had the idea of taking stock of our knowledge on the subject. The resulting papers are being published in three volumes, of which this is the earliest to appear. The other two are tentatively titled *The City in Late Imperial China* (edited by Professor Skinner) and *The Chinese City Between Two Worlds* (edited by Professor Skinner and Mark Elvin). These three volumes in turn form part of the larger series Studies in Chinese Society, on which particulars are given opposite.

Eight of the papers in this book were originally presented at a research conference held in St. Croix, Virgin Islands, at the end of 1968. Sponsored by the Subcommittee on Chinese Government and Politics and the Subcommittee on Research on Chinese Society of the Joint Committee on Contemporary China of the Social Science Research Council and the American Council of Learned Societies, the St. Croix conference was attended by some twenty scholars from the United States and Great Britain. The following China specialists, some of whom gave papers on pre-Communist urbanization, also participated in discussions relevant to this volume: David D. Buck, Mark Elvin, Stephan Feuchtwang, Morton Fried, Edward Friedman, Bernard Gallin, Shirley S. Garrett, Winston Hsieh, Rhoads Murphey, John C. Pelzel, Irene B. Taeuber, and Richard W. Wilson. Norton E. Long and Charles Tilly helped us to place China's urban problems in a comparative and interdisciplinary framework; as will be plain to readers familiar with their writings, I have drawn heavily on their ideas in my Introduction. Sophie Sa Winckler and Edwin A. Winckler served as rapporteurs and produced a superbly edited conference record.

When the decision was made to publish the St. Croix papers in two volumes, it seemed desirable to round out this one on the Communist period with additional essays. We accordingly invited John Gardner and Lynn T. White to prepare essays on urban youth and recent Shanghai developments, respectively, and by good fortune also obtained Christopher Howe's paper, which had been written for another conference. Other invited papers, as well as some delivered at St. Croix, had to be excluded for various reasons, notably my concern with keeping the book as short and as integrated as possible.

The preparation of the manuscript for publication also benefited from a cooperative effort. I am deeply grateful to Marion Bieber and Gerry Bowman for carrying the heavy burden of editorial and secretarial assistance, and to Anne Murray of Stanford University Press for her work on the manuscript. I have had help on my Introduction from Muriel and Jess Bell, John Philip Emerson, Gardel Feurtado, B. Michael Frolic, Paul Harper, Victor Li, Seiichiro Takagi, D. Gordon White, and others. The index was ably prepared by Norma Farquhar, and the maps by Karen Ewing. Finally, I am indebted for financial support for my own research and editorial work to the London-Cornell Project for East and Southeast Asian Studies and to Stanford's Institute of Political Studies and Center for East Asian Studies.

It is a sad commentary on our times that none of the authors represented in this volume has actually set foot in a city in Communist China. Western scholars who have are few, and our efforts to bring one or two of them to St. Croix were unfortunately unavailing. Thanks to Professors Long and Tilly, our attempts to be comparative were somewhat more successful, though chiefly in the sense of showing us how little we knew. We were most successful of all at being interdisciplinary. At St. Croix historians, anthropologists, and other social scientists made important contributions to every paper. The book itself contains the work of two legal scholars (Jerome Alan Cohen and Victor H. Li), two sociologists (Ezra Vogel and Janet Salaff), an economist (Christopher Howe), and a demographer (John Philip Emerson). The rest, all political scientists, by no means worship at the same methodological altar.

I am not altogether happy with the book's title. Despite our efforts to concentrate on what has happened in Chinese cities as such since 1949, too often we have had to work with data that blur the distinctions between national and local, urban and rural, propaganda and reality, policy and result. I must also acknowledge the many gaps in our coverage—especially in respect to economic and social institutions—and concede that we have not always escaped the biases found in the published record. I have tried in my Introduction to make up in part for some of these shortcomings, but I fear with indifferent success.

The endpaper map requires a note of explanation. It is based on information of different dates, there being no single date on which our information was sufficiently good on all points of interest. We accordingly give provincial boundaries as of late 1968 and city size as of the end of 1957. Information on urban size is taken photographically from a U.S. Government map, and we have chosen not to make the spellings of place names on this map rigorously consistent with those elsewhere in the book. Thus the map must be used with caution for any purpose other than its primary one, which is to show the main areas of population concentration and the relative intensity of Chinese urbanization in the Communist era.

It is customary in books published in Mainland China—those on urban affairs included—to ask for the reader's help and criticism. We too would welcome the assistance of our readers as we begin what may prove to be a long journey.

J.W.L.

*December 1970*

# Contents

# Contributors

JEROME ALAN COHEN, Professor of Law at Harvard University, is the author of *The Criminal Process in the People's Republic of China, 1949–1963: An Introduction* (1968), and the editor of *Contemporary Chinese Law: Research Problems and Perspectives* and *The Dynamics of China's Foreign Relations* (both 1970). He is currently completing a study of China's theory and practice of international law.

JOHN PHILIP EMERSON received his M.A. in East Asian Studies from Harvard University in 1955, and studied Japanese economic history in Japan and Taiwan in 1956–58. Since 1958 he has been employed by the U.S. Bureau of the Census, Foreign Demographic Analysis Division, to make studies of the Mainland China labor force. He is the author of *Nonagricultural Employment in Mainland China: 1949–1958* (1965).

JOHN GARDNER did his graduate work at the School of Oriental and African Studies, University of London, from 1962 to 1966. Since 1966 he has been Lecturer in Government at the University of Manchester. He has carried out research in Hong Kong and Japan in 1963–64 and 1968, and is now writing a book on the consolidation of Communist control in China in 1949–54.

PAUL F. HARPER received his Ph.D. in 1969 from Cornell University. He did research in Taiwan and Hong Kong during 1964 and 1965 on trade unions in Communist China, and has written various articles on the roles of the unions. He has taught at Hofstra University since 1966, where he is Assistant Professor of Political Science and Chairman of the Asian Studies Program.

CHRISTOPHER HOWE has been on the staff of the School of Oriental and African Studies, University of London, since 1963. His main research interests have been the labor market and the character of economic development in urban China. His book *Employment and Economic Growth in Urban China, 1949–1957* will be published in 1971.

YING-MAO KAU is Assistant Professor of Political Science at Brown University. He received his undergraduate education at National Taiwan University and did his graduate work at Cornell University, conducting research in Hong Kong in 1965–66. Currently he is completing a book on Communist China's bureaucratic and political development.

JOHN WILSON LEWIS is Professor of Political Science at Stanford University. His publications include *Leadership in Communist China* (1963), *Major Doctrines of Communist China* (1964), and *The United States in Vietnam*, with George McT. Kahin (1967); and he has edited *Party Leadership and Revolutionary Power in China* (1970). His principal current research on China deals with urban political development in Tangshan.

VICTOR H. LI received his J.D. in 1964 from Columbia Law School, where he is now Assistant Professor of Law. He is also a J.S.D. candidate at Harvard Law School. In 1965 and 1968 he did field research in Hong Kong on his dissertation topic, political-legal work in Communist China. His paper in this volume is a part of his dissertation.

JANET WEITZNER SALAFF is obtaining her Ph.D. in sociology from the University of California, Berkeley. In 1967–69 she did fieldwork in Hong Kong for a dissertation on the impact of changes in social structure on family formation, age of marriage, and fertility in Mainland China. In 1970 she joined the Sociology faculty of the University of Toronto.

EZRA F. VOGEL, Professor of Social Relations at Harvard University, received his Ph.D. from Harvard in 1958 and since 1961 has been associated with the East Asian Research Center there. He is the author of *Japan's New Middle Class* (1963), *Canton Under Communism* (1969) and numerous articles on Communist China, and co-editor of *A Modern Introduction to the Family* (rev. 1968).

LYNN T. WHITE III is a graduate student in political science at the University of California, Berkeley. From 1967 to 1969, he held a Foreign Area Fellowship to work in the Far East, especially at Universities Service Centre, Hong Kong. He is now working on his dissertation at the Center for Southeast Asian Studies of Kyoto University, Japan.

THE CITY
IN COMMUNIST CHINA

# Introduction: Order and Modernization in the Chinese City

JOHN WILSON LEWIS

This volume deals principally with the Chinese Communists' policy toward the city since 1949; its four-part division reflects the successive phases of that policy. During the early years of Communist rule, the emphasis was on the establishment of law and order. In the mid-fifties, with order well established, the party turned its attention to plans for economic and social modernization, plans in which cities played a leading role. By the early 1960's, the growth of China's urban bureaucracy, together with the priority given industrial development, was threatening the values of the revolutionary leadership. Mao Tse-tung responded by purging those he held responsible and calling for new and more truly revolutionary forms of urban organization and industrialization. The result was a national crisis whose repercussions are still being felt. The essays that follow analyze these developments, and in doing so suggest that the changes taking place in the modern Chinese city continue to defy Mao's revolutionary doctrine.

The role of the city in that doctrine has often been misunderstood. Although the Communists' revolutionary strategy prior to 1949 had called for winning rural bases first, their ultimate target was always the cities.[1] The party under Mao initially announced its intention of shifting to an urban-centered strategy at the Seventh Plenum of its Sixth Central Committee in April 1945.[2] The plenum's landmark resolution on party history sought first to explain and justify the years in the wilderness, and then to anticipate the impact of the new political line:

Only now, in the final stage of the War of Resistance against Japan, when the army under our Party's leadership has grown strong and will grow still stronger, is it correct to place work in the Japanese-occupied cities on a par with work in the Liberated Areas, actively to prepare all the conditions for annihilating the Japanese aggressors in the key cities by co-ordinated attacks from within and without and then to shift the centre of gravity of our work to these cities. This will be a new change of historic significance for our Party, which shifted the centre of gravity of its work to the countryside with so much difficulty after the defeat of the revolution in 1927.[3]

Four months later, when the war against Japan ended, this change had already begun to take effect, with Communist cadres throughout the Liberated Areas studying the experiences of officials who had run the few small cities and large towns controlled by the Communists during the war. Over the next four years, 1945–49, Mao expressed an increasing concern with developing the industry, commerce, and finance of the urban places held by his troops.[4] The key to the control and development of cities, he argued, was the creation of a united front, a strong local coalition within which there would be a gradual transition to complete Communist rule.

The magnitude of the immediate task facing the Communists' urban cadres in 1949 for a time overshadowed all other policy considerations. Decades of warfare and neglect had left China's cities in wretched shape, their economies near collapse, their social and political institutions decaying or defunct. In the circumstances, cadres in the cities had no choice but to set aside their Yenan heritage and accommodate to established ways of getting things done. The party line on classes indicates the direction this accommodation took. Although Mao was later to denounce his second-in-command, Liu Shao-ch'i, for propounding a conciliatory policy toward "class enemies" in the cities,[5] it was Mao himself who urged this policy in 1949. Cautioning his subordinates against the notion that the revolution was to benefit only the poor peasants and farm laborers, he exhorted them to shed all vestiges of the peasant guerrilla mentality and set about learning the complex techniques of city management.[6] It was in reference to mastering urban problems that Mao in February 1949 first called for the army to be a school, a notion resurrected years later during the Cultural Revolution. And in March 1949, a month set aside for his soldiers to study city administration, he delivered his famous report to the Second Plenum of the Seventh Central Committee calling for a continuous revolution, proclaiming a shift in the revolution's "center of gravity" from the countryside to the city, and authorizing a broad coalition of urban classes to join the Communists in power. Though generally optimistic, the report ended by cautioning the revolutionaries against the dangers of city life and closer relations with the bourgeoisie.[7]

As this volume shows, Mao also has repudiated any urban policy that favors the city at the expense of the countryside. What is sometimes taken as his "anti-city bias" is understood correctly only in the context of his persistent aspiration to link the city and the countryside in a way that benefits them both. The implications of this aim have emerged slowly, however, and even yet are uncertain and subject to change.

Unfair as it may seem to attack Liu Shao-ch'i for supporting policies in the 1940's that were accepted at the time by all disciplined Communists,[8] Liu and other leading party officials did in fact take positions that tended to create an urban culture of a sort Mao later found abhorrent. One way or another, the early policies of the People's Republic enabled urban cadres to exploit the countryside to the cities' advantage. Even programs to transfer surplus cadres to the rural people's communes or to stem peasant migration to the cities served to perpetuate the city's superiority by excluding potential troublemakers from its precincts. Campaigns to "support the countryside" were often no more than a smokescreen behind which the city walled itself off from the deepening agricultural crisis. Indeed, the municipal administrative system of the 1950's linked the bureaucrats of one city far more closely to those of other cities than to their comrades in nearby villages and market towns.[9] This bureaucratic network expanded rapidly, moreover, and like all bureaucracies became preoccupied with its own survival. City officials sneered at their country cousins and consciously enjoyed the comparative luxury of city living. In making the city a prime target during the Cultural Revolution, the Maoists had numerous real grievances in mind.[10]

In launching the Cultural Revolution, Mao sought above all to divest city dwellers of their penchant for specialization and their acceptance of fiscal incentives, a money economy, intellectual standards, and formal bureaucracy.[11] Urban elitism and indifference to the rural masses, he argued, must give way to rural-urban cooperation and urban service to the countryside. One effect of the Cultural Revolution has accordingly been to undermine the urban stability that was given top priority in 1949.

## Law and Order in the Chinese City

The initial formulation of the Communist party's urban goals stressed pacification and reconstruction. Order was to be guaranteed by the People's Liberation Army and the police; the concurrent resumption of economic production would help assure public acceptance of their control measures.[12] City governments and party committees were formally entrusted with maintaining order throughout their jurisdictions, which included rural areas. Although much has been made of Mao's dissatisfaction with the government's post-Liberation security goals and his theoretical preference for "struggle,"[13] he applauded those goals in the first years of the People's Republic and helped perfect the techniques for attaining them.[14] When public order was threatened even in later years, Peking sanctioned the use of ruthless measures, including purges and witch hunts, against counterrevolutionaries and variously labeled criminal elements. In practice, repression has been as common under the Maoists as under the bureaucrats they have purged.

Theory and practice diverged, too, when the government's laws and regulations for achieving public order were applied on the local level. Since 1949 there have been recurrent cycles in the handling of the urban populace, with periods of intensive mobilization alternating with brief periods of relaxation. It is accordingly difficult to generalize about the effects of the law in overcoming urban disorder, as Jerome Cohen shows in his essay on the regulations dealing with mediation of civil disputes. These regulations were vague and incomplete; they made no distinction between the city and the countryside, or between small cities and large. At central party headquarters the mediation rules adopted in 1954 after four years of experimentation appeared to be flexible, but their application at lower levels suffered on the one hand from rigid formalism and on the other from confusion caused by national control campaigns that had been launched without respect to their potential social impact or to local differences in public participation and compliance. The mediation committees examined by Professor Cohen might have provided a direct link between the judicial bureaucrat and the populace, and thus have served as a testing ground for revolutionary legal principles in the cities. Had "mass line" concepts truly prevailed, the administrative bias in favor of procedural tidiness might have been overcome. Instead, an underlying official distrust of unregulated participation by the citizenry in the work of the mediation committees prevented Peking from expanding their jurisdiction and from giving mediation clear precedence over litigation. Nevertheless, even before the Great Leap Forward of 1958 downgraded bureaucracy and made mass line procedures more common at the lower levels, the number of cases before the mediation committees grew. Apparently the traditional popular avoidance of the courts and local support for mediation helped offset official biases.

As Professor Cohen shows, the role of law in civil conflict under the Communists had roots in Chinese tradition and even in Kuomintang legal practice.[15] Communist mediation rules, like earlier written codes, were used by officials to protect themselves against accusations by their superiors, and in practice disputes were settled not by resolving the point at issue but by making it too costly for the disputants to continue the argument. Since the Communist officials who wrote the laws had no fundamental quarrel with the Kuomintang's essentially European type of legal system, and since they found it expedient to retain most Kuomintang lawyers and judges, no radically new approach to civil disorder was possible. Laws regarded as temporary expedients gained institutional immortality, and revolutionary doctrine gave way to a formal legal apparatus.

Although foreign visitors regularly praised the orderliness of China's cities in the 1950's and early 1960's, the Maoists in the Cultural Revolution repudiated the former reliance on the courts and the police to deal with private disputes, delinquency, crime, counterrevolutionary activity, and other forms of disorder.[16] Indeed, they saw any exclusive reliance on the law as itself counterrevolutionary. Industrialization by legal edict, for example, leading as it does to the proliferation of dictatorial organs, inevitably puts the law in the rightful place of revolutionary doctrine as the essential instrument of social change. If the alternative to this prescription for stagnation is disorder, well and good, so only that the revolution be advanced.[17]

The difficulty of this formulation, as we have seen, is that proponents of a continuing revolution have a fundamental need for order as well as "revolutionary struggle." Communist policymakers, even those identified as Maoists, concede as much: they assume that the law has a role to play, but they have yet to decide on the legal institutions that best promote revolutionary goals. As Professor Cohen suggests, the mediation committees were caught between competing but overlapping theories of law as a coercive restraint and law as an instrument of social change. The other essays in Part I, by Victor Li and Ezra Vogel, deal with these respective emphases in Chinese Communist theory and practice.

Professor Li's paper is a case study of the law enforcement structure in Hui-yang *hsien* (county). Crime as defined in the West was apparently not a serious problem in Hui-yang; a surprisingly small security force policed the county seat of 60,000 and a hinterland population of some 450,000. The Red Guards have charged Liu Shao-ch'i with seeking to set up an independent police establishment of the traditional sort, and to reduce the number of police, in accordance with his theory that the class struggle had come to an end.[18] Whatever the merit of this charge, the police force in Hui-yang was of the sort Liu allegedly favored. Its functions were largely the traditional crime control functions (though crime in China of course included political deviation); its social and ideological reform functions were negligible. Moreover, despite their priority in cadre recruitment programs, the police ended up consisting largely of society's dregs. The low quality of the police in turn decreased their authority, except (as Professor Li shows) during periods of relatively high centralization, when authority accrued to them as representatives of the national government in Peking.

The case of the Hui-yang police illustrates one kind of problem the Communists confronted when they took over the cities in the late 1940's. Many able cadres were unwilling to become policemen in places like Hui-yang unless they could count on promotion to more prestigious positions in larger cities. The growth of police professionalism after 1949 made recruitment less difficult, but at the price of a breakdown in local ties between the public security force, other government agencies, and the populace. Caught up in the Cultural Revolution without a base of popular support, the police became one of its major victims.

The essay by Ezra Vogel deals with the other side of the law, its uses and consequences for social change. As seen from Peking in the 1950's, there was little need to differentiate among crimes except in the degree to which they could ramify and threaten the building of socialism. The severest sanctions fell on offenders whose crimes were seen as having the greatest social significance. As so often happens, the new sanctioning mechanisms soon acquired a life of their own and became part of a larger system for regulating the entire social environment.

This development was but a symptom of a more fundamental transformation. The Communists' security apparatus at the time of the takeover had directed its activities against war criminals and those who resisted Communist rule. Within a few years, its mission had become to control the instability caused by Communist programs themselves and to create a general climate of compliance. The new security programs had the unintended effect of discouraging innovation and encouraging concealment and collusion. It seems probable in the circumstances, as Professor Vogel suggests, that cadres in the cities had all they could do simply to maintain order. Thus we observe the increasingly dominant role of security officials (army officers after the Cultural Revolution) in urban life, and an increasingly doctrinaire quality in the government's approach to social order.

*Leadership and Bureaucracy*

In theory, the establishment of urban order was a temporary means of mobilizing the Chinese populace to build a socialist state; party and government bureaucracies were but temporary expedients to this end. In practice, the bureaucracies soon developed ends of their own and formidable means of pursuing them. As might be expected from the urban location of the large majority of cadre offices, most of these ends and means favored the city at the expense of the countryside.

The city of course benefited from the jobs and money generated by the expanding political bureaucracy, as well as the accompanying improvements in housing, welfare, and transportation. Yet this expansion brought additional problems in a number of localities. Peking maintained that cadres at the national level should "grasp the big power" and delegate the "little power" to cadres at lower levels.[19] But in a city it was hard to distinguish between the two kinds of power, especially since in nearly all large and medium-sized cities national, provincial, hsien, and municipal cadres worked side by side. As a result, the urban cadre tended to assimilate himself to the politics of the national capital. Locally the cross-pressures caused by rapid growth and the fusion of national and urban bureaucracies complicated the urban cadre's calculations, and involved him willy-nilly in the national power struggle of the 1960's.

His confusion was aggravated by the inappropriateness of the urban models that Peking used in approaching the problems of the Chinese city. As Franz Schurmann has remarked, the Chinese leadership has been unable to "bring about a new sense of community to replace the anomie inherent in modern cities, with their crowded tenements and mixed populations."[20] China is no worse in this respect than other countries undergoing rapid urbanization; its leaders must be blamed not for failing to solve the problem, but for insisting on a solution that does not work. Urban cadres who try to apply Peking's community model in their work find it vague and self-contradictory. They have no way of telling, for example, whether a given level of community autonomy will be regarded as appropriate or excessive by Peking, or even to what extent personal effort on their part to fulfill the party's plans will be considered loyal service and to what extent particularism. Whereas Mao has often affirmed the need for greater local autonomy, he simultaneously has repudiated the values and group norms that would support such autonomy or make it more than momentarily legitimate for the urban cadre. The game of politics in urban China is played according to changing rules. Inconsistently applied standards baffle municipal officials and cloud their field of choice. The emergence of the local community, however measured, has more often been the product of what Banfield calls "social choice"—the accidental result of group actions—than of skillful leadership.[21]

Unsure of the proper balance between leadership and popular voluntarism, unsure how to treat the populace on a mass line basis, China's

urban cadres have typically withdrawn into their own institutional
world.[22] This world has its compensations, among them a good life for
its inhabitants. As the city's bureaucratic structures proliferated in the
1950's, so did the cadres' perquisites, which came to include membership
in exclusive clubs, special schooling for their children, good jobs and
admittance to special shops for their wives, and access to restricted communications, including uncensored news of the outside world.[23] In time
urban cadres insulated themselves from the people they were meant to
lead, and from the problems they were supposed to solve.

Ying-mao Kau's essay on the growth of urban bureaucracy in the first
decade and a half under Communism offers a generalization of data
found in other papers in this volume. In the early years, perhaps the
main pressure on urban cadres was that of reconciling the values of a
revolution fading into memory with the daily demands from Peking and
their more immediate worlds. These tensions gave rise to two notable
urban campaigns in the 1950's: the "three-anti" (*san fan*) campaign to
erase corruption, waste, and "bureaucratism,"[24] and shortly thereafter
the "five-anti" (*wu fan*) campaign directed against urban businessmen
and their supporters in the bureaucracy.[25] The duration and specific
targets of these campaigns varied from city to city, and in some places
the two campaigns merged into one. Localism tended to be a more serious issue in the cities farther from Peking, which suggests that the
purges accompanying the campaigns were part of a planned readjustment of national as well as local power relationships. Almost everywhere, however, the more astute bureaucrats apparently manipulated
these campaigns to their own advantage, using officially sponsored
purges to consolidate their power within the bureaucracy and extend its
reach within the city. Both anti-bureaucratic campaigns thus paradoxically ended in bureaucratic expansion and an inflated demand for "qualified" cadres to fill the newly vacated slots. Although a massive recruitment of officials from 1949 through the early 1950's had been required
simply to staff the posts vacated by Nationalist officials, the three- and
five-anti campaigns created so many new openings that hiring standards
had to be lowered to fill them. Threatened by the campaigns, the bureaucracy contrived not only to protect itself but to accelerate its expansion and its members' promotion.[26]

As Professor Kau notes, the apparatus for recruiting officials soon
gained a pivotal position in the Chinese political system. Organization
and propaganda departments were established, and a shortened training process introduced. Regular channels of upward mobility were
created, and with them lasting group associations and natural lines of

influence. By the mid-1950's this self-sustaining process had resulted in overrecruitment and potential factional struggle, but little progress was made in slowing it down. The rate of bureaucratic growth ceased to have any relationship to the rate of economic development, or to a coherent national plan for developing cadres. By the time Peking took steps to reassign surplus urban cadres to jobs in the countryside, the mechanisms for resisting fundamental change were far too strong for moderate reforms to succeed. Even during the most intensive antibureaucratic campaigns city officials could be found proclaiming the need for more cadres, and temporary contractions of the bureaucracy during campaign periods were commonly followed by months of active recruitment. Small wonder that the Maoists have spoken of "two lines"—theirs and the bureaucrats'—as fundamentally opposed approaches to the problem of state-building in China.[27]

Although Maoism as it is now understood did not become a major factor in state-building until the mid-1960's, strong pressures did counter the bureaucratic wave. In the early 1950's the emphasis on law and order left city administrators relatively little room for maneuver. The forms of urban control used by the Japanese occupiers and the Kuomintang, notably the *pao chia* system of collective responsibility,[28] were continued, with real power given first to military control commissions and then to party-dominated civilian governments. Follow-up regulations provided for an urban administration with functional bureaus as well as for elected councils of representatives. Gradually there emerged an integrated system, described by Janet Salaff in Part IV, which was built pyramid-like from residents' groups and committees, to street offices and public security stations, and thence to the organs of the district (*ch'ü*) and municipal governments. Officials in the governments were jointly responsible to elected congresses, to higher-level administrations, and most especially to the relevant party office. Yet this apparatus was regularized in 1954 as part of a highly publicized effort to democratize the entire system following the promulgation of a state constitution earlier in the year.[29] Greater emphasis was given to popular participation in government, and citizens were encouraged to make their views known by visiting public offices, writing letters to officials, and getting actively involved in civic affairs.[30] In a typical report of the period, local offices were described as "close to the people":

You'll find [the street office] a hive of activity. It's the first place a citizen goes when he has a problem, a suggestion, or when he wants something done. If he wants to get married, off he goes to the street office for registration. If a family are at loggerheads, the street office will arbitrate. Somebody is taken

ill: the street office gets the ambulance. Somebody's roof leaks and the landlord is awkward: the street office gets things done. There is always someone
on duty all round the clock.[31]

This phase of constitutionalism and mass-line democracy was followed
in 1957 by more explicit central direction and an insistence on discipline
in the form of an increased role for the party and its political cadres.
This injunction lasted until 1966, when lower-level officials were suddenly required to subordinate themselves not to the party organization
but to the infallible guidance of Chairman Mao, and were denounced
for their earlier "confused compliance" with party directives and their
"slavish mentality."[32] The recurrent insistence on obedience either to a
distant party Central Committee or to Mao's rather delphic pronouncements has of course played havoc with the status of officials in both the
cities and the countryside.

With their formal authority recurrently undermined, wise bureaucrats
have found it expedient to conceal their views and interests behind the
slogans of the hour and protestations of admiration for Mao. But the
course of the Cultural Revolution suggests that nearly autonomous networks of influence not unlike those found in Western cities continue to
operate throughout urban China.[33] Successful city officials normally
combine close relationships with the capital with a genuine talent for
problem-solving; model officials on urban committees adopt a stance
of modesty and service while shrewdly hammering out decisions in the
midst of "struggle" meetings. All this is part of what Norton Long has
called the "ecology of games."[34]

Although we know little about the actual conditions of the urban
"game" in China, the heart of it is undoubtedly coalition-forming and
intergroup bargaining. Coalitions are always considered temporary; authorized struggle among them usually involves very concrete, long-
standing urban problems, ranging from production to welfare. The most
intense conflicts, however, seem to arise when the power of the coalition
itself is at issue and the rights of any party to it are challenged. The
Maoists have emphasized that the bargaining process should yield both
a realistic outcome and a new unity among the initial competitors, or
"three strands tightly twisted into one rope," to cite a slogan of the late
1960's.[35] Ideally, the bargaining process also features mass criticism, but
such criticism must be disciplined and in the public interest.[36] In practice
this means that a number of issues of interest to the student of urban
affairs—those involving personal relationships and informal groups—
seldom get discussed publicly.

The question of just how urban leadership operates in China is a particularly important one because Mao believes that only new styles of leadership can reverse bureaucratic growth in the cities. His call for mass-based political leadership and for "better troops and simpler administration" was meant to reduce the influence of urban party bureaucrats, particularly at the middle levels, and to increase the power of those with strong ties to the countryside as well as to Peking. Mao's concept of linkages within a social system allows for a minimum of bureaucratic structure and rejects the notion of long-term specialist training for cadres. Since his system has proved difficult to institutionalize, it is not clear exactly how the cities have been run since 1966, except that coalition-building and competitive bargaining seem to have played an even more significant role than before.

Paul Harper's study of the efforts of Chinese labor unions to educate workers for leadership positions in management, factory administration, and the Communist party illustrates both the problems of institution-building and the dramatic consequences of the rapid expansion of the urban labor force discussed in Part III by John Philip Emerson and Christopher Howe. The unions appear to have been highly responsive to the requirements of industrialization in the cities, and to have generally ignored plans and policies emanating from Peking. Although the unions played a large part in mobilizing and educating workers in the 1950's, they apparently did so in quest of higher output and more efficient management rather than for political reasons. Indeed, in the first decade the unions may well have done more than the Communist party to change the course of urban life and industrialization. To the extent that some of the changes in question can be legitimately described as "revisionist," the Cultural Revolution may be said to have abetted the cause of revisionism by its emphasis on putting greater authority in the hands of the urban proletariat.

Professor Harper describes how the unions identified and educated workers for leadership positions following Mao's 1949 injunction to rely on the proletariat in the cities. The training of growing numbers of industrial workers brought about major changes in their status and forged a solid link between the unions and the party. More and more urban bureaucrats were recruited from union ranks, and many of these recruits rose to positions of power and responsibility. The training of urban workers brought them into conflict with entrenched technical elites, many of them poorly trained, who occupied specialist or managerial positions in business, industry, and the political apparatus. The Cultural Revolution subsequently upgraded many experienced workers in the cities at the expense of technical experts and high-level managers.[37]

Conflicts of this sort are treated at length in my essay in Part II on commerce, education, and political development in Tangshan, which explores tentatively the systematic relationships at the local level within which political conflicts were worked out. To a certain extent the urban bureaucracy of Tangshan, like that of many other Chinese cities, could remain isolated from local political problems so long as it had bases of support elsewhere, notably in Peking. During the Great Leap Forward, however, as Tangshan cadres were driven to depend on local political resources, they had no choice but to establish and nurture alliances in the city and its hinterland. Such alliances upset the existing urban political structure and the arrangements that had worked in the years before 1958. The resulting redistribution of power forced threatened groups in Tangshan city to align themselves directly with village leaders, and worked considerable economic and social hardship on the intermediate hsien towns in the Tangshan region. People from those towns later formed the core of the "radical" forces set loose in Tangshan during the Cultural Revolution.

The attack on the Tangshan Establishment during the Cultural Revolution was led by young people, who sought to destroy whatever they considered unprincipled or personally disadvantageous. Their behavior raises questions about the educational process that have echoes throughout this volume, as well as questions about leadership and bureaucracy that young urban radicals are raising throughout the world. In the Cultural Revolution students denounced the bureaucratic mentality of municipal leaders while demanding government measures that would have required augmented, not diminished, bureaucratic power. The confusion found in discussions of participation and power in Western literature, both popular and academic, also beset the Red Guards in China's cities. They were inclined to see the geographic scale of an operation as inversely related to the possibility of meaningful participation: that is, the smaller the scale, the greater their chances for exerting influence. But one lesson of the Cultural Revolution was that the dispersion of power, though it might well lead to increased local autonomy, could dramatically reduce the access of the powerless to the mechanisms of decision.

Mao, who has dealt with this problem on several occasions, has concluded that decentralization, properly conceived, guarantees centralized rule. What is needed, he wrote in 1956, is to increase the power of the regions and "promote a consultative style of work with the regions."[38] One advantage of decentralization in his view is that it prevents local bureaucracies from becoming self-serving organizations linked only to the center. Much of his opposition to the Liuist model of urban politics stemmed from his conviction that, paradoxically, its reliance on centralized party control promoted local-level machine politics. Ironically, the reappearance of former urban officials in large numbers as "liberated cadres" in 1969 and 1970 suggests that Mao's remedy was largely ineffectual, and that the roots of local bossism go deeper.

## Modernization in the Chinese City

Communist leaders agreed from the outset on the indispensability of industrialization and the importance of political and social factors in development, but there were differences between them on the proper direction and acceptable costs of modernization.[39] Until the Great Leap Forward of 1958, the debate was tempered by the common expectation that changes in political institutions would not threaten Communism's basic principles or require a major reorganization of the party itself. Specifically the argument centered on the optimum rate of economic development, the correct social locus of development, and the appropriate political mechanisms for monitoring and rectifying personal attitudes during the transition to an industrial economy. The debate quickened after 1958, and the leadership became polarized.

Although most Communist leaders appear to have agreed that the burden of industrialization should fall equally on the rural and urban sectors,[40] no one knew how China could achieve this goal and still keep industrialization moving. Despite repeated calls in the 1950's for cities to share their advantages with surrounding towns and villages, the city's superiority as a place to live remained obvious to all. Peasants continued to pour into the city in what Peking called a "blind influx."[41] According to figures in John Philip Emerson's paper, the urban population grew from over 77 million in 1953 to 99.5 million in 1957 and to 130 million in 1961. Travel permits, area-specific rationing cards, the "sending down" of cadres, enforced population registration—nothing stemmed the tide.

Although China's cities clearly benefited from Communist policies in the 1950's, Mr. Emerson questions the extent to which Peking's manpower planning actually furthered the goals of industrialization. His paper investigates the education and employment of China's urban labor force in plan and in practice. As he demonstrates, revolutionary standards and preconceived or Soviet systems for schooling and employing the labor force proved more important to Peking's planners than economic facts. Distrustful of city standards and professionally trained personnel on ideological grounds, many leading Chinese Communists were unable to approve of the modernization schemes advanced by non-Communist experts.

Mr. Emerson concentrates on the demographic aspects of the Communists' predicament. He shows that the Communists understood the importance of their urban labor policies, but applied them without understanding how a given plan and a given outcome were related. The various kinds of population regulations were not just crude or misapplied, but misconceived; they resulted from a failure to comprehend the basic characteristics of the city and the effect of an urban industrial program on other nationally determined programs. In discussing these difficulties, Mr. Emerson sheds light on the deficiencies of a command economy and demonstrates how the effects of urban social organization undercut political planning.[42] Central planning is difficult enough in the best circumstances in a country as large and diverse as China; it is impossible when only a handful of experienced statisticians are available and there is no overall economic model against which to assess problems as they arise. The Communists could not agree on such fundamentals as a tolerable rate of population growth, educational priorities and standards, and the permissible ratio of high to low incomes. A number of important demographic developments took them completely by surprise, shattering their conviction that one way or another their plans would prove out.

Education became a particularly frustrating sphere for Communist planners. For one thing, revolutionary ideology and moral values notwithstanding, entrance examinations necessarily favored the urban bourgeoisie, and increasingly so as a student progressed from lower to higher levels. Even more troublesome, however, was the problem of group attitudes, particularly among young people. Each of the government's many shifts in manpower policy produced a different type of educated Chinese, with the result that the last twenty years have seen not just one or two educational generations but many generations separated by sharp divisions.[43] Mr. Emerson concludes that the Communists' many educational blunders have left them in a state of shock, unable to cope with realities all the more unpleasant for being largely unforeseen. In his view, the unsettled questions of attitude that Mao considers the most important of all for the country's youth will persist in bedeviling Communist leaders for the foreseeable future.

Mr. Emerson would be the first to concede the difficulty of saying much about the Chinese city on the basis of aggregate statistics for the whole country. Christopher Howe illustrates some of the difficulties in his study of manpower data for the city of Shanghai. This metropolis, the object of several other studies in the volume, provides an excellent example of how deceptive aggregate statistics can be even at the municipal level. Urban growth has been only dimly understood in China, and comprehensive statistics for so-called key indicators may well fail to include information vital to determining the probable success of a proposed policy. Dr. Howe's analysis reveals how the problems of unemployment, job opportunity, and sectoral employment in Shanghai are distorted by such figures.

Furthermore, as the Shanghai data show, the categories used in national plans obscure the workings of change and provide no adequate basis for measuring the impact of any given policy on the cities. What is meant, for example, by "city" and "countryside" in these plans? It is one thing to relocate residents of Shanghai in China's far west and quite another to relocate them in nearby suburbs, yet in both cases they are being "sent to the countryside." The expansion of municipal boundaries in the mid-1950's made it possible for urban-rural migration to go unreflected in the statistics on "urban" manpower despite its potentially significant impact on the affected population.[44] Communist policies since the Cultural Revolution have tried to take such factors into account. An effort is being made to transform backward areas near cities by introducing improved agricultural techniques, part-time education, and small-scale industry. In accepting the increased local autonomy that followed the Cultural Revolution, China's leaders have partially come to terms with the problems of demographic planning on a national scale.

The new emphasis reopens the question of how equal the urban and rural sectors should be, and how closely their destinies should be linked. For more than a decade industrial planners presumed a definite break between the city and its hinterland; despite the actual overlapping of the two worlds, particularly in the more modernized areas of China, their plans called for the integration of the city on the one hand and of the rural collective on the other. John Gardner's essay, which illustrates how this system affected youth, lends support to the Maoists' charges that the pre-1966 model of education gave far better opportunities to urban than rural youth and failed to give due weight to the cognitive effects of this built-in inequality. As Mr. Gardner notes, the anger given expression by the Red Guards had its cause in Communist policy. He argues that the Maoist strategy seeks to remove this cause by eliminating differences between town and country, workers and peasants, and mental and manual labor. Unlike the "Liuist view," with its emphasis on production quotas and the setting of economic priorities by urban elites, the Maoist program seeks to expand opportunity and political consciousness along with production. This shift has created a clash between "two lines" of education, a clash that Mr. Gardner considers in the light of the half-work half-study program and the response to it. In an important sense the Cultural Revolution was a "struggle to determine the destiny of the young," whose collective anger unquestionably bore out Maoist criticism of the Communist programs that had brought things to this pass. But the Cultural Revolution also revealed the essential naïveté of the Maoists, who tried to effect fundamental attitudinal changes without slowing down the complex process of industrialization.

The Howe and Gardner papers indirectly raise a number of other questions about the modernization of the Chinese city. How has modernization affected the urban economy? How is it organized? To what extent do municipal officials seek to plan and manage the economy? How successful have they been in planning for welfare, housing, and public health? How does the city dweller's standard of living compare with the peasant's? How much say do municipal officials have in decisions that affect their cities?

These questions are not easily answered. The state of China's urban economy has proved as perplexing to the Communists as it has to scholars in the West.[45] Chinese planners have differed over incentives, organizational techniques, managerial principles, and the role of planning itself. Prior to 1966, their debates—e.g., on regulating trade by means of networks of wholesale cooperatives and warehouses and on the use of rationing to control consumption—generally indicate a preference for a nationally uniform regulation of state-owned sectors of the economy.[46] Since 1966, the leadership has been readier to accept local variations and to recognize that the imposed solution of one urban problem often simply creates another one.[47]

We have been discussing planning for the urban economy as part of the national economy. What about planning for the city itself, which did not get under way until 1955?[48] The 1955 plan for urban development was drawn up after debates over the definition and nature of cities on the one hand, and on the ideal size and location of the cities on the other. The provisions of the plan were as follows:

1. Observing the principle of economizing funds and rationalizing distribution, provincial and municipal authorities should make over-all plans for new cities, for cities which must be reconstructed or which will be enlarged to prevent guideless building and over-concentration of populations.

2. Observing the policy of giving priority to industrial construction and industrial production, all public utility construction projects in new cities and cities being reconstructed or enlarged should make timely provision for the needs of new and reconstructed enterprises and enterprises which are expanding production in the fields of water supply, drainage, roads, bridges, etc. At the same time, taking into consideration the needs of over-all city planning,

public utility construction projects should be got going at a rate dictated by the degree of their importance and urgency so as to avoid any waste which might result from incorrect planning.

3. Provincial and municipal authorities should make full use of the potentialities of urban public utilities with their existing equipment, and, as local financial resources permit, acquire such new equipment as is needed to satisfy the immediate, urgent needs of the urban working people.

4. Provincial and municipal authorities should exercise stricter control over the expenditure on city construction, and draw a proper distinction between allocations for public utilities, and investments in ordinary municipal construction. Certain funds for urban development and maintenance should be allocated as needed from local revenue.[49]

According to one source, cities were to be kept relatively small and the emphasis was to be on creating new towns and building up potential urban centers in China's interior.[50] In 1956 Mao confirmed this interpretation: "From now on, the greater part of heavy industry—90 per cent or more—should be established inland so that the distribution of industry may gradually be evened out to insure the rational distribution of industry throughout the country. There is no question in this regard. However, part of the heavy industry must be built and expanded along the coast."[51] After 1956 a great deal of attention was given to the development of both coastal and inland cities, the creation of new towns, and the upgrading of such west China cities as Urumchi, Lanchow, and Paotow.[52] In general, urban planning was to be carefully monitored for its impact on security and national growth,[53] but strangely Mao vetoed the idea that the masses should debate urban plans. They would supervise the personnel, not their policies.[54]

Beginning about the same time, detailed attention was given to the improvement of urban living conditions. Typical studies discussed municipal construction, hygiene, pollution control, and urban living standards in general. Reports on land use, schools, crime, and accidents appeared in city newspapers, along with a great many articles on the urban proletariat as such. As Table 1 shows, industrial workers increasingly dominated the urban labor force. Housing for urban workers received priority attention in the First Five-Year Plan (1953–57), with prime consideration given to locating their dwellings near factories.[55] Welfare programs for workers were also emphasized, and some were notably successful, as Joyce Kallgren has shown in her study of urban social welfare.[56]

Perhaps the most publicized of Peking's innovations in public health and welfare was the series of campaigns, most of them launched just before major holidays or during the summer, to rid the country of flies,

TABLE 1. NONAGRICULTURAL EMPLOYMENT BY MAJOR SECTORS
(*Per cent*)

| Sector | Communist China | | Soviet Union |
| | 1952 | 1957 | 1928 |
| --- | --- | --- | --- |
| Industry | 32% | 38% | 45% |
| Construction | 2 | 4 | 8 |
| Transportation | 14 | 14 | 12 |
| Commerce | 33 | 24 | 9 |
| Government and other services | 19 | 20 | 26 |

SOURCE: Alexander Eckstein, Walter Galenson, and Ta-chung Liu, eds., *Economic Trends in Communist China* (Chicago: Aldine, 1968).

NOTE: For Communist China, Industry consists of manufacturing, mining, and fishing; Construction is basic construction; Commerce includes finance, banking, and insurance; and Government and other services includes personal and professional services and water conservation.

rats, roaches, mosquitoes, and other disease-bearing pests. These campaigns produced substantial results, but in so doing inevitably widened the gap between urban and rural health standards.[57] In the 1960's Mao began to complain about the urban bias in the Ministry of Public Health, which he said "only works for 15 per cent of the entire population.... At the present time the system of examination and treatment used in the medical schools is not at all suitable for the countryside.... We should keep in the cities those doctors who have been out of school for a year or two and those who are lacking in ability. The remainder should be sent to the countryside."[58] During the Cultural Revolution, Mao's demands led to a nationwide movement to train "barefoot doctors" for the countryside and to give peasants preferential access to urban medical facilities.

Mao's complaints about medical care were part of his overall attack on the city dweller's continued superiority in standard of living. Table 2 shows the difference between urban and rural living standards in the mid-1950's. In the first decade of Communist rule, for which we have relatively reliable figures, the purchasing power (real wages) of the urban populace rose steadily.[59] During the years of crisis in the 1960's, some scholars believe that rural living standards declined, both absolutely and relative to urban standards. Whatever the difference between the two may be today, continued denunciations of the city's advantageous position suggest that it remains great.

The economic changes of the 1950's had direct consequences for urban class structure.[60] Urban classes—once neatly classified into "bureaucratic" or "national" bourgeoisie, petty bourgeoisie (including intellectuals), and working class—shifted and began to merge. Income ceased to be an accurate measure of status; the low-status class of

TABLE 2. RELATIVE INCOME AND EXPENDITURES OF URBAN WORKERS AND PEASANTS

| Category | Urban workers and employees | Peasants | Percentage difference |
|---|---|---|---|
| Per capita income, 1955 (current yüan) | 102 | 94[a] | 8.5% |
| Per capita expenditures, 1955 (current yüan) | 97 | 89[a] | 9.0% |
| Per capita consumption of food grains, 1956–57 (kilograms) | 282.4 | 258.9 | 9.1% |
| Per capita consumption of cotton cloth, 1955 (meters) | 11.4 | 8.8 | 29.5% |

SOURCE: Nai-ruenn Chen and Walter Galenson, *The Chinese Economy under Communism* (Chicago: Aldine, 1969).
[a] Excludes handicraft products made by peasants for their own use.

former capitalists, for example, received relatively generous interest payments for nationalized property.[61] The "bureaucratic" bourgeoisie suffered as a class immediately after Liberation, then flourished for a year or so while the government offered official encouragement to private industry and business, and finally were all but extinguished by the five-anti campaign after 1951, the rapid socialization of private enterprise in the cities in late 1955, and the anti-rightist campaign of 1957. Was China experiencing proletarianization and the "withering away of classes"? It was not, according to the Maoist leadership in the Cultural Revolution. Arguing that class was ultimately a matter of attitudes and behavioral style, they emphasized the importance of "class" struggle among Chinese of roughly the same economic status.

Another brief triumph of ideology over practical considerations was the 1959 movement to establish urban people's communes.[62] The idea behind this movement was to create a new form of urban community by integrating industry, commerce, education, household activities, and, where appropriate, agriculture. Although as of July 1960 some 1,064 urban people's communes with some 55.5 million members were reportedly functioning, the frantic activity and highly publicized model programs of this movement proved to be short-lived.[63] Years later, during the Cultural Revolution, Liu Shao-ch'i was blamed for errors in judgment at the time of the urban communes, but the causes of their failure ran deeper. The commune concept tended not only to fragment the modern sector of the economy along residential lines, but to sharpen the division between the city and the countryside.[64] Ideologically as well as economically the urban commune proved to be a step backward; the attempts to increase the self-reliance of cities merely reinforced the divisions that Mao and other revolutionary leaders were striving to eliminate.

During the mid-1960's there were experiments with a different economic unit, the "economic region" discussed in my paper on Tangshan. The urban commune had proved economically too small and politically too divisive; the solution to both these problems, it was thought, was a region uniting cities, towns, and countryside. Bureaucratic and other variations in these regional units—the term "economic region" (*ching chi ch'ü yü*) was used only in a limited number of places—have made for unavoidable disparities in rates of economic development in different parts of China, but Communist leaders are apparently willing to pay this price. Another difficulty is the tendency for regional planning to result in gross disparities in distribution, a problem that could be critical in times of famine or national upheaval. Indeed, region-wide development may be an unattainable ideal in a rapidly modernizing society, and efforts to force the process may well end in weakening China's cities without a commensurate strengthening of the countryside.

It is perhaps equally important that the economic region, being neither clearly urban nor clearly rural, is difficult for cadres to conceptualize and manage. The Chinese press since the Cultural Revolution rarely speaks of the city or region as such, but confines itself to particular factories, businesses, schools, or government bodies. The Communists' extraordinary difficulty since the Cultural Revolution in formulating a legitimate role for the municipal revolutionary committees and creating viable regional institutions indicates their uneasiness in dealing with the new larger-scale units. What evidence we have suggests that beneath the rhetoric of revolution city-based bureaucracies continue to operate, but now extend their influence to a broader range of activities, including rural ones. Again one notes a disparity between theory and practice, similar to the one that helped spark the struggle in the cities in 1966.

### China's Urban Crisis

At the outset of the Communist period development was seen as city-based and nationally planned. The countryside got the leftovers, despite the place of honor promised the peasant in the social and political hierarchy. The peasant's frustrations were matched, however, by the unhappiness of the urban bureaucrat, whose performance was evaluated by national standards that were generally insensitive to his local situation. For a time ambitious young people in the cities applauded Peking's development strategy, but by the mid-1950's even privileged groups felt threatened by programs that called on the young and the unemployed to leave the cities for a Spartan existence in the mountains and deserts of western China.

These anxieties were turned into feelings of hostility against the Communist leadership during the Great Leap Forward, and in succeeding years urban groups, especially the intelligentsia, gave expression to widespread discontent by means of passive resistance and a wave of underground protest literature.[65] The central authorities' bureaucratic response merely accentuated the discontent, while symbolizing for Mao the ineffectiveness—or even collusion—of party and government officials in the crisis. Under the intense pressures of the time, interest-type groups were formed and battle lines drawn.[66] When Mao told students not to be afraid to make trouble and informed his colleagues that "a few months of disturbances will be mostly for the good," he set loose emotions long pent up in the cities. The urban crisis became what Lin Piao called a "nation-wide civil war without guns." By the middle of the Cultural Revolution the qualification "without guns" had ceased to apply.

To a large extent the crisis appeared to turn on conflicting priorities, policies, and political doctrines, but for the city's populace more practical questions were at stake. For city dwellers what counted was not ideological but personal: housing, welfare, job training and placement, land use for factories and parks, and the like. Nothing in their behavior justified Mao's optimistic assumption that the predictable outcome of political upheaval was a national political renaissance. It may be true, as Ezra Vogel has written, that changes in city life were effected less "by technological development than by the reestablishment of order, government-sponsored housing, government rationing, socialist transformation, and the organization of the citizenry into small groups."[67] What is certain is that each of these policies was accepted or modified by city dwellers in accordance with its effect on their immediate family or group.[68]

Janet Salaff discusses the impact of the Cultural Revolution on urban residential communities, and Lynn White in the succeeding essay explores some of the major issues in China's urban crisis in the light of Shanghai's experience. By 1965, the residents' committees set up in the 1950's had grown introverted and inert, and many were run by small-time bosses. Professor Salaff examines the pressures in the Cultural Revolution that led to the seizure of power from established urban leaders and to a series of campaigns, meetings, and study programs intended to create a new participatory political environment at the municipal level. Her findings bear out the importance of the grievances of the urban young, especially those who had been shipped to the countryside, in touching off the rebellion. The Cultural Revolution was largely confined to the cities and their suburbs.[69] Gaining the allegiance of the urban population was an immediate goal of the Maoist leadership, which had precipitated the power struggle not so much to remove individual officials as to halt the fundamental trend toward urban and bureaucratic dominance and to build up broad-based institutions for "continuing the revolution." It is only in this sense that the Cultural Revolution might be considered revolutionary, which is not necessarily to say irrational. As many readers will observe, much of the effort described by Professor Salaff to increase the participation of Chinese city dwellers in the political process echoes themes in the writings of such American urban commentators as Norton Long and Jane Jacobs.[70]

The most distinctive institution to come into existence during the Cultural Revolution, the revolutionary committee, officially symbolizes these aspirations for a mobilized urban citizenry.[71] How successful these committees have been in increasing participation we do not know. Mass movements for the criticism of class enemies, which were spreading at the time the revolutionary committees were formed, were joined in late 1968 by campaigns urging the populace to prepare for war; both movements perpetuated the atmosphere of fear and crisis in which the committees' efforts might be expected to thrive.[72] On the other hand, the reorganization of urban workers in 1970 in such a way as to raise the status of veteran workers, whose experience and productivity were once more considered of value to the revolution, seemingly marked a trend away from revolutionary innovation and a tendency to limit the scope of popular involvement in urban political affairs.[73] If any generalization is possible in the present confusion, it is that workers whose positions were consolidated before the Cultural Revolution are probably willing to accept a moderate level of disruption and political agitation either as a reasonable price for their favored position or as the inevitable concomitant of the national campaigns to propagate Mao's thought and prepare the nation for war.[74]

The costs of this continuing tension, Professor Salaff notes, have been high, and pressures have accordingly mounted to ensure public order and state security. Although the call for law and order heard in 1949 has not been revived, "criminal" suspects are often labeled "class enemies" with the same emotional intensity and meet the same end in public denunciation, trial, and punishment. The newly emerging security agencies have also been used to manage population movements and to help run cities. At first the army bore much of the burden. Indeed, its political role in the late 1960's closely resembled its role in the late 1940's, except that whereas in the 1940's the army worked hand in glove with the party, in the 1960's its allies were more often teams of police, "revolutionary cadres," and "revolutionary residents." Conceivably, this high degree of popular participation in the control network may lead to greater popular support for such controversial programs as the one for sending urban youth to the countryside. One cannot even guess, since the line between persuasion and coercion is once more blurred.

In many respects, the Cultural Revolution derived from the crisis of modernization so familiar to students of social change everywhere. The remarkable aspect of the Cultural Revolution was neither its rhetoric nor its violence, but the fact that the Maoists were willing to gamble the country's entire future on their utopian vision of the new society. Lynn White's study of Shanghai is a case history of that gamble. The four types of institutions Mr. White discusses—security-military, residential, educational, and workers'—include groups that function as political actors, some of which form parts of larger political systems. Conflicts have raged within and between the four types of institutions, whose mutual and conflicting interests cannot readily be disentangled. The groups formed under such conditions exhibit distinctive relationships between leader and follower, and these distinctive traits determine the pattern of city politics and influence city social structures as well. What separates a group from other groups and keeps it separate is as important to its leader as his ability to maintain ties with other groups; yet while separateness strengthens the leader's position, it weakens the group's by increasing the danger of conflict with other groups.

Although the Chinese penchant for organization has long been strong in the cities, the rapidity and unevenness of urban change in recent years have badly complicated things. Communist ideology is not much help, except to the extent that its ambiguity can let a resourceful cadre escape the pressure of uninformed dogmatic prescriptions. Of course ambiguity may also lead to confusion, resentment, and rebellion, and add fuel to a conflict once it breaks out. Once an open conflict exists, its dynamics and those of the organizations to which it gives rise may force the leadership into formulating new decisions and goals that are essentially unideological and unrelated to their original social aims. The result is both increased complexity and the structuring of urban politics for conflict. Such is the logic of the crisis in Shanghai, Mr. White believes, and perhaps in other Chinese cities as well.

## Prospects for the Chinese City

What do the essays in this book tell us in a general way about the city in Communist China? It is apparent that the bureaucracy in any large city between 1948 and 1966 was a composite of several levels of administration, both rural and urban. The city administration occupied a middle position in the national bureaucratic hierarchy; it had to juggle and negotiate the priorities relayed to it from above and look after the city's needs as such and the needs of its members. In the circumstances, it was often hard to tell whether a given political decision reflected the requirements of the city, the surrounding region, the central government, or the city administration itself.[75]

Whether the Cultural Revolution created additional complexities in urban political life or simply exposed long-standing political relationships that for twenty years were successfully hidden behind a façade of doctrinal unity, we cannot be certain. Whatever the explanation, one does have the impression that the increase in local autonomy since 1966 has led to less infrastructure, less planning, more diversity, and greater vitality in Chinese urban life today than at any time since the Communist takeover.

The new developments do not in themselves alter the fundamentals of city life for the individual citizen, and are by no means all in the direction of increased political participation. In the city of Peking itself, for example, the national press in the fall of 1969 noted a surprising spread of the so-called small-group mentality, a disposition to remain aloof from government and to oppose the incursion of one's neighbors into affairs that had been happily turned over in the past to party cadres or other local officials. The *Jen min jih pao* of September 12, 1969, complained:

Those who work for the small group always confine themselves to a narrow circle. They call those in their own group brothers and look upon them as "bosom friends," but avoid or discriminate against those revolutionary comrades who do not belong to their small group, regarding them as "aliens." It seems from their point of view that the fewer the people the better, and the smaller their circle the better.

City dwellers were seemingly just as reluctant to leave their private spheres following the Cultural Revolution as in the years of central party direction.

The attitudes of urban dwellers toward recent political programs are also conditioned by painful memories. For one thing programs to send the "urban idle" to the countryside remain in effect; and whereas their purpose, especially in the smaller cities, has generally been to tie the city more closely to nearby areas rather than to transport individuals to distant places, the effect is no less traumatic.[76] Then, too, the closer relationship of cities and countryside does not strike Chinese as a particularly novel or attractive change. Traditional Chinese cities were arranged in a patterned network of internal and external relationships, many of which have broken down in the past century of social turmoil and warfare.[77] The attempt to establish regional networks may help erode the insularity of cities within a given region and encourage cooperation among them; but there is also the danger of reverting to a regional fragmentation of the sort that prevailed in the warlord era. Any significant change in this direction would almost certainly bring many city dwellers to press for precisely the kind of centrally controlled push toward modernization from which their leaders have retreated.

Confusing and problematic as Chinese urban policy has been, it has its good points in the minds of many city dwellers. The official preference for rapid change, the autonomy of a number of authorized political groups, and the leadership's norms permit considerable popular spontaneity and local initiative. Nor is the government's role reducible to meddling and manipulation. In the Chinese urban system governments do meddle, but their cadres have learned that there are genuine social limits to politically induced change. The government may act as arbiter and mediator in the competition between local interest-type groups, but the government itself is divided into different groups and factions some of which have local ties and independent bases of support.

Indeed, the move toward "politics in command" and the adulation of Chairman Mao may well portend less rather than more government interference in the city. As several essays in this volume stress, the current model of urban governance places unprecedented emphasis on direct citizen participation. Since 1966 the word has gone out to the cities that politics is no longer an elite affair. Officials, experts, and professionals are all being told to work with and pay heed to the masses. A typical injunction to the nation's municipal revolutionary committees reads as follows:

The old arrangement whereby each standing committee member [of the revolutionary committee] was in charge of one particular field of work was done away with to free him from day-to-day routine. Instead the members have been divided into three groups. One takes part in productive labor. Another is to stay with selected basic units to guide and help the work there. The third group remains in the office. The three groups are rotated at regular intervals, so that everyone has a chance to go to the grassroots level.[78]

This system recalls arrangements introduced during the Great Leap Forward, when the energies of city-based officials were diverted to the countryside and the cities were allowed to go their own way.[79]

Periods of permissiveness, however, have never lasted long in Communist China. The chief threat to the present system is the utopian strain in Mao's view of leadership, with its emphasis on resisting the pressures of modernization.[80] Development occurs, Mao believes, when societal routines are disrupted and local groups are pitted against one another in "revolutionary struggle." The evidence does not support him. The result of struggle can simply be rancor, or the cementing in place of hostile groups geared for conflict. Under these conditions politics not only may not take command, but may so sap the vitality of the system that no lasting solutions are possible. The recent role of the Chinese military in urban politics and administration is not reassuring in this respect. Ironically, it appears that Mao's pursuit of a "natural" order emerging from political struggle could lead to precisely the bureaucratic authoritarianism he so abhors.

Perhaps the most fascinating aspect of Communist China's urban experiment is the attempt to realize in hundreds of cities at different stages of industrialization an ideal of local self-reliance and rural-urban cooperation that is only idly discussed in the West. In Chinese cities where the experiment is taken seriously, and there are many, what is being sought is a wholly new model of urban society. Mao has described it this way: "The localities should consider ways of setting up independent industrial systems. First of all [economically] coordinated regions, and afterward a number of provinces when conditions permit, should all set up relatively independent even though dissimilar industrial systems."[81] In places bent on realizing Mao's ideal of regional self-reliance, major efforts are under way to spread the benefits of science and technology,[82] to develop efficient small-scale factories, to combine labor and learning, to overcome people's fear of innovation, to cultivate a new type of management, and to make people care. Modernization according to this ideal, Mao believes, requires a spirit of revolution, a spirit whose components are militancy, self-sacrifice, daring, and improvisation.

The whole Maoist concept of regional community (or modernizing "base areas") depends on a mobilization of the urban populace and a rapid multiplication of social contacts between cities and their hinterlands.[83] In turn this places heavy demands on all urban facilities. Despite official trumpeting of the peasantry's special virtues, the aim of the present Chinese leadership is much more to urbanize the countryside than to rusticate the city. That the countryside will in fact be urbanized seems likely enough. That this will happen soon, or in line with the Maoist vision, seems considerably less likely.

# PART ONE

# Law and Order in the Chinese City

# Drafting People's Mediation Rules

JEROME ALAN COHEN

According to the traditional American view, mediation is the process by which a third person intervenes in an effort to reconcile two contending parties. This formulation, which fails to recognize the extent to which American mediators, at least in disputes affecting the public interest, bring pressure on reluctant parties to accept an unsatisfactory settlement, is too narrow a definition of "mediation" to apply to the Chinese situation. I have written elsewhere that

> the term "mediation," which for our purposes is synonymous with "conciliation," refers to the range of methods by which third persons seek to resolve a dispute without imposing a binding decision. The Chinese mediator may merely perform the function of an errand boy who maintains contact between parties who refuse to talk to one another. At the other end of the spectrum, he may not only establish communication between parties, but may also define the issues, decide questions of fact, specifically recommend the terms of a reasonable settlement—perhaps even give a tentative or advisory decision—and mobilize such strong political, economic, social and moral pressures upon one or both parties as to leave little option but that of "voluntary" acquiescence.[1]

For millennia the Chinese have preferred unofficial mediation to official adjudication. After the Manchu dynasty was overthrown in the 1911 revolution, the new republican government made the first of what was to become a long series of attempts by twentieth-century Chinese regimes to build on this traditional preference by enacting legislation

I am grateful to Mrs. Fu-mei Chang Ch'en for her valuable assistance in reviewing my analysis of the contemporary sources and in introducing me to the historical materials. I have also benefited from the criticisms of other colleagues, especially Benjamin Kaplan and Frank Münzel.

designed to institutionalize extrajudicial mediation under official auspices. In 1913 it created a Commercial Arbitration Bureau whose principal task, despite its title, was to mediate commercial and business disputes.[2] In the 1920's, when various warlords contended for national and regional power, experimentation with new forms of out-of-court mediation continued. Especially noteworthy was the legislation establishing "anti-litigation associations" in Shansi province, the domain of warlord Yen Hsi-shan.[3] The Nationalist government, which ruled most of China from 1928 to 1949 and which continues to exist on Taiwan, issued a spate of statutes, regulations, interpretations, and decisions in an effort to adapt traditional mediation practices to serve the goals of a modernizing China.[4] The Communist regime, while further modifying the nature of traditional practices to suit the needs of a revolutionary system, has made popular mediation a major instrument of its legal policy.

This essay will analyze how the Chinese Communist leadership chose to meet the difficult problems involved in establishing a mediation system when in 1954 they promulgated the only rules that their regime has ever made applicable to the entire nation. Specifically, we will inquire about the extent to which these rules, which were issued after five years of Communist control of China's cities, reflected the party's urban experience rather than its earlier preoccupation with the administration of rural areas. Because of the inaccessibility of China to foreign scholars and the lack of detailed Chinese studies of mediation, our knowledge of actual mediation practice is fragmentary,[5] but what can be gleaned from published sources and emigré interviews suggests that the mediation system that was functioning on the eve of the Great Proletarian Cultural Revolution of 1966–69 was not very different from that contemplated in 1954,[6] although political and economic changes in the intervening period stimulated a variety of ideas about mediation and experiments with it. Thus the rules are worthy of our attention even today. They not only tell us something of the contemporary Chinese view of mediation, but also give us an insight into the Chinese view of the legislative process.

### Background of the 1954 Rules

Like other Chinese Communist legislation, the Provisional General Rules of the People's Republic of China for the Organization of People's Mediation Committees (Provisional Rules)[7] did not spring full-blown from the heads of draftsmen, but were the product of widespread experimentation. Disputes were mediated in Communist-held territories long before 1949, but we know little of the details, and the relative paucity of documentation suggests that developing a mediation system was not then a matter of high priority with Mao and his associates. An important Communist legal official asserted that the party began to give the matter increasing attention during the period of the Sino-Japanese War (1937–45),[8] during which it extended its rule from its capital at Yenan to other remote revolutionary areas, eventually having authority over approximately ninety million people.

By the early 1940's the party had articulated a policy for settling civil disputes that placed greater emphasis on mediation than on adjudication.[9] As part of what was proclaimed to be the "new democratic workstyle" developed during the Yenan period, attempts were made to establish mediation organizations that would enable the masses to participate in settling disputes under government supervision. The mediation regulations of the various revolutionary bases deserve careful comparison with each other and with contemporaneous Nationalist efforts, because of their sophistication, their diversity, and the differing manner in which each regulation evolved in response to local circumstances. In this essay, however, we can simply refer to this body of pre-1949 norms in order to understand the extent to which alternative possibilities might have been known to those who designed the mediation system in 1954. We shall refer particularly to the pertinent Nationalist regulations of the day and to those of two of the principal Communist-controlled areas: the Shensi-Kansu-Ningsia Border Region (Shen-Kan-Ning or SKN) and the Shansi-Chahar-Hopei Border Region (Chin-Ch'a-Chi or CCC).

When Communist armies took over the major cities of China in 1949, party leaders confronted the same question with respect to mediation organizations as they had with respect to other institutions that had evolved in response to the primitive conditions of life among the peasantry: to what extent would institutions have to be altered to suit the more complex circumstances of the nation's urban residents? Although the creation of appropriate means of settling disputes was not as urgent a problem as the suppression of counterrevolution, it was nevertheless important.[10] Wholly apart from considerations of national security, the party faced a difficult legal situation in the cities. The chaotic conditions accompanying the collapse of Nationalist rule appear to have spawned more than the usual number of disputes in the period just prior to Liberation, and the inevitable hiatus in government during the Communist takeover had led to the accumulation of large numbers of unadjudicated civil cases. The backlog of pending cases increased after the takeover, when the party simplified judicial procedures and lowered litigation fees as part of its publicized policy of making the courts more accessible to the people than they had been under previous regimes.[11] Effective extrajudicial mediation could help to reduce the caseload and thereby alleviate grievances. Moreover, having brought the masses into mediation as part of their successful effort to win popular support in the rural areas, party leaders were eager to employ similar tactics in the cities.

Of course, in the rural revolutionary areas citizen participation in especially designated mediation institutions had not precluded mediation by other organs and persons; this was also to be the policy in the cities. Court personnel were particularly exhorted and trained to engage in mediation, and "mediation sections" were established at the district level in the government of certain large cities, including Peking. In addition, other bureaucrats, policemen, members of the party and the youth league, work supervisors, union officials, and participants in semi-official local groups such as the residents' committees and the women's associations were also expected to include mediation among their duties whenever the need arose.[12] In the cities, as in the rural revolutionary areas, the party continued to experiment with ways to enlist the masses in specialized mediation organizations and roles. In many places people's mediation committees were set up.[13] In others, citizens designated as mediators served as part of the local residents' committee. In still other cities, activists among the masses were selected on an ad hoc basis to mediate certain types of disputes.[14] A 1950 directive even instructed judicial cadres to try to establish comrades' courts within government organs and social organizations in order to mediate and arbitrate interpersonal disputes.[15]

The stock of these experiments with popular mediation fluctuated with the political developments of the day as well as with local circumstances. For example, the "judicial reform" movement of 1952–53 revived sagging interest by spurring legal cadres throughout China to lead the masses in organizing small groups and committees for mediation.[16] When in the spring of 1953 the Second National Judicial Conference announced a new policy that emphasized the role of law in national economic construction and proclaimed as a major goal the establishment of people's mediation committees in all of China's cities and administrative villages, a uniform system of extrajudicial mediation appeared to be at hand; draft rules on the organization of mediation committees were even presented to the conference.[17] Yet before the end of 1953, during the "five too many" movement that sought to eliminate unnecessary organizations, in many places mediation committees were abolished as superfluous or ineffective.[18]

The actions taken during the "five too many" movement and the delay of almost a year in promulgating the draft rules that had been presented to the judicial conference suggest serious doubts about the utility of mediation committees. Even the *Jen min jih pao* editorial that welcomed the 1954 promulgation of the Provisional Rules appeared to be defensive. It conceded that in the past some people's mediation committees had not behaved in accordance with the principles now set forth in the Provisional Rules:

They applied pressure to the parties or resorted to "holding a struggle meeting," "passing by a show of hands," and other rough methods to coerce the parties into accepting and carrying out the reconciliation "agreement." Or else, they did not dare to use appropriate criticism-education against the erroneous views of the parties and adopted a compromising attitude. As a consequence, mediation failed or the reconciliation agreement did not accord with policies, laws, and decrees, or it impaired the interests of the other party. Some other mediation personnel mistakenly thought that the people's mediation committee was a judicial organization of the first level with powers equal to those of the people's court. Consequently, there arose forbidden phenomena such as "no suit may be brought unless mediation has been tried," "restrict the bringing of suits," "cases cannot leave the village," "if you want to bring suit, you must be introduced by the district or village," and treating the reconciliation agreement as a judgment and forcing the parties to carry it out.[19]

It admitted that some committees had been ineffective, but argued that this was "mainly because local people's courts and governments were deficient in providing them with leadership. One certainly cannot, because of this, completely deny the role of the people's mediation committees."[20] The virtues of the committees were appreciated by the inhabitants, the editorial claimed, for in places where the committees had been formally abolished they nevertheless continued to function, and in some instances the populace persuaded the cadres to restore the formal status of the committees. According to the *Jen min jih pao* the Provisional Rules "more concretely defined the nature, tasks, scope of jurisdiction, and the organizational and operating principles of people's mediation committees, thus providing the committees with a clear and definite basis for conducting their work."[21] This, it implied, would put an end to the difficulties that had plagued the committees.

How much guidance, then, did the Provisional Rules actually provide? And how different were they from regulations that the party had enacted a decade earlier to meet the needs of a rural population?

## Goals, Organization, and the Selection of Committees

The Provisional Rules began by stating that people's mediation committees were being established for the purposes of "promptly resolving disputes among the people, strengthening the people's patriotic observ-

ance of the law, and promoting the internal unity of the people in order
to benefit production by the people and construction by the state."[22]
The authoritative interpretation supplied by the *Jen min jih pao* editorial gave the reasoning that underlay this brief statement.[23] Although
the various social reform movements led by the party had enhanced the
people's political consciousness and law-abiding nature and had thereby
reduced the number of disputes among the masses in comparison with
pre-Liberation days, the masses believed that under the new regime the
government and courts belonged to them, and thus they did not hesitate
to burden these institutions whenever disputes arose. Therefore "the
number of cases received by basic-level governments and courts has risen
year-by-year." Failure to resolve these disputes promptly and correctly
would adversely affect public order and production. Yet neither in the
cities nor in the countryside could the government and the courts handle
the volume of disputes. If they did attempt to do so, the *Jen min jih pao*
went on, government officials would "be unable to concentrate their
strength on leading the people in the various kinds of production and
construction, and basic-level courts will be unable to concentrate their
strength on dealing with major cases." Moreover, even if administrative
and legal personnel could devote all their time to mediating disputes,
this would "pile up cases as before and thus cause the masses to be dissatisfied." Furthermore, resort to official agencies for the resolution of
disputes would cost the masses and the state "an incalculable loss in
money and production time." The solution to the problem was to adopt
"an effective organizational form and work method" for handling disputes among the masses, and experience had demonstrated the excellence of the mediation committees, whose members would be familiar
with local conditions and could quickly and conveniently settle disputes.
This would enable both the masses and the officials to devote their energies to more productive pursuits. The committees would also have two
other virtues that were more than incidental: they would allow the
masses to increase their participation in the governing of China, and
they would constitute powerful instruments for indoctrinating the
masses in the revolutionary laws and values of the regime.

Although Article 4 of the Provisional Rules provided that in the countryside, the administrative village was generally to be the unit of operation for each committee, it was vaguer concerning the cities. There a
committee might serve either "the area under the jurisdiction of a public
security station or the street." Since a public security station in a city
might police an area containing twenty to thirty thousand people
whereas a street might have fewer than one-tenth that number, the

choice of unit of operation was obviously likely to affect the magnitude of the committee's tasks. Yet the Provisional Rules offered no criteria for determining how the choice was to be made. According to Article 4, each committee was to be composed of between three and eleven members, although nothing was said about the basis on which the exact number was to be fixed; presumably it was to vary with the size, the population, and the volume of disputes of the unit of operation.

In providing for the selection of committee members by indirect election, Article 5, like the preceding article, was less precise with respect to the cities than with respect to the countryside. In the cities, members were to be elected "by representatives of the residents, under the direction of the basic-level people's government." In the countryside they were to be elected by the people's congress of the administrative village. In both cases there was to be an annual election, members were permitted to be reelected, and the committee chairman and the one or two vice-chairmen were to be chosen by and from committee members. Article 5 made no urban-rural distinction in giving criteria for choosing committee members; it simply conferred eligibility on "all those among the people whose political appearance is clear and who are impartial, linked with the masses, and enthusiastic about mediation work." It authorized the electing institution to recall and replace any committee members who "violate the law, are derelict in their duty, or are unfit to discharge their duty."

If we compare these provisions for the organization and selection of citizen mediators with the regulations of the Shen-Kan-Ning and Chin-Ch'a-Chi areas and the Nationalist government, we find that they resemble more the Nationalist regulations than the early Communist ones. Although early legislation regularizing the government of the Chin-Ch'a-Chi area had provided for mass mediation committees that were to be elected by village assemblies,[24] the mediation regulation adopted in 1942 abolished these committees and assigned mediation to each village government's committee on civil administration. The village government was authorized to invite fair-minded persons and cadres from its village and other villages to assist it, and government and mass organization cadres from higher levels could also take part "on their own initiative or upon invitation." But the "rights and responsibilities" relating to mediation were those of the village government.[25] Because this system apparently overburdened village officials and failed to inspire the confidence of the disputants, in 1944 a new plan sought to relieve the government of operational responsibilities for mediation as much as possible and to give it more of a supervisory role. Actual mediation was ordinarily to be carried on by mediators who were to be selected not by the government but by the parties themselves.[26] The 1943 Shen-Kan-Ning regulations also contemplated that mediation would normally be conducted by nongovernmental personnel who were convened on an ad hoc basis. The parties themselves were authorized to invite neighbors, friends, relatives, or representatives of a mass organization to evaluate the dispute and suggest an appropriate method of settlement. If this proved unsuccessful, they could apply for mediation by government agencies that could, "when necessary," invite "fair-minded gentry" from local mass organizations to help with the mediation on an ad hoc basis.[27] Nationalist law, by contrast, provided for permanent mediation committees composed exclusively of "fair and upright persons" from the community who would be elected by the local assembly.[28] With respect to selection of committee members, the only significant difference between Nationalist law and the 1954 Communist rules was that the Nationalists prescribed that members had to "possess a knowledge of law" as well as the confidence of the people, whereas the Communists emphasized political purity and links with the masses.[29]

### Training, Time Commitment, and Compensation

To use committees of citizens for mediation raises questions about whether committee members should receive training for their task, should serve on a full-time basis, and should receive compensation for their services. The 1954 rules were vague on all these matters. Their only references to training simply required the committees to "conduct their work under the guidance of basic level people's governments and courts" (Article 2), and called upon those agencies to "strengthen their guidance and supervision over mediation committees and also help them in their work" (Article 10). Thus, the extent to which Communist mediators were to remain untutored amateurs—politically reliable but legally unsophisticated—was unclear. The only reference in the Provisional Rules to the time commitment of members was in Article 8: committees "shall conduct their work during periods of production leisure." It is uncertain whether this merely meant that committee members were not to disrupt the production activities of the masses or whether it also meant that committee duties were not to take members away from their own production obligations. The second meaning was probably intended, but even this interpretation would not exclude the possibility that unemployed members might serve full-time.

Although Article 7 prohibited mediators from "corruptly accepting bribes" as well as practicing favoritism and other abuses, the question of legitimate compensation was left open; Nationalist legislation specifically answered this question by providing that mediators were to serve without pay and were to be prohibited from collecting compensation from the parties or levying other charges except for expenses incurred in carrying out inspections at the request of the parties.[30] It was probably well understood, especially in the light of previous Communist practice, that members of "mass mediation organizations" were not to receive compensation unless this was specifically prescribed. Not long after the rules were promulgated, the party's legislative draftsmen demonstrated their ability to authorize "subsistence allowances" for members of related mass organizations, the city residents' committees,[31] so it was unlikely that the failure of the Provisional Rules to mention compensation was inadvertent. Similarly, although the rules were also silent about how miscellaneous expenses of mediation committees were to be met, the problem of expenses of city residents' committees was explicitly dealt with in the legislation that established them.[32] This legislation integrated with mediation organization into the residents' committee structure and thus provided subsistence allowances for mediators who were members of the parent residents' committee. It also assigned the burden of other mediation expenses to the residents' committees. To the extent that this scheme failed to provide subsistence for mediation committee members, it necessarily excluded persons who had to support themselves from serving in more than a part-time capacity, and it enhanced the likelihood that housewives and retired people would play important roles.

## Scope of Jurisdiction

Despite the importance of the scope of jurisdiction of the committees for the administration of justice, the rules were also quite vague about this question. According to Article 3, the committees were to mediate "ordinary civil disputes among the people." This formulation differed from that found both in Shen-Kan-Ning, which like Nationalist law authorized mediation in all civil disputes,[33] and in Chin-Ch'a-Chi, which authorized mediation in civil disputes over obligations, rights over things, family relationships, and succession.[34] Apparently the phraseology of Article 3 sought to indicate that civil disputes between a state entity and a collective entity or between a state or collective entity and individuals were not within the jurisdiction of the mediation committees, although the term "among the people" could even be read more narrowly to suggest that disputes involving members of one of the disfavored "enemy" classes, such as landlords and rich peasants, might also not be appropriate work for the committees. The modifier "ordinary," a typically broad Communist legal term, seems to have been inserted to make clear that the parties to important, complex, or politically sensitive disputes were not to resort to such extrajudicial mediation.[35]

Article 3 also provided for mediation of "minor criminal cases." Again, the choice of words, though imprecise, was hardly casual. Since criminal offenses challenge public order and sometimes even the survival of the state, to draw the line between offenses that the state can safely leave to the handling of unofficial or semiofficial local groups and offenses sufficiently important to require handling by state agencies has been a problem in all modern societies, in practice if not in theory. Plainly, every government has an overriding interest in punishing certain offenders regardless of the wishes of the victim or the local group. This problem has been explicitly recognized in Chinese legislation at least as far back as A.D. 1291, and traditional statutory prescriptions have varied over the centuries.[36] In the twentieth century the anti-litigation legislation of warlord Yen Hsi-shan, for example, authorized extrajudicial mediation of all but homicide cases.[37] The Nationalist regime took a much more restrictive view of which criminal cases were appropriate for mediation, although it experimented a good deal to try to find a suitable formulation. Pre-1949 Nationalist regulations prohibited mediation in all criminal cases except specified offenses, such as certain crimes involving public morals, family relations, personal safety, and property.[38]

Ma Hsi-wu, a Chinese Communist judge who attained prominence in the Yenan period, claimed that the Nationalists did not enforce this prohibition but allowed the wealthy and powerful to evade criminal prosecution by resorting to mediation even in murder cases and in cases where women and children had been seriously harmed; according to Ma, by spending some money an offender was able to persuade the victim or his relatives not to pursue the case.[39] However, despite this belief that Nationalist practice was unfair and contrary to the interests of the community, the Communists in Chin-Ch'a-Chi adopted the same approach as the Nationalists, although the offenses that were noted in Article 5 as appropriate for mediation differed in some respects from those on the Nationalist list. Article 2 of the Shen-Kan-Ning regulation, on the other hand, took a somewhat more expansive approach, authorizing mediation in all criminal cases except for 23 categories of offenses.

That Communist draftsmen became dissatisfied both with prohibiting mediation except for specified offenses and with authorizing mediation except for specified offenses was suggested by the more general formulation of the February 1949 regulation of the North China People's Government; it authorized mediation "in ordinary, minor criminal cases, but not in those cases where public order of state and society has been harmed or where there has been relatively serious harm to rights and interests of individuals."[40] By 1954, experience had apparently convinced the Communists of the futility or undesirability of attempting even to that extent to spell out the scope of the mediation committee's criminal jurisdiction.[41]

## Relationships Between Mediation and Litigation

The question of whether mediation was to be a prerequisite to litigation, like the question of the scope of the mediation committee's jurisdiction, involved the fundamental problem of the allocation of competence in the governmental system in a rural or an urban setting. To the extent that extrajudicial mediation was made a prerequisite to litigation, it obviously increased the importance of the role of the mediation committees, lessened the workload of the courts, and required disputants to look in the first instance to their fellow citizens rather than to the courts for a remedy. Although legislation during the Mongol dynasty (1279–1368) and an imperial edict issued early in the Ming dynasty (1368–1644) made extrajudicial mediation a prerequisite to litigation in various categories of relatively unimportant cases, neither the Ming code nor that of the Manchu dynasty (1644–1912) contained such a provision.[42] Nevertheless, during the nineteenth century such traditional local groups as clans and guilds continued to adopt and enforce rules requiring their members to exhaust group conflict resolution procedures before taking their dispute to the government magistrate, and the magistrates themselves often reinforced this practice by sending the disputants back to their groups if they had not exhausted group procedures. Similarly, despite the fact that both Yen Hsi-shan's anti-litigation regulation and Nationalist law prohibited mediation committees and judges from denying parties direct access to the courts,[43] social practice continued to deviate substantially from these norms.[44]

Pre-1949 Communist legislation was ambivalent about whether there was to be free access to the courts or whether preliminary resort to extrajudicial mediation was to be required. The Act for the Protection of Human Rights and Property Rights, which was promulgated in Shen-Kan-Ning in 1942 as part of the Communist program to promote "new democracy" and legality, guaranteed disputants complete freedom to vindicate their rights in the courts without prior mediation.[45] Yet the mediation regulation enacted in Shen-Kan-Ning shortly thereafter ambiguously stated in Article 2 that "Mediation should be carried out in all disputes in civil cases." Although Ma Hsi-wu has written that this provision was not intended to restrict direct access to the courts, many cadres read it literally and had to be corrected.[46] Article 2 of the 1942 Chin-Ch'a-Chi regulation plainly prescribed that mediation was to be a voluntary matter in all cases, but subsequent Chin-Ch'a-Chi legislation required parties to try mediation prior to litigation in most civil cases and in various types of minor criminal cases.[47]

The 1954 rules, by comparison, provided that mediation was not to be compulsory in any case. Article 6(2) stated that "Agreement of both parties must be obtained and mediation may not be coerced." From the context it is clear that this language meant not only that parties who have entered into mediation may not be coerced into making an agreement, but also that parties may not be coerced to enter into mediation and may bypass it. The *Jen min jih pao* editorial that elucidated the meaning of the rules confirmed this.[48] Furthermore, Article 6(3) stated: "It must be understood that mediation is not a procedure to which resort is necessary in order to bring suit. The parties may not be prevented from bringing suit in the people's court on the ground that they did not resort to mediation or that mediation was unsuccessful."

The rules were silent, however, about whether resort to litigation was a bar to mediation, despite the fact that pre-1949 Communist legislation had devoted some attention to the problem. The Shen-Kan-Ning regulation (Article 6) stated: "Even if the matter is already under the jurisdiction of the legal organs, mediation . . . may be carried out, whether the matter is being investigated, tried, appealed, or executed." Moreover, in addition to authorizing the courts themselves to undertake mediation, it also permitted them (in Article 11) to refer cases to extrajudicial mediation. It failed to make clear, however, whether such a reference— which would have been tantamount to compulsory mediation if made without the consent of the parties—required their consent. Article 4 of the Chin-Ch'a-Chi regulations provided for mediation "at any time," even though litigation was pending, and Article 6 also authorized reference to extrajudicial mediation in civil litigation, in certain minor criminal cases, and in certain violations of police regulations tried by the police, but only with the consent of the parties and only "before court judgments and police decisions are made."

## The Conduct of Mediation

The Provisional Rules offered little guidance about how mediation was to be conducted. Article 6(1) constituted a general admonition that "mediation must be conducted in compliance with the policies, laws, and decrees of the people's government." There were, to be sure, some specific constraints placed upon mediators in addition to the prohibitions against coercing the parties and obstructing their access to the courts contained in Article 6(2) and (3). As previously mentioned, Article 7 prohibited mediators from "corruptly accepting bribes or practicing favoritism and other abuses," and it also prohibited "punishing the parties or taking them into custody" and "engaging in any oppressive or retaliatory conduct against the parties." But positive instruction on the techniques and procedures of mediation was minimal. Apart from its ambiguous command to conduct work during periods of production leisure, Article 8 merely enjoined mediation committees to "attentively listen to the opinions of the parties . . . penetratingly investigate, study, and clarify the circumstances of the case . . . and conduct mediation with a friendly and patient attitude and in a reasoning manner." And Article 3 simply authorized committees, in the course of mediation, "to conduct propaganda-education concerning policies, laws, and decrees."

Nothing was said, for example, about whether the parties to a dispute were to be heard together or separately; whether mediators were permitted to take the initiative in entering a dispute rather than to wait for a request by the parties; or whether the mediators were to carry out their work in a designated place. Nor did the rules take account of the special circumstances of conducting mediation in cities rather than in rural areas, in different regions of the country, or among minority nationalities. In general these matters were also not mentioned in the pre-1949 Communist and Nationalist regulations, although they had dealt with a number of other aspects of mediation that were ignored by the rules.[49]

The 1943 Nationalist mediation law had covered certain problems not mentioned by any Communist legislation. Article 16, for example, provided that, when necessary, the victim of a crime or his representative could request local government officials to inspect his wounds and investigate other physical circumstances pertaining to the crime in order to make a record of evidence that might not otherwise continue to be available. Article 14 required a member of a mediation committee to withdraw from handling a dispute in which he or one of his household family members was involved, in order to guarantee the parties an unbiased hearing, and it also made clear that mediation was not to be conducted by a single mediator but by a majority of the committee. Article 12 specified that the parties might apply for mediation either orally or in writing, stating their names, sexes, ages, addresses, and a summary of the facts; the local government was to forward this information in written form to the mediation committee.

The 1942 Chin-Ch'a-Chi regulation, which despite a primitive environment and wartime conditions represents the most sophisticated mediation effort of Communist draftsmen, set forth several provisional measures that could be taken in mediating disputes that had not yet been taken to court. Article 19 provided that at any time prior to the conclusion of mediation in a dispute over the infliction of bodily injuries, the party who had inflicted the injuries could agree to "assume necessary medical responsibilities," without prejudicing the outcome with respect to other aspects of the settlement. An equally interesting provision in Article 20 stated that in civil disputes involving the maintenance of relatives, if the party seeking mediation were unable to support himself, the other party would be required to offer him the necessities of life during the period of mediation. And a party to a civil dispute over obligations or rights over things was authorized in Article 21 to ask the local court to order a provisional attachment or disposition of another party's property pending the conclusion of mediation, thereby preventing the other party from frustrating the mediation process by disposing of assets before a settlement was reached.

The Chin-Ch'a-Chi regulation also made an effort to deal with the question of representation of the parties. In Article 8 it authorized other persons to act on their behalf during mediation, sparing them the inconvenience or embarrassment of dealing directly with the mediators or each other, but it required the parties to appear and express their agreement when a settlement was reached.

Both Chin-Ch'a-Chi and pre-1949 Nationalist law took up the problem of devising appropriate institutional means for settling disputes between persons from different areas, a problem that had plagued traditional Chinese society.[50] The Chin-Ch'a-Chi regulation prescribed in Article 7 that mediation of both civil and criminal disputes should be conducted by the mediation unit operating in the area where the defendant resided, thereby sparing him the pressures of possibly biased mediators. The Nationalist regulation, however, permitted the parties to agree to mediation in either area; if they could not agree on an appropriate committee, Article 6 specified that any mediation of civil disputes was to take place where the defendant resided, but that criminal matters were to be mediated where the crime was committed.

Another point neglected by the 1954 rules but not by pre-1949 regulations was whether mediation should be subject to any time limitation. The Chin-Ch'a-Chi regulation stated that the period for mediating a dispute that had not yet been taken to court or to a public security bureau could not exceed seven days; a time limit for terminating the mediation of a dispute that had already been taken to one of the legal organs was not set; but Article 10 provided that whenever a mediation period prescribed by one of the legal organs had ended or the trial date had arrived, a single five-day extension of the time for mediation might be granted, presumably by the legal organ. The Nationalist regulation, in contrast, did not reflect any concern about promptly ending mediation but sought instead to assure a prompt beginning. It required mediation to get under way in civil disputes within ten days of receipt by the committee of the parties' application and in criminal disputes within a five-day period; at the request of the parties, a ten-day extension was made permissible in civil disputes.[51] Both of these approaches reflected a desire to prevent either the mediators or one of the parties from delaying resolution of the dispute.

Apart from the previously mentioned prohibition of punishment, detention, or retaliation against the parties, the Provisional Rules did not specifically limit the remedies that mediation committees might approve as a basis for settling disputes. Yet the 1943 Nationalist regulation had provided in Article 18 that, except for compensation for loss suffered by a party to either a criminal or a civil dispute, mediation committees were to permit no property or physical sanctions to be imposed. And the Shen-Kan-Ning regulation had offered more comprehensive guidance on remedies. It stated that reconciliations could be based on a gesture of regret, an oral apology, or a written admission of fault. Compensation for damages and the payment of money for support were also authorized, as were "other customary forms for settling disputes, but not those that violate good customs or involve superstition." To make it clear that the mediators were not rigidly circumscribed in their discretion, Article 3 added that the various remedies might be resorted to alone or in combination and that in simple disputes where the parties did not insist on any specific terms as a basis for settlement the mediators were not to be limited to these remedies.

## Compliance

The statement in Article 6(1) of the rules that mediation had to be "conducted in compliance with the policies, laws, and decrees of the people's government," was a broad enough requirement to include substantive rules of law as well as informal procedures and customary remedies, an approach similar to that in Article 14 of the Chin-Ch'a-Chi regulation, which stated "If the terms of the settlement are in violation of the government's prohibitions, are against good morals, or involve criminal conduct, it shall be void from the start." Although existing "policies, laws, and decrees of the people's government" were grossly inadequate in prescribing detailed norms for China's citizens, they did regulate many aspects of life. The significance of requiring that all extrajudicial settlements be reached within the confines of official norms should not be underestimated. As the *Jen min jih pao* emphasized in hailing the advent of the rules, no "unprincipled mediation" was to be permitted, compromises based on "the erroneous views of the parties" were banned, and mediators were to use "appropriate criticism—education" so that reconciliations were based on official principles.[52] Especially in view of the Chinese people's traditional preference for mediation over litigation, this subjection of mediation to official principles represented an important step toward forcing traditional social practice to conform to the norms of the revolutionary regime.

Of course, it is one thing for the state to declare that settlements contradicting official norms are illegitimate, but it is quite another to make this declaration effective. The rules reflected an awareness of this enforcement problem, for as we have seen, they provided for the selection of mediators who would be responsive to government norms and the replacement of those who failed to adhere to them (Article 5), and they called upon basic level people's governments and courts to "strengthen their guidance and supervision over mediation committees and also help them in their work" (Article 10).[53]

The most thorough means of assuring compliance with prevailing norms of substance and procedure clearly would be to officially review every mediation committee's handling of every dispute, whether or not a reconciliation was achieved. The rules did not make clear, however, whether so burdensome a process of review was contemplated. What they did make clear was that the courts rather than the local government agencies were charged with principal responsibility for undertaking whatever review there was to be. Article 9 stated: "If, in mediating cases, mediation committees violate policies, laws, or decrees, the people's court shall correct or annul the action." But the rules failed to indicate how the people's court was to learn about a mediation committee's violation. Was a court representative to review the handling of every dispute? Of every reconciliation? Of only those reconciliations brought to the court's attention by one or both parties or the mediation committee?[54]

The rules did not require notification to the courts or any other government agency of the outcome of mediation. Article 8 merely stated that "successful mediation of a case may be registered, and, when necessary, the parties may be given a certificate of mediation." This left a number of questions unanswered. In what circumstances was registration appropriate, and where was registration to take place? In what circumstances was it "necessary" to issue a mediation certificate, and what was to be the content of the certificate? Furthermore, what was the legal significance of registering a successful mediation, of issuing a mediation certificate and, indeed, of settling a dispute through mediation with or without registration and certification? These questions had a vital bearing both on the efficacy of official review of mediation and on the rights of the parties. Yet nothing was said about them.[55]

As in so many other instances, the silence of the rules cannot be attributed to oversight, for the pre-1949 legislation had sought to deal with many of these matters. The 1943 Nationalist law, for example, provided an opportunity for official review of every dispute handled by a mediation committee and placed primary responsibility for this review not with the courts but with the local government. In instances when mediation was successful, in addition to requiring the committee to issue a certificate to the parties as proof of the reconciliation (Article 5), the Nationalist regulation in Article 15 required the committee to send the local government office a report listing the names, sexes, ages, and addresses of the parties, a summary of the facts, and the date of reconciliation; the local government office was in turn to send copies of the report to the county government and to the competent court for their records. Even in instances when mediation proved unsuccessful, a similar report explaining why mediation had failed was to be filed. The Nationalist regulation's only explicit reference to judicial review concerned the disposition of cases that were already before the court at the time that an extrajudicial settlement was attained: Article 3(1) provided that in civil cases an application had to be made requesting the court to dismiss the litigation, and Article 4 stipulated that in criminal matters the complainant had to withdraw his complaint. Nothing was said about whether the court was to scrutinize the legality of the reconciliation on these occasions, and, if so, how extensive its review was to be. Although the regulation was silent on this point, full opportunity for judicial review presumably would be presented if a party brought suit either to enforce the agreement or to seek a declaration of its validity; there was no reason to believe that an extrajudicial reconciliation was any less a contract than any other agreement.

The Shen-Kan-Ning regulation was less comprehensive than Nationalist law with respect to the official review of mediation, probably because of the role it assigned to local government personnel in the actual mediation process. Article 8 of the Shen-Kan-Ning regulation required mediators to give the parties to a successful mediation a certificate as evidence of their reconciliation. According to Article 9, the certificate was to outline each party's version of the facts of the dispute, describe the basis on which a settlement had been achieved, state that no coercion had been used and that the agreement was voluntary, contain the full names and the signatures, seals or fingerprints of the parties, the mediators, and the scribe who drew up the documents, and list the date and place of reconciliation. However, the regulation made no provision for official scrutiny of the validity of the reconciliation certificate except with respect to disputes that were already being processed by one of the legal organs (presumably either the procurator or the court or their equivalents). In such disputes the mediators were instructed in Article 8 to send a copy of the certificate to the pertinent legal organ and to request dismissal of the cases. The legal organ was instructed immediately to examine the certificate, but the scope of its review was limited to the single question of whether the dispute was one that was properly subject to extrajudicial mediation. If it was not, the reconciliation agreement was to be quashed. If the dispute was properly subject to mediation, according to Article 10, the case was to be dismissed. Like Nationalist law, the Shen-Kan-Ning regulation appeared to leave open by implication the possibility of full judicial review if a party subsequently sought to bring suit over the agreement.

The Chin-Ch'a-Chi regulation presented the draftsmen of the 1954 rules with a different model for judicial review of extrajudicial reconciliation. Like both the Nationalist and the Shen-Kan-Ning regulations, it required the issuance of a certificate when mediation was successful (Article 11), and if the dispute had already gone to litigation, its Article 13 provided for submitting the reconciliation data to the legal organ that possessed the file, in order to terminate the litigation. Like Nationalist law also, it neglected to state what the scope of the legal organ's review was to be in such cases. But, unlike both its Nationalist and Shen-Kan-Ning counterparts, the Chin-Ch'a-Chi regulation did not leave open the possibility that full judicial review might be obtained by a party who subsequently decided to sue on the agreement. It specifically endowed the out-of-court reconciliation certificate with "the same effect as the record of a compromise made in the course of a judicial trial," and it authorized the parties to request compulsory execution of its terms "unless the certificate is invalidated through examination."[56] Unfortunately, it failed to specify what was to be the scope of the examination that would determine the validity of the certificate. The regulation in its Article 15 did authorize a party who claimed that the reconciliation had been based on fraud or duress (within six months from the time of discovery of the fraud or escape from the duress) to request that the certificate be quashed. But whether a party against whom compulsory execution was being sought might attempt to show that the agreement was void because its terms violated government prohibitions, good morals, or the criminal law was uncertain though likely.[57] It was less likely that other grounds, such as a violation of prescribed mediation procedures, could be subject to review in execution proceedings. That the Chin-Ch'a-Chi draftsmen intended to treat out-of-court settlement not as a mere contract but as the equivalent of a court judgment was made plain by the provision that, after an out-of-court settlement had been reached, no litigation on the matter was to be allowed.[58] Apparently the reconciliation certificate was invested with such authority because, in addition to being approved by the parties and the mediators, it was also required to bear the official seal of the village administration, a requirement that was probably thought to guarantee substantial official review of the settlement.[59]

## Other Agents of Dispute Resolution

Apart from calling on basic level people's governments as well as courts to strengthen their guidance and supervision over mediation committees, the Provisional Rules did not mention whether any other agencies were to play a supervisory role. Following the legislation promulgated at the end of 1954, urban street offices and residents' committees appear to have taken over the local government's direct responsibility for supervising mediation committees.[60] Although frequently other institutions in the cities, especially the public security stations, also tended to exercise a kind of de facto review over the work of mediation committee members, there was no reference to this in the rules. Nor was there any reference to the role of the Communist party. Moreover, despite the fact that the Shen-Kan-Ning regulation had been drafted to govern all types of mediation activity—by friends, relatives, neighbors, mass organizations and courts, as well as by government cadres—the rules purported to embrace only the activities of one institution, the mediation committees. Nothing was said about the mediation efforts of policemen, judges, other officials, residents' committee leaders, party or youth league members, and the staffs of unions and women's organizations. Undoubtedly the silence of the rules left the mediation committees free to act even while other agencies were engaged in mediating the same dispute, just as these agencies might seek to resolve a dispute that was already before a mediation committee. It was far from clear, however, to what extent the mediation efforts of these other agencies were to be subject to the procedural and substantive prescriptions embodied in the rules.

*Conclusion*

Does this study vindicate the claim of the *Jen min jih pao* that the rules provided people's mediation committees with "a clear and definite basis for conducting their work"? The rules did provide a basis for meeting certain problems, such as how the committees were to be organized and how their members were to be selected, whether resort to mediation was a prerequisite to litigation, and whether disputes were to be settled in accordance with substantive law and policy. By and large, however, the rules offered little guidance on a surprising number of important and complex questions. They were either vague or silent about the training and time commitment of committee members, the scope of committee jurisdiction, and many aspects of the mediation process. And they shed little light on the means of reviewing the work of the committees and on the relation of the committees to other agents of dispute resolution.

Furthermore, with two minor exceptions, the rules failed to reflect the enormous differences between rural and urban conditions in China. The two exceptions, the provisions for selecting the unit of operation and the membership of urban mediation committees, were somewhat more imprecise than the provisions governing the same tasks in the countryside. Otherwise the rules made no urban-rural distinctions. They constituted a brief, vague, loosely structured effort to provide only the broadest outline for the nationwide organization of mediation committees.

One should not infer from the brevity, imprecision and omissions of the rules that in 1954 the Chinese Communist Party lacked the legal skills required to draft legislation capable of providing greater guidance. As a comparison with pre-1949 Chinese mediation legislation makes clear, not only the Nationalist efforts but also those of Communist draftsmen in Shen-Kan-Ning and especially in Chin-Ch'a-Chi were far more sophisticated than the Provisional Rules. Indeed, the Communist regulations of the early 1940's dealt with legal problems that the Nationalists had overlooked, even though during that period Communist control was confined to relatively primitive rural areas. How then can we account for the fact that the rules, instead of reflecting the more complex conditions that the Communists encountered after taking over the cities of China, emerged as what would be regarded from a Western point of view as a rather simplistic, inadequate document? The answer is probably rooted in the evolving Chinese Communist view of the legislative process.

The past decade—from the Great Leap Forward to the Great Proletarian Cultural Revolution—has witnessed a dramatic decline in China's legislative output and a concomitant lack of interest in legislation on the part of China's leadership. During Communist China's first decade, however, and particularly after the inauguration in 1953 of the period of "large-scale and planned economic construction," many Chinese leaders, including some who have recently fallen from power such as Liu Shao-ch'i and P'eng Chen, recognized the importance of developing comprehensive codes of law.[61] But they were careful to state that the process of developing "strong and complete" sets of laws would have to be a slow one. According to this view, the way to formulate legislative change is to begin by introducing the innovation on an experimental basis in a number of areas; as P'eng Chen put it, "by reporting and synthesizing the typical experience of various places, systems and legal procedures will be gradually formed and then gradually developed from simplicity into complexity, from general rules into detailed rules, from separate laws and regulations into a complete set of criminal and civil law."[62] This process of gradual development was described by one of the few Chinese legal treatises:

Preliminary drafts of many of our country's important laws and decrees, including criminal laws and decrees, were presented by the state's leadership nucleus, the Chinese Communist Party, after examination and study of the actual work, summarizing of the people's experience in struggles, and concentration of their revolutionary will. Afterwards, the party sought opinions from people in various walks of life that gradually were incorporated into the drafts. After discussion and revision by state organs, some of these, still in draft form, were transmitted to local state organs and people's organizations down to the county and administrative village levels, and the masses were roused to conduct discussions. Other drafts were put into effect experimentally for a given period; they then became formal laws and decrees after further scrutiny and passage by legislative organs of the state.[63]

The Provisional Rules represented an intermediate step in this process. They were, after all, merely "general rules" (*t'ung tse*) that were prescribed by the principal executive agency of the era, the Government Administration Council, and not a "law" (*fa*) enacted by the then official legislator, the Central People's Government Council. And they were specifically entitled "provisional." In these circumstances it is perhaps not surprising that the rules were as incomplete as they were.

Undoubtedly the rules were also influenced by a related aspect of the Chinese attitude toward legislation. Even the relatively few "laws" that were officially promulgated during the first decade of the People's Republic were largely general and incomplete, reflecting the belief of some

Chinese leaders, including Chairman Mao, that law should never be so detailed as to "bind the hands and feet of the masses," a euphemism for constricting the party's freedom of action.[64] This lack of a strict set of laws also gave full play to the leadership's penchant for virtually ceaseless tinkering with institutions, a penchant that was subsequently indulged with respect to mediation.[65] Moreover, in a country as vast, diverse, and changing as China, there are obvious advantages not only for the ruling elite but also for the society as a whole in the enactment of laws that are flexible enough to permit innovation and a wide variety of local implementation. The inadequacies of national legislation in providing guidance for the hundreds of thousands of Chinese mediators has been compensated for by the promulgation of norms by lower-level units such as city governments, by mediation committees themselves, and by less formal means such as newspaper editorials, pamphlets, radio broadcasts, meetings, and personal instruction.[66] All these ways of communicating norms are much more readily adaptable to changing conditions than is national legislation.

Although the Provisional Rules provided relatively slight guidance to Chinese mediators, the foregoing discussion of their content and background shows the complexity of both the problems and the earlier Communist solutions to them. Simple as the 1954 rules were, this was how urban mediation as well as rural mediation was to be organized. That the Chinese Communists have made little or no distinction between rural and urban problems in their legal guidelines is interesting in itself. Unfortunately, no research has been done on the extent or kind of differences there were in actual administration between city and rural mediation. But, as previously emphasized, the very simplicity of the 1954 rules allowed for flexibility in interpretation and application according to specific local conditions. Other papers in this volume will discuss how such flexibility contributed to the growth of local autonomy in Chinese cities.

# The Public Security Bureau and Political-Legal Work in Hui-yang, 1952–64

VICTOR H. LI

This chapter is part of a larger study of the political-legal system in Hui-yang *hsien* (county).[1] It focuses on the public security system, although there is also some discussion of other organs such as the court and the procuracy. Particular attention is paid to the organization, scope of activities, and work methods of the public security apparatus, the relation of this organ to the party, and the relation of lower- and upper-level cadres within the public security system itself. Although some reference is made to public security at the city level in Hui-chou and in the rural areas, this chapter is concerned primarily with the hsien-level public security bureau. By studying the personnel of this bureau, I try to identify the types of persons who enter public security work, their career patterns, and the principal channels of vertical mobility.

The pages that follow cover the period between the fall of 1952 and the summer of 1964 with greater emphasis on the later years. The beginning date is chosen because the initial transition and land reform present very different problems and can be treated separately. In addition, this period marks the end of the three-anti and five-anti campaigns, the beginning of efforts to reorganize and strengthen the public security system, the beginning of the land reform reinvestigation campaign, and the arrival of the "southbound" cadres.

The study ends in 1964 partly because the division of Hui-yang into two hsien, Hui-yang and Hui-tung, and the conversion of Hui-chou from a *chen* to a *shih* (a municipality, and hence taken out of the jurisdiction of the hsien) provide a clear and reasonable line of demarcation. More important, and realistically, my data begins to become ambiguous and sketchy at this point.

Hui-yang hsien is located approximately one hundred miles north of
the China–Hong Kong border in Kwangtung Province. It is bounded by
Pao-an hsien and Ta-ya Bay on the south, Tung-huan hsien on the west,
Hui-tung hsien on the east, and the East River on the north.[2] This area
is basically agricultural, producing sugar cane, peanuts, and fruit in
addition to the usual rice, vegetables, pigs, and poultry. There also is
some industry, mainly food processing plants and factories supplying
various agricultural needs.

The hsien has a population of roughly half a million. Sixty thousand
persons live in the hsien seat of Hui-chou, and the rest are scattered
throughout the hsien in ten towns and many villages. The majority of
the inhabitants are Hakka; there also is a large number of Punti, and a
small group of persons of Ch'ao-chou origin. A substantial portion of the
population appears to have some overseas Chinese connections.

Several rivers traverse Hui-yang, the most important of which is the
East River. These waterways make Hui-yang a major transportation link
for southern Kwangtung. They also, however, pose a constant flood
threat. Severe floods causing great damage have occurred almost every
year, and much local effort and resources are expended in water conservancy and control work. The city of Hui-chou is situated on the East
River along five lakes, including the famous West Lake. The West
River, a tributary of the East River, divides the city in half, forming
the Bridge West (or West of the Bridge) section and the Bridge East
(or East of the Bridge) section. This city is the administrative center
for the area. All hsien and city-level government and party organs are
headquartered here. A number of special district (*chuan ch'ü*) organs
are also located in Hui-chou, including the Party Area Committee
(*tang ti wei*), the Special District Office (*chuan ch'ü kung shu*), the Special District Public Security Section (*chuan ch'ü kung an ch'u*), and the
Intermediate Level Court. In addition, several contingents of the People's Liberation Army (PLA) are stationed on the edge of the city, and a
major military airfield is located at P'ing-t'an several miles to the east.

Hui-chou also is the commercial and cultural center for the hsien. It
contains two large markets where local products may be sold. The
People's Bank and other state trading organs and enterprises have
branches in the city. In Hui-chou there are several industrial establishments, the most important of which is a sugar refinery, and a number
of other smaller food processing plants, a cement plant, two printing
plants, several factories for the manufacture and repair of light machinery, and an electrical power generator. There also are a number of

schools, including an upper middle school and a nursing school, and several hospitals, clinics, and convalescent homes.

## The Public Security, the Procuracy, and the Court

As envisioned by the state constitution of 1954, political-legal work is divided among the public security system, the procuracy, and the court, and carried out within the framework of a system of checks and balances.[3] In administering the criminal process the public security bodies maintain order, apprehend criminals, and conduct investigations of criminal activity.[4] The findings then are handed over to the procuracy. The procuracy conducts an investigation of its own, and if it feels that the evidence is sufficient, files a complaint with the court.[5] During the trial, the procuracy acts as prosecutor; after judgment is rendered, it may, on behalf of the state or the accused, protest the decision to a higher court. In addition, the procuracy also has the duty "to see that the law is observed by persons working in (local state organs) and by all citizens," as well as "to see that the investigatory activities of investigation departments conform to the law" and that "the judicial process of people's courts conforms to the law."[6] After a complaint is filed with the court, a further preparatory investigation is carried out by a member of the judiciary. The entire matter is then fully reviewed at the trial. On the basis of all available information, the court, "administer(ing) justice independently, subject only to law," decides the guilt or innocence of the accused and fixes the penalty.[7]

It is quite clear that this theoretical model of the legal process never became fully operational in China, and was perhaps hardly implemented at all.[8] In Hui-yang, for example, the procuracy did almost nothing, and the court often was little more than a rubber stamp in criminal cases. Thus, in practice, the administration of the criminal process was handled almost entirely by public security apparatus without the active participation of the other two political-legal organs. The inactivity of the Hui-yang procuracy is fairly easy to demonstrate. Since its establishment in the latter part of 1955, the number of persons working there never exceeded five and dropped to as few as three.[9] A staff of this size cannot handle a great volume of work.

The procuracy plays a small role in investigating criminal cases and in deciding which ones will be brought to trial. As stated above, a case is not normally submitted to the procuracy until public security cadres have completed their investigations and have reviewed the findings several times. On receiving the case, the procuracy usually only casually rechecks the findings of the public security organs. Even more detrimental to the work of the procuracy is the power of public security officials to impose administrative (*hsing cheng*) sanctions on their own authority.[10] These can be very severe; for example, a person can be sentenced to "rehabilitation through labor"—a kind of forced labor—for a term of up to three years (and possibly six years, if after the first term the offender has not yet been "rehabilitated"). Through the use of such administrative sanctions, the public security organ, if it wishes, can dispose of all minor and doubtful cases without the participation of the procuracy or the court. Thus, it is possible that only the most serious and clear-cut cases ever reach the procuracy and the court. Where this occurs, there is little opportunity for the procuracy to dispute the findings of the public security officials or to exercise any form of prosecutorial discretion.

The decline of the Hui-yang procuracy, or perhaps more accurately, the failure of the procuracy to develop into a viable and important political-legal organ, can also be seen in the career patterns of the procurators. The first group of persons appointed procurators were cadres of relatively high status and ability, including a senior party official, two demobilized PLA officers, and a former public security station chief. After about a year, these persons were transferred out of procuratorial work and replaced by cadres of lesser status and experience. By 1964, the chief procurator was a former youth league worker, and his staff consisted of a demobilized PLA corporal, a former accountant in the hsien tax bureau, and a former accountant for the public security bureau who was not even a party member. As the quality of the personnel declined, so did the importance of this office.

The Hui-yang court did not fare much better than the procuracy. Since usually only straightforward criminal cases were submitted to the court, there was little possibility for disagreement over the facts or the law. Consequently, there was very little for the court to decide. It became less of a decision-making body and more of a forum where a case was publicized and the official imprimatur was placed on the findings of the public security. The Hui-yang court had particular problems with its personnel. Many of the members of the judiciary during the years immediately after Liberation were holdovers from the Nationalist regime. During the 1952 three-anti and five-anti campaigns, most of these men were accused of corruption and purged.[11] In addition, the first president of the court, who was concurrently deputy party secretary for the hsien, was removed in 1953 for being too lenient with landlords during land reform[12] and for allowing widespread corruption in his organization. The judges who took over after 1953 were unable to do much better. Of the 22 persons (forming about three-fourths of the total number) who were judges or assistant judges in the Hui-yang Basic Level Court between 1953 and 1964, seven were purged. One man who had been trained under the Nationalists was declared a rightist in 1957 for advocating judicial independence. Three were removed in 1960 for refusing to take part in agricultural labor. (These four men were college educated; I know of only one other person in the entire hsien political-legal apparatus who had a college-level education.) In addition, one man was removed in 1958 for submitting exaggerated reports, and another was arrested for raping his baby-sitter. Finally, even Yeh Chi-ming, who was elected president of the court in 1955, through the publicity of the election campaign was recognized by a member of the masses as a former Nationalist army officer.[13] Many of the other judges were not persons of high status, and five were not party members, an unusually high percentage for this level of government. Some judges were assigned to the court after demotion or as a punishment. Li Tun, the first public security bureau chief, was transferred out of public security work and made president of the court just prior to his removal by the "southbound" cadres in 1953. Wu Wei-kuang, a former chief of the secretariat of the public security bureau, was reprimanded and fined for improperly carrying out his work, and then was demoted to the position of assistant judge in the court. Similarly, Li Ta-ch'eng, the first chief of the Bridge East Public Security Station, was declared a corrupt element in 1952, and demoted to the level of assistant judge. The court was also used as a place to which senior officials could be "kicked upstairs." In 1964, the president, Ch'i Ch'i, and vice-president, Ku Po, were former senior public security cadres whose educational level and ability were too low for public security work. The court was a fashionable but harmless place to assign them.

## Organizational Structure of the Hui-yang Public Security Bureau

Details of the organizational structure of the public security bureau help explain the scope and quantity of public security work, and give an insight into how this organ regarded the relative importance of its various functions. Furthermore, through an examination of the organizational structure of the bureau, the places and offices where decisions were made and the methods used by higher-level cadres to control their subordinates can be identified.

Immediately after Liberation, a public security bureau patterned generally after the former police bureau of the Nationalists was established. A major reorganization took place in the winter of 1953, followed by

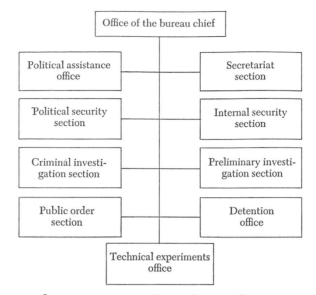

ORGANIZATION OF THE PUBLIC SECURITY BUREAU

several more changes over the next few years. The organizational structure and functional division of the bureau during the middle and late 1950's and the early 1960's is briefly described below.

*Office of the bureau chief.* In the early years, this office consisted of a chief and a deputy chief. As the size of the bureau grew, the number of deputies increased to between two and four. Normally, one deputy took care of the day-to-day operations of the bureau, and the others were in charge of the public security sector offices.[14] One deputy had the additional duty of acting as liaison to the other political-legal organs. Beginning in 1960, there was also one deputy in charge of political work within the bureau.

*Political assistance office (cheng chih hsieh li pan kung shih).* Until 1953, this office, manned by seven cadres,* was called the personnel section. It had the important job of maintaining files on the history and political attitudes of all the public security cadres. It also handled job assignments and transfers.

---

* The number of persons employed in each section is an approximation, given only to suggest the amount of work normally handled by that section. In practice, a number of persons were assigned concurrently to more than one section. Moreover, whenever a section needed help, additional persons were assigned to it on a temporary basis.

*Secretariat* (*mi shu ku*). This ten-cadre section was in charge of finances, statistical compilations, and paper work. It also served as the communications center for the bureau. Before the establishment of the procuracy in 1955, it had the additional function of acting as "prosecutor" in criminal trials.

*Political security section* (*cheng pao ku*). Also called the No. 1 Section, this section of twenty cadres was in charge of all cases involving foreign agents and spies, counterrevolutionary activity, and reactionary activity.* It was particularly busy during the early years, but after 1952 it handled only about a hundred cases a year. (1962 was an exception: the caseload doubled when the number of persons who were caught trying to escape to Hong Kong increased greatly.) Most of this section's cases involved attempted escapes to Hong Kong and rumormongering, although there were also several spectacular instances of capturing enemy agents. Before 1953, this section together with the internal security section was known as the investigation section (*tiao ch'a ku*).

*Internal security section* (*nei pao ku*). Also called the No. 2 Section, this eight-cadre section handled united-front work, including cases in which foreigners, overseas Chinese, and intellectuals were involved. It also dealt with cases where a member of the "five (or four) elements" or some other person already suspect had committed a second crime. Most of the work of this section appears supervisory rather than investigatory in nature.

*Criminal investigation section* (*hsing chen ku*). This section of ten cadres investigated the common crimes, including homicide, arson, rape, assault and battery, criminal negligence, and sale of narcotics. Thefts of more than 15 yüan and smuggling or tax evasion over 70 yüan constituted the large majority of the cases, although during the early years corruption was also an important item. The total caseload varied greatly during the years. Before 1953, this section handled well over a thousand cases a year; this dropped to less than five hundred for each of the years from 1954 to 1960. With the bad economic conditions of the early 1960's, the number of thefts rose sharply, dropping again in 1963 to the level of the

---

* The political security, internal security, criminal investigation, and public order sections often are referred to as the four "specialized sections" (*chuan ku*) or "investigatory sections," since they are in charge of investigation work. The number of cases handled by each of these sections is, at best, a rough approximation. Crime statistics are notoriously manipulable to show whatever one wants to show. This is especially true here, since they are based on the memory of one informant and since the definition of what constitutes a "case" is not entirely clear. As with the number of cadres in each section, the figures on crime are given only to suggest the amount of work a particular section handled.

late 1950's. Before 1953, this section was a part of the public order section.

*Public order section (chih an ku).* This section was called the "garbage section," since its 13 cadres took care of everything that was not specifically assigned to another section. This included household and travel control, fire prevention, traffic direction, issuing of permits for special occupations and events, and general supervision of antisocial persons who had not committed a specific offense. This section also investigated antisocial acts that were not "crimes," including thefts and tax evasion below the monetary amount mentioned above and attempted escapes to Hong Kong by persons who were not politically suspect. This section had the largest caseload of all, usually handling from one thousand to three thousand cases a year.* Most of these offenses were attempted escapes, violations of household registration regulations, and violations of various "misdemeanor laws," such as the Security Administration Punishment Act (SAPA).[15] There were also a number of cases of gambling, drug addiction, and violations of currency controls.

*Preliminary investigation section (yü shen ku).* This section, staffed by ten cadres, was charged with conducting a second investigation of cases where criminal proceedings might be instituted. Before it was established in the spring of 1956, its work was handled by members of the detention office, and even in 1964 the section was situated in the detention office headquarters. Members of this section were also stationed at the labor reform camps and at the collection camp (*shou yung so*) to review the cases of the inmates.[16]

*Detention office (chü liu so).* This office had charge of prisoners and other persons awaiting final disposition of their cases. Its staff of ten cadres operated three detention cells, two labor reform camps, and a collection camp.

*Technical investigation office (chi shu hua yen shih).* This six-cadre office carried out medical, chemical, and other scientific investigations on behalf of the investigatory sections.

*Other sections.* Two other sections were set up for a period and then abolished. Supervision of security work in the factories was originally handled by the internal security section, but in 1955 a separate protection section (*pao wei ku*) was formed to take over this work. This section was abolished for a brief period in the spring of 1957 but was re-

---

* As discussed below, many public order cases are resolved at the station or sector office levels. Cases disposed of at the sector level are included in the statistics of the public order section. Thus, it is not possible to say how many of the cases reported by the public order section are actually investigated and resolved by that section.

established later that year when control over a number of factories was decentralized from the special district to the hsien level. In April 1960, it again was abolished, and protection work reverted to the internal security section. A border protection section (*pien fang ku*) was established in 1957 to handle problems of guarding the border and preventing escapes, work that had previously been handled by the public order section and the public security stations located in the border areas. This section was abolished in April 1960; in its place, a border protection work department (*pien fang kung tso pu*) was formed by the hsien Communist party committee, and in the winter of 1962 a public security border protection subbureau was formed to take over the work of border protection.

## The Public Security System Throughout the Hsien

*Sector offices* (*p'ien pan kung shih*). In addition to the main office in Hui-chou city, the bureau operated "suboffices" throughout the hsien. The hsien was divided into five sectors, and a sector office was established in each.[17] Depending on its size and location, each sector office had a staff of five to fifteen persons. The sector chief was a high-ranking bureau officer, usually a deputy bureau chief or a section chief. Except for several months during the 1955 *su fan* campaign (to purge the bureaucracy as well as to attack counterrevolutionaries) the sector offices did not assume an important role in public security work until after 1957. After that time, they supervised all public security work within the sector and were the channels through which the bureau and the lower-level public security organs communicated.

*Public security subbureaus.* There were two subbureaus in the hsien, one in Hui-chou city and the other along the coast at P'ing-hai. The Hui-chou subbureau had a staff of about twenty, who supervised the work of the four public security stations in Hui-chou. After 1957, basic policy decisions were made by the sector office for Hui-chou, and day-to-day operational control was exercised by the subbureau. When it investigated cases, the subbureau was under the leadership of the appropriate investigatory section.

The P'ing-hai subbureau was established in 1962 to assume charge of border protection work. There were six public security stations under its jurisdiction. In practice, the subbureau's staff of 15 was in charge of cases involving border protection, while the sector office in Nien-shan supervised the ordinary police work of the public security stations in the area. The P'ing-shan subbureau also had jurisdiction over an inspection station (*chien ch'a chan*) located in the port of Kang-k'ou. This station

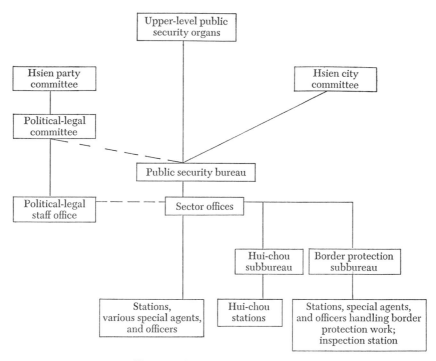

HUI-YANG PUBLIC SECURITY SYSTEM

was staffed by six public security cadres who assisted the commodity inspection office and the foreign trade control office in their work.

*Public security stations (p'ai ch'u so).* In 1964 there were 14 public security stations in the hsien, four in Hui-chou and the others in the larger market towns.[18] The Bridge West and Bridge East stations in Hui-chou were established at Liberation by taking over the former Nationalist police stations. The other stations were formed later, mostly in the 1952 drive to "establish the police system."

The station staff varied in size, ranging from 24 cadres in the Bridge West station, which covered the most important government and commercial centers, to four cadres in a station situated in a rural market town. In the larger stations, there were a chief, a deputy chief, and sometimes a political director (*cheng chih chih tao yüan*) who was in charge of political work within the station. One or two relatively senior cadres (called *nei ch'ün*) handled such internal administrative work as managing finances, compiling data and preparing reports, and maintaining the personal files of the residents in the area. There may also have been a few cadres with no specific assignments who helped investigate the more serious cases. The rest of the cadres were designated "household patrolmen" (*hu chieh ching*) and were assigned particular "beats." Each patrolman was responsible for virtually everything that occurred in the area under his control: he not only had to maintain order and enforce the law, but also had to look out for the general welfare of the inhabitants and see that government policies were implemented.[19] In the smaller stations, the division of labor was much less clear. The chief took care of most administrative matters, and the others filled in wherever needed.

*Public security special agents* (*t'e p'ai yüan*) *and officers* (*yüan*). The stations, situated in the towns, generally did not extend into the rural areas. Therefore the bureau assigned about twenty special agents and ten officers to handle public security work in the various communes and state farms. The special agents were of the same rank as station chiefs, and the officers were of slightly lower rank.[20] These cadres usually lived in the communes, although a few were concurrently assigned to a station. Although they were paid out of commune funds and considered to be commune officials, their professional (*yeh wu*) activities as well as their assignments and transfers were controlled by the bureau.

*Fire brigade.* The fire brigade, located in the Bridge West portion of Hui-chou, had forty members. Strictly speaking, firemen were part of the public security system, but in practice this group was fairly autonomous and stayed apart from the cadres involved in actual police work.[21]

*Summary of public security personnel.* It is difficult to get an accurate count of the number of cadres in the public security system, since many persons held more than one position concurrently. A station chief, for example, might also be a special agent and also be attached to the sector office. However, a rough personnel count follows:

| | |
|---|---:|
| Bureau, including five sector offices | 130 |
| Two subbureaus | 35 |
| Fourteen stations and one inspection station | 90 |
| Special agents and officers | 30 |
| Fire brigade | 40 |
| Total | 325 |

This relatively small public security force was responsible for the order and safety of a hsien populace that exceeded 500,000 in 1964.

## Channels in Public Security Work

Normally a case arose when a complaint was lodged by an individual, either in person or by depositing a letter in one of the many complaint boxes located throughout the hsien. A case might also be discovered by a local public security cadre or reported by a member of one of the mass organizations that assisted him. Whenever possible, the matter would be handled on the spot, through "mediation" by the local public security cadre. Most minor disputes and arguments were disposed of in this manner (according to the rules and procedures discussed by Jerome Cohen in this volume).

The more serious cases were reported to the station chief, who could settle claims arising out of traffic accidents and other tortious acts, and could impose the administrative sanctions of criticism, warning, and reprimand against minor antisocial activities. Under the Security Administration Punishment Act, the sanctions of monetary fine and detention had to be approved by the bureau or subbureau,[22] a requirement that was often ignored or more frequently evaded by informally assigning an offender (or having him "volunteer" for) extra work and study details under the supervision of a public security cadre or a local activist. Cases disposed of at the station level were reported to the bureau only in periodic summaries and as statistics.

Serious cases and still unresolved cases were usually reported to the bureau by means of a telephone call followed by a short written memorandum. Before the summer of 1957, the station chief communicated directly with the investigatory section that had jurisdiction over the case; homicides, for example, were reported to the criminal investigation section. After 1957, reports were sent to the sector office that had jurisdiction over the station. Stations under the jurisdiction of a subbureau sent duplicate reports to the subbureau and the sector office. As stated earlier, the sector office usually made basic policy decisions, leaving the supervising of routine activities to the subbureaus.

In minor cases in which the investigation had been completed and the facts were clear, the sector office could dispose of the matter by imposing the sanctions of monetary fine or detention. Serious cases and those that required investigation beyond the capacity of the local station would go to the appropriate investigatory section. The sector office might join the investigation, although this occurred infrequently, since the staffs of the sector offices were too small to do much more than keep in touch with the cadre in charge of the investigation and urge him to work harder and solve the case quickly.[23]

When more than one section was involved (as in a criminal case with political overtones), all relevant sections would be informed. In addition, any section that felt it ought to be included might enter the case on its own initiative. On the whole, the various sections worked together fairly well, and there were few serious clashes or disagreements. Public security cadres seemed to feel that they were members of a "family" and hence tried to cooperate with each other, a feeling that was enhanced by the constant transfer of personnel from one section to another, with the result that a cadre did not develop strong identification with one section to the exclusion of the others. Moreover, members of one section frequently were called on to assist in the work of other sections. Indeed, functional divisions were not at all clear among the personnel of the sections, and often a person's job assignment was a statement more of his rank (such as deputy section chief) than of his function.[24] Of course, how well the various sections worked together depended ultimately on the personalities of the persons involved. Not surprisingly, the ability to get along with one's co-workers was an important criterion for professional advancement.

The investigatory section assigned a senior cadre to oversee each case. In carrying out his work, this cadre might call on the local station, subbureau, and other sections for assistance. With the completion of the investigation, a detailed report was submitted to the section chief and sometimes to the sector office and subbureau as well, all of which might study and comment on the findings and the investigation methods. On the whole, both the investigation by the senior cadre and the review by the section chief were quite careful and thorough. Although public security cadres sometimes acted in a high-handed manner toward the masses, they seem to have been conscientious about their duties. For both professional and ideological reasons, they worked hard to ascertain the "truth" in each case, sometimes spending what seems to have been an inordinately large amount of time, energy, and resources even on trivial matters.

After the chief of the investigatory section had given his approval, cases that might require the bringing of criminal charges were sent to the preliminary investigation section; all others were submitted directly to the office of the bureau chief. The preliminary investigation section then reviewed the case and submitted a report on the facts and the law to the office of the bureau chief, together with a recommendation for action. If there were discrepancies between the findings of the preliminary investigation section and the investigatory section, the two sections would discuss the issue, and if necessary, they would conduct a reinvestigation.

All cases handled by the investigatory sections and the preliminary investigation section eventually reached the office of the bureau chief to be reviewed once again. Because of the limited manpower of this office, however, this review consisted only of reading through the files to spot obvious errors and omissions. Most of the cases sent back for further investigation involved matters that, in the view of the office of the bureau chief, called for a different political interpretation of the facts and therefore an alternate line of reasoning. A large majority of the decisions on cases was approved by the bureau chief. In cases requiring the imposition of some punishment, he would order an administrative sanction[25] or recommend that the procuracy institute criminal proceedings.

Even after the decision had been made to impose an administrative sanction, there often was another chance for review within the public security system. Members of the preliminary investigation section were assigned to the labor reform camps and the collection camp. Their primary duty was to investigate pending cases, but they also reviewed objections voiced by inmates over the handling of their cases or the appropriateness of their punishments. Similarly, almost every winter, a "work group for the clearance of accumulated cases" was formed in the public security bureau, consisting of several members of the preliminary investigation section and several high-ranking cadres from other sections. Although this group was concerned mainly with disposing of unsolved cases that had arisen during the year, it also looked into completed cases in which the offender had expressed dissatisfaction.

### Problems Encountered in Public Security Work

From the foregoing description, one might conclude that public security work functioned smoothly and efficiently in Hui-yang. That was more or less true in the sense that public order was maintained and the criminal process was administered with a minimum of force and error. However, there did arise several serious problems that can be summed up in the terms "localism," "careerism," and "professionalism." These three problems were intricately interwoven with each other and are often difficult to sort out, but they all tended to contribute to the evolution of the Hui-yang public security system into a small "independent kingdom," or at least into a system that developed tendencies of becoming independent of the party and upper-level public security organs.

Localism in the Hui-yang public security organs involved antagonism, and sometimes even ill-will, among the cadres. The local cadres—by this I mean persons from Hui-yang or one of the adjoining hsien—resented the fact that a disproportionate number of the top positions were filled by nonlocal persons, particularly non-Cantonese. During the period covered here, 15 nonlocal cadres worked for at least part of the time in the Hui-yang public security system. This number included eight (out of a total of 12) bureau chiefs, one deputy bureau chief, and six section chiefs or deputy chiefs. There was also resentment that nonlocal cadres seemed to have greater opportunities for promotion and advancement. Bad feeling existed as well within the group of local cadres, dividing those who tried to curry favor with their nonlocal superiors and those who would not. This was particularly serious after 1960, when a number of persons having little or no public security experience were transferred into public security work. Localism did not appear to have involved competition between the local area and higher levels for resources. Perhaps such competition did occur in the party organization, where in a similar fashion the top positions were held by nonlocal persons having a greater degree of allegiance to the center.

Closely related to the problem of localism was careerism. The local cadres, particularly those who had been in public security work for many years, seemed to have felt frustrated over the lack of opportunities for upward mobility. Of the 77 local cadres who held at least the position of deputy section chief for a time within the period covered by this chapter, only six were eventually promoted to public security work at the special district level or in Canton. (These 77 plus the 15 nonlocal cadres discussed earlier constitute about 80 per cent of the total number of Hui-yang public security cadres of this rank.) In contrast, five of the 15 nonlocal cadres were promoted to higher-level public security work. Promotion to higher levels was unlikely, as was promotion within Hui-yang. The more senior cadres were still relatively young persons who typically entered public security work soon after Liberation and by 1964 were only in their forties. Of the 92 middle- and upper-level cadres discussed here, none had retired, and only one had died. In addition, after the mid-1950's there was little further expansion of the public security system. Thus, none of the top positions was likely to become vacant, and few new ones were created. Openings did occur as cadres were purged, but as mentioned earlier, after 1960 some of these positions were filled by persons having little or no experience in public security work, not by promoting public security cadres from the lower ranks.

The third problem, again closely related to the other two, was professionalism or departmentalism. The growth of a sense of community and togetherness within the public security system is not hard to understand. Public security cadres had great power and prestige. They wore a distinctive uniform and dealt with matters from which all other persons were excluded. In addition, most cadres had been in public security work for many years. For example, the 77 local cadres in the middle and upper ranks had been in such work for an average of nearly ten years each. For 49 of this group, their entire career pattern consisted of joining public security work at or soon after Liberation and rising through the ranks. As cadres such as these became more experienced, the feeling grew that nonprofessionals, including those in the party, should not interfere in public security affairs.

The three problems of localism, careerism, and professionalism caused major troubles for the Hui-yang party and the top public security officials. Apparently as the public security cadres realized that there would be little further career advancement, they became less oriented toward the party and the upper-level public security organs that had control over career advancement. Instead, these cadres became more concerned with consolidating and protecting their own positions by establishing ties of mutual support, assistance, and protection with others in the hsien public security apparatus. These ties were strengthened by feelings of friendship, years of dealing with each other, a bias against the nonprofessionals, and, among the local cadres, resentment against the nonlocals. Particularly strong bonds, or even cliques, formed among the local cadres who had been in public security work for many years and centered around the deputy bureau chiefs and the section chiefs. Twelve men had been chief of the Hui-yang Public Security Bureau.[26] Of these, only three were local persons. The pattern is very different at the deputy bureau chief level. Of the ten men who have occupied this position since 1950 (and there are several deputy chiefs at one time), four were in high public security positions in Hui-yang for over ten years and four others for over six years. Only two were not local people—Yüan Chen-shan and Wang Chiu-ming, the only deputy chiefs to be promoted to chiefs in Hui-yang. A similar local bias existed for the seventy persons who were section chiefs and deputy chiefs. Of this group 41 had been in public security work since the early 1950's, and all but six were local persons.

Thus, it appears that whereas there was a great deal of shuffling and transferring at the bureau chief level, the levels immediately below were manned by cadres with strong local ties of long duration. These persons probably were influential in public security affairs, since they were both experienced and familiar with local conditions. The bureau chiefs, in contrast, not only were outsiders, but also tended to be stationed in Hui-yang for short periods only. Probably the most important consequence of the formation of these ties was that public security cadres became very reluctant to criticize or inform on each other. They were unwilling or unable to carry out rectification campaigns within the hsien public security apparatus itself. Several times between 1951 and 1962 the party or the upper-level public security organs had to import outsiders to Hui-yang to conduct these campaigns.

A number of rectification campaigns have been carried out within the Hui-yang public security apparatus. The first took place in 1951, when the holdovers from the Nationalists and new cadres who had bad class backgrounds or doubtful histories were removed. A number of others were criticized and demoted in 1952 during the three-anti and five-anti campaigns. The next purge occurred in late 1953, when a group of "southbound" cadres came from the north and took over all the positions of leadership in the hsien.[27] The former leaders were criticized for their policy of "peaceful land reform"; the first secretary, a deputy secretary who was also president of the court, and the hsien chief were removed; Li Tun, the first bureau chief, was transferred to the court, and removed soon after; a general rectification campaign was carried out within the public security apparatus as well as in other government organs; supporters of the former leaders were criticized or removed, and many promotions were given to supporters and favorites of the "southbound" cadres.

This purge did not solve all problems. During the winter of 1954, preparations were begun for the su fan campaign of the next year. Kao I-ju, the second bureau chief and a "southbound" cadre, was unsuccessful in collecting materials for a rectification campaign within the public security system. One informant said two of the deputy bureau chiefs (both of whom had held this position since Liberation) resisted Kao's efforts; another informant said that it was Kao's own fault, since he was barely literate. In any case, Kao was transferred to another post, and a cadre was sent by the provincial party committee to be acting bureau chief and to prepare the campaign materials. This man left in early 1955 after the completion of the preparation of materials. A short time later, Chang Yung-lu, a party secretary with no previous experience in public security work, became bureau chief. Chang carried out the su fan campaign, during which two deputy bureau chiefs, a section chief, and a number of lower-level cadres were removed. Chang returned to party work immediately after the completion of the campaign.[28]

The same pattern was repeated in the anti-rightist campaign. In June 1957, Liu Shou-k'ai, a party secretary with no previous experience in public security work, became bureau chief. Although the former bureau chief was not removed immediately, power was in the hands of Liu. Liu returned to his party post in December 1957 after the completion of the first stages of the campaign, and Teng Hua-chang, a demobilized PLA officer who had been in public security work since 1953 but who also maintained strong ties with the party, became bureau chief. By the spring of 1958, all persons who were deputy bureau chiefs prior to the anti-rightist campaign had been transferred away,[29] and seven other section chiefs or deputy chiefs were demoted or removed from political-legal work. Although Teng held the post of bureau chief for the next four years, it appears that he was unable to bring the public security apparatus under firm control. He was an aloof man who concerned himself more with party work than with running the public security system. Once again it appears that the deputy bureau chiefs, the section chief, and deputy chiefs managed to retain operational control.

Another shake-up occurred in late 1960 and in 1961 when a chief of the public order section stole money from the bureau safe, issued exit permits to himself and several of his friends, and escaped to Hong Kong. Teng, enraged, instituted a severe rectification campaign. The central government declared Hui-yang to be "backward" in political work; Teng and Ch'ang Sheng, who had been first secretary of the hsien party committee since 1956, were transferred away soon after. Wang Chiu-ming, a former PLA officer who joined public security in 1953 and who had been deputy bureau chief for a period, became bureau chief. Between the end of 1960 and early 1962, all deputy bureau chiefs, 11 of 14 section chiefs and deputy chiefs, and a number of lower-level cadres were replaced. Three of these former middle- and upper-level cadres were sent to engage in agricultural work, five were removed from political-legal work entirely, and the others were transferred to work in other hsien.

In earlier shake-ups in personnel, the replacements usually were men of the same mold as their predecessors. That is, local cadres who had been engaged in public security work in Hui-yang for a number of years were promoted. The group promoted to middle- and upper-level positions between 1960 and 1962 was quite different: whereas the two new deputy bureau chiefs were still of the old mold, seven of the 11 new section chiefs and deputy chiefs did not join public security work until after 1956, and nine of the 11 had been engaged in other government or party work for a considerable period of time before assuming their public security posts.[30] It appears that the party was trying to appoint to leadership posts in the public security system persons who had not developed strong ties within the system and who had attachments and loyalties to the party. It remains to be seen, of course, whether these new men would remain amenable to party influence after a period of time. Further research might reveal that after attaining their positions, they too would begin to develop strong ties and loyalties to the public security system at the expense of their ties to the party.

One other problem the top Hui-yang public security officials encountered was the difficulty of finding high quality cadres. Of the eighty section chiefs and deputy chiefs, for example, 26 were eventually purged or demoted, three for political reasons, seven for having doubtful histories, eight for professional incompetence, two for corruption, two for rape, and one for publicly fighting with his wife. In addition one escaped to Hong Kong. (There are also two cadres for whom the reason for demotion is not known.) This is quite a motley crew.[31]

### Attempts at Coordination and Control before the Anti-Rightist Campaign of 1957

In addition to manipulations of the leadership personnel described above, a series of structural and organizational changes were tried in an effort to improve coordination and control of political-legal work.[32] During the early years after 1949, there probably was not much difficulty in coordinating the work of the various political-legal organs. The procuracy had not yet been established, and the court was still not fully developed. With the promulgation of the constitution in 1954 and the accompanying propaganda extolling the importance of the court and judicial independence, however, conflicts between the public security organs and the court increased. These were compounded the next year when the procuracy was added. A further complication arose when the difficulties with the su fan campaign indicated the need for greater party influence over the public security apparatus.

One of the hsien party secretaries (almost always the man who concurrently was the public security bureau chief) usually was in charge of all political-legal work in the hsien, including the resolution of disagreements among the political-legal organs. In order to increase efficiency and improve party supervision over the work of the political-legal organs, Chang Yung-lu (the party secretary who became public security bureau chief during the 1955 su fan campaign) established the political-legal committee as a subordinate organ of the hsien party committee. The political-legal committee consisted of ten to fifteen high-ranking persons engaged in political-legal work. These included the public security bureau chief and several other public security officials (usually most of the deputy bureau chiefs), the chief procurator, the president of the court, the commanding officers of the military units stationed in Hui-yang, and sometimes the hsien chief. In addition, there were several high-ranking party officials. The committee was chaired by the party secretary in charge of political-legal work. At monthly meetings all matters relating to political-legal work, including disagreements among the political-legal organs, were discussed. Because of the infrequency of meetings, however, this committee was not able to exert much influence over political-legal work.

In the winter of 1956, the political-legal staff office (*cheng fa pan kung shih*) was established to carry out the day-to-day work of the committee. Before the anti-rightist campaign, the chairman of the committee was also the chairman of the staff office; thereafter a separate cadre headed the office. In the beginning, its functions were limited, and the number of workers did not exceed two full-time and two part-time cadres. In practice, the court, the procuracy, and the public security organs sent regular reports on all their cases to the staff office for compilation and transmittal to the hsien party committee. The staff office might state its opinion on how a matter should be handled but generally did not take part in actual political-legal work except when the party committee became dissatisfied with how a few major cases were being handled. On the whole, the staff office was a communications channel, not an operational body.

During the Hundred Flowers period of 1957, a number of criticisms arose concerning political-legal work.[33] For one thing, no one really understood what the procuracy was supposed to do. In addition, the public security people were annoyed that the court would sometimes ignore their recommendations and decide cases on its own. The court, in return, felt that public security cadres were overbearing in their attitude and relations. Everyone was unhappy over this "each on his own" policy among the political-legal organs. A number of people were also unhappy over the staff office; its functions were not clear, but it had the ear of the party committee. Finally, many people complained about the lack of rules defining the limits of power of the public security apparatus.

*The Anti-Rightist Campaign to Summer 1959: the Redefinition of Political-Legal Work*

The anti-rightist campaign brought about many changes in political-legal work. Some were responses to criticisms raised during the Hundred Flowers period; others were accelerations of tendencies that had already existed for several years. These changes led to greater supervision of political-legal work by both the party and the upper-level public security cadres and to better cooperation among the court, procuracy, and the public security apparatus.

After becoming public security bureau chief in June 1957, Liu Shou-k'ai enlarged the political-legal staff office to eight full-time cadres, and urged them to take a greater role in political-legal work. Rather than merely acting as an information conduit, the staff office actually participated in the investigation and disposition of cases. At the same time, the sector offices of the bureau were also enlarged, and they assumed active supervision of all public security work within the sector. Being responsible directly to the office of the bureau chief, the sector offices provided a means by which the sections of the bureau could be supervised or, when necessary, bypassed.

As might be expected, there was a period of considerable confusion and blurring of the lines of command. The lower-level public security personnel had to report to the staff office, the sector office, the appropriate investigatory sections, and perhaps a subbureau. All of these organs might issue orders, often contradictory ones. The staff office (being a part of the hsien party committee) and the sector office (being an arm of the office of the bureau chief) had precedence in rank, but their staffs were too small and sometimes too inexperienced to provide adequate leadership. Nevertheless, they were jealous of their power and tried to participate in every case, with the result that often nothing was accomplished. In addition, there were considerable tensions between these two offices.

Beginning in late 1957, a series of steps were taken to simplify and rationalize political-legal work.[34] The most dramatic move was to shift the offices of the chief procurator and the president of the court to the public security bureau.[35] Physical proximity made it easier to discuss and resolve disagreements; moreover, the greater power of the bureau chief was made abundantly clear, and he was able to have his way in most matters.

Relationships among the staff office and other public security organs were redefined. A lower-level public security organ reported only to the sector office, which then transmitted the information to the staff office and the appropriate investigatory sections. The staff office did not participate in the actual investigation of cases, although it could supervise the work of other organs. The sector office could participate in the investigation of cases, but the general principle was that "cases should be left to the appropriate investigatory sections."

The staff office also reexamined procedures in political-legal work and issued a number of new uniform rules. For example, after 1957, only the bureau chief could order the detention of a suspect.[36] Similarly, the system of financial control was revised, and the manner and form of reports submitted by public security stations were revamped to a large degree. With the assistance of the internal security section, the staff office also reviewed the files of all cadres in political-legal work to decide who were not needed or not wanted and therefore should be transferred to agricultural work. In addition, the staff office rechecked materials on all persons with doubtful or unclear histories; about 150 such persons were punished or held for further investigation.

It is ironic that in some ways the period following the initial antirightist crackdown may have been the time when the "rule of law"—in the sense that there are clear and publicized rules that were obeyed by both officials and the masses—was strongest in China. With the issuance of the new uniform rules by the staff office, and the promulgation of national regulations, such as the Regulations Governing the People's Police, the SAPA, and the Decision of the State Council Concerning Some Problems in Rehabilitation Through Labor, more clearly defined rules existed than ever before.[37] The staff office took special interest in seeing that the new rules were obeyed. One section chief was demoted, for example, when in violation of the Arrest and Detention Act he ordered the detention of a suspect without first obtaining the approval of the bureau chief. There also was an attempt to publicize the law. The only articles (except for descriptions of mass trials) that directly discussed law in the *Hui-yang pao* appeared during this period. On September 4, 1957, a fairly lengthy article discussed the meaning of law and the role it plays in supporting the socialist development of the nation. In October, a series of five articles gave the text of the SAPA, together with pictorial explanations. Unfortunately, whatever may have been accomplished in this period was undone by the Great Leap Forward that began the following year.

*Summer 1959 to 1964: Increase in Party Control*

The changes introduced before 1957 were directed primarily at coordinating the work of the court, the procuracy, and the public security system. Between 1957 and 1959, efforts were made to improve the quality of and increase party influence over political-legal work. The changes that occurred in 1959 and 1960 were concerned primarily with establishing party control over the political-legal organs, especially the public security apparatus.

Although the staff office was a party organ, before 1959 most of its members were affiliated closely with the public security system. They tended to favor the interests of that system and defer to the wishes of the senior public security cadres. In 1959 and 1960, the size of the staff office was expanded to about 12 cadres. Several relatively senior public security cadres were transferred out of the staff office, and nine new men were appointed. Of these, three had no ties with public security: two were party officials, and the third was a member of the procuracy. Four of the other six were young men who joined the public security only two or three years before and who were activists within the party. All members of the staff office were given commissions (*wei ling*) directly from the hsien party committee and were told that from that time they were responsible only to the party committee.

During the earlier years, the staff office often sent a cadre to check on the work of the sector offices. Beginning in late 1959, a member of the staff office was stationed permanently at each sector office, usually as the second in command. This person reported directly to the staff office, and issued orders in the name of the staff office. Although he usually did not participate in the actual investigation of cases, he closely supervised the work of the sector office and the subordinate public security organs. The staff office members became quite powerful, since they were the agents of the party committee and could complain directly to that body. As far as I know, this pattern continued into 1964.

A number of questions that can be the focus of further research and consideration are raised but not fully dealt with in this paper. For example, what are the effects on the administration of the criminal process of having a relatively inactive court and procuracy? Does this inactivity mean that the public security system has almost unbridled power, or does this lead to some other organ, such as the party, taking over the task of supervising and reviewing public security work? In the latter case, does the new supervisory organ develop definite procedures for soliciting, accepting, and processing complaints from the masses, as well as a specialized staff to handle this work? If not, does the lack of definite procedures and the use of nonspecialized staff hinder or facilitate the work of controlling the public security and providing redress for grievances?

We might also ask how effective are the various internal checks carried out within the public security system itself? As we have seen, a criminal case may be handled or reviewed by eight or more groups related to the public security system before finally being disposed of. Do these different levels tend merely to support the others' findings and recommendations without much question, or do they really provide adequate safeguards for an accused person against arbitrary or erroneous actions? Are some levels of review more effective than others? Do some public security cadres constitute a fairly separate group who (although they have strong departmental affiliations and loyalties) feel that they can and ought to correct any mistakes committed by their colleagues?

A different set of questions arises with respect to the question of the "independent kingdoms." I have suggested a number of influences that

give rise to this phenomenon within the Hui-yang public security system. As a cadre's position becomes more permanently fixed, he develops increasingly stronger ties with the local community and especially with other cadres in the same department at the same level. Do
"independent kingdoms" in other localities, departments, and levels develop for the same reasons? If not, can a pattern be identified that indicates why particular factors are important in particular types of organizations?

I have also suggested that although the Hui-yang public security apparatus exhibited some tendencies to be independent from upper-level
public security organs, the most important struggle was against the
attempts of the hsien party committee to assert control over public
security work. This is illustrated by the fact that the persons assigned to
take over the public security bureau during the 1955 su fan campaign
and the 1957 anti-rightist campaign were hsien party secretaries, not
upper-level public security officials. Similarly, Teng Hua-chang, the
man who became bureau chief after the anti-rightist campaign, was a
cadre with several years of experience in public security work, but a
person who also had especially strong ties with the party. Did the party
have similar difficulties with other departments? Were the difficulties the
same at higher levels of government? Do the departments and organs
that try to assert independence from party control have common characteristics?

More generally, is China's bureaucracy a pyramid of many "independent kingdoms"? If so, how do the various kingdoms that exist in different localities, departments, and levels interact with each other? The
problem is considerably more complex than one that merely involves
competition between the center and the local area. Each level sometimes
competes and sometimes cooperates with the levels above and below
itself. Within each level, there are similar tensions among the party and
the various departments. Even within a particular unit such as the Hui-
yang public security apparatus, there probably are smaller cliques and
more subtle independent tendencies.

Answers to these questions will yield insights into the nature of Chinese society and the Chinese political process. They may help explain
many of the developments of the past twenty years and may shed some
light on the causes and effects of the Cultural Revolution.

# Preserving Order in the Cities

EZRA F. VOGEL

The term "public security" is not just a euphemism to give a more attractive public image to a police apparatus. It symbolizes a particular approach to controlling deviance in society, an approach that stresses the maintenance of public security and public order over the preservation of law.*

The Western conception of "law and order" is a dualistic one with inherent tensions.[1] Law presupposes an orientation toward justice, toward the equitable application of fixed rules. The application of law is governed by regulations about due process, the collection and evaluation of evidence, the treatment of suspects, and the manner and severity of sentencing. Legal processes are activated when a claim can be made that a law has been violated. The maintenance of order is governed by a different set of considerations that involve preventing disruptions by investigating, restraining, and apprehending potential troublemakers. Unlike legal administrators, police administrators may take an interest in

---

* This is an interpretive essay that draws on Chinese Communist newspapers, magazines, Red Guard papers, other documents, and interviews with a sizeable number of former residents of China, including several former public security officials. The most intensive data for this paper are drawn from research on Canton, described more fully in my *Canton Under Communism: Programs and Politics in a Provincial Capital, 1949–1968* (Cambridge, Mass.: Harvard University Press, 1969). Because the general pattern described here is reflected in national directives and in the accounts of former Chinese residents from other localities, there is reason to believe that the basic patterns described here are found in cities throughout China. Furthermore, despite the temporary lapse in order caused by the Cultural Revolution, there is no indication that there has been any lasting change in the approach to public order or in the organizational structure for preserving order. In the countryside, the approach to public security is similar, but there is generally a lower level of governmental activity, of administrative sophistication, and therefore of public discipline.

a potentially disruptive situation even before a claim is made that laws have been violated. Recent studies in Western countries make it clear that most cases of law violation never reach the courts and that decisions by the court are affected by a number of questions other than technical legal ones. Yet even in the handling of cases that do not get to the courts, policemen in Western countries are constrained by past decisions of courts and by court norms for handling violators.

The Communist Chinese do not conceive of the same conflict between law and order. Their efforts to maintain order are not constrained by law or by a legal administration differentiated from the public security administration.[2] Despite abortive attempts to establish an independent judiciary based on the Soviet model of the early 1950's, few cases ever reached the courts, and those that did were selected more to provide moral instruction than to reach verdicts. By 1958 even these efforts to separate legal from public security administration were essentially abandoned.

Historically the failure to develop an independent legal system derived in large part from the incapacity of the government to ensure justice throughout the society. The government operated offices in the larger cities, but the staff was too small to provide protection to the citizen from trespass by fellow citizens. Most cases of theft, assault, and property damage never came to the attention of the government.[3] The government perpetuated the teaching of Confucian morality, but it could enforce this morality only selectively by publicizing certain important cases to deter the public from similar disregard of morality. Administrative officials had an elaborate machinery for handling problem cases and preserving a minimum of order, but there was no independent or universal legal system.

Without an independent judiciary to evaluate administrative encroachment on due process, the Chinese have been less restricted in responding to individual cases than have administrators in Western nations, and there has developed a rational system that depends not on bureaucratic rules but on the evaluation of the effects of individual cases. China has a long history of sophisticated political administration; thus the efforts to maintain order have perhaps been more thoroughly rationalized in China than in any other country in the world. The typical citizen has had only a vague notion of how this system works, for its success has depended in part on his incapacity to take part in the decision, but the public security official has been explicitly taught the practices that embody the rationalized approach to maintaining order.

## Calculating the Threats to Order

Unlike the application of criminal law in the West, in Communist China the case opens not when a "crime" has been committed but when a person or a group is considered a potential threat to order. Public security officials in China thus take much more initiative in searching out potential cases of deviance. They observe a person for his expressions of ideas as well as for his behavior. A citizen under scrutiny is not simply being tried for a crime but for any predilections, any associations with other suspicious persons, any circumstances in his life that might lead him to disrupt social order. He is subject to complex judgments concerning the degree of his alienation from the system or from certain segments of society, his capacity for doing damage, and the restraints and sanctions that would reduce his threats to order. The cadre has to make judgments far more difficult than mere applications of a rule.

When a potential troublemaker is being evaluated, one of the most important considerations is the effect of his behavior or thoughts on other people. Those who witness a deviant act or have special information about the suspect are questioned not only to ascertain the guilt of the suspect, but to understand the impact of the crime on witnesses and others who heard about the crime. The concerns are whether or not others might be motivated to commit similar crimes and what steps are necessary to deter them. It follows that a major task of public security cadres is to investigate and write reports on the mood of various segments of the population.

The speed and seriousness with which a case is handled is determined by the difficulty of the task of restoring public order and instilling confidence in the government's competence. If, for example, large numbers of people witnessed an armed robbery, public security officials would feel compelled to respond almost instantly by announcing a "solution" to the case and apprehending a suspect before all the facts were in. The officials might in fact continue the investigation after the public announcement until they had apprehended the true wrongdoer, but even if they discovered an error they would not publicize it. They would privately take steps to detain and punish the real wrongdoer. Some kind of gesture would then be made to the scapegoat, who would be released. No public statement would be made that might lessen the public's respect for the capacity of the regime to deal with public disturbances.

If the general public mood is tense and the possibility of widespread disorders great, public security officials not only act with greater speed

and severity but launch special publicity efforts to contain small disorders. If, for example, a person sells something on the black market
when the black market is not a serious problem, the case would be
handled in a low key. If black-market activities become more severe, the
regime takes greater initiative in investigating black-market activities,
apprehending offenders, and punishing them more severely. If the problem is especially severe authorities would launch a publicity campaign
to see that the public is aware of the seriousness with which the regime
regards the case.

In the case of a severe problem, it is common for the public security
officials to launch showcase trials. A showcase trial is not a trial in the
Western sense where a decision is held in abeyance until the end of the
proceedings. The decision is reached in advance; the purpose of the
"trial" is to teach a lesson, to help create a mood in which people are
annoyed at the wrongdoer, likely to criticize and report a similar case,
and afraid of committing such an act themselves. Such cases are handled
systematically throughout a city. In Canton, for example, a very large
trial would be held in Sun Yat-sen Memorial Hall, the largest auditorium
in the city. Each major group in the city would send representatives to
attend the meeting, the number of representatives attending being dependent on the involvement of members in similar problems. After a
large showcase trial, representatives report the results of the trial to their
local groups and neighborhoods, and other forms of communication such
as radios, newspapers, wall posters, and theatrical groups are mobilized
to make certain the message is conveyed.

Public security officials concerned with the impact of a case on the
public give careful consideration to a wrongdoer's popularity. If, for
example, a famous and popular person were involved in a minor offense, public security officials would be hesitant to prosecute at all, since
an attack on such a person by crystallizing opposition among his followers would create more problems than it would solve. In such a case, the
person involved would be warned or invited to attend a brief study
period, and encouraged to set a good example. Possibly the public security officials would make veiled threats of what might happen if the
person did not "rectify" his thoughts and behavior. If such a person
openly resisted the regime on an issue of importance and his resistance
were known to a number of people, the public security officials would
have no choice but to attack, taking great care to discredit him and his
friends and associates severely. There would then follow a character
assassination designed to convince the public of the accused person's
selfishness and at the same time the government's compassionate con-

cern. The attack would be continued until those not directly involved were persuaded that he was selfish, pursued pleasures, or was unsympathetic to ordinary people and to the government or party. Despite the defamation of the person's character, the regime tries to avoid harsh punishment of a well-known deviant so as to prevent friends of the accused from becoming resistant to the regime.

In general, public security officials have exhibited great confidence in their own capacities and have not hesitated to move when threats to order arise. Nevertheless, when the public mood is one of widespread alienation, as in the severe food shortages of 1959–61, the public security officials cannot tighten their control immediately without risking an uncontrollable situation. At the time of some mass campaigns such as collectivization and communization, public security officials are so overextended by their many responsibilities that they cannot possibly attend to all problems that might disrupt the social order.

In the first years after takeover, before the limits of the regime's capacities could be specified with any clarity, some ambitious public security officials tried to control almost all expressions of dissident thought as well as dissident action. Because the essential task in maintaining order is deterring future cases of disorder, public security officials in China do not distinguish action from thought as sharply as do enforcement officials in the West. A person who might commit a serious crime is treated much more harshly than a person who has already committed a small crime. Yet in general, deviant action is considered more serious than deviant thought simply because it creates a greater disturbance to public order.

Because the regime cannot possibly prevent or control all cases of deviant thought and action, it must have clear priorities. Aside from the distinctions based on the extent of impact on others perhaps the most fundamental distinction is made between political crimes that reflect or contribute to basic alienation to the regime and personal crimes that are essentially irrelevant to political attitudes. A person who insults an official or damages government property is treated far more severely than one who insults a private citizen or damages private property. Public security considerations, then, are subordinated to the general political goal of maintaining appropriate respect for the government, just as the public security apparatus is subordinated to the party. The Chinese public security apparatus, unlike that of the Soviet Union under Stalin, was clearly subordinated to the party, at least prior to the Cultural Revolution.

One political purpose that is regarded as particularly important in the handling of cases is the maintenance of the class line. Wrongdoers from bourgeois and landlord classes are in general treated much more severely than workers and peasants. And beyond the severity of sanctions, the cases from the "wrong social classes" are also given much more publicity than those from the "good social classes." Even when a member of a "good social class" is criticized, his behavior is explained in terms of influences from the "wrong social classes." Thus, the handling of cases is used to publicize the wickedness of the "wrong" classes and the virtue of the government in defending the interests of the workers and peasants.

Public security officials concentrate their efforts much more in the cities, where dissident thought can have much greater impact and dissident groups can cause much greater damage than in rural areas. The thoughts of urban cadres, intellectuals, and especially those responsible for the written word are taken much more seriously than the dissident behavior of peasants far from the center of power. Although a commune may have only one or two public security cadres, an urban area of comparable population would have a local police station with a sizeable staff.

In calculating potential social disruption, public security officials differentiate special occasions from ordinary occasions. A large public parade or celebration, for example, can provide an unusual opportunity for dissidents to cause trouble. Hence, potential troublemakers are commonly rounded up by local police officers and kept under close observation away from any large public events. On the eve of a large celebration or demonstration, controls are tightened and threats are issued to potential deviants to reduce the chances of trouble.

The handling of any single case is subordinated to the general effort of preventing disorders. It is standard procedure not to arrest a suspect immediately; his relations with others can thus be observed, and the activities and contacts of a network of people could be known and dealt with if necessary. When such a network is uncovered, the whole network would be raided simultaneously to ensure that none escapes. Questions of residence, transfer, job assignment, or study programs are all affected by the possibilities of collecting information about anti-regime activities. Those involved in major cases might be allowed to continue their contacts so that all possible information might be gathered; in minor cases the members of a group who are in some way resistant to authority might simply be dispersed to various localities where they can have no contact with each other.

The major sanction used by Chinese police, like police elsewhere, is coercion or threat of coercion. But the Chinese Communist police make an effort to play down coercion and to gain the positive cooperation of the citizenry through normative appeals to patriotism and the necessity of preserving an orderly society, a sentiment that is widely shared by people who have observed much disorder. When, in the course of investigations, it is found that some segments of the population do have complaints about material conditions or about special injustices, the public security officials in collaboration with other organs of government may make some special concessions to the wrongdoers or potential wrongdoers at the same time as they tighten the coercive controls. Whatever technique is used, the dominant consideration is how to reduce the likelihood of further disturbances.

The complex judgments required for the maintenance of order offer many opportunities for lower-level officials to commit errors. In particular, the vagueness of rules provides no clear guidelines for determining when mutual favors between low-level policemen and local citizens should be considered improper. Higher-level officials try to keep fairly tight control over the lower-level officials, not simply to prevent corruption and misinterpretation of rules but to reduce the likelihood of the lower-level officials alienating certain portions of the population that might therefore cause further disturbances. When disturbances do arise, the local public security officials responsible for that jurisdiction are held responsible to a considerable extent for not having done everything possible to prevent such disruptions.

Many elements in the Chinese system can also be found in the practices of Western enforcement systems. In cases of drugs, prostitution, and groups plotting to overthrow the government, enforcement officials do take the initiative in searching out cases even before a crime has been reported. In the case of juvenile offenders, complex considerations concerning motivation, background, and potentialities are more important than the application of strict rules. Yet the Chinese enforcement practices are much more single-minded and systematic in their overall efforts to maintain order.

## Special Campaigns

Although public security work has a consistent logic that has not changed greatly over time, the actual effort of public security officials in China is subject to an ebb and flow that corresponds to the ebb and flow in other areas of Chinese society. The cycle of attack and relaxation is a reflection of the persistent efforts of Chinese Communist leaders to launch all-out efforts to remold and transform Chinese society, and of the need for some recuperation before launching a new attack.

These special assaults, known as "campaigns," are designed not only to apprehend people who have caused disturbances but to deter others who might be inclined to create them. When a campaign begins, all those most guilty are suddenly apprehended and placed in custody for criticism, struggle, and possible punishment. The campaign is in keeping with the Chinese Communist tradition of using such cases as a form of public education, extolling morality, and warning against undesirable thought and conduct. Campaigns do have a powerful effect in deterring citizens from causing trouble even during lulls between campaigns. The citizenry can correctly assume that officials will be keeping notes, recording instances of incorrect thought and behavior. When the officials discover such instances in the lull between campaigns they do not necessarily act on them. The instance is noted and kept on file for possible use later. The citizen, unable to differentiate those things for which he may be punished from those for which he will not be punished, behaves with due caution.

In the twenty years since the Communists came to power, it is possible to distinguish three general circumstances in which campaigns to preserve order have been launched: as an effort to eliminate disorderly remnants from pre-Communist society, as a response to rising disorder, and as an accompaniment to other political and economic campaigns.

In the early years after takeover the Communists launched a series of assaults on organized crime that stood in the way of their efforts to establish order. The timing of these assaults was a function of the readiness of the local officials to launch the attack, and the order of the attacks was based on the severity of the problem. First, remnants of Kuomintang (KMT) troops were cleaned out, and then KMT officials and sympathizers. This beginning was followed first by the "democratic reform" movement, an assault on old labor gangs and secret societies, and then by a series of assaults on networks of vice involving prostitution, drugs, gambling, extortion, and petty thievery. In each case, the public security officials first made as detailed investigations as time would allow; they then launched lightning attacks to apprehend the offenders. Those considered most dangerous were killed. Others were detained, subjected to reform, and when released, placed under close supervision.

These campaigns operated almost according to a schedule, but the second type of campaign, the response to disorders, occurred when large segments of the public became sufficiently bold to risk disregarding official pronouncements. They occurred at the time of the Korean War when businessmen and government officials were profiteering from the shortages and heavy government procurement, in 1957 when intellectuals were becoming too outspoken in their challenge to party authority, and in 1959 when high officials were resisting some of the aspects of the Great Leap Forward. In the winter of 1960 the attack extended to local officials in the rural areas, and beginning in late 1962 there was a series of attacks against black marketeers, officials who were making personal profit at public expense, and those who resisted the Maoist efforts to achieve mass mobilization. These campaigns were designed not only to punish particular targets but to increase the general level of public discipline.

Preventive campaigns are inaugurated when other campaigns might alienate certain segments of the society. When cooperativization was undertaken in 1955–56 and when communization was undertaken in 1958, "auxiliary campaigns" were launched in the public security field to ensure that dissident elements alienated by the new program would not be able to sabotage it. In late 1960 and in 1961, as organizations underwent retrenchment and people were transferred to lower-level positions, there was a similar public security campaign to inhibit the activities of alienated elements.

A campaign to tighten public discipline requires not only an overwhelming control over the instruments of force but a minimum of acquiescence on the part of the general populace. In the period of 1960–61, because of severe food shortages as a result of failures in the Great Leap Forward, even this degree of public cooperation was lacking. So alienated was the general population that it was difficult to apprehend those guilty of petty deviations in the black market without arousing uncontrollable opposition. But as the situation eased because of an increase in the availability of food and other supplies the regime was able to impose the level of discipine that it had previously achieved. Thus the mood of the general public sets outside limits on the ability of the regime to launch a campaign that would restore order.

The initial effect of campaigns of this type is to restrain excessive acting out and to restore a measure of discipline. The problem with the campaign approach is the danger of a relapse once the peak of a campaign passes. The regime tries to ease the problem by not announcing the end of a campaign, but this has reduced value as the public becomes more sophisticated in discerning the relaxation of official pressures. Before a campaign is discontinued the officials make certain that it has reached all elements of the population. The more serious political rectification campaigns against certain elements of the population end up as milder programs of rectification (known as socialist education campaigns) directed at other groups of the population. Once a campaign slows down in the less affected elements of the population, an attempt is made to institutionalize some safeguards to ensure that the population continues to take heed of government pronouncements. Thus it is common for a campaign to end as soon as new education or propaganda programs or departments are established in school and work units to ensure that the message of the campaign is not forgotten. Despite these efforts, the decline of discipline after the peak of a campaign is inevitable, since the tension and the severity of sanctions cannot be maintained at such a high level.

The early campaigns were conducted in a spirit of ebullient and naïve optimism, for many officials genuinely expected that they would virtually eliminate crime and political opposition for all time. In its effort to wipe out every single trace of opposition the campaign was thus an instrument of revolutionary utopianism. As time went on the political rectification campaign was an institutionalized feature of the political process. Campaigns were no longer aimed at eliminating disorder for all time but at restoring a higher level of order.

## Organization for Deterrence

At all levels of political organization in China public security considerations have been given high priority. Within a municipality, however, the lower the level of government, the greater the predominance of the public security apparatus.* Even prior to the Cultural Revolution at the municipal level the public security bureau had an undue influence within the party because such a high proportion of public security officials were party members. During the period immediately after takeover and during the Cultural Revolution when the army rather than the party had ultimate authority, the public security apparatus had great influence because so many security officials had once been high military officials.

Yet at the municipal level, the highest of the three levels of government in a large city, the public security bureau is only one among many large bureaus subordinated to municipal government. At the second level, the district (ch'ü), the public security branch bureau is not only comparable in size to all the rest of district government but entirely independent of the district government, reporting only to the municipal public security bureau. At the lowest level, the precinct, the dominant organ is the public security or police station (p'ai ch'u so), which

---

* See the chapter by Victor Li for a discussion of the municipal-level public security structure. See also Ko-wang Mei, "Police System Under the Chinese Communist Regime," *Issues and Studies*, II: 2 (Nov. 1965), 31–41.

is directly under the district public security branch bureau. Several years after takeover the precinct government office ( *chieh tao pan shih ch'u*, literally the "street office") was officially separated from the precinct police station, but in fact the precinct police station is much larger than the government office. Most important precinct business is handled directly by the police station, and if any important problems are involved, even routine administrative affairs handled by the precinct government office are ordinarily cleared through the police station. In smaller cities, there is no district organization, and the local police stations report directly to the municipal public security bureau. The police dominate the lowest level as they do in larger cities.

The preeminence of the security apparatus at the lowest levels of government reflects the importance the regime attaches to the control of the population and the efficacy it expects from organizational means. Wary of unorganized masses and spontaneous organizations, in their efforts to gain control over organizations the Chinese Communists have chosen to work through face-to-face natural groupings. In Imperial China and in the KMT period, the *pao chia* system ( of ten households mutually responsible for each other's good behavior organized into ten groups of ten households) was an effort to enlist nongovernmental structures to keep peace when the government lacked the formal structure to maintain peace by itself. The formal pao chia system was merely the best-known case of the pervasive notion that groups and leaders of the groups should accept responsibility for the good conduct of members. Leaders of clans, guilds, home-town associations, and neighborhood associations were all held responsible for the proper conduct of members. In essence, what the Communists have done in the city is to expand downward the municipal police organization and to give it more authority in supervising informal associations. Since clan, guild, and home-town associations are no longer important in the life of the Chinese city, the government concentrates on the most important natural groupings, the work and neighborhood networks and, in the case of students, the student groups.

Within the work organization, the hierarchy—whether it be a section, branch, or independent cooperative—is also responsible for supervising the worker's behavior whether or not it is related to his job. Each large unit employs officials concerned with security, either full-time security officials or trusted persons with other work assignments who work with unit heads in supervising workers. Supervision on the job is obviously easier than in the neighborhood.

For urban persons not employed or in attendance at schools, surveillance is provided by neighborhood organizations,[4] primarily the precinct police station. The local police station is divided into a number of beats, with a single policeman in charge of each. Each beat, which typically has about three to four hundred households, has its own residents' committee (*chü min wei yüan hui*) with a full-time director, typically a woman who lives in the neighborhood and works under the guidance of the policeman assigned to that beat. Each residents' committee is in turn divided into a number of small groups or lane committees (the Chinese terminology for which differs from area to area). The head of each small group, which is designed to include fifteen to forty households, is commonly the representative of her group on the residents' committee. The small group and residents' committees vary greatly, but some of them perform many functions: administration of rationing, street maintenance, dirt or snow removal, supplemental schooling and literacy training, sewing and cottage industries, welfare and funeral assistance. The residents' committees reached their peak of activity in 1960 during the urban commune period, when in many cities they became the centers for organizing local mess halls, day-care centers, and handicraft shops. After the decline of the urban commune, some residents' committees retained some of these functions; many were transformed into "service stations" to help residents with such tasks as sewing and child care; with decentralization and retrenchment in 1961, some took over low-level "people operated" (i.e. private) schools for neighborhood children; and others returned to a reduced level of activity.

The sine qua non of the neighborhood organization is the registration of the members of each household at the local police station. Although precise regulations have varied, visitors who stay more than a few days are to be reported to the local police. Local residents away from the area for more than a few days are similarly to be reported. The policeman, who makes his rounds daily, consults with the leaders in the residents' committee and the small groups as well as with party members, former soldiers, and other trusted people who may live in the neighborhood.

The policeman's explicit responsibility for managing the civil affairs of households helps increase his familiarity with the conditions on his beat. He generally supervises all the nonpolice activities—the rationing, lost and found, health inspections, fire inspections, neighborhood work, and schooling activities—although these affairs can also be handled by nonpolice officials of the precinct street offices, which were under a district's civil affairs section. Indeed the civil affairs section supervises these activities even when the street offices are part of the precinct police station. But placing them under the policeman's charge helps ensure that the policeman has familiarity with all the details of the households on his beat and ensures the primacy of security considerations.

In carrying out his rounds the policeman relies heavily on the members of the residents' committee, but he usually also relies on young "activists." The local activists, commonly youths aspiring to be Communist Youth League members or league members aspiring to be Communist party members, are of invaluable assistance to the policemen in identifying problems before they lead to disruptions of order. These activists are the most thorough and motivated of rapporteurs for the policeman, and the typical policeman makes a point of encouraging their cooperation.

Theoretically all residents' committees are to have a "security and defense committee" (*chih an pao wei wei yüan hui*) composed of the reliable elements living in the committee's jurisdiction, and each small group within the residents' committee is also to have a security and defense "small group." The accompanying list based on the city of Canton in late 1955 gives some idea of the average population served by each of these committees.[5]

| Neighborhood organization | Number |
| --- | --- |
| Precinct police stations | 54 |
| Security and defense committees | 675 |
| Security and defense small group committees | 6,992 |
| Canton municipal population | 1,717,000 |

In fact, it was difficult for the local policemen to keep these as functioning committees. However, even if he did not have a functioning committee, the policeman cultivated activists on his beat who could be relied upon to report unusual activities or cases of individual alienation.

With this neighborhood control structure, it is possible to supervise problem cases with special rigor. People who have committed crimes, who belong to "bad classes" (former landlords, businessmen, and rich peasants), rightists, those with relatives living overseas, and those suspected of harboring hostility toward the regime may be classed as "controlled elements" (*kuan chih fen tzu*) and subjected to special surveillance. They may be restricted, for example, from going out at night, from traveling far from the neighborhood, or from having visitors. They may be required to attend special meetings, to write reports of their daily behavior, and to sign in at the local police station at regular intervals. In all these tasks, the residents' committees and lane committees can assist the policeman in seeing that the "controlled elements" have met their obligations and to some extent the committees can be held responsible. Such an organizational structure gives the enforcement officials an extremely effective device to prevent deviance, a device that is not possible in Western systems even for vices where enforcement officials take more initiative.

So effective is the local surveillance of one-time wrongdoers and citizens from the "wrong class background" that local activists and security defense committees are correctly advised that the greatest dangers come not from those already under surveillance but from citizens not previously suspect. They are instructed, therefore, to pay special attention to any signs of newly developed dissatisfaction. The very success of these local activists makes their task more difficult, for local citizens are especially cautious to see that signs of disaffection are not expressed in the presence of activists.

In addition to the activists there are many specialized full-time public security officials: a motorcycle corps attached directly to the central public security office in the city patrols the streets watching for signs of trouble; secret police agents in the guise of regular workers are assigned to such places as bus stations, wharves, train stations, and airports, where trouble might occur; some small shops located in critical places are operated directly by the public security apparatus; and special security officials are assigned to take part in other governmental activity, in the market, in dealing with overseas visitors, businessmen, and others who might be suspect.

The crucial link between the public and the security apparatus is the local policeman, who keeps records of deaths, births, and changes of residence and files special reports on the controlled elements (variously known as the "five bad elements" or "four bad elements"), on suspected secret agents, reactionary propaganda, public disturbances, and thought retraining programs. His daily notes on neighborhood happenings are essential to the files at the district police station and the higher levels of the public security apparatus.

## Labor Camps and Deterrence

Labor reform, a criminal sanction, is officially distinguished from labor reeducation, a noncriminal sanction: a person guilty of a criminal act is sentenced for a specific term of labor reform; a person who has improper or questionable thought but is not considered a criminal may be assigned to an unspecified period of labor reeducation. In fact labor reform camps are virtually indistinguishable from labor reeducation camps. The labor reform sentence is more specific, although in practice it may be radically changed, depending on the social situation and the "progress" of the laborer.

The assumption on which labor camp policy is based is not that the punishment should fit the crime but that the environment should be manipulated until the inmate learns to stop saying or doing anything that would disturb the social order. Physical and mental pressures are continued until a person's spirit of resistance is broken. The major activity, productive labor, is reflected in the names of the camps: X Sugar Mill, Y Enterprises, Z Industry. Offenders are sometimes assigned to urban enterprises, but more often they are sent away from the city to X Farm or Y Mining Company. Whether in a factory, a farm, or a mine, laborers commonly join in hard physical labor for ten to twelve hours a day on food rations that are less than the average Chinese adult's rations. After work hours the laborers spend several hours in political study and discussion with eight to ten of the people they work and live with. The members therefore have adequate material from their work and personal relations for the daily mutual criticism and self-criticism that accompanies political study. Cadres who lead these discussion sessions are skilled in the creative use of "contradictions" between prisoners to enhance the psychological pressure on those most inclined to resist. Those who fail to bend are subjected to greater hardships or additional burdens: cold food, reduced rations, more difficult work, or longer hours. In contrast, the worker who shows "progressive" attitudes and freely criticizes his fellow prisoners on lines approved by the leaders will be granted additional privileges. Although the Western term "brain-washing" is excessive, these manipulations do have the desired effect on prisoners.

Within the camp the intensive control over group activities and discussion ensures that prisoners have little opportunity to plan or incite resistance. Prisoners are forbidden to discuss the facts of their cases, to talk in dialects unknown to guards, to read any materials not supplied by the camp, to keep any cash, gold, jewelry, or other goods that might be sold if they escaped. If they need to go to the bathroom at night, they must announce their intention to the guard. Incoming or outgoing mail is inspected in the prison office to weed out any criticism of the camp, however indirect. In some camps at least, it is common for a prisoner to be restricted to one visitor a month. A visit with a relative is often limited to thirty minutes, and it takes place in the presence of a cadre fluent in the dialect of the prisoner and his visitor.

The last promise that is extracted from a person being discharged from a labor reform or reeducation camp is that he will not repeat any of his misbehavior and will avoid expressing "bad thoughts." Before he departs he is lectured on the virtue of selflessness and warned that he will remain under observation and will have to prove himself by good behavior. His local work or neighborhood units are asked to pass on reports of his attitudes and behavior after discharge, and the man himself is sometimes required to make periodic reports of his activities and "thought" to the local police. The observations of emigrants from mainland China bear out the conclusion that ex-prisoners are very cautious and are unlikely to become recidivists.

In brief, in Communist China, unlike the United States and many Western countries, not only is the concern for order pursued systematically and thoroughly, but there is great coordination between all units in the society to this end. Penal and police administration are closely coordinated to ensure that ex-prisoners are closely supervised by the police. There are no pockets of private organizations with their own policing, and police supervision penetrates quite thoroughly into nongovernmental organizations. There are no separate jurisdictions of national secret police, state police, and municipal police. The higher levels supervise police activity at the lower levels. Thus the program to maintain order is unrestrained either by laws or by jurisdictional separatism.

## Pressures for Formal Rationalization Before 1966

In their single-minded pursuit of the maintenance of order after 1949, the Chinese Communists avoided any formal rationalization of their enforcement procedures that would eliminate their flexibility. China's rulers were not bound by rules; rather rules were used and adapted by rulers. Still the Chinese Communists have not been immune from a variety of pressures for a more formal rationalization of existing practices in the form of codified law.

One source of pressure for codification was the sheer quantity of work. In many political campaigns, the processing of cases fell months behind. Under the heavy load of campaigns the security apparatus commonly borrowed cadres from other units, but the capacity for borrowing was limited by the number who were sufficiently trustworthy and by the needs for cadres in other fields. When outside cadres less familiar with public security work helped process cases it was still more important to have specified guidelines, since they could not be familiar with the profusion of informal practices that regular staff members followed. But in campaigns, even regular staff members had to use rules of thumb to cope with their heavy load quickly.

A second pressure for formal rationalization came from public demand for equity. The Communists did not radically alter the traditional expectation of the masses that they would not be included in or informed about decision-making processes. Typically, the citizen, frightened of possible wrong-doing, tried to develop a more precise notion of what was expected of him. He knew that he must not steal, attack people, gamble, engage in prostitution. But there was a wide range of behavior that could or could not be considered deviant. He sought greater predictability and was upset when surprised by sanctions that were arbitrarily applied. In a state of uncertainty, he suffered from a diffuse anxiety that forced him to behave with great caution toward any authority. This was an attitude seldom discouraged by the officials, even at the time of the annual "love the people" campaign, when the regime encouraged better relations between public security officials and the general public. Nonetheless the regime could not completely ignore the public desires for greater specification of rules if only for the reason that the state itself was the employer, directly or indirectly, of much of the population; if the populace, and especially technically skilled persons, became too alienated as a result of unfair treatment, they could work less energetically or even stop working. This problem was demonstrated clearly in 1956–57, when the government issued appeals to highly skilled professionals who had been alienated by the excesses of the 1955–56 campaign against hidden counterrevolutionaries.

Typically the people could not express their sense of inequity directly, but their concerns, and especially the concerns of elites, could be expressed by well-placed cadres. When these feelings were voiced by cadres who themselves sensed inequities the pressures were difficult for decision-makers to resist.

A third pressure for rationalization came from officials who had to make the complex decisions about the application of sanctions. Because the range of considerations for decision-making was so broad and the scope for judgment so great, lower-level officials were often criticized for their decisions. Indeed, at the end of almost every major campaign, from land reform through communization and the Cultural Revolution, officials were subject to severe sanctions for the excessive harshness of their decisions during the campaign. Yet during the campaigns they were subject to even greater pressures to take a firm line. Officials had some means of reducing their risks: they could pass on difficult cases to their superiors; they could use terminology and justifications that had come straight from higher levels. But since it was not possible to eliminate their risks, they were among the most effective advocates of more specific rules that would protect them from being criticized for errors. In its first two decades the regime was able to resist these pressures for formal rationalization, for the moral consensus that led to the codification of laws in the West was lacking in revolutionary China. The emergency nature of campaigns and revolutionary change allowed for varying sets of norms and for harsher judgments without rules and without the protection of individual rights. Under these rapidly changing conditions, there was no stable consensus that might lead to the codification of laws. One effect of the lack of codification was to give the authorities more leeway in the treatment of political opposition. Since political opponents in contemporary China were by no means a loyal opposition, those who held power were reluctant to regularize procedures that might protect their opponents. Totally discrediting political opponents was a far more effective way of dealing with them than punishing them only when they had committed specific crimes. It is not surprising that the more secure officials, unlike their underlings seeking protection, were reluctant to further codification of rules and regulations. Nevertheless, the public security apparatus could not handle its many cases without some standard procedures. The result was a compromise in the mid-1950's over codification: the most common problems and public security techniques were codified as guidelines for cadres, but the guidelines were not binding and not publicized. Thus, the general public, not knowing these guidelines, could not afford to disregard any orders from local authorities.

In the years since 1949 the limits of political power have been gradually more clearly perceived and implicitly accepted.* Distinctions between activities necessary and unnecessary for the preservation of order have been drawn more sharply. In more recent years minor cases in which governmental and party prestige was not at stake were handled quickly and routinely or dismissed entirely. The early revolutionary enthusiasm for enforcing a new and thoroughgoing morality on the entire population gradually gave way to a greater willingness to over-

* As we have said, there is no indication that the Cultural Revolution led to any lasting change in the approach to public order or the organizational structure for preserving it. On the contrary, the seriousness of the disruptions and the difficulty of stabilizing society in the wake of the Cultural Revolution make it unlikely that the concerns with public order will give way to a more thoroughgoing bureaucratic code for handling offenders.

look minor problems of minimal political relevance. The regime ignores, for example, minor cases of marital infidelity when political issues are not at stake. In short, during the first twenty years of the Communist regime in China, public security practices were increasingly rationalized to maintain order, though they were not formally rationalized as laws.

# PART TWO

# Leadership and Bureaucracy

# Patterns of Recruitment
# and Mobility of Urban Cadres

YING-MAO KAU

Ever since the Chinese Communist Party moved from the countryside to the cities to take over political and administrative control of the nation in 1949, it has been confronted in a unique way with the problem of bureaucratic development. Realizing the important role that the bureaucracy played in administrative control and the party's critical weaknesses in bureaucratic organization and administrative manpower at the time of takeover, Mao Tse-tung launched urgent mass campaigns of "institution building," party construction, and cadre recruitment. He appealed anxiously and urgently to the rank and file of the party, who were then pouring into the cities to fill bureaucratic posts en masse:

All cadres should learn how to be good at managing industry and commerce, good at running schools, newspapers, foreign affairs, good at handling problems relating to the democratic parties and people's organizations, good at adjusting the relations between the cities and the rural areas and solving the problems of food, coal and other daily necessities, and good at handling monetary and financial problems. . . . If we do not pay attention to these problems . . . we shall be unable to maintain our political power, we shall be unable to stand on our feet, and we shall fail.[1]

In spite of such urgent calls to build a strong administrative bureaucracy, his ambivalence toward the budding bureaucracy was immediate and clear. He openly expressed his fear that "certain moods may grow within the [bureaucracy and among the cadres]—arrogance, the airs of a self-styled hero, inertia and unwillingness to make progress, love of pleasure and distaste for continued hard living."[2] The routinization

I wish to express my special thanks to Pao-min Chang, King Chen, Philip E. Ginsburg, John W. Lewis, Norton E. Long, Pierre M. Perrolle, G. William Skinner, Ezra F. Vogel, and Lea E. Williams for their valuable comments and suggestions on an earlier draft of this paper.

of bureaucratic operation, Mao apparently felt, would inevitably erode the revolutionary spirit of the cadres, the egalitarian style of work and living, and the ascetic ethic of diligence and frugality. The introduction and institutionalization of new bureaucratic norms would ultimately reorient cadres to a different set of attitudes and values. Moreover, a full-blown bureaucracy might even generate its own course of development and render itself insensitive to political control. The development of events in Communist China has generally confirmed Mao's fears.[3]

In the past nineteen years of Communist China's political and bureaucratic development, subtle tensions and open conflicts between the revolutionary leaders who are determined to pursue their ideological goals and the growing bureaucracy have been evident. The periodic massive rectification campaigns, the organizational retrenchments, the political purges, and so on, are clear symptoms. The violent attacks on the party and state bureaucrats at all levels in the course of the Cultural Revolution clearly indicate such tensions and conflicts. As the bureaucratic establishment grows more complex and institutionalized, the trend toward routinization and functional autonomy within the bureaucracy independent of the political leadership's normative aspirations and priorities seems to become stronger.[4] This trend in fact became so strong during the early stage of the Cultural Revolution that the Maoist leadership found itself unable to control the bureaucracy through normal channels of command. As a result, the leadership had to bypass the bureaucracy and appeal to extrabureaucratic forces such as the Red Guards, the revolutionary masses, and the military to help purge the firmly entrenched bureaucrats from without.

The conflicts and the associated tensions between the thriving bureaucracy and the political leadership in Communist China, though dynamic and at times dramatic, have not yet received attention commensurate with their significance. Nor have such phenomena been understood correctly in terms of the deeper and more fundamental conflict in social roles and political perceptions between the bureaucrat and political leader.[5] In this essay I shall first present a macroscopic analysis of the recruitment and mobility patterns of urban cadres with special reference to their cyclical organizational expansion and contraction, and then relate these patterns of behavior to problems of the nation's bureaucratic and political development.[6]

### The Cadre Shortage in the Early Years

According to Nationalist government sources, there were about two million government officials and functionaries in China in 1948 that might be considered rough equivalents of what the Chinese Communists call "state cadres" (*kuo chia kan pu*).[7] When the Communists assumed administrative responsibility for the whole country in October 1949, the party, according to An Tzu-wen, then minister of personnel, had only 720,000 qualified cadres available for administrative tasks.[8] This acute shortage of state cadres meant that the new leadership was unable to fill almost two-thirds of the cadre posts with men of its own choice. The need for cadres was particularly critical in the cities, where state organs, schools, and public enterprises were concentrated. The shortage also meant that for purposes of control there was a low ratio of cadres to population—only one cadre for every seven hundred citizens.[9]

In his report on the situation in the southwest region in 1950, Liu Po-ch'eng complained that the new government was able to make only 30,000 new appointments, filling a mere 17 per cent of the region's 180,000 cadre posts.[10] In the northwest, a region that the Communists had liberated much earlier, the conditions were no better. A report of the Northwest Bureau of the Central Committee suggested that in the spring of 1950, the party was able to fill only from 10 per cent to 30 per cent of all cadre posts in various sectors of the region.[11] This acute shortage was clearly reflected in Mao's urgent appeals to turn the "fighting force" of the People's Liberation Army (PLA) into a "working force" for government administration and also in his repeated directives to the Communists to "lay down what they were familiar with" and "start to learn new skills of national reconstruction."[12]

Even though the party had a membership of approximately 4.5 million in 1949, apparently the majority of party members were either in the army or had neither the required ability nor the training to qualify as cadres. In view of the unique background of the Communist movement in China prior to 1949, this cadre shortage in 1949 was not surprising. The long period of rural activity and guerrilla warfare before takeover had forced the party to recruit heavily from the poorly educated peasantry. Before 1949, men were recruited mainly because of their political enthusiasm and loyalty to the cause rather than because of their professional competence or expertise. Moreover, party members were first and foremost trained as guerrilla fighters and revolutionaries, not as administrators and bureaucrats.[13]

When the party assumed responsibility for the cities, other difficulties were added to these unique rural-oriented circumstances and the leadership's emphasis on guerrilla strategy. Not only were well-trained and highly educated cadres of urban background in short supply; the cities required cadres with a high standard of technical knowledge and professional training for complex and specialized urban tasks. This clearly rendered the already limited supply of cadres still less adequate. Although during the war of resistance against the Japanese the party was able to recruit a small number of better-educated urban students and intellectuals by appealing to anti-Kuomintang sentiments and rising nationalism,[14] there apparently was no urgent need at the time to train them for city-oriented tasks. Moreover, as evidenced in the rectification campaign of the early 1940's, these urban students, intellectuals, and patriots, showing little clear ideological commitment to the cause of Communism, were not politically trusted by the party.[15]

The shortage was further aggravated by the sudden great demand for cadres following the Communist takeover. During the Nationalist years state officials were needed only to man governmental organs. After the Communist takeover, however, cadres were needed not only for the expanded state and party bureaucracy but also for a large number of heretofore nongovernmental enterprises and organizations now taken over from the Kuomintang, the "imperialist agents," and other "class enemies" in the cities.

If the number of party members available in the cities at the time of takeover can be taken as a rough measure of the critical condition of cadre supply in the cities, the data in Table 1 are highly instructive. In a city of 1.5 million population like Canton, for instance, only a hundred party members were reported to have been there at the time of Liberation. The case of Canton might be rather extreme, but even in cities such as Peking, Sian, and Mukden which were liberated much earlier, the ratios of party members to population in 1949 were still no higher than 0.34 per cent. The overall ratio of 0.17 per cent for the five

TABLE 1. PARTY MEMBERSHIP IN SELECTED CITIES, 1949

| City | Population | Number in party | Party membership as percentage of population |
|---|---|---|---|
| Peking | 1,603,000 | 3,350 | 0.21 % |
| Mukden | 1,121,000 | 3,773 | 0.34 |
| Sian | 503,000 | 1,015 | 0.20 |
| Canton | 1,414,000 | 100 | 0.007 |
| Liuchow | 194,000 | 145 | 0.07 |
| Total | 4,835,000 | 8,383 | 0.17 % |

SOURCES: Population data taken from Morris B. Ullman, *Cities of Mainland China: 1953 and 1958* (Washington, D.C.: Bureau of the Census, 1961), pp. 35–36. For Peking's party membership, *Hsin Hua yüeh pao* (New China monthly), II: 3 (July 15, 1950), 505–6. For Mukden, *Shen-yang jih pao* (Mukden daily), Sept. 14, 1956. For Canton, *Kuang-chou jih pao* (Canton daily), Sept. 27, 1959, in *Survey of China Mainland Press*, No. 2152, p. 22. For Sian, John W. Lewis, *Leadership in Communist China* (Ithaca, N.Y.: Cornell University Press, 1963), pp. 114–15. For Liuchow, *Liu-chou jih pao* (Liuchow daily), Apr. 12, 1957.

cities sampled was certainly much lower than the national average of 0.83 per cent in 1949.[16]

Data available on the proportion of party members among the bureaucratic leaders of the Wuhan Municipal People's Government in 1950–51 are illuminating. Of the 43 so-called "high-level cadre posts" at the bureau-head level and above—including the mayor, deputy mayors, staff office heads, bureau directors, and commission chairmen— 39 (91 per cent) were assigned to party members.[17] At the middle level, among approximately two hundred section heads (*k'o chang*) and their equivalents, the proportion of party cadres dropped to only about one-fourth of the total number (24 per cent). The fact that the party cadres virtually monopolized the high-level posts does not, however, necessarily suggest that there was no shortage of qualified cadres at higher levels.[18] Indeed, as became clear during the *san fan* (three-anti) and *wu fan* (five-anti) periods, a number of the early top appointees in Wuhan were only semiliterate, with so little administrative ability and professional competence that the party eventually found it necessary to dismiss them from their high offices.[19]

In Shanghai, according to P'an Han-nien, a deputy mayor of the city, a similar condition prevailed.[20] At the time of takeover the shortage of cadres in the city was so acute that the new government even appealed to all "politically pure" Nationalist officials and functionaries to stay on their jobs, with the guarantee of "three originals"—original job, original rank, and original pay. As late as 1952, 70 per cent of the city's leadership posts at the division-head (*ch'u chang*) level and above were still occupied by nonparty cadres. The Municipal Party Committee of Shanghai also complained that in 1952 over 80 per cent of the city's 1,367 elementary schools were still unable to organize party branches because of the shortage of cadres who were professionally as well as politically qualified in these schools.[21]

The shortage of cadres seemed to be particularly serious at the middle level. At the higher level, the number of cadre posts was normally small and could be filled relatively easily. At the lower level, though the number of posts was large, as Chang P'ing-hua, secretary of the Wuhan Party Committee remarked in 1950, "The political and technical requirements at these levels were lower, so activists who have sustained the test of one or two mass movements should be recruited quickly in large numbers into the lower-level leadership."[22] It was at the middle level that the problem of cadres became particularly critical, for the number needed was large, and the party apparently found it difficult to compromise on political and professional qualifications. The party

seems to have felt that ordinary activists were not professionally qualified for the middle-level leadership posts, and many of the professionally competent intellectuals and former officials were not acceptable
politically.

Aside from the problem of quantity, the quality of cadres was also
a problem. Fragmentary press reports on the quality of the cadres who
were hastily recruited early on were sometimes appalling. A substantial number of lower-level cadres and party members did not even
know how to read and write: a report from Tangshan city revealed,
for example, that in 1950 a special cadre school was set up for the
training of illiterate cadres.[23] In a class of 603 newly recruited cadres,
347 had attained the fourth-grade level of literacy after one year of
training, and the remaining 266 reached only the second-grade level.
In the spring of 1951, it was further reported that the municipal party
committee had inaugurated a program aimed at providing literacy training for at least half of the illiterate party cadres in industry and mining
and for one-third of those in the suburban areas.[24]

### Massive Recruitment to Meet the Shortage

To meet the critical need for improvement in the supply of cadres
in the early years, the leadership adopted two approaches. They retained the services of old personnel, particularly those who were involved in technical and professional functions. And they recruited and
trained new cadres on a massive scale, through mass movements for
instance.

Since the days when the party had begun to move from the countryside into the cities, Mao Tse-tung and the top leadership had repeatedly emphasized the hard reality that "the cadre situation in the nation
today is that we have too few, and not too many, cadres."[25] On the eve
of the nationwide victory in 1949, the central leadership laid down four
basic principles with regard to the old personnel of the Nationalist
government. (1) The leadership at all levels should win over all technicians and specialists in the government organs and state enterprises,
persuade them to cooperate with the party, and let them continue to
work in their original posts with peace in heart. (2) Competent administrative personnel should also be retained and allowed to stay in
their original jobs. Reassignments and transfers were permissible only
when there were surpluses of manpower. (3) Incompetent personnel
may be demoted, sent away for reeducation, or dismissed, but this
should be done only on the basis of individual merits, and not in a
wholesale manner. (4) "Reactionaries" and Kuomintang agents whose

counterrevolutionary activities were firmly proved should be thoroughly purged.[26]

In order to prevent the abuse of power by party cadres persecuting old personnel in the name of "political clean-ups," the Northeast Bureau of the Central Committee, for example, in the summer of 1948 directed that the military control commissions and public security bureaus should exercise "unified control over the arrest of class enemies and the confiscation of their property," and warned of severe punishment for violators.[27] Military representatives dispatched to various organs and enterprises in 1949 were instructed to make sure that the party's policy toward "retained personnel" was correctly carried out.[28] Reaffirming the "three originals" policy for retained personnel, Ch'en Po-ta declared in 1949 that "as long as they are faithful to their official duties and do no sabotage, their peace and security should be guaranteed."[29] The mayor of Shanghai, Ch'en I, even went so far as to promise that "regardless of their ideological differences with the party, the retained cadres may even receive preferential treatment, should they be prepared to break with their past completely and support the people's government."[30]

Repeated appeals such as this from the party itself appear to have had some success in checking excessive political purges and winning the support of old personnel and retaining their services. In Shanghai, for example, according to P'an Han-nien, a deputy mayor, roughly 70 per cent to 80 per cent of old Nationalist personnel continued to work faithfully at their jobs in the early years.[31] When the First National Conference of Party Secretaries met in the summer of 1951, Li Wei-han, director of the United Front Work Department of the Central Committee, renewed the call to party secretaries to "respect and learn from the nonparty experts and administrators with modesty and to help the nonparty cadres exercise their administrative functions and authority with dignity."[32]

While managing to retain the services of a large number of old administrative personnel and technical experts through a variety of methods—material incentives, appeals to patriotism, technique of the "united front," and coercion—during the early years, the party also launched massive drives for recruitment of new cadres in the cities. In a period of about three years between October 1949, and September 1952, according to An Tzu-wen, then minister of personnel, the party recruited nearly three million new cadres, increasing the number of cadres from 720,000 to 3,310,000.[33] These new recruits were brought into the government from three major sources: 1,730,000 (57.7 per cent) were workers and peasants who emerged as activists in the mass movements; 1,200,000 (40.1 per cent) were members of the party and the PLA, and "progressive elements" among the retained personnel who had gone through short-term training; and 66,000 (2.2 per cent) were graduates of the regular institutes of higher education. Thus over half of the new cadres were worker and peasant activists who emerged from such mass movements as the Resist-America and Aid-Korea campaigns, the production competition, and the san fan and wu fan campaigns conducted in the cities. The san fan campaign (1951–52) alone produced as many as 374,500 new cadres in a short period of four months.[34] In Tientsin, for example, 8,994 industrial workers and shop clerks (including 1,692 women) were promoted to cadre status during the campaign,[35] while in Mukden 3,908 workers were assigned cadre posts.[36] It was also reported that 1,740 cadres in the factories of Shanghai had moved into "more responsible posts," and 1,126 workers under the East China Textile Administration had been appointed to cadre positions during the same period.[37] The posts these workers and activists received were mainly at the lower levels, as group leaders (*tsu chang*) and subsection heads (*ku chang*). Apparently their limited education and professional training failed to qualify these people for advancement beyond these levels.

A second major source of recruitment was the short-term training institutes such as the people's universities, political training institutes, party schools, and various vocational training classes.[38] These institutions were established by the new leadership in the cities to provide training for middle-level cadres for a period ranging from a few months to a year. They served either to technically train party and demobilized PLA cadres who were already in leadership positions but had few job-oriented skills or to offer political and ideological courses for the professionally qualified retained personnel who lacked knowledge of Communist doctrine and policies. Moreover, these training institutes also served as an effective screening device for the party to put the political loyalty and professional ability of all prospective cadres under close scrutiny for a period of time. The three major training institutes operating in north China in 1948–49—the North China People's University, the North China Revolutionary Cadre Institute, and the North China Military Cadre School—were typical of short-term training institutes. In early 1949, the Central Committee assigned these three institutes the task of training 17,000 cadres to be sent to the south each year, in addition to producing 25,000–30,000 middle-level cadres for duty in north China.[39] When the Communists gained control in central and south China, institutions of this type were established virtually in all cities under the auspices of party and government organs at the regional, provincial, and municipal levels. By mid-1952, the widespread network of training institutes had produced as many as 1,200,000 middle-level cadres for the new government, representing roughly 40 per cent of the total of new cadres.[40] This method of turning a large number of people with a wide range of qualifications and talents into state cadres, through short-term political or technical training, proved to be an effective and economical approach to the cadre shortage.

A third major source of cadre recruitment was the institutions of higher education, notably the regular colleges and universities in larger cities. College graduates as a block of highly trained and technically competent manpower constituted an ideal source of recruitment; in fact, as An Tzu-wen noted with satisfaction, as many as 99.4 per cent of all the 1951 college graduates were recruited into various state organs and enterprises, and "the great majority of them, after a period of practical training, have become the backbone of the cadre corps."[41] The leadership clearly considered the institutions of higher education in the cities the best sources for recruiting quality cadres and specialists. However, according to An Tzu-wen, this group was too small in number and the process of their training was too slow and costly. Indeed, in the first three years of Communist rule, regular colleges and universities produced only 2.2 per cent of the recruits. Thus, while recognizing the leadership role of the college graduates in the bureaucracy, the party always emphasized the importance of recruiting cadres on a large scale through other channels to meet the needs of the lower and middle levels.[42]

## From Shortage to Overrecruitment

By mid-1952 the number of state cadres had surpassed the two million estimated as the total under the Nationalist government before its downfall. Moreover, as An Tzu-wen indicated in his 1952 report, the strength of cadre forces by late 1952 had met the basic needs of the government. By 1953, therefore, the central government began to urge caution in expansion of administrative organs and promotion of cadres at various levels, particularly those in the urban sector.[43] An editorial in the *Jen min jih pao* in 1955 confirmed that during the second half of 1953 and the first half of 1954 the people's governments at various levels had selectively removed over 150,000 incompetent and unneeded cadres.[44] In 1954–55, the central leadership even reversed its earlier policy of "bold recruitment and promotion" by initiating a policy of "curtailment

TABLE 2. NUMBER OF STATE CADRES, 1949–58

| Year | Number of cadres | State cadres as percentage of population | Average annual growth |
|------|------------------|------------------------------------------|-----------------------|
| 1949 | 720,000 | 0.13% | |
| 1952 | 3,310,000 | 0.58 | 863,333 |
| 1955 | 5,270,000 | 0.86 | 653,300 |
| 1958 | 7,920,000 | 1.21 | 883,333 |

SOURCES: For 1949 and 1952, *Jen min jih pao* (People's daily), Sept. 30, 1952. For 1955, *Hsin pao* (New news, Djakarta), Sept. 25, 1956. For 1958, see *Chung-kuo ch'ing nien pao* (China youth daily), Jan. 30, 1958.

and adjustment," and in 1956–57 a drastic measure of "bold retrenchment and reduction" was introduced.

Signs of the reversal in official policy began to appear in 1954, when the State Council issued the first in a series of directives warning all state organs to curtail recruitment and streamline organizations "voluntarily."[45] In spite of these warnings, the momentum of bureaucratic recruitment and expansion continued to advance after 1954, as shown in Table 2.[46]

Data available on the growth of the municipal government bureaucracy of a number of large cities are highly instructive. The Municipal People's Government of Canton, which may serve as a typical case, had a cadre force in late 1949 of approximately 1,000, both party and nonparty. (See Table 3.) In the period of fifteen months between January 1953 and March 1954, the number of cadres within the municipal government increased by twice as many as it had between 1950 and 1952. In 1953 alone the number of bureau and division directors was reported to have grown by 142.5 per cent and that of section chiefs by 115.4 per cent; and over the next three years this figure continued to expand, in spite of the 1956–57 campaign for organizational retrenchment and personnel reduction. Thus during the first eight years of Com-

TABLE 3. CADRES IN THE CANTON MUNICIPAL GOVERNMENT, 1949–57

| Year | Number of cadres | Annual increase rate |
|------|------------------|----------------------|
| 1949 | 1,000 | |
| 1954 | 4,500 | 70% |
| 1957 | 7,750 | 24 |

SOURCES: For the 1949 and 1954 figures, see *Nan fang jih pao* (Southern daily), Mar. 18, 1955. For the 1957 figure, see *Kuang-chou jih pao* (Canton daily), Feb. 25, 1957.

munist rule, the cadre force in the Canton municipal government expanded by 675 per cent, showing an average expansion rate of 84.4 per cent per year.

Fragmentary press reports on the numbers of cadres in other cities generally confirm this trend toward rapid expansion. In 1956, the Peking municipal government, for example, was reported to have roughly 10,000 cadres at the section-head level and higher;[47] the figures for the Nanking and Mukden municipal governments for 1957 were 4,832 and 6,500, respectively.[48] It should be noted, however, that the figures given above are limited to cadres of the municipal governments only. If cadres of other state organs and enterprises located in the cities were included, the figures would certainly be much higher, as Table 4 shows. In 1951, Tientsin was reported to have nearly 43,000 state cadres in various state, provincial, and municipal organs and enterprises within the city, excluding local cadres at the street level generally known as *chieh tao kan pu* (street cadres). On the eve of the great retrenchment campaign in 1957, the number of the state cadres of all types in Wuhan reached nearly 100,000.[49] These and other fragmentary data indicate that by 1957, before the retrenchment campaign, the average ratio of state cadres to city population in large cities might have been as high as 4 per cent.

Equally striking with the fast increase in state cadres in the urban sector over time was the rapid growth of street cadres, who operated at the level of street offices, residents' committees, and residents' groups. As the state expanded its welfare programs and extended its administrative control down to the grassroots units in the post-Liberation period,

TABLE 4. STATE CADRES IN SELECTED CITIES, 1951–65

| Year | City | Population | Number of cadres | State cadres as percentage of population |
|------|------|-----------|------------------|------------------------------------------|
| 1949 | Canton | 1,414,000 | 2,000 | 0.2% |
| 1951 | Tientsin | 2,500,000 | 42,483 | 1.7 |
| 1952 | Chungking | 1,700,000 | 60,000 | 3.5 |
| 1957 | Wuhan | 2,000,000 | 98,700 | 4.9 |
| 1957 | Canton | 1,800,000 | 60,000 | 3.3 |
| 1957 | Chengchow | 720,000 | 26,126 | 3.6 |
| 1959 | Shanghai | 7,000,000 | 100,000 | 1.4 |
| 1965 | Canton | 1,900,000 | 30,000 | 1.6 |

SOURCES: For Tientsin, *Jen min jih pao* (People's daily), Oct. 21, 1952. For Chungking, *Hsin Hua jih pao* (New China daily), Mar. 29, 1952; the figure included military cadres in the city. For Wuhan, *Ch'ang-chiang jih pao* (Yangtze daily), Dec. 24, 1957. For Canton, see *Kuang-chou jih pao* (Canton daily), Sept. 27, 1959, and *Yang-ch'eng wan pao* (Canton evening news), Dec. 12, 1965. For Chengchow, *Ho-nan jih pao* (Honan daily), Dec. 10, 1957. For Shanghai, *Jen min jih pao*, Mar. 22, 1959.

TABLE 5. STREET-LEVEL CADRES, 1957

| City | Population | Number of street cadres | Street cadres as percentage of population |
|------|-----------|-------------------------|-------------------------------------------|
| Tientsin | 3,220,000 | 39,000 | 1.2% |
| Shanghai | 6,900,000 | 100,000 | 1.4 |
| Canton | 1,840,000 | 29,482 | 1.6 |
| Mukden | 2,411,000 | 65,380 | 2.7 |
| Peking | 4,010,000 | 150,000 | 3.7 |
| Total | 18,381,000 | 383,862 | 2.1% |

SOURCES: For Tientsin, *Ta kung pao* (Impartial, Peking), Dec. 7, 1957. For Shanghai, *Chieh fang jih pao* (Liberation daily), Mar. 3, 1957. For Canton, *Kuang-chou jih pao* (Canton daily), Oct. 17, 1959. For Mukden, *Shen-yang jih pao* (Mukden daily), Sept. 15, 1957. For Peking, *Pei-ching jih pao* (Peking daily), Dec. 15, 1957.

government personnel and activities at the street level also quickly expanded. This was particularly striking in 1954–55, when the State Council standardized the city's neighborhood organizations across the nation; in 1956–57 they augmented their functions and personnel in conjunction with the reorganization of public security substations and the socialist upsurge movement. During these campaigns, a large number of former spare-time street activists and volunteers were made full-time or half-time paid local cadres (see Table 5).

If the average ratio of 2.1 per cent based on a limited sample given in Table 5 does not deviate too much from the actual average ratio for all cities, there were roughly 1,932,000 street cadres among China's 92,000,000 urban population in 1957. Thus, cadres of all affiliations at all levels in urban China as a whole constituted at least 5 per cent of the total urban population in 1957.[50] To put it differently, the total number of cadres of all types, state and local, administrative and technical, operating in the cities in 1957 may be conservatively estimated at 4,600,000, or one for every twenty members of the urban population.

Just as the initial shortage of cadres in the cities was reflected in the scarcity of party members available in that sector, so the increase in the number of urban cadres after 1949 was reflected in the growth of party membership in the cities. As Table 6 shows, the average ratio of party membership to population in the cities sampled was only .17 per cent in 1949, barely one-fifth the national ratio of .83 per cent. From this low starting point, the party stepped up its membership recruitment in the cities by assigning priority explicitly to urban workers, students, and intellectuals.[51] In Mukden, for instance, the party membership increased twenty times between 1949 and 1956, and Sian showed a gain in 1959 of sixty times the 1949 membership.

TABLE 6. GROWTH OF PARTY MEMBERSHIP IN SELECTED CITIES, 1949–59

| City | 1949[a] | | 1956 | | 1959 | |
|---|---|---|---|---|---|---|
| | Number | Percentage of population | Number | Percentage of population | Number | Percentage of population |
| Shanghai | | | 152,000[b] | 2.3% | 240,000[c] | 3.4% |
| Peking | 3,350 | .21 % | | | 257,000[d] | 6.2 |
| Mukden | 3,773 | .34 | 76,683[e] | 3.1 | | |
| Canton | 100 | .007 | | | 60,000[f] | 3.2 |
| Sian | 1,015 | .20 | | | 63,724[g] | 4.6 |
| Liuchow | 145 | .07 | 4,000[h] | 2.3 | | |
| Sample average | | .17 | | 3.2 | | 4.4 |
| National average[i] | | .83 | | 1.7 | | 2.2 |

SOURCES:

[a] National ratios and population data are drawn from Morris B. Ullman, *Cities of Mainland China: 1953 and 1958* (Washington, D.C.: Bureau of the Census, 1961), pp. 25–35. Sources for data in the 1949 column may be found in Table 1 above.

[b] *Jen min jih pao* (People's daily), July 14, 1956.

[c] *Ibid.*, July 1, 1959.

[d] John W. Lewis, *Leadership in Communist China* (Ithaca, N.Y.: Cornell University Press, 1963), p. 114.

[e] *Shen-yang jih pao* (Mukden daily), Sept. 14, 1956.

[f] *Kuang-chou jih pao* (Canton daily), Sept. 27, 1959, in *Survey of China Mainland Press*, No. 2152, p. 22.

[g] Lewis 1963, p. 114.

[h] *Liu-chou jih pao* (Liuchow daily), Apr. 12, 1957.

[i] Franz Schurmann, *Ideology and Organization in Communist China* (Berkeley and Los Angeles: University of California Press, 1966), p. 129.

Taking the data on the cities sampled as a whole, by 1956 the average ratio of 3.2 per cent for these selected cities stood at almost twice the national ratio of 1.7 per cent. In the following three years, the rapid rate of recruitment continued. By 1959, the average ratio in the cities sampled had risen to 4.4 per cent, continuing to maintain a 100 per cent lead over the new increased national ratio of 2.2 per cent. Projecting these findings (presented in Table 6) to China's urban population as a whole, party membership in the cities probably totaled approximately 2,800,000 in 1956 and 4,400,000 in 1959. In other words, by 1959 the ratio of party members to the urban population had reached the level of one party member for every 23 urban residents.

## Causes and Consequences of Overrecruitment

Normally, expansion of the government bureaucracy in developing nations can be considered a function of the modernization process and the increasing involvement of the state in that process, particularly in states oriented toward socialism, where the governments plan and control much of national life.[52] In this light, the general trend toward organizational and personnel expansion in Communist China's administrative bureaucracy since 1949 is not unusual; what appears to have been unique in the Chinese case is the pattern—the rate and course—of its development.

The rapid growth of the cadre force, which increased by about a thousand per cent in ten years,* indeed raised the basic question of whether or not such a rate of expansion was justified by the rate of China's socioeconomic development during the same period. As early as 1954, the State Council had concluded that "the high recruitment rate cannot be justified by the rate of expansion of state functions and the nation's economic growth."[53] It demanded, therefore, that "such an excessively fast expansion of personnel and structure of state organs and enterprises should be checked.[54] Data on economic growth in China available in the West tend to support the conclusion reached by the State Council. From 1952 to 1958, China's gross national product was estimated to have increased only by 46.4 per cent (from 75.6 to 110.7 billion yüan),[55] a rate much lower than that of the cadre expansion in the corresponding period (139 per cent).

An explanation of the rapid expansion of cadre forces, therefore, has to be found elsewhere. To begin with, China's deep-rooted bureaucratic tradition, in which it was the goal of "all the talented to become officials," appears to have been a significant factor.[56] This time-honored tradition may have become still more compelling under Communist rule, when the state had eliminated the private economic and educational sectors and incorporated all nongovernmental organizations into its bureaucratic system. In this way the expanded and unified state bureaucracy virtually monopolized the channels of political, social, and economic mobility. Under these circumstances, men who were motivated to move ahead—be they aspiring to personal advancement, or dedicated to public service—had little choice but to join the all-encompassing state bureaucratic system. Thus, the circumstances and tradition, reinforcing each other, appear to have made the rush for bureaucratic posts ever more intense after the Communist takeover.

The great disparity in the standard of living and in the availability of limited modern amenities between the urban and the rural sectors apparently also contributed to a one-way flow of cadres. Under Communist rule, urban wages remained much higher than farm wages: as

* It should be noted that these figures must have included personnel of former private enterprises who were incorporated into the state's unified bureaucratic system as a result of the socialist transformation of these capitalist enterprises. The increase of this type, which simply switched private posts to cadre posts, ideally should be differentiated from the expansion through recruitment of new blood into bureaucratic service. However, no data are yet available for such a differentiation.

late as 1956, the average industrial worker in the cities earned three to five times more than the average peasant in the rural sector (569–1039 yüan, in contrast to 185 yüan per year).[57] Furthermore, the cities offered a great variety of modern facilities, material comforts, and educational opportunities that the rural areas could not match. Cadre posts in the cities generally involved prestigious office work and other nonmanual jobs and also offered better opportunities for upward mobility in the bureaucratic hierarchy.[58] In a country like China, where society had long placed a great symbolic value on holding government posts in the administrative center, the attraction of the city can hardly be over-emphasized. Thus, it was still common under Communist rule for urban cadres to avoid rural assignments, and for rural cadres to seek posts in the urban bureaucracies, for cultural reasons.[59]

The reorganization of the administrative system of rural China in 1955–56 demonstrated clearly how various cultural and economic considerations motivated cadres to move into the city bureaucracy and how the bureaucrats at higher levels tried to accommodate large numbers of upward-moving cadres for a variety of reasons, organizational aggrandizement, for one. In conjunction with the party's move to simplify administrative organs, the State Council ordered in December 1955 the abolition of the 19,000 rural districts (*ch'ü*) and the amalgamation of the 210,000 *hsiang* into larger administrative units. The move was popularly known as the "abolish ch'ü and amalgamate hsiang" (*ch'e ch'ü ping hsiang*) movement.[60] In the course of this reorganization movement, as an article in the *Jen min jih pao* pointed out, "few cadres of the abolished hsiang and ch'ü governments volunteered to work in the enlarged hsiang governments or to go down to the newly organized agricultural producers' cooperatives. Everybody demanded to work in the *hsien* governments and hoped to move into a larger city in the future."[61] A local party secretary frankly confessed: "During the movement, those who were assigned to office work or managerial jobs in towns and cities smiled with content, while those who were sent to organize cooperatives and work with the masses in the field thought they were doomed."[62]

Survey data on Hunan, as revealed by the *Jen min jih pao*, show that the rush for government posts in the cities became quite serious as early as 1954, even before the rural administrative reorganization was put into effect in the province. In that year, cadres newly promoted from the hsiang level were found to constitute 70 per cent of the ch'ü cadre force, and those promoted from the ch'ü level occupied 50 per cent of hsien cadre posts.[63] During the reorganization movement in 1956, most hsien governments increased their personnel by at least 30 per cent in order to accommodate over 100,000 cadres moving up from the now defunct ch'ü and hsiang governments, a move that inevitably pushed more lower-level cadres into higher-level governments in large towns and cities. The same survey found that 66 per cent of special district (*chuan ch'ü*) cadres and 35 per cent of hsien cadres had moved into the provincial-level organs and their subordinate enterprises in large urban centers in the course of the reorganization movement. Reports on the movement of rural cadres into the cities in other provinces generally confirm the pattern found in Hunan.[64]

This rapid influx of cadres from the lower to the higher levels, and from the rural to the urban areas, resulted in such major bureaucratic crises as the weakening of leadership at the lower levels, and an increase in financial and manpower waste with a breakdown of organizational efficiency at the higher levels. The flow of rural cadres into the urban areas during the 1956 *ch'e ch'ü ping hsiang* movement is a case in point. An editorial in the *Hsin Hu-nan pao* (New Hunan news) squarely placed responsibility for the weakening of the leadership in the countryside on the erratic movement of cadres. It declared:

In the past several years, we have transferred many cadres from the lower-level to the higher-level organs for the purpose of strengthening the leadership of the upper governments. The policy is basically correct and essential. However, many local organs failed to give due attention to needs at the lower levels. Consequently, too many cadres were transferred upward too fast. This has created not only the problem of a "heavy head with light feet" in our administrative structure but also disruption of leadership continuity and stability at the lower levels. Our problem is too many cadres at the top and too few at the bottom.[65]

Indeed, during the push for the "upsurge of socialism" in the countryside in 1956–57, the leadership found that few cadres working at the village level were competent to advance the formation of higher-level agricultural producers' cooperatives and to consolidate their operation. As a result, the central government was compelled to send a large number of cadres from the higher-level organs in conjunction with the massive organizational *ching chien* (retrenchment) and personnel *hsia fang* (downward transfer) movements in order to strengthen the rural leadership and to sustain the agricultural collectivization movement.

The rapid upward movement of cadres also created serious problems for the upper-level administrative organs in the cities. As Teng Hsiao-p'ing pointed out in his report to the Third Plenum of the Eighth Central Committee in 1957, the excessively rapid expansion of state bureaucracies had created budget drains, waste of manpower, a growth of "bureaucratism" and "careerism," a trend to organizational self-aggrandizement, and the deterioration of administrative discipline and efficiency.[66]

A survey of the personnel structure of the government organs conducted by the Office for Correspondence and Materials of Statistical Work of the State Statistical Bureau in 1955 revealed that there was tremendous overstaffing and ineffective use of manpower at all levels of the state organs. In the nation as a whole, about one-third of all administrative employees were "nonproductive" personnel.[67] Also, the State Council complained that the maintenance of state cadres alone cost as much as 9.6 per cent of the national budget in 1955, almost twice the 5 per cent ceiling planned by the leadership.[68] Aside from the financial and manpower problems, the concentration and overstaffing of cadres in the cities also created a host of other problems, such as the breakdown of organizational discipline and morale and the tendency for the "productive" cities to erode into "parasitic" cities (a development that Mao feared and repeatedly cautioned against). An indictment of bureaucratic deterioration in the retraining division of the labor bureau of the Shanghai municipal government in 1955 provides an example:

New offices are more crowded than ever. But over half of the 61 cadres in the division have not received any work assignment for at least half a year. . . . Work that should and can be done by one cadre is now divided among four or five or even ten persons. Worse still, no one is in charge, and no one is responsible. The cadres ordinarily spend hours reading newspapers or just gossiping every day. When they get bored at the office, they go out wandering in the streets in the name of "business coordination" or "field inspection." The morale of the division has dropped so low that two cadres were specially assigned to show movies eight times a month in order to cheer up the bored cadres.[69]

Stories such as this were quite common in both the local and the national press in the mid-1950's.[70]

### From Recruitment to Retrenchment

The leadership's dilemma over administrative bureaucracy started in the early days of the Communist regime, as we have seen. In 1949 the party urgently appealed to its rank and file "to learn how to administer and lead the cities," and also warned them to be on guard against the "sugar-coated bullets" of the "bourgeois vices."[71] During the 1951–52 *san fan* campaign conducted in the cities, the leadership purged about

4.5 per cent (approximately 100,000) of the state cadres as corrupt and incompetent.[72] During 1953 and 1954 the leadership once more trimmed the fast-expanding bureaucracy by 150,000 cadres, sending them out of their urban posts.[73] However, these moves appeared to be sporadic and not a systematic effort to control the expansion of bureaucracy.

It was in the early spring of 1955 at the national conference of the party that the leadership formally began to push for systematic control of bureaucratic expansion.[74] Following the conference, the leadership launched a strong press campaign to expose the evils of excessive recruitment and concentration of cadres in the cities, and demanded that all state organs and enterprises develop plans for systematic readjustment and reduction in personnel.[75] In late 1954 the State Council instructed state organs at all levels to form special "commissions on organizational tables" to work out concrete programs for organizational readjustment and retrenchment in the cities.[76] Despite the hue and cry of press editorials in 1955, the bureaucrats' inertia and resistance to the reform remained firm and strong.

The formation of commissions on organizational tables did not really get started on a large scale in major cities until June of the following year. Moreover, even where the commissions were set up and tentative plans for reorganization and retrenchment were announced, little action toward implementation took place. In Peking, for example, Chang Yu-yü, a deputy mayor, reported that a commission on organizational tables had been organized for the city in July 1955, with the purpose of eliminating 50 per cent of the municipal government personnel, as instructed by the city's party committee.[77] But no indication of progress of the commission's work was reported in the Peking-based *Jen min jih pao* during the next twelve months.

To attack the bureaucratic inertia once more, the State Council issued another stern directive in December 1955 demanding that all government organs immediately put their retrenchment plans into effect and stipulating that the tasks of simplification and reduction at the national level should be completed by January of the following year, and at the municipal and other local levels by February.[78] The directive also ordered that retrenchment in the managerial bureaucracy of industrial and commercial enterprises should be carried out in the same manner after the retrenchment in the administrative bureaucracy of government organs. Under the intensified pressure from the top, most municipal governments and their commissions on organizational tables did begin to announce plans for simplification of organizations and to criticize the evils of overexpansion.[79] But throughout the year, the reluctant bureaucrats appear to have again succeeded in ignoring the leadership's directives. A stalemate and inaction again prevailed: plans were loudly publicized and declarations issued, but as before no real progress toward implementation was reported in the local press.

A number of cities even continued to proclaim the shortage of cadres and to insist on the need for "bold" recruitment. Canton, for example, declared in September 1956 that the city still needed 2,200 administrative cadres and 5,600 technical cadres in the following year, despite the fact that in that year 3,900 cadres were reported to have been promoted from the ch'ü and other lower levels.[80] Adding to confusion of this sort, an editorial in the *Jen min jih pao* on June 11, 1956, declared, contrary to its earlier stand:

In early 1956, about one-third of the leadership posts in Peking were still unfilled. During the first quarter of the year (January to March), over 2,200 cadres of section-chief level or higher have been promoted. This effort has brought the number of unfilled posts down to one-tenth of the original. But the problem of cadre shortage still exists in some units.[81]

To deal with evasive maneuvers of the bureaucracy, the State Council flatly notified all organs in November 1956 that "from the very date this notice is received, government organs at all levels must immediately cease setting up any new organizations, adding any personnel, and filling any vacancies."[82] And by early 1957, the leadership had apparently reached the conclusion that in order to break the bureaucracy's inertia and its stance of self-preservation a more drastic measure in the form of mass movement would have to be introduced. The pressure for a mass campaign began to build up in the spring, and the momentum for retrenchment and simplification reached full swing in the summer. By the fall, virtually all government organs and state enterprises were reported to have been compelled to retrench from 30 per cent to 50 per cent of their personnel. (See Table 7.)[83]

Reports on the development of campaigns in specific cities and organs illustrate the mood and momentum of the movement. In Canton, for example, the original plan drawn up in December 1956 called for the elimination of 20 per cent of the municipal cadre force.[84] Two months later the target was raised to 25 per cent.[85] (See Table 8.) As the movement surged ahead, various organs began to compete with one another in setting ever-higher targets, presumably trying to show that the higher the target, the more "advanced" the unit. By September the 30 per cent to 40 per cent retrenchment rate had almost become the minimum.

In Peking, as in Canton, where a shortage of cadres had been re-

TABLE 7. ORGANIZATIONAL RETRENCHMENT OF STATE CADRES IN
SELECTED CITIES, 1957

| Report date | City | Number of cadres retrenched | Number as percentage of total cadres |
|---|---|---|---|
| Sept. 1957 | Canton | 20,000 | 33% |
| Oct. 1957 | Tsinan | — | 40–50 |
| Nov. 1957 | Sian | 2,425 | 41 |
| Nov. 1957 | Peking | 21,000 | 30–50 |
| Dec. 1957 | Chengchow | 9,100 | 30–40 |
| Dec. 1957 | Tatung | 10,000 | 40 |
| Dec. 1957 | Wuhan | 32,900 | 33 |

SOURCES: For Canton, *Kuang-chou jih pao* (Canton daily), Sept. 27, 1959. For Tsinan, *Ta chung jih pao* (Mass daily, Tsinan), Oct. 25, 1957. For Sian, *Shan-hsi jih pao* (Shensi daily), Nov. 27, 1957. For Chengchow, *Ho-nan jih pao* (Honan daily), Dec. 10, 1957. For Tatung, *Shan-hsi jih pao* (Shansi daily), Dec. 20, 1957. For Peking, *Jen min jih pao* (People's daily), Nov. 17, 1957. For Wuhan, *Ch'ang-chiang jih pao* (Yangtze daily), Dec. 24, 1957.

TABLE 8. RETRENCHMENT PLAN OF CANTON CITY, FEBRUARY 1957

| Sector | Percentage of cadres to be reduced |
|---|---|
| Industry | 40% |
| Finance and trade | 26 |
| Culture and education | 21 |
| Transportation | 25 |
| Capital construction | 21 |
| Political and legal system | 10 |

SOURCE: *Kuang-chou jih pao* (Canton daily), Feb. 25, 1957.

ported in the previous year, a reduction of about 40 per cent occurred in all organs by the end of 1957.[86] The cases of the retrenchment of the personnel and religious affairs bureaus of the municipal government, as reported by the *Jen min jih pao* in detail, demonstrated clearly the process and intensity of the campaign. After having gone through three progressive stages of retrenchment in 1957, both bureaus found their working forces drastically reduced and their original administrative subdivisions completely abolished. (See Table 9.) Even large bureaus such as those for commerce, handicrafts, and light industry, which normally maintained several thousand cadres each, were reported to have reduced their personnel by 62–66 per cent in October.[87] Although a large number of those who were retrenched during the campaign had presumably managed to return after the radical campaign mood was eased, such drastic retrenchment as this was by no means exceptional.[88]

By March 1958 in the nation as a whole, according to An Tzu-wen,

TABLE 9. RETRENCHMENT UNDER THE PEKING PEOPLE'S COUNCIL, 1957

| | Personnel Bureau | | | Religious Affairs Bureau | | |
|---|---|---|---|---|---|---|
| Stage | Section | Number of cadres | Percentage staying | Section | Number of cadres | Percentage staying |
| Original | 7 | 60 | 100% | 4 | 16 | 100% |
| First stage | 3 | 32 | 53 | 0 | 9 | 56 |
| Second stage | 0 | 17 | 28 | 0 | 4 | 25 |
| Third stage | 0 | 8 | 13 | | | |

SOURCE: *Jen min jih pao* (People's daily), Nov. 29, 1957.

then director of the Organization Department of the Central Committee, more than 1,300,000 cadres had been separated from their urban bureaucratic posts at higher levels and transferred downward to the countryside and factories.[89] If the 30 to 50 per cent reduction in all cities reported in the local press can be accepted, the total number of cadres retrenched would have been about 2.6 million, considerably higher than the official figure given by An Tzu-wen.[90]

*From Ching Chien to Hsia Fang*

The ching chien campaign of 1957 was designed mainly to reduce personnel, to simplify organization of the upper-level organs in the cities, and to reassign the retrenched cadres to permanent posts at basic levels in the countryside and factories. As a directive of the State Council issued in December 1955 explained, "the purpose of the campaign is to correct the serious problem of inflated and redundant organizational structures and of the waste of manpower and resources on the one hand, and to improve administrative efficiency and leadership at the lower levels on the other."[91] Thus the 32,000 cadres reported to have been eliminated in Wuhan in 1957, for example, were all reassigned to work at the basic levels of hsiang governments, cooperatives, and factories.[92] Cadres transferred during the campaign were told to "make up their minds to settle down, establish households at their new posts, and work there with peace in heart."[93]

In late 1957, following the Third Plenum of the Eighth Central Committee in October, a new dimension was added to the ching chien movement. In a keynote speech to the plenum, Teng Hsiao-p'ing, general secretary of the party, called for the sending downward of more cadres "to take part in productive labor and work with the masses" on a short-term basis.[94] In the following months, a new movement called hsia fang (sending cadres downward) emerged alongside the ching chien movement. By the spring of 1958, the hsia fang movement had generally merged with the ching chien and had even become the dominant form of the campaign by the end of the year.[95] Though the two movements were similar and complementary in many aspects, hsia fang was designed primarily to transfer cadres downward on a temporary basis, for periods ranging from several weeks to a year. Moreover, the aims of hsia fang were more concerned with rectifying the city cadres' eroded ideological outlook and renewing their "mass viewpoint" through the practice of manual labor for production and close contact with the masses.[96]

The hsia fang campaign reached a peak in May and June of 1958, when Chairman Mao himself and other top leaders did manual labor for many days alongside workers at the construction site of the Shih-san-ling Water Conservancy Project on the outskirts of Peking.[97] On September 28, the Central Committee and the State Council issued a joint directive formally "requiring all cadres to take part in manual labor for one month each year."[98] This hsia fang campaign lasted throughout the radical years of the "communization" movement and the Great Leap Forward. Official statistics released by the *Jen min jih pao* in 1959 stated that over 1,300,000 cadres were sent down to work in the production workshops and fields and to live with the masses for at least a month. Among them, 257,700 cadres (20 per cent) stayed at these levels for over a year.[99] In Shanghai it was reported that over 100,000 cadres did physical labor at the basic levels for one to three months.[100]

The hsia fang movement had tapered off gradually by 1960, as the leadership retreated from the radical policies of the Great Leap Forward and the people's communes. The movement, however, was revived in a slightly different form, known as *tun tien* (squat on the spot) in 1964–65.[101] A large number of urban cadres were once again sent down from the upper organs, often in teams, to do physical labor, live with the masses, and carry out the socialist educational campaign as had been done during the earlier hsia fang movement. But this time the hsia fang cadres were instructed to "squat" in a specific unit or organ for an extended period of time to conduct "investigation and research," and to "learn about and solve problems with the masses right on the spot."[102] The tun tien movement, therefore, appears to have been designed to combine the functions of both the ching chien and hsia fang campaigns, with a new emphasis on strengthening the supervisory role of the upper-level cadres and tightening the bureaucratic chain of command.

The process of cadre recruitment and mobility in urban China's bureaucratic development after the Communist takeover demonstrates a distinct pattern of behavior—a pendulum-like movement between contrasting types of campaigns, namely, the recruitment and retrenchment of urban cadres.

The acute shortage of qualified cadres in the cities in the early years motivated the leadership to launch movements urging cadre recruitment and bureaucratic construction in order to satisfy the manpower and administrative needs of the new government. Although the basic needs were met by 1952, the institution-building and recruitment movement, with a momentum of its own, eventually became unresponsive to the leadership's control and ran to the other extreme of excessive expansion of personnel and organizational self-aggrandizement from 1953 to 1956. To cope with this situation, the leadership was compelled to launch a new movement of the opposite nature to counter the growth of bureaucratic organization and the excess of personnel. The ching chien (1957), hsia fang (1958–59), and tun tien (1964–65) movements did succeed in reducing the number of upper-level cadres in the cities by transferring them to the lower levels for permanent or temporary assignments. Nevertheless, in the times between these movements, when radicalism subsided and the leadership stressed orderly administrative control, the retrenched organizations and cadres moved quietly to reclaim the power and influence they had lost during the mass movements. From the vantage point of the Cultural Revolution, the current violent campaign against the bureaucratic establishments would appear to be another pendulum-like swing, an attempt to check the resurgence of the bureaucratic forces.[103]

Looking at this sequence of movements, one finds that bureaucratic development in Communist China and the Maoist leadership's policy toward bureaucracy over time shows a clear pattern of challenge-and-response alternation, a pattern characterized by the use of the mass movement as an instrument for implementing policy. Clearly the mass movement was a powerful and effective method of achieving policy objectives, but it consistently took on a momentum and an independent course of development of its own, which eventually became difficult to control. Thus, although the mass movement could effectively cure many bureaucratic ills, it tended to "overcure," so to speak, and to create a host of other ailments often no less serious than the original ones. As a result, successive mass movements always became necessary.

The massive recruitment campaign of the early 1950's indeed solved the problem of the cadre shortage. But the massive treatment applied resulted in bureaucratic inflation, manpower waste, budgetary drains, and the breakdown of administrative efficiency. The drastic "dosage"

of the ching chien and hsia fang movements, which involved the transfer of perhaps more than three million urban cadres from the upper
organs in the cities to assignments in the countryside from 1957 through
1959, seems to have played a role in providing the impetus for the excesses of the Great Leap Forward and the "communization" movement
in the late 1950's.[104] The hsia fang cadres, generally more "advanced"
and "progressive" ideologically than their rural counterparts, and free
of local kinship ties and vested interests in new local assignments,
tended to act more radically and freely than local cadres. Furthermore,
they knew that their chances of returning to the cities depended on
their performance in the countryside. Thus the hsia fang cadres often
became deliberately radical and aggressive in order to win special recognition for their "revolutionary merits" and qualify to regain their urban
posts. In this way the massive ching chien and hsia fang movements
seem to have created an atmosphere of radicalism in the countryside in
1957–58, which in turn apparently set the stage for the nation's radical
push in 1958–59.[105]

Here again the pattern of "overkill" was evident. The hsia fang movement, although it was designed to eliminate organizational evils and to
strengthen the rural leadership and revolutionize the cadres, was obviously carried away by its own momentum. As a result, the hsia fang
cadres from the cities in a way "overstrengthened" and "overrevolution-
ized" the rural leadership.

The Cultural Revolution appears to represent another pendulum
swing in the Maoist leadership's effort to harness the resurging bureaucracy and make it politically responsive and free from the evils of "bureaucratism." The unsuccessful attempts to achieve such objectives
through the socialist education and the "four clean-ups" campaigns in
1962–65 apparently led the leadership to mobilize such extrabureaucratic forces as the Red Guards and revolutionary rebels to attack the
party and state bureaucracies during the Cultural Revolution. With the
battle cry of "thoroughly smashing all bureaucratic structures,"[106] the
revolutionary committees emerged as new organs of power and began
in early 1967 with the support of the military to "seize power" from
bureaucrats at all levels.[107]

In mid-1968 a new movement of ching chien and hsia fang appears to
have been set in motion in conjunction with the political purge and
power seizure then in progress. Mao was reported to have issued a series
of new directives on ching chien earlier in the year, instructing all
organs to launch a new simplification and retrenchment movement according to the "eight-character principle" of *hsia fang, ho ping, ch'e*

*hsiao, ching chien* (sending cadres downward, amalgamating overlapping organizations, abolishing superfluous organs, and streamlining inflated structures).[108] The Red Guards and revolutionary groups were told to make sure "the movement is carried out thoroughly with all seriousness and on a large scale, and not superficially with a perfunctory attitude on a small scale."[109]

After July 1968, the new ching chien movement emphasized publicizing model cases in the press and on the radio.[110] In September, many revolutionary committees in cities had claimed to have succeeded in reducing their organizational structures and cadre strength by 40–70 per cent by sending tens of thousands of "surplus" cadres to the countryside and factories.[111] Although the final outcome of the Cultural Revolution and its impact on cadre redistribution and structural reorganization in the cities remain to be seen and analyzed, the similarities in the pattern of development between the 1956–58 ching chien and hsia fang campaigns and the current one are striking. It seems clear that the Chinese bureaucratic system is undergoing another period of convulsion as Mao determines to try once more his egalitarian model of bureaucratic development.

# Trade Union Cultivation of Workers for Leadership

PAUL F. HARPER

In many developing nations, trade unions have assumed a significant role in the process of urbanization. In the developed nations, unions have historically been involved in a variety of activities during the course of industrialization, but today in the West, the collective bargaining process between labor and management is viewed as the main legitimate activity of a union. Although unions do engage in political activity to varying extents in the West, this is generally considered a means to an end; the goal of the unions is the betterment of the workers through higher wages, better working conditions, and fringe benefits. Trade unions in developing nations, in contrast, have often appeared to stress political action at the expense of economic advancement for their members.[1] Frequently the unions are closely tied to and even led by a political party, with economic welfare appearing to take a secondary position to efforts on behalf of nationalism, anti-imperialism, or some party ideology. Unions in the developing nations are generally less autonomous structures in the polity than their Western counterparts. Furthermore, they serve a wider range of functions than do the unions in the developed nations.

According to Eisenstadt, the most important "ecological manifestation" of modernization has been the process of urbanization, the concentration of people in urban areas where specialized economic and professional activities are centered.[2] Some concomitant aspects of this process of urbanization have been closely related to functions performed at least in part by the unions: achieving the commitment of the industrial labor force, or "performance and acceptance of the behaviors ap-

This study was made possible in part by funds granted by the Carnegie Foundation of New York through the London-Cornell Project at Cornell University.

propriate to an industrial way of life";[3] the breaking down of the traditional, village, and kinship ascriptive criteria of status and the developing within the urban and factory context of less rigid, more achievement-
oriented social strata;[4] the replacement of the preindustrial peasants'
acceptance of scarcity with a recognition of opportunity and rewards
for achievement in a context of technological change;[5] and the "allevia-
tion of labor unrest that is caused by the frictions created in the transition from a preindustrial society to an industrial one." To benefit from
industrial civilization, workers must become members of organized urban communities and submit to industrial discipline. Despite the apparent preoccupation with political activity, unions in developing nations
are indeed concerned with these social and economic functions and in
bringing about "orderly processes of transition to industrial life."[6]

Another quite important concomitant of urbanization, and the one
that interests us most here, is an "upsurge of social mobility through
occupational, educational and political channels."[7] The unions in China,
as in various other developing nations, function as a channel for imparting industrial skills, educating, politicizing, and selecting workers
for advancement into the urban and national leadership structures. In
the developed Western nations, unions are sometimes a channel into politics and some unions provide the training necessary for workers to move
from unskilled to skilled labor status; but rarely do unions in the West
assume very broad educational chores, since the labor forces already
have a relatively high educational level. In most developing countries,
the unions and management must deal with large numbers of minimally
educated, often illiterate workers. In China, the unions have also assumed this educational function, but under the pervasive Communist
regime the aims and techniques of the unions in cultivating workers for
leadership in China's industry and cities may differ from those of unions
in non-Communist developing nations.

Trade unions in Communist political systems are considered the mass
organizations of the workers. A Communist party cannot itself be the
organization of the workers, since it is by its own definition the vanguard of the working class, a party of elites. Thus the party works
through mass organizations that link it to the various classes and sectors
in society, passing on the ideology to the masses while seeking to integrate those masses into the political system and legitimate the party's
leading role. Leading cadres of the mass organizations are also members of the Communist party, often in leadership positions in the political elite, and in their "transmission belt" role perform a two-way function: not only do they link the party with the masses, but they also

represent the particular interests of their sector in party councils. Being closer to a given group in the population than the party, the mass organization serves to pinpoint and train the "advanced" individual for recruitment into the elite.

In China's cities, there are several mass organizations for various sectors of the society. We are concerned with the trade union, the link between the Chinese Communist Party (CCP) and the proletariat, the mass organization that educates and indoctrinates the workers and channels the more talented and politically reliable amongst them onto the path of leadership in industry or the party. According to the orthodox theories of Communism, the workers are the leading class in society; Mao and his peasants notwithstanding, the CCP after 1949 sought to "proletarianize" itself by increasing its working class component, to bring reality into line with doctrine.

The unions in China are under a single umbrella organization, the All-China Federation of Trade Unions (ACFTU). The basis of organization is the enterprise, mine, or institution, not the craft. Thus all the workers in any unit, whatever their occupation, belong to the same primary organization. There are a total of 16 national industrial unions, with vertical levels of leadership upward from the primary unit through the city ward, the city, the province, and the national committee of the union to the ACFTU. In addition to vertical rule, local trade union councils at the city and provincial levels provide leadership over all primary units under their geographical jurisdiction, whatever industrial unions those primary units might belong to. Leaders of the industrial unions and the trade union councils at the various levels are frequently among the leading party figures in a city or province.

Party, government, and union leadership roles often overlapped in the early 1950's. In some cities, such as Shanghai and Wuhan, the chairman of the municipal trade union council was also deputy secretary of the municipal CCP committee while concurrently holding various leading government posts. The importance of the local trade union councils diminished after 1953 with the rise of the industrial unions and the stress on specialization, but this relatively powerful centralized union structure led in turn to increasing pressure for more independence from the party in local union operations. Since the decentralization of CCP power to regional levels in 1958, the local trade union councils became again the most significant channel for party leadership of the unions.[8]

The basic level, or primary, trade union organization, which is the focus of this chapter, is the foundation of trade union work. Any factory,

mine, or institution with ten or more members can form a primary organization. General meetings of the union members in the primary organization elect a committee to direct the union's work in a plant; in large
enterprises, committees at the workshop or office level constitute the
basic level organization. Production work is considered "the most important task" of these primary organizations, but they also are expected,

under the leadership of the party and the upper levels of the trade unions,
to educate and organize the broad worker masses, to raise their class consciousness and technical levels, to inculcate new labor attitudes, to organize
labor relations, and to ensure the fulfillment of the national plan, at the same
time actively paying attention to improving the workers' labor and livelihood
conditions and to protecting the daily welfare of the workers.[9]

The educative roles assigned to the trade unions are concisely stated
in the constitution of the trade unions of China. "The trade unions of
China are the mass organization of the working class led by the party
and are the transmission belt between the party and the masses. Under
the people's democratic dictatorship, the trade unions are a school of
administration, a school of management, and a school of Communism
for the worker masses."[10] These educative roles are the means by which
the unions have in the long run contributed most to the urban leadership and to the modernization of the society as a whole, for industrial
workers, more conversant with the rational orderly procedures and requirements of industrialization than the revolutionary guerrilla fighter
or the peasant, have been selected and trained for cadre positions in
the cities.

### The Union as a School for Management

The only conspicuous failure in these roles for the unions has been
as a school for management. Success in this role would demand a growing democracy within industry, with workers learning to manage their
enterprise—to supervise the administration of the factory and to make
decisions about the allocation of funds, the distribution and reinvest-
ment of profits, the choosing of supervisory personnel, and other issues
of management. Democratic participation in management need not imply the anarchist strains marking syndicalist movements of the past, but
it certainly entails more than pro forma discussions and ratification by
the masses or their representatives of decisions made at the top, as has
been the case in China.[11] Workers' councils in Yugoslavia provide perhaps the closest thing to a model for industrial democracy in a Communist state today.[12]

In China, the unions have not been able to implement effectively and persistently a system of democratizing the management process in the factory, for efforts to bring the workers into management have foundered on changes in the party line. In the early years, the "labor-capital consultative conference" in private enterprises did bring workers and unions into the making of management decisions,[13] and the 1950 "rules of procedure for settling labor disputes" added teeth to the workers' powers by making the final arbiters of disputes in private industry the trade union–dominated local labor bureaus.[14] But these tools had lost their efficacy long before the nationalization of all industry in 1955–56. In 1956, Lai Jo-yü, then chairman of the ACFTU, spoke to the Eighth Congress of the CCP on the need for the unions to begin functioning as a school for management, declaring that the workers' representative conference in the factory had "in general become a platform for cadres only, and so has lost its significance."[15]

Following the Eighth Party Congress, Lai Jo-yü and the trade union leadership, with party approval, began to develop plans to bring workers realistically into management participation. The workers' councils of Yugoslavia were studied. At the end of May 1957, workers' representative congresses with some genuine powers were proclaimed in a *Jen min jih pao* editorial as an organ to be set up in all state enterprises.[16] Within a few weeks, however, the anti-rightist campaign of 1957 was in full swing, and the workers' congresses were stillborn. A similar effort to reinvigorate the unions as schools for management was begun in some places in 1965 with an overhaul of the workers' congresses, which were still dominated by administration cadres.[17] But this movement fell under the impact of the Cultural Revolution. At the present time, although workers serve on the revolutionary committees running the factories, it is at least arguable that the objective of the Cultural Revolution in the factories has not been so much to provide mass supervision over management as to destroy the old managerial apparatus. In any case, the unions are not the leaders in the movement and cannot be considered successful in their role as schools of management.

## The Union as a School for Administration

The Chinese trade unions' performance as a school of administration for the workers has been much more effective than their performance as a school for democratic management. One function of the unions is to train or at least select for training workers who show leadership qualities or some aptitude for more generally responsible tasks than production line duties. As the mass organization of the workers, the unions have become the most important vehicle for identifying and thrusting upward outstanding members of the proletariat who can serve the system in supervisory or administrative positions.

Besides identifying the potential administrators, the trade unions function as a school for administration in another manner. They are responsible for organizing and operating technical and cultural education in the factories. Through the spare-time education system in the enterprise and, to a lesser extent, through short-term study programs, the unions have provided schooling that has not only increased the technical capabilities of China's workers, but has also established an educational foundation that has enabled many workers to rise into supervisory and technical-expert staff positions.[18]

Workers' education has long been considered essential by the Chinese Communists in their plans for national development. At the Second Plenum of the Seventh CCP Central Committee held in March 1949, when the "shift of gravity" from the village to the city was made explicit and official as the CCP line, the working class was designated as the core group on which the party was to rely in its struggle to build a new China.[19] But the leading role of the proletariat in China could hardly be achieved without a veritable revolution in the levels of production and productivity. Changing the "backward state" of the cultural, scientific, and technical level of the workers became a "task of decisive importance."[20]

Official cognizance of this need was taken in June 1950, when the Government Administration Council issued the "Directives on Developing Spare-Time Education for Workers and Staff Members,"[21] in an effort to develop an adult education program. The unions in the enterprises were assigned the task of carrying out this program. But spare-time schools in the factories developed rather unevenly until the mid-1950's. Political education received initial priority and was the main thrust of union work in the spare-time schools during these early years, for union cadres were best qualified at that time to work in the political sphere, imparting to the workers a sense of the proletariat's new leading role and "mission" in the new social order. Cultural studies, which were to be "similar to the main courses in regular primary and middle schools," and technical classes grew slowly. The factory management soon took over the running of cultural and technical education, with emphasis on literacy and lower-primary-school classes and on such popular technical study as master-apprentice contracts.[22]

The state of China's proletariat at the time of the establishment of the People's Republic of China cannot realistically be described as ready for rapid modernization of the economy. In terms of size, it was hardly adequate to the task: industrial workers in 1949 numbered three million, and the total number of "workers and employees" was eight million, less than two per cent of the population.[23] Lack of education among the workers kept the technological potentialities of the proletariat at a low level; the Communists have declared that the proportion of literates in the proletariat at that time was only 20 or 25 per cent. Working long hours for low pay with little job security, the proletariat was exploited under the Kuomintang, which was dominated by cliques somewhat less than sympathetic to the labor movement. Social welfare policies for workers were low on the scale of priorities, and the inflation of the 1940's struck as hard at wage earners in industry as at the middle class. Thus the Communists had a ready audience for their propaganda, which extolled the virtues of the proletariat and offered hope for a better life.[24]

Some sense of the situation facing the new leadership in those early years is given in an article discussing technical education in Peking factories;[25] written in April 1950, it describes the content of technical education in the enterprise and draws a picture of the difficulties facing these programs, difficulties not easily reduced in the first half dozen years of Communist rule. Practical work was stressed, with demonstrations and lectures on plant machinery, reading and drawing blueprints, and "on the spot" lectures and demonstrations. The early years were a time when basic skills were at a premium, and practical knowledge offered immediate rewards. Little attention was paid to theory, although some classes in the fundamentals of science were instituted from the beginning: arithmetic, and sometimes algebra and geometry were taught to the young apprentices and unskilled workers, as well as some basic physics relevant to the work of the factory. It was noted, though, that "at present, the achievements of these classes are still very small."

The master-apprentice system was a source of conflict and tension in a plant. Skilled workers were reluctant to impart their knowledge— partly because of attitudes developed in the days when an elderly worker could be replaced by a newly trained and stronger young apprentice—and they jealously protected their status in the plant. Apprentices, for their part, were often "cocky," even to the point of refusing to fetch tools. Such attitudes only made the master workers even less inclined to share their knowledge and experience. Political education of both groups eventually helped relieve the tension, as did a system of bonuses to encourage skilled workers to publicize their skills.

At another level, the problem of too many other activities, a difficulty that persistently plagues spare-time education, was felt. In the face of meetings constantly called by the party, administration, trade union, and Communist Youth League, attention paid to technical education classes wanes.

For example, in certain factories, Monday and Wednesday are trade union small group activities days, Friday is party day, Tuesday is league day, and Thursday and Saturday are for political education; and then suddenly there is even cultural education. These activity periods and the time for technical education conflict. Not only is there no attention paid to technical education; technical education must yield to some unnecessary activities. There is even a feeling that technical education must not be dealt with too long, for that would mean being an obstacle to trade union work and political education.[26]

The pressures on time demanded by such activities in the early years would build up and then ease periodically, contributing to the uneven development of cultural and technical education in the factories until 1956.

To indicate the scope of trade union education for the workers prior to 1956, some comparative data are available for 1954. Of the 18,809,000 "workers and employees" in China that year,[27] slightly over three million, or 12 per cent, were attending some sort of spare-time education course. In all, 953,000 workers were studying in technical classes, with over 100,000 workers engaged in full-time technical study at some point during the year.[28] Efforts to train the workers varied from industry to industry, with the coal-mining industry and its union developing one of the more comprehensive systems of education during the early years. By the end of 1955, each mining center on the mainland had at least one spare-time school for the miners.[29]

Generally, however, spare-time cultural and technical education for workers "lagged far behind the needs of [China's] industrial construction, agricultural cooperativization, and technical reform" until 1956.[30] A National Work Conference on Spare-Time Education for Industrial Workers, held in December 1955, outlined the major problems facing the union-operated spare-time schools in the factories at that time: slow establishment of a complete range of schooling; lack of study time for the workers; few qualified teachers; and lack of funds.[31] Cadres in local governmental education departments tended to ignore or deprecate spare-time schools and their teaching staffs. Trade union cadres as well as management and Communist Youth League cadres who helped run the schools were accused of a negative approach when they complained that there was too great an antagonism between study and production. They were aware of the conflict between the need for immediate production success and the need to raise the workers' technical levels, an effort being served by the spare-time schools.

A concerted and sustained effort by the Communist leadership and particularly by the unions began after this 1956 conference and continued through the Great Leap Forward. The attack on illiteracy received first priority in the first half dozen years; after 1956 a more elaborate program was established, with many plants setting up classes from primary school through the university level. The Great Leap Forward brought rapid expansion not only of industry and the industrial working force, but also of the industrial education system. The unions were barely able to cope with the heightened pressures, and serious competition arose between production and study. Industry-centered education continued to expand until it reached its peak in 1960, when 25 million workers were reportedly enrolled in and attending spare-time classes in the factories.[32] But the nationwide crisis of 1961, which affected all phases of life and the economy in mainland China, halted and almost destroyed workers' education. Even the best spare-time education programs in Chinese industry suffered nearly complete disruption as a result of changes in production, shifting of workers to other jobs or to the farms, and an attitude of antipathy toward educational duties among the cadres as organizational confusion spread and production quotas rose.[33] However, even at this low point, skeletal cultural and technical education programs were maintained. Workers' education was slowly and laboriously rebuilt so that the proletariat was once more supplying trained administrative personnel for the industrial sector at the time of the Cultural Revolution.

The reported figures for workers' enrollment in spare-time classes in Tientsin show clearly the course of workers' education during the last decade. This largest industrial city in northern China had stressed these programs for several years and was apparently more successful in obtaining results from workers' education than most other industrial centers. In the spring term of 1958, somewhat more than 200,000 Tientsin workers were enrolled in spare-time classes. Then the Great Leap Forward gathered momentum and over 420,000 workers enrolled for the fall 1958 term.[34] The peak was reached in mid-1960, when more than 800,000 were reportedly in class.[35] Then the culmination of Great Leap problems struck Tientsin's industries. Although no figures have been released for workers' education in Tientsin during 1961, disorganization must have been fairly complete, for the number of workers enrolled in 1962 (whether in the spring or fall term, or both, is not stipulated) had plummeted to less than 70,000. In 1963, enrollees almost doubled, rising to 130,000, and it was claimed that one half of all Tientsin workers had now reached at least the junior middle-school level of education.[36] By February 1965, after consolidation and reorganization of the various spare-time schools in the city, 140,000 were said to be studying in 330 schools.[37] The trade unions were beginning to function again as a school for administration with some semblance of their former capability. Thus in a city of approximately four million inhabitants, as many as 800,000 workers were in spare-time classes at one point, though the scope of enrollment fluctuated with the political exigencies of the moment.

In December 1965, shortly before the Cultural Revolution brought all formal educational processes in China to a halt, Peking announced that the future form of schooling in China would be part-work part-study schools for all. At a conference on part-work part-study education that was addressed by Lu Ting-i and at which both Chou En-lai and Liu Shao-ch'i "gave important instructions," it was decided that the work-study experiments carried out in some cities on a trial basis since 1964 would become the model for all schools.[38] This was not to be a crash program; the system would be instituted over ten years, including five years of further experimentation and another five years of "populari-zation." A *Jen min jih pao* editorial of December 11, 1965, served as the directive ordering wide experimentation with the part-work part-study scheme, especially in urban areas: this type of school was to provide the "fundamental revolution to put into effect Comrade Mao Tse-tung's theory on education," the idea that education must serve proletarian class politics and be combined with labor.[39] Thus could "red and expert" revolutionary successors be assured for the building of the modern China. The new program was to be modeled on the experiments pre-viously carried out by the unions. Along with the cultural and technical classes run on a spare-time basis, the unions had experimentally imple-mented a program of half-work half-study integrated with the factories in some cities after 1958 and especially aimed at young apprentices. Most such schools closed following 1960, but some struggled on, as did the regular spare-time education programs. By the beginning of 1964, industry had been sufficiently stabilized to enable industrial education to be reinstituted in a "careful, down-to-earth manner."[40] The decision announced in December 1965 to transform all of China's education to a part-work party-study formula may well have been reached at a Janu-ary 1964 national conference on workers' spare-time education, at which recent efforts were reviewed and future tasks laid out. A *Kung jen jih pao* editorial of January 26, 1964, declared that: "In the coming two years, we must actively develop spare-time education for workers on the basis of consolidation."[41] Thus the national part-work part-study system announced 23 months later may be viewed as a planned outgrowth of this experimental facet of workers' spare-time education.

Secondary technical schools and universities received primary attention during these two years of trial. During 1964 the spare-time system at these levels was expanded. The initial techniques varied widely; the union running a school in a large factory would allow other factory workers to attend, or several unions would coordinate a school run jointly by several factories, or municipal education authorities would set up a city-wide school or conduct a "television university," as in Peking and Tientsin. Responsible authorities for these schools might be trade unions, factory management, or local education officials. Time spent in school varied: short-term courses with the workers detached from production were not favored, although they did exist; half-and-half schedules were common, especially as 1965 went on; and other combinations were tried, such as the Shanghai Spare-Time Industrial College's 24 hours of class per week, 16 of which were counted as working time.[42]

The system of part-work part-study schools was further expanded in 1965, following extensive publicity in late 1964 and the official encouragement in Chou En-lai's speech to the Third National People's Congress in December 1964.[43] Sometime toward the end of 1964 the Central Committee issued an unpublished but occasionally quoted directive encouraging the establishment of part-work part-study schools.* All these factors brought about a rapid extension of the system; as the fall semester began, Shanghai alone enrolled 50,000 students in 350 work-study schools.[44] The student body included both recent graduates of primary and junior middle schools and older workers, who hoped for promotion as their skills increased. The schools concentrated for the most part on one vocational area, although the general subjects of the middle-school curriculum were also taught; cultural and basic scientific courses were simplified under the pedagogical policy of "less but better," which omits portions of a subject as it is taught in the conventional full-time schools.[45]

By the end of 1965, following the official announcement of the policy

---

* Terminological confusion arose with the new emphasis on part-work part-study schools. The Chinese term for these schools in the urban areas was *pan kung pan tu*, the same term by which the half-work half-study system instituted in 1958 had been known. This term had later been applied almost wholly to the agricultural middle schools; see Robert D. Barendsen, *Half-Work Half-Study Schools in Communist China* (Washington, D.C.: Office of Education, 1964). But with the 1964 decision to extend experimentation with the education system, pan kung pan tu became the term applied once again to the urban industrial schools; their counterparts being established in the rural areas were known as *pan nung pan tu*, part-farming part-study schools.

to convert the whole of the educational system to the part-work part-study model being emphasized in industry, the new program was rapidly being established alongside the expanding older spare-time system in the factories.[46] But then came the Cultural Revolution and with it the demise of cultural and technical education in industry. Even though industry was spared great upheaval until the end of 1966 when the Red Guards moved into the factories, spare-time study in 1966 had been spent largely on Mao's thought. Since 1967, the workers have been caught in the maelstrom of the Cultural Revolution, and there is no indication that spare-time cultural and technical education still exists in any systematic, regularized form. It has given way to the demands for political and ideological study and activity. It may be that we shall eventually learn that a skeletal program has been maintained, as during 1961–62; at the moment there is no evidence that workers are receiving formal schooling to aid in their advancement into administration in the urban areas.

### Union Effectiveness as a School for Administration

The effectiveness of the unions as a school of administration for the proletariat cannot be evaluated in terms of the spare-time cultural and technical education system alone. Although this has been the most important technique for identifying, selecting, and grooming workers for promotion to administrative posts, even before the spare-time education system was instituted, the unions were performing this function.

Prior to the establishment of the Chinese People's Republic, Liu Ning-i, then ACFTU vice-chairman, could note that the unions were already functioning as a school for administration. In the earlier controlled northeast particularly, the workers were thrust into responsible positions. Liu wrote in August 1949 that 4,431 workers on the Manchurian railways had been promoted to some sort of administrative post and that over 90 per cent of the administrative personnel in the Harbin Railway Plant were ex-workers.[47] Railroad workers have always been considered a key object of CCP solicitousness and, comparatively speaking, were a politically reliable group from which to draw leading personnel in the first days after the Communists took over an area. The ACFTU also drew on this pool for its own leaders. Liu noted that, besides workers promoted to railway administration, some 600 workers on the Manchurian railways had become cadres in the trade union apparatus. Two years later, another 12,000 workers in the railways were filling such leadership posts as station masters, section chiefs, and departmental heads in offices and yards.[48] The railway system perhaps exhibited the greatest degree of worker mobility into responsible positions during the initial period of Communist rule, but the same process was occurring in other industries. In 1950 alone, over 7,000 miners were promoted to positions as managers, section chiefs, or mine technicians.[49] The Wuhan Municipal Trade Union Council, when it compiled statistics after May Day 1951 on workers in the city who had become cadres, found that although most had moved into trade union cadre posts, over a hundred Wuhan workers had become superintendents or assistant superintendents, and a similar number had been given posts as engineers or technicians in the city's industries.[50]

It is hardly likely that this spurt of upward mobility for ordinary workers in the early years was wholly attributable to trade union training. It was part of the Communist party's policy in industry and would surely have been attempted on a doctrinal basis even had there been no unions. Nonetheless, it was the unions, working closely with the party, that provided the organizational means for finding worthy and politically reliable workers. Indeed, the unions functioned as a school for administration in a much more literal sense: many workers promoted to administrative posts had first proven themselves in some responsible or approved trade union activity. Leading producers and activist workers would be incorporated into the cadre structure of the unions, where trade union leaders (most of whom were also CCP members) could more easily evaluate them. Many of these promotions followed or were followed by training in specialized cadre schools, which were mostly designed to give the promising worker or newly appointed cadre some acquaintance with general management problems or technical training, depending on the post, plus some intensive political education. Particularly in the northeast, such schools were operating before Liberation: the Workers Political College in Mukden, the Polytechnic Institute and the Railway School in Harbin, and the Mining Institute serving the Penki and Fushun coal mines in Liaoning, as well as the North China Workers School in Tientsin.[51]

Over time, however, it was the spare-time cultural and technical education carried on in the enterprise outside production hours that enabled the trade unions to carry out their school of administration role. Even during the years 1950–56, when the unions were accused of paying inadequate attention to technical and cultural education, some notable successes were achieved. Earlier we noted that the coal mining industry set up a comprehensive spare-time education program; from 1949 through 1953, the system trained 21,541 cadres for administrative or trade union posts, including 3,552 engineers and technicians.[52] The spare-time education programs at the Anshan Iron and Steel Works trained some 24,000 specially skilled or "technical workers" (*chi shu kung jen*) in the years prior to 1956 and promoted 740 technical workers to be technicians (*chi shu yüan*) or engineers and another 593 workers to be managers.[53] Such instances demonstrate that some unions very effectively fulfilled their function of training proletarian leaders for industry from the beginning.

Over a longer time span, the cumulative results of this industry-centered schooling have made substantial contributions to the achievement of trade union goals and national economic goals. The average educational level—and thus the potential technological level—of industrial workers has risen markedly. In 1949, between 75 and 80 per cent of China's workers were illiterate; a decade later, the number had dropped to 20 per cent. By November 1959, approximately nine million workers had reportedly reached a middle-school educational level,* and over 400,000 were at the college level.[54] These two groups represented about a quarter of the total industrial working force.[55] By 1964, Peking said the proportion had risen to 40 per cent.[56] During the January 1964 conference on workers' education, it was stated: "In the past three years especially, and in spite of relatively difficult economic conditions, the development of spare-time education for workers kept at a steady pace."[57] Although all evidence certainly belies that statement for 1961, the years 1962 and 1963 had witnessed a more careful, flexible approach, without the stress on quantity marking the Great Leap Forward era. The *Jen min jih pao* was consequently able to claim that from 1959 to 1962 the industrial education system had graduated over one million workers from primary classes, half a million workers from junior middle-school classes, approximately 100,000 workers from senior middle school, and over 15,000 from the workers' spare-time universities.[58] Considering the general difficulties during much of that four-year period, this was no mean accomplishment to add to earlier efforts.

The spare-time schools cannot be given complete credit for the workers' rising educational level. The labor pool for industry also is better educated. Personnel departments in some modern factories and mines took advantage of this opportunity to raise the plant's educational level rapidly by hiring only those already having at least a primary- or middle-school education.[59] Nevertheless, the rising educational level of the workers and their heightened administrative skills are also certainly

* It should be remembered that reports of students "reaching middle-school level" do not necessarily mean completion of secondary-school studies; rather, the student has studied in one of the six grades comprising the middle-school level.

attributable in part to the spare-time schools, as well as to higher recruiting standards. The number of workers attending these classes rose
from 760,000 in 1950 to over three million in 1954.[60] By August 1960,
as noted above, 25 million workers were enrolled in factory classes. The
increasingly vast number of workers attending classes over the years
would indicate that, simply by sheer weight of participation, the industrial spare-time school system has been a crucial and dominant factor
in raising the educational level of the workers.

Beyond the long-range effects of union-run industrial education, the
unions play the key role in thrusting forward the best producers among
the workers and cultivating them for advancement. The Chinese Communists have come to regard the socialist emulation drive, or labor
emulation, as the main method of improving production.[61] Hundreds of
thousands of China's workers have been designated or elected "labor
heroes," "model workers," or "advanced producers" in the last two decades, and thousands of factories or production units have won flags,
banners, cash, or national recognition for their performance in labor
emulation drives.[62] National conferences have been held to honor and
publicize these individuals and groups and their achievements. It has
been the task of the unions, particularly at the bottom levels in the factories and cities, to focus attention on such persons and their work and to
urge other workers to emulate their feats. The model workers are natural
objects not only for propagandizing but also for recruiting. They are
ideal targets for advancement by the leadership, well beyond the original realm of industrial production. The case of Yüan Kai-li, a skilled
worker in the No. 2 Mill of the Shanghai Steel Works, though perhaps
a somewhat extreme example, illustrates the way the Chinese Communists have co-opted model workers into positions of leadership in the
urban apparatus as well as in industry.[63] During the period October
1950–May 1951 he held the following posts within the mill: production
team leader, member of the mill's trade union executive committee,
member of the mill's production committee and the factory management committee, and "propaganda officer for the party." He was simultaneously being started on the path of urban leadership outside the mill:
he was deputy director of the mill's committee for elimination of counterrevolutionaries outside the mill, a worker representative on the Shanghai People's All-Circles Representative Conference, people's representative from Yangtsepoo (his residential district), and a vice-chairman of
the new Municipal Central District Consultative Conference.* In this

* Since Yüan was still ostensibly a full-time worker, these many posts played
havoc with his record. Half the posts entailed a meeting at least once a week, last-

fashion, China's "labor heroes" have moved into positions of leadership in the cities, sometimes into too many positions. Ambition on the part of the worker matching the desires of the leadership to exploit the worker who has proven himself is the only requirement. Some model workers have risen to positions of municipal, provincial, and even national importance. The *Kung jen jih pao* ran biographical sketches of many of the 79 "labor hero" delegates to the Eighth Trade Union Congress in November and December 1957. Other model workers have over time come to hold important posts in the union structures; Liu Ying-yüan, for example, rose from "labor hero" status in a Harbin power plant in 1948 to be the ranking official of the Water Conservancy and Electrical Workers Union at the time of the Cultural Revolution.

The overall effectiveness of trade union performance in selecting promising workers for promotion and helping management to educate the workers has important implications not only for the industrialization process but also for the development of the party. Unsullied or only lightly touched by the bourgeois conventional schools, such ex-workers are by definition from the doctrinally pure proletariat and may be said to have been formed in an ideal Communist mold. Exploited and without much hope for advancement before 1949, they are easily reminded by the Communist party of the tribulations of pre-Communist days. They have offered some visible evidence for the Communist contention that the industrial workers are the leading class of China. They might be considered the most vivid examples of the plausibility of being both fully "red and expert." And yet their "redness," which stood the test well when they showed their loyalty to the party against the intellectuals in 1957, is not necessarily or even probably a Maoist revolutionary "redness." Although the Communist press today does not provide specific evidence of the attitudes of different groups of cadres in industry, the unmistakable impression is that all types of cadres in the industrial system have been attacked during the Cultural Revolution. There is no reason why the loyalties of the industry-bred cadres should turn to the visionary values and norms formed in and appropriate to the guerrilla years in Yenan. The trade unions, in schooling these men for administration, instilled attitudes that were not revolutionary, but professionally industrial.

---

ing anywhere from two to ten hours. He often worked a night shift, spent the whole day in meetings, and then napped during the next shift. His production team's record dropped way behind others as time went on, and his status actually became counterproductive; his worker peers came to regard him as a "model worker of attending meetings," and his case was finally used as an example of unwise "over-utilization"of the model worker.

*The Unions as a School for Political Education*

Of all the trade unions' educative roles, that as a school for Communism is usually considered the most important. Political education at both formal and informal levels has been the backbone of workers' education in Communist China and has been the keystone of efforts in industry by the CCP. Attention to cultural and technical education in the factory and trade union responsibilities and control for it have shifted more than once, but political education has remained central even though emphasis on this program has fluctuated according to party policies. In some future era in China, Communist values may well be taught to young children by their parents, but at present the Chinese proletariat is still backward and must be taught as adults the tenets of Marx, Lenin, and Mao. This has been a task delegated specifically to the unions, under the guidance of the party.

Political education constituted a major effort of the unions during and immediately after the final period of the civil war. The ACFTU reported on May Day 1950 that "the most urgent problem facing the trade unions following the liberation of each city" had been raising the political consciousness of the workers by class education.[64] The immediate need in this early period was to give the workers an elementary schooling in the doctrine of class struggle and their role in the new society. This intensive political education in industry preceded the implementation of systematic workers' education in all fields. The 1950 "Directives on Developing Spare-Time Education for Workers and Staff Members" assigned responsibility for all phases of education in the plants to the ACFTU and clarified the educative and administrative roles of the unions, management, and local governmental spare-time education committees. Management's role was limited at the outset to supplying facilities for the schools, but, as classes were slowly set up, the responsibilities were split: the unions handled all phases of political education and organized the whole spare-time educational system in the plant, whereas the teaching of cultural and technical studies was turned over to management.

A large part of the initial stages of political education has actually been conducted in the trade union–organized small group at the production team level, supplementing classroom studies. But the formal classes, taught by union and party cadres, never ceased in the factories after 1949, although the amount of time expended has varied according to the party's changing policies. The proportion of political education in the factory's spare-time classes during a relatively quiet period of development may be seen in the schedule of a model factory in the northeast.[65] There were six hours of political study and an equal number of hours of cultural education per week; the political study included one hour of inspection and discussion of the trade union small group's work on the production line, three hours of discussion on the current political mass movement, and two hours of systematic study of Marxism-Leninism.

*Kung jen cheng chih k'o pen* (Textbook on Politics for Workers), a widely used text in political studies first printed in 1950, suggests the content in the initial stages of workers' political education, each brief chapter forming the basis for a lesson.[66] Beginning with chapters on class struggle and the exploitative society, the text then moves on to the "new democratic revolution" and the fall of the Kuomintang, the need for restoring production, and the relations between the proletariat and the CCP. The position of the workers and their responsibilities as the leading class in constructing a new China are expounded; a simple explanation is given of how workers in state-run enterprises are now the masters and how workers in private enterprises must protect their own welfare by paying attention to production. "The new attitudes toward labor," which a worker should acquire in a socialist state, outlines the acceptable lines that a politically astute worker should adopt. And the text's last chapters explain the role of the trade union in the workers' lives. A simply written, unsophisticated text, this would initiate workers unacquainted with Communist ideology into some understanding of the slogans and lines of the party.

More advanced stages of political education are a challenge for both the cadre and the worker. In his workaday world of realities, the worker must face inconsistencies between what he has learned concerning his position in society and the problems with which he must struggle in his daily routine. Intensive shock drives to meet production quotas can be mentally and physically exhausting; his income may drop through reorganization of workers' grades or wages, or, as in the Great Leap Forward, by the payment of wages partially in kind. The state, in which the worker is declared to be the leading element, makes its decisions on the basis of the nation as a whole, and the immediate material interests of the workers are rarely, if ever, wholly consonant with the interests of the state. To resolve such apparent contradictions, the party seeks to teach the working class to "consider all problems from the point of view of all [of China's] 600 million people and not only those of a section of the people,"[67] and the trade union cadre in his educative role can and often does become the central actor in the attempted resolution of such contradictions. As the worker's political consciousness and education advance, the cadres seek to make him understand the ultimate necessity under Marxism-Leninism for the worker to bring his interests into total accord with the interests of the state. The politically advanced workers may be encouraged to devote more time to ideological study, as a prelude to induction into the Chinese Communist Party or the Communist Youth League.

When the CCP launches mass movements or embarks on a new line, an intensification of political education accompanies it. Inevitably, the increased efforts expended on political study during such a mass campaign conflict with the usually increased production demands accompanying the campaign. Union cadres are caught in the middle as they seek to emphasize both. Most notably in the Great Leap Forward, many enterprises responded to these stresses as the economic squeeze tightened after 1959 by reducing the hours for spare-time education. But the sector of the education program that suffered was the cultural and technical side, not the political education. Indeed, a *Kung jen jih pao* editorial of April 28, 1961, suggested that the proper step would be more or less to eliminate the hours spent in cultural education, so that added time could be given to politics. Nonetheless, since the ranks of the industrial labor force had swelled so extraordinarily in the Great Leap,[68] the union role as a school for Communism was partly or wholly neglected in many places. When the initial enthusiasm generated by the Great Leap Forward waned through 1959 while production goals remained high, the apolitical attitudes and values of the new workers created problems for management and unions. This was especially marked in new industrial areas, where the proportion of workers drawn from a peasant milieu was relatively high and where workers lacked the labor discipline and political consciousness of the workers transferred from the cities. The Communist leadership viewed their lack of political indoctrination as a crucial factor impeding the attainment of Great Leap Forward targets.[69] Although it is understandable that party, management, and trade union cadres would try to shift the blame for the nonfulfillment of the unrealistic quotas of the Leap onto noncompliant new workers, it is significant that such arguments were not used in the more industrialized cities of the east coast. There the long-time political education of the urban workers had created a working force amenable and flexible enough to adapt to the vagaries of the party line. Political education was felt to be so important for the new workers in the frontier areas that large chunks of time were devoted to a crash program of three months for political training by the unions in Sinkiang. In the end, of course, even political education was quite unable to alter the actualities of economic chaos wrought by the Leap Forward.

## Union Effectiveness as a School for Communism

The best measure of union effectiveness in its role as a school for political education would be a detailed study of the working class component in the CCP, but information of this sort is relatively rare, at least on an aggregate national level. We can extrapolate from the available data a sense of union performance in building class consciousness and in identifying and helping recruit potential leaders from the urban workers into the political elite.

The Chinese Communists have concentrated on recruiting workers at only three points in the party's forty-nine-year history: in 1925–27, sporadically through 1950–57, and since 1968. But not since 1927 has the CCP been truly a party of the proletariat. The high tide in the Chinese labor movement between May 30, 1925, and April 12, 1927, was a period of rapid expansion in the party, when it grew from less than a thousand members to 57,967 members represented at the Fifth Congress in April 1927.[70] A majority, 53.8 per cent, of these Communists in 1927 were workers.[71] Many of these workers were also leaders in the trade unions of China, often having been union leaders affiliated with the Kuomintang; they came into close contact with the CCP during the period of collaboration, and many joined the CCP as the Kuomintang became more rightist and labor became more leftist. During these two years, the CCP not only led political activities in the labor movement but was also able to dominate the movement toward the end, with its 30,000 worker-members strategically placed in unions under the All-China Federation of Labor.

But never again has the working class been so well represented in the CCP. The decimation of the "white terror" after April 1927 eliminated most workers from the party's ranks. After rebuilding the CCP in the guerrilla bases, the Communists claimed that approximately 10 per cent of the members were of working class background, but only a fraction would actually have been engaged in light industry in the Soviet areas. Although the CCP never entirely lost contact with the labor movement in the cities, even after the Long March and Yenan, the little influence the party had retained with the workers after the "white terror" was dissipated in the obtuseness of the "Li Li-san line." Mao's reorientation of the party to a guerrilla peasant movement completed the shift away from the cities and the proletariat. Still, even during the years in the wilderness the city had never been dismissed by the party leaders; in

China the city remains the center of social, economic, and particularly political activities.[72] As Communist armies brought nearer the day when the CCP would rule China, the party faced its tasks with a leadership of largely urbanized intelligentsia and a membership overwhelmingly peasant, and as the cities fell to the People's Liberation Army a change in the party's composition became inevitable. Once victory had been achieved, the shift was made complete. As the governing party, the CCP could now select from the whole range of social classes; it returned to the orthodox Marxist priorities. Peasants were to be ignored in favor of industrial workers. In his June 1950 speech to the Third Plenum, Mao called a halt to all expansion of the party in rural areas. Instead, attention was paid to "systematically recruiting politically conscious workers into the party and to expanding the proportion of workers in the party."[73] The CCP then set about bringing its class composition more in line with Communist doctrine, a stress that remained the official line through 1954.

The CCP, not intending to blindly expand its working class membership, has favored a cumulative process. The unions first embrace the workers en masse, bringing them into the union branch. Then, after a suitable period of political education, the workers differentiate themselves according to degree of political activism, production abilities, and enthusiasm. The unions must cultivate such activists, usually by engaging them in trade union cadre positions or activities, to school them as Communists and prepare them for selection into the party, just as the unions in their role as schools for administration select and train the capable workers for industrial administrative posts. Some mass campaigns, such as the three- and five-anti movements, have been particularly useful in identifying the political activists, but in the long run it is the unions routinely functioning as a school for Communism that heightens the "correct" political consciousness of the workers.

The first step in raising the workers' political awareness—bringing them into the union—has distinct advantages for the workers: the social welfare and labor insurance programs run by the union, the clubs and social activities, the sanatoria and vacation resorts maintained by the unions and charging members only nominal fees, all cost the union member only 1 per cent of his monthly wages as dues.[74] Unpleasant aspects of industrial life in China, such as shock drives or meetings held after working hours, apply to all workers, whether in the union or not. Yet interviews in Hong Kong reveal that even in modern sectors of the economy pockets of resistance to joining the union were still being met in the late 1950's. Sometimes earlier experiences with company-run unions, in which the workers rarely saw any benefits from their dues, had created a totally antagonistic attitude toward all unions. And whereas pressures on the trade union cadre or activist would be great to persuade patiently such an individual that he should join the union, the pressures against literally forcing him to join, by dint of threats, for instance, would be equally strong: the sense that the worker should voluntarily join the mass organization has been carefully preserved. The greatest cause for resistance to joining, it seems, was often simply those monthly dues of 1 per cent of the wages. To some household budgets this seemingly negligible sum might appear crucially important; for others, it was a case of union propagandists never having convincingly presented a picture of the long-range benefits.

Thus, when old unions were taken over or new ones were organized by the ACFTU, not all workers and employees would join and not all would be reached in a more than cursory manner.* The initial chore of the unions was to bring in as many workers as possible, so that workers' understanding of Communism in China could be more rapidly and systematically enlarged. Membership in the ACFTU rose from under 1.5 million in 1948 to slightly over ten million in 1952. From 1953 until 1956, membership rose only from 12 million to 13.7 million, while industry underwent a period of consolidation (and while the party turned from its emphasis on recruitment of workers to recruitment in the countryside to consolidate its rural control after 1954). In the first year of the Great Leap Forward, union membership stood at 17.4 million; at the end of the experiment, in 1960, at 20 million; and it had risen to 22 million on the eve of the Cultural Revolution.[75] Figures for workers attending spare-time classes over the years, which would mostly include political education classes even if cultural or technical courses were not available, suggest that most union members have consistently undergone political indoctrination.

The next step for the unions was, and is, to encourage potential leaders. Being a trade union activist or serving in a trade union cadre position is a way station on the path of upward mobility into the party. For the ambitious worker, activism in trade union work is a primary option

---

* Not all trade union organizations understood the need to incorporate all the workers into the trade union in order to educate them in Communism. Some units permitted only workers with a clean history, proper class background, and demonstrated political activism to join the union. These units were accused of operating on the basis of "closed-doorism" or "exclusionism" (*kuan men chu i*) because the union cadres "had no experience, but possessed a rural village viewpoint." See, for example, *Ho-nan jih pao* (Honan daily), Mar. 25, 1950. The phenomenon of "exclusionism" in several unions was attacked by the ACFTU and the party that spring.

and probably the best way of demonstrating his suitability for selection into the political elite. Thus the unions also serve their own cadre recruitment needs while preparing working class recruits for the party.

A New China News Agency release of February 1950 illustrates the early emphasis the union placed on this function.[76] It stated that in Wuhan, for example, one-fifth of the city's 210,000 workers and employees were union members; of these 41,000-odd members, 4,720 were being trained as "worker cadres" (that is, for various administrative posts), of which approximately 1,200 were receiving such training and cultivation by serving as trade union committee members. In Tangshan, 17,800 of the total working force of 82,000 had become "backbone elements" in the union organizations. Of the nationwide total of 12,454,000 union members in 1954, over one-fifth of them (2,730,000) were noted as "taking an exceptionally active part in the work."[77] The same proportion continued into 1958.[78]

Mass campaigns provide a more dramatic and concentrated instance of the unions as a school for Communism. Probably the most effective of all such campaigns in quickly thrusting forward activists and generally educating the working class in the operational doctrines of class struggle were the three-anti and five-anti campaigns of 1952. In 1951, the terrorism and harshness of the "suppression of counterrevolutionaries campaign" and the propaganda accompanying a "democratic reform movement" in the trade unions had served an educative purpose, but the campaigns of 1952 personally involved tremendous numbers of the workers. John Gardner points out that one out of ten workers in private firms in Shanghai became activists to the extent of participating in work brigades mobilizing the proletariat during the five-anti campaign.[79] Although both the anti campaigns were largely directed by the party, the trade unions became the key organization in, and in fact led, the five-anti movement.[80] During this campaign, union organizations were set up in all private enterprises in some cities.[81] The trade union cadres organized investigation and "strike the tiger" teams of workers, which then mobilized all workers who could be reached to denounce their employers' corrupt practices. Gardner concludes that the five-anti campaign in Shanghai was sufficiently effective to raise the class consciousness of the city's workers to a point where the complex network of interrelationships that had characterized the city's socioeconomic life were dichotomized, with the workers finally pitting themselves against their erstwhile patrons, the owners.

The reform of basic level trade union organizations begun in the 1951 democratic reform movement was carried to fruition in the five-anti campaign, providing an opportunity for workers who had been active in the campaign against businessmen to be placed in union cadre posts or specified for further cultivation. In Tientsin it was noted: "The newly elected cadres are all trade union cadres, trade union members, or activists whose class stand was firm in the five-anti, who are positively united with the workers, and who firmly struggled with criminal capitalists."[82] Although we cannot directly correlate trade union mobilization and education of the workers during the three- and five-anti campaigns with recruitment into the CCP, great numbers of workers took the first step on a political career in the union apparatus and thence into city or party leadership during these mass movements.

The test of the unions' effectiveness as a school for Communism is measured in the number or proportion of workers taken into the party. Entry into the political elite, however, is determined by a number of factors other than the degree of political understanding that the union has imparted to the worker, not least among which is the CCP's changing view of what sort of educational, occupational, or class groups it wishes to recruit. Despite Marxist doctrine, the CCP really favored the workers as a source of recruitment only during the first years of the regime, when the proportion of industrial workers in the party was extremely small. In the mid-1950's emphasis returned to the peasants; then for a brief time the intellectuals were favored; and after the Great Leap Forward emphasis once again settled on the peasants as the most politically reliable source, especially the peasants indoctrinated in the People's Liberation Army in the 1960's.[83]

Since the Twelfth Plenum of the Eighth Central Committee, held in October 1968, the party has again promulgated a line stressing the centrality of the industrial working class to China's continuing revolution. Mao specifically declared that "the party organization should be composed of the advanced elements of the proletariat." The communique issued at the plenum laid down a new recruiting policy: "Take into the party fresh blood from the proletariat—above all, advanced elements with Communist consciousness from among the industrial workers."[84] Then, Lin Piao in his political report to the Ninth Party Congress in April 1969 explicitly reaffirmed the preeminence of industrial workers in the CCP's plans for building the party.[85] Reflecting this new emphasis, at least 26 members of the Central Committee newly elected at the Ninth Congress have been identified as workers or model workers, and most of these are full rather than alternate members. Since there are still many members whose backgrounds are completely unknown to Western observers, it seems probable that even more than these 26 are

PARTY AND UNION MEMBERSHIP, 1948–65

| Year | Trade union membership | Party membership | Worker party members |
|------|------------------------|------------------|----------------------|
| 1948 | 1,448,228 | 3,065,533 | |
| 1949 | 2,373,938 | 4,488,080 | |
| 1950 | 5,070,024 | 5,821,604 | |
| 1951 | 7,297,857 | 5,762,293 | 360,000 |
| 1952 | 10,002,901 | 6,001,698 | 450,000 |
| 1953 | 12,100,188 | 6,612,254 | |
| 1954 | 12,454,091 | 7,859,473 | |
| 1955 | | 9,393,394 | |
| 1956 | 13,728,685 | 10,734,384 | 1,502,814 |
| 1957 | 16,300,000 | 12,720,000 | 1,740,000 |
| 1958 | 17,400,000 | | |
| 1959 | | 13,960,000 | |
| 1960 | 20,000,000 | | |
| 1961 | | 17,000,000 | |
| 1963 | 20,800,000 | | |
| 1965 | 22,000,000 | | |

SOURCES: Trade union membership data are from: *Chung-kuo kung jen* (Chinese workers), 4 (Feb. 1958), 7; *The Chinese Trade Unions*, 3 (1959), 8; Bruno Di Pol, "Position of Trade Unions in Communist China," *Avanti*, Dec. 3, 1960, in *Joint Publications Research Service*, No. 6631, p. 14; "Some Facts on Trade Unions in China," *China Reconstructs*, 5 (May 1963), 27; "Trade Unions in China," *The Society For Anglo-Chinese Understanding News*, Jan. 1966, p. 1. Party membership figures are from John W. Lewis, *Leadership in Communist China* (Ithaca, N.Y.: Cornell University Press, 1963), pp. 110–11. The last column, CCP members who were also workers, is from *Jen min jih pao* (People's daily), Apr. 25, 1953, and Lewis 1963, p. 108.

workers who have been suddenly elevated to the Central Committee. Just as Mao concentrated on the workers to change the nature of party membership in 1949, so has he turned to the workers following the Cultural Revolution. But the workers, indoctrinated by union cadres rather than revolutionaries over the years, and committed to the party, may not be the revolutionary successors Mao seeks.

A glance at the growth of trade union and CCP membership as outlined in the table shown above suggests that the two grew simultaneously, with an ever greater proportion of the party being from a worker background. As we have seen, this seeming correlation is not at all the case. In the most recent occupational and class status breakdown of the party, made in 1957, "workers" accounted for only 1.74 million CCP members, 13 per cent of the total party membership.[86] And inasmuch as recruitment emphasis shifted to the peasantry after 1957, it seems unlikely that this proportion has risen significantly in the last decade, even given the shift after the Cultural Revolution.

We may assume that any worker who is a CCP member has also joined the trade union in his enterprise and retains that membership, even if he no longer really takes an active part in union work. Thus, if the 1,740,000 party members who were workers in 1957 were also all trade union members, then 10.7 per cent of all union members were also party members. This is not a particularly high proportion of the union membership to have been recruited into the party; however, this does not suggest so much that the unions have been lax in their role as a school for Communism as that the CCP has emphasized recruitment among other groups than the proletariat when mass recruitment drives were going on. Shifting party priorities and the absence of a mass drive after 1954 to absorb workers (except for efforts since 1968) chiefly account for the relatively small proportion of trade union members who have become party members.

Other figures for workers in 1957 suggest a somewhat higher ratio of union members nearing entry into the political elite. Of the 11 million "industrial workers" in 1957 (specifically, workers in light and heavy industry, transport and communications, and construction), 13 per cent were members of the CCP and another 29 per cent were members of the Communist Youth League,[87] a connection that heightened the possibility of eventual acceptance into the party. This youth league figure indicates a much higher rate of success on the part of the unions as a school for Communism than consideration of the proportion of CCP members alone. All these figures for 1956–57, furthermore, show a higher proportion of union members moving into the political elite than in earlier years. The only other national data available, for the years 1951–52, show that in 1951, as the party began its character change by emphasizing careful recruitment of the proletariat, only 360,000 or 6.3 per cent of CCP members were workers. Assuming that all were also trade union members, this figure represented approximately 5 per cent of the union memership.[88] In 1952, the number of workers who were CCP members was 450,000, or 7.2 per cent; rapid expansion in the trade unions following the five-anti campaign meant that this constituted only 4.5 per cent of the total union membership.[89] Thus between 1951–52 and 1956–57, there was an average annual increase of approximately 1.5 per cent in the proportion of union members who also became CCP members.* We must note, however, that although no data are avail-

* In 1952, there were also 650,000 workers in the New Democratic Youth League, the predecessor of the Communist Youth League; see *Jen min jih pao* (People's daily), Apr. 25, 1953. Together with CCP members, this represents 11 per cent of the trade union membership of that year. Hence the 42 per cent of all industrial workers who were members of either the league or the CCP in 1957, as noted above, is further evidence of increasing success for the unions in educating the workers in Communism during these years.

able after 1957, this proportion has most probably not continued to increase. The changed party policies emphasizing recruitment of peasants since 1958 has perhaps kept the proportion of trade union members in the party at about the 1957 levels or, even more likely, caused that proportion to decrease, and the shift in emphasis since 1968 has probably not yet had an effect.

Some scattered data suggest the patterns of worker recruitment into the party. In the northeast region, much of which was already controlled by Communist armies in 1948, approximately 80,000 workers were CCP members in 1949, and by 1952, another 50,000 had joined.[90] These 130,000 workers constituted nearly 30 per cent of all workers in the party in 1952—a figure that reflected the headstart the northeast region had in industrial reconstruction due perhaps to the efforts of Kao Kang to build and consolidate his party power base there. Whatever the cause, the industrial northeast provided a disproportionately large number of workers for the party in the years when Kao ruled in Manchuria. There is no evidence about how these northeast workers fared in the purge following the crushing of the Kao-Jao clique in 1954.

The pattern of worker recruitment into the party was predictably uneven in different cities in the years immediately after 1949, for some had only recently been taken over by the Communists whereas others had had a reasonably effective underground or nearby CCP organization operating for some time before Communist capture,[91] and the Communists proceeded cautiously in cities such as Shanghai at first.[92] Organization of the workers in Tientsin into the trade unions was rather rapid, since this, like the northeast region, was a favored area for worker recruitment into the party. The workers of Peking also received early attention, probably because the capital city was considered a showcase and a model. At the end of March 1950, nearly 60 per cent of all the workers and employees in the city (exclusive of personnel in state and municipal organs) were members of a union; one-tenth of the more than 190,000 union members were being cultivated as trade union cadres at the level of small group leader or above.[93]

As we have seen, many workers entering the party already held some leadership position, usually at a low level such as production team chief. The team leader or deputy leader who becomes an activist in some campaign or, in industry, in a production drive, is most likely to have his membership application favorably received. The unions can ensure that the themes of Communism are learned by all the workers and goad some among them to become political activists, but the party has also been concerned with including those with proven administrative or technical skills within its own ranks to meet the demands of managing a modernizing economy.[94] Such a policy naturally leads to an overrepresentation of industrial cadres, as compared with rank-and-file workers, within the party. In 1956, Li Hsüeh-feng, then director of the Central Committee's Industry and Communications Work Department, stated in his speech to the Eighth CCP Congress: "At present, the number of party members in enterprises has reached 10 to 20 per cent of the total number of workers and staff, while most of the cadres are party members."[95] In some enterprises, particularly those which the leadership considers critical to China's industrial progress, the party members in some production teams constitute a majority of the workers. Less critical enterprises, particularly those concerned with consumer goods, have a lower proportion of the workers as CCP members, although youth league membership could reduce the disparity here. Furthermore, the ordinary worker is automatically favored for promotion to cadre status posts after being accepted into the party, simply by virtue of having entered the political elite and, therefore, by definition having been recognized as a vanguard element.

The effectiveness of union performance in the role of school for Communism, then, cannot be denied. Although party policy sets effective limits on the ultimate test of the unions in this role by controlling the number of workers who can enter the CCP, the persisting efforts of the unions over the years in political education have schooled the main body of the proletariat well.

The trade unions in their educative roles have contributed signally to the modernization process in Communist China and have been instrumental in shaping the composition and style of urban leadership. By being on the whole successful in their efforts as schools, the unions have demonstrated that under a tightly controlled Communist political system the unions can function better than in most other emerging societies in furthering concomitant aspects of urbanization and industrialization.

The apparent minimal degree of labor unrest in Communist China can be ascribed to the effective performance of the trade unions. The frictions produced in the transition from a preindustrial society to a modern industrial nation have been mitigated by the unions, working for the most part in close cooperation with the CCP. The unions have been the organ through which industrial discipline has been taught and imposed, the agent for eliciting a commitment to organized urban and industrial life. This has chiefly been effected not because the unions have been an agent of coercion or brainwashing, but because they have functioned as a welfare organization and as channels of mobility for the workers.

As schools for administration, the unions have raised the cultural and technical levels of millions of Chinese workers. Most developing nations rely on the regular school system to perform this function, and for most nations the method is slow. No nation has sought to implement a spare-time education program for a rapidly expanding proletariat on so massive a scale as China. Probably no comparable program has succeeded so well in raising the overall level of the workers' skills and educational attainments as China's, despite the slow start and the pause following the Great Leap Forward. As a result, Chinese industry has a large corps of administrators with solid experience on the production line, but with sufficient cultural and technical education to hold their own in a traditionally education-conscious society. It is the unions who have laid this foundation for the future by running the spare-time courses, by identifying and grooming the more capable to move into administrative and technical posts, and even by experimenting with part-work part-study urban schools that may yet provide the model for the regular Chinese education system.

If the unions have been a key means of activating labor, of providing a channel for mobility, they have also been the organization through which the Communist leadership has maintained control over this crucial sector of Chinese society. The expectations of material benefits and upward mobility have been instrumental in legitimizing the system and raising productivity during periods of normalcy. During periods of mass movements, when moral or ideological exhortation replaces material incentives, the unions' political education provides the channel for the ideological driving force. Political education has also brought some workers directly into urban and industrial politics as workers were recruited into the party—often by way of the union structure itself. The unions swung the workers behind the new political system in the course of a few years and replenished the party's ranks when policy allowed. Political education in general has, in fact, been so effective that the workers were well aware of the one area of failure for the unions—as schools of management. Not until the Cultural Revolution, if then, have the workers truly had a say in the management of the state's enterprises. But the compensations accorded to what has once again become the leading class in the official party view have been immense. In terms of material benefits, social status, and mobility, the workers in the cities have been a favored class since 1949.

To what extent the workers believe themselves to be "masters of the state" is irrelevant; the workers as a whole have tendered solid support to the CCP as the leading body of the Chinese polity. There is no evidence of disaffection from the party by a significant part of the industrial workers even during times of deepest disturbance. The workers supported the CCP against attacks by the intellectuals in 1957. Again, unlike the peasants, workers were not rioting in the hard days of 1961. And the old-line party organization received strong support from industrial workers in the Cultural Revolution. Generally speaking, the Maoist's revolutionary visions and ideology have been rejected by the workers, but ties to the object of the Maoist attacks, the party and the industrial bureaucracy, remained firm. Much of the credit for consolidating the proletariat's loyalty to the CCP must go to the unions. It is both the material advancement of the workers and the routine education in the non-Maoist tenets of Communism over the years that has produced the workers' commitment to the party organization and to its goals of a modern, socialist, and ordered society. In these ways, the unions have functioned well as schools for administration and for Communism. It remains to be seen whether or not an infusion of fresh blood from the proletariat will change Communism as practiced by the CCP. The past work of the unions suggests that the workers will continue to bring orthodox Communist attitudes rather than Maoist visions to the party.

# Commerce, Education, and Political Development in Tangshan, 1956–69

JOHN WILSON LEWIS

Tangshan has ranked as one of China's leading industrial centers since the 1920's. Occupying the area bounded by the Kailan coal basin in eastern Hopei, the population of this municipality exceeded 800,000 people in 1958,[1] and may well have reached more than one million before the flow of in-migrants was stopped and then reversed in the early 1960's. Just prior to the Great Leap Forward, Tangshan was one of twenty or so "medium-sized" Chinese cities with between 500,000 and 1,000,000 inhabitants. Sustaining their livelihood and the area's economic expansion were large nearby deposits of coal, bauxite, and limestone; crucial too was Tangshan's strategic location in the expanding commercial network of the north and northeast. Resources and location not only underlay the economic growth of the area from the late-nineteenth century onward; they also dictated the social and political character of the community.

This chapter deals with selected aspects of the crucial relationship between economic and political development for the thirteen-year span from 1956 to 1969. Although a great deal is known about the earlier development of Tangshan,[2] past events in the city can be analyzed best in terms of the data for the period immediately preceding and during the Cultural Revolution. The evidence of the past decade, though weak and of dubious value in some respects, provides insights into the links between sectors of the urban society on which data for the earlier years is almost totally lacking.

Central to the subjects of urban society and political development in China are questions about the legitimacy and degree of autonomy of urban institutions. Under what conditions, if any, have local political structures acquired more than the minimal independence needed to operate as conduits for central-level authorities?* Under circumstances of greater independence, how do these structures gain the support needed to withstand pressures from the center? Is the dependence of a city on its immediate hinterland a factor, as seems to have been the case in the autonomy of some Western cities?[3] Can the makeup of the base of support for the urban leadership be compared to the contending elements found in urban politics elsewhere—i.e., does a full-fledged urban bureaucracy develop from the need to balance competing interests and form them into ad hoc coalitions?

## Tangshan in the 1950's

In attempting to reach even tentative answers to these questions, it is necessary to establish a baseline against which the evidence of the most recent years might be considered. Since relevant monographic studies are only now being written, such a baseline must be set forth tentatively.

The small amount of published work on Chinese cities[4] and on Tangshan in particular[5] would suggest that cities undergoing rapid industrialization after 1949 were subject to the expected strains and breakdowns that result from the transformation of peasants into miners and factory hands.[6] At the same time the recent history of Tangshan reveals that popular reaction to these problems was reasonably muted and often constructive. The community was stable, workers' real income was increasing, the leadership was considered to be legitimate by a vast majority of city dwellers, and, as far as we can tell, a great many peasants in the surrounding countryside would have preferred to live in the city rather than on their collective farms.

A key element in this positive attitude seems to have been the ability of the educated young to rise in the bureaucratic-political system. Sustaining their upward mobility, educational institutions in Tangshan had grown in step with the urbanization and industrialization of the 1950's and through extension-type programs had reached into deprived areas of society, particularly to the poor and old, who never before could have

---

* Gideon Sjoberg notes: "A critical issue in industrial-urban orders concerns the amount of autonomy the local community can wield in an industrial-urban society. We hypothesize that the range within which urban communities can function effectively is rather wide, although it may be narrower than in the preindustrial, civilized society. It is difficult to specify with precision what is the optimum 'balance,' or point of equilibrium, between the opposing structural requirements. Given our present state of knowledge, we may have to be satisfied with delineating, through the use of 'negative cases,' the boundaries to feasible centralization and decentralization." "Cities in Developing and in Industrial Societies: A Cross-cultural Analysis," in Philip M. Hauser and Leo F. Schnore, eds., *The Study of Urbanization* (New York: John Wiley, 1965), pp. 240–41.

expected to receive any formal education. Equally important, the great majority of youth by 1956 could anticipate securing satisfactory positions after leaving school and could model their careers on those of successful leaders from Tangshan—both those who had fought in the Communist revolution and those who had graduated from the Tangshan Engineering College (*T'ang-shan kung hsüeh yüan*). Here were ready contrasts to the conditions of Tangshan social life prior to the Communist occupation of the city in December 1948.

The educated were not the only ones who felt a sense of well-being. The industrial workers and miners had also progressed steadily in the first decade of Communist rule. Later this period was to be referred to as one of "revisionism" and "economism," a not inappropriate label, since by the mid-1950's the principal incentives for hard work consisted of higher pay, promotion, and public recognition. All available data indicate that Tangshan's authorities had gone unusually far in improving the workers' livelihood with stress placed on job safety, social welfare, in-service training, and construction of new housing and recreational facilities. No one would contend that this burgeoning coal, steel, and cement town was a paradise, for one had only to walk a few blocks from any of the major factories and pitheads to find slums, antiquated transportation systems, and in some sectors acute poverty, but the contrast between 1948 and 1956 apparently was perceived as being so sharp that few seemed to have been disposed to express resentment concerning the difficulties that remained to be solved. The Communist leadership recognized, moreover, that any blatant attempts at suppression of incipient discontent would have constituted a tactical blunder. If one can believe stories from the *Tangshan Labor Daily*,[7] the grievances that might have escalated into widespread discontent were aired, almost continuously, in ubiquitous small study groups (*hsüeh hsi hsiao tsu*)[8] formed in neighborhoods, factories, mine shafts, and schools.

The occupation of the city by Communist troops in 1948 and the use of police-state methods, of course, complicate this assessment of popular support. By the mid-1950's, the Communists had reorganized the urban populace into residents' committees and street offices under the guidance of local police stations. The paternalism in their early policies was matched by a rigid, though masked, authoritarianism in the areas of public security and the distribution of power. Continuing the surveillance system (*pao chia*) introduced by the Japanese in the 1940's and perpetuated by the Nationalists after the war, Communist cadres systematically extended their jurisdiction, wiping out the traditional areas of solidarity and autonomy that had survived earlier dictatorial suppression as well as the eroding effects of the industrialization process itself. By 1956, the many urban organizations, associations, and guilds based on common place, occupation, surname, or school ties, for all practical purposes had been subverted or destroyed.

The position of the party leadership that had taken over Tangshan, moreover, helped neutralize any activist tendencies at the local level. Although the urban bureaucrats had no natural competitors of their own in the city, neither did they have a basis for creating a locally autonomous bureaucracy there. Rather they facilitated the orders from above and carried out the control and political missions determined by Peking. Each cadre in the city was virtually dependent on national-level decisions. As a transient element within the rigid framework of central administration, his urban world bore little relation to his arena of power. With luck Tangshan was a rung on the promotion ladder, but the chance slip of a subordinate or a decline in factory output could mean the abrupt end to a cadre's career.

At this time, too, the larger cities were fully integrated in the centrally directed economic network. Like many cities of its size and location along the national rail system, Tangshan at this time was relatively independent of its own hinterland* but was considered virtually a satellite city of Peking and Tientsin in the larger commercial network of the north. In such an economic system, individual cadres were also in continuous flux. This turnover and the broad undifferentiated character of their functions seldom allowed them to specialize, despite the bias toward professional expertise and specialization then underlying the slogan "red and expert."[9] In short, the city in 1958 was dependent on the center, which manipulated Tangshan's affairs without particular concern for its historical uniqueness or special problems.

## Commercial Reorganization and the Creation of the Tangshan Economic Region

The campaign in 1960 to establish communes in China's urban places seems to have had virtually no effect on Tangshan. Indeed I can find no reference to the actual creation of communes in the municipality's nine districts. No refugee interviewed as yet has had knowledge that any substantial reorganization took place during the urban commune movement, although there was a great deal of discussion in mid-1960 as the movement for urban communization gained momentum.

---

* As a larger study of Tangshan will show, one aspect of this independence was a lack of correspondence between the two cadre systems, one for city and one for special district. The latter handled only rural problems and did not serve as a mobility channel for urban cadres. The next level of control above Tangshan was the province, not the Tangshan special district.

This is not to say that the city's life was not seriously disrupted by the Great Leap Forward, which accompanied the rural commune program. The emphasis on frantic production with amateurs and political cadres in command and the mobilization of large numbers of people to labor on special projects was as prominent in Tangshan as elsewhere in China. What does not seem to have happened in Tangshan, however, is the cutting off of the city from its suburban or rural hinterland by the creation of urban communes. Rather the very reverse occurred as Tangshan became a model in early 1958 for the creation of a commercial exchange system on the basis of the Tangshan special district, which in 1969 consisted of two municipalities and twelve *hsien*.[10]

This district set the pace in the movement, which was apparently limited to selected more modern areas, for expanding the economic control of each district seat (in this case Tangshan city) over all urban and rural places under its jurisdiction. The circulation of commodities was adjusted to accord with the arrangement of political units (municipality, hsien, commune, brigade, and team) in the district. Because many of these units had no natural marketing relations with one another, the power and influence of city cadres had to be brought to bear to establish connections where none had existed before.

As a result of this reorganization the Communist cadres of the municipality and the special district were forced to work together. The urban leadership, however, carried greater weight by virtue of the key position given the city in the commercial exchange system. The buying and selling of commodities within politically defined boundaries accentuated the disruption that in 1958 had accompanied the installation of the uneconomic rural communes across the boundaries of the traditional peasant marketing areas. Increasingly as the commune structure in the rural areas broke down throughout 1959 and 1960 the city elite was called on to make more detailed decisions concerning the local distribution of goods and services. Moreover, as the national economic crisis spread, the emphasis in its decisions shifted to arbitrating among local interests as a way of maintaining order. In playing the role of mediator among competing village interests in a condition bordering on famine, the city officials, of course, faced increasing intransigence from local cadres at the same time that demands for performance mounted from Peking. As a result, the Tangshan elite in the early 1960's gained experience in dealing with a large number of local problems, though the cumbersome political system through which it worked added to its vulnerability and denied it any real measure of autonomy.

Its chance to remove these strictures came in 1962. At the Tenth Plenum, the Central Committee of the Chinese Communist Party ap-

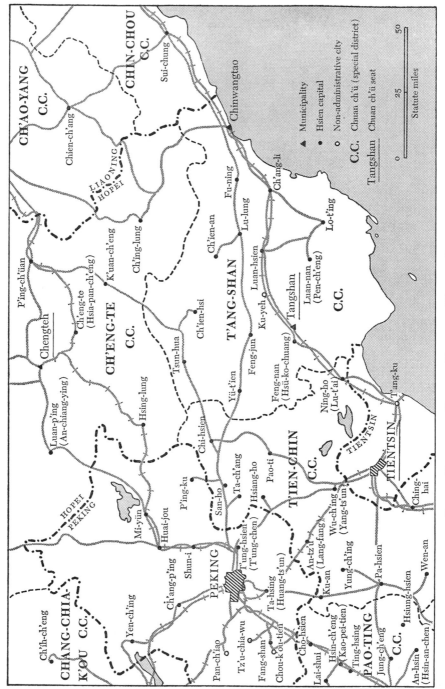

SPECIAL DISTRICTS IN EASTERN HOPEI AND WESTERN LIAONING, 1969

proved the still secret "Decisions Concerning the Question of Commercial Work."[11] These decisions stipulated that each industrial city should have its own "economic region" (*ching chi ch'ü yü*).[12] Each such region was to take shape according to the "natural" marketing pressures, and in this respect the regions would not depend on, but were to supersede, the previous district-based administrative hierarchy as the basic unit for commercial exchange. Tangshan was chosen as the model place to lead in the formation of economic regions in the more modern areas of China.

Begun in December 1963, the complete reorganization of the Tangshan commercial system required fourteen months.[13] During this time, those who previously had argued for the distribution of commodities according to the administrative hierarchy of the district were criticized and either induced to go along or denounced. Their arguments that it would be difficult to master market trends were belittled as feeble excuses for maintaining a prominent role for uneconomic units, particularly the hsien town.

In the course of the controversy an alliance emerged between the rural villages and Tangshan city against the hsien authorities. Both partners in this new coalition in Tangshan pressed hard for the new commercial system while the hsien opposed it. In the year-long debate, moreover, the Communist press provided them with the rationale for their common front. The emphasis on "mass line" leadership uniting city and countryside and on the unity of politics and economics gave ideological support to their closer relationship. As one newspaper put it "The infusion of political work into economic work means to penetrate into the production process, into the circulation process, into scientific experiments, and into the daily life of workers and employees and amongst their families."[14] Furthermore, this integration of city and village leaders depended on the decisions of the Tenth Plenum and thus acquired a special force in the fields of finance and trade work. An important later development was that even the trade unions and educational authorities used the new commercial system to relate their plans for the city with what was going on in the villages around Tangshan.

Comparative transportation costs were the principal determinant in the creation of the boundaries for the Tangshan economic region.[15] Prior to the Tenth Plenum and under the 1958 system, industrial commodities from the Manchurian city of Shenyang (Mukden) that were needed in the eastern part of the Tangshan special district had first to be sent to Tangshan city and then to be reshipped over the same railway lines back to the district's eastern cities. A similarly uneconomical situation prevailed in the southwest part of the special district in the

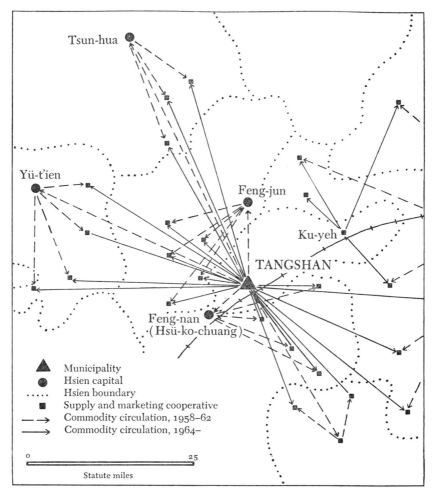

Tsun-hua

Yü-t'ien

Feng-jun

Ku-yeh

TANGSHAN

Feng-nan
(Hsü-ko-chuang)

▲ Municipality
● Hsien capital
..... Hsien boundary
■ Supply and marketing cooperative
— ➔ Commodity circulation, 1958–62
——➔ Commodity circulation, 1964–

0                                        25

Statute miles

CIRCULATION OF COMMODITIES IN THE TANGSHAN ECONOMIC REGION
Source: *Jen min jih pao*, May 19, 1965

case of goods shipped to and from Tientsin. In these cases, Tangshan city's marketing functions as established in 1958 were simply too extensive to service economically the entire political district. The economic limits of the Shenyang and Tientsin markets could be and were computed purely in terms of relative costs,[16] although some news articles also insisted on the need to define economic regions according to levels of modernization defined on the basis of "geography, communications, and production."[17]

While encroachment on the Tangshan district was occurring from the two cities of Shenyang and Tientsin, internal factors within the district were also helping shape Tangshan city's economic region. For example, it was seen that four other market cities along the railway in the district—Ku-yeh, Luan-hsien, Ch'ang-li, and Chinwangtao—could have supply and marketing cooperatives at the same level as Tangshan's.[18] In April 1964, the Tangshan leadership decided that 56 basic-level supply and marketing cooperatives should go beyond hsien boundaries to procure goods directly from the most accessible of the five principal market cities, including Tangshan city itself. Thus five economic regions were gradually replacing the old district-based commercial system.

At the same time, it was agreed that the Tangshan city market was organized irrationally when its goods had to pass through hsien-level markets before reaching cooperatives at the lower level. These cooperatives in turn were strengthening their own autonomy as their relevant commercial areas were coming into alignment with the standard marketing areas.[19] Given the existing transportation net, the city could send goods directly to the lower-level cooperatives without shipping them first to the hsien town. The same would be true of the other four market cities that were forming their own economic regions.

By these arrangements for the new commercial regions around these larger cities the workload of the intermediate hsien-level commercial establishments was abruptly reduced.[20] As a result, hundreds of hsien-town businesses were shut down. Their workers were transferred elsewhere;[21] most went to the local-level cooperatives, and a few were able to relocate in the growing urban centers such as Tangshan. According to the Communist press,[22] as the "five principal market cities along the railway line have greatly increased their wholesale tasks, they are separately converted into substations. . . . Personnel are increased appropriately." In sum, an alliance of more "natural" local systems, the larger urban-based commercial system, and the marketing communities "nested" within it, was developing at the expense of the politically based units, particularly the hsien.[23]

One immediate result of this reorganization was the creation of a genuine sense of loss in the hsien. Some expressed this loss in terms of the
change of routine, fearing "that it will upset normal business operations
and cause loss in work."[24] Others felt even more antagonistic and actively opposed the change. It is for this reason that the reorganization
of commodity recirculation in Tangshan was called primarily an ideological revolution, one requiring intensive reeducation of the affected
workers. Particularly hard hit were the cadres who expressed "great
apprehensions."[25] These cadres, it was recognized, "fear that they would
suffer loss, that they would face additional trouble, and that the interests of their own areas and their own unions would be jeopardized."

There is no doubt that their fears were justified. Commercial workers were rapidly demoted or dismissed as the authorities responsible for
the economic region worked to "simplify operations" at the hsien level
and to gain overall control of the finance and trade system.[26] Grain and
oil distribution were taken out of hsien hands.[27] Banks were reorganized
to close hsien branches, as were all processing industries, wholesale outlets, businesses, and relevant political structures.[28] Step by step, the
Tangshan bureaucracy was reaching into areas where it had a more
"natural" role to play, and as a result all urban structures were gaining
additional powers. Looking at the goods pouring in from the city to the
local supply and marketing cooperatives, peasants in the economic region reportedly exclaimed: "Ah, our place is truly turning into a 'small
Tangshan.' "[29] Evolving in the midst of a national economic crisis and
the consequent loss of central administrative direction, Tangshan was
acquiring an independent base of power.

### The Worker-Peasant System

These circumstances were not alone in shaping the political development of Tangshan. Along with the creation of the Tangshan economic
region two other interrelated changes were producing important repercussions. The first, a direct result of the loss of economic function for the
hsien town, was the movement of unemployed workers into the rural
communes or into Tangshan city.[30] The national program for handling
these workers was called the "worker-peasant system" (*i kung i nung*).[31]
The second change affected education. In the towns, educated youth
could no longer be assured of jobs, and as a group these young people
comprised a large part of the unemployed workers who were to come
under the worker-peasant system. In cities such as Tangshan, urban
youth were being transferred from the city to reduce population pressure and to guarantee stable career prospects for a smaller number of
students graduating from high schools and colleges. Formal education

was cut back as a part-work part-study program gained official sponsorship. The two developments thus altered the fate of workers, some who had only recently been students, and of urban intellectuals only slightly younger than those who had automatically received good positions in the years from 1954–56. Each of these two developments will be described briefly. This section deals with the worker-peasant system.

The creation of economic regions modeled on the Tangshan pilot region added to an already growing surplus labor force in the hsien towns.[32] Viewing this force as one to be mobilized for officially determined labor tasks, the government experimented with ways to handle these workers in the context of the economic regions. The cities and the countryside in turn viewed these workers as a force to be exploited, although considerable apprehension was expressed that their entrance into other job markets would jeopardize the positions of urban and village workers. What resulted was a plan to regulate these unemployed by regimentation into migrant labor bands. These would undertake "work and farming by rotation,"[33] and during 1965 they were used in unskilled jobs in more than thirty different trades in the cities and in seasonal occupations on the farms.[34]

At the urban level, factories and mines absorbed most of the displaced workers from the hsien laboring force. Many were hired to do menial tasks, as cart pushers, warehousemen, and general helpers under the supervision of the regular laborers. Others were assigned to mobile task forces to keep the commercial system functioning while it was undergoing the major reorganization into economic regions.[35]

There were thus two different kinds of laboring forces within the cities. One, made up of regular workers, comprised the more stable laborers; the other was composed of the temporary workers.[36] The existence of two categories of workers, moreover, immediately made it possible for factory heads to fire workers from their permanent staff who were considered undesirable for any reason whatsoever. The result was the creation of two threatened groups of workers—one in the city and the other from the hsien—that were played off against one another by the management of factories and mines and by the political leadership. Salaries were particularly subject to manipulation, for the regular labor force were paid for the same jobs at a higher rate than the employees under the worker-peasant system.[37] Later this system was to be denounced as a device by which the bureaucracy under Liu Shao-ch'i divided the workers into two strata with great differences created between them.[38] In the Cultural Revolution, the workers under the worker-peasant system were described as having "had no seniority and their contracts could be extended without any limit. Their work was not fixed

and when they got older [they could be let go]. . . . Under this system
a few 'mandarins' could direct everything as they wished and get the
best of everything. They set themselves up as dictators. Anyone who
did not fit in with their ideas could be dismissed arbitrarily."[39]

The opportunities for discrimination became almost endless. One
favored technique was to send peasants into the factories as cheap labor
and to weed out higher paid factory hands and deliver them to the
countryside. Moreover, pressure on individuals was increased because
during the inaugural period of the economic regions, as part of a movement to reduce pressure on the cities, the dependents of recently arrived
workers were sent back to their native places in the countryside.[40]
Workers and peasants both were later to compare this system to the
hated contract labor system that had been so prominent a feature of
manpower practice in the Nationalist period.[41] As that earlier period of
labor unrest had provided fuel for agitation, so this period of the economic region and worker-peasant system was to create the basis for
new political activism.

Leadership for one such force came from lower-level cadres, who in
the various movements for cadres to become ordinary laborers found
themselves rubbing shoulders with the highly dissatisfied laboring men
or with the peasants. Particularly active in this respect were workshop
cadres who began to form close relationships with their subordinates.[42]
Cadres were almost immediately pressed into political roles by workers who viewed them as channels to express grievances; the handling
of these grievances in turn provided a way for the cadres to attract personal supporters and to form small groups for political pressure. Evidence in the Hopei press suggests that such political groups were common in Tangshan and that later they provided the basis for the formation of factions.

Generally speaking, the pressure that characterized the worker-peasant system came to be centered on cities such as Tangshan. It was the
urban leadership that now had links to the countryside and that was the
most strategically placed to cope with the competing interests. Increasingly these interests were expressed in ways determined according to
categories created by the worker-peasant system. The peasants, the
hsien-level workers, and the regular workers in the Tangshan region
had three different points of view that were being expressed and organized on an interest basis.

As would be expected, the most conservative of these views was expressed by the regular workers in the Tangshan factories and mines
as well as by the older, more stable peasants in the villages at the lower

levels. Since it was these older peasants and the permanent working force groups that had the most ready access to the Tangshan leadership, they not only joined forces, as suggested above, but they also exerted the greatest influence over the urban leadership.

In this the trade union cadres played a strategic role,[43] and later it was charged that the unions had followed a policy of "production, livelihood, and education in one with production as the center."[44] It became clear after the purge of the trade union leadership that the union cadres had worked to protect their own working force at the expense of the migrant workers under the worker-peasant system.[45] Making use of such Communist-sponsored mechanisms as the workers' clubs, the trade unions were able to draw in their own supporters and control them for maximum effectiveness in the political bargaining that was occurring at all levels in the economic regions.[46] Inexorably Tangshan politics were coming to display the features of "bossism" and coalition bargaining so frequently found in the politics of cities in modern Western societies.

### Movement of Urban Intellectuals

Closely related to these changes in the labor system were changes occurring in education. At this time statements such as this were frequent: "The related departments therefore expressed the view that, to enforce the labor system of work and farming by rotation, it would be necessary first of all to go through an ideological revolution, to put the thought of Mao Tse-tung persistently in command, to organize the broad masses of workers to study earnestly the instructions of the CCP Central Committee on two labor systems and two education systems, and to increase their ideological consciousness."[47] These statements made clear that the two-track system in education closely corresponded to the two tracks in the worker-peasant system.[48]

As the Tangshan economic region was coming into existence in 1964 and 1965, a campaign was being mounted throughout China to establish schools on a half-work half-study basis. At the First Session of the Third National People's Congress in December 1964, Chou En-lai stated that instructions had come from Liu Shao-ch'i to continue this two-part educational system, one full-time and the other based on part-time study and part-time work.[49] By the end of 1965, it was revealed that more than 40 million students in China were attending the half-work half-study system, and there were strong indications that this form of education was being increased.[50] The regular system spawned elitism and protectionism as did the regular system of workers. Emphasis was placed on the best students, and any troublemaker or less qualified student could expect his school authorities to waste no time in shifting him into the part-time educational network often in conjunction with the worker-peasant system. Increasingly, therefore, the half-work half-study system of education became associated with a form of punishment and was clearly considered less desirable because it offered only minimal opportunities for later career advancement.[51] This was particularly true because the students associated part-time education with the hated worker-peasant system.

Although it is beyond the scope of this paper, the lot of former urban youth dispatched to the village level was especially unfortunate. On the one hand, the peasants considered them part of the worker-peasant system and thus subject to exploitation on the job.[52] The peasants could justify the maltreatment of these urban youth on the grounds that they were equivalent to landlords for the simple reason that they had come from cities.[53] Urban origin and landlord background were often considered equivalent, an especially dangerous juxtaposition because of the severe purge of "landlord elements" then going on in the countryside under the socialist education campaign.[54] These youngsters in turn became the ready tools for the village cadres who, for a price, would protect them and keep them from being branded as landlords. In many places, moreover, efforts to protect urban youth in the countryside took the form of recruitment into the party itself, which made the party units seem especially alien and threatening to the peasantry.[55] Perhaps the greatest irony of the situation was that the peasants despised the students because they believed that the former urban youth were back in the villages because they had not made the best of their opportunities in the cities: "The division between city and countryside is perpetuated from generation to generation by the fact that rural children who go to the city for education return to the countryside after graduation."[56]

Turning back to what was going on in the city, the two educational tracks were gaining importance in the political process that was emerging with the creation of the economic region. Job placement and education clearly went hand in hand.[57] A directive passed by the unemployment conference of August 25, 1964, noted that during the third five-year plan "industries in the cities can only accommodate five million people, and there is a problem of employment for more than six million people."[58] The senior elite in the cities used the regular educational system to foster its own successors and to take care of the children of its own cadres.[59] It also made educational opportunities available to its most active supporters as a way of rewarding them.

It was later to turn out that the half-work half-study system was to have significant consequences in the struggle that emerged during the course of the Cultural Revolution. Many of the workers in the factories and mines in 1964–65 were becoming eligible for education under the part-time system. This learning, of course, raised their expectations and increasingly brought them into conflict with people in the regular system of education who received almost automatically higher status and better-paying jobs. By 1966 the workers could only see that their part-time education was leading no place, and that the factory and mine alone profited from their additional training. Their sense of hostility in this regard was accentuated because of the mounting pressure on the labor force from the migrant workers. Thus student workers in such part-time schools as the Kailan Mines Correspondence School in Tangshan increasingly expressed their antagonism within the very groups that were acquiring political significance in the economic region.[60]

## Workers, Intellectuals, and the New Urban Polity in 1965

As one consequence of these developments, the Tangshan political administration had been transformed into a full-fledged bureaucracy by 1965. No longer were governmental units in the city simply channels connecting the all-powerful center with the obedient localities. Rather, in the language of the Cultural Revolution, there were "many centers."[61] Tangshan itself was one, and its bureaucratic structure reflected the multiplicity of subcenters within the city and economic region.

The potential for this development of autonomy can be traced back to the way the economic region was formed. In creating the region one of the demands that was met was the urban cadres' that their "rights should be restored."[62] They insisted that these rights include the authority to direct political and economic work associated with the commercial systems. This link of politics and economics throughout the natural marketing system, as we have seen, was to give them the mechanism to expand their control in an independent fashion throughout the Tangshan economic region. They were also to achieve support for this maneuver from the lowest levels. In 1963 the members of the local supply and marketing cooperatives had attempted to reorganize their trading patterns along more economic lines only to be rebuffed on several occasions by the hsien authorities.[63] Finally the director of a local grain station decided to test the language of the mass line by mobilizing support for the desired changes. He thereupon bypassed the hsien cadres to enlist the support of the Tangshan city authorities. The director even told the hsien-level cadres: "If you do not approve our request, we are prepared to report the matter to the provincial party committee." The result of these tactics was to force the hsien cadres to retreat. What had been feared by the hsien officials was that the creation of the Tangshan economic region would place the "urban viewpoint in command." Their fears, as it turned out, were justified.

In the new urban polity the municipal party committee played a crucial role;[64] at the center of the "many centers," it took responsibility for solving problems and easing the conflict among the various interests. "Politics in command" at this time meant party cadres in command, and thus the municipal party committee assumed a role in all of the aspects of economic and social life undergoing the most rapid change in these several years.

The party was not only at the hub of this conflict system; it was also seen to be biased on one side by many of the inhabitants of the economic region. The municipal party committee appears to have understood the widespread dissatisfaction and even the potential for opposition throughout the region, and accepted the responsibility for this by attempting to promote a more positive spirit toward the regional organization through ideological reform campaigns.[65] As one article put it: These campaigns would enable everyone to "understand the means of organizing a unified socialist market."[66] Many workers and students remained unconvinced, however, and later were easily persuaded that the reason for the party's actions in creating the economic region was to strengthen its base of power at their expense.[67] Their beliefs were reinforced by the party's base of authority becoming so heavily dependent on what appeared to be conservative elements throughout the region. On the eve of the Cultural Revolution in Tangshan, therefore, the party was in an extremely difficult position, unable to deal effectively with the many problems in the economic region and vulnerable to the attack on its position that was to be mounted by the Maoists.

### Tangshan and the Cultural Revolution

The fate of the Tangshan political system during the upheaval of the Cultural Revolution years is only gradually becoming clear. Given the autonomy of the urban leadership in the economic region that existed on the eve of the Cultural Revolution, the political leaders of Tangshan for many months not only had the power to resist inroads on their authority but had the foresight politically to insulate themselves from outside scrutiny. As a result, the sources on Tangshan provide only sporadic, though important, glimpses into the course of events from late 1966 to 1969. For this reason no attempt will be made here to describe step by step the specific transformations that occurred; rather we will present only a broad outline of what happened.

First, it seems clear that in the Cultural Revolution the previous urban bureaucracy was destroyed. The economic region ceased to exist as a formally approved system, and the top bureaucratic elite in the city that had manipulated that system was purged. However, the successor bureaucratic apparatus, organized within a new political environment, kept many of the essential attributes discussed in the context of the Tangshan economic region. The "new" polity in the area retained elements of autonomy. It linked urban and rural elements at the expense of the hsien and continued to depend on the city of Tangshan. The outlook of the replacement leadership remained conservative. The urban bureaucracy that came into existence in the aftermath of the Cultural Revolution no longer dealt with the kind of conflict that the earlier Tangshan leadership faced, and to this extent it became more of a regulative body within the terms of the prevailing political condition of China. By 1969 the system was more administrative, with military control attempting to ensure the existing distribution of power locally.

Although the former political apparatus in Tangshan was largely destroyed, the previous coalition of regular workers and older peasants survived and, with the army, gained control of Tangshan. This so-called "revolutionary" coalition, or three-way alliance, not only eliminated the threat of the more radical lumpen-proletariat and students who had been its previous competitors, but in replacing the former Tangshan political elite moved to denigrate the regular educational system and put all aspects of education under its own control. This led to a situation in which the regular workers in Tangshan's mines and factories could remove the upper-echelon scientists and technicians trained in the old technical schools, including those graduated from the prestigious Tangshan Engineering College.

What follows is an attempt to suggest how and why this situation came about. For purposes of brevity, three principal stages in the political developments after 1966 will be discussed: the upsurge of the hsien worker-peasant groups and disadvantaged students as allies in the nationally sponsored Red Guard movements begun late that year; the counterattack of the more entrenched urban proletariat who apparently could foresee that the assault on the elite would eventually come to include themselves; and the reestablishment of control and the creation of a new political mechanism under the label of a revolutionary committee.

The first phase was one of violence as the previously disaffected students and hsien worker-peasant elements sought to take revenge upon the urban and village elite whom they considered their enemies. Egged on by the slogans of the Red Guards and feeling justified by the radical bent of the Cultural Revolution, these disaffected elements struck out at the previously identified foe. As in other industrial cities of this size, the effects of the actions of the Red Guards seem to have come late to Tangshan. Although the Central Committee at its Eleventh Plenum in August 1966 had authorized the carrying out of the Cultural Revolution in "large and medium cities,"[68] the early rampages of the Red Guards seemed to have been confined, in this area of north China at least, to Peking and Tientsin.

But when the assault came in December it was carried out with extreme bitterness. The national-level documents that are available make clear that youth—students and workers caught by the worker-peasant system and the reorganization of education—were in an ugly mood. In attacking the urban bureaucracy they felt justified to retaliate by beatings, sit-ins, personal harassment, and in some cases executions. The wave of violence unleashed the hostilities stored up in the aftermath of the previous reorganizations.

Also set loose in the city were the contract and temporary workers who had been shuffled about under the worker-peasant system.[69] Their grievances were no less strong, their spirit of vengeance no less fierce. The young worker-peasant elements, under the guise of attacking Mao's enemies, penetrated factories to avenge past wrongs, or if at village level, set out to destroy the old peasants who had persecuted them. In some places, particularly around Shanghai, the victims were "dragged out" and handed over to the populace in the hsien towns who took particular delight in destroying those who in their eyes had damaged their communities.[70]

A central target at this time was an old peasant by the name of Wang Kuo-fan,[71] who later had an important role in the creation of the Tangshan Revolutionary Committee. The nationally known leader of the "paupers' co-op" in the Tangshan economic region, Wang had been singled out seven times in the 1950's by Mao Tse-tung for special commendation.[72] Thereafter his co-op and eventually the Chien-ming commune, which he was to lead, were taken as national models and given continuous publicity.[73] During the course of this first stage of the Cultural Revolution in the Tangshan economic region, however, Wang Kuo-fan was driven from power and subjected to intense criticism and personal abuse.[74] Similarly in the Tangshan mines "veteran workers" came under attack after the leading cadres in the former Tangshan municipal party and governmental apparatus disappeared in the onslaught.[75] The mines were said to be "seriously affected by anarchism."

At the height of the Cultural Revolution, the previously disaffected hsien-level workers and peasants and their student allies almost attained full power in Tangshan. In doing so, however, they not only smashed the former political apparatus there, but came close to bringing the city's economic and social order to a state of near collapse. Under these extreme conditions the older workers and peasants who had worked together in the Tangshan economic region now began to cooperate for their own defense, and simultaneously their leaders sought ways to create and expand their base of political power. These were the conditions that ushered in the second phase.

In the months that followed, not only was the assault of the radical elements turned back with order being restored, but a leadership coalition based on the more conservative urban and village groups began to form. It was this elite that was to work out the terms for an alliance with the People's Liberation Army (PLA) and eventually for the creation of the Tangshan Revolutionary Committee.

In February 1967 the central authorities under Mao awoke to the chaos that their policies had wrought. As part of a series of moves they issued directives aimed at checking the activities of the Red Guards' groups that had been encouraged to undermine authorities in the cities but that had now begun to turn their attacks against the top command in Peking itself.[76] Concerned by the loss of "market control" brought on by the self-seeking revenge of the radicals, Peking denounced them as "reactionaries, speculators, and profiteers." The *Jen min jih pao* added: "They make use of extensive democracy under proletarian dictatorship to undermine the socialist market, to counterattack, to settle accounts . . . and to carry out capitalist restoration activities."[77] In particular, the temporary, contract, rotation, and piece workers had begun to form national-level federations under the general title of National Rebel General Corps of Red Laborers.[78] Though some evidence suggests that Madame Mao herself had encouraged this to take place,[79] there is no doubt that by February this organization was considered a threat, and it was ordered dissolved. At the same time an abortive effort was made to reopen schools, and generally speaking to restrain the activities of the rampaging Red Guards throughout China. In these circumstances the Central Committee on March 18 dispatched a letter to all revolutionary workers and cadres instructing them to oppose "small group mentality, anarchism, the tendency to seek the limelight, economism, and selfishness."[80] Peking's emphasis shifted to control, labor, discipline, production, and order. Summing up, a Central Committee directive of early 1968 stated:

With regard to temporary workers, contract workers, workers working by rotation, and workers supplied by outside contractors [all these coming under the worker-peasant system], the center is prepared to make reforms according to different circumstances and after investigation and study. Before a new decision is taken by the center, none of them shall be changed to the status of permanent workers. . . . None of the temporary workers, contract workers, workers working by rotation, and workers supplied by outside contractors are allowed to form independent organizations. They must not exchange experience and establish revolutionary ties with one another or organize visits of personnel to the higher level. If they have problems, they should report to the local revolutionary committee.[81]

In the countryside, PLA units in the Tangshan area were deployed to contain the "counterrevolutionary activities" of those who had previously manned the radical organizations themselves or had been "hoodwinked" into becoming associated with the once-sanctioned radical elements.[82] In Tangshan, as one article in the *Kuang ming jih pao* makes clear, the hapless persons defeated by the army had promoted economism and distribution of the public welfare funds, reserve funds, and production funds.[83] In the aftermath of one such struggle in the Tangshan economic region in February, for example, village leader Wang Kuo-fan was restored to power in his commune, and the Paupers' Rebellion Regiment led by worker-peasant radicals was subdued.[84] It was only Mao's praise of Wang's paupers' co-op on seven occasions between 1955 and 1959 that had saved the peasant official during the attacks of the radicals, and in February Wang was able to use his national reputation to strike back at those who had earlier turned on him. Since many of the members of worker-peasant groups were the very urban youth the peasants had earlier identified as "landlords," this now became the basis for attacking the "radicals" as tools of reaction.

With the tide turned, a new urban coalition began to form around an alliance of the more conservative veteran workers, lower-level technical personnel, peasants, and the army.[85] PLA unit No. 4555 played a particularly important role in this respect by backing the political maneuvers of veteran miners in Tangshan's Kailan mines.[86] Any considered or labeled troublemakers were hustled out of town. Stability and order became the watchwords of the local organs of power throughout the city.

As viewed by the center, the extreme localism implicit in these new arrangements was considered threatening to its revolutionary aims, though temporarily at least beyond its control.[87] The *Chieh fang chün pao*, for example, denounced the prevalence of a so-called "guild mentality" as a "kind of feudal ideology unfavorable to the proletarian revolutionists for forming great alliances at present according to different factories, different systems, different units, and different departments."[88] In Tangshan it was those with just such a guild mentality who were responsible for restoring order to the city and who joined forces to create a revolutionary committee in January. Later Peking was again to describe trade organizations in the cities as an obstacle to the formation of revolutionary alliances,[89] but in Tangshan these organizations were the basis for the officially approved revolutionary alliances. When the revolutionary committee was founded on January 11, 1968, it was made quite clear that a combination of trade organizations of the factories and mines backed the urban committee.[90] At the Kailan mines, for example, the coal miners had earlier formed a revolutionary committee of their own, in which the older, more skilled workers were given a powerful role to play.[91] Representatives from the Kailan committee then met with PLA representatives and other group delegates to plan the Tangshan revolutionary federation.

One of the most interesting aspects of the new Tangshan committee was the role of Wang Kuo-fan of the paupers' co-op.[92] Brought in as the deputy chairman of the Tangshan Revolutionary Committee, Wang by his very presence symbolized the coalition of the more conservative forces, and in particular showed the degree to which the tacit alliance between Tangshan city and the villages comprising the economic region had acquired the more permanent attributes of a power coalition. Wang, who had been expelled during the heyday of radicalism, now was brought into the city to help run it, at the same time that he was allowed to continue as head of his own commune.[93]

### The Tangshan Political System in 1968

With the creation of the revolutionary committee on January 11, 1968, and the Hopei Provincial Revolutionary Committee the previous month, a new political system began to emerge for Tangshan.[94] The relationship of these committees to each other and to Peking, however, remained unclear, although the high ratio of military personnel made the revolutionary committee structure in north China resemble the transitional military occupation immediately after the Communist victory in 1949. Thus, despite its appearance of stability, the political system of 1968 could be considered only one in a series of types of urban organizations to develop in Tangshan in the last decade, and probably not the last.

As we have suggested, the more conservative social forces set in motion with the creation of the Tangshan economic region in 1965 and 1966 came to exercise dominant political authority in concert with PLA officers on the revolutionary committee. A brief description of these forces, especially in the realm of education and labor, will demonstrate the continuities as well as highlight the distinctive aspects of the 1968 urban political system.

In July of that year, Mao Tse-tung issued a nationwide directive concerning the Cultural Revolution in education. The text read as follows:

It is still necessary to have universities; here I refer mainly to colleges of science and engineering. However, it is essential to shorten the length of schooling, revolutionize education, put proletarian politics in command, and take the road of the Shanghai Machine Tool Plant in training technicians from among the workers. Students should be selected from among workers and peasants with practical experience, and they should return to production after a few years' study.[95]

Throughout the rest of the year, a series of statements trumpeted new educational directions, particularly a form of scientific and technological training tailored for ordinary workers and peasants.

Two aspects of this national educational program deserve special comment because of their influence on Tangshan. First, the national campaign on scientific and technological education emphasized the training of workers on the job. The propaganda with respect to the Shanghai Machine Tool Plant heralded the breakthrough to power of technicians who had been blocked for years by pompous superiors trained in Western methods and theoretical engineering.[96] They were particularly bitter toward engineers who had diplomas from the large modern schools. Summing up their feelings was this typical statement:

Politically, the reactionary bourgeois technical "authorities" have become infamous, and their technical incompetence has become fully exposed. In the past the capitalist-roaders did their utmost to idolize the reactionary "authorities" and advised the young technicians to learn from them, "measure up" to them, and "work hard in order to become engineers." The mentality of many young technicians has now undergone considerable change.[97]

The Cultural Revolution was propelling to power lower-echelon staff whose part-time training had brought the same political expectations as a college degree.

A feature of this shift in Tangshan was the public criticism of graduates of the "regular-track" schools, who had been allied to the now discredited party cadres. These were the students who had taken advantage of their connections, it was said, to avoid labor service in the countryside, or who had only done so on a temporary basis in order to establish their credentials for selection or promotion to higher positions. In the summer of 1968, a mounting national campaign to send these students permanently to the countryside found echoes in Tangshan.[98] The Kailan miners, capitalizing on their political triumph, thereupon approved the half-work half-study educational system as the dominant one, and in Tangshan news of the regular educational system disappeared from the press.

In late October, these same miners made the headlines as models in the nationwide campaign for the transformation of education.[99] The story was told of the damaging role that the older senior engineers at Kailan had played. Charged with suppressing the "creative power and intelligence of the more skilled coal miners, the former engineers at Kailan had rejected the introduction of worker-invented laborsaving devices and had brought in foreign-made machines that waste electricity and fail to increase production." A typical description of the change that occurred included both praise for the People's Liberation Army, which had helped remove the old leadership from power at Kailan, and a rebuke to the "engineers" who were foreign-minded and relied on "foreign stereotypes." In one Kailan pithead the "technical authorities" were belittled for having "massed a large group of college graduates to tackle the job, but these intellectuals were divorced from production and sat in their offices looking up technical data and drawing blueprints. After three months of work they still had no idea of how it should be done. Later the electricians at the pit bottom drew on their practical experience and successfully devised a central control box for four transporters." Galvanized into a political force by the onslaught of the temporary worker-peasants and the students in 1967, the Tangshan coal miners and factory hands who had remained united under the pithead or workshop cadres now took charge of the educational apparatus, relegated the regular school system to a secondary position, and ushered the better-educated elite and students out of town. Organized into 380 short-time training classes, the Tangshan miners comprised one of the largest "student bodies" in the city's educational system.[100]

Thus, highly organized groups of laborers won a strategic advantage in the course of the Cultural Revolution in Tangshan.[101] The new managerial staff at the coal mines, moreover, had used its pivotal position to take charge of the commercial network that to some extent remained intact during the purge in the economic region. Although we cannot be sure that all systems in the Tangshan region remained operative, fragmentary evidence indicates that the city still traded directly with the villages on the basis of the economic region as well as with other cities, whereas the hsien remained isolated and in a state of decay.[102] In Kailan the staff took over planning for the transportation of coal in the region and utilized the commercial network to support its political power.[103]

Within the framework of the revolutionary committee in Tangshan the "revolutionary masses" consisted of more conservative people who had survived the radical stage of the Cultural Revolution and were able to reach an agreement among themselves with the backing of the People's Liberation Army. Incorporated into the natural economic system, this most recent administrative structure had a reach and a degree of authority that exceeded any of the previous Tangshan bureaucracies. The power of that structure was more "centralized" within the city as men such as Wang Kuo-fan were co-opted to run the urban-based system from its center.[104]

By eliminating its competitors who had fallen by the wayside in the purge, this bureaucracy was far less complex than the one that had emerged in the economic region.[105] In Tangshan, the alliance of workers, peasants, and army men in keeping with the slogan "simplify administration" had reduced the apparatus built up by "an upper class" of educated managers and powerful party cadres to deal with competing interests. The new bureaucracy was more of a regulative one, maintaining stability and gradually extending its authority into all sectors of the economic region.[106]

The three bureaucratic structures that administered Tangshan from 1956 to 1969 typify three different kinds of power arrangements.[107] These may be profitably summarized here in order to highlight their differences and to explain aspects of Tangshan's political development after 1956.

The Tangshan political system of the mid-1950's may be seen as a component of a larger national hierarchy. To the extent possible, that hierarchy neutralized the exercise of independent political power within Tangshan. Gerrymandered political boundaries worked against the political leadership of more "natural" units, such as the marketing systems, and helped ensure policy control from Peking. The Tangshan city trading system at this time was largely independent of its immediate hinterland but could attain virtually no political autonomy because of the impediments to specialization and the continuous turnover of cadres as determined by Peking. The system of government for Tangshan at this time did not bestow power on political incumbents, although the elite in the city had substantial status and thus were ready candidates for provincial or national leadership posts.

Following the Great Leap Forward, and with the creation of the Tangshan economic region, a more complex political system developed. Cadres of the city and the villages were the beneficiaries of the redistribution of power in the economic region, but because the total product available for distribution was declining, there was apparently no sense that their lot was improving. To the leaders at these two levels, it must have seemed that they were simply distributing the goods and values of society on a fair and equitable basis. To those at the hsien level, however, the system appeared to be highly redistributive and to their acute disadvantage. On the one hand, the result of the distributive aspects of the political system were to lead to coalition politics and, on the other, the importance of maintaining the city and village against the still-powerful hsien apparatus reinforced the power position of senior cadres. The various elements of workers and peasants, having shared interests in some areas, aligned politically to divide benefits they already had; at the same time they allowed themselves to be manipulated or coordinated by urban bosses in order to forestall any losses to their competitors from the hsien.

Because of the breakdown of the national-level system at this time, the urban polity associated with the economic region moved very far in the exercise of independent decision-making. The interest group aspects of political life, it appears, were overlooked by Peking as long as production increased and party rule remained firm. Apparently convinced that no single contestant would (or could) win out permanently or engage in a form of competition that would irrevocably jeopardize Peking's authority, organs of the central government encouraged the ongoing political combat. In the context of its policy of decentralization, this could be viewed as the "testing" of new political relationships as the basis for a revision of the "superstructure." With the collapse of the party-led bureaucratic structure in the Cultural Revolution, this test was abruptly terminated.

What emerged from the 1966–68 upheaval was a regulative system for the governance of Tangshan. Ironically, it had a greater potential for locally based bureaucratism than either of the two previous Tangshan political systems. The first, it will be recalled, was relatively neutral in power terms and, under the center's direction, quite stable. The second was characterized by more active conflict and shifting coalitions within the bureaucracy. The factor of shared interest gave the national system a general appearance of stability but also convinced Mao that its organizational orientation was self-defeating or "revisionist." The post-1968 Tangshan system was no longer so neutral, and stability was maintained by political balancing and military force. The distribution of power was considered final, however, and decision-making theoretically mirrored the politics of regulative agencies that simply adjudicate according to prearranged deals rather than in terms of competing interests.

Yet Tangshan's autonomy over the long run would depend on the willingness of the center to allow politics in places such as Tangshan to take their own course. As we have suggested, the aspects of "guildism" and conservatism appeared highly threatening from Peking's point of view, and the revitalization of the natural commercial systems under the city could only be considered a direct contradiction of the goals of the Cultural Revolution. The very possibility of a reversal by Peking—a turn of events that seemed likely—prompted local revolutionary committees to take preemptive moves against potential, though weak, adversaries whom the Maoists might some day mobilize. The working out of norms for the continued harmony of the three participating groups in the Tangshan Revolutionary Committee was thus aided by the threat of Peking's power.

This system, like its immediate predecessor in Tangshan, more directly integrated city and countryside, but it brought representatives of the two into an army-controlled power system. The revolutionary committee was thus inherently unstable. Operating together, the two civilian groups might have had sufficient power to offset a complete army take-over, but the effectiveness of this power was reduced because the elite was no longer so geographically dispersed. Rather, its members had become more concentrated in Tangshan city itself, making the civilians easy targets for the army. Although this concentration strengthened the role of the city in the local political system, it also made its leadership subject to episodic upheavals and to the continuing manipulation or "logrolling" by persons fearful of loss of position.

The role of education in this urban polity magnified the impact of short-run political manipulations. Having become a fundamental part of the power transformations after 1956, the educational system reflected the contemporary political balance with great accuracy. With each political shift, everyday education was thrown into a state of turmoil. Career calculations had an unpredictable life span, generating uncertainty for a whole generation of Chinese youth. Socialized in conflict, these young people might eventually be expected to contrive so-cial restraints or rules of political fighting in the atmosphere of perma-nent crisis. Until a common agreement was reached on these rules, however, each shift would take on a more totalistic, ideological mean-ing that would accentuate hostilities and destroy common understand-ing.

Furthermore, the links between politics, education, and the commer-cial system made the whole system unusually susceptible to tensions associated with the modernization process itself. Since no one could be sure of the source of these tensions, political caution would dictate that each partner in the three-way alliance assume that any change might undermine his political standing. In a complex and disruptive way, commerce, education, and political development had merged. Where most political decisions should have had minimal repercussions on the distribution of power, as one would assume in a regulative system, every decision would in fact have the most profound consequences because of the links in the system and the instabilities in the three-way power relationship. A vast gap thus existed in Tangshan between the daily requirements and the ultimate consequences of urban politics.

# PART THREE

# *Modernization in the Chinese City*

# Manpower Training and Utilization of Specialized Cadres, 1949–68

JOHN PHILIP EMERSON

In a stationary or slowly growing economy, like China's before 1949, levels of skills and utilization of manpower may not be matters of great urgency. However, in an underdeveloped economy for which rapid development is planned, as in China since 1949, training and utilization of manpower are vital to the continuing achievement of rapid growth, and hence are of much greater importance. Planning for manpower training and utilization and the implementation of the policies required to realize such plans are difficult under the best of circumstances. When revolutionary changes are taking place in social, economic, and educational institutions, effective manpower planning and policy-making may be virtually impossible.

Because the necessary statistical data are lacking,[1] no attempt is made here to analyze the training and utilization of the large and heterogeneous groups of nonspecialized cadres who held administrative positions in the party, the government, and other organizations in Communist China.* The training and utilization of specialized manpower in urban areas is discussed generally in terms of the urban manpower available for specialized training, the training policies and programs relating to specialized personnel, the ways in which specialized cadre positions were filled, and some of the problems encountered in efforts to meet the demand for these cadres. In an attempt to show the links between the urban population base, education, and the modern sector

---

* This essay is based mainly on demographic, educational, and labor statistics; accounts of the development of educational, labor, cadre, and general economic planning; reports of plan results; and evaluations of these reports—all from Chinese Communist sources. With few exceptions, the statistical data presented apply to the country as a whole; no attempt has been made to present data by region, province, city, enterprise, etc.

of the economy, and the degree of success achieved by the Chinese Communist regime in training and utilizing professional and semiprofessional personnel, I also try to answer such questions as: what proportions of students in secondary and higher education were supplied from the urban population base? To what extent did the secondary and higher educational systems meet First Five-Year Plan demands for professional and semiprofessional manpower? How were the graduates of secondary and higher educational institutions utilized in industry, construction, transport and communications, education, public health, and other branches of the modern sector of the economy of Mainland China?

## Manpower and Educational Policies

The five-year and annual labor and cadre plans drawn up by the State Planning Commission (SPC) between 1953 and 1959 were detailed statements of particular aspects of the party's overall manpower policies. As parts of the national economic plans they established quotas of specialized cadres to be assigned to the various branches of the economy included in these plans and served as authorization for individual training programs undertaken by the educational and industrial ministries. In the period of economic rehabilitation (1949–52) specialized cadres received little attention in official statements on manpower policy. At that time the major objectives of Chinese Communist manpower policy were: to supply the nonspecialized cadres needed by the new regime to serve as administrative staff and to carry out the land reform program; and to provide employment for the urban unemployed. Cadre training programs were developed by the Ministry of Personnel, sometimes jointly with the Ministry of Education, and under the Ministry of Labor employment centers were established in the larger cities. During the next five years, the training of specialized cadres did become a major aspect of manpower policy. The goal of this training was to supply the engineers, technicians, and other specialized personnel needed for First Five-Year Plan projects and for the twelve-year development plans for scientific research, agriculture, medicine, and several other professional fields, drawn up in 1956. Between 1956 and 1958, the SPC tried to make greater use of the types of labor, cadre, and educational planning then in use in the Soviet Union so that there would be a continuous flow of newly trained, specialized personnel to meet planning requirements. In addition, the party adopted a policy of preferential treatment toward those already trained—engineers, university professors, and other teaching professionals—by increasing their salaries and adding other material incentives to ensure better use of their talents toward the achievement of national goals. During the Great Leap Forward such preferential treatment was largely abolished, and the trend toward increased specialization and more elaborate division of labor was replaced by a drive for maximum industrial and agricultural production through the greater use of unspecialized labor under the direction of professionally unqualified party officials. During the years 1961–65, manpower policies generally aimed at raising productivity and improving the quality of production in industry. Labor specialization and material incentives were again used as means to achieve these goals. Since the start of the Cultural Revolution, policy on the training and utilization of specialized manpower has been eclipsed by more immediate political concerns, as have most other aspects of economic policy.

Educational policy since 1949 has been subordinated to the goals of manpower policy and has been shaped in terms of the domestic political and economic objectives of the regime. In the 1949–52 period, educational policy aimed both at creating a socialist educational system with a corps of teachers loyal to the party line and capable of teaching the subjects required to master modern technology, and at training nonspecialized personnel as bureaucrats. The training of specialized personnel seems to have been a secondary consideration. Development of such a system continued to be a major preoccupation throughout the period of the First Five-Year Plan, when the party also enjoined educational authorities to copy the Soviet systems of higher and specialized secondary education. During the Great Leap Forward educational policy was reduced to conforming to the "general line," which included a drive to achieve universal primary education (six years) throughout the country and universal junior-middle-school education (nine years) in urban areas. In secondary and higher education the "general line" required that conventional curricula be converted to work-study programs in which half or more of the school year was spent in work outside the classroom; in addition, school enrollments and teaching staffs were greatly expanded. From the collapse of the Leap in 1960 until 1966, educational policies were concerned with quality rather than quantity, a concern reflected in the slogan "fewer but finer." Near the end of this period an effort to make work-study programs the standard form of education in agricultural middle schools was aborted by the Cultural Revolution. In 1966 came the most radical change in 17 years of educational policy: Mao decided to abolish the existing systems of secondary and higher education on the grounds that they were "bourgeois" and "revisionist." Accordingly, the schools were closed.

During much of the last twenty years, centrally determined political objectives have had a positive effect on the training and utilization of professional and semiprofessional manpower; but at other times their impact has been devastating. Most foreign observers agree that the policies that led to the halting of inflation and to sustained increases in economic production in the first three years of Communist rule benefited the great majority of Chinese, including the professional classes. The upturn in the economy in the years 1949–52 enabled the regime to undertake a rapid expansion of schools at all levels and of all types of medical facilities, as well as to give employment to millions in industry, construction, transport and communications, and other branches of the economy. During this period, nonagricultural employment rose by an estimated 40 per cent.[2] The First Five-Year Plan provided a continuity in basic economic policy that has been lacking in the years since 1957; it also initiated programs for training specified quotas of professional and semiprofessional manpower and marked the beginning of specialized manpower planning. The party policy, adopted at the start of 1956, of fully utilizing the talents and experience of leading engineers, educators, scientists, doctors, and other professionals seemed to signify that party leaders recognized some past mistakes in the use of available professional skills. In particular, the excessive political repression of many highly trained people during the 1955 campaign against potential counterrevolutionaries was recognized.[3] These benefits did not survive the start of the Great Leap Forward early in 1958. Not until the early 1960's did the party again explicitly recognize professionals as a group whose talents and skills entitled them to special responsibilities and rewards.

Among the party policies that in my opinion militated against the utilization and training of specialized manpower was the land reform policy. This was the first major domestic program carried out by the Communists after they seized power. Under this program some members of landlord families were sentenced to penal servitude, "labor reform," or execution, and most of the others were deprived of their property and civil rights and barred from most kinds of employment, regardless of their professional or educational qualifications. In the drives against counterrevolutionaries in 1951 and 1955, many people, including professionals, were convicted on the basis of false charges or without evidence, or were given excessive punishments, as party leaders afterwards admitted. Among the chief targets of the rectification campaign in 1957 were teachers, scientists, engineers, doctors, and other professionals who had criticized party or government cadres during the Hundred Flowers movement. Many were sentenced to terms of labor reform or removed from professional positions and given clerical or menial work. Under the "general line" during the Great Leap, little attention was given to utilizing the skills of professionals; party officials who had replaced the professional managers of industrial plants were primarily concerned with maximizing physical output and furthering the political activism (participation in mass campaigns) of their subordinates. Professional training was suspended by the Cultural Revolution. Not only were secondary and higher schools closed, but all existing curricula were abolished, and few, if any, had been completely restored by the end of 1969. Teachers were among the earliest targets of vilification and abuse by Red Guards. The only professionals who seem to have escaped Red Guard excesses were the scientists, engineers, and technicians working under military protection. Such have been the principal policies of the regime toward professional and semiprofessional manpower during the last twenty years.

## Demographic Characteristics of Manpower in Urban Areas

The urban population of China contributed far more than its proportional share of students to secondary schools and higher educational institutions. Among the rural population, adults from landlord and rich peasant families, who had been educated and were most able to afford education for their children, were largely disenfranchised by the land reform. And their children, as members of landlord families, were excluded from many educational opportunities. Furthermore, much of the peasantry was illiterate and lived in extreme poverty. In addition, because rural primary and secondary schools in general were inferior to those in urban areas,[4] students trained in them were much less likely to pass the competitive entrance examinations that determined who would be included in the quotas of students admitted to the next higher level of education.

According to a State Council resolution passed in 1955, urban areas were defined for statistical (as distinct from administrative) purposes as (1) places that had 2,000 or more inhabitants and were county (*hsien*) seats or municipal government centers or areas in which 50 per cent or more of the population were engaged in nonagricultural work; (2) places that had 1,000–2,000 inhabitants of whom 75 per cent were employed in nonagricultural work; (3) important communications centers, educational and research institutions, and (with some exceptions) health centers.[5] This definition was said to have been nearly the same as the de facto definitions used in a 1952 employment survey and in the 1953 census.[6] So far as is known, the definition has remained unchanged. The extent to which the definition was adhered to in practice is not known.

The urban population figures presented in Table 1 are official figures.

TABLE 1. POPULATION OF URBAN AND RURAL AREAS IN
MAINLAND CHINA, 1949–61

*(Absolute figures are year-end and are in thousands)*

| Year | Total | Number | | Per cent | | Rate of growth[a] | |
|------|-------|--------|--------|----------|--------|-------------------|--------|
|      |       | Urban  | Rural  | Urban    | Rural  | Urban             | Rural  |
| 1949 | 541,670 | 57,650 | 484,020 | 10.60% | 89.40% | —[b] | — |
| 1950 | 551,960 | 61,690 | 490,270 | 11.12 | 88.88 | 107.00 | 101.29 |
| 1951 | 563,000 | 66,320 | 496,680 | 11.78 | 88.22 | 107.50 | 101.31 |
| 1952 | 574,820 | 71,630 | 503,190 | 12.46 | 87.54 | 108.00 | 101.31 |
| 1953 | 587,960 | 77,670 | 510,290 | 13.21 | 86.79 | 108.43 | 101.41 |
| 1954 | 601,720 | 81,550 | 520,170 | 13.55 | 86.45 | 104.99 | 101.94 |
| 1955 | 614,650 | 82,850 | 531,800 | 13.48 | 86.52 | 101.59 | 102.24 |
| 1956 | 627,800 | 89,150 | 538,650 | 14.20 | 85.80 | 107.60 | 101.29 |
| 1957 | 646,530 | 99,500 | 547,030 | 15.39 | 84.61 | 111.60 | 101.56 |
| 1958 | — | — | — | — | — | — | — |
| 1959 | — | — | — | — | — | — | — |
| 1960 | — | 120,000 | — | — | — | — | — |
| 1961 | — | 130,000 | — | — | — | 108.33 | — |

SOURCES: *1949–56:* Data Section, "1949–56 nien wo kuo jen k'ou t'ung chi tzu liao" (Statistical data on China's population, 1949–56), *T'ung chi kung tso* (Statistical work), 11 (June 14, 1957), 24, in *Extracts From China Mainland Magazines*, No. 91, p. 23.

*1957:* The 1957 year-end urban population was 38.9 per cent larger than the corresponding figure for 1952 according to Hsüeh Cheng-hsiu, "Shih lun she hui chu i ch'eng shih jen k'ou ti tseng ch'ang ho kung nung yeh sheng ch'an fa chan chih chien ti kuan hsi" (A tentative discussion of the relationship between socialist urban population growth and industrial and agricultural production development), *Kuang ming jih pao* (Bright daily), Oct. 7, 1963, p. 4.

*1960:* "In the last three years the population of urban industrial and mining areas has increased by about twenty million," from "Ch'üan tang tung shou, ch'üan min tung shou, ta pan nung yeh, ta pan liang shih" (Let the whole party start to work, the whole people start to work, to farm, to raise grain), editorial, *Jen min jih pao* (People's daily), Aug. 25, 1960, p. 1.

*1961:* Ch'eng Shih-fu, Cheng Hsiao-sui, An Yung-yü, and Chou Kan-shih, "Kuan yü chü chu ch'ü kuei hua she chi chi ko wen t'i ti t'an t'ao" (An inquiry into several problems of residential area plan design), *Chien chu hsüeh pao* (Journal of architecture), 3 (Mar. 30, 1962), 1.

[a] Preceding year = 100.

[b] — = no information available.

Whatever the defects of these data, the figures at least show the magnitude and direction of population change in urban areas as seen by Chinese Communist officials.[7] The official data for 1950–52 were estimated by the State Statistical Bureau on the basis of assumed overall urban population growth rates of 7 to 8 per cent per year. From 1953 through 1956, urban population data were based on the 1953 census and the urban population registration system.[8] The indicated average annual rate of growth for the entire period 1949–57 is about 6.4 per cent; the actual rate may well have been higher since during these years large numbers of migrants entered the cities without registering, despite frequent attempts by the regime to restrict migration to the cities.

For 1958 and later years the regime has not published any urban population figures that can be identified as being based on reports from the registration system. There were many reports that exceptionally large rural-to-urban population movements took place in connection with the Great Leap Forward production drives in 1958, but the only published estimate of total urban population since 1957 is an undated figure of 130 million, first cited in March 1962.[9] This figure is assumed to be an estimated total for year-end 1961, although Chinese Communist officials have cited it in later years with no indication of a reference date.[10] This figure and the one for 1960 imply an average increase rate of more than 7 per cent per year for the years 1957–61. In 1964, the regime instructed its public security apparatus to conduct a new population investigation,[11] but no results of this operation have ever been published; unlike the 1953 population census and the efforts to establish urban and rural population registers, the 1964 investigation was never mentioned in the Mainland China press. Attempts to estimate changes in the size of the urban population since 1961 can hardly be more than exercises in conjecture. The assignment of many graduates of urban middle schools and higher educational institutions to rural or border areas, widely publicized in the press in 1964 and 1965 and again in 1968 and 1969, suggests that the rate of urban population growth may have fallen below earlier levels. However, the partial breakdown of civil administration caused by the Cultural Revolution seems to have weakened controls over population movement so much that migration was relatively unrestricted. There is no way of knowing how these two contrary influences have affected recent urban growth.[12]

Urban population growth results from natural increases and net in-migration. Available data do not permit an accurate estimate of how much of the growth of the urban population is attributable to each of these factors. Natural increase rates have been given for seven large cities for the years 1952–56, all but one of which are above 3 per cent,[13] or about one and one-half times the official natural-increase rates for the total population of Mainland China;[14] but the rates for these cities cannot be taken to represent the rates for the urban population as a whole. According to one official estimate, net migration from 1952 through 1957 amounted to eight million persons, or about 40 per cent of the urban population increase for those years.[15]

Between 1949 and 1960, rural-to-urban migration was sustained by social upheaval and depressed economic conditions in the countryside combined with higher levels of living and a wider range of economic opportunities in the cities. The land reform and the drive against suspected counterrevolutionaries in the early 1950's, the compulsory induction of peasants into agricultural producers' cooperatives in 1955 and

1956, and the amalgamation of the cooperatives to form rural communes in 1958 produced a succession of social, political, and economic crises that disillusioned large numbers of the rural population and destroyed their traditional ties to the land. Many migrants came from landlord and rich peasant families, and, because they were far better educated than the average peasant, would have been more likely to migrate even in normal times.[16] But the great majority of rural-to-urban migrants were young male peasants with little or no education, attracted to the cities by economic opportunities.

Migration was heaviest in years when job opportunities in the cities were the greatest. In 1953, the first year of the First Five-Year Plan period, rural-to-urban migrants accounted for more than 70 per cent of the increase of 2.45 million workers and employees, according to a vice-chairman of the State Planning Commission.[17] In 1956, peasant migrants made up one-third[18] of the increase of 2.24 million workers and employees.[19] The crash construction and production drives of the Great Leap Forward in 1958 caused by far the largest worker and employee increase in the history of Communist China—nearly 21 million persons —for the most part in urban areas;[20] in that year there were more than ten million rural-to-urban migrants.[21] Many migrants probably left their homes not only in search of economic opportunity but also to escape from life in the new rural communes. The strength of the forces that prompted peasants to migrate is evident in the fact that the movement continued in spite of the official prohibitions and measures against migration enforced by the public security police and the periodic expulsion from the cities of large numbers of migrants.[22] Although official spokesmen referred to the rural-to-urban movement as a "blind drift," urban economic opportunity was not merely an illusion conjured up in the peasants' minds. Many peasants were interviewed and hired by recruiters from urban construction enterprises and industrial plants. Others were given travel documents and letters of introduction by officials of their cooperative or township to help them find jobs in the cities. By 1958 the cooperatives were entering into contracts with urban enterprises to supply the labor of specified numbers of peasants at specified wage levels,[23] usually well below the wages paid to urban workers. The contract labor system was officially sanctioned on the grounds that it prevented peasants transferred to cities for short periods from becoming permanent urban residents,[24] and has continued in use to the present, apparently on a greatly expanded scale. During the Cultural Revolution a controversy arose over the widespread use of contract labor instead of permanent workers in industry, transport, and construction.

Permanent workers feared that their jobs would be taken from them by contract labor from nearby rural communes.[25]

Official concern over urban population growth was based on the consideration of urgent practical problems. During the period of the First Five-Year Plan, employment problems were the commonest cause for alarm over rural-to-urban migration,[26] although housing shortages, the demand on public utilities, schools, hospitals, and welfare services, and the problem of supplying consumer goods were also frequently mentioned.[27] The agricultural crisis of 1959–61 made the supply of food grains to urban areas the most acute problem for urban planning and administration.[28] All of these considerations had political overtones, though officials usually avoided giving the impression in public statements that the regime was worried about the possible political consequences of excessive urban population growth.[29]

During the First Five-Year Plan period about one million persons on the average were added each year to the working-age population* in urban areas from the urban population alone; in addition at least 800,-000 working-age rural people migrated per year.[30] These figures imply an average annual total of 1.8 million new job seekers in urban areas, but the increase in the number of urban workers and employees is estimated at less than 1.5 million each year.[31] The Chinese Communists have not published any data on the total number of workers and employees for the years following the Great Leap Forward in 1960. There is no reason to think that workers and employees have increased significantly during these years. At the same time the size of the urban working-age population has presumably been growing steadily, and the annual increase should now be about two million. The failure of urban job opportunities to keep pace with the rising demand for employment may explain the regime's insistence on relocating various urban groups during the 1960's.[32]

The policy of relocating urban residents has been in force more or less continuously since the 1950's. Almost without exception the relocations have been involuntary. In the early 1950's relocation was reserved for those judged guilty of offenses or crimes against the regime, who were sentenced to fixed or indefinite terms of labor reform in rural and frontier areas. The rural and frontier areas chosen by the regime for resettlement were deficient in such public services as housing, schools, and health facilities. Following a heavy influx of peasants into the cities in 1954, a year of unusually severe hardships in rural areas,

---

* Working age is considered to be 16–60 years for men and 16–55 years for women.

a major effort was made in 1955 to return migrants to their native villages. Some 700,000 were expelled from Shanghai and Tientsin alone. This drive was given as the explanation of the unusually low rate of increase (1.6 per cent) shown in official figures of the urban population for 1955.[33] In 1956 the regime ordered graduates of urban schools who had originally come from rural villages and who were not going to continue their education to return to their villages. In the following year the categories of students eligible for assignment to the countryside were expanded to include the graduates of urban schools who were not going to continue their education and could not find jobs. In addition, demobilized servicemen and dependents of military personnel in urban areas, most of whom came from peasant families, were required or encouraged to return to their native villages. In 1957 more than one million administrative cadres from the central and provincial administrations were "sent down" to township units or agricultural producers' cooperatives.[34] These assignments lasted from one month to more than a year. The program for transferring students out of the cities was expanded in 1958 as part of the "general line" of the Great Leap. Millions of young people were sent to mountainous areas or wastelands to work on reclamation projects. Most of these projects seem to have been shortlived, since very few claims of lasting success were made in the press. It seems likely that most of the young people involved soon drifted back to their urban homes. And despite its magnitude, the forced out-migration from the cities was more than offset by the continuing in-migration of peasants.

After the collapse of the Great Leap Forward, food shortages in 1960 became so serious that the regime again began to expel large numbers of people, apparently in an effort to relieve the pressure on urban grain reserves: a total of "more than ten million" peasants reportedly were returned to rural areas during the last quarter of 1960 and the first quarter of 1961.[35] As in earlier years, urban residents with peasant backgrounds were the first group to be rounded up. There were reports of jammed railway stations in 1961 and early 1962 as the mass exodus continued.[36] Reducing the urban population was the fourth of ten "urgent tasks" of economic readjustment set out in the April 1962 policy statement of the Third Session of the Second National People's Congress.[37] Official plans evidently called for cutting the urban population back from 130 to 110 million.[38] Again, large numbers of school graduates were sent to the countryside or to remote border areas. In the early 1960's most of these were primary- and middle-school graduates without any prospect of continuing their formal education, but at least by

1965 increasing numbers of college graduates were among the outward bound.[39] These assignments were extremely unpopular among students. Reports from China during the Cultural Revolution suggest that during the chaotic movement of millions of Red Guards from city to city many former students took advantage of the breakdown in travel restrictions to return to their urban homes.

During the first-five-year-plan period most students in higher educational institutions came from urban households. In 1955, midway through the period, although the urban population made up only 13 per cent of the total population of Communist China (see Table 1), students from urban households accounted for 75 per cent of all the students enrolled in these institutions. The predominance of urban students was also evident in enrollments at lower educational levels; 50 per cent of middle-school students and 25 per cent of primary-school students were from urban households.[40] One reason for the preponderance of urban students was the significance of family background in determining access to education above the primary level. In 1955, 71 per cent of all students in higher education and 31 per cent of all general middle-school students came from families officially classified as not of worker or peasant "class origin."[41] The great majority of these families were said to be members of "the exploiting classes or petty bourgeoisie," which were chiefly urban but probably made up less than 30 per cent of the total urban population.[42] There was roughly one student in higher education for every twenty to thirty of these nonworker-nonpeasant families; the ratios were one student per hundred urban families and one per 1,800 rural families.[43] These ratios existed in spite of the facts that tuition for secondary and higher education was free and that substantial state funds were available for cost-of-living scholarships to students from poor families.[44] Not only were the students from worker-peasant families disadvantaged with regard to enrollment for higher education, but they were also less likely to be enrolled in the better institutions. According to an education planner, the proportions of students of worker-peasant origin were smaller in institutions located in large cities and higher in provincial and municipal normal colleges and agricultural and forestry colleges—which were generally located in smaller cities and were often inferior to the major institutions in quality of education.[45]

In 1961 enrollments in higher educational institutions were almost three times higher than they were in 1955.[46] The proportions of students from urban and rural households are not available, but it was reported that in 1961 only one-third of the students came from nonworker-nonpeasant households, and the rest came from worker-peasant households.[47] These proportions mean that there were nearly six times as many students of worker-peasant origin in 1961 as there had been in 1955 but only about one-third again as many students of nonworker-nonpeasant origin. This almost complete reversal of the ratio of nonworker-nonpeasant to worker-peasant students reflects party policies that stressed the admission of more workers and peasants to higher-education institutions in the years following 1955, but it may also reflect the impossibility of rapid expansion in enrollments without broadening the population base from which the increased enrollments come. Probably a large part of the increase consisted of the children of workers and therefore still represented urban households, but it is also likely that the proportion of students from rural households increased significantly too.

Barring major catastrophes, the rate of natural increase will probably continue to be higher in urban areas than in rural areas, at least in the immediate future. In both urban and rural areas, the larger cohorts of young people born since 1949 are or soon will be reaching the child-bearing ages, a trend that would increase the crude birth rates even if there were no change in age-specific fertility levels. This increase may be further augmented by the recent sudden increase in marriage rates, which can be expected to cause a rise in age-specific fertility levels. There are reasons to believe both these factors at present affect the urban more than the rural population. Since the urban mortality rate will probably remain low, a sharp upward trend in the natural increase rate is very likely. Such a rise may bring renewed central pressures for adoption of policies concerning contraception, abortion, sterilization, and delayed marriage, but past campaigns do not seem to have been very successful despite the intensive propaganda efforts of a comparatively effective administrative system. Until the civil authority undermined by the Cultural Revolution has been restored, there is not much chance that future campaigns to reduce the birth rate will be more successful than those of the past. The only immediate and practical method of controlling or reversing urban population growth is planned relocation of some part of the urban population in rural areas. Since for most urban residents in China the move from urban to rural communities involves a decline in living standards and an increase in personal hardships, large-scale relocations cannot be conducted on a purely voluntary basis. Yet forcible relocation can be permanently successful only if the security police and other organs of civil control have sufficient power to prevent substantial backflow from the resettlement areas. At the end of 1969, they did not seem to have the requisite degree of control. Lacking such control, the flow of rural-to-urban migrants can be expected to continue as long as the cities offer better wages and generally better living conditions than the rural areas. If food shortages become acute, as they did in 1960–61, rural residents may again flock to the cities to share in the emergency grain supplies distributed to urban residents. If the economy resumes its growth at rates comparable to those of the time of the First Five-Year Plan, rural-to-urban migration may once more be encouraged by official policies, and a period of rapid urban growth might ensue. In short, it appears that only a catastrophe severe enough to make the cities less habitable than the rural areas could reverse the pattern of voluntary rural-to-urban migration that has prevailed, except for brief intervals, from 1949 to the present in China.

## Education Planning

Between 1949 and 1965, the two major objectives of party education policy were to provide political indoctrination for all students and to train as many as possible of the professional and technical personnel deemed necessary in state plans for expanding the economy.[48] Education planning was part of the overall plan for manpower training and utilization—which also included plans for labor use and cadre training. As in planning for production, construction, and labor, the Chinese Communists followed Soviet models in planning for education. Education planning was almost nonexistent before 1953[49] and only reached a very limited stage of development during the First Five-Year Plan period.[50]

For higher educational institutions and technical middle schools the education plan included estimates of the number of students who would pass qualifying examinations and be admitted to school or college (outlined by level of school and by length of course); the number of students expected to graduate, by level of school; and the number of students who would be enrolled at the start of the school year. Separate estimates by length of course were made of the number of graduate (research) students in Mainland China* and the number that were to be sent abroad for specialized study. Starting in 1956, spare-time students in higher educational institutions and specialized secondary schools were also to come under the plan. General middle-school and primary-school education plans provided estimates of the numbers of schools, classes, students to be admitted, students to graduate, and

---

* Graduate students are called research students in Communist China probably because at almost no time have there been advanced degrees toward which these students could work.

students in school at the start of the school year. The middle-school plan also included estimates of the number of new middle-school teachers available for hiring and the number needed, estimates that were to be based on plans for new schools, classes, and courses.[51]

During the height of the Great Leap Forward in 1958, central education planning was virtually abandoned as local party secretaries were allowed to set up "schools" at all levels by the hundreds of thousands.[52] Since the collapse of the Great Leap in 1960, there are indications that the central authorities reasserted at least a measure of control over education in the early 1960's,[53] although very little has been published in the Chinese press about education planning. From available data on higher educational institutions (see Tables 2 and 4) it is clear that a decision was made in 1960 or early 1961 to reduce enrollments in these institutions by admitting fewer first-year students. This decision obviously reflected a major change in educational policy and indicated that some form of education planning was still going on. Planning apparently lasted until the schools were closed toward the end of 1966, after disruptions by newly formed Red Guard contingents made it impossible to operate the schools as educational institutions. Subsequently, leading Maoists have stated that most curricula in use before the closing of the schools were to be abolished and replaced by totally new courses of study.

The training of cadres in professional and semiprofessional specialties was the task of higher and specialized secondary education institutions, which were organized and developed after Soviet education models of the mid-1950's. This extremely utilitarian training, which was generally for specific occupations, included only a very small proportion of the total number of students in Mainland China, never exceeding 2 per cent of all the students enrolled or 3 per cent of all the students who graduated during the First Five-Year Plan period.[54] Thus relatively few persons were trained for specific kinds of work, whereas large numbers were given formal education that was not in any sense job-training; still the regime has been unable to make full use of even the small number of trained specialists.

## The Educational System and Manpower Training

To reach higher educational institutions, students first had to pass through a primary school system of a four-year junior- and a two-year senior-primary school and a secondary school system of junior- and senior-middle schools, three years in each. Completion of junior-middle school was required for admittance to specialized secondary schools, and annual entrance examinations were used to select the quota of students admitted to first-year classes of both specialized secondary schools and higher educational institutions.[55] Specialized secondary schools were of two major types: technical middle schools, which gave secondary-level instruction in many areas of study in which the higher educational institutions offered specialties, and normal schools, which trained primary-school teachers. Higher educational institutions included comprehensive universities, polytechnical universities, engineering and industrial colleges, normal colleges, and colleges specializing in agriculture, forestry, fisheries, medicine, and veterinary medicine. The first three types of institutions were classified in terms of the number of faculties; the comprehensive universities had the most and the industrial colleges the fewest. Each faculty was responsible for teaching a prescribed number of specialties. After the reorganization of higher educational institutions in 1954–55, all of the courses required for a specialty (the rough equivalent of a college major) were prescribed and most of them were in applied sciences. Only students studying to be teachers of natural sciences and of humanities were allowed to take more general courses such as physics, chemistry, or history.

By the end of the First Five-Year Plan period in 1957, the courses offered, the teaching personnel, and the size of enrollments in higher educational institutions and specialized secondary schools were radically different from what they had been in 1949. The changes were due largely to several major reorganizations of education. Following several programs of thought reform for teachers, privately run schools at all levels were transformed into state-run institutions under the jurisdiction of the Ministry of Education. The changeover in higher education was completed by 1953 and in general and specialized secondary education by 1955, when only a few privately run primary schools remained in operation.[56] During this period, most teachers in higher education were subjected to thought reform at least once. Minister of Education Tseng Chao-lun reported that in 1951 a thought reform program had been developed among teachers in higher education, the equivalent for teachers of the much publicized "three-anti" campaign among government administrative officials and the "five-anti" campaign among private industrialists and businessmen.[57]

A series of attempts to standardize existing higher educational curricula began in 1952 and culminated in the wholesale adoption of a Soviet system of academic specialties in most fields of study during 1954–55.[58] Under this system there were seven fields of study—engineering, natural sciences, liberal arts, agriculture, medicine and pharma-

cology, economics and finance, and political science and law—that together offered a total of 173 specialties.[59] By the 1956–57 school year
the number had grown to 313, among which were 181 specialties in
engineering alone,[60] the same number offered in the Soviet Union at
that time.[61] The specialties taught in technical middle schools were
also modeled on those taught in Soviet specialized secondary schools.

From the last years of the First Five-Year Plan period until the closing
of the higher educational institutions in 1966, higher and specialized
secondary education in Communist China continued to follow Soviet
models. Because large numbers of Chinese engineers and technicians
had to be trained to operate Soviet-designed factories and machinery
assembled in China, the Soviet educational system was an appropriate
model during the First Five-Year Plan period; it also freed Chinese educators from the need to devise their own courses of study. They simply
translated Soviet textbooks and course materials verbatim. But at the
same time, the adoption of Soviet curricula meant that Chinese Communist educators had to provide teachers qualified in a great number
of new specialties, a requirement that was impossible to meet and was
therefore a cause of numerous problems.

Another problem that evidently grew more serious as the need for
specialists increased in the last years of the First Five-Year Plan period was how to locate and develop enough technical middle schools.
The problem seems to have originated soon after 1949 in the attempt
of each industrial ministry to train in its own schools the technicians
needed for its own expanding operation. By 1957 it had become increasingly apparent that the ministries individually were unequal to this
task. The timber industry and water conservancy ministries, for example, found that they could not train even the small number of machinery, electric power, and railway technicians they needed. The First
Ministry of Machine Building could not meet even its own needs for
machinery technicians in 1957. The Ministry of Coal needed technicians
trained in sixty to seventy specialties, but its own technical middle
schools could provide training in fewer than twenty. The training in
the technical middle schools run by local government administrations
was even more unsatisfactory than that in the schools of the central
ministries, with the result that locally administered plants and other
enterprises were chronically short of technical personnel.[62] Few junior-
middle-school graduates were able to gain admittance to the technical
middle schools administered locally, and those admitted had an extremely limited choice of specialties. For example, in 1957 in Anhwei,
besides a fairly large number of specialized secondary schools that

trained medical and public-health technicians, there were only four agricultural schools, and only one teaching forestry, one tea-leaf processing, and one electric-power specialties. At that time, in this predominantly rural province there was very little opportunity for specialized secondary training even in agricultural specialties, not to mention industrial ones. Some local Anhwei authorities said that to provide a satisfactory solution to local demands for technical skills, schools offering industrial specialties would have to be established in urban areas before factories and other modern enterprises were built.[63]

Enrollment in higher and specialized secondary education more than doubled during the First Five-Year Plan period.[64] The total of 441,000 students enrolled in higher education was higher by a few thousand than the plan target for 1957, and the figure of 778,000 in specialized secondary education exceeded the plan target by more than 100,000.[65] Enrollment in higher education in 1957 was 127 per cent greater than the 1952 figure; in specialized secondary education it was 22 per cent higher. This expansion strained existing resources of personnel and school facilities, and necessitated first-year enrollments larger than the number of students graduating each year from the general middle-school system. The higher education plan called for the enrollment of 510,000 new students in universities and colleges during the years 1952–56, but during this period only 370,000 students graduated from senior-middle schools. Not all of these students took the higher education entrance examinations, and of those who did, not all passed. To make up the deficit, 840,000 persons outside the educational system were invited to take the entrance examinations. These included government employees, primary school teachers, specialized secondary-school graduates, young persons whose formal education had ended earlier, demobilized servicemen, overseas Chinese students, and so-called young "intellectuals" from industrial and commercial enterprises. All were given three months' paid leave to prepare for the examinations, and if they failed, they could return to their old jobs.[66] The great differences in levels of education among those admitted to higher educational institutions during these years were said to have had an extremely adverse effect on the quality of education offered.[67] In discussing Second Five-Year Plan requirements, Premier Chou En-lai said in 1956: "At present, the greatest difficulties in developing and raising the levels of higher and specialized secondary education are the shortage of teachers and low quality of the students."[68] Although middle-school enrollments rose sharply[69] in accordance with First Five-Year Plan specifications,[70] the numbers of senior-middle-school graduates failed to satisfy the higher

TABLE 2. UNDERGRADUATE ENROLLMENT IN HIGHER EDUCATION BY FIELD OF STUDY, 1949–60 AND 1965

| Year | Total | Engineering | Agriculture | Forestry | Economics and finance | Political science and law | Medicine and public health | Physical culture | Natural sciences | Education | Humanities and social sciences | Fine arts |
|---|---|---|---|---|---|---|---|---|---|---|---|---|
| 1949 | 116,504 | 30,300 | 9,800 | 600 | 19,400 | 7,300 | 15,200 | 300 | 7,000 | 12,000 | 11,800 | 2,800 |
| 1950 | 138,470 | 38,462 | — | — | — | — | 17,414 | — | — | 13,312 | — | — |
| 1951 | 155,402 | 48,517 | — | — | — | — | 21,356 | — | — | 18,225 | — | — |
| 1952 | 191,500 | 66,600 | 11,300 | 2,200 | 22,000 | 3,800 | 24,700 | 300 | 9,600 | 31,500 | 13,500 | 3,600 |
| 1953 | 212,200 | 80,000 | 12,800 | 2,600 | 13,500 | 3,900 | 29,000 | 1,100 | 12,400 | 40,000 | 14,200 | 2,700 |
| 1954 | 253,000 | 95,000 | 12,800 | 3,100 | 11,200 | 4,000 | 33,900 | 1,900 | 17,100 | 53,100 | 18,300 | 2,600 |
| 1955 | 287,700 | 109,600 | 17,300 | 4,000 | 11,400 | 4,800 | 36,500 | 2,300 | 20,000 | 60,700 | 18,900 | 2,200 |
| 1956 | 403,200 | 149,400 | 30,700 | 5,700 | 12,800 | 7,100 | 45,900 | 2,700 | 24,900 | 98,800 | 22,500 | 2,600 |
| 1957 | 441,200 | 163,000 | 33,800 | 6,100 | 12,000 | 8,200 | 49,100 | 3,200 | 38,700 | 114,800 | 19,600 | 2,500 |
| 1958 | 660,000 | —a | — | — | — | — | — | — | — | — | — | — |
| 1959 | 810,000 | — | — | — | — | — | — | — | — | — | — | — |
| 1960 | 955,000 | — | — | — | — | — | — | — | — | — | — | — |
| 1965 | 695,000 | — | — | — | — | — | — | — | — | — | — | — |

SOURCES: *Totals: 1949–51:* Ministry of Higher Education and Ministry of Education, "Development of Numbers of Students at Each Level of School Throughout the Country and a Comparison with Pre-Liberation [Conditions]" [Sept. 1954], *Jen min chiao yü* (People's education), 10 (Oct. 1954), in *Survey of China Mainland Press* [hereafter SCMP], No. 939, p. 27. *1952–58:* State Statistical Bureau, *Wei ta ti shih nien—Chung-hua jen min kung ho kuo ching chi ho wen hua chien she ch'eng chiu ti t'ung chi* (The great ten years—statistics on economic and cultural achievements in the People's Republic of China) (Peking: Jen min ch'u pan she, 1959), p. 170.

*1959:* "Press Communique on China's 1959 Economic Progress," *New China News Agency,* Jan. 21, 1960, in SCMP, No. 2186, p. 6. *1960:* Chūgoku kenkyūjo (China Research Institute), *Shin Chūgoku nenkan, 1962* (New China yearbook, 1962) (Tokyo: Kyokutō shoten, 1962), p. 296. *1965:* V. Z. Klepikov, "Sud'by narodnogo obrazovaniya v Kitaye" (Ways of public education in China), *Sovetskaya pedagogika* (Soviet pedagogy), 8 (1968), 133–34.

*Figures by field of study: 1949, 1952–57: Guia de la Nueva China* (Guide to new China) (Peking: Foreign Languages Press, 1958), p. 207. *1950 and 1951:* Ministry of Higher Education and Ministry of Education 1954.

a — = no information available.

education plan admission requirements in 1954 and 1955, because middle-school plans had made no allowance for dropouts.[71] Consequently too few graduates of senior-middle schools applied for admission to higher educational institutions in both 1955 and 1956.[72] Plans to expand senior-middle-school enrollment in 1956 were hampered because the number of junior-middle-school graduates was smaller than had been planned; according to the Minister of Higher Education, the total would be barely large enough to meet the admittance quota in 1957.[73] These shortages of junior-middle-school graduates also adversely affected enrollment plans for specialized secondary schools, since completion of junior-middle school was normally required for admission to these schools.

The Second Five-Year Plan period began in 1958, just before the Great Leap Forward. Some 300,000 persons were admitted as first-year students to higher educational institutions, causing a 50 per cent jump in enrollment (see Table 2).[74] Probably at least half of the new students were recruited outside the general middle-school system and were therefore below the regular admission standards.[75] Although expansion was less rapid in the next two years, enrollment in higher education continued to grow, reaching a peak of 955,000 in 1960, 45 per cent above the 1958 figures. By 1962 enrollment had declined by between 100,000 and 200,000 students[76] to below the level that had been anticipated when the Second Five-Year Plan was under discussion in 1956.[77] Thus, instead of a gradual increase in enrollment in higher education, Great Leap policies had caused an overexpansion that had to be scaled down later. The decline in enrollment continued during the next three years, and by 1965 there were only 695,000 students in higher education, less than three-fourths of the number in 1960. This trend meant that the number of persons admitted as first-year students had dropped to about 100,000 a year, roughly the number admitted in 1957. Since this figure is unquestionably much smaller than the number of students graduating from senior-middle schools by 1965, the quality of the students admitted to higher educational institutions may have been rising.

The data shown in Table 3 suggest that engineering, the field of study of 36.5 per cent of the graduates of higher educational institutions, was given the highest priority during the period of the First Five-Year Plan. Education ranked second in importance as a field of study, producing 25 per cent of all graduates. Other areas were far less important. Economics and finance accounted for only 10.9 per cent of the graduates, medicine and public health for 9.6 per cent, humanities and social sciences for 7.6 per cent, agriculture and forestry for 5.7 per cent,

TABLE 3. GRADUATES OF HIGHER EDUCATIONAL INSTITUTIONS,
PLANNED AND ACTUAL, 1953–57

| Field of Study | First Five-Year Plan target figures | Reported number of graduates | Reported number as percentage of target figure |
|---|---|---|---|
| Total | 283,000 | 269,000 | 95.1% |
| Engineering | 94,900 | 98,197 | 103.5 |
| Agriculture and forestry | 18,800 | 15,444 | 82.1 |
| Economics and finance | 25,500 | 29,373 | 115.2 |
| Medicine and public health | 26,600 | 25,918 | 97.4 |
| Physical culture | 2,800 | —[a] | — |
| Natural sciences | 13,800 | 12,072 | 87.5 |
| Education | 70,400 | 65,525 | 93.1 |
| Humanities and social sciences | 21,600 | 18,987 | 87.9 |
| Fine arts | 3,800 | — | — |

SOURCES: Target figures: *Chung-hua jen min kung ho kuo fa chan kuo min ching chi ti ti i ko wu nien chi hua, 1953–1957* (First Five-Year Plan for the development of the national economy of the People's Republic of China in 1953–1957) (Peking: Jen min ch'u pan she, 1955), p. 120.
Number of graduates: State Statistical Bureau, *Wei ta ti shih nien—Chung-hua jen min kung ho kuo ching chi ho wen hua chien she ch'eng chiu ti t'ung chi* (The great ten years—statistics on economic and cultural achievements in the People's Republic of China) (Peking: Jen min ch'u pan she, 1959), p. 172.
[a] — = no information available.

and natural sciences for 4.9 per cent. The burden placed on education by the training demands of the first plan is indicated by the assignment of about 40 per cent of all graduates to teaching positions. Almost all of the graduates in the natural sciences, education, humanities, and the social sciences, and some of the graduates in the other fields of study were given such assignments. But the number of college graduates so assigned was still too small to relieve the acute teacher shortages in higher and secondary education.[78]

Although the 556,000 students admitted to higher educational institutions during the First Five-Year Plan period were 2.4 per cent more than the plan called for, the 269,000 students reported to have graduated during the period were 4.2 per cent fewer than the plan target.[79] Numbers of graduates exceeded plan requirements only in engineering and economics and finance. Graduates trained for teaching represented only about 93 per cent of the plan target, and graduates in agricultural subjects 82 per cent. A leading education planner ascribed these failures to faulty planning that made no allowance for dropouts, and to extending the course length in some comprehensive universities and engineering colleges from four to five years, thus delaying graduation and reducing the number of graduates.[80]

In the Second Five-Year Plan period the proportion of graduates assigned to teaching increased as the Chinese Communists tried to provide enough teachers to handle the greatly expanded enrollments in higher educational institutions and secondary schools. The number of persons trained in agricultural specialties also increased (see Table 4). Of the 608,000 graduates during the period, well over 40 per cent were trained in teaching, 28 per cent in engineering, 10 per cent in agriculture and forestry, 8 per cent in medicine and public health, and not quite 13 per cent in other fields.[81] By 1963, the proportions by field had changed again, perhaps because the need for teachers in higher educational institutions, and possibly also in secondary schools, had lessened after at least three successive years of declining enrollments. Of all graduates, 38.5 per cent were in engineering, probably not more than 33 per cent in teaching, 12.5 per cent in medical and public health work, 8.5 per cent in agriculture and forestry, and less than 12 per cent in other fields.

The number of engineers by specialty group (see Table 5)[82] shows clearly the priority given to the needs of heavy industry during the First Five-Year Plan period, when heavy industry was to receive most of the funds for industrial investment[83] as well as 50 per cent of the engineering graduates of higher educational institutions. Among the engineering specialty categories, machine and tool manufacture was assigned the largest number of engineering students. This group was to account for 20.4 per cent of all engineering graduates. Mining and electric power followed with 8.0 and 7.9 per cent, respectively, and chemical technology, metallurgy, and electrical products manufacturing specialties trailed with 5.4, 3.4, and 1.8 per cent. Engineering specialty groups used largely in support of heavy industry included construction[84] and geology, in which about 25 and 10.5 per cent, respectively, of all students were to graduate.

No way has been found to determine how closely the actual numbers of graduates matched the plan target figures for various specialties; but they probably did match fairly closely in specialties that had been taught in China before 1949 and not so closely in the fields of engineering introduced after 1949. (To provide faculties for teaching in the newer branches of science, the new China University of Sciences and Technology was opened in Peking in 1958. It was staffed for the most part by Academy of Sciences personnel and had 13 departments.)[85] In 1958, one specialist in education planning said that despite the great demand for metallurgists there would be only 662 students of metallurgy graduating in 1959, none of whom had specialized in

## TABLE 4. GRADUATES OF HIGHER EDUCATIONAL INSTITUTIONS BY MAJOR FIELD OF STUDY, 1949-65

| Year | Total | Engineering | Agriculture and forestry | Economics and finance | Medicine and public health | Natural sciences | Education | Humanities and social sciences | Other |
|---|---|---|---|---|---|---|---|---|---|
| 1949 | 21,000 | 4,752 | 1,718 | 3,137 | 1,314 | 1,584 | 1,890 | 2,521 | 4,084 |
| 1950 | 18,000 | 4,711 | 1,477 | 3,305 | 1,391 | 1,468 | 624 | 2,306 | 2,718 |
| 1951 | 19,000 | 4,416 | 1,538 | 3,638 | 2,366 | 1,483 | 1,206 | 2,169 | 2,184 |
| 1952 | 32,000 | 10,213 | 2,361 | 7,263 | 2,636 | 2,215 | 3,077 | 1,676 | 2,549 |
| 1953 | 48,000 | 14,565 | 2,653 | 10,530 | 2,948 | 1,753 | 9,650 | 3,306 | 2,615 |
| 1954 | 47,000 | 15,596 | 3,532 | 6,033 | 4,527 | 802 | 10,551 | 2,683 | 3,276 |
| 1955 | 55,000 | 18,614 | 2,614 | 4,699 | 6,840 | 2,015 | 12,133 | 4,679 | 3,406 |
| 1956 | 63,000 | 22,047 | 3,541 | 4,460 | 5,403 | 3,978 | 17,243 | 4,025 | 2,303 |
| 1957 | 56,000 | 17,162 | 3,104 | 3,651 | 6,200 | 3,524 | 15,948 | 4,294 | 2,117 |
| 1958 | 72,000 | 17,499 | 3,513 | 2,349 | 5,393 | 4,645 | 31,595 | 4,131 | 2,875 |
| 1959 | 71,000 | —a | — | — | 10,000b | — | — | — | — |
| 1960 | 135,000 | — | — | — | — | — | — | — | — |
| 1961 | 160,000 | 50,000 | 10,000 | — | 20,000 | — | 45,000 | — | — |
| 1962 | 170,000 | 50,000 | 20,000 | — | 17,000 | 11,000 | 56,000 | — | — |
| 1963 | 200,000 | 77,000 | 17,000 | 3,000 | 25,000 | 10,000 | 46,000 | — | — |
| 1964 | 200,000+ | — | — | — | — | — | — | — | — |
| 1965 | 170,000 | — | — | — | — | — | — | — | — |

SOURCES: *Total and by field of study; 1949-58:* State Statistical Bureau, *Wei ta ti shih nien—Chung-hua jen min kung ho kuo ching chi ho wen hua chien she ch'eng chiu ti t'ung chi* (The great ten years—statistics on economic and cultural achievements in the People's Republic of China) (Peking: Jen min ch'u pan she, 1959), pp. 172, 174.

*1961:* "160,000 Chinese College Students Graduate," *New China News Agency* [hereafter NCNA], Aug. 2, 1961, in *Survey of China Mainland Press* [hereafter SCMP], No. 2554, p. 16.

*1962:* "170,000 College Graduates in China This Summer," NCNA, Aug. 29, 1962, in SCMP, No. 2813, p. 18.

*1963:* "200,000 Graduates from Institutes of Higher Learning Throughout the Country in 1963 About to Take up Posts of Reconstruction of the Motherland," NCNA, Aug. 11, 1963, in SCMP, No. 3040, p. 6.

*Total; 1959-60:* "Big Advance This Year in Number and Quality of Chinese Graduates," NCNA, Sept. 4, 1960, in SCMP, No. 2335, p. 13.

*1964:* "More Than 200,000 Graduates in the Nation to Go into Employment," *Chung-kuo ch'ing nien pao* (China youth daily), Aug. 13, 1964, in SCMP, No. 3288, p. 4.

*1965:* "Take the Road History Wants You to Take," *Chung-kuo ch'ing nien pao,* in SCMP, No. 3523, p. 6.

*Medicine and public health; 1959-60:* Derived from calculating the difference between the 110,000 doctors and pharmacists graduated from medical colleges during the first 14 years of the regime and the sum of reported numbers of graduates by year. The total of 110,000 is reported in Ch'ien Hsin-chung, "Chinese Medicine: Progress and Achievements," *Peking Review,* Feb. 28, 1964, in *Selections From China Mainland Magazines,* No. 409, p. 35.

a — = no information available.
b Combined total for 1959 and 1960.

TABLE 5. PLANNED ENROLLMENTS AND GRADUATIONS BY ENGINEERING SPECIALTY GROUPS, 1953–57

| Specialty Group | Planned enrollment, 1953–57 | | Planned number of graduates, 1953–57 | | Planned enrollment, in 1957 | |
|---|---|---|---|---|---|---|
| | Number | Per cent | Number | Per cent | Number | Per cent |
| Total | 214,600 | 100.0% | 94,900 | 100.0% | 177,600 | 100.0% |
| Geology and prospecting | 17,500 | 8.1 | 10,000 | 10.5 | 12,500 | 7.1 |
| Mining and management | 16,000 | 7.4 | 7,600 | 8.0 | 12,400 | 7.0 |
| Electric power | 15,500 | 7.2 | 7,500 | 7.9 | 13,300 | 7.5 |
| Metallurgy | 10,000 | 4.7 | 3,200 | 3.4 | 8,900 | 5.0 |
| Machine and tool manufacture | 54,100 | 25.2 | 19,300 | 20.4 | 46,100 | 26.0 |
| Electric motors and supplies manufacture | 9,400 | 4.4 | 1,700 | 1.8 | 8,800 | 5.0 |
| Chemical technology | 10,600 | 5.0 | 5,100 | 5.4 | 9,100 | 5.1 |
| Papermaking and lumbering | 700 | 0.3 | 600 | 0.6 | 600 | 0.3 |
| Light industry | 4,400 | 2.0 | 3,300 | 3.4 | 3,600 | 2.0 |
| Surveying, drafting, meteorology, and hydrology | 4,600 | 2.2 | 2,100 | 2.3 | 3,500 | 1.9 |
| Building construction and city planning | 37,400 | 17.4 | 25,100 | 26.4 | 28,200 | 15.9 |
| Transport, posts, and telecommunications | 9,600 | 4.5 | 4,700 | 5.0 | 8,500 | 4.8 |
| Others | 24,800 | 11.6 | 4,700 | 4.9 | 22,100 | 12.4 |

SOURCE: *First Five-Year Plan for Development of the National Economy of the People's Republic of China in 1953–1957* (Peking: Foreign Languages Press, 1956), pp. 179–80.

casting, smelting, and refining furnaces, automated installations, non-ferrous metals, or metal rolling and heat treatment of nonferrous metals. Graduates specializing in electrical equipment production were expected to number only 400 and those in mining only 700, half as many as had graduated in 1958. There were to be none in mine surveying. Graduates specializing in electric power would be only half the 1958 total, including only eighty specialists in thermal power plant installation and none in hydroelectric plant installation.[86]

*Utilization of Professional and Semiprofessional Manpower*

The utilization of professional and semiprofessional manpower can be thought of as beginning with methods of allocation. In countries with market or mixed economies, the labor market is the principal means of allocation, reflecting consumer preferences to a large extent. In countries whose economies operate on Marxian principles, the labor plan is the means of allocation, and the state determines the priorities. The labor plan, the cadre training plan, and the education plan together constituted the central planning for manpower training and utilization for the modern sector of the Chinese Communist economy, at least until the Cultural Revolution. Insofar as they could, the Chinese Communists followed Soviet models in drafting their overall manpower plans, and local administrations modeled their planning on that of the central administration. Plan results, summarized in State Statistical Bureau economic communiques and statistical abstracts, formed the basis against which Chinese Communist planners measured the degree of success attained in fulfilling plans and on which they made plan adjustments or drew up new plans.

In mid-1955 the labor plan was limited to state industry, some jointly run "state-private" industrial plants, capital construction, railways, and the centrally administered postal and telecommunications systems. The private sector was completely omitted, as were also state-private transport, almost all state-private enterprises not under the jurisdiction of the industrial ministries, and all enterprises and organizations in the nonproductive branches of the economy. The nonproductive branches included finance, banking, and insurance; education, cultural affairs, and public health; government administration; mass organizations; urban public utilities; and meteorology. In 1956, with the socialization of the private sector largely completed, the labor plan was expanded to include all state-private enterprises, the few remaining private enterprises, and the nonproductive branches with the exception of mass organizations.[87] This expansion brought some 2.3 million more workers and employees under the national economic plan, raising the total to 22.4 million workers and employees at the end of 1956,[88] more than 90 per cent of the total number.[89]

The labor and wage plan covered four target areas: labor productivity increases in the material production branches of the economy; numbers of workers and employees by branch of the economy; the average wage; and the wage bill.[90] The last three targets included overall figures as well as subtotals for each of the six categories of workers and employees then in use.[91] The labor and wage plan served as the basis for the cadre training plan,[92] which consisted of estimates of the number of engineers, technicians, and other professional and semiprofessional personnel needed and expected to be available for the plan period. Prior to 1956 the cadre training plan included: the numbers of new workers and employees needed and the sources of these additional personnel; the numbers of workers already hired who were to be trained for higher level positions; the methods of raising levels of worker skills; the numbers of apprentices to be recruited and students to be enrolled in factory training programs and worker technical schools; and the numbers of persons required who had completed higher or specialized secondary education. The first item in this list consisted of estimates that were not considered operational figures. The second included estimates for the three kinds of worker training used at that time —apprentice training, factory training classes, and worker technical schools. The fourth item, concerned with apprentices and students, was intended to prevent completely unplanned recruiting of students at local levels of government administration, and the fifth item concerned facilitating the allocation of graduates to jobs. In 1956 and 1957, the contents of the plan were modified. For example, the last section was to be dropped entirely in 1956, since it duplicated a section of the education plan.[93] Other changes and refinements in the cadre training plan indicate that near the end of the First Five-Year Plan period the State Planning Commission was continuing its efforts to adapt Soviet models to meet Chinese needs.[94] An authoritative SPC article in 1955 described cadre planning as even more defective than labor and wage planning,[95] which the SPC sharply criticized in 1957.[96] That cadre planning was defective in 1955 is not surprising, since at that time the statistical basis for it was very poor.[97]

Although Chinese Communist planners recognized that long-range planning was essential for successfully meeting the demand for professional and semiprofessional manpower,[98] in February 1956, one year after the draft of the First Five-Year Plan had been presented to a national party conference, a vice-chairman of the SPC said that such planning did not exist.[99] In short, the Chinese Communists did not succeed in developing an effective basis for planning the allocation of professional and semiprofessional manpower during the years before the Great Leap Forward for which Chinese Communist analyses of planning problems are available. During the Great Leap economic planning on the Soviet model was all but abandoned, and the statistical system on which planning had been based was seriously damaged. In 1962, Director Wang Ssu-hua of the State Statistical Bureau (SSB) indicated that the labor reporting system had not recovered from the damage it suffered in 1958.[100] There is still no evidence that prior to the Cultural Revolution this system ever regained even the moderate level of efficiency it had achieved by 1957. Since manpower planning of the kind described above cannot be better than the statistics on which it is based, planning in the 1960's probably was not as good as it had been in 1957.*

Given the shortages of trained manpower that existed during most of the period under discussion, demands for such personnel were bound to conflict; few could be met entirely, many could be met only partially, while some could not be met at all. The extent of the shortages and some of the ways in which they were met are indicated by the qualifications of persons in professional and semiprofessional work. Some of the reasons for the failure to eliminate shortages are revealed in the kinds of job assignments given to persons with professional and semiprofessional qualifications; others are shown in the manner in which persons in professional and semiprofessional positions were utilized on the job.

In 1955, 75 per cent of all urban specialized cadres were teachers, engineers, and technicians. Medical and public health personnel accounted for 15 per cent, and the remaining 10 per cent included cultural affairs personnel (propagandists, librarians, radio and museum personnel, journalists, and editors). In 1956–57 the number of specialized cadres in urban areas grew from 1.5 million to 1.9 million, a 27 per cent increase. Primary-school teachers, engineers, and technicians accounted for more than 90 per cent of the increase. In the two years of the Great

---

* My account of developments in labor and cadre planning up to 1958 is based almost entirely on articles published in *Chi hua ching chi* (Planned economy), the official bulletin of the SPC. This was the agency that was ultimately responsible for all economic planning and for reviewing plan results. Such reviews form the basis for most of my comments on professional and semiprofessional manpower utilization. Where authors who were not SPC officials are cited (Chou En-lai, for example), it is almost certain that their remarks were based on analyses and reviews by the SPC, the SSB, or the National Economic Commission after its establishment in 1956, since these were the three principal agencies that made economic evaluations on a national scale.

Leap Forward, the total grew to approximately 2.3 million, an increase of only 17 per cent.

During the First Five-Year Plan period, the allocation of engineers and technicians by branch of the economy seems to have corresponded roughly to the growth of employment in each branch. Activities grouped under the heading of capital construction absorbed 50 per cent of the engineers and technicians added to the nonagricultural labor force during the period (building and installation work took 85,000 persons, survey and design 50,000, and geological survey 25,000), and industry added 117,000 persons, or 35 per cent. Water conservancy, transport, and communications accounted for most of the remaining 15 per cent. Roughly half of the engineers and technicians added to industry were hired in the electric power, coal, textile, and papermaking branches, although these branches employed only 28 per cent of all industrial workers and employees in 1956. A large proportion of the remainder probably were employed in the infant petroleum industry and in the few large iron and steel, machinery, chemical, and cement plants then in operation; a small proportion went into the food processing, metalworking, nonferrous metals, building materials (other than cement), and timber industry branches.[101] In 1958, when many new plants were rushed into production ahead of schedule to help meet Great Leap Forward targets, 70 per cent of the 122,000 new engineers and technicians were allotted to industry,[102] a proportion twice as large as that for the First Five-Year Plan period. During and after construction, the ratios of engineers and technicians to workers assigned to First Five-Year Plan projects were much higher than those allotted to existing enterprises not included in the First Five-Year Plan as construction projects.[103]

Because of the acute shortage of persons who had completed engineering specialties in higher or specialized secondary education during the first ten years of the regime, many persons who lacked the formal educational qualifications were placed in engineering and technical positions. Most of these were not graduates of higher educational institutions with engineering training, but they had worked for some time in a plant or enterprise before they were promoted or transferred to engineering or technical positions. A technician who had not completed higher education could be promoted to the level of engineer or else be transferred to an engineering position without a formal promotion. Similarly, after completing on-the-job training a worker could be promoted or transferred to the level of technician.[104] Such persons are the Chinese equivalents of *praktiki* (practicals) in the Soviet Union.[105] Of the 609,000 persons in engineering positions in 1955, 374,000, or 61 per

cent, were practicals.[106] According to the cadre plan, their number was
to increase to 432,000 at the end of the First Five-Year Plan period in
1957, but would then make up only 54 per cent of the total number of
persons in engineering and technical positions.[107] In industry, the number of certified engineers and technicians increased from 58,000 in 1952
to 125,000 in 1955.[108] Of this increase, 30,000, or 45 per cent, had been
promoted from worker to technician.[109]

The practice of filling positions requiring professional and semiprofessional skills with persons who lacked the educational qualifications
extended into most if not all professional fields. According to SSB statistics, there were 29,000 more doctors and pharmacists practicing Western medicine in 1955 than in 1950,[110] although only 15,000 students
graduated from medical colleges between 1949 and 1954 (see Table 4).
Of the 50,000 doctors included in the September 30, 1955, census of
state-sector workers and employees, only 49 per cent had completed
higher education. Among the 1,632,000 persons reported as teachers in
the same census, 136,000 had completed higher education, the required
level of educational attainment for middle-school teaching, and 714,000
had completed secondary normal school, the minimum educational requirement for primary-school teaching. At that time there were nearly
1.6 million teachers in primary and secondary schools (excluding teachers in higher education).[111] In 1956, 1.1 million primary-school teachers, or 61 per cent, were credited with having completed secondary
normal school or junior-middle school.[112] Of junior-middle-school teachers in 1957, only 48 per cent met the educational qualifications for
teaching; among senior middle-school teachers the proportion was much
higher, 83 per cent.[113] But few of the 460,000 persons hired as teachers
in order to facilitate the enormous expansion of school enrollments in
1958[114] could have met the educational requirements for the teaching
positions they filled.

It would be a mistake to suppose that, just because of such acute
shortages, the relatively few specialists available were well utilized
during the First Five-Year Plan period and during subsequent periods
when the need for technical skills in the economy was explicitly recognized in party policy statements. Many serious misjudgments were made
in allocating manpower and assigning jobs, with the result that there
was a general underutilization and misuse of professional and semiprofessional manpower. Near the end of the First Five-Year Plan period
this situation was uncovered by SPC analysts, whose findings were
based not only on the SSB 1955 census of state-sector workers and employees but on other statistical surveys.

In 1956, a large number of party leaders and government administrators felt that the misuse of the most highly trained professional and semiprofessional personnel then working in China was so widespread that it warranted a complete review and revision of party policy.[115] It was in that year that the National Economic Commission had been established to draft and review annual national economic plans; thus it was responsible in general for the allocation of graduates of higher educational institutions and specialized secondary schools. The Ministry of Higher Education, together with the industrial and other "business affairs" ministries in charge of industrial and other higher education institutes, formulated actual work assignment plans, while the personnel offices of higher educational institutions made actual individual assignments.[116] One error that the National Economic Commission made was to allocate to plants not yet built or not in operation newly graduated professional and semiprofessional personnel, who found no job or place of work when they reported for work.[117] The personnel offices of the Ministry of Higher Education and other ministries frequently assigned graduates to work that was unrelated to their training; for example, graduates in metal cutting and processing were assigned as Russian language tutors, graduates in metal forging and casting as labor administrators, and graduates in Russian language as teachers of physical culture. Such disregard for the specialty training of graduates appears to have been particularly flagrant in the personnel offices of the industrial ministries.[118] Even if the upper administrative levels made correct allocations and assignments, their work could be and often was nullified by misassignments at lower levels. For example, a graduate in structural engineering assigned to an engineering enterprise might be given clerical work to do. During the years 1953–56, more than 5 per cent of the graduates assigned jobs requested reassignment,[119] a figure that probably understates the actual frequency of incorrect assignments. Ignorance of how to request reassignment, fear of reprisals from superiors for making such a request, and passive acceptance of an unsuitable assignment are among the reasons that the number of reported misassignments would have been smaller—probably much smaller—than the number of actual misassignments.

Not all faulty utilization of professional manpower could be ascribed to errors in assignment; some of it was due to poor organization of work. Correcting defects in work organization was one of the chief objectives of the 1956 wage reform. At the time of the reform, Minister of Labor Ma Wen-jui described the disparity between the salaries and duties of engineers and technicians as follows:

The salary levels of the overwhelming majority of technical personnel in enterprises have not been assigned on the basis of the professional duties for which the personnel are responsible but according to their titles and grades as engineers and technicians. The result is that the salaries they receive bear no relation to the duties they perform, and this does not help strengthen their sense of responsibility for production management. At the same time, technical personnel, some of whose responsibilities are heavy and some light and whose contributions to the enterprise vary in importance, receive the same salary simply because of title and grade. This is not rational. This wage reform in addition to giving comparatively large salary increases to technical personnel . . . will in general put into effect a salary system based on duties performed.[120]

Ma's description of the organization of work is amplified in an article on industrial salaries:

Before the 1956 wage reform job titles were vague, job responsibilities illdefined, and professional duties and salaries not in line. This was especially true of engineers and technicians. Their salaries were not determined by the professional duties for which they were responsible. Many of them had no fixed work positions and had no definite responsibilities for production, but functioned only as "advisers." Such circumstances greatly weakened their sense of responsibility for production.[121]

The 1955 census of state-sector workers and employees revealed that 63,000 qualified engineering graduates of higher educational institutions were employed as technicians. According to Chou En-lai, many of them were performing the duties of engineers, and many should have been promoted to the level of engineer.[122] They constituted 20 per cent of the 322,000 persons who at that time had obtained the occupational title of technician.[123] The extent of the failure to utilize professionally trained personnel at the job level for which they were qualified was shown in a 1956 SSB survey which found that of the 98,000 graduates of higher educational institutions who had been classified as engineers and technicians only 22,000, or 22 per cent, were employed as engineers. The remaining 76,000 were employed as technicians—14,000 more than the graduates thus employed in 1955. Graduates of specialized secondary schools apparently were even less successful in obtaining jobs commensurate with their training. A vice-chairman of the State Planning Commission stated that these conditions "clearly were wastes of trained manpower."[124]

The extent to which mistakes in allocation and assignment led to gross misuse of trained manpower is further indicated by data from the 1955 census of state-sector workers and employees. The number of graduates of higher educational institutions and specialized secondary schools who had not obtained technical occupational titles of any kind— that is, who were not employed in either technical or engineering work despite their academic qualifications—included 11.7 per cent of all those who had completed higher education engineering specialties and 17.8 per cent of all specialized secondary engineering graduates.[125]

*Prospects for the Future*

One way to look at the future of training and utilization of specialized manpower is in terms of the overall effects on these activities of urban population growth since 1949. The Chinese Communists never succeeded in reducing to acceptable levels either the rate of natural increase in the urban population or rural-to-urban migration. Consequently, as the pressure of urban population growth mounted, they relied more and more on the strategy of relocating in rural areas members of the urban population who were considered surplus. As the relocations increased during the 1960's, the regime became progressively less selective of the types of population that were transferred out of the cities. In the 1950's, only urban groups classified by the regime as nonproductive were targets for relocation; after the Cultural Revolution almost no occupational groups in urban areas were exempt. Except during the Cultural Revolution, relocation was mandatory for most of the graduating students in urban areas who could not find employment in the cities. After the Cultural Revolution, large numbers of medical and other professional and semiprofessional personnel, as well as administrative cadres, were also sent to rural areas. The relocation of these groups represented the abandonment of the party policy, adopted near the end of the First Five-Year Plan period, of making the most effective possible use of specialized manpower. The training of specialized manpower was halted when the schools were closed in 1966, on the grounds that the old courses of study were revisionist Soviet curricula, and it had not been resumed to an appreciable extent by the end of 1968. The tentative proposals made by leading Maoists since the end of the Cultural Revolution for new courses to replace the old Soviet curricula all point to shorter periods of training and a reduction in specialization in schools at all levels. If these proposals are implemented, students in higher education in the next few years probably will receive less technical training than did their predecessors of the past twenty years and will not be trained for specific occupations as the latter were. For this reason students in the early 1970's may have less definite career expectations than did students in the last two decades. Thus, on the one hand, they may be more willing to accept whatever work they are assigned, even if it takes them to rural areas. On the other hand, a general scarcity of career opportunities may produce greater frustration among youth than was felt in earlier years.

There are several reasons for thinking that utilization of specialized manpower may be even less effective in the early 1970's than it was during the Great Leap Forward—when the earlier policy of effective utilization of specialized manpower and the conventional forms of management were abandoned. As long as mass transfers of urban students to rural areas continue, graduates are unlikely to be given the jobs for which their specialized training may have qualified them. The so-called revolutionary committees that took over the management of some industrial plants after the Cultural Revolution abolished conventional management methods and staff functions and stopped using engineers and technicians in a professional capacity. It seems unlikely that the regime will try to resume systematic and rational utilization of specialized manpower as long as the "thoughts" of Mao, with their inherent preference for political participation over technical expertise, control domestic policy in Communist China. Any efforts by economic planners and managers to return to a more pragmatic approach would probably be denounced as revisionist. The overall effect of Maoist policies, which amount to a virtual rejection of modern technology, will be to retard industrialization and the development of modern occupations and services in urban areas.

# The Level and Structure of Employment and the Sources of Labor Supply in Shanghai, 1949–57

CHRISTOPHER HOWE

In this study I explore the possible use of materials relating to specific cities as a means of measuring both the size and structure of the urban labor force and the sources of urban labor supply in modern China. This information may illustrate changes in the urban labor market during the period 1949–57 and during the longer period 1926–57.

Of the estimates of employment that can be used to throw light on the development of the urban labor market, I shall consider first those of John Philip Emerson (published prior to his essay in this volume).[1] Emerson's work is without question one of the most professional and painstaking pieces of research that has been done on the Chinese economy since 1949. However, in many ways Emerson's work has limited value for students of the urban labor market, for I think it can be shown that his final data have limitations that justify an attempt to find alternative approaches to the problem of quantifying China's urban employment experience. The first difficulty with Emerson's data is that they are concerned principally with the whole of the nonagricultural work force. Hence they include persons resident in rural areas and engaged in such activities as construction work, water conservancy, fishing, trade, services, education, and various kinds of government and party work. Since such persons form a majority of all those engaged in nonagricultural employment, it is immediately obvious that analysis of employment of this kind can have only a restricted value to those concerned with the analysis of economic change and of the labor market in urban areas.[2] It is particularly difficult to use these data in conjunction with urban demographic data and with qualitative information in order to construct a coherent picture of urban population and employment. It is true that the juxtaposition of Emerson's data with other material on urban areas is often suggestive and interesting, but by definition precise conclusions are precluded.[3]

The second difficulty posed by Emerson's data is their admitted inaccuracy. Emerson is fully aware of this problem, but some users of his work do not always appear to have been so. Emerson's work, basically a reconstruction of official data, reflects the inadequacies of such data. The official data are defective in two respects. First, the slow development of a centralized and effective statistical system precluded the collection of comprehensive and consistently defined employment data, particularly in the early 1950's. Indeed, according to Emerson, it was admitted that adequate estimates of employment were unobtainable right up to the end of the First Five-Year Plan.[4] Information on the public sector was, of course, fairly comprehensive, and there was also considerable information on persons classified as "workers and staff" (people who are basically wage earners), who were in the private sector until 1956.[5] Apart from these categories comprehensive information did not exist, a failing that resulted in substantial underreporting, which is reflected in Emerson's data. Moreover, this deficiency and general unreliability was made particularly serious by the inclusion of data from rural areas, where statistical organization was most primitive and the problems of occupational differentiation most difficult. The second major source of underreporting in the official data is the absolute exclusion from employment surveys of persons in certain types of occupations, in particular people engaged in some of the traditional trades and services—capitalists (a category that included persons employing labor in very small-scale enterprises), tutors, servants, persons doing religious work—and others doing jobs that the authorities regarded as unproductive or socially harmful. Apart from these deliberate exclusions, the official figures are unlikely to contain systematic information on those engaged in illicit economic activities.

To some extent Emerson has been able to allow for these omissions in his estimates; in particular he has data on persons engaged in traditional transportation. However, as he makes clear, his figures must reflect the biases in the official data, and therefore substantially understate actual nonagricultural employment. By using Ou Pao-san's prewar data Emerson has estimated that his figure for nonagricultural employment for 1949 is about 27 per cent below the actual figure. He estimates that for 1957 the undercount had dropped to 11 per cent.

Turning from Emerson's work, I now consider the set of estimates of Ta-chung Liu and Kung-chia Yeh. It is an indication of the degree of uncertainty surrounding the national data that these estimates con-

flict seriously with those of Emerson.[6] The degree of divergence between the two estimates is illustrated by comparing the basic figure for
total nonagricultural employment. Emerson's figure is 39,667,000 for
1957; raising this by 11 per cent in accordance with Emerson's estimate
of the undercount in his data, we have a figure of 44,000,000, which
compares with Liu and Yeh's estimate for the same year of 64,000,000.
Differences of this magnitude between competent scholars throw doubt
on the feasibility of any national manpower estimates. A detailed examination of the two sets of estimates makes it clear that Liu and Yeh's
calculations are much more ambitious than any of Emerson's, and that
their results are given in a form that in principle is more useful analyti-
cally, in particular because they offer a systematic breakdown of employment and unemployment that uses the urban-rural dichotomy.
However, the reliability of the data is what is crucial, and the only
means of appraising this is by comparing the methods employed in
arriving at the estimates. Here the contrast between the two sets of
data is very instructive. Whereas Emerson departs as rarely as possible
from the official figures and thus has difficulty obtaining satisfactory
results, Liu and Yeh start from a small collection of pre- and post-1949
data, which by making a number of assumptions they convert into a
detailed series of estimates for all major categories of employment.* In
some ways, therefore, Liu and Yeh's results are less satisfactory than
Emerson's, for although Emerson's results are incomplete and difficult
to analyze they give us valuable positive information. Liu and Yeh, by
contrast, give a brilliant, internally consistent account of what reality
may have looked like; but ultimately one has more admiration for their
skill than confidence in the detailed accuracy of the finished product.

In addition to these reconstructed Western estimates of employment,
we have some official data on urban labor supply. The crucial figures
here are those contained in Sung P'ing's famous article on employment
published in 1957.[7] In this article Sung P'ing furnishes us with estimates
of the natural increment to the urban labor force and an estimate of
the total migration from rural to urban areas up to 1957. Clearly these
figures are of vital importance for any estimate of urban labor supply,
and it is possible to use them in conjunction with data on employment

---

* Two important but unsubstantiated assumptions made by Liu and Yeh are
that there was a constant relationship between agricultural output and agricultural
population for the years 1933–57 (this assumption is used to obtain population data
from production data for the period 1952–57); and that the employment rate
among male nonagricultural workers was the same in rural and in urban areas.
No evidence is offered for either of these crucial assumptions, and both seem improbable to me.

and other matters. Unfortunately, however, we cannot have much confidence in their accuracy. The figure for the increment to the labor force is a net figure that appears to assume that members of the existing force retire in accordance with the official regulations. But there is much evidence that this was not the case; indeed, until the new retirement regulations were produced in 1958, the retirement regulations applied by law only to enterprises with more than one hundred employees, and they even contained built-in material incentives for workers and staff to resist retirement.[8] Sung P'ing's data on migration hardly inspire more confidence than the data on the natural growth of the labor force. We know that much migration was illicit, and that it was periodically reversed. But we have no means of estimating how these considerations affect the data. Clearly Sung P'ing's data are crude estimates; they are better than nothing, but they are of very limited analytical value. Perhaps the greatest reason for dissatisfaction with the national data is that they are national, and that they are therefore aggregates of significant regional variations. In the context of extreme variation in resource endowment, of differential development in the prewar period, and of the discriminatory development policies of the First Five-Year Plan, significant differences in urban China's demographic, employment, and economic development are bound to have occurred. It is therefore possible that, in the aggregate, the national data conceal almost as much as they reveal.

In view of the apparent difficulties in producing national data and of the limited analytical usefulness of such data even if they are produced, it seems worthwhile to try to reconstruct a statistical picture of some aspects of urban labor force changes using data from individual cities. This approach eliminates many of the difficulties encountered in estimating and handling highly aggregated data. Employment data from individual urban areas may be used in direct conjunction with demographic and production data. With the addition of systematic qualitative information of the kind available for many cities, it is possible to build up a coherent, if sometimes sketchy, picture of individual urban economies. The population, migration, and employment data available for some cities are more detailed and probably more accurate than national data on these subjects; they are certainly superior to data that include or are derived from information that includes figures from rural areas. Thus, although specific urban studies may be less ambitious than attempts to survey and analyze data for all urban areas, they have the advantage that they may often furnish answers to more complicated and interesting economic questions than more general surveys.

A further reason for considering the study of individual surveys worthwhile is the extreme inadequacy of statistical data for all urban areas in China in the prewar period. Indeed, the data are so inadequate that it seems impossible that a satisfactory comparison between the prewar and postwar periods can ever be produced. Yet if our understanding of the problems and our appreciation of the significance of the economic performance of the later period are ever to be adequate, we must be able to compare the two periods. If this is impossible at the national level, we can try to achieve something at the local level by studying cities where the materials for the earlier period exist, even though their interpretation is often difficult. I had hoped that it might have been possible to construct a detailed picture for a number of cities, but this proved too difficult, and it seemed best to concentrate on one city, Shanghai.

There are several reasons for selecting Shanghai. First, there is an exceptional availability of newspapers and of other sources of data; for example, four main daily newspapers and a number of important journals are published in the city, and these tend to contain articles of special relevance to Shanghai's development. A second reason for looking at Shanghai was the probability that the data would have an accuracy above average even for urban areas. The Shanghai city administration had had considerable experience in statistical work; in the period before the war against Japan, the Bureau of Social Affairs of the Shanghai city government undertook a number of pioneering surveys of the city's industrial structure and of the effect that industrialization was having on population, employment, and living standards. This experience, together with the higher than average degree of literacy and the general sophistication of the city, gives grounds for confidence in any data produced by the municipal government. Third, materials are available that give information about the prewar period, thus making a comparison of the pre- and post-1949 periods possible. The results for Shanghai are, of course, interesting in their own right. In the First Five-Year Plan the city accounted for approximately 20 per cent of all of China's industrial output and was a significant producer in both heavy and light industries.[9] In terms of population, in 1957 Shanghai was the largest city in China and still accounted for 7 per cent of total urban population.

Apart from this, although one must bear in mind that no city can be considered typical, Shanghai's experience of economic change in the 1950's was not abnormal, nor was it even an extreme example of any of the types of urban development that can be identified in these years.

The city was not one of those designated for rapid expansion, as were some of the older Manchurian cities and the new cities in the northwest. But neither was it like cities such as Chungking, where special factors led to completely untypical forms of change. If this attempt to produce a statistical picture of some aspects of the Shanghai labor force is judged not wholly credible, perhaps it may be considered to have advanced our knowledge by identifying yet another limit to the study of the Chinese economy.

In Tables 1 to 9 below we present data on total employment and its structure in Shanghai in 1957, together with supplementary data derived from the basic Table 1 and introduced for comparative purposes.

TABLE 1. THE STRUCTURE OF NONAGRICULTURAL EMPLOYMENT
IN SHANGHAI, 1957

| Category | Number employed (in 1,000's) |
|---|---|
| *Industry* | |
| modern factories | 770 |
| workshops | 129 |
| Total | 899 |
| *Handicrafts* | |
| peripatetic and household | 38 |
| workshops employing fewer than ten persons | 71 |
| individual handicraftsmen and others | 149 |
| Total | 258 |
| *Other small-scale production* | 30 |
| *Construction* | 30 |
| *Transport and communication* | |
| old (pre-1956) public system | 57 |
| pedicabs | 40 |
| carts | 80 |
| Total | 177 |
| *Stevedores* | 33 |
| *Commerce* | |
| old private sector stores | 221 |
| peddlers | 240 |
| old public sector commerce system | 72 |
| Total | 533 |
| *Banking* | 25 |
| *Food and services* | 50 |
| *Education* | 72 |
| *Health* | 30 |
| *Government, mass organizations, and other (residual)* | 281 |
| Total | 2,418 |

The quality of the data is inevitably uneven, but doubtful figures can usually be identified fairly easily; for the more firmly based data numerous cross-checks are possible. The general picture suggested by the estimates is almost certainly authentic, and in conjunction with other data a number of conclusions can be drawn from it.

The number in employment at the end of 1956 was reported as 2,390,000.[10] To obtain a figure for 1957 we add 110,000 for additional employment in 1957, and deduct 82,000 for jobs estimated to have been "lost" in that year. The "lost" category is made up of: (1) an estimated halving of the basic construction work force, which in 1957 was only 30,000; (2) 6,000 jobs that disappeared when cadres were sent to the countryside; (3) 46,000 jobs estimated to have been lost on the assumption that one third of the peasants who returned to the countryside had some sort of employment before being returned. This figure for 1957 represents an increase of about 1 per cent over the figure for 1956, a figure almost exactly identical to Emerson's estimate of the increase in all nonagricultural employment in the same period. We have assumed that agricultural employment in the rural suburbs of Shanghai is not included in the data presented here. The total agricultural population in 1957 was reported as 400,000.[11]

The total number of workers and staff in workshops and factories at the end of 1957 was given as 970,000, of which 200,000 were in workshops. We also know that in 1954 there were 71,000 workers in handicraft workshops in the private sector employing fewer than ten persons. This number has been deducted from total factory and workshop employment. The use of the 1954 survey as an indication of employment at the end of 1957 is open to question, since it is known that employment in this sector suffered some decline in the mid-1950's. Against this, however, we would argue that the upsurge of 1956 and the continuing high level of small-scale production, both licit and illicit, in 1957 probably implies a recovery of employment in this sector at least to the 1954 levels; it is certainly difficult to make sense of the total numbers reported in employment unless handicraft production was employing people on the scale indicated for 1954. The more difficult problem is that of trying to sort out the changing organizational forms of small-scale production.[12]

The figure for handicrafts in Table 1 is based on materials from the 1954 national survey of the individual handicraft industry.[13] This survey was wider in scope than its title indicates, as the general breakdown in the table shows. The third subdivision under handicrafts includes 20,000 handicraftsmen already in cooperatives. The evolution of the forms of small-scale and handicraft production was complex, and is difficult, if not impossible, to discuss with confidence. In general, it appears that in the socialization of late 1955 and 1956, individual crafts-men were put into conventional cooperatives, and the small workshops became public-private enterprises. However, these distinctions were not always clear, and thousands of workers moved in and out of handi-craft organizations according to the dictates of the economic situation and of the prevailing political atmosphere.

In addition to individual and cooperative handicraft production, we know that there were substantial numbers engaged not only in small-scale production but also in services as part of unemployment relief work and in illicit production. These forms of employment increased in 1957, but it is impossible to judge the extent to which this was at the expense of employment in official cooperatives, if at all. It may have been sim-ply a substitute for household handicraft employment that could not be incorporated into the ordinary cooperatives. The maximum figure given for employment in relief groups and in illicit organizations in 1957–58 was 40,000. We have reduced this to 30,000 to allow for some double counting. We have assumed that the authorities made allowance for these types of employment in their estimates of total employment, since the purpose of quoting a figure for total employment in the article referred to was to show employment change in its most favorable light.[14]

The numbers employed in construction in Shanghai probably fluc-tuated very sharply as they did at the national level. Throughout the 1950's the average figure seems to have been constant. We have a figure of 33,000 for 1950; in 1954 construction employment declined greatly and at least 10,000 construction workers were transferred to other em-ployment; in 1956 employment apparently increased sharply, but in 1957 the number reported in construction work was once more 30,000.[15]

The national survey of workers and staff in 1955 reports a figure of 57,000 for employment in public sector transportation. The figure for pedicab men is for 1958, whereas the figure for employment in other nonmechanized transportation is for 1957. The last two figures must be treated with caution, but there is no reason to think that they are over-estimates. On the contrary, it is reported that many of the peasants returned to the countryside in 1957 had illicitly engaged in pedicab and transport work, so the figures may be understatements. During the 1950's the process of converting rickshaws to pedicabs was completed. It is interesting to compare the figure of 40,000 pedicab men with the figure of 50,000 rickshaw men in Shanghai in the late 1920's.[16]

The only data on the numbers normally engaged in stevedore work are those given for 1950. One possible guide to employment change would be any indication of changes in the volume of foreign trade that passed through Shanghai. We find two references that claim substantial increases in trade, but both of them use 1950 as their base year. In this year stringent foreign trade controls reduced activity and caused a third of the regular stevedore work force to be unemployed. Trade rose sharply in 1956 and 1957, but the evidence suggests that the number of experienced stevedores was not easily increased, especially in 1956. We assume, therefore, that there was no net increase in the number of stevedores over the whole period.[17]

The figures for commerce are taken from several apparently reliable articles published in late 1956 and early 1957.[18] The figure for food and services is given in *Hsin wen pao* for August 15, 1957. The figure of 72,000 for employment in education and the figure for health are derived from an article of March 8, 1957.[19]

The figure of 25,000 for banking is a 1950 total. Conflicting forces influenced the net change in employment in this category up to 1957. Although the take-over of private banking at the end of 1950, accompanied by pressure for rationalization, reduced employment, in late 1952 it was government policy to make enterprises retain redundant personnel until alternative employment could be found. Later in the 1950's employment in banking on a national scale increased markedly.[20] We have assumed, therefore, that by 1957 the numbers employed in the banking system were as great as in 1950.

The final estimate in Table 1 is a residual figure that should be treated with the reserve appropriate to all residuals. The only information on employment in government and mass organizations we have is indirect, from a report that estimates the total number of cadres and "nonproductives" (staff) in Shanghai as 470,000. (This is the number of persons who were liable to be sent to the countryside or demoted to productive work in the *hsia fang* campaign of 1957.) If we deduct our estimate of 281,000 from this figure we are left with 189,000 cadres and nonproductives, which represents about 9 per cent of the work force, a reasonable figure, for we know that this was almost exactly the proportion of cadres and staff in industry alone.

The following pages present eight additional tables; Tables 2 to 4 are based on Table 1.

TABLE 2. THE STRUCTURE OF EMPLOYMENT IN SHANGHAI, 1957

| Category | Number employed (in 1,000's) | Percentage of total employed |
|---|---|---|
| Agriculture | 160[a] | 6.2% |
| Factory production | 770 | 29.9 |
| Traditional production | 417 | 16.2 |
| Transport and communications (including stevedores) | 210 | 8.1 |
| Construction | 30 | 1.2 |
| Commerce | 533 | 20.7 |
| Food and services | 50 | 1.9 |
| Government, education, health, banking, and other | 408 | 15.8 |
| Total | 2,578 | 100.0% |

[a] Assuming that 40% of the rural population was employed in agricultural work.

TABLE 3. THE STRUCTURE OF NONAGRICULTURAL EMPLOYMENT IN SHANGHAI, 1957

| Category | Number employed (in 1,000's) | Percentage of total employed |
|---|---|---|
| Total production | 1,187 | 49.1% |
| (Factories or workshops employing ten or more persons) | (899) | (37.2) |
| Construction | 30 | 1.2 |
| Transport (including stevedores) | 210 | 8.7 |
| Commerce, food, and services | 583 | 24.1 |
| Government, education, health, banking, and other | 408 | 16.9 |
| Total | 2,418 | 100.0% |

TABLE 4a. NONAGRICULTURAL EMPLOYMENT IN SHANGHAI BY
TRADITIONAL SECTOR, 1957

| Category | Number employed (in 1,000's) | Percentage |
|---|---|---|
| Workshop industry | 129 | 12.3% |
| Handicrafts (including other small-scale production) | 288 | 27.5 |
| Transport | 120 | 11.4 |
| Commerce[a] | 461 | 44.0 |
| Food and services | 50 | 4.8 |
| Total | 1,048 | 100.0% |
| Total as percentage of total employment, both modern and traditional | | 43.4% |

[a] This figure undoubtedly includes a few persons employed in stores that should be classified as modern. But since the average number of workers per enterprise in this segment of commerce (i.e., of persons working in stores) was fewer than four, it seems reasonable to include all the old private-sector commerce in the traditional sector.

TABLE 4b. NONAGRICULTURAL EMPLOYMENT IN SHANGHAI BY
MODERN SECTOR, 1957

| Category | Number employed (in 1,000's) | Percentage |
|---|---|---|
| Industry | 770 | 56.2% |
| Construction | 30 | 2.2 |
| Transport and communications (including stevedores) | 90 | 6.5 |
| Commerce | 72 | 5.3 |
| Education, health, banking, government, and other | 408 | 29.8 |
| Total | 1,370 | 100.0% |
| Total as percentage of total employment, both modern and traditional | | 56.6% |

TABLE 5. PERCENTAGE OF EMPLOYED IN URBAN INDIA, 1961,
CONTRASTED WITH DATA FOR SHANGHAI, 1957, BY
INDUSTRIAL CATEGORY

| Category | India | Shanghai |
|---|---|---|
| Agricultural pursuits | 11.9% | 6.2% |
| Mining and quarrying | .8 | — |
| Manufacturing (including household) | 28.7 | 46.0 |
| Construction | 3.8 | 1.2 |
| Trade and commerce | 16.5 | 20.7 |
| Transportation, storage, and communication | 8.1 | 8.1[a] |
| Other services | 30.2 | 17.8[b] |
| Total | 100.0% | 100.0% |

SOURCES: India data from *Fact Book on Manpower* (New Delhi: Institute of Applied Manpower Research, 1963). Shanghai data from Table 1, with the addition of 160,000 in agricultural employment based on the assumption that 40% of the city's rural population was employed
in agricultural pursuits.
[a] Includes stevedores.
[b] Includes food and services, education, health, banking, government, and other.

TABLE 6. THE STRUCTURE OF EMPLOYMENT IN SHANGHAI, 1926–27

| Category | Number employed | Percentage of total employed |
|---|---|---|
| Food manufacturing | 22,596 | 1.8% |
| Handicrafts | 226,900 | 18.1 |
| Domestic service | 66,617 | 5.3 |
| Tobacco factories | 36,020 | 2.9 |
| Local transport | 68,500 | 5.5 |
| Municipal government | 149,480 | 11.9 |
| Railways | 6,740 | .5 |
| Textile industry | 246,390 | 19.7 |
| Printing | 36,445 | 2.9 |
| Chemical industry | 33,760 | 2.7 |
| Metallurgical industry | 39,500 | 3.2 |
| Artistic and craft work | 29,300 | 2.3 |
| Shop employees | 272,440 | 21.7 |
| Sailors | 6,800 | .5 |
| Construction | 10,830 | .9 |
| Other | 1,008 | .1 |
| Total | 1,253,326 | 100.0% |

SOURCE: *Dai yonji zenkoku rōdō daihyō taikai ni teishutsu seru Shanhai sōkōkai no hōko-
kusho* (Report from the General Labor Union of Shanghai on its activities, May 1926 to May
1927), translated into Japanese by Taicho Mikami *et al.* (Osaka: Kansai Daigaku Tōzai Gaku-
jutsu Keykyūjo shiryō shūkan, 1962), p. 38.

TABLE 7. NONAGRICULTURAL EMPLOYMENT IN SHANGHAI BY
MAIN CATEGORIES, 1926–27 AND 1957
(*per cent*)

| Category | 1926–27 | 1957 |
|---|---|---|
| Total production | 51.3% | 49.1% |
| (Factory production) | (24.1) | (31.9) |
| Construction | .9 | 1.2 |
| Transport | 6.0 | 8.7 |
| Commerce, food, and services | 27.0 | 24.1 |
| Government, and residual | 14.8 | 16.9 |
| Total | 100.0% | 100.0% |
| Absolute totals | 1,253,326 | 2,418,000 |

SOURCES: For 1926–27: as Table 6; the estimate of factory employment is based on the survey of the Shanghai factory labor force in 1929; the figure for 1929 has been adjusted downward using data on capital equipment installation in the cotton industry as an indicator of industrial activity and employment change in Shanghai industry, 1926–27 and 1931; see D. K. Lieu, *The Growth and Industrialisation of Shanghai* (Shanghai: China Institute of Pacific Relations, 1936), pp. 344–45, 422.
For 1957: see notes 11–20; the figure for employment in factories excludes employment in workshops in order to make it as comparable as possible with the estimate for 1926–27.

TABLE 8a. THE STRUCTURE OF EMPLOYMENT IN THE
SHACK AREAS OF SHANGHAI, 1949

| Category | Percentage of total employed |
|---|---|
| Industry | 37.1% |
| Communications and transport | 24.4 |
| Other workers and staff | 14.7 |
| Small traders | 20.3 |
| Other | 3.5 |
| Total | 100.0% |

TABLE 8b. THE STRUCTURE OF EMPLOYMENT IN THE
SHACK AREAS OF SHANGHAI, 1960

| Category | Percentage of total employed |
|---|---|
| Industry | 65.2% |
| Communications and transport | 16.0 |
| Commerce and services (workers and staff) | 14.3 |
| Handicrafts | 1.7 |
| Other (workers and staff) | 2.8 |
| Total | 100.0% |

SOURCE: *Shang-hai p'eng hu ch'ü ti pien chien* (The transformation of the Shanghai shack areas) (Shanghai: Jen min ch'u pan she, 1965), p. 66.

TABLE 9. PERCENTAGE OF TOTAL POPULATION EMPLOYED, UNEMPLOYED, OR
NONPARTICIPATING IN THE LABOR FORCE IN THE SHANGHAI
SHACK AREAS, 1949 AND 1960

| Group | 1949 | 1960 |
|---|---|---|
| Employed | 53.7% | 75.4% |
| Unemployed | 17.5 | 0.0 |
| Nonparticipating | 28.8 | 24.6 |
| Total | 100.0% | 100.0% |

SOURCE: *Shang-hai p'eng hu ch'ü ti pien chien* (The transformation of the Shanghai shack
areas) (Shanghai: Jen min ch'u pan she, 1965), p. 65.

What conclusions can be drawn from the figures given in these
tables? First, we estimate that the number employed in 1957 was equal
to 35.8 per cent of the total population—a decline from the figure of
45.2 per cent for 1926–27.[21] This represents a substantial decline in employment participation, and it implies a long-term increase in the total
cost of producing a given level of goods and services in the city. This
decline in employment participation can be explained by a number
of factors in evidence in the 1950's. It is probable that demographic
changes resulted in an increase in the proportion of persons not of
working age, i.e., those who were physically incapable of work. Official
data on age structure are not available, but we have sufficient fragmentary evidence to be able to estimate that the percentage of persons
fifteen years old or younger in the total population of Shanghai was
29 per cent in 1930; 28.7 per cent in 1949; and 34.6 per cent by 1957.
The last figure is probably a minimum, since evidence of age structure
in the Shanghai suburbs shows that in these areas the persons in this age
group accounted for between 40 and 50 per cent of the total population.[22]

In addition to demographic factors, policy decisions on the employment of women and children were also important determinants of participation in the 1950's. According to a 1931 survey, women accounted
for 51.2 per cent of the factory labor force and children over fourteen
for 10 per cent. In the textile industry women and children were particularly dominant, accounting altogether for 78.7 per cent of all workers.[23] In the very early days of the Communist regime the policy on
child labor was that immediate abolition was impractical, although the
long-term aim was to eliminate it.[24] By 1955 in the public sector at least,
employment of persons under eighteen years of age accounted for only
1 per cent of those employed.[25] It seems probable that this sharp decline
in child participation was caused by unemployment pressures, which

converted the humane, long-term policy into a necessary, short-term expedient. The above data and argument are national, but it seems probable that similar phenomena are at least a partial explanation of the decline in employment participation in Shanghai.

Female participation was the subject of a series of policy cycles, both at the national and at the local level in Shanghai. These cycles coincided with fluctuations in output and employment. Since the underlying strategy was for an increase in female participation in the labor force, the government took active steps to encourage such participation, especially in periods of economic upswing. However, in periods when the level of economic activity was not high, policy toward female participation was reversed. The precise effect of this policy cycle in the period 1949–57 is unclear, but it appears that although female employment between 1931 and 1957 increased absolutely, the female share of the factory labor force declined from 51 per cent to 45 per cent.[26]

A third factor relevant to participation is the growth of the higher education system (upper-middle schools and universities), which must have had the effect of removing ever-increasing numbers of young persons from the labor market. These numbers, of course, are only important if the intake into the educational system of persons of working age is growing, for if the system is static, the outflow of graduates equals the inflow of new entrants. In the period to 1957, the national data indicate that the number of participants in the educational system was increasing; this must have had an effect on labor force participation.[27]

The final explanation of the decline in employment participation is increased unemployment. The data available for the pre-1949 period do not enable us to make satisfactory comparisons with the late 1950's. However, we can make an estimate of male unemployment for 1957, based on the following steps. The total population of Shanghai was 7,200,000,[28] of which "regular" (*ch'ang chu*) nonagricultural population totaled 6,000,000.[29] Of the population aged sixteen years or more (3,930,000),[30] the number of males was 2,160,000.[31] Thus, the total male labor force (i.e., 2,160,000 plus 50 per cent of temporary and illicit migrants) totaled 2,560,000. In 1957 there were 500,000 females[32] in a nonagricultural employment total of 2,418,000. The total number of males employed in 1957 was 1,918,000. Thus, male unemployment in 1957 (net of educational retention) totaled 560,000.[33] The final total of 560,000 is clearly substantial, being in excess of 25 per cent of the total male labor force. The only legitimate reduction that we have been unable to estimate is the allowance for workers of retiring age who had actually retired. But, in view of available age structure data, it appears improbable that retirements could account for more than 120,000 men. Furthermore, taking into account the reported difficulties of persuading workers to retire as well as the flexibility of upper-age participation limits in traditional forms of employment, the actual figure could be much lower. Moreover, it must be noted that this estimate of unemployment has, by definition, excluded consideration of females of working age who were not in the labor force in 1957 but who were willing and able to enter it. Qualitative evidence from the late 1950's indicates that there were many women in this position.[34]

Let us now look at the structure of employment as shown in Tables 1 to 9. In Table 1 we have absolute figures for nonagricultural employment divided into twelve main categories. Within some of these groups further subdivision has been attempted in subsequent tables. In Table 2 we introduce a figure for employment in agriculture (in the rural suburbs of the city) that enables us to group employment into eight main divisions. In Tables 4a and 4b we break down employment into traditional and modern sectors. In general the distinction here is in terms of scale of organization; the traditional sector is approximately coterminous with the private, small-scale sector as it existed before the socialization of 1956. In Tables 5 to 9 we attempt to find data that can be used for comparative purposes. Thus in Table 5 we have used data for all urban areas in India in 1961 for comparison with Shanghai; and in Tables 6 and 7 we have included data on employment structure in Shanghai in 1926–27, from which, with caution, a few comparisons may be drawn. Tables 8 and 9 attempt to describe the changing employment experience of inhabitants of the slum areas of Shanghai. Apart from the general lack of credibility of these last data, the peculiar nature of the sample of the population that they represent prevents us from making much use of them. It is nonetheless interesting to see the Shanghai employment picture as the Chinese see it, or would wish us to see it.

To draw some conclusions from these tables, we shall begin by considering the importance of production and industrial employment. From Table 3 it can be seen that production accounts for nearly half of total employment, and industrial production for 37.2 per cent, including the modern factory category, which in itself accounts for 31.9 per cent of the total. Although a lack of data makes systematic comparison of the relative importance of industrial employment between Shanghai and other cities impossible, we can compare industrial employment as a percentage of national urban population with the Shanghai data expressed as a percentage of Shanghai population. The Shanghai percentage is 12.5 per cent, which compares with a national average of about 8 per cent.[35] Thus, unless the relationship between total and employed population in Shanghai is very abnormal, the conclusion must be that industrial employment in the city is comparatively high. The comparison of the share of employment in all forms of production in Shanghai and in all Indian urban areas also suggests how exceptionally large this area of activity was in Shanghai, for whereas in the Indian cities production accounted for only 28.7 per cent of employment, for Shanghai the comparable figure was 46 per cent. The comparison of the 1957 Shanghai data with those for 1926–27 indicates that the relative importance of employment in production has remained approximately the same. However, the aggregate data conceal the growth of the factory category. Over the whole period 1929–57, the employment of workers and staff in factories can be estimated to have grown at 3.3 per cent per annum. Between 1929 and 1949 the figure was 2.4 per cent, and between 1949 and 1957 it was 5.8 per cent.[36] The effect of the growth was to raise the share of factory employment from 24.1 per cent to 31.9 per cent, as Table 7 shows. It is interesting to note that within the factory category the share of the textile industry in total employment declined from approximately 60 per cent in 1931 to approximately 34 per cent in 1957.[37]

We have no satisfactory data to measure changes in employment in traditional production in Shanghai. The traditional sector accounts for only a third of total employment in production in 1957, and it seems probable that the absolute level of employment in this sector remained about the same in the 1950's, although it was subject to intense fluctuations. The importance of commerce was still considerable in 1957. It accounted for 20 per cent of total employment and 44 per cent of traditional sector employment. (See Tables 2 and 4.) Taken together with food and services, the importance of commerce between 1926–27 and 1957 fell slightly, as indicated in Table 7. But the condition of the basic data is such that this decline cannot be regarded as certain; it seems probable that although there were fluctuations in these areas in the 1950's, they did not grow in relative importance between 1949 and 1957.

We have estimated that transportation accounted for 8.7 per cent of nonagricultural employment in 1957. Although it is interesting to note that the relative importance of employment in transportation in Shanghai appears to be exactly the same as in Indian cities in 1961, there can be little doubt that the level of employment declined relatively, and possibly absolutely, between 1949 and 1957, for in the mid-1950's there were numerous reports of unemployment among workers in the traditional sector. This decline was caused partly by the mechanization of the transportation system and partly by the decline in the foreign and tourist population in the 1950's.

Finally, apart from industry, there appears to have been an increase in employment in education, health, banking, and government. This development is suggested by Table 7, in which the share of these categories is shown to have increased from 14.8 per cent to 16.9 per cent between 1926–27 and 1957. Moreover, a comparison of official data for 1949 with estimates for 1957 suggests that there was a decline in government employment between the late 1920's and 1949, followed by rapid growth in the 1950's amounting to 14 per cent per annum compound. Hence total 1957 employment in government was about three times as great as it had been in 1949.[38]

In order to estimate the number of persons who entered the labor force between 1949 and 1957, it is necessary to make some assumptions about the age structure of the population at the beginning of the period. In the absence of more satisfactory data, we have used detailed age structure data for the population of Greater Shanghai in 1930 and adjusted this in the light of data for 1947.[39] Applying this prewar age structure to the 1949 population, we estimate the natural addition to the labor force to have been 645,000 between 1949 and 1957.

The migrant addition to the labor force requires that a number of assumptions be made about the working status of persons involved in the massive flows of population in and out of Shanghai during the 1950's. Reported immigration amounts to 1,820,000 persons, of whom 1,000,000 migrated before April 1955 and the rest in 1956 and 1957. It is assumed that 50 per cent of these were seeking jobs.[40] The gross addition to the labor force can therefore be put at 910,000. The question of emigrants is not so simple. Emigration for the whole period is reported at 1,080,000, a total that can be broken down as shown in Tables 10 and 11. The 1,080,000 total of emigrants[41] includes persons sent to open new land, as well as 10,000 persons who were sent to labor reform in 1950, a figure that may well correspond exactly to the "unspecified balance" in Table 10. The figures in Table 10 may be compared with

TABLE 10. EMIGRANTS FROM SHANGHAI, 1949–57

| Category | Number (in 1,000's) |
|---|---|
| Persons assigned to employment in other cities | 260 |
| Persons returned to work in rural areas | 780 |
| Persons sent to open new land | 30 |
| Unspecified balance | 10 |
| Total | 1,080 |

SOURCE: Article by Hsü Chien-kuo, Wen hui pao (Cultural exchange news), Jan. 7, 1958.

those obtained by summing the annual data present in Table 11, namely 258,000 for persons assigned to other cities, 750,000 for persons sent to rural areas, and 50,000 for others, giving a total of 1,058,000. The slight discrepancy between the total given in Table 10 and that derived from Table 11 is probably accounted for by the return of refugees in 1950, but figures on that movement were not published at the time.

Using our data for immigration cited above, we arrive at a figure for net immigration into Shanghai, in the period up to 1957, of 740,000.

With the help of Tables 10 and 11 we can estimate the effect of the emigration on the labor force. It is assumed that persons assigned to work in other cities, sent to open new land, or sent to labor reform were members of the labor force. Since those who returned to rural areas were nearly all peasants being returned to their homes, it is assumed that 50 per cent of them were members of the labor force. Thus the total loss to the labor force from emigration amounted to 690,000, leaving a net gain to the labor force of 220,000.

TABLE 11. EMIGRATION FROM SHANGHAI, 1949–57
(*in 1,000's*)

| Category | 1949 | 1950 | 1953 | 1954 | 1955 | 1956 | 1957 | Aggregate |
|---|---|---|---|---|---|---|---|---|
| (1) All persons assigned to work in other cities | | 16 | 24 | 30 | 59 | 123 | 6 | 258 |
| (2) Skilled workers, staff, and cadres sent to other cities | | (16) | (24) | | (23) | | (6) | (69) |
| (3) Persons returned to rural areas | 50 | | | | 560 | | 140 | 750 |
| (4) Persons sent to open new land | | | | | | | | 40 |
| (5) Persons sent to labor reform | 10 | | | | | | | |

The figure for 1949 is from "Almost 50,000 refugees have been organized and returned (to their homes in the countryside)," *Chieh fang jih pao* (Liberation daily) [CFJP], Aug. 21, 1949.

Figures in row (1) for 1950 and 1953 are in or derived from "Shanghai industry helps national construction," *Wen hui pao* (Cultural exchange news) [WHP], Aug. 27, 1954, and "A large batch of skilled workers in the city give in their names to participate in national key-point construction," WHP, June 22, 1954. The figure in row (5) for 1950 comes from "More than 10,000 men just off to open waste land," CFJP, Mar. 7, 1950.

The 1954 information is from "220,000 workers sent from Shanghai to take part in construction in various places," *New China News Agency* [NCNA], Sept. 16, 1957, and Sung Li-wen, "Report on the implementation of the Shanghai National Economic Plan in 1956 and on the Plan for 1957," *Hsin wen pao* (Daily news) [HWP], Aug. 28, 1957.

For 1955, sources for the three figures are as follows: Row (1), Sung Li-wen; Row (2), to Mar. 1956, "[The Shanghai Municipality Communist Party] decides that future Shanghai industry will be fully and rationally developed," CFJP, July 27, 1956; Row (3), Chang Jui, "Some views on Shanghai's population and area," WHP, Feb. 11, 1957.

The figure for 1956 is from "220,000 workers sent from Shanghai to take part in construction in various places," NCNA, Sept. 16, 1957.

The first two figures for 1957 are all cadres. See "A new high tide of cadres being sent down to the countryside from Shanghai," WHP, Jan. 3, 1958. The third figure comes from "Almost 140,000 returned to rural production," HWP, Dec. 20, 1957.

In the "Aggregate" column, row (4) is from "The Kansu consolation organization holds a consolation conference," CFJP, Feb. 13, 1957. This article refers to the activities of an organization responsible for keeping in touch with the Shanghaiese working in Kansu Province.

TABLE 12. SOURCES OF LABOR SUPPLY IN SHANGHAI, 1949–57

| Sources | Total (in 1,000's) | Percentage of total |
|---|---|---|
| Natural addition to the labor force | 645 | 48% |
| Migrant addition to the labor force | 220 | 16 |
| Unemployed | 495 | 36 |
| Total | 1,360 | 100% |

We now have estimates for the addition to the labor force of natural growth and migration. To this we must add the total number estimated to have been unemployed in 1949 and the number who lost employment between that year and the end of 1957. The combined total for these classes of person is 671,000;[42] from this, however, we must deduct something for the number of these persons who would have reached the age of sixty by 1957, and who may therefore be considered as having retired. Using prewar age structure again, this figure is put at 176,000.

From the data given in Tables 1 to 12 we can estimate the relative shares of the three sources of labor supply between 1949 and 1957. These are shown in Table 12.

We have made no allowance in Table 12 for persons retained in the educational system because educational retention is significant only if in the long run the educational system is expanding more rapidly than the rate of growth of population. The most important feature of Table 12 is that the share of migrant labor in the total labor supply is smaller than might have been expected, for although Emerson, using Sung P'ing's data, puts the migrant share of labor supply during the First Five-Year Plan period at 45 per cent, our figure for 1949 to 1957 in Shanghai is only 16 per cent. To some extent the difference is accounted for by the fact that immigration was less important between 1949 and 1952 than in the later period. But the data raise two other interesting possibilities. It may be that Sung P'ing's data take insufficient account of the importance of outflows of population in the First Five-Year Plan period, for if one uses the gross inflow figure to estimate population or labor-supply changes, the overall picture is completely different from that suggested in this paper. Alternatively, it may be that the hsia fang campaigns in Shanghai were more effective than in other cities. If so, the results presented in this paper underline the value of geographical disaggregation for obtaining an accurate understanding of the character of Chinese economic development.

# Educated Youth and Urban-Rural Inequalities, 1958–66

JOHN GARDNER

One of the most distinctive features of the early stages of the Cultural Revolution was the wave of youthful violence and vandalism that erupted in China's cities in the summer of 1966. Violence itself, mental rather than physical, was not a new phenomenon, for since 1949 it had been an intrinsic part of the Chinese political process. Generally, however, it had been institutionalized, manifesting itself through a series of well-prepared, highly organized, and disciplined mass campaigns directed against carefully specified social groups.

The violence of the Red Guards, however, differed in some respects from what had gone before. Its most striking characteristic was that it gave every appearance of being spontaneous. The Red Guards themselves had appeared with dramatic suddenness and without well-defined organization and leadership. What direction there was consisted principally of direct communication between senior political figures and the Red Guards themselves. In the early months of their activity especially, they operated with considerable freedom, often selecting their own victims for criticism, interrogation, and even physical attack. Calls issued by members of the Maoist leadership to refrain from excesses were frequently ignored, and even the increasing involvement of the People's Liberation Army in 1967 was unable to stop all outbursts of violence and "anarchism" that persisted into 1968. The violence was also unusual in its wide range of victims chosen. The Red Guards attacked not only senior "capitalist roaders" within the Chinese Communist Party but also many urban dwellers who in some cases were classified as "bourgeois" for such trivial reasons as wearing European clothes and adopting Western hairstyles. Frequently, Red Guards indulged in acts of wanton destruction, taking the view that to "get rid of the old" it was necessary to burn ancient books and smash antiques.

This "righteous anger of the masses" was not, then, inspired solely by judicious "stage-management"; many young people were expressing their dissatisfaction with "the system" and the inequalities of it. The data that have appeared since the Cultural Revolution confirm trends detectable in skeletal outline in the 1960's, trends that by 1966 had resulted in a certain loss of revolutionary momentum as Chinese society developed pockets of privilege and deprivation. These inequalities were both geographic, in the sense that the urban areas were being favored at the expense of the rural areas, and social, in the sense that certain groups were entrenching their positions as a new "upper class" while others were finding their "lower-class" status confirmed. As far as the young were concerned the major determinant in role allocation was education, and in the 1960's the educational system was one of the principal factors responsible for the uneven distribution of rewards.

Between 1958 and 1966 China's leaders were far from united over educational strategy. In these years there were considerable fluctuations in educational policy reflecting not only shifts in the power balance between rival factions offering alternative educational choices but also changes of attitude by individual party leaders. Although a rigid polarization of attitudes was not necessarily present throughout the period, two distinct approaches to educational policy were in conflict.

One of these may be termed the "Maoist" strategy, which was rural-oriented and egalitarian, viewing education as the means by which the "three major differences" between town and country, worker and peasant, and mental and manual labor could be rapidly eliminated. To achieve this end it was necessary to ensure that the educational system paid proper attention to three considerations. First, educational opportunity should be available to as many people as possible, particularly to those living in rural areas. If necessary, "positive discrimination" was to be applied to ensure that the poorest, and thus almost by definition the most politically "advanced," benefited. Instead of treating education as a competitive process by which the most able were selected and trained as an elite, the Maoist approach was intended to cultivate all-around and modest skills in as many people as possible, seemingly taking the view that two mechanics were worth more than one engineer.*

---

* One of the main advantages of the Maoist strategy was that it permitted flexibility. Those with all-round skills could be moved relatively easily from post to post to suit the needs of the economy at any given time. On the other hand, higher education can impede such flexibility. As one writer has noted: "One of the dangers in modern economies is that formal schooling can introduce certain dysfunctional rigidities, a fetishism of titles, certificates and diplomas. Skilled artisans are worth

Second, education was to be closely related to the needs of production. Courses were to be short, and "superfluous" material such as undue emphasis on pure theory was to be omitted. As far as possible theory and practice were to be united by the establishment of a system based on half-work half-study principles.

Third—and of utmost importance—education was to foster "political consciousness," which in its broadest sense meant the selfless desire by citizens to "serve the masses" and the state and forgo egoistic ambitions. In part such values were to be inculcated by intensive ideological instruction, based primarily on Mao's writings; accordingly, educational institutions were required to make adequate provision for students to participate in political activities. Beyond this, however, manual labor, apart from its productive importance, was seen as the key to instilling these values and bringing about successful social integration and rapid social change. The notion that the educated should engage in manual labor—an unusual idea in any society—is particularly novel in the Chinese context, where the educated had traditionally treated physical work with contempt; but from Mao's point of view it was a prerequisite for the development of a new leadership style. By working in the fields and factories, the educated would develop an appreciation of the problems facing the masses and would be encouraged to use their skills to solve them. Instead of acting as remote "experts" directing the peasants to implement innovations, and thus likely to cause resentment if not noncompliance, they would be able to "lead from within" by example and persuasion. While teaching they would themselves be taught, so the theory ran, and would not become "divorced from the masses." Hence the educated would act as agents of rapid social and economic change. Because of their education, and not in spite of it, they would enthusiastically make their careers in the villages, and use their talents to cause a cultural and economic transformation; thus the gap between town and country would narrow and ultimately be closed.

Mao's romantic and revolutionary vision was not shared by all his colleagues, let alone by all those who were involved in educational work. Many subscribed to an urban-oriented, elitist view that for convenience may be called the "Liuist" approach, for its major proponent allegedly was Liu Shao-ch'i. It is clear that Liu was receptive to this approach,

---

more to a society than briefless lawyers. The concern for standards becomes a preoccupation with token certificates. The curricula can become conservative, and insistence upon these rigidities aggravates the inelasticities in the supply of labor." Graham E. Johnson, "Education, Manpower and Development: Developmental Marxism and Chinese Practice," unpub. paper, Cornell University, 1968, p. 14.

but its actual implementation was the particular concern of two other members of the Central Committee. One of them was Lu Ting-i, director of the Central Committee's Propaganda Department, the party organ responsible for the supervision of educational work; the other was Yang Hsiu-feng, minister of education throughout most of the period under consideration. These men, together with many senior cadres and party and nonparty intellectuals, preferred a model more in line with Soviet experience, which had been the dominant influence on Chinese education in the 1950's. Their approach tended to be based on economic arguments rather than on the social-ethical ones used by Mao, taking the view that scarce resources should best be spent on creating an educated elite of "professionals," a shock-force of such specialists as scientists, engineers, and administrators, who could lead China on the road to modernity. Proponents of this view argued for educating the most talented to a high level, and consequently were happy to preserve and develop the full-time schools and universities. Access to education, particularly higher education, was to be determined primarily by academic ability, a policy that favored urban children from middle-class families. Political considerations were by no means ignored, but were measured by a youth's willingness to obey the party and its affiliated organizations rather than by his revolutionary enthusiasm or the poverty of his family. The importance of production was similarly seen largely in economic rather than political terms. Labor activities, although prescribed for students, were generally limited to a few weeks a year and were not to interfere with study.* Ideological instruction was not stressed to the degree it was in the Maoist strategy, and its content was based less on Mao's works than on more general Marxist-Leninist principles of obedience and discipline. According to this view political activism was no substitute for professional knowledge.

The support that the Liuist approach enjoyed in educational circles in the 1960's impeded and thwarted Mao's attempts to launch an educational revolution. Furthermore, whatever economic success the urban-oriented and elitist model had, it failed socially in Mao's eyes, for it preserved existing inequalities and created new ones. My purpose here is to examine this conflict in Chinese education between 1958 and 1966 in order to understand the frustrations that drove many youths to respond so violently to Mao's slogan "rebellion is justified." It has been argued that the Red Guard movement was in a way analagous to the

---

* In this context it is worth noting that the average Chinese university student probably gave no more time to labor activities than many Western students give to their vacation jobs.

roughly contemporaneous "student revolts" in the United States and Western Europe. In both cases an educated and indeed privileged stratum of young people rejected the society of their elders in general and of "politicians" in particular, which they saw as "exploiting," "brutal," "unequal," "hypocritical," and "egoistic"; in its place they desired a society based on a more selfless, collectivist, and vaguely "proletarian" ethic of their own. There is some validity to this comparison, for idealism is a force that should never be discounted in the activities of the young, and particularly of students. Yet to accept this as a total explanation of the Red Guard movement would be to read only the left-hand pages of the history book, for many of those in revolt, including students, were among the deprived. A number of Red Guards were youths who were unable to gain access to the educational system and its rewards and students who found themselves unable to compete successfully. Not all of those mouthing Maoist slogans were inspired by Maoist motives; there was, for example, more than a hint of self-seeking in cries for the abolition of examinations. Thus in addition to its idealism, the Red Guard movement was an expression of envy by which the "have-nots" took their revenge on the "haves."

Briefly, in this essay I am concerned with four themes related to the educational process. I begin by discussing the Maoist strategy of educational development as expressed in and after the Great Leap Forward, particularly as manifested in the advocacy of a half-work half-study system of particular value to the rural areas. I then examine the urban-based and elitist alternative, which successfully prevented the full implementation of the former. The third section analyzes one of the major consequences of this conflict, namely the use of the rural areas as a dumping ground for urban youths who failed to meet the exacting standards demanded by educational institutions in the towns. Finally, I examine briefly the role of the Communist Youth League, the organization that should have played the major part in instilling revolutionary values in the young but that instead became a principal cause of social stratification, biased, as it was, in favor of the cities. I do not attempt to cover all aspects of Chinese education (no consideration is given to spare-time education, for example) or all areas of privilege and deprivation affecting young people (for example, the great inequalities between the contract workers and the regular trade unionists of urban China are not discussed).[1] It is hoped, however, that this discussion will demonstrate the extent to which Chinese youth was divided by 1966 and particularly how this division was part of a wider rural-urban dichotomy, for the Cultural Revolution has been yet another occasion of the countryside being pitted against the cities, with Mao, as the apotheosis of revolutionary, peasant-based values, once again attacking the "decadent" and privileged urban centers.

Because this study relies heavily on Red Guard data, a statement of caution is in order. It must be admitted that Red Guard allegations are sometimes completely incorrect. The authors of Red Guard tabloids are not professional journalists or scholarly purists. Thus, the charges they make are occasionally partly or wholly inaccurate, and the time at which certain events took place may be wrongly recorded, so making it difficult to check against other contemporary accounts of what happened. Furthermore, Red Guard authors themselves were sometimes confused about the correct "line" on a given policy at a given time. Thus an attack on some "bourgeois" deviation of Liu Shao-ch'i may be supported by a quotation from Liu of impeccable Maoist orthodoxy. Moreover, because these are polemical writings designed to portray Mao's opponents in the worst possible light, remarks made by "Liuists" are frequently quoted out of context, a very easy matter given the preference of China's leaders for policy statements to cover all contingencies (a preference that although flexible, results in statements of considerable ambiguity). One example of such malicious distortion involved the charge that Lu Ting-i was guilty of proclaiming that "those who work with their minds govern others, those who work with their hands are governed by others"; in his celebrated 1958 speech, "Education Must Be Combined with Productive Labor," Lu did indeed use these words, but what the Red Guard tabloids do not point out is that Lu was quoting from Mencius and was doing so specifically to attack and refute this view. Another common use of distortion was the practice of generalizing on the basis of a particular deviation or utterance. In its most extreme form this resulted in Liu Shao-ch'i being branded personally as the author of almost every anti-Maoist statement and policy, but the same tendency occurred at all levels.

On the positive side, Red Guard data possess qualities often lacking in official reports. Since Red Guard tabloids were generally produced by students writing about their own institutions, they provide a wealth of first-hand information on the situation at the local level. Moreover, they reveal a great deal about the views of individual party leaders, for information was "fed" to the Red Guards by influential members of Mao's "Cultural Revolution Group." In order to attack almost three-quarters of the members of the Eighth Central Committee, for example, it was necessary for Mao and his close supporters to provide far more convincing evidence of wrongdoing than was revealed in the hastily scribbled and ephemeral wall-posters stuck up by Red Guards in the summer of 1966. Thus in discussing the organization of "investigation projects," Chou En-lai stated: "If you can submit the projects, I'll support you and supply you with the material. This is because you must have sufficient material if you are to criticize, discredit, and repudiate politically, ideologically, theoretically, and organizationally the top party person in authority taking the capitalist road and the handful . . . in your units."[2]

It is clear, then, that although Red Guard data must be used with circumspection they are of great value, especially if certain safeguards can be observed. If a charge is made repeatedly by a number of tabloids and is then given further recognition by publication in the "official" press, or if it is acknowledged as correct by a member of the Maoist leadership, it should naturally be taken more seriously than if it is an isolated accusation made in one tabloid and then never seen again. As far as the data on education go, they are generally repetitive. The time to which the accusation refers is also important: charges made against a senior party leader based on his activities since 1958 are more believable than those based on his behavior in the 1920's. The best check on Red Guard data is to look at contemporary accounts to see if they contain evidence to confirm or deny the Red Guard charges made several years later. As far as the general themes pursued in this study are concerned, such evidence does exist. It is known that Chinese education in the early 1960's swung away from the Maoist path of 1958; it is known that China had developed a degree of social stratification and that urban residents enjoyed many advantages denied to the peasants; it is known that many urban youths, particularly educated ones, regarded living and working in the villages as little short of purgatory. This knowledge was provided both by refugee accounts and by admissions in the official press at the time. What was not known until after 1966 was the extent of general dissatisfaction and, particularly, the dissatisfaction of senior party leaders with Mao's policy prescriptions.

Between 1958 and 1966 the Chinese press was studded with references to resistance from individuals with "bourgeois" views. With regard to education, for example, those who believed in "intellectual development first" and "the one-sided quest for higher education" were frequently mentioned. However, the claim that such ideas were held only by "some individuals" or "a few comrades" was readily accepted by observers accustomed to thinking of the Chinese leadership as an exceptionally united and cohesive elite. Swings in policy were viewed primarily as pragmatic responses to the exigencies of the situation, responses to which all leaders subscribed. Though in many instances this was no doubt a valid interpretation, it obscured the fact that there were real factions within the top leadership of the Chinese Communist Party. The Red Guard data are, therefore, a valuable corrective. Unfortunately, it is not always possible to find detailed confirming evidence. Some of the directives and, more commonly, the policy statements quoted by the Red Guards do not appear to have been published openly or, if they were, are extremely difficult to locate because of inadequate or incorrect references. Public figures in all countries like to make "off-the-cuff" and "off-the-record" statements, and refugee data confirm that China's leaders are no exception. Thus in the last analysis I have been forced to rely on what appears to be "reasonable"; in the following analysis this principle has been adopted, particularly when I depend entirely on Red Guard accounts.

## The Maoist Strategy of Half-Work Half-Study

Mao's desire to revolutionize education, which was an integral part of the Great Leap Forward of 1958, arose from his dissatisfaction with developments that had taken place in Chinese education since 1949. The Chinese Communists had developed an educational system based on a three-tier structure of primary, secondary, and tertiary schooling. The primary schools offered a six-year course; junior- and senior-middle schools each provided a three-year course that was either general or technical. The tertiary level embraced all institutions of higher education, generally providing courses of a range and nature similar to those of the Soviet Union. In addition, a number of schools provided primary- and secondary-level education to adults. The principal influence on Chinese Communist education during the decade following 1949 was that of the Soviet Union. During the period of the First Five-Year Plan particularly, education was closely related to the needs of economic development; there was an emphasis on "useful" subjects, frequently taught according to Soviet curricula and with the use of translated Soviet textbooks. During this period the numbers receiving education at all levels increased dramatically, as did the percentage of students coming from humble backgrounds.[3]

Mao's view of the situation, however, was not entirely favorable. The development of education based on the Soviet model had forced the regime to utilize the skills of intellectuals, many of whom, "bourgeois" in both origin and outlook, had revealed their lack of political purity in the Hundred Flowers campaign of 1957; continued reliance on them obviously endangered the values of the young. Moreover, despite improvements since 1949, the educational system still disfavored children from poorer backgrounds. In 1957–58, for example, just over one-third of the students at the tertiary level were from proletarian families. Hence, Mao found it necessary to press for radical departures in educational policy. At an enlarged meeting of the Central Committee held in Chengtu in March 1958, he argued against unnecessary reliance on the Soviet model,[4] calling for a system more in line with China's needs; subsequently this theme was given considerable attention at a series of conferences convened by the Politburo between April and June.[5] As a result of these deliberations, a new educational policy emerged, embodied in a "Directive on Educational Work" issued jointly by the Central Committee and the State Council on September 19, 1958.[6]

In essence, the new line stressed the importance of making education universal, of guaranteeing that it served the needs of the proletariat and was closely related to productive labor. In concrete terms, two measures were deemed essential. First, regular schools were to establish farms and factories in order to become fully integrated with the productive process. Second and more important, however, factories and cooperatives, particularly in the rural areas, were to establish their own schools to provide education for their members. Such schools were generally to be run on a half-day or alternate-day system so that study could be combined with normal work. This "educational revolution" was implemented in the autumn of 1958 with the official support of all senior party leaders, including Lu Ting-i, who delivered a major speech on the subject at the time.[7] Whatever doubts may have been felt about the wisdom of rapidly expanding the school system, none were expressed publicly; the atmosphere of euphoria that characterized all aspects of the Great Leap Forward was not to be disturbed.

The arguments underlying the propagation of the half-work half-study system were perfectly rational. It is estimated that in 1957 there were some 150 to 200 million children of elementary- and secondary-school age in China, of whom about 71 million were receiving full-time education. Of these some 64 million were in elementary schools, while most of the rest were in junior-middle schools.[8] Despite the rapid advances made since 1949, therefore, many children, particularly in rural areas, were receiving little or no education, and chances to progress beyond elementary level were strictly limited. Universal full-time education, with the massive capital investment involved, was clearly beyond the means of an underdeveloped country with a large proportion of its population in the school age group. Consequently, the half-work half-study system had much to commend it. Its advocates hoped that it would bring junior-middle-school education within the reach of many peasant youths who would otherwise be deprived. By providing them with basic skills, closely related to practical work, the economic and cultural level of the villages could be raised, so lessening the gap between town and country. And, it was believed, the fact that students would spend half their time working meant that the costs of education would be partly or totally defrayed. Accordingly, in 1958 and 1959 the drive to expand education was instituted with "great fanfare," with major attention focusing on the creation of agricultural half-work half-study schools. In April 1960, Yang Hsiu-feng, minister of education, was able to claim that over 30,000 had been set up (roughly one to each commune), with a total enrollment of nearly three million students.[9]

From their inception, however, many of these schools ran into difficulties. One problem was the recruitment of teaching staff, for the enormous shortage of trained teachers forced the school administrators to rely on people whose "cultural level" scarcely equipped them to teach the young. Fortunate schools were sometimes able to enlist the services of senior-middle-school graduates or elementary-school teachers; others, however, were manned by elementary-school graduates, cadres who had been sent down to the countryside, local cadres, and even peasants. As a result, the academic standards of these schools were generally far inferior to those of the full-time urban schools. Consequently, morale in the rural schools was often low, and it was officially admitted that in some places "the hearts of the teachers and students were not in the schools." This second-rate status was clearly illustrated in a *Kuang ming jih pao* article that stated elementary-school graduates would "cheerfully apply" to enter agricultural middle schools if they failed to secure admission to the full-time schools. A further problem was the overoptimism of the idea that such schools could be run on a shoestring budget; most of them were unable to approach self-sufficiency by running their own labor projects.[10]

The schools also had to contend with considerable criticism from persons who were prone to "bourgeois" attitudes, including cadres and educators. It was officially admitted that in 1958 some people had derided the schools as "schools for beggars, inadequate and inferior." Others even questioned the wisdom of bothering to provide education for workers and peasants and believed that the schools were wasting time better spent at productive labor. Such negative views gained ground during 1960 and 1961 as the disasters of the Great Leap Forward continued to be felt, and positive articles in the official press ceased to appear for a time.[11] When favorable reports once again began to appear in late 1961 and early 1962, significant changes in the half-work half-study system were taking place. Many of the schools had been reorganized: instead of teaching on a half-day or alternate-day basis, they had switched to the system of giving full-time education during the slack agricultural season, generally providing students with only five months of education a year. For the remaining months students worked in the communes, where they were supposed to engage in a little study on their own, teachers being assigned to specific areas to visit students and tutor them occasionally. Thus the teachers, in addition to being of poor quality, were at a further disadvantage, for under this system they had to teach all subjects to all students in a given area. Moreover, the principle of self-sufficiency disappeared; students now paid for their education out of their wages from the communes.[12] Reorganization, however, was not the only change in the system. In many areas the agricultural middle schools were in the process of being closed down altogether by the end of 1961. Despite the lack of adequate official information at the time, scattered statistics revealed that the number of such schools was dwindling rapidly. For example, in Kiangsu province, where the experiment had started in 1957, there were 2,200 schools reported in April 1960. By November 1961 the number reported was only 1,500.[13] Data that have emerged in the Cultural Revolution fully confirm this trend and, indeed, indicate that the whole idea of providing education for the peasant youths was attacked with considerable success in the "three bad years," 1959–61.

What might be termed the "bureaucratic backlash" was carried out with the full support of many leading party cadres. Red Guard allegations have accused these men of having always been opposed to the half-work half-study system, and it is probable that a number of them were. Many of them, however, were probably cadres who had welcomed the scheme originally but had changed their minds when the lack of careful planning that characterized the Great Leap Forward began to result in excesses and dislocations in all spheres, including education. Faced with the economic crisis produced by the Leap, which undoubtedly weakened Mao's authority within the CCP, the regime began to "back-pedal" on many issues; not only the agricultural middle schools but also other schemes of extending education to the rural areas were judged as wasteful and unproductive luxuries that were to be shelved at least for a time.

Thus in Szechwan, China's most populous province, Li Ching-ch'üan, first secretary of the provincial party committee, in 1959 described Mao's educational revolution as a "frightful mess that has lowered the quality of education." He argued that the schools had been set up too hastily, had reduced the pool of available labor, and were a waste of money. In 1960–61, with his approval, all but two of the agricultural middle schools in Szechwan were closed down, as were a number of other schools in the province. Although middle schools, particularly half-work half-study schools, were the main targets, the elementary schools were also badly affected, almost 48 per cent of all primary school children being "chased out." In addition to this, campaigns to stamp out illiteracy and to carry on spare-time education were brought to a halt. It is claimed that nearly five million primary- and middle-school students were abruptly deprived of their education by the closure of their schools. The percentage of children attending primary and middle schools fell back to the 1955–56 figure and, in some *hsien*, even to pre-Liberation levels. Whereas in the immediate post-Leap period some 80 per cent of school age children had been attending schools in the province, by the end of 1961 the figure had fallen below 30 per cent in some areas.[14] Where schools were allowed to continue, Li took measures to reduce the number of students. Following the party Central Committee's Ninth Plenum in January 1961, Li distorted the principle of "readjusting, consolidating, filling out, and raising standards" by driving overage students from the schools. Furthermore, he "increased the miscellaneous expenses of primary and middle schools," presumably by denying them state subsidies, and insisted that "whoever goes to school provides his own money and grain." By requiring students to bear the full cost of their education, Li ensured that many of them were forced to leave.[15]

The situation in China as a whole was little better than in Szechwan. According to one account published during the Cultural Revolution, "incomplete statistics" for 1962 showed that the number of agricultural middle schools was reduced "at one stroke" from 22,600 (with a total of 2.3 million students) to 3,715 (with a total of 260,000). Large numbers of primary schools were also closed with the result that the number of school age children attending schools dropped from over 80 per cent in 1958 to only 56 per cent, the main dropouts being the children of workers and peasants. With the exception of Kiangsi, where devotion to Maoist principles led to the establishment of a half-work half-study university (to be discussed below), provincial party officials, aided and abetted by a number of cadres at the center, had succeeded in dismantling most of the agricultural middle schools by the end of 1962.[16]

In 1964, however, there was a revival of the half-work half-study system in both rural areas and towns. This move was closely associated with the reappearance, both physically and ideologically, of Mao Tse-tung. In September 1962, Mao had addressed the Tenth Plenum of the party Central Committee and had called on his colleagues to "never forget the class struggle." At that particular time Mao's charisma was decidedly on the wane, and senior party officials had quietly ignored him while attempting to pursue "revisionist" policies designed to rectify the Maoist "adventurism" of the late 1950's. By 1964, however, the position was changing; Lin Piao's reforms within the People's Liberation Army once more gave Mao a power base that could not be ignored when he raised demands for radical change. This he did in February 1964, when he called for the educational revolution to be implemented.[17] Moreover, the gradual improvement of the Chinese economy, a result of the measures taken in the early 1960's, may well have led other leaders to give some support to the idea that the half-work half-study system should once more be implemented.

Beneath the apparent unanimity on the issue of half-work half-study schools in 1964, however, there was considerable conflict. Mao himself envisaged a system whereby education would not be narrowly academic but would be of a more general nature, closely related to practical work, a system in which students would overcome their contempt and dislike for labor by actively engaging in it and in which careful ideological education (based on Mao's works) would foster selfless "proletarian" ideals of dedication to the cause of socialist construction. Such a system in Mao's eyes was infinitely superior to one based on full-time education, in which students were constantly in danger of being influenced by "bourgeois" and "revisionist" ideas, and was gradually to replace it.[18] Many of Mao's colleagues, however, argued that full-time schools, giving specialist education, should be protected. Red Guard attacks on Lu Ting-i, for example, allege that he argued in favor of academic education and claimed that "it is inevitable that the differences between manual and mental labor will continue. Therefore, some people will inevitably go in for more advanced studies. You cannot keep them down." He is also supposed to have argued that "it is perhaps wrong to label as 'bourgeois' people who give first place to intellectual development."[19]

As a result of these conflicting attitudes, a "two-track" system of education was set up in 1964. The half-work half-study system was seen by many not as a superior innovation with which to replace existing institutions, or even as "separate but equal." In the eyes of many cadres and "the masses" themselves, half-work half-study schools were inferior institutions designed to provide a limited education for the children of peasants and workers or to serve as preparatory establishments to "feed" the full-time system. The principal advantage of such schools in the eyes of many senior cadres was that they were cheap. Thus Liu Shao-ch'i, who made numerous speeches in favor of the establishment of the system in 1964, supposedly stated that "those who cannot afford the full-time system must make do with the half-day system, and since full-time schools are limited, half-day schools should be run to provide schooling."[20] Students at the half-work half-study schools followed the full-time syllabus, with one significant exception: they learned only half as much. Instead of studying subjects closely related to practical work, learning was by rote and teaching was based largely on "dead books." The "bourgeois" emphasis on "intellectual development first" resulted in students becoming "revisionist seedlings with only technical knowledge, seeking to climb up the ladder by means of this technical knowledge."[21] The study of Mao's thought, that necessary corrective to selfish individualism, was not stressed.

Whereas Red Guard charges have attempted to portray this debasement of Mao's noble vision as the work of those determined to keep the children of peasants and workers "in their place" by providing them with only sufficient education to equip them for minor white collar and semi-skilled occupations, numerous articles published in 1964 and 1965 reveal that the problem was far more complex. One of the difficulties besetting the system was that many local cadres and teachers refused to accept Mao's evaluation of it. In a typical confession, one cadre admitted that his supervision of teachers of a work-study primary school had been "approached from the angle of it being the preparatory class of the full-day schools." He further stated that he had regarded the idea of work-study schools as "abnormal" and the full-day schools as "rational"; consequently "though outwardly I helped operate the work-study school, actually I exploited it to build up the fortunes of the full-day school."[22]

Thus cadres and teachers, convinced of the inferiority of the half-work half-study schools, encouraged students to progress to full-time schools and did not try to make the work-study schools distinctive and adequate institutions in their own right. In this they were acting in accord with many rural parents who saw in the new schools an opportunity to participate in the educational process through which their children could progress to higher things. Theirs was the age-old dream of "having a son become an official." For example, in one Shantung commune, of 1,420 students who enrolled in a half-work half-study primary school, 65 per cent subsequently transferred to the full-time system. Among these were a number of children from families with above-average living standards and labor power and fewer children. Such families undoubtedly originally intended to give their children full-time education and simply used this school as an academic spring-board from which to compete successfully for scarce places within the full-time system.[23] Many children from poor and lower-middle class families were also encouraged to go to full-time schools. Teachers encouraged parents to transfer their children by telling them that "studying a whole day is better than studying half a day." Thus parents were faced with a dilemma: if children devoted themselves to studies the parents lost some much needed labor power; conversely, if children continued to help their parents in the fields, they were unable to compete successfully against classmates from richer homes. An example of the problem is the case of a full-time school in Hsing-ning hsien in Kwangtung. There, because the school authorities pursued a policy of trying to qualify as many students as possible for higher education, the school terms were long and fixed, with the result that the holidays did not coincide with the busy farming seasons and children from the poorer peasant families lost schooling while helping their parents.[24] Even success at full-time school brought problems for childen from the poorer peasant households. Many students became "divorced from agricultural production and from rural realities." Their expectations rose, and they became unhappy with their lot as laborers in rural areas. Moreover, in many instances, the "book knowledge" they had received was of little value to the communes.[25] Thus a situation common to many underdeveloped countries developed, in which the education system produced large numbers of youths who, though convinced of their own superiority, possessed skills of limited value and hence were condemned to lives of dissatisfaction.

As an educational system in its own right the work-study system had a very limited appeal even to peasants who had no other educational opportunities. For example, in 1965 one youth pointed out that when he had proposed to enter a half-work half-study school, his neighbors had advised him against it, "saying that I wouldn't get anything out of it and that no one with a future would attend this kind of school. They said that to both study and take part in labor was nonsense. If you really want to learn then you can't take part in labor. If you want to be a laborer then there is no need to go to school."[26] Evidently Mao's dream of an educational system producing "educated laborers with socialist consciousness" was not shared by many of those among "the masses" in whom he had such faith.

Consequently, in 1965 rural education was a source of considerable frustration. The failure of the half-work half-study concept to gain wide support meant that the prestige of the full-time system remained undiminished. Because there were few full-time schools in the rural areas, many peasant youths could not pursue goals that required formal academic training. Even primary-school education was unavailable in many areas. The situation throughout rural China was typified by an article describing the position in Heilungkiang, which noted that "at present the development of rural primary-school education is still very unbalanced, a fairly large number of school-age children, mainly those of poor and lower-middle peasants, are not attending school, and some people are still ideologically averse to the development of half-work half-study primary schools."[27]

Before discussing the urban-based and elitist educational system that dominated China in the 1960's, consideration must be given to the case of the Kiangsi Communist Labor University, which was established in August 1958. The pinnacle of the half-work half-study system, *Kung ta* as it is known, continued to function throughout the 1960's, and has become something of a model for the educational experiments being advanced in China's universities at the present time. An examination of this institution reveals clearly both the strengths and weaknesses of Mao's educational theories. The fullest account of the work of Kung ta has been made by Liu Chün-hsiu in a report published in the *Jen min jih pao* in April 1965.[28] Liu, who was both principal of the university and the secretary of the provincial party committee, noted that the university had been established for the specific purpose of "developing production, building up the mountain areas, and building new socialist villages." Unlike "bourgeois" universities based on the Mencian belief that "those who work with their minds govern others, those who work with their hands are governed by others," it was an institution whose gates were open to the children of workers and peasants and to rural basic-level cadres.

At the outset the university was of considerable size. In addition to a main campus in Nanchang, it had 88 branches and 14 affiliated technical schools scattered throughout Kiangsi by 1959. In 1959–60 almost 50,000 students from nine provinces in addition to Kiangsi were attending. The general policy of curtailing education in 1961–62 had reversed the early expansion of Kung ta, but Liu reported in 1965 it was operating 47 campuses with an enrollment of 14,000 students. From the time of its foundation, Kung ta was actively engaged in productive work. Liu claimed that in the space of six years it had built 35 farms and managed 45,000 *mou* of farm land, 20,000 of which had been reclaimed. It had developed 31 afforestation schemes and managed more than 400,000 mou of forest land. In addition, the university operated 46 factories. Of the 47 campuses, ten had become self-sufficient or had achieved a surplus in grain and in financial assets by 1965, and seven were "fundamentally self-sufficient." A further 18 were partially self-sufficient in grain production and completely financially self-sufficient; the remaining 12 were partly self-sufficient in both grain and financial assets.

Because of this orientation toward production, Kung ta had greatly assisted the provincial authorities by helping to develop mountain areas, by building villages, and by supporting state construction. By 1965 the university had reforested 352,000 mou of land, cut down 100,000 cubic meters of timber and 400,000 stalks of bamboo, and sold the state one million *chin* of surplus grain. "Outstanding success" had also been achieved in improving low-quality and barren land and in raising the quality of seed strains. Between 1962 and 1965, 13,000 graduates had been sent to the "agricultural front," where they worked as basic-level cadres and technicians, many of them in forestry work. In addition to possessing valuable agricultural skills, Kung ta graduates were imbued with the selfless spirit of serving the masses to the utmost of their abilities. It was claimed, for example, that 24 graduates assigned to carry out surveys on a reclamation farm "feared neither severe cold nor blinding heat; they climbed over mountains and hills, scrambled on cliffs, and forded streams, circled every mountain, went to places where others had never gone to investigate; in the daytime they made surveys, and at night they drew charts. They went out early and returned late; they ate the wind and slept on the dew."[29] Because of their superior political consciousness, Kung ta graduates did not adopt the attitude of lecturing to the peasants or ordering them to make improvements. Instead, since they had no objection to physical labor, they taught by example. In short, unlike the city-trained university graduates, those of the Communist Labor University were able both to integrate with the masses and to make a substantial contribution to economic development in the villages.

Reports about the curriculum of the university and the length of the courses offered gave the impression that Kung ta was able to provide reasonably thorough and advanced training in subjects closely related to the rural economy. The curriculum was based on the economic needs of the state in general and of Kiangsi in particular, the subjects taught mainly being agriculture, forestry, livestock breeding, fishing, agricultural machinery, and veterinary science. In some branches local needs were served by the provision of courses on such subjects as the care of silkworms and orchards. Most students enrolled for a four-year course, roughly half of which was spent on "study"; since the university's teaching was based on the principles of "the essence only" and "study with a mind to use," it seemed at first glance that the university might well be offering the sort of advanced training offered in agricultural colleges elsewhere. This, however, was not the case, for the actual duration of formal training was far less than two years. In his report, Liu Chün-hsiu stated that the university emphasized "on-the-job training," to unite theory and practice, an aspect of the program that seems to have counted as formal "study." In this context it is interesting to note an account by a refugee who had taught at Kung ta. Published in November 1965[30] under the uncompromising title "Kiangsi Communist Labor University is a Reclamation Farm," the article claimed that faculty members were expected to teach while laboring side-by-side with their students, who were kept in the fields most of the time. After such activities, both teachers and students were expected to engage in the study of politics, an expectation that obviously reduced still further the amount of time available for formal instruction.

Apart from the time limitations on formal training, standards were affected by the fact that both teachers and students were an extremely heterogeneous and generally poorly informed group. A minority of teachers were graduates of full-time schools at various levels, but many were simply either cadres who had been "sent down" to the countryside or reassigned army officers. Most of the students were of peasant and worker origin, and few possessed more than primary education when they entered Kung ta. Claims that Kung ta was an institution of university level, then, were simply untrue. Although there is no reason to doubt that low-level agricultural skills of value to graduates assigned to the communes as basic-level cadres were taught, these could hardly be regarded as a product of higher education. This was a widely recognized judgment at the time, and Liu Chün-hsiu complained that since its establishment the Communist Labor University had "constantly" met with resistance from those imbued with "bourgeois" thought—not only intellectuals who scorned physical labor and emphasized book-knowledge but also persons associated with the university itself. As Liu admitted, "some cadres and teachers in the school itself believed that work at Kung ta was low-class, so they were not at ease there; some students also felt that it was not glorious to study there, so their attitudes toward study were not stable."

Although by 1965 similar institutions had been established in Shantung and Kwangtung, it is apparent that many senior party leaders were not prepared to accept them as models worthy of emulation. Although they were doubtless prepared to treat them as useful training schools in which to teach peasants elementary techniques, they were certainly not willing to accord them university status. Thus, writing in 1964, one authority on the half-work half-study system noted that as far as he could determine "these 'universities' never have been explicitly endorsed as national policy in a hortatory editorial in the *People's Daily*."[31] In the years preceding the Cultural Revolution, therefore, most rural youths were denied the opportunity to pursue educational goals beyond the lowest levels. Where education was available through the half-work half-study system, it was often of such poor quality that it proved unattractive. Good education remained a preserve of the towns.

## *The Urban-Oriented, Elitist Approach*

In 1960, there were indications that certain senior cadres in educational work were beginning to question the validity of Mao's educational revolution of 1958. The speeches at the time continued to praise the innovations of the previous two years and called for their further implementation, but, almost imperceptibly, slight changes of emphasis revealed that certain modifications of policy were in the offing. Both Yang Hsiu-feng and Lu Ting-i made speeches to the Second Session of the Second National People's Congress in April of that year. In his address Yang warned against the hasty implementation of major reforms and stated that those concerned "should take the complexity of the reform program into full account and carry it out in a prepared, systematic manner." Though he continued to emphasize the need to universalize education, Yang also argued that "we should try our best to raise the standards of selected schools to higher levels." In his speech, Lu Ting-i made a number of references to schools that were making good academic progress and so were raising the quality of education. He also spoke of the need to look after teachers properly, and stressed that they should be accorded respect because of the difficulty of their work.[32]

By 1961, as the havoc caused by the Great Leap Forward continued to be felt, the movement against the educational revolution swelled. Beyond the drive to reject the half-work half-study system, the movement led to demands for quality in place of quantity. Increasingly, academic talent rather than political purity was favored, and the success of any given school was measured by the number of graduates it sent on for higher education.

Those who demanded educational improvement did not so much advocate a concentration of resources within the full-time sector as stress the need to give better facilities to the best of the full-time schools. Appeals to "talk less of universalization and more of elevation" were given full support, it is alleged, by Lu Ting-i, who in October 1962 proposed that certain full-time schools be developed to function "like a pagoda to enable the students to gradually enroll themselves in higher institutions as well as to train diverse experts."[33] Two months later provincial and municipal authorities were instructed to select such "little pagodas," which were then given a disproportionately large share of state resources, including good staff–student ratios, so that they could concentrate on educating outstanding students.

The favorable conditions prevailing in these schools have been described in a report on their operation in Shantung, where the provincial educational authorities introduced a plan for their development in May 1963. Here, some 36 middle schools (less than 4 per cent of the provincial total) and 162 primary schools were chosen. In middle schools, the time allotted for teaching and study was to be not less than nine months of the year; in primary schools it was to be slightly longer. Labor requirements were minimal, middle-school students being required to devote only one month a year to it, and primary-school students a mere two weeks. In practice this meant that "labor" was largely confined to the cleaning of the school premises.[34] By the standards of the half-work half-study schools, these "pagodas" were lavishly equipped. One school in Shantung had its old one-story building replaced with a construction of two and three stories, which was fitted out with brand new furniture; the school's used accouterments, which were only a year old, were handed down to an ordinary school. Its building program was carried out with unnecessary extravagance, for in addition to "new decorative walls and an iron gate," each classroom was provided with "a Soviet-type platform with a glass blackboard and six fluorescent lamps." The expenditure on this school alone amounted to more than 200,000 yüan.

One of the interesting aspects of the Chinese political system highlighted by the Cultural Revolution has been the extent to which senior cadres have been personally involved with the establishment of "key points" and "models" in all fields. Education appears to have been no exception, for many of these schools appear to have enjoyed the patronage of influential party bureaucrats. Thus in Peking, for example, the No. 22 Middle School was singled out for special treatment by Chang Wen-sung, who headed the Department of Education of the Peking party committee. Here education was organized on the basis of the "four selfs"; namely, self-selection of teaching content, self-determination of hours, self-choice of association, and self-awareness and self-volition, under which the school authorities implemented a highly academic approach to study. Mao's writings and other political documents were excluded on the grounds of length and language; teachers refused to use political material in their lessons. The status of older and presumably "bourgeois" teachers was enhanced by the school's insistence that younger teachers learn from them. The school's "experience" was publicized by the municipal party committee through articles in *Pei-ching jih pao* and *Ch'ien hsien,* and also by means of radio broadcasts.[35]

Many of the favored schools were well-established institutions, having been set up during the Republican period or even earlier and, as such, had strong traditions of academic excellence. For example, Peking's No. 25 Middle School was an "old educational glory" with a history going back over a century. Despite the takeover in 1949 the school had remained in the hands of "bourgeois authorities" and continued to inculcate "bourgeois" values. Its reputation caused the municipal party committee to use it as an experimental school based on the Soviet model. According to a Red Guard account, its ten-year course was characterized by "lots of books, lots of subjects, lots of preparation, lots of lectures, lots of study, lots of recitation and memorization. Little was taught about class struggle, there was little study of Mao Tse-tung's thought, there was little contact with the workers and peasants, little labor, and little recreation ... or rest."[36] Students were encouraged to aspire to higher education, to be ambitious, and to take the branch road of putting academic standards and grades first.

Since early academic success depends very largely on environmental factors, it is not surprising that schools whose admissions policies were based largely on "intellectual" criteria recruited overwhelmingly from a very small section of the community. A case in point is No. 2 Experimental Elementary School in Peking: before Liberation this school catered "exclusively for young ladies and gentlemen of the capitalist class," numbering Mme. Wang Kuang-mei and her brothers and sisters among its alumni; after 1949 it retained its elitist position by means of entrance examinations. Although several thousand children sought admission every year, few were successful. In 1964 there was only one worker's child in the school, the rest of the pupils being the children of senior cadres, "democratic personalities," and high-level intellectuals and cadres in general. The children of senior cadres were in a particularly privileged position because for them entrance examinations could be waived. Among the students who attended this particular school were the children of Liu Shao-ch'i, Yang Shang-k'un, Po I-po, Chiang Nan-hsiang, and Lin Feng. Such children were placed in separate classes and given a special educational program. The school authorities, reportedly with the special permission of Liu himself, recruited its own staff without reference to higher authorities, and the classes of top cadres' children were allocated the best teachers.[37]

The question of the education of senior cadres' children is a particularly important one, for it reveals clearly the very human issues underlying the debate about the "correct" educational policy for China. Whatever their views on education in general, many members of the increasingly routinized and urbanized party bureaucracy were determined to promote an elitist system for the benefit of their own children. The provision of schools either entirely or largely for the children of cadres had begun in the border areas before Liberation. After 1949 they had been established in the major cities, where they became models for the policy of "complete Sovietization" supposedly advocated by Liu Shao-ch'i. Some leaders, including Mao Tse-tung, Chou En-lai, and K'ang Sheng had argued from the early 1950's that such schools should be absorbed into the ordinary educational system, but they had been opposed, particularly by the party committee of Peking, in which city such schools were of course most prevalent. In 1955 the schools had been criticized by "revolutionary comrades" in the primary education bureau of the Ministry of Education, who had argued that they were extremely expensive and moreover produced graduates who regarded themselves as "new aristocrats." The municipal party committee's Department of Education, however, insisting that Peking, being the capital, was a special case, not only retained the existing schools but set up new ones. Furthermore, in 1958 and thereafter as a result of Soviet influence, Khrushchev's 1956 call for boarding schools was apparently taken up by Liu Shao-ch'i, who announced that such schools were fully in accord with true Communism and thus should be established for cadres' children. These schools existed not only for the civilian bureaucracy, but also for the PLA until they were abolished by Lin Piao in 1963.[38]

Apart from the emphasis on formal academic training, one very interesting feature of "schools for cadres' children" and, indeed, for "pagoda" schools in general was the emphasis on foreign languages. At a time when Mao himself was becoming increasingly nativistic, many of his colleagues had retained or had developed an internationalistic outlook and regarded the study of foreign languages as an essential part of elitist education. In 1961 a number of foreign language schools were promoted under the auspices of Lu Ting-i and, probably, Ch'en I. On Lu's instructions, these schools were encouraged to accept cadres' children, and the number of such students increased by over 85 per cent in a short time.[39] Foreign languages were of more than intrinsic value, however, for they were one of the subjects included in the entrance examinations of many of the more prestigious universities. Moreover, they were not taught in many ordinary full-time schools; hence students from these institutions were at a further disadvantage in competing with graduates of the "pagodas" for university places.[40]

Thus the full-time schools in general, and the "pagodas" in particular, were an affront to Mao's views of what education should be. The students of these schools were unable to take part in the "three major revolutionary movements," for they were "tied down" in the classroom and "studied behind closed doors." Whereas the children of workers and peasants attended inferior schools—if they attended schools at all—and were given only the basic education necessary to equip them for low-level roles, the "new aristocrats" were encouraged to pursue selfish goals by way of academic achievement. Moreover, their schools provided havens for "bourgeois" intellectuals, for the insistence that teachers must have considerable experience, high academic qualifications, and rich and specialized mastery of their subjects as well as pedagogic skills naturally favored men who had themselves been trained in "bourgeois" institutions and who had little sympathy with Mao's concepts of education and the relevance of politics. Bourgeois values became institutionalized and manifested themselves in ways familiar in the West, even to the extent of many schools holding annual "speech days" when former students who had gone on to distinguish themselves were invited to a reunion at which they were held up as models for emulation.[41] Therefore, by the mid-1960's, China's full-time schools, particularly the "pagodas," were still producing large numbers of graduates whose aspirations were virtually identical with those of their contemporaries in the West. In April 1965 a report on graduates of primary and middle schools in the city of Hangchow presented what was obviously a typical picture: it noted that "there are still quite a few students who are unable to see correctly the relationship between the desires of the individual and the needs of the state." Far from wishing "to become the kind of intellectual youth who engage in plowing and planting," many took the view that "study is the only lofty occupation" and that "the road to officialdom is study."[42]

Many urban students, still feeling that success was a question of gaining admittance to a university, knew that the best way to achieve this was by hard academic work, rather than by political activism. As one educational journal observed in an article on the "one-sided pursuit of higher education," in the passing of university entrance examinations "what plays the primary role is still intellectual education. There are few people who fail to gain admission because of inadequacies in their moral or physical culture, but the majority of failures are due to poor intellectual attainment."[43] Consequently, those who were able scrambled to compete for university places in the cities. If successful, they were able to prolong their student life for as much as eight years during which time the pattern of study reinforced and developed the attitudes already inculcated in primary and middle school.

Higher education had enjoyed protection since the Great Leap Forward. This had been afforded not only by bourgeois intellectuals but by very senior figures in the field of university administration such as Yang Hsiu-feng, Chiang Nan-hsiang, and Lu P'ing, who themselves enjoyed the support of men in the highest echelon of the party, including, it is alleged, Liu, Teng Hsiao-p'ing, Lu Ting-i, P'eng Chen, and Ch'en I.[44] Although the "educational revolution" of 1958 appears to have had a limited impact on higher learning at the time, the universities were given considerable encouragement during the "three bad years." In particular, the above-mentioned "clique" produced in September 1961 "sixty articles on higher education," a policy prescription that was the antithesis of Mao's ideas in its stress on the need for professional competence at the expense of political consideration.[45] In order to train specialists "of the sort needed for socialist construction" students, "especially good students," should be encouraged and helped, the document emphasized. The "mistaken viewpoint of belittling book-knowledge" was to be overcome, and anything that impeded education, such as "excessive production, excessive scientific research [practical work], and excessive social [political] activities," was to be stamped out. It was asserted that "instruction is the basic factor"; students, therefore, were to devote themselves to their studies. The role of the teacher, whatever his class origin, was enhanced. Students were specifically forbidden to use "the method of hostile struggle" against teachers and were told to "learn with humility" from old teachers. Teachers were told that their basic function was to give serious instruction, and their promotion prospects depended on "the manner in which they gave their instruction, the quality of their instruction, and their academic standards." As a result of this, teachers were encouraged to forgo involvement in politics, and to pursue the "white and expert" road of self-advancement.[46]

The "sixty articles" did contain a call to strengthen the party's leadership in the field of higher education. This, however, was not intended to accord any primacy to the thought of Mao Tse-tung but was a manifestation of the "Liuist" belief in the primacy of organization and discipline.[47] The purpose in fact was to ensure that higher education was conducted in accordance with the wishes of senior party members concerned with the administration of the tertiary sector, who thus secured the right to vote and veto "revolutionary" innovations that might be put forward. Thus, *"in a word, the brakes were put on."*

While the "sixty articles" were being prepared, their substance was revealed in a speech made by Ch'en I to the graduating students of Peking's institutes of higher learning.[48] Delivered on July 1, 1961, this speech was published, in a somewhat revised form, in *Chung-kuo ch'ing nien pao* in August and was later carried in *Chung-kuo ch'ing nien.* Ch'en dealt at length with the relationship between "red" and "expert" and came down heavily in favor of expertise.

Our socialist construction requires every kind of talent. One kind is people who specialize in doing political work; they take political work as their specialization. There are others who are engaged as specialists in different fields, for example, in industry, agriculture, literature, geology, mining. . . . Generally speaking, the job of institutes of higher learning is to study various kinds of specialist knowledge and make students become expert in their own field. Therefore political schools make the study of politics primary, whereas specialist schools make the study of specializations primary.[49]

Ch'en went on to stress that both Marx and Mao were specialists, polymaths who had acquired expert knowledge in many different fields. He also used the examples of Central Committee members and foreign office personnel to demonstrate the need for professionalism. Although he stated that it would be wrong to regard political and professional study as diametrically opposed, he warned that "red" must not replace "expert" and stressed the need "to emphasize specialist study at the present time," for if students neglected specialized study in favor of political and labor activities China would remain "forever backward" in science and culture. In his desire to protect and develop specialist education Ch'en even adopted the heretical idea that "red" and "expert" were one and the same. He argued that the "political task" for a student was to work hard at his specialization; the higher his political consciousness the more he would understand the need for specialist study. He argued that it was the institution's political task to nurture specialists and drew the astonishing conclusion that "wherever a school has students who study their special subject well, then that school is putting politics in command in a good way." He went on to request that political activities be "suitably arranged" so as not to encroach on time allotted to academic study, advising students to emulate the great scholars of the past by becoming so immersed in their work that they would "forget to eat and rest."

He then asked that graduates be given every assistance to utilize fully their special skills in the service of the state, condemning the tendency in some units to brand as "white specialists" those who dedicated themselves to their work. It would be erroneous, he argued, to judge a man's "standpoint" by the amount of time he spent in political activities. Indeed, as long as he made contributions to the motherland's construction, specialists were to be given every encouragement. Genuine "white specialists" who served the enemies of the people had, he claimed, been largely eliminated by the mass campaigns of the 1950's and were no longer a real danger. Finally, Ch'en turned to the subject of ideological reform and pleaded that a gentle and gradual approach be adopted, observing that erroneous ideas could not be changed in a few weeks and young people could not be expected to reach the high standards of the true Marxist in a short time. Using himself as an example, he pointed out that despite forty years of service to the revolution his own thought was not entirely Communist, but contained elements of Confucian, Mencian, and bourgeois ideology. Ch'en specifically mentioned students from "exploiting families" in this plea for tolerance and argued that the "theory of taking account of class origin alone" was incorrect. He reminded his audience that many Central Committee members had come from the upper and middle classes and that it would be wrong to discriminate against young people from such backgrounds, since they had no choice in the matter of their birth, the influence of the ideology of the "exploiting classes" had diminished considerably, and there was nothing to prevent them from becoming true revolutionaries.

The ideas expressed in the "sixty articles" and in Ch'en's speech were widely publicized throughout urban China. Ch'en himself carried them as far afield as Kweiyang, where in 1962 he addressed a conference of cultural and scientific workers and delivered what he later confessed amounted to an "unprincipled eulogy of intellectuals" that greatly overrated them, failed to emphasize the need to rectify their ideology and so provided sustenance for those who were determined to resist reform. He also made a number of speeches on the study of foreign languages, in which as foreign minister he had an obvious interest. In this connection he has admitted, "I never stressed politics but heavily emphasized specialization, thus encouraging the tendency among some people to ignore politics. These speeches were openly published and spread poison throughout the country; their influence was very bad."[50] Teng Hsiao-p'ing was also prominent in emphasizing skill rather than political considerations. In 1961, he publicly described the "sixty articles" as a "good document" and the following year again stressed the need for professionalism when he made his memorable remark at a meeting of the Central Committee of the Communist Youth League that "it doesn't matter whether a cat is black or white; if it catches mice it is a good cat."[51]

Given such encouragement, many of China's better universities and institutions concentrated on quality rather than quantity—a development evident from the numerous Red Guard allegations concerning the more prestigious institutions. The China Medical University (formerly Peking Union Medical College), for example, introduced an eight-year course in 1959 fully in keeping with the reputation as a center of academic excellence it had enjoyed in the Republican period, when many of its graduates had held office under the Nationalists. The syllabus at the university was highly academic, with little importance being attached to politics. Indeed, one regulation specifically forbade the reading of newspapers and Mao's works in the time reserved for private study. Formal lessons on political matters constituted only 3.5 per cent of the total study time and even then the "thoughts of Chairman Mao" were given scant attention, since "self-cultivation and the like" were the main objects of study.[52] The course itself was an extremely difficult one, designed to give a broad, deep training. The three-year premedical course included training in natural science theory as well as foreign languages to prepare students for scientific research. Students were also required to follow the same mathematics, physics, chemistry, and biology courses as those in engineering institutes and departments of chemistry and biology. If successful, students then embarked on an equally comprehensive formal medical course that left no time for productive labor or political activities. The average time devoted to study was 15 hours a day, so it is scarcely surprising that students had little contact with the masses.

Such exacting standards meant that the entrance requirements were weighted in favor of students who came from "good" families and who had attended the "pagoda" schools of the towns. According to one report of students enrolled between 1959 and 1962, only 5 per cent were from worker and peasant families whereas 30 per cent were the children of "top intellectuals" 5 per cent of "bourgeois elements," and 5 per cent of "landlords, rich peasants, counterrevolutionaries, bad elements, and rightists." The family background of the other 55 per cent was not stated, but presumably included the children of cadres, white-collar workers, overseas Chinese, and other nonproletarian elements. Moreover, students of humble background had a much higher failure rate at the university. Approximately one-third of the students of worker and peasant families who had enrolled in 1958 for premedical courses at other colleges and who subsequently transferred to China Medical University were dropped within two years of entering, as were one-half of the party members in this category. Of 12 students of the 1961 class dropped during their premedical course, 11 were the children of workers, peasants, and (presumably low-level) cadres.[53] A further damning indictment of the university, in Mao's eyes at least, was that it ignored completely the medical needs of rural China. Allegedly this was due to the university's adoption of the "Liuist" view, which "consistently opposed the orientation of medicine serving the vast rural population, claiming that health work must be made a success in the cities before health work in the countryside could be dealt with effectively." Consequently, the university authorities invented the theory of "indirect service to the 500 million peasants" and paid no attention to people with common ailments in the rural areas. Instead students acquired a great deal of knowledge of limited value. They learned too much theory, specialized in "high-class diseases" rather than common ones, and learned to operate expensive and sophisticated equipment that could only be found in large urban hospitals. Such skills were no preparation for work in rural clinics nor, indeed, were they expected to be, for as some professors told their students, "Do you think we train you for eight years just to turn out country doctors?"[54] In any event, none of the graduates (of whom there were only fifty by 1967 because of the length of the course) were assigned to rural posts. In this specific instance, then, it is difficult to counter the charge that "in the last analysis 'indirect service to the 500 million peasants' meant 'direct service to the bourgeoisie' and the theory of 'cities before the countryside' meant 'refusal to serve the poor and middle peasants.' "[55]

During the 1960's it appears that some cadres did criticize the system at the China Medical University but were rebuffed by Lu Ting-i, who, "speaking falsely in the name of the Central Committee," announced that "it is not permitted to discuss the question of whether or not it [the eight-year course] should go on or not." Indeed, the university became a model for emulation, and in 1962 the "urban, lordly Ministry of Health" decided to lengthen the course of study in all medical colleges group by group.[56]

In the years following the Great Leap Forward such developments became commonplace. Men such as Lu P'ing of Peking University, Chiang Nan-hsiang of Tsinghua, Chu Shao-t'ien of Wuhan, and Ch'eng Chin-wu of Peking Normal University, used their positions both as principals and, more important, as secretaries of university party committees, to manipulate organizational and disciplinary procedures to curtail such radical changes as had occurred in 1958 and to suppress those responsible for such innovations. Thus at Wuhan, some members of the faculty had introduced a half-work half-study system in certain departments in 1958. Chu Shao-t'ien's arrival as principal and secretary of the party committee in 1961, however, led to a rapid reversal. Denouncing the situation as "chaotic," Chu insisted on restoring the "normal order of the curriculum" and closing down the offending departments. Li Kuo-p'ing, the professor of mathematics, was attacked for having supported the 1958 changes, and the "backbone elements" involved were, in many instances, transferred elsewhere, their posts being taken up by Chu's own intimates who were brought in from outside. Following this Chu implemented "revisionist" policies. Aided by Ho Ting-hua, the deputy principal, who was later to be dubbed "the Teng T'o of Wuhan," Chu was able to resist the wishes of the Hupeh party committee by resorting to that traditional technique of Chinese politics, "open obedience and secret violation."[57]

The reaction against the primacy of political considerations, which resulted from the failures of the Great Leap Forward, caused many institutions to reduce the amount of time spent on political study and, in some cases, to ban political material from the classroom. At Peking University some formal courses based on Mao's works were eliminated, and it was recommended that they should be a subject for voluntary study only. The story of the professor of oriental languages who refused to permit the inclusion of the "thought of Mao Tse-tung" in lectures on the grounds that "Marxist-Leninists cannot master the Arabic language" may well be apocryphal, but it reveals clearly the attitude of many Chinese intellectuals at the time.[58] In a number of institutions of higher learning political study and political activity appear to have hardly been given lip service. At the South-China Engineering College in Canton, for example, a ten year (1963–73) plan for the training of faculty members was drawn up following the transmission of the "sixty articles" to the lower levels. Although a lengthy document, the only consideration given to political and ideological matters was in the form of a "simple reminder to teachers at all levels that they should support the leadership of the party and socialism and [should] willingly devote themselves to the cause of socialism." The plan made no mention of the study of

Marxism-Leninism, the writings of Mao Tse-tung, current affairs, or the party's general and specific policies. Nor did it refer to the importance of "holding high the great red banner of the thought of Mao Tse-tung, creatively learning and applying Chairman Mao's works, his three 'constantly read articles,' and taking an active part in the three major revolutionary movements."[59] Instead of emphasizing the need to remold teachers' ideology, the plan stressed the importance of "respecting and worshiping professors" and was, it is alleged, "a black program for fostering intellectual aristocrats lording it over the working people and behaving like pompous bureaucrats."[60] The plan did, however, specify in the most minute detail the qualities deemed desirable in a teacher: pedagogic skill; skill in production; a thorough knowledge of the literature on one's subject, particularly theory; knowledge of a foreign language; and mastery of a specialized field of scientific research. Chang Chin, the college principal, told young teachers that unless they concentrated on their work they would be unable to find posts in the best schools; other senior members of the faculty pointed out that promotion depended far more on completing a dissertation than on political and ideological status. Teachers who devoted time to political activities were warned that it would harm their careers. One teacher was told that "you can hardly make a living by counting on politics alone. You have to study hard behind closed doors. Don't move about here and there. If you are not professionally sound, even the general party branch can't do much in keeping you [in your job]."[61] Consequently, many young teachers became obsessed with the possibility of being "weeded out" and gave up political and social activities in order to concentrate on their professional work. What was true of staff in institutes of higher learning appears to have been true also of students training for teaching posts at lower levels. At Peking Normal University, for example, Ch'eng Chin-wu, the principal, also stressed the acquisition of professional skill.[62]

In many universities demands to shorten courses were successfully resisted; in fact, they were frequently lengthened, often along the lines of courses in Soviet institutions. Some special short-term courses were dropped, and the usual four-year course was extended to five, six, or even more years. Allegedly, this was done with the blessing of Lu Ting-i and was in accordance with his "reactionary" theory that "the first and foremost task of education is to impart knowledge."[63] Such an extension took place at Tsinghua University, where Chiang Nan-hsiang, a P'eng Chen appointee, since 1952 had been applying ideas derived from the model of the Soviet University of Science and Technology, including the introduction of a five-year degree course. In 1959, the course was lengthened by a further year. Chiang argued that "students should be fostered carefully and early and [should be] given a long period of training as Ulanova and Mei Lan-fang were trained." Accordingly, he restricted political activities, dissuading students from studying Mao's works and from taking part in such campaigns as the "socialist education movement." Chiang saw Tsinghua as a center of academic excellence geared to the production of "high caliber cadres" and "red engineers." In 1964, he opposed Mao's Spring Festival instructions and insisted that they did not apply to science and engineering courses. Moreover, in September of that year he introduced a "three-stage rocket" system to train outstanding specialists. Selected students were given a two-year preparatory course at the middle school attached to the university, after which the formal university course lasted only four years. On graduation, however, good students were admitted to a two-year course to prepare them for advanced work, and on satisfactory completion of that they entered graduate school for a further three years. Hence, despite the claim that the degree course was being shortened, good students were actually receiving up to nine years of university education.[64]

In terms of academic achievement, it appears that the emphasis on quality and the need to produce an elite produced good results, particularly in science and engineering. By the mid-1960's, some 800 research institutes were operating in China, of which 305 specialized in life science, 205 in physical sciences, and 271 in engineering. Writing in 1966, Geoffrey Oldham, an authority on Chinese science, noted that qualified visitors were impressed by the large number of young scientists at work and were in agreement that "the majority of these young scientists were bright and eager, and showed an excellent grasp of their research problems." Indeed, "in a few branches of the physical sciences the Chinese work [was] probably on a par with the best in the world."[65]

Yet the social consequences of this were hardly encouraging to anyone who wished to build a radically new social order, for as Mao saw it, the universities were contributing to social stratification and were training an elite motivated by selfish ambition. One of the major consequences of the reemphasis on professionalism was a reduction in the number of university students from worker and peasant families, and a corresponding increase in those from the families of senior cadres and the "exploiting classes." Moreover, students who came from humble backgrounds and who had sometimes gained admission on political rather than academic grounds, were far more likely to be "weeded out"

or at least forced to repeat a grade. Thus at Peking University the number of students from worker and peasant families fell from nearly 67
per cent in 1958 to only 38 per cent in 1962, while the number of students of "exploiting class" background more than doubled in the same
period. Many of the university's professors were contemptuous of proletarian students, referring to them as "coarse teacups not amenable to
fancy carving" and resenting the fact that such students had obtained
university places by means of "ladders." Of 237 such students admitted
to the eight departments of natural science in 1958 only 45 graduated
with their original class, the others having been expelled or held back.[66]

In 1962, some 5,000 students classified as being of worker, peasant,
or soldier class were expelled from higher schools in Peking alone, and
another 5,000 were forced to repeat a grade. At Peking Technical College more than 800 of the 919 cadres and military men sent there as
students were "weeded out," as were 200 at Tsinghua. Of 108 students
expelled from the Peking Commercial College, some 94 per cent were of
working-class origin. Some 380 of the 867 students at the Peking Electrical College were forced either to repeat a grade or leave, the majority
being the children of workers and peasants.[67]

A particularly backward step, from the Maoist point of view, was that
some institutions specifically established after 1949 to educate proletarian students were, in the 1960's, "captured" by the bourgeoisie. The
Shanghai Institute of Mechanical Engineering, which grew out of the
Shanghai Technical School for Machine Building established under the
First Ministry of Machine Building in 1952, is a case in point. At the
time of its inception considerable attention was being paid in Shanghai,
and throughout urban China, to the training of a proletarian elite following the three-anti and five-anti campaigns of 1951–52. Consequently, the
institute's first group of students included 2,181 workers, peasants, and
basic-level cadres who had been "steeled" in the campaigns. In 1960,
however, the institute used the "pretext" of "equal opportunity to everyone according to results in the entrance examinations" in order to raise
standards. As a consequence of this, only 17 children of workers and
peasants were admitted, 14 of whom were forced to leave because of the
examination system.[68] This trend continued until 1966. Han Suyin, a
well-informed and favored visitor to China, has written: "Investigations
into the universities and senior middle schools in the cities provided a
shock; after 17 years of socialist China, over 40 per cent of the students were still from bourgeois, ex-landlord, and capitalist families, even
if these were only 5 per cent of the population."[69] Naturally, the class
composition of the student body varied widely from institution to in-

stitution. At a comparatively obscure university, in a backward province, proletarian students obviously had a better chance; thus Han Suyin was told that in 1962 over 80 per cent of the students at Yunnan University were of worker and peasant origin. At the more prestigious universities, however, the student body was likely to include many students from nonproletarian families. Indeed, she was told that in early 1966 90 per cent of the students at the Shanghai Music Institute were of bourgeois or petty bourgeois origin.[70] Since music is a subject unlikely to appeal to the children of workers and peasants, bourgeois domination in such a field is not surprising. Nevertheless, a Red Guard report on the number of worker and peasant children in certain leading institutions in Peking on the eve of the Cultural Revolution, shows clearly that in many fields they were extremely underrepresented. Thus at the Movie College only 30 per cent were of proletarian origin; at Peking Normal University only 25 per cent; and at Peking No. 2 Medical College and Peking Electrical Institute only 17 per cent.[71]

The selfishness typical of many graduates, whatever their class origin, was clearly revealed in a confession (published in December 1965) by a man who had graduated from the East China Normal University that year and would have received all his higher education since 1960. He admitted that, like many of his contemporaries, his thought had been dominated by the "three gets" attitude: "get by in politics, get good at your profession, and get on well in life." For this young man, as no doubt for many others, political involvement meant no more than being careful not to oppose the party or socialism. Apart from this obvious safeguard he felt that he could concentrate on his career, for, as he told his friends, "the promising graduate need not fear a ragged gown," for "he has learning in his belly."[72] Instead of wishing to dedicate their lives to serving the masses, graduates able to impress the university committees of party cadres and professors that determined job assignments could often hope to pursue reasonably satisfactory careers as "high caliber cadres" or "red engineers," to use Chiang Nan-hsiang's words. As such they could expect a good standard of living, since within the system there was a relatively wide range of differential salaries and perquisites.[73] Moreover, they could remain in the cities, where not only were living standards higher but promotion prospects were also better than in the rural areas.[74] Thus their contact with the masses, particularly the rural masses, was minimal. At university they had been protected from involvement with workers and peasants, and this continued afterward, for, as one accusation notes, they were able to go direct from school to government institutions as cadres without going to the fields to help peasants plant and harvest crops.[75] Not surprisingly, during the Cultural Revolution a number of these favored people complained that because of the educational system "they were no longer willing to go to places abounding in hardship."[76]

It must be remembered, however, that such highly educated youth constituted only a small part of the urban population. Most young people in the cities had little chance of advancement either because they lacked talent or because the system prevented them from developing any they did have. Indeed, in the 1960's, many of them even lost the right to live in the cities.

### "Down to the Villages and Up to the Mountains"

The movement to send young people away from the cities began in December 1955, when Mao recommended that those who could should go to the villages to work. The campaign became a constant feature of Chinese life after the Great Leap Forward, and by 1964 some forty million young people had been sent "down" to the villages.[77] Unlike the more general policy of making students and bureaucrats engage in productive labor at regular intervals usually in villages a few miles from their town, this campaign frequently involved the transfer of youths over vast distances into areas with different climatic conditions, customs, and dialects. Perhaps the most striking example of this has been the drive throughout the 1960's to send Shanghainese to Sinkiang.

The reasons for this policy have been varied. In simple socioeconomic terms the urban areas were unable to absorb and provide adequate career outlets for their vast young population. Strategically, too, a rationale existed, in the sense that frontier regions, particularly Sinkiang and the ominously named "great northern waste" of Manchuria, required an influx of Han Chinese settlers. As conceived by Mao, however, the principal aim of this policy was to expedite the removal of the "three major differences" between town and country, mental and manual work, and worker and peasant. By sending millions of youths with some elementary-school, middle-school, or even higher education to "integrate themselves" with rural society, Mao envisioned a rapid raising of the peasants' cultural standards and an accelerated rate of rural economic development facilitated by the ability of these youths to undertake relatively low-level technical work as well as to use their literacy and numeracy skills as teachers, book-keepers, and accountants. By such a process, it was argued, a genuine social unity would develop between town and country that would eventually result in the creation of "Communist man," for the educated youths would not only teach, but learn from the peasants. Moreover, they not only would acquire peasant skills, but would become politically "pure." As in the "Yenan days," the village was to be the crucible of revolution in which a new generation of successors would be produced. The problem of educated youths sent to the villages was one of the greatest significance. Mao's grand design, by which this movement would play a major role in the elimination of urban-rural differences was so inadequately implemented, and indeed distorted, that by 1966 the conflict between the peasant and the urban dweller appears to have been as prevalent as ever.

The actual concept of sending millions of youths to the countryside does not appear to have met with any great resistance. There seems to have been a high degree of unanimity on the need to use the countryside as a reservoir for the burgeoning youthful population that could not be provided with careers in the towns. What is evident, however, is that many of those involved with the young disagreed with Mao over the exact purpose of sending them in the villages and the means by which the plan was to be implemented. In the 1960's, many teachers and cadres took the view that the cream of China's youth was to be exempt from this policy; they were to stay in the towns and receive the advanced education that would equip them for specialist work in the bureaucracy and industry. Thus one Red Guard charge notes that "the old educational system and Liu's movement of going to the countryside are twins. Their only difference is that the latter is serving the former. The higher grade schools take away students who are 'excellent in both conduct and study,' whereas the movement of going to the countryside takes over the remnant 'refuse' who are 'poor in conduct and study.' "[78] Furthermore, in some instances, cadres used the countryside as a dumping ground for the political undesirables among the young. Youths who either because of their own activities or because of family background belonged to the "five bad elements" (*wu lei fen tzu*) were encouraged or coerced to make their lives in the villages. Some cadres told them, "You should find a sweetheart in the countryside. It does no harm for you, who are eighteen or nineteen years old, to get married early; otherwise the organization will not support you and will discard you."[79] Others said that youths from bad backgrounds could become cadres in the rural areas. But whereas the countryside was used at times as a means of punishment, and whereas some cadres appear to have used "sending down" as a cynical means of ridding the towns of troublesome "social youth," the policy was seen by some as a means of "saving" urban youth. It is likely that many urban officials viewed the rural and border areas as a land of opportunity, where those unfortunate enough to carry a poor "status" (*ch'eng fen*) could redeem themselves by working hard in the Chinese equivalent of Botany Bay. Whatever the motivation behind the policies of such officials, the policy itself was to prove a disastrous failure.

Another distortion of the correct Maoist line was found among urban cadres who accepted the principles of sending down well-educated and talented youths but on a temporary rather than a permanent basis, viewing the process as a form of national service that would entitle those participating to accelerated career advancement afterwards. Liu Shao-ch'i himself is alleged to have expressed this view while addressing a forum of students in Hsüchang in 1957, telling them that after three to five years in the countryside they would know all that the peasants knew, and moreover, would be "cultured" as the peasants were not. Consequently, they would rapidly become hsien cadres, then cadres at the provincial level, and could even go on to become members of the Central Committee.[80] The idea that the villages were merely a stepping stone to better things was obviously contrary to Mao's wish that urban youth should go to the country for life, to devote themselves unconditionally to the job of integrating with the peasants.

Coupled with the attempt to portray the movement "down to the villages" as a means of personal advancement was the attempt to present rural life in a highly idealized manner—a revolutionary Canaan flowing with milk and honey. Thus in 1963, youths in Chiangmen city in Kwangtung were mobilized to go to T'ai-shan Breeding Farm where, they were promised, the benefits offered included "all the oyster oil you can eat. You shall be given several packs of cigarettes and one catty of wine every month. At most you shall be required to work for three to four hours a day. You shall receive thirty-five yüan in wages monthly. You may return to Chiangmen after four years."[81] Other youths from this city were sent to San-shui at the same time. According to the cadres in charge of mobilization, "San-shui Agriculture Farm has tall buildings, cars and tractors. . . . It is very near Canton. Every Sunday you may go to Canton for pleasure." According to those who were sent and who managed to return to urban civilization in the course of the Cultural Revolution, San-shui "was an uninhabited place overgrown with wild grass; there were only several worn out straw sheds."

Resettlement cadres enlisted the support of urban teachers to assist them in painting a rosy picture of rural life. In 1964 the Chiangmen Resettlement Office organized teachers to go to the countryside to investigate conditions there. After a tour of scenic spots, they informed their students that "you should have no worry about going to the countryside. You have everything there. The scenery is beautiful, transport is convenient. The pay is very good. When you go out at night you need not carry a flashlight. There the peasants have no culture, and how much they need you!"[82] Some accounts of life in the villages did stress the hardships involved, but most tended to gloss over them.

Red Guard attacks on the personnel responsible for such policies naturally portray them as men inspired by the most cynical of motives. It is important, however, to recognize the extreme pressure under which such people worked. It has been pointed out frequently that Mao's "mass-line" techniques, with their emphasis on persuasion and education, naturally only work when the policy advocated can be seen to be beneficial to those called upon to enact it. Clearly, any teacher or cadre faced with the task of persuading "educated youths" to sacrifice their whole lives in the most primitive conditions could obviously hope to succeed with only the most idealistic minority. Given Mao's faith in "the masses," however, any failure to implement policy was the responsibility of the cadre concerned. Consequently, the fear of incurring the disapproval of superiors drove many cadres and teachers not only to exaggerate the attractions of rural life, but also to coerce students to leave the cities. By such means they were able to present their superiors with admirable statistics of youths transferred to the villages. For example, in 1965 a "new mobilization" system was instituted at certain middle schools in Chiangmen. Students awaiting the results of the entrance examination to senior-middle school were harassed by tactics designed to make them "volunteer" for the villages, including demands that they surrender their residence cards under penalty of not being given notification of their examination results. They were also told that if they failed the examination they would not be given jobs in the city. In some schools principals and teachers wrote adverse reports on recalcitrants who refused to volunteer. Thus in the Chiangmen *Hua ch'iao* (Overseas Chinese) Middle School, the principal warned that, "those who refuse to go to the countryside are counterrevolutionary and shall never be given jobs."[83] Elsewhere, youths were also threatened with a change in their official class status if they resisted. Sometimes parents were threatened with dismissal from their jobs if they failed to persuade their children to leave the cities. Often, of course, coercion consisted simply of "prolonged mental torture" whereby a number of teachers concentrated on small groups of fourteen- or fifteen-year-old students, exhorting them constantly until they "volunteered" to go.[84] On occasion, quotas were made up by sending to the villages the very young, the frail, and the sick. Thus in Hunan, of 33 students sent to Lo-pai-yen Agricultural Farm in

Fu-shan, two suffered from rheumatic inflammation of the joints, four from stomach disorders, three from anemia, three from hepatitis, one from dropsy, and two from chronic appendicitis. In Chen-kuan *chen* (town) in Ch'a-ling hsien, Hunan, ten students were taken from the second year of junior-middle school to make up the required number. Among these were youngsters under thirteen, many suffering from various diseases including hepatitis, nervous disorder, and high blood pressure.[85]

The Chinese press frequently presented the "educated youth" in the villages as making major contributions to rural life, integrating with the peasants, earning their gratitude, and easily overcoming any hardships and difficulties encountered, the last point frequently being played down in any case. Thus a letter published in the Canton *Yang ch'eng wan pao* on February 17, 1965, described the experiences of Canton students in the villages as "not only a tense militant life but also a pleasant program coordinated with literary and artistic propaganda for politics and production that paves the way of changing the local customs and mores." In a detailed account of the activities of a group of students from the No. 2 Middle School of Canton who had gone to a commune in 1964, the article described the youths' contribution to the commune in smug paternalistic terms. Although "learning from the peasants" was mentioned, what the youths had done for the villages was emphasized: they had performed revolutionary dramas, taught revolutionary songs (including "Commune Members Are Sunflowers"), read newspapers to the peasants, carried out propaganda against "superstitious practices," and helped the poor and lower-middle peasants to carry water, cook food, sweep up, and cut animal fodder. No great difficulties were faced, all problems were speedily overcome, and the youths claimed that "during the several months of our settlement in rural villages, we have not stopped singing or joking."[86]

No doubt a number of youths from the towns were able to adjust to rural life and had the skill and motivation to make reasonably satisfactory careers for themselves. Sometimes they were well-received by the peasants and were able to become activists. Thus, a report on 2,200 "educated youths" from Amoy who went to rural areas in 1963 claimed that more than 260 of them had been rated as "five good workers," "six good commune members," advanced producers, or labor models. Ninety of them had been selected as leaders or deputy leaders of production teams, and many of them had joined the party or the league. Some were even elected as delegates to the hsien people's congress.[87] Other reports frequently mentioned that urban educated youths were given jobs as teachers in rural schools.[88]

Many, however, were not so fortunate, as accounts published during the Cultural Revolution have revealed. Whatever motivated educated youths to go to the rural areas, whatever the inducements or pressures used in the name of mobilization, it is evident that many of them suffered enormous privations in the villages. Literally millions of these youths flooded back to the towns in and after 1966 under the pretext of "making revolution," and their obvious feelings of grievance were manifested both in the violence of the attacks on those they blamed for their fate, and in their reluctance and indeed refusal to return to the countryside despite countless calls from the Maoist elite that they should do so.[89] Although it is likely that the accounts published by these youths are probably exaggerated somewhat, as with most Red Guard data, there is no reason to doubt the substance of the allegations.

Apart from the normal hardships of peasant life, educated youths often suffered from discrimination at the hands of the peasants and, on occasion, the local cadres. Not only did the peasants feel obvious resentment at the prospect of extra mouths to feed; the newcomers became a target for the peasants' hostility and feelings of envy toward city dwellers. The policy of sending down the academically second-rate, the politically undesirable, and the weak provoked a rural reaction that branded all educated youths as social misfits. In April 1962 one youth complained in a letter to *Chung-kuo ch'ing nien*: "After going back to the village, to my complete surprise, some villagers spoke badly of me behind my back. They said that those who returned to the rural areas for productive work were either people who have lazed around not working properly, or people who had made mistakes."[90] A good example of the way local cadres tended to regard educated youths as bad elements sent to the countryside for punishment is provided by a report from Hunan. There, the "top capitalist of Ling-ling hsien" stated that "young intellectuals come here to be remolded."[91] When one youth asked to what class young intellectuals belonged, a cadre of the Tung-shan-ling State Farm "pulled a long face and answered, 'The majority of young intellectuals are landlords' puppies. Your sons will also be landlords; your grandsons will still be landlords.'" Similarly, in a Kwangtung commune a cadre observed that good people did not come to the countryside; he told youths that "99 per cent of you are beyond salvation. You came here because you could not make a living in Chiangmen city."[92] Consequently, in many areas educated youths were not permitted to really integrate and were treated as a pariah caste. In Mu-chou commune, Kwangtung, one cadre told members that educated youths were of bad origin and were used to city life. They had been sent to the countryside to be remolded and therefore, he said, the poor and lower-middle peasants were to supervise them. In the Li-ts'un production brigade outside of Chiangmen educated youths were put to work along-side the "five bad elements," and at San-shui Agricultural Farm a "labor reform team of youths who arrived in the countryside" was established, putting youths in exactly the same category as prisoners undergoing "reform through labor" (*lao kai*) under police supervision.[93]

Sometimes youths were forbidden to exercise their "political rights." Thus in Ch'a-ling hsien they were forbidden to join the militia, or put up wall posters (*ta tzu pao*); at the onset of the Cultural Revolution, the Huang-pu brigade of Mu-chou commune refused to let them join Red Guard organizations and when they raised the matter in a poster, the brigade officially labeled them as rowdies, giving them the status of "social youth."[94] Peasant hostility could even manifest itself in attacks based on superstition. Thus, during the socialist education movement in Tung-shan-ling, a work team included the name of Wang Cheng-ming, an educated youth, in the list of class enemies who were to be struggled against. When friends asked why "small Wang" had been singled out, a peasant replied, "we do not need to have any data in order to struggle against Wang Cheng-ming. His pair of eyes is good evidence that he must be an anti-socialist element!" The unfortunate Wang had excep-tionally large eyes, a bad omen according to local superstition.

Because of the hostility they encountered, these youths were frus-trated further by not being permitted to use the limited technical skills they possessed; in one case from Hunan, for instance, the educated visitors, delighted to hear that their production brigade was to buy a pump, felt that their knowledge was to be used at last. The secretary of the commune party committee, however, quickly dispelled their illu-sions. Addressing the poor and lower-middle peasants he pointed out that "there are some sixty young intellectuals in your brigade, the great majority of whom are children of landlords and capitalists. We could not feel safe if the pump were placed under their control. We poor and lower-middle peasants must brace ourselves up and handle our own business by taking good care of the pump. Don't allow them to make use of their culture to push us aside." Because of this "we young intel-lectuals had no right to have anything to do with the pump. Sometimes when we stood closer to look at it or touch it, commune members watched us with their vigilant and antagonistic look. . . . Sometimes, when we heard the pump work for a while then stop for repairs we silently drew a sigh."[95] Often, of course, frustration was simply due to the great shortage of anything approximating mechanization in many communes. In a letter in *Chung-kuo ch'ing nien pao* on August 1, 1963, one youth complained:

Day in, day out, I am chained to the farm, with a hoe or a sickle in my hand. I work under the sun in the daytime and have the moon for company at night. I am indeed unfortunate and have no future at all. Are we creating a powerful society with modern industry, science, and culture? Can we say we are doing this when we have such primitive tools as hoes, sickles, and broken carts pulled by decrepit oxen?[96]

The educated youths also suffered economically. Apart from the fact that the standard of living in the rural areas was lower than in the cities, they were the victims of discrimination in pay. No doubt this partly reflected their inability to undertake the exhausting physical work to which the peasants were inured and their inability (either because of outright prohibition or the general absence of "sophisticated" machinery) to use what technical skills they possessed, but in fact they were sometimes paid at lower rates than local commune members. Thus in Mu-chou it is alleged that youths did the same kind of job as the peasants but received only 80 or even 60 per cent of the work points given to local workers. In this commune, moreover, ordinary members were credited with work points when they attended meetings (presumably political) whereas educated youths did not.[97] A breakdown of wages earned by members of the "mountain hawk" youth team at Tung-shan-ling reveals that sometimes youths were unable even to pay their way.[98] Five youths working there in December 1966 were charged a total of seven yüan for food each, yet not one of them earned more than 2.51 yüan. They ended up owing more than they earned. As a result of this system many were forced to borrow either from their parents or from the farm, where they were thus rapidly reduced to a state of virtual peonage. Some youths at Tung-shan-ling acquired debts ranging from 100 yüan to 600 yüan in four years. A youth who raised the matter of debt was told by a cadre, "It doesn't matter at all. If you can't pay the money, your son will; if your son can't, your grandson will." To try and break this vicious circle some young people undertook additional occupations such as working on private plots or fishing at night. Needless to say, overwork in bad conditions affected their health; in T'ai-shan youths who could not work because of illness were treated as absentees, losing two days' pay for one day's absence. In Hsiang-p'ing commune,

some fifteen- and sixteen-year-old girls were forced to marry early because of their inability to earn a living wage.[99]

A combination of hard work, atrocious conditions, inadequate pay,
lack of medical attention, and indifference or hostility from rural cadres
and peasants caused widespread illness—and occasionally death—
among young intellectuals. It was reported that 300 youths sent to the
Hsia-pa-shui area of Hua hsien in Kwangtung, allegedly by T'ao Chu,
were required to use river water for cooking, washing, and bathing. As
a result over 80 per cent of them became ill with rashes, high fever, dry
cough, eye diseases, and dysentery.[100] Youths who tried to leave the
countryside without authority were liable to suffer beatings and even
death at the hands of the peasants, and instances of girls being seduced
or raped have also been recorded. A final problem facing young intellectuals was the difficulty of finding a suitable spouse. The case of girls
forced to marry peasants for economic reasons has been mentioned. In
addition to this, the problem faced by young men in finding wives of
an equivalent level culturally was one mentioned by official sources as
early as 1957.[101]

Consequently, the educated youths came to constitute what was possibly the most explosive element in Chinese society. Sharing with the
peasant youths the general lack of opportunity for career advancement
vis-à-vis the "intellectual aristocrats" of the cities, they suffered from
the additional disadvantages we have mentioned. Having experienced
city life, and having been "rejected" by the system, they, more than
most, were a frustrated and disappointed group. Though it will take
considerable time before detailed analyses of Red Guard violence and
factionalism find their way into print, it seems reasonable to assume that
where anarchism has occurred, there will have been youths who have
returned from the countryside.

### The Role of the Communist Youth League

The attack on the Communist Youth League and its replacement by
a host of Red Guard organizations in the summer of 1966 seems inex-
plicable at first glance, for the league had always enjoyed a role as the
leading auxiliary of the party.[102] Moreover, since 1964 particularly, its
voice had been strident in support of Mao's policies to revitalize the
Chinese polity. In a detailed analysis of *Chung-kuo ch'ing nien*, the
league journal, James Townsend described its role in 1965 as that of a
"vigorous propaganda organ," its pages being dominated by three
themes apparently in accord with Mao's wishes:

One of these was glorification of the thought of Mao Tse-tung, stressing its usefulness in solving problems of any nature and its importance as the guide for all revolutionary action. Another was "serving the poor and lower-middle peasants," a theme which extolled the revolutionary class character of these groups and the ideological value of maintaining close contact with them. For intellectual youth, "serving the peasants" meant respecting them as people, demonstrating personal concern for their problems, and assisting them in education and the acquisition of modern knowledge. The third theme was glorification of physical labor in rural and mountain areas, and its slogan was, "One must revolutionize through labor."[103]

Underlying this apparent display of loyalty, however, there was a hard core of resistance to the pursuit of revolutionary goals. Policies implemented by the league since the early 1950's had caused it to develop into a rigid organization whose members often had a vested interest in the maintenance of the status quo and had no desire to be "revolutionized." As Townsend has observed of *Chung-kuo ch'ing nien*, "the printed page is easily changed to meet the demands of the times. An organization cannot transform itself so easily."[104] Moreover, as numerous examples from the Cultural Revolution have shown, because a policy was publicly advocated in official journals, it was not necessarily implemented or carried out without distortion.

Senior league cadres, whose sense of self-preservation was heightened by the renascence of Maoist ideals (through the medium of the People's Liberation Army, which was evident by 1964), gave lip service to Mao's instructions and then ignored or sabotaged them. An examination of the league's activities up to and in the mid-1960's provides information that demonstrates clearly why the organization became a target in 1966. Specifically, the factors responsible for the demise of the league were four-fold: it had failed to break away from its urban orientations; it had ceased to be a militantly class-conscious organization; its cadre policy had deadened revolutionary fervor; and it had given support to the "revisionist" educational policies implemented throughout urban China.

The strong urban bias of the league had been noticeable since the early 1950's when it had concentrated on building up organizations in the cities, and had neglected the rural areas. This, of course, was perfectly consistent with party policy at the time. However, because the league was a minuscule organization in 1949 that expanded enormously in the early 1950's, urban representation increased at a much faster rate than it did in the party itself, which in 1949 was already a large organi-

zation of overwhelmingly peasant membership with a much more cautious recruitment policy. In December 1951 the league's first secretary
had pointed out that only 52 per cent of league members were peasants
(at a time when peasants constituted over 85 per cent of the population). On the other hand 34 per cent were industrial workers and over
11 per cent were intellectuals.[105] Despite fluctuations, urban overrepresentation remained a noticeable feature of league membership as, increasingly, it did in the party. In 1959, the league announced that total
membership stood at twenty-five million, of whom only thirteen million
were in the rural areas.[106] This lack of interest in the countryside was
again confirmed in 1964, when it was reported that only 13 per cent of
rural youth were in the league.[107] Since in the previous year there were
about one hundred million rural youths in the age bracket eligible for
membership, it would appear that the number of rural youths in the
league had scarcely increased since 1959.[108] It is thus quite clear that
the benefits accruing from membership in the league were more readily
available to urban youths than to young peasants. The absence of hard
statistical data for the 1960's makes an accurate assessment impossible,
but it seems probable that in the early 1960's the average city youth was
three times as likely to be a league member as his rural counterpart.[109]

As for the class basis of recruitment, up to 1965 the league apparently
refused to admit any significant number of young people from the families of "bad elements" such as landlords, rich peasants, counterrevolutionaries, rightists, and criminals. However, the emphasis on political
purity favored not only industrial workers but two urban groups whose
revolutionary enthusiasm could not be taken for granted. First, there
were the children of senior cadres, who being of the "right background"
were able to gain admission relatively easily. This new privileged class
included many youths who assumed that they were automatically endowed with revolutionary virtue and, indeed, had virtually inherited it.
In the Cultural Revolution such youths sometimes formed "reactionary" Red Guard organizations to defend the status quo; as one critic put
it, they held the view that "if your father was a revolutionary, you're a
good son of Han; if your father was a counterrevolutionary, you're a
rotten egg." Second, there were the young intellectuals, many of whom
were from nonproletarian backgrounds; they were favored because of
the need for expertise. Many in this category were probably "careerists"
who sought league membership to give them an aura of political respec-
tability otherwise denied to them because of their class background.
By 1966 a majority of university students were league members, as were
many students in the senior-middle schools.[110] Hence by the 1960's, the

league had a number of members, particularly in the cities, who were inclined to see themselves as members of an elite organization; if the members showed the appropriate obedience and respect, membership would result in privileged roles in the society including, of course, enhanced opportunities to join the party itself. The lack of revolutionary fervor among league members had reached such a stage by 1964 that it was the cause of considerable concern to people like Mao who were dedicated to the belief that China could only be transformed by the inculcation of selfless ideals in the young. In one of the many editorials devoted to the matter, the party's theoretical journal pointed out the dangers facing the young:

The imperialists abroad headed by the United States pin their hope on the "peaceful evolution" of China through the degeneration of our third and fourth generations. *Who can dismiss this view as entirely groundless?* ... Now, in every sphere of life in China there is the class struggle with the overthrown reactionary classes plotting to stage a comeback. There are frantic attacks by the old and new bourgeoisie and degenerate elements who, like the imperialists and reactionaries abroad, are fighting and resorting to every means to win the younger generation from the proletariat and lead them onto the nonrevolutionary or counterrevolutionary path.[111]

Although not expressly stated, it is apparent that the league and its deficiencies were uppermost in Mao's mind at this time. Hu Yao-pang, the first secretary of the league, admitted in 1964 that "evil and degraded" elements had crept into the organization.[112] The league also admitted that it was desperately underrepresented in rural areas, and an attempt to rectify this situation and to revitalize the league was made in 1964.[113] The Ninth National Congress held in the summer of that year elected a new central committee and so brought some new blood into the leadership, although a number of members elected in 1957 and even in 1953 were reelected. The Ninth Congress also revised the constitution of 1957, which had been promulgated when the New Democratic Youth League was transformed into the Communist Youth League and which, significantly, had ignored the guiding role of Mao's thought, preferring to stress orthodox Marxism-Leninism. In 1964 the thought of Mao was restored to its rightful place in the ideological pantheon.[114] The league authorities were also required to vigorously support the movement to train "revolutionary successors," Mao's blueprint for preserving and continuing the revolution.[115] To further this movement, members were urged to participate in a number of ideologically oriented campaigns, the most important being the drive to "learn from the People's Liberation Army," the closely related "emulate

Lei Feng" movement, and, of course, a campaign to study the works
of Chairman Mao. Furthermore, the league called for the energetic expansion of its organization in the rural areas.[116]

Despite the widespread publicity given to Maoist policies in the pages
of league publications and in the speeches of officials, many youths refused to respond as readily or as speedily as Mao desired. In part this
was because appeals to "emulate Lei Feng" or to "serve the poor and
lower-middle peasants" were unlikely to appeal to relatively sophisticated and educated urban youths bent on advancing their careers. In
addition to this, however, there was the question of leadership. The evidence suggests that the league's basic-level cadres were often uninterested in pursuing Maoist goals and that senior cadres, particularly in
the cities, were often willing to actively oppose them. At the basic levels
the league organization was suffering from considerable rigidity by the
mid-1960's. Instead of being young selflessly motivated activists closely
involved with their members, many basic-level cadres had become "old"
time-serving bureaucrats interested in their own careers and unwilling
to involve themselves in activities that might lead to instability.

Since the 1950's the league had been faced with the problem of cadres
clinging to office, remaining in their posts long after they had reached
the normal "retirement age" of twenty-five. In March 1964, a Communist
Youth League work conference had addressed itself to the matter, calling for the retirement of overage members, particularly those with
cadre jobs, and stressing that the correct policy for staffing league organizations was "to promote young cadres boldly."[117] Yet eighteen months
later a discussion in the league newspaper, accompanied by calls for
a new policy of asking old cadres to step down and for the principle of
"one man one job" to be adopted, revealed that earlier appeals had
often fallen on stony ground.[118] This discussion, which was based on
"readers' letters," was published in November 1965; it hinged on the
fact that "in the past" a few people had monopolized a disproportionately large number of responsible positions in the league. One letter
from a Peking university student pointed out that some people had
started their "official" careers in primary school, where they had held
posts in the Young Pioneers, the party's organization for children under
fifteen. After that they automatically progressed to posts as league
cadres, continuing to advance up the league hierarchy until they left
university. Similarly, a Shenyang middle-school student complained
that a few favorites monopolized the available cadre posts, many holding several concurrently, so denying to other (and younger) youths the
chance to "develop leadership talents." It was also noted that many

league cadres, not surprisingly, had developed airs of "cadre superiority." They were, moreover, reluctant to "lose face" by making way for new men. If demoted, some cadres became upset and embarrassed because "they think the other students despise them, and they resent the new leadership."

The presence of status-conscious cadres who had given long service to the organization, and who in many instances had opted for political involvement at a very early age, not only helps to account for the organization's preference to continue operating through well-established and familiar bureaucratic procedures rather than to energetically effect radical change. It also indicates that by the mid-1960's the league was alienating some of its younger members by being unable to offer them the opportunities for advancement that it had offered in the 1950's. Whatever their motivations in seeking cadre posts, many politically ambitious youths, especially those who were "late developers," had little opportunity to advance because of the "bottleneck" caused by older or more senior cadres. Although it was stated in February 1966 that many league branch committee members were under twenty years of age, it is clear that in many instances old cadres refused to surrender power.[119]

There was, however, a certain irony in this situation that added to the league's difficulties, for the dissatisfaction of those who were unable to secure cadre roles was matched by the demoralization of cadres who could not opt out of an "activist" existence. In a stimulating discussion of factors influencing career choice in China, Michel Oksenberg has rightly observed that:

the more one opted for and secured the goals offered by the political system, the more difficult it became to opt out of an active involvement in political life and to pursue successfully those goals found outside its realm. . . . As a result of drifting into the "activist" role as a teenager, and then securing membership in the league, it was possible for Chinese to find themselves deeply enmeshed in politics, with little recourse but to sustain the level of activism necessary to retain the position they had attained.[120]

Within the league, as elsewhere in the Chinese political system, there were very real disadvantages in pursuing political goals and exercising political office. The discussion on office-holding mentioned above stressed that some cadres' health and studies had suffered because of the long hours they had to spend on league work. In February 1966 the league paper provided evidence that some cadres were clearly dissatisfied. During the campaign to "emulate Chiao Yü-lu," a number of league cadres confessed to having "previously" held erroneous ideas. Thus one youth admitted that he had been waiting for the day when he could "graduate" from league work to something higher, and another said that he had seen "no future" in work as a league cadre and wanted to continue his studies as a technician. A particularly interesting statement was made by a cadre from Chungking Architectural College who confessed that he had always been dissatisfied with work in the league, believing that as a university graduate he was entitled to something better. However, being bound by party discipline he was forced to continue working in a post he disliked.[121] Significantly, such confessions revealed that by 1966 career opportunities for which educational qualifications were a necessity were proving to be attractive alternatives to those based largely on political work. Youths who through political activism had been given the opportunity to acquire some education wished to go further academically; similarly, educated youths who had joined the league to demonstrate political responsibility appear to have later resented the time and energy spent on political involvement. Thus it seems clear that many of the league cadres entrusted with the work of implementing Mao's policies at the "grass roots" level were either uninterested or incapable of turning themselves into a revolutionary "shock force."

At higher levels, there was active opposition, for many league leaders, particularly those at the central and municipal level in Peking, were men who either had defended and developed the "revisionist" educational policies of the 1960's or had been influenced by those involved and thus had an interest in maintaining the status quo. In league work, as in party affairs, Peking especially became a hotbed of "revisionist" and "bourgeois" ideas on which the thought of Mao had little effect. The league's municipal committee was controlled by P'eng Chen's party committee, some of whom were active in disseminating anti-Maoist ideas among the young, particularly among the students of Peking, which boasted some three hundred middle schools in addition to its numerous institutions of higher education.[122] Teng T'o, for example, enthusiastically built up support among young intellectuals and was a regular participant in student discussions and youth forums.[123] Under his influence the league's municipal committee recommended that league cadres and young people generally should read the "poisonous weeds" put out by Teng and his friends, particularly "Three Family Village," "Front Line," and "Evening Chats at Yenshan."[124] Lu P'ing and Chiang Nan-hsiang, both of whom were ex-members of the league's central committee, made use of Sung Shih, deputy director of the Department of Higher Education under the Peking party committee, to advance their influence with the municipal league organization. Under such pressures the municipal committee supported the preservation of the "old" educational system and resisted demands that it be revolutionized. A major figure in this resistance was Wang Chia-liu, deputy secretary of the league municipal committee, who had been active in league work in the capital since 1954 and had been elected to the league's central committee in 1957. A specialist in university work, Wang was antagonistic toward any attempt to increase the amount of time students were to give to Mao's works, having no faith in "shouting empty slogans." Wang did not so much object to political education per se; rather he believed that Mao had little to offer the intelligent and educated. Thus he argued that "those of low [cultural] level should study Chairman Mao's works, and those of high level the classics of Marx, Engels, Lenin, and Stalin." It is claimed that he even dared to call into question the legitimacy of Mao's teachings by asserting that they were not truly Marxist-Leninist, a view common enough outside of China, but rarely voiced within.[125] Wang also objected to the time-wasting disorder that resulted from an overemphasis on political activities. Tolerant of such traditional values as friendship, which blur class lines, he stated that "class struggle must not be vulgarized, and class education must not be brought up everywhere." He especially opposed the teaching of politics in time better spent on academic study: it was "asking far too much to require junior-middle-school students to study Chairman Mao's works, and anyway why is it necessary to cultivate middle-school students into little politicians?" The municipal league committee similarly refused to propagate the thought of Mao by means of emulation campaigns and to implement the movement to "emulate Lei Feng," on the grounds of "formalism." The committee would not publicize the experience of a league branch that had placed the thought of Mao in command and, instead, ran an editorial in the municipal party newspaper to promote the experience of a rival branch that had not stressed Mao's guiding role. In the same vein, the committee in 1964 attempted to make Peking's No. 4 Middle School into a model where there was no class struggle.[126]

Although the most vicious and detailed attacks on the league have concentrated on the activities of the Peking municipal committee, the central committee itself did not go unscathed during the Cultural Revolution. A lengthy article by "proletarian revolutionaries" of the central organs of the league laid the blame for its deficiencies on Liu Shao-ch'i, who supposedly had been in direct control of the league since 1953. Some of the charges against Liu (and his "handful" of agents in the league's central committee) are identical to some leveled against him in connection with his work in the party itself. Thus he has been held personally responsible for the omission of Mao's thought from the 1957 constitution and has been accused of preaching his "docile tools" theory in and after 1958 in order to impress upon members the need to obey the organization unquestioningly.[127] Three other charges against him are particularly relevant to this study. First, Liu and his supporters in the league's central committee are accused of having fostered "bourgeois egoism" among league members; we have seen that such an attitude undoubtedly existed among many youths, and the league authorities failed to curb it. Second, they are charged with preaching the doctrine of "intellectual development first" in educational work. Again, such a view was certainly prevalent; indeed, in 1965 the central committee through its journals was taking the line that political and productive activities be suitably institutionalized so as not to interfere with students' academic work.[128] The third charge, that class struggle was ignored, is of special interest, for the league authorities on the eve of the Cultural Revolution openly pursued policies that (with the benefit of hindsight particularly) were obviously at variance with Mao's wishes. In 1965, a year after the league had called for expansion in the rural areas, a massive recruitment drive brought 8,500,000 youths into the league. It was claimed that this influx was possible because of the young's success in studying Mao's works and in participating in the three great revolutionary movements.[129] However, although the bulk of the new members were peasant youths, a small but significant number were children from upper-class families; in 1965, the league had instituted a campaign calling on its members to integrate with and so "educate" backward elements and children from politically dubious backgrounds.

A typical editorial, published by the league newspaper in April 1965, dealt with a factory in Tsitsihar in Heilungkiang, where there were fourteen youths from such families. It was explained that league members had regarded such youths and their parents as "birds of a feather" and had adopted the "mistaken attitude" of keeping their distance from them. This viewpoint was unjustified, it was argued, for "the great majority" of such youths were willing to take "the road of socialism" and had not participated directly in exploitation. Consequently, "we cannot regard them as elements of the exploiting class." Instead, "to unite with and educate them, win them over and transform them, is a responsibility of the league that should not be shirked."[130] Moreover, on numerous occasions in the first half of 1965 the league journal reassured such youths that they were welcome to join.[131] This "soft line" on doubtful elements might, at other times, have been in accord with Mao's belief in a person's ability to change his class standpoint if suitably "remolded," but it hardly fits with either the fear of "degeneration" among the young—so evident in Mao's attitudes at the time—or the extremely severe and exaggerated criteria used in class analysis in the early stages of the Cultural Revolution. Moreover, according to Red Guard allegations, far from instituting a vigorous policy of ideological education in 1965, the central committee of the league advocated a policy of "liberalization" by which people could voluntarily study Mao's works as they wished and for as long as they wished.[132] A Japanese journalist who visited league headquarters in October 1965 "noted the reluctance of the organization's leaders to discuss Maoist ideology except in the most perfunctory way."[133]

Apparently, then, some members of the league's central committee came to see little value in the concept of class struggle and were prepared to drop it altogether. Before the Cultural Revolution began Michel Oksenberg suggested that the recruitment of upper-class children into the league was motivated by a desire to prevent their becoming "alienated."[134] Subsequent events seem to justify that interpretation; the existence of a large number of people who believed that class struggle among the young was of no particular importance may have been what finally made Mao feel that he had been betrayed by the league, forcing him to look elsewhere for organizations to lead the young.

The Cultural Revolution was the product of many factors, and none was of greater importance than the struggle to determine the destiny of the young, particularly as that struggle manifested itself in terms of education. In 1966 teachers and cadres responsible for the propagation of "revisionist" and "bourgeois" educational ideas became one of the major targets for attack by the militant Red Guard factions, as did "reactionary" students who had a vested interest in the preservation of the status quo. One of the earliest victims of the Cultural Revolution was Lu Ting-i (although his "crimes" were by no means confined to the field of education). The persecution of Yang Hsiu-feng was so intense that he was driven to commit suicide. In educational institutions at all levels, "bourgeois authorities" were humiliated, and the schools were closed down.

Out of the chaos of 1966 and 1967, a new revolutionary educational system is emerging, one designed to produce "intellectual laborers endowed with socialist consciousness." The "bourgeois trick" of entrance examinations has disappeared, and the children of workers and peasants are being favored by a policy of relying primarily on class background and political consciousness as criteria for admission. The cur-

ricula of schools and universities are being revised to ensure that all
courses are no longer than necessary and are fully integrated with productive labor, so that the educational system may at last serve the interests of the proletariat. As far as possible the content of education,
even in such "abstract" subjects as mathematics, is being taught in
political terms. Throughout the new system runs the Maoist leitmotiv
that the purpose of education is to provide a little skill and a great deal
of political motivation. The object of emulation is no longer the parasitic "expert" from China Medical University, bent on a satisfying career in the big city, but the "barefoot doctor," a peasant youth equipped
with rudimentary medical knowledge, whose commitment is so total
that he is able to accomplish miracles in public health work in China's
villages.

For social scientists accustomed to thinking of modernization, and the
even more nebulous concept of "development," in terms of models derived from Western, Soviet, and Japanese experiences, it is difficult to
evaluate the Maoist attempt to solve China's problems without recourse
to an urban-based elite of specialists. In economic terms particularly,
it is difficult to see how rapid and sustained economic growth can be
achieved by Maoist methods. In political and social terms, however, it
may be argued that Mao is one of the few leaders in the underdeveloped world attempting to deal seriously with problems that are largely
ignored elsewhere. The problem of an urban elite divorced from rural
realities is by no means restricted to China, and perhaps the greatest
sign of Mao's originality is that he is genuinely attempting to eradicate
the "three major differences." In terms of China's social history no goal
could be more truly revolutionary.

# PART FOUR

# China's Urban Crisis

# Urban Residential Communities in the Wake of the Cultural Revolution

JANET WEITZNER SALAFF

In the atmosphere of competing political interests and demands that was created by the Cultural Revolution many issues concerning the quality of urban life and the problems of administering China's cities have come to the fore. One such issue, the difficulties of extending political control over and mobilizing the residential populace, is the focus of this study.

The development of urban residential administrative organs under Chinese Communist control has been a dual process involving the extension of administrative control and the encouragement of political mobilization in the neighborhood within the limits of this control. Chinese urban dwellers in general have become enmeshed in a network of civic and political groups since Liberation, but it is only certain sectors that have participated in the household-based residents' committees that are our main concern here. Chinese Communist urban administration has been guided by two principles of administrative and political organization. The first is functional, based on employment; the second is geographical, based on place of residence. Thus such persons as union members, office workers, and students are organized at their places of employment or study. Others such as housewives, children, unemployed youths, and retired workers are organized in the neighborhoods in which they live. The two organizational settings have not been equally effective in involving their members in the political process. In factories the daily interaction of workers stimulates the formation of informal cliques and groups. Given such a basis it is fairly easy for each worker to be integrated into a small group (*hsiao tsu*) that formalizes and controls small, face-to-face groups in sections of the factory. Residents are organized into similar small groups that may overlap or coincide with informal neighborhood and visiting patterns, but residents lack enduring structural ties, such as those based on work arrangements, that can compete with the bonds of kinship. Their basic allegiance, therefore, has been to the family unit rather than to the small group. This organizational problem—the lack of a satisfactory parallel organizational form that involves residents in political activities to the same extent as factory workers or students—was to be confronted during the Cultural Revolution.

In the early 1950's, following the upheavals of civil war, party work in the cities was concerned with extending administrative and political control to lower levels. In 1949 the Communists unified urban administration by eliminating the *pao chia*, a mutual responsibility policing system that had been inherited from the Nationalists and the Japanese occupation regime. By the end of 1954 the Communists had worked out a dual administrative framework based on the public security station (*kung an p'ai ch'u so*, or, more commonly, *p'ai ch'u so*) and the street office (*chieh tao pan shih ch'u*, usually shortened to *pan shih ch'u*).[1]

The public security station, which represented the lowest level of the hierarchy of the municipal bureaucracy, was an administrative and policing agency. Its main tasks—generally similar to European and Japanese police stations—were to register the population and to keep public order, which included not only the checking of criminal activities but also the maintenance of files on dubious or suspected residents. The station also served as a center for household registration and food rationing, and it processed applications for the special rations that were needed for travel out of the city. In its policing function, the public security station administered only relatively minor sanctions; the handling of major crimes was referred upward to the divisional headquarters. A dozen or more patrolmen handled traffic control and covered law and order beats. The role of the unarmed "Uncle Policeman" was not considered coercive; in fact he depended on a close relationship with residents for their assistance in security work in the neighborhood.[2]

The street offices were a parallel organization, for their administrative boundaries generally were the same as those of the public security stations. Their purpose was to mobilize the residents within the area for political activities and thus to strengthen the party's political control at the basic level. These offices became the lowest level of civil government (nonpolice) units in the city, and were operated by paid cadres assigned by the district branch of the city government. The cadres took over responsibility for registering vital statistics, which were passed on to the security station. They also handled the distribution of food ration coupons, supervised the work of mass organizations, assisted in the mediation of disputes, and disseminated propaganda.

### The Residents' Committees Before the Cultural Revolution

Under the jurisdiction of each street office were an unspecified number of residents' committees (*chü min wei yüan hui*), usually between ten and twenty. Not staffed by the street office and not official organs of the municipal administration, the committees were considered "autonomous mass organizations" that were headed by elected, unpaid, activist volunteers. Before the development of the residents' committees, when the authorities wished to mobilize the citizens for a particular campaign, special ad hoc committees for the purpose had been set up. The already existing mass organizations (for women, youth, etc.) were of course also expected to join in these campaigns. There was no clear separation of powers between the various mass organizations and the ad hoc committees, so the problem of "multi-headed" leadership was an inevitable result. Once the committees were set up, political participation was, in principle, to be developed through them under the direction of the street offices.

The residents' committees routinely carried out a large number of essential day-to-day services. First, they were charged with supervising the social service and welfare tasks of the residents. Second, they were to transmit and enforce government decisions and also to transmit citizen complaints "upward." In the large cities, where residents' committees were better organized, certain members were permanently responsible for the welfare tasks, which ranged from running nurseries, organizing handicraft work for unemployed residents, and supervising "livelihood service stations" (homemaking, sewing, mending, laundry) to operating an employment office. The residents' committees also played a crucial role in maintaining public order.[3] As early as the Yenan period, the Communists had encouraged mediation of civil disputes; in March 1954, mediation committees were formalized under the public security stations and street offices in each section of the city, with members drawn from the residents' committees. The committees were to hear local disputes and marital and family squabbles. In place of legal sanctions, they were to be able to use social pressure. (The extra-legal family conciliation courts in some American counties also try to "talk people back together.") The residents' committees were also linked to the public security organization by a security and defense committee (*chih an pao wei wei yüan hui*, sometimes shortened to *pao wei hui*), which was charged with reporting any suspicious activities in the neighborhood. These two committees—one for mediation and the other for public security—recruited members from each residential small group.

Subordinate to the residents' committee, each small group was made up of fifteen to forty contiguous households that elected a chairman and one member to represent them on the residents' committee. The function of the small group, like its counterpart in a factory or office, was political education. Political directives were passed down during group meetings, which served as the main channel for mobilizing the residential population. The well-organized public health campaigns, for example, were carried out by street office mobilization of the residents through their small groups. During the birth control campaigns of 1957–58 and 1963–64, the public health cadres propagandized birth control in the neighborhoods by working with the small groups; small group leaders and neighborhood women's representatives also went from door to door because some women would not attend meetings. It was through the small groups that the residents exercised their franchise in the district legislative body, the district people's congress (*ch'ü jen min tai piao ta hui*). Principally a symbolic and legitimating body, it meets only twice a year, chiefly to elect the members of the district people's council, who in turn make the real decisions at the district and street office levels.[4]

The vertical bureaucracy of the Chinese city is typically set up along the following lines. A large city of more than 100,000 (or sometimes of more than 50,000) is divided into districts (*ch'ü*), which are divided into subdistricts (*fen ch'ü*), each of which has one public security station and one street office. The street office has a permanent staff of up to seven persons appointed by the district, who direct and assist the residents' committees in the subdistricts, of which there may be as many as seventeen. Every family is normally required to send one member to a small group. Each small group elects a representative to serve on the residents' committee, and functional units and offices in each subdistrict also send representatives to sit in on the meetings of the residents' committee. (Politically disenfranchised residents—e.g., the "five-bad elements"—could and did attend small group meetings, but could not vote.)

Examples from several major cities can be taken as typical of urban residential organization throughout China. Shanghai was divided into ten districts. In Lu-wan district the residents' committee of Shuang-chang Lane has been described as typical. It comprised about a thousand households, from which six hundred persons were eligible for membership in the neighborhood organization. They formed 46 small groups. During the Cultural Revolution, this committee became one of the earliest organizers of a "revolutionary residents' committee."[5] Peking's central city had four districts. Ch'ung-wen district contained 288 residents' committees and was noted for activity in the Cultural Revolution.[6] Canton was divided into seven districts, which were subdivided according to this scheme. A typical street office in Yüeh-hsiu district contained about 15 residents' committees, each one responsible for five to six hundred households. Each residents' committee was further broken down into ten or more small groups, each with ten to fifteen members.*

## Pre-Cultural Revolution Leadership Style and Patterns of Resident Participation

Urban residents were encouraged to participate in political activities and to present their views through the small groups. They elected the group officers who led their activities and served on the residents' committees. Independent of the municipal administration, the residents' committees were intended to be the legitimate channel of the residents' political expression. This contrasted with the operations of the street offices, which were staffed by cadres appointed from above. An original goal of this residents' organization was to encourage the potential neighborhood leadership and to recruit a continual flow of new activists. In fact, the residents' committees and their leaders were tied tightly to the party structure and did not exercise power separately from it.

The system of indirect elections served to make the leadership of the neighborhood organizations dependent in part on the approval of the street party committee, and even to concentrate this leadership in the hands of party members. In the selection of the small group leaders, politically responsible activists—often retired workers and old party members—were recommended by the street party committee leadership. The party members in the small group introduced a slate of candidates; it was possible to campaign for an independent candidate, but

---

* Neighborhood associations in cities are not unique to Communist China, but are basic units of other Socialist nations' urban centers. The Cuban Committees for the Defense of the Revolution (CDR) are somewhat similar to the small group structure in China and the residential committees. The CDR membership is not limited to urban residents; committees are found in economic units throughout the country, and by 1963 the CDR contained one-third of Cuba's adult population. Similar in function to the residents' committees in Chinese cities, they perform both political and social work. Depending on the particular political campaigns in progress in Cuba, the CDR emphasize political education, political control and surveillance, and political mobilization. They also perform social service and welfare tasks, anti-illiteracy drives, public health work, cultural activities, and community development. For a discussion of the political functions of the CDR, see Richard R. Fagen, *The Transformation of Political Culture in Cuba* (Stanford: Stanford University Press, 1969), pp. 69–103.

since residents often believed, or knew, that the residents' committees had less connection with their lives than did the party, the proposed nominees were usually elected. The flow of new activists and talent into leadership positions may in fact have declined after the 1958–59 mobilization of the urban commune movement in the neighborhoods.[7] That movement tended to strengthen the local elite's informal control over leadership positions, and it enabled established local political bosses to fill and control nonparty leadership positions down to the street level. This style of political recruitment became a target during the Cultural Revolution, when the street organs were reshaped in order to eliminate the influence of established political figures.

The residents' committees had been organized some fifteen years before the Cultural Revolution, and in some cities the only substantial structural changes in community administration that had occurred happened during the 1958 urban commune movement. During periods of political consolidation after the Great Leap Forward, the residents' committee leaders did not emphasize mass mobilization. Their channels of communication and leadership tasks were fixed routinely at the officer level, over the heads of the residents. As in other "old" organizations, the leaders had more of a commitment to the administrative structure of their organizations—the patterns of activities and statuses, their salaries or social rewards—than to the political goals of the organization.[8] When the Cultural Revolution struck the neighborhoods with a new definition of political participation, most neighborhood cadres did not respond flexibly and found themselves under attack for putting survival of their organizations ahead of new political goals.

The residents' committees were only able to draw a minority of the total populace of available residents to attend meetings and participate in activities. Every household belonged to one small group, and thus to a particular street office. But only people not employed elsewhere were required to attend irregularly scheduled meetings of the small group, whose tasks were minimal anyway. Each household in the district sent one member (perhaps an old woman or a child) and the small groups, according to informants, became an arena of the very old, who used this as a gossiping ground and were encouraged to spy on others' activities. Although there were genuine activists in the residential groups, such persons considered themselves rare, and spoke wryly of their ineffectiveness in trying to integrate the personal lives of the residents with the high moral and political standard they thought the nation should attain.

The failure to integrate the unemployed was particularly striking. For instance, in Canton during recent years population growth and faulty industrial planning left an estimated one-half of the junior-middle-school graduates without places in senior-middle schools. A further two-thirds of the senior-middle school graduates did not continue on to the university.[9] According to an informant from Canton, between 60 and 80 per cent of these in recent years failed to find jobs.[10] Though attempts were made to send about one-fourth of them to rural areas,[11] many returned to the city. The others hunted for handicraft work through the residents' committee labor service stations. Added to this number were many housewives who wanted jobs to supplement their incomes but could not find them and so retreated into their family groups. The small group meetings did not discuss the livelihood questions that might have aroused the interest of members. The dissatisfied group of unemployed later sought to remove from the residents' committee leaders who did nothing to improve the employment situation. At the same time, the enthusiasm of the enrolled students could not be tapped at the residential level because primary- and middle-school students were already organized at their schools. The structure was built to pull members out of their private family living space, but interest in leadership had been discouraged among residents, and there was little opportunity for residents to become activists.

## The Impact of the Cultural Revolution on the Neighborhoods

On the neighborhood level the Cultural Revolution resulted in an increase in the political involvement and participation of residents in community activities along fairly specific lines. First, the former administrative structures that had been bypassed or overrun during the Cultural Revolution were revamped provisionally to encourage an increase in residential political participation, although there were still limits on the type of political activities performed. Second, new and intense types of political study meetings were established that functioned not only to stimulate radical change but to control it within bounds. Third, ad hoc administrative changes in the system of policing and public security were made, aimed at increasing the revolutionary residents' powers of self-policing to cope with the chaos created by the movement and to establish an atmosphere of security. We turn now to a discussion of these developments, finally noting the effect of the Cultural Revolution on family solidarity and on the involvement of the family in the political system.

The first goal of the Cultural Revolution in the neighborhoods was to elicit criticism and expressions of repudiation of the political style of the street party committees. Although the residents had long been organized into political groups through which they were to express their opinions, concern for the political consequences of criticism had inhibited them. In many cities, the Cultural Revolution provided the first opportunity in ten years for residents to raise personal and local problems. The residents were eager to criticize the lane cadres, the nearest political authority figures to them, but they still were afraid to attack the street party committees. The demands of the residents, who were mostly housewives, concerned the economic or political treatment of their families; moreover, the political stance they took in the neighborhoods was often influenced by the alliances made by their husbands in work units and by their children in schools.

Many urban residents protested the moving of urban workers and students to rural villages and frontier and border regions. Shanghai residents protested this policy early in the Cultural Revolution, since for over ten years large numbers of Shanghai youths had been sent to the villages to do physical labor. For example, at the time of the Cultural Revolution, two thousand Shanghai youths were working in a forestry station in Anhwei. The policy of sending groups of Shanghai students to particular parts of Chekiang, Anhwei, and Sinkiang allowed them to communicate while they were outside of the city; thus they supported one another's grievances and by 1966 were easily persuaded by local provincial authorities to leave en masse. After following the exciting course of the movement in Shanghai from afar, they abandoned their rural posts and returned to the city, with the encouragement of local cadres.[12] Reacting to the flood of returned youth, urban neighborhood cadres organized residents to urge their children to go back again, and in each Shanghai district a revolutionary rebel headquarters of the Revolutionary Parents of Shanghai Aid Sinkiang Youth was formed. The Cha-pei district parents, for example, were reported to have gone to the train station to see off their children who were returning to Sinkiang.[13] But the climate of the times also allowed parents to reverse the orders; many complained that their children had been mistreated in Sinkiang by the workers' construction corps,[14] and they petitioned the Shanghai revolutionary committee to demobilize their children so that they could return to Shanghai "as soon as their terms were filled" (even though there were, however, no fixed terms of service for youths in the border regions). In some neighborhoods they protested to the lane cadres, holding them personally responsible for ensuring their children's return.[15]

Residents also demanded hearings to review the political status of their families. Although some complaints concerned the classifications of 1952, the most frequent were calls to review the changes in status that had been promulgated during the four clean-ups campaigns (*ssu ch'ing*) two years before.[16] The preoccupation of the protagonists in the Cultural Revolution to "correctly" classify the class status of people in authority[17] raised hopes among families that were dissatisfied with their class labels. Posters and petitions flooded rehabilitation centers of the work units of the revolutionary committees.[18] Accusation meetings were held in the newspaper reading groups, at which lane cadres were criticized for the political treatment they had meted out over the years.[19] In the Hung-k'ou district of Shanghai as early as December 1966, residents held meetings in which the lane party cadres had to bow their heads and confess to mistreatment of the families accusing them. Such confrontation meetings to avenge "blood debts" grew more numerous during the periods known as "adverse current of capitalist restoration" in Shanghai during the spring of 1967, and probably during the "evil wind of reversal of verdicts" in the following year. The "revolutionary rebels of Cha-pei police station" reported on one neighborhood accusation meeting that was dominated by a woman of undesirable class background, who scolded the cadres: "In the past you fought against our father, today it is your turn!"[20] Accusations against lane cadres became so numerous that a meeting was held by the preparatory committee of the Shanghai Nan-shih district security bureau on February 11, 1967, to check those who acted against lane cadres under the pretense of avenging blood debts; and one man was arrested to set an example.[21]

A residential neighborhood's political stance was generally influenced by the affiliations of the breadwinners and students there. Neighborhoods in which numerous workers were employed in a local factory, or in which there was a school, tended to support the dominant factions in these units, and students and workers frequently propagandized the residential areas to solidify support. Changchun revolutionary rebel organizations held street debates to encourage residents to come into the Cultural Revolution on their side.[22] In some cities Red Guards joined the residential newspaper reading groups. Some Shanghai factory workers found themselves under attack in one lane meeting as representatives of the "men in power";[23] the reason for this may have been that the female residents were influenced by husbands belonging to rival factions.

In some areas housewives and unemployed youths demonstrated to protest the scarcity of employment in the neighborhood service stations. These complaints were similar to those expressed in the Red Guard papers of the time by part-time and contract workers in factories. Local street cadres attempted to deflect these demands into political channels. Furthermore, many residents were angered by the excesses of the Cultural Revolution. They held lane cadres responsible for the return of any money and belongings that had been confiscated by Red Guards during the "destroy the four-olds" movement. Residents formed vigilante groups to halt petty crime, to guard their homes, and to stem black-marketing.

For some residents, political participation was stimulated by such grievances. But the criticism and repudiation of party officials could not be solidly based on such local and short-term problems. Nor could lane cadres or People's Liberation Army officials bypass the residents and issue unilateral orders calling for political struggle against the local elite, because such a political changeover needed popular support and some form of legitimacy. The problem was to find a way to arouse the residents without allowing spontaneous and complete popular formation of policy. Thus the timing and the nature of neighborhood political reorganization, to which we now turn, was important. In particular, we will discuss the functions of the study classes on Mao thought, which were the characteristic organizational form designed to stir up and at the same time contain residential participation during the Cultural Revolution.

### Reorganizing Neighborhood Administration

Since the Cultural Revolution began in Shanghai, this movement to seize power faced the initial problem of activating political participation in China's largest and most sophisticated city. But in all urban areas for which data on the timing of the formation of neighborhood revolutionary committees are available, successful attempts to overcome the political vacuum in the administration of residential areas were made only after revolutionary groups were formed at municipal levels. In most cities the "productive" units—factories, schools, hospitals, and offices—established alliances first, building support from the bottom up for the provincial and municipal revolutionary alliances. Neighborhood or street residential reforms in Shanghai, Canton, and other cities followed the establishment of municipal and district alliances by at least two months. This time sequence suggests a definite reliance on support from revolutionary alliances in work units and on the municipal and district levels.

We can trace the development of revolutionary committees in Shanghai's neighborhoods, the first city to set them up. The first district revolutionary committee was established in the centrally located Huang-p'u district, the location of the people's park where many rallies were held. The first revolutionary residents' street committee in Shanghai, set up in May 1967, was on Ku-ling Road in a densely populated area of

Huang-p'u district. The establishment of this revolutionary street committee helped consolidate the alliance at the higher level of the street
office, which in turn influenced the establishment of other residential
committees under it. The next district in Shanghai to form a revolutionary committee, on April 7, 1967, was Ch'ang-ning district, to the
west of Huang-p'u district in central Shanghai. A month later the district's first residential revolutionary committee was set up on Hsin-hua
Road. Close proximity to Huang-p'u, which became a model of "advanced achievements," greatly facilitated the establishment of committees in Ch'ang-ning, whose cadres sent over representatives to study the
example of Ku-ling Road.[24] Thus, from the center of the city to the
periphery (P'u-t'o district on the outskirts was the last), Shanghai's ten
districts and their neighborhood revolutionary committees were set up,
a process that with some difficulties took one year.

Other major cities followed Shanghai's example. In Canton the municipal revolutionary committee, set up in March 1968, was followed
after four months of study by the first revolutionary street committee
on T'ai-k'ang Street.[25] Finally, smaller cities, *hsien* centers and *chen*,
followed the example of each provincial capital. In September 1968,
however, it was stated that "the iron broom of revolution has not yet
reached the towns." Hankow Radio chided revolutionary organizers by
saying it was not true that because most of the residents in towns were
old people, the weak, the women, and the children, it was difficult to
organize them; and it was not true that the masses of people did not
have much concern about politics and that their standard of struggle
was very low. Political activists were urged to overcome the notion that
"the people in towns lag behind."[26]

When the street revolutionary committees were finally in the process
of being set up, they were guided by politically reliable persons from
rebel groups outside the neighborhoods. Shanghai may have had more
spontaneous residential organization than other cities, for alert cadres
organized study classes there as early as November 1966, but in most
other cities the decision to push the Cultural Revolution into the neighborhoods came from the municipal revolutionary committees. In Harbin, for example, the municipal revolutionary committees held a meeting to discuss the necessity of, and means of, carrying the Cultural Revolution into the neighborhoods. After these meetings loyal street cadres
and participants in the neighborhood revolutionary mass organizations
were exhorted to hold residential mass criticism and repudiation meetings, run study courses, and seize power in the residents' committees.[27]
The formal political links these neighborhood mass organizations had

with workers' rebel and Red Guard alliances outside the neighborhoods
are not clear. The criticism and repudiation meetings took the form of
street debates of residents and cadres so that "people with different
opinions would speak up in public," and those who harbored doubts
about the movement could express them in the open. Residents would
release pent-up grievances against the existing power structure, inspir-
ing others to join in and support a power change.[28] Those voicing politically regressive ideas would probably find themselves criticized. Criticism and repudiation sessions were a means of liberating most cadres.
Street cadres were to engage in self-criticism admitting their mistakes;
they generally deflected criticism from themselves to the top men in
authority. They would then allow themselves to be reeducated by the
liberated cadres and masses. In Shanghai's Ku-ling Road two-thirds of
the street cadres exposed and denounced their own past attitudes and
leadership styles, and then joined neighborhood revolutionary mass organizations. These criticism and repudiation meetings were also used
to purify mass organizations that had advocated erroneous policies and
to prepare the way for the formation of provisional power organs in
residential areas.

In early 1968 activists and representatives of grass-roots revolutionary residents' organizations were fairly influential in the residential administration, but this was to be temporary. The expansion in numbers
of committee members at first added to their influence, but the movement to simplify administration in mid-1968, followed by the settlement
of some residential population in the countryside starting in the winter
of 1968–69, reduced their numerical representation. Moreover, the new
neighborhood mass revolutionary alliances were given representation
in the revolutionary street committees and street offices only while the
Cultural Revolution was in progress; their disbandment meant that residents no longer had independent informal power bases from which to
exercise their influence in the new administrative organ.

Shanghai's first residential revolutionary committee in Ku-ling Road
illustrates the relative representation of different local interests. In
March 1968 the revolutionary street committee had 22 members, representing a constituency of 11,000 households, or 46,000 people. This
committee included sixteen representatives of various local mass organizations; three were representatives of the district organizations of government workers; three others represented local revolutionary organizations. Of the 22, sixteen were women, and sixteen were party members.[29]
In this case, there was an equal number of representatives from revolutionary organizations and workers' rebel groups, which suggests that
the revolutionary residents were given considerable power. In other

residential committees, however, public security representatives were present; in such cases the sheer number of representatives of outside alliances—workers and public security representatives—would set real limits on the influence of the locally recruited revolutionary activists in the residents' committees.

The degree of influence of the activists also varied over the course of the Cultural Revolution. Early on, the process of electioneering was not rubber-stamping but was accompanied by street debates and critical wall-poster advertising of merits and defects. In one reported case where the local cadres had criticized the party committee and unilaterally seized power without involving the revolutionary activist residents, cadres were later forced to concede some power. The revolutionary residents' committee of Hsin-hua Road, in Shanghai's Ch'ang-ning district, which had been staffed by the preparatory committee of local cadres, found themselves forced to relinquish their monopoly of positions by adding representatives of revolutionary organizations. Revolutionary residents used the same arguments made against the old power structure to attack the new one, complaining that the street three-in-one residents' committees were as bureaucratic as before, "monopolizing everything" and "lacking trust in the masses." They were able to force the revolutionary committee cadres to hold a meeting attended by representatives of revolutionary residents, at which revolutionary residents were selected to participate in an enlarged revolutionary committee.[30]

This did not solve all the problems of representation, for the residents were at a disadvantage in participating with experienced cadres.

Elected members of the revolutionary committee, the revolutionary residents were both happy and worried. They were happy because the laboring people had won emancipation under the leadership of Chairman Mao and the Communist party and had also grasped power. They were worried because they belonged to a low cultural level, were slow of speech, and feared that they could not do their work well. Some representatives even thought of themselves as "supporting actors," thinking that they came from the alley and were inexperienced in leadership work and that it would be better to let the cadres of residents' organs play the leading roles. Some other representatives thought of themselves as "temporary workers," thinking that they came from among the residents and were not cadres and that they might be regarded as a cadre today but would become an ordinary resident when they moved to another place tomorrow.[31]

In decision-making the residential representatives thus clearly lacked the political influence of the party members, workers, and public security officials in the new residents' committees.

The political goal of the Cultural Revolution in the neighborhods was to bring residents more closely into the municipal political system by encouraging residential participation in the political movement, whereas the residents' committees were reorganized to better respond to and control the residents. The criticism and repudiation of street party committee members and local cadres was couched in terms of eliminating their bureaucratic work style. Rebels spoke of "maintaining close contact with the masses." Leadership had found that total control of decision-making from the top resulted in a disaffected populace.

The most fundamental principal in the reform of state organs is that they must keep in contact with the masses. The revolutionary leading cadres of this residents' committee formerly suffered from China's Khrushchev's bourgeois reactionary line and were influenced by old work styles and old rules and conventions. In doing something they acted slowly and shifted responsibility to others, and the general office shifted the responsibility to the party committee. Everything had to be "studied" or "discussed." The contact with the masses was relatively poor.[32]

The provisional three-in-one political form was itself seen as one structural means to facilitate mass residential participation in policy execution. The "unified leadership" of the residents' committees allowed for the bypassing of some steps in the transmission of directives, but such a system depends on transmitting directives in mass meetings, and popular receptivity tends to be relatively high when a movement is in progress. What happens after the movement is always a question.

Formerly, when some work was arranged for the residents' committees, its secretary, chairman, and members first met to discuss the questions and the cadres unified their thinking before "forcing" this work on the residents; this assignment had to go through many levels and complicated formalities. Now whenever a task arises the revolutionary committee would call a congress or an enlarged meeting of its members, in which the representatives of revolutionary cadres, the public security organ, and revolutionary residents take part, so that this task goes through fewer levels and is assigned to the grassroots level straightforwardly, quickly, and accurately. Ordinary residents also join in the leadership of the residents' committee and behave as "masters of the house," thus guaranteeing the close relationship between the revolutionary committee and the masses.[33]

The party members also came under attack for having monopolized political decision-making without giving even an appearance of seeking out the opinions or approval of the residents; this had inhibited resident involvement and identification in street political work. There were two ways of dealing with the party monopoly of political roles: one was to decentralize the operations of the residents' committees; the other was to send cadres to special "May 7" cadre schools to engage in manual labor and self-criticism.*

Formerly, when a secretary of the party residents' committee visited the residents his assistant accompanied him issuing orders, and he assumed the airs of the master. At present, the committee chairman and members and the ordinary cadres go to the residents' groups and homes to consult the masses of the residents on the work to be done.[34]

The Hsin-hua Road Revolutionary Committee (Ch'ang-ning district, Shanghai), started this trend of paying door-to-door visits and listening to the views of the masses. Similarly, representatives at district levels were also to take personal responsibility to transmit directives down to the streets, bypassing the formal channels of communication within the bureaucracy.

Formerly, China's Khrushchev and his agents in Shanghai, such as Ch'en P'ei-hsien and Ts'ao Ti-ch'iu, blocked Chairman Mao's directives at different levels. Sometimes they transmitted the directives with a part of the contents held up, so that a pigtail that was assigned at the top level would be reduced to a single hair when it reached the grass-roots level. At present the revolutionary committee transmits Chairman Mao's latest directives to the grass-roots level directly.[35]

In sum, the revolutionary residents' committees incorporated several structural reforms that worked to decentralize the political processes and to increase the involvement of residents in political processes. The three-in-one format brought worker and public security representatives into the committees in greater numbers; thus the residents' committees were tied into the municipal system. More characteristic of the administrative reforms encouraging residential political participation was a critique of leadership styles. In such ways, the revolutionary committees were not only expanding residential participation in policy execution but retaining control over policy formation.

## Political Study and Political Participation

Political study had a role in stimulating political reforms in the neighborhood by creating an area of political participation considered proper by the leadership under Mao. Political study also functioned to resolve

---

* As the Cultural Revolution drew to a close, schools for the reeducation of all cadres were set up, in accordance with the directive that all cadres should in turn do manual labor. Schools for cadres existed before; this one emphasized common activities with the peasants through labor, rather than political study alone. Ten thousand cadres of the Shanghai area were attending school by October 1968. One school that housed 3,000 in rotation was investigated by Han Suyin in "A May-Seventh School for Cadres," *Eastern Horizon*, VIII: 6 (Nov.–Dec. 1969), 6–15.

factional disputes and to bring the Cultural Revolution in the neighborhoods nearer "completion." The struggle for power was aroused, controlled, and channeled largely through the Mao Tse-tung thought study classes, which all residents were required to attend.

Started as voluntary classes organized by lane cadres and adapted to the former structure of the residential small groups, the study classes changed in form and content between 1966 and 1969. One early report of such classes was in Yenan Street, Ching-an district, Shanghai, where alert lane cadres organized newspaper reading groups to develop criticism against the district party committee. Forty of the 680 families living in the lanes joined in organizing the study groups, which also supervised the fifteen residents identified as five-bad elements during the "destroy the four-olds" movement.[36] There were, however, limitations to the early newspaper reading groups, since they contained the same residential households as the small groups. Some families were chiefly interested in revenge against their lane cadres, and others were as delinquent in attendance as they had been before. These small groups were superseded by a "flexible variety of forms," with an emphasis on total and intense involvement of the entire residential populace.

With the residential small groups finally abandoned, classes were organized along social and demographic lines rather than by residence. Some were composed entirely of women, primary-school children (called "little Red Guard fighters"), or retired workers. In others, the evening study sessions were attended by whole family units, and family study within the home also became popular. This type of study class differed significantly from the pre-Cultural Revolution neighborhood small group, because now family members confronted each other. The more involved youths and workers could influence the less involved housewives, and family resistance to the Cultural Revolution could be more easily overcome. Additionally, these study classes were put in the hands of trusted leaders, for a fair number of the former small group leaders were influenced by "the bourgeois line" and had to be reformed. The size of the study classes exceeded that of the former neighborhood small groups: in Lu-wan district of Shanghai, for example, each of the original 46 residents' groups were enlarged so that the total number was reduced to 25, a change that might have been due to leadership shortages.[37]

Street meetings and debates were thus followed by political study, a structured and more intense form of criticism and repudiation.

There are two methods in general use [for political study]. One is to use Chairman Mao's teachings in combination with the residents' sufferings in old

China to refute the revisionist theories of China's Khrushchev. . . . The other method is through struggle meetings that expose the crimes of the diehard expropriated landlords and rich peasants, counterrevolutionary elements, bad elements, and rightists. Through the exposure and condemnation of crimes of these class enemies, the residents uncover and condemn the crimes of China's Khrushchev in his attempt to bring about a restoration of capitalism in China.[38]

The method of political study that involved using Mao's teachings in combination with the residents' sufferings evoked emotionally charged memories that were then transferred to the current situation. The second method—calling forth hatred of crimes suffered in the past and then accusing individuals of responsibility for these crimes—was directed against the street party administrators whom the populace was previously afraid to attack. One retired workers' circle read four quotations per meeting, and each worker contributed stories and anecdotes from his own life to illustrate the quotation. In this manner residents were encouraged through study activities to attack and criticize the party committee members.

The readings, which consisted of Mao's sayings, the "three widely read pieces," and specific directives, were suited to the many political tasks at hand. From late 1966 through 1967 the readings were meant to encourage the residents to rebel. Mao's thought, dealing with the relations between the leaders and the led, contained general prescriptions and tools to encourage the residents to formulate opinions and find fault with the established bureaucracy. Each directive had a target related to the struggle process of the period. Mao's directive of May 8, 1967, for example, was used the next month when Shanghai neighborhood discussion groups were organized more widely;[39] its themes were the importance of overthrowing the power holders in the neighborhood; how to distinguish the people in authority taking the capitalist road; encouragement for the street dwellers themselves to carry out revolution without relying on the cadres, Red Guards, or workers; the need to reform the public security substation; and the importance of continuing struggle against the five-bad elements. The readings provided the basic framework of accepted values within which people were brought together to discuss specific problems. Although the problems were defined from above, the study sessions did not involve rote repetition. The form of face-to-face interaction, one widely understood from past small group experience, was used to replace factional fighting. The process of study, of application, and of criticism was a powerful tool, for decisions emerging from the study sessions were binding.

The process of political transformation in the neighborhoods was slow because of the residents' reluctance to attack the party's authority. One year after the establishment of the Shanghai Revolutionary Committee, the task of criticizing the old-guard leadership had still not been completed in the Shanghai neighborhoods, even where the provisional revolutionary three-in-one residential associations had been formed:

The remnant influence of the counterrevolutionary revisionist line put forth by China's Khrushchev and his agents in Shanghai . . . is deeply rooted and widespread throughout this city, particularly in the streets and neighborhoods. . . . The handful of capitalist roaders in leadership organizations, such as neighborhood party committees, neighborhood administrative offices, and other organizations above this level have not yet been completely overthrown. . . . Many bad elements . . . hoodlums, delinquents, reactionary bourgeois people, and other types of bad people are still taking shelter in the dingy corners of the streets and neighborhoods.[40]

The criticism sessions created problems in addition to the misdirected rebellion against local-level cadres in early 1967. Criticism sessions encouraged neighbors to express longstanding grudges that were not easily resolved and that sidetracked the process of criticizing party officials. It was reported from Hankow that criticism and self-criticism sessions created so much factionalism that:

old friends and neighbors fell out and in many cases refused to speak to each other for more than a year. Almost in desperation the "lane committees" invited soldiers from the People's Liberation Army to visit them to try and straighten out what had become a serious tangle. In the end, they accepted the advice of the soldiers to abandon their enjoyable habit of vocal criticism of each other and to replace this with vocal self-criticism for a trial period. The upshot was a speedy reconciliation and formation, overdue, of the now famous "three-in-one" combination. The district, in fact, has never really returned to mere criticism as a way to get things done.[41]

Thus the nature of the study sessions changed in 1968 to single out more precisely those to be attacked and to lay the bases for these attacks. In the summer of 1968 neighborhood study sessions like those in the schools were taken over by the People's Liberation Army (PLA), worker propaganda teams, and retired workers, and the study sessions became more frequent. The soldiers and workers endeavored to connect the sessions to the other cultural revolutionary activities in the neighborhoods and to overcome emergent factionalism.

Political study has continued to play an important role in the neighborhoods. Generally each important political directive is studied at least once in the residents' study groups. One form of ideological study that was continuously applied to consolidate the results of the Cultural Revolution after the power struggle was called "heart-to-heart talks." These were conducted in productive units and elsewhere to overcome animosity between the factions that took control and the cadres and others who had joined losing factions.[42] Worker propaganda teams in effect divided the factions, reasoned with them separately,[43] and removed the few die-hard agitators.[44] In this manner power struggles in the neighborhoods were apparently brought to completion.

## Rebuilding Public Security in the Neighborhoods

Illegal migrants and unregistered residents working in underground jobs lived fairly easily from the black markets or their families' help prior to the Cultural Revolution, but in the wake of this political movement there was a tightening of security and new policing forms were introduced.

The Cultural Revolution disrupted formal and informal mechanisms of political control in the neighborhoods. The usual day-to-day tasks of neighborhood public security substations—population registration, traffic control, and the issuing of rations—were no longer carried out in most cities by early 1967, after the security stations were taken over because of their support for the local party committees. With the changes in power structure in the residents' committees, the security defense committees and the mediation committees, which had been the informal means of maintaining order and resolving disputes in the neighborhoods, also ceased to function. Party members, local-level cadres, and activists who had participated in these security and mediation committees lost their personal authority during the criticism and struggle against them. The disruption of both formal and informal mechanisms for maintaining the collective order in the neighborhoods prevented them from halting chaos in the streets.

Although the extent to which the residents themselves took up arms is not clear, factional fighting is known to have spread from schools and factories to the residential areas in the summers of 1967 and 1968 in Kwangtung and elsewhere. In July 1967 the water and electricity supplies and the phone service were cut off in Canton; and in August 1967 transportation and communications facilities in Kwangtung were disrupted.[45] Residents put up blockades, and curfews, looting, petty theft, bicycle thievery, pickpocketing, and muggings were serious threats to the populace.[46] The disorder created further urban problems: shortages of goods—especially of cloth and coal—were reported, due in the main to transportation bottlenecks; in the following winter, water and power shortages, resulting from sparse summer rains in Kwangtung, forced rationing of electricity in Canton. This inconvenience, which would normally have been tolerated, renewed anxieties born of the previous year's experiences.

When the public security stations, confronted with their loss of political authority, stopped making household checks, large numbers of people entered the city and lodged with relatives in search of better opportunities. Some were ex-landlords who had fled difficult rural conditions, but the majority were youths who had been sent down to villages before the Cultural Revolution. Their parents harbored them without the necessary residence permits.

The first attempt to deter unrest, violence, and petty theft in the neighborhoods was made by the PLA, which established military control committees to manage public security. In Canton this occurred in February 1967, but the army did not assume responsibility for security until mid-1967. In some places the army attempted to confine urban disturbances without taking a position, but in other areas the army purposefully tilted the balance toward one of the less extreme revolutionary organizations. The fact that before 1967 PLA recruits were rarely stationed far from home may have involved them in local factionalism.[47] When Mandarin-speaking units from outside the province were transferred to Canton, they seemed to enforce the ban on violence more impartially. Measures to keep the PLA impartial included a ban on their purchase and reading of Red Guard newsletters.[48]

Individual cities and even small areas within them had independent solutions to violence in the neighborhoods beginning in late 1967 and early 1968. In May 1968 in Kwangtung, Nanchang, Peking, and Shanghai revolutionary rebel factory groups organized "workers picket teams" to reestablish order in the area. They worked with five- to ten-member Red Guard teams from colleges and universities, touring the neighborhoods in units, wearing their own badge and insignia, armed with knives and tasseled clubs. Two teams were formed in Canton—the Workers Picket Team, organized by the East-Wind faction, and the Peace and Order Picket Team, which represented the factory workers of the Red Flag faction. There were 5,000 members of these teams in Canton in May and June of 1968, apparently as a result of Peking's concern to have a peaceful spring fair. Organized under the army,[49] they nevertheless had trouble keeping order because the two teams were drawn into factional struggles and were suspended soon after the fair. Shanghai Radio announced on January 19, 1968, that in response to the vocal demands of the residents, a specially created "Shanghai municipal command for rectifying traffic order" would take responsibility for highway traffic inspection, the enforcement of traffic control, and the improvement of street order.[50]

With the establishment of revolutionary committees in the neighborhoods, concern for restoration of public security came to the fore. This was desirable both to halt violence and to establish political control. The revolutionary committees now combined police work and civil enforcement of the criminal process. The presence of public security representatives in the neighborhood revolutionary committees facilitated the formation of "three-in-one" public security enforcement teams, composed of representatives of the police, the revolutionary cadres, and the revolutionary residents.[51] In Canton similar provisional security committees were formed from early 1968, composed of public security, army members, and workers' picket team representatives. Any arrests made by members of these security teams in the neighborhoods were to be agreed upon by the unit as a whole. Housewife residents also organized their own unarmed teams to keep an eye on strangers in the committee areas and to clean up the streets. These teams performed such routine policing tasks as checking bicycle and pedicab licenses and ownership and regulating vendors' activities. Farmers from suburban communes who brought vegetables and poultry to the free markets and charged prices much higher than those of previous years were branded as "profiteers"; and middlemen who bought produce from them to resell at higher prices were called "speculators." First-time offenders who then sold their goods to the state were not otherwise punished. Nonetheless, widespread speculation continued unabated because of shortages of many goods. In the spring of 1968, teams like the workers' and students' committees were organized to search out unauthorized residents of the city, a task previously performed by neighborhood security committees and people's police. Door-to-door searches were carried out, and in study groups members were urged to send such interlopers back to the countryside. Many avoided detection, however, by wandering from relative to relative. The search teams did not survive beyond the spring because their opponents claimed they were being used by members of one faction to control members of other factions.

The reestablishment of security work was characterized not only by the setting up of ad hoc mechanisms for policing purposes, but also by changes in the atmosphere of sanctioning that were reminiscent of the mass law enforcement "line" of the 1958 Great Leap Forward.[52] Concern for bringing the Cultural Revolution to an end and for using the problems of law enforcement to prove to the residents that there was a need for control by a "mass dictatorship" was as pressing as the call for the apprehension and conviction of lawbreakers. There were several units established for this purpose. In Canton, in July 1968, the workers' provost corps (*kung jen chih an chiu ch'a tui*), drawn from factories, was organized to locate and isolate reactionary elements from neighborhood organizations and units. Members of the corps later returned to their factory jobs, where they may have been the forebears of the 1969 "red sentry" movement in factories, which was organized to locate opposition to the way the Cultural Revolution was being concluded. Neighborhood residents' committees set up "dictatorship of the masses" teams, with informal sanctioning powers paralleling those of the former public security committees. These were three-in-one combinations of retired workers, workers' dependents, and neighborhood cadres, in which the militia and employed workers participated as "advisors," and the Red Guards served as "vanguards." Only those with proper class and political backgrounds could participate in this policing system, which was organized hierarchically: neighborhood residential committees contained "dictatorship of the masses" committees; the alleys and lanes had branch committees; and teams were located in residents' discussion groups. Seventeen branch committees were formed in Shanghai's Luwan district, controlling 102 dictatorship teams.[53]

The emphasis on residential policing contrasted with the previous formal sanctioning by the police, the judicial mechanism, and the public procuracy, now considered by the rebels as "legalistic."[54] The public security stations were accused of having formerly distrusted the masses and of having worked in an "atmosphere of high secrecy." Mass dictatorship used the sanctioning processes as a political weapon as much as a means to control criminal behavior. Political suspects were to be held locally, controlled, and reeducated (rather than being sent up to the public security stations); and their children were to "separate themselves" from their parents and be educated by the movement. The formal mechanisms for dealing with political suspects were thus bypassed.

Residents considered that there are three great advantages to be gained by retaining the enemy in the local area to be kept under surveillance and remolded by the revolutionary masses. (1) The masses of residents take care that surveillance and remolding are carried out, thus giving the masses excellent training in enhancing their ability to distinguish class enemies. (2) Local residents are most knowledgeable about the class enemies, and can best help with surveillance and remolding. (3) One-sided activity can only deal with isolated cases; implementing the policy of surveillance and remolding can, through those enemies already exposed, lead to an unearthing of class enemies hidden more deeply.[55]

Referred to here as "one-sided" was the previous method of channeling security work through the public security station; under the new system the politically reliable residents were to control the cases that were to reach the public security stations. Also reminiscent of the Great Leap Forward is the combination of public security work and procuracy in a single unit.[56]

These reforms of the security system grew out of the intense atmosphere of Mao study, which mobilized the public to locate and condemn deviants. In the struggle and criticism sessions, residents were to step forward to report on others.

An old woman who had been afraid to expose the sabotage activities of bad elements became bold enough to struggle against the class enemies. . . . Some of the masses ferreted out the hiding place of a counterrevolutionary from the slim clue offered by a bayonet . . . a reactionary capitalist was apprehended through an incident of digging in the middle of the night; a landlord element was discovered based on deductions made from a teacup; and a slip of the tongue in an altercation between two sisters led to the unearthing of a merchant landlord.[57]

Mass dictatorship was also seen as a means to involve the residents even further in the movement, as in three study groups of a Shanghai residents' committee.

Formerly the residents revelled in quarrels with one another and in playing card games. When study classes were set up very few of them joined in the study, and class enemies made trouble. Later when the masses were mobilized to struggle against the handful of class enemies, the condition of these groups has changed remarkably. Fewer people now quarrel, the habit of playing card games has changed, and more people are taking part in study.

As a consequence of this vigilance there was a "people's radar" in each lane.

In the past when a gust of wind blew in society the waves would rise to three feet high in the alleys. . . . The exercising of mass dictatorship is like installing a "radar" in every street and posting a "sentry" in every alley. Once the masses of revolutionary people are armed with the invincible thought of Mao Tse-tung, no enemy, no matter how sinister and cunning he may be, can find a place to hide himself.[58]

In contrast to public security work, mediation work was not reorganized during the Cultural Revolution because dispute resolutions were less critical politically than public security problems. Perhaps, too, cadres were afraid to make decisions for fear of attack. The revolutionary committees also lacked the manpower and experience to carry out mediation work.

The preoccupation with security was not limited to the residents' committees. It was duplicated in the "red sentry" movement in the factories during the spring of 1969 and in the organization of children as Red Guard fighters to report on suspicious activities in the neighborhood and at home. The ability of such a mass dictatorship to operate requires that urban residents accept an atmosphere of marked public conformity. This may not persist in China for long, in spite of the three-in-one structural reforms in neighborhood security organization or reforms to the security stations. The final stage in reestablishing political control in the neighborhoods commenced in winter 1968–69, when public security officers began to round up large numbers of urban dwellers to send them to the rural areas.

## The Practice of Political Labeling

During the Cultural Revolution revolutionary rebels and Red Guards scrutinized the political history and the current behavior and attitudes of all figures in managerial and administrative positions in productive and administrative units. Their attack on "leading cadres" in authority was a call for the renewal of the egalitarian ideal of Yenan in work and life styles. They sought to abolish social inequalities that grew out of differential pay patterns and different levels of status and power. The investigation and accusation of cadres and party members was tantamount to passing political judgment on them; with the bypassing of formal channels for such accusations political labels were used as the chief weapon in the factional struggles.[59] Thus, the political struggle had a widespread impact on the economic and political positions of many urban dwellers.

The differences in pay between managers and workers, though less extreme than in other socialist countries, were resented.[60] Apart from actual wages, managers had been rewarded with bonuses in the forms of access to a better version of services (such as improved schooling for their children, better dormitory housing, cadres clinics, and health services) or liberalized application of schemes available to others, such as retirement plans. Such benefits were particularly important in an economy of scarcity and were particularly resented by revolutionary rebels who advocated that they be eliminated, and that administrators be motivated on the job by nonmaterial incentives.[61] The violent political-ideological attack on the material differences of rank has resulted in the closure of special services and has depressed the standard of living enjoyed by cadres and their families.

Another concern of the rebels was that urban political and economic units should develop a bureaucracy with a generalist approach and flexible behavior. The responsibilities of managers or workers were not to be confined to the narrow technical specifications of their job definitions. Managers and teachers of engineering, for example, should know how to operate the machinery, thereby strengthening their identification with workers. Similarly, workers should know how to be technicians and to manage and direct. The principle that recipients of services should know how to run these services was applied in the neighborhoods. This concern with flexibility affected the neighborhoods in several ways. Social services to the neighborhoods were decentralized to reduce the number of required administrators and to allow for residential management. Some former managers and administrators were sent to the countryside or to special "May 7" cadre schools to do manual labor and to study, and some were placed in the ranks of their organizations. Although cadre salary levels were to be frozen during the Cultural Revolution, pressure for cadres to accept voluntary salary cuts and thereby to demonstrate their political attitudes toward the Cultural Revolution resulted in great economic hardship for many cadre families. The permanent adjustment of the differentiated salary scales has not yet been determined. To ease their sudden salary loss those sent down to serve with the workers may have been granted "transitional" pay, similar to that granted to rural primary-school teachers. It is likely, however, that their salaries will be cut to match those of their co-workers.

The effects of political attacks on cadres and their families were as serious as economic deprivations. Before the Cultural Revolution political judgments or labels—with their consequent social, economic, and political discrimination against the accused—were applied to a small proportion (less than 5 per cent of the total population) and only after some formal procedure. The process of political attack during the Cultural Revolution by mass accusation, mass collection of materials, and the facile passing of judgment led to an indiscriminate and sometimes vicious use of political labels. This process served in part to justify the Cultural Revolution as the continuation of the Chinese revolution. Since current attitudes and behavior were seen as related to family and personal social class history, those who were to be struggled against had their dossiers searched for evidence of a bad class background and bad political affiliations. Those in positions of authority with bad class backgrounds were automatically suspect as antiproletariat and disloyal to Mao, and they were not allowed to join revolutionary groups.[62] Archival material was collected against any in particularly senior positions. However, because class background did not correctly explain current behavior, new terms were devised; the consequent expansion of labeling and the passing of political judgments by one faction against another meant that large numbers of people had their records searched and some who were accused had their careers and reputations damaged. In the early stages of the Cultural Revolution, party committees in schools accused and judged the Maoists; Red Guards in turn were urged to rebel against these party committees, but where the rebels were not strong enough, cadres would preemptively accuse them.[63]

The impact of political accusations on the accused and on their families undoubtedly will be long-lasting. Although the rebels were later ordered to burn archival material, they did not always comply. Attempts to have the verdicts reversed were not granted everywhere, and the records may remain. The common act of searching homes of suspect persons produced a stigma that would not be removed quickly and that would incriminate the entire family of the accused.

### The Decentralization of Services to the Residential Areas

When the power struggle of the Cultural Revolution was over, local residential cadres experimented with the decentralization of urban services to the neighborhoods. The intent was both to minimize costs and to increase the political content of the services. The labor and self-administration efforts of residents were to substitute for municipal funding and control and for staffing by bureaucrats, who had come under political attack. The decentralized model presupposed a productive base such as a factory or commune that could provide an alternative to central financing and staffing, and where such a base was lacking, the various goals of economic efficiency, expanded services, and political control were not easily achieved through resident administration. The school system and the system of medical services, in which there are clear economic limitations to successful decentralization, provide cases in point; in these cases, some alternative forms of resident participation and control may have been worked out.

In December 1968, the *Jen min jih pao* published reports of model schools run by residents' committees, suggesting how neighborhoods or a combination of lanes and productive units could join to run neighborhood schools.[64] The worker-propaganda teams stationed in residential areas would establish the schools, but since the workers could not remain permanently without crippling industry, retired workers would take over to sit on administrative committees with neighborhood cadres and other residents. Such a system was considered appropriate for primary schools in particular, since young children remain around the home during the day. The schools would truly be a means toward "uniting the family, the society, and the school." Community-run schools would assist the curriculum transformation that was in progress and would be a means of implementing the production-linked applied education programs. Workers were to participate in the education process by giving lectures, thereby releasing teachers for their required productive labor. However, since there were not enough outlets for the labor power of all the students and teachers available in the residential areas, some were recruited to do public sanitation work or to participate in new neighborhood consumer services. In some cases it was possible to have schools linked to productive units so that the students could do shop work, but this type of school was not feasible on a mass basis, for even in Shanghai the students, who outnumbered the workers, would simply swamp the factories.

The decentralization of the school system along these lines presumably would permit greater political and ideological control over the educational process. Narrowing the content of the education, deciding the curriculum in residential newspaper reading groups, and tying education to the applied and productive process would tend to curb the critical and creative potential of children. The educational process has come to involve more study of Mao's thought, which received relatively little emphasis in primary and lower-middle schools before 1966. Teachers, too, have been required to reform their thinking in worker-run study courses.[65] In this atmosphere education means the adoption and application of existing knowledge; apparently the regime thinks that the country cannot afford to provide for youth a period of intellectual and social differentiation.

Workers' control also has affected the treatment of students, particularly those who are the children of workers. The result of having cadres and workers participate in the administration, teaching, and judging of students was that teachers—who were mostly of nonworking class origin—could not give grades based solely on academic achievement. Workers' children were to have the opportunity to compete "more equally" with professionals' children. The schools would also exercise political direction over the residents by assigning students to participate in political study groups in which they would examine their parents' political behavior. This was proposed as a solution to the inadequacies of residential small groups.

Residents' committees have apparently had difficulty raising adequate funds on their own to support the decentralized school system. Unlike the factories or rural collectives, for which decentralized operation of the school system was initially designed, residents could raise funds only through handicraft workshops. Students could not easily earn their own keep or fund the school by working in the workshops, for these lacked enough remunerative work even for the residents. Financial difficulties may prove insurmountable. What is likely to survive of the new decentralized form is not the self-sufficient economic structure of the rural schools in an urban setting, but the representative aspect—the continued participation in school administration and staffing by residents, neighborhood cadres, and retired workers, and the increased participation by students in neighborhood activities.

Medical services, similarly subjected to decentralization, had deteriorated during the Cultural Revolution when the ministries of health, education, and culture were attacked and as the medical units themselves underwent a revolution in their ranks. Factionalism had been rampant, with clinics sometimes refusing patients of opposing factions. In the reorganization of medical services in the fall of 1968, large groups of doctors were sent to the countryside to serve in local-level clinics or in mobile teams doing propaganda and healing work. The depletion of the urban medical corps and the loss of several classes of medical students beginning in 1966 increased inadequacies in urban medical care. The main motivation for the decentralization of urban medical services, however, was to politicize the doctors and other medical professionals and to integrate them with the ranks of their profession. The model decentralized urban public health facilities were designed to reduce the work load of urban district hospitals and neighborhood clinics by training an auxiliary medical staff for outpatient medical care. Clinics serving residential areas adjusted their services to maintain current levels or to improve preventive medical services without increasing costs.

Shanghai's Huang-p'u district Ku-ling Road section hospital (in the same neighborhood that was a model for administrative reforms) was a model in health reforms, and one of the first to send doctors to the countryside.[66] Remaining doctors and staff, adjusting their practice to neighborhood conditions, felt impelled to go out in the neighborhood to do their outpatient care as proof they were serving the people, and they went from door to door in the factories, stores, alleys, and lanes. Some doctors temporarily moved into workers' homes to study Mao's works with them and to further politicize their thinking. The hospital began a program to train new personnel to serve as medical workers and to equalize hospital work tasks: nurses and orderlies were trained to diagnose and treat common illnesses; doctors in turn were to learn patient care. Political value was placed on the doctors' visibility in serving the people. The attack on the medical professional style led to doctors being trained in nurses' duties and being required to practice in improvised surroundings. The role of the medical professional, then, like that of the factory manager or leading cadre, has changed; he is to be a generalist, not a specialist, and is to perform the same kind of work as his subordinates.

In other neighborhoods, in order to save municipal funds, residents (mostly wives of workers) have been trained and organized into voluntary medical and health teams. In one Nanchang neighborhood, fourteen women were said to have learned in the neighborhood clinic how to treat such recurrent illnesses as bronchitis and inflammation of the middle ear, charging only for paper work and medicines.[67] Such examples of local "self-help" have received a great deal of publicity. We would guess that these women were supervised by a trained medical worker who would direct them to refer people with more serious ailments to the clinic. At any rate, much of the medical work they were responsible for was preventive. The extension of Nanchang's public health services to the streets was seen as one step in that city's improvement of services to the residents through decentralization. Neighborhoods operated vegetable centers that each served a thousand families, whose clerks went from house to house to study the needs of the residents—particularly the elderly, the ill, those who were nursing mothers, and families where both the husband and wife worked—and to deliver food to them. This service was apparently an extension of the neighborhood service stations, and students participated in the centers to serve their periods of productive labor. Residents in other streets set up stalls to increase the number and variety of services available to residents and handicraft workers in the neighborhoods.

The decentralization of services cannot be interpreted narrowly as an economic measure, however; the social isolation of housewives and families was recognized with renewed concern as the difficulties in involving women in the new politics were overcome. There was a concomitant political component to most of the reforms, especially in the concern to politicize administrators and to involve residents in the operation of the residents' committees in their area.

### Political Participation and Family Solidarity

In the course of the Cultural Revolution the *Wen hui pao* editorials repeatedly exhorted residents to participate actively. It was suggested that the street cadres' delay in seizing power grew out of the inability of the residential organization to stimulate political participation among residents who devoted much time to family activities. Neighborhoods were characterized as "dead corners" that greatly slowed the scheduled criticism and repudiation of urban party members and restricted family members' full participation in the movement. The *Wen hui pao* suggested that political study sessions should serve the double purpose of stimulating immediate political changeovers and politicizing family members by cutting in on family solidarity.

Such an approach was not new. Many regimes have had difficulty eliciting political participation from people who would rather withdraw into their own private lives and occupational worlds. The structural basis of the traditionally tight Chinese family had, of course, been altered since Liberation: the marriage law, land reform, and the socialization of private enterprise in the cities had abolished, or at least greatly weakened, the traditional rules and rituals of marriage, the limitations on rights and decision-making powers of women, the legal ties of property inheritance, and family control over job opportunities. The effect of these changes was to reduce greatly the controls that the family had over its members.

Political campaigns to integrate the family into the polity have complemented legal and administrative reforms at three times in China's recent history. During the campaign to implement the marriage law, parental control over the choice of a marriage partner was an issue. The anti-rightist campaign in 1957 and the four clean-ups campaign in 1963–64 were directed toward limiting the influence of class background on the political and social attitudes of the younger generation.[68] Prior to 1966, however, the preferred way of changing authority relations in the family was by means of propaganda and education, not by struggle.[69] Children from worker and peasant backgrounds were taught to respect their parents and to convince them of new ideas with patient explanation. For example, if a bride's parents demanded that she have a dowry, she was to talk them out of this traditional demand; since the parents were of the same class background as their children, they could surely be won over by reason. Children from exploiting class backgrounds, however, were to break off relations with their families.

With the Cultural Revolution came the concern that the existence of a tight family authority structure and the patterned relations of social deference and obligations between generations and sexes in working-class families might hinder political participation by youth and women. Thus the aims were to tightly integrate the family into the polity and to cut in on family relationships and solidarity. Changes in the meaning of political participation accented these aims. There have been periods (the early 1960's, for example) when political activities were less emphasized in China, but during the Cultural Revolution, the Maoists—who sought a greater politicization of the populace—gained ascendancy and tilted the *kung ssu* (public-private) balance toward reducing the permissible amount of privacy at home, at work, with friends, and with neighbors. In other words, "public mindedness" was expanded at the expense of "privatism." One of the first events of the Cultural Revolution in the neighborhoods illustrates the way a hitherto private sphere was redefined as public. During the "destroy the four-olds" campaign in August 1966, students were given a green light to intrude into the residents' homes to smash "old ideology, old thoughts, old habits, and old customs." They searched homes for gold bars, expensive watches, copies of the Chinese classic *Shui hu chuan,* and land title deeds. In the process, the residents were subjected to the full force of students' aggression. If the door was locked to a private dwelling, the students posted notices of the time they would return. If the members of the household attempted to stop them, the students would break in and beat and kick the residents, fit them with "instant conical hats," and parade them through the streets. Workers' homes were also entered, but in a more restrained manner. In addition, the few private shops that did not belong to the joint public-private cooperatives were closed down for several days.

The students represented forces intent on bringing political activities into the family homes. Their organized strength was based on their concentration in one physical locus (in dormitories of middle schools, colleges, and universities) separated from the constraints of family bonds and disapproval. With the assistance of the public security station files, they located and aimed first at the "five-bad elements," a recognizable and acceptable target. After the bad elements had first been selected for attack, the common tactic was to launch a wider campaign in the neighborhood.

The redefinition of the meaning of political participation could be seen in the progressive elimination of the distinction between the residents' working and leisure hours and activities. The model resident was seen as one who gave his private time for the improvement of the collective. Hobbies were criticized if they were of an antisocial nature; after-hours production for private consumption was considered selfish. One old Hankow resident renounced his morning physical exercise of *t'ai chi ch'uan,* to sweep the residents' committee meeting halls.[70] The way of stimulating such voluntarism was to arouse emotions through political study and the recollection of ills suffered under the old society. When the memory of past exploitation at the hands of class enemies aroused high emotional feelings, new demands were introduced. After evoking bitter memories and reading *Serve the People,* retired worker Uncle Wang let loose his pet birds and rabbits and volunteered to regularly clean up the meeting hall of the residents' committee, thus demonstrating his new concern for the neighborhood as a community.[71] The economic function of voluntarism as a mechanism to fill nonpaying jobs is obvious.[72] In comparison to the early 1960's, the period of the Cultural Revolution witnessed a greater emphasis and value placed on promoting voluntarism for economic purposes as well as on developing activism for its own sake. The stress on volunteer political participation encouraged the nonparty member to participate in the residents' committee. He was to demand power and influence equal to that accorded old-time street cadres and the street party members. Politics was not to be linked to one's position in the bureaucracy or office. This emphasis on the right to criticize and to bring down political leaders and party members had an obvious political function in the power struggle.

Even when residents were not volunteering their time in collective activities their private thoughts were supposed to concern political affairs. Housewives were directed to turn their attention from cleaning and child-care to national and international affairs. In order to induce this reflection every evening the family members were to join classes on Mao's thought, which discussed the "new revolutionary morale."

The evil influence of feudalism, capitalism, and revisionism has penetrated quite deeply in our families. Although it has been wiped out considerably since the Liberation, this situation has not been completely changed. As a result families often become a "dead corner" in various mass movements, and a shelter for bourgeois thinking. . . . In the past when family members gathered together they spent most of their time gossiping. Now when they are together they discuss matters concerning the Great Proletarian Cultural Revolution.[73]

In this political atmosphere, relationships in the family were held up for examination. Criticism of family members who had tried to remain out of politics was encouraged.

Some party members and cadres who perform well while on duty in their own work units act differently as soon as they return home. Not only do they fail to encourage their own family members to participate in study courses, but they try to prevent them from attending such classes. This is an extremely shameful selfish idea and also a double-dealing tactic. Family members should rebel against such persons and refuse to obey them until they admit that they are wrong.[74]

Youths frequently supported political factions different from those supported by their parents. If parental authority was being used to oppose their children's ideas, young Maoists should be encouraged to rebel.

Over thousands of years our family relations have been that the son obeys what his father says and the wife obeys what her husband says. Now we must rebel against this idea. . . . We should make a complete change in this. . . . It should no longer be a matter of who is supposed to speak and who is supposed to obey in a family, but a matter of whose words are in line with Mao Tse-tung's thoughts. . . . If a grandfather's words are not in line with Mao Tse-tung's thought it is absolutely justified for his grandson to rebel against him.[75]

The demand that the "family head system" be abolished and children allowed to "voice their opinions" was one of the "hundred examples of destroying old things" drawn up by Peking Red Guards.[76]

Family study of Mao's works was used to challenge excessive parental authoritarianism. During this family interaction process, young children and daughters-in-law were encouraged to examine their family relationships and to criticize those in authority in the family for any excessive use of power. Youths reported beatings by parents; mothers-in-law were criticized for ordering and demanding compliance, husbands for dinnertime demands. The youths challenged parents for being house-proud: cleaning up the community was to come first. The fact that parents often held back family members from political participation was one source of this examination of family relationships, but the family relationships were also examined as a means of weakening their bonds and tying the members to the polity. How much were family relationships and solidarity weakened because of this ideological approach? Although every family member had to participate in Mao study, this was not a continuous process; families participating several times and manifesting a good attitude could be excused from further study until the next directive was issued, for there was a shortage of leaders and groups. Family study in the home was generally done only by the activists, who were then made models for behavior by others. The vast majority of families may not even have participated in the process of examining their authority structure.

Greater inroads on familial solidarity may have resulted from political and economic changes. The struggle against persons for their political attitudes caused tension in the families of a number of residents. One indicator of familial strain is divorce applications. Although we lack statistics on divorce rates, it is notable that during the Cultural Revolution damaged political identity (or political attacks on one's spouse) was considered grounds for divorce. For example, a Canton high-school teacher was under attack as a "capitalist roader" who had successfully hidden his landlord family background from the students; during his trial and subsequent incarceration, humiliation, and confession, his wife moved back to her mother's house in Swatow and tried to file for a divorce. Such cases were too numerous to be dealt with by the Red Guards, and the mediation committees had ceased functioning, so it was ruled that matters requiring mediation, such as rehabilitation of social class, application to restore income, divorce procedures, and applications for welfare, were to be postponed until the conclusion of the Cultural Revolution.[77] Since the accepted view during the Cultural Revolution was that a person was "guilty" until he took positive steps to clear himself, the lack of mediation facilities has further damaged the solidarity of families. Although sociologists have noted that families typically fall back on the assistance and security of family relationships during times of war and chaos, the impact of the Cultural Revolution on family solidarity in urban residential areas would seem to have been to lessen family ties.

Structural reforms of neighborhood services and political-ideological education during the Cultural Revolution drew neighborhood residents into wider and more intense community activities. The expanded interpretation of political participation functioned initially to justify and accomplish goals to seize power, even though residential neighborhoods had been termed "dead corners" early in the Cultural Revolution because in many cities residents lagged behind worker rebels and Red Guards in helping to implement political change. But political participation by the residents soon became a goal in itself. Residents engaged in political debate, criticism, and struggle against the leadership's bureaucratic work styles, and they began to take greater initiative in self-administration. Public security work involved mass alerts for political nonconformity, with residents reporting on those who exhibited adverse political behavior. Residents were supposed to administer the newly decentralized social services and take responsibility for community activities.

The purpose of this emphasis on residential community activities was not only to ease overburdened community services and to aid the municipal or national budget; by drawing residents more into community activities, alienation from the local power structure would be decreased. Thus emphasis on residential performance of local activities was accompanied by a stress on correct political attitudes, which residents often demonstrated by giving voluntary service to the community and engaging in daily political study. The combination of decentralization of urban administrative apparatus and intensification of local political controls was the solution of the Cultural Revolution to the problem of maintaining political commitment in the complex, differentiated urban setting of a developing society.

# Shanghai's Polity in Cultural Revolution

LYNN T. WHITE III

Shanghai is not a sovereign level of politics, and cultural revolution is not ordinary politics. Each of these two aspects of our title poses a dilemma of method; each allows us to generate theory from lively events.

The first dilemma arises from the fact that Shanghai is only a region within a state. Modern political scientists often point out that the old concept of sovereignty must be decentralized, but they have not yet found a method to match that hope. In other fields than political science, it has often been possible to talk about regional levels of self-continuing, interlocking, nested complex systems, and to build larger national systems that include and relate the levels harmoniously. But political levels can be willful; they can inspire local loyalties. Nations and cities have policies, and individuals act; but their combined behavior cannot be explained just from any one level's "needs." Functional definitions fail when there are so many autonomous sources of them together. "System" and "level" are in practical contradiction. For our present topic we must use old terms more loosely to acknowledge sovereignty and system over many strata. If we can play this gambit, then behavior of nation, region, and person might be explained in a grammar which allows both their dependence and their independence. Morals, which inhere in personal and local as well as societal levels, might be rescued from society's firmest clutches. Political system might become polity while remaining scientific.

The author extends thanks to the Foreign Area Fellowship Program, Universities Service Centre, and Berkeley's Center for Chinese Studies. These institutions provided indispensable support for the writing of this essay, although there is no connection between their policies and its contents. Warm thanks are extended to many colleagues at the Universities Service Centre in 1969, and to John Lewis and Anne Murray, for their comments on earlier drafts of this paper.

The second dilemma arises from the intended revolutionary nature of the events we shall study in Shanghai. The slow cultural revolution in our own country, and the changing identities of our own groups, have led Americans to reemphasize that a type of data that enables social science is data about ideas, "phenomenological" data, based on the similarity between ourselves and the actors whom we study. We can rehearse our objects' meanings in our own minds. In natural science, that procedure is not possible. In the past we tried to ensure accuracy by basing our methods on natural science. These older methods gather some information that explains behavior, and they deny us an obvious advantage in obtaining other information that explains behavior. When the meanings of data are anyway unclear because the tests we can run are limited (as for Shanghai), then either single kind of information is too small a base on which to build toward likely accuracy.

To be realistic, as well as clear, about Shanghai's Cultural Revolution, we will need to use balanced methods. We must allow new units of analysis as players and new perceived motives for plot. We will try to use a *system of political levels* and a *phenomenological science*—despite the tensions even in those phrases.

We are not going to prejudice events with theory first, although neither is more important here. Shanghai's Cultural Revolution can be seen scientifically, which means exactly that it can be seen through two instruments. One is heavily structured by assumptions; the other is more free of them ("impartial") to find what parts of perceivable data the more structured tool may miss. Testing and theory-building are not essentially different. The degrees of their structuring cannot diverge as much for study of this topic as of others, but the method here is still scientific. The more natural, less organized tool will be used first. It will group facts around four types of institutions which were prominent in Shanghai's Cultural Revolution: (1) military and public security institutions, which are armed; (2) institutions for conveying political information to and from urban residents; (3) educational institutions; and (4) labor-recruitment institutions, including apprenticeship education. This list does not claim to exhaust all of Shanghai's institutions.

Each of these will be examined as it changes over time. Attacks on leaders came in waves, first at middle and fairly high political levels, later at other levels. These waves were not simultaneous in all geographical areas of the city; and they were not simultaneous in all circles, as the movement's "cultural" label implies. Shanghai institutions can nevertheless be scanned chronologically in terms of their roles in the city's past politics, in the period prior to "power seizure," during cultural revolutionary struggle, and after that when the nature of the new government began to emerge.

## Shanghai's Armed Institutions

Shanghai's armed control agencies strongly affected the city's other institutions during the Cultural Revolution. On organization charts, China's Ministry of Defense has some control over its four services of land, sea, air, and military public security units; over various militias set up in coordination with schools, unions, and communes; and over the civilian public security units, which at all levels above the subdistrict public security station (*p'ai ch'u so*) are led by a soldier who concurrently holds a leading post in miliary public security at the same level.[1] But this coordinated unity is very much an ideal. The division between army, militia, and police in Chinese cities is nothing new. Canton merchants in 1847 set up China's first modern militia—in order to protect their shops from looting, not to help the mandarins or dynastic army accomplish any larger, patriotic purpose.[2] When the Red Army took over Shanghai in 1949, it detailed its own units to do patrol work, and it gave no important job to the militias that had already been established in Shanghai by workers. Country soldiers were easily bedazzled by the metropolis. They could have been employed in the south to help fight a continuing civil war; but they became police for Shanghai.

Local organizations did not cease to organize civilian militias; the army needed and used their help to do that after Liberation. Many paramilitary programs for civilians, like the exercise program of the Shanghai Sports Committee in 1955, were organized for civilians in these years.[3] The decentralized Great Leap period, especially the summer of 1959, saw a special effort in Shanghai to send college students, workers, and local government officials to camps both on and off military bases,[4] and similar programs—with similarly local, joint civilian-military sponsorship—continued into the 1960's.[5] Shanghai urban militias were organized by *ch'ü* (administrative districts), and ch'ü-level governments had some role in controlling them.[6] The ideal of army administration of all military activity did not pertain in fact. The army and local groups set up joint organizations, and used them in separate ways. An example of really complex jointism, sponsored by the army, occurred in 1964 when no fewer than 12 disparate Shanghai organizations—ranging from the Movie Bureau to the women's federation to the medical society—organized a Youth Eyesight Protection Commission. Its purpose was explicitly stated to be in part military.[7] It was chaired by Ch'en Lin-hu, who later became a member of the Shanghai Revolutionary Committee; and it was one of many organizations which championed the "learn from the People's Liberation Army" movement in Shanghai at that time.[8] This historic alliance between national army and urban militias—a relationship which involved both friction and affiliation—later affected the main armed-control-system battle of the Cultural Revolution, which united the two of them against Shanghai's party police.

Long before the Cultural Revolution, Shanghai's local police stations were brought under firm Communist political control; but the process was surprisingly slow. In a series of different campaigns, policemen who had worked for the Kuomintang were fired from their jobs.[9] The party waited a long time before associating itself too closely with a renovated public security system, apparently because the duties of Shanghai's police, carried over from the earlier period of military administration, remained unpopular. The party's efforts to overcome this distrust were generally unsuccessful. There is no need to list specific acts of repression by the Shanghai Public Security Bureau against all sorts of dissidents in the dozen years before 1966. Later tirades against the bureau are the best data on this subject anyway, because they show how earlier feelings affected later action. Attacks on the Shanghai Public Security Bureau were almost liberal, and evidently democratic; critics accused the bureau of having substituted, for mass struggle, a "dictatorship by the few," by a small band of police-technicians. They compared the bureau to Soviet OGPU secret police and called it a foreign import.[10] Because the relevant data are secret, it is difficult to prove conclusively that the Shanghai Army Garrison and the Shanghai Public Security Bureau were in opposition to each other before the Cultural Revolution. The civilian-military movements of the mid-1960's and their associated joint organizations served to reinvigorate army interest in matters that had previously been the preserve of public security organs. The party was inextricably connected with public security because the political-legal secretary (*cheng fa shu chi*) of a party committee was usually also head of the local public security force. These two, combined intimately in this way, prevented the formation of any groups in opposition to the party.

Early Cultural Revolution directives provided legitimacy for the founding in Shanghai of many new workers' and students' groups that could usurp the authority of party and public security forces. It gradually became obvious in 1966 that these directives were subversive of the public security system because they did not require such groups to be controlled as before. These directives—especially the "sixteen points" of the Central Committee's August plenum—confused and neutralized public security cadres, and so left party organizations open to attack, which in Shanghai became most intense during the "January Revolution" of 1967. The tenth demand of the January 8 "Urgent Notice" explicitly linked the local public security bureau with the municipal party committee, and enjoined them both to obey the new political power on pain of "immediate punishment."[11]

Neutralization of public security offices, the control agencies having the closest contact with ordinary Shanghai residents, precipitated a crisis that quickly prompted the People's Liberation Army (PLA) to intervene in particular areas, because the spontaneous organization of new groups disrupted vital public services. On the morning of December 30, 1966, someone at the Shanghai North Station turned off electricity governing all stop-go beacons along both mainline railways to Nanking and to Hangchow. These lines were not restored even to irregular, unscheduled service until at least January 10.[12] The city's general supply of electricity was also threatened because of a coal shortage caused by delays in internal shipping and on the dock. When public security controls were relaxed, for example, in the Sixth Dock District in November 1966, no fewer than eight separate longshoremen's groups appeared spontaneously in that single area. A joint organization combining these eight was created in January, but it failed to halt fragmentation. Two alliances sprang up to post "big characters" against one another. The army sponsored self-criticism meetings among these two; but apparently because the criteria for criticism were still ambiguous in directives, the groups split further apart. The military, completely frustrated in this first attempt on that dock, then threw support to some quite different groups there. Under army auspices, they formed another Sixth Dock District coalition, which later proved so unreliable it had to be dissolved by the Shanghai Revolutionary Committee. Only after extensive direct participation by "army comrades" was the Sixth Dock District Revolutionary Committee finally formed.[13]

The need for army control was not limited to public utilities and economic bottlenecks. Examples could be multiplied, but we shall give only one more here: on February 14 the PLA sent 300 soldiers to K'ung-chiang Middle School, which had an enrollment of only 1,800. It is in Shanghai's eastern district of Yang-p'u, where "new towns" have been constructed since 1958,[14] and many cadres' families live. Although some of the students "seized power" for army-approved purposes, other student groups would not readily submit to a new centralized authority after the old one had been destroyed.[15] The destruction had allowed some genuine democracy of an anarchic, freewheeling sort at low levels, but military persuasion was then used to help restore some order.

A Shanghai Military Control Commission (*chün shih kuan chih wei yüan hui*) was formed sometime before February 1967 to create a new armed control institution. The founding of this commission was not announced, but apparently it had two related functions: (1) to organize, along with civilians on the Shanghai Revolutionary Committee, at least nominal "power-seizures" and "three-way alliances" and when necessary to direct the use of soldiers in those processes; and (2) to revive the relationship between the army and the urban populace by training an enlarged workers' militia to take over the immense job of patrolling Shanghai, a costly task now that the public security organization had been demoralized. Beginning in July and August, instructions of the party Central Committee condoned formation of "civil offense, armed defense" units "under" the Shanghai Revolutionary Committee "with the help of" local PLA units. At first these troops were armed with wooden clubs, the classic weapon of police.[16] As late as September, Chiang Ch'ing praised the PLA itself, for directly "supporting the left" at a series of factories and docks in Shanghai;[17] but about that time the new militia began to engage in sporadic "revolutionary actions" to deal "heavy blows" to "enemies of the new political power."[18] To provide officers for these forces and to fill street-level bureaucratic posts, the Shanghai Army Garrison set up training schools for new leaders at the lower levels. These leaders were often either too timid or too independent for the army's taste, if the publicized example of a Hsü-hui district factory militia head is typical: the garrison party committee decided to send some of these local group leaders through the training program a second time, to try again.[19] Meanwhile, the marriage between army and urban militia was as unstable as ever. Differences between Shanghai's major newspapers, the *Chieh fang jih pao* and the *Wen hui pao*, from mid-1967 to mid-1968 can be partially interpreted in terms of it. One *Wen hui pao* editorial openly declared that "revolutionary masses" ought to play a bigger role on committees, and have more representatives, than the army.[20] The military, for its part, felt pressed to bring together civilians who were hopelessly divided into groups. Throughout the first half of 1968, for example, naval units, which were quite active with civilians, led "mass criticism and repudiation" sessions against Liu Shao-ch'i to help unify (on that distant issue) the groups within an important Shanghai shipyard which had already formed its revolutionary committee the previous October.[21]

Fragmentary evidence suggests that there may possibly have been sharp disputes within military circles in east China concerning the extent to which they should intervene among civilian groups. The more "expert" air force (and possibly navy) units in the area may have been more eager to restore order than was the land army. A sibylline article in the organ of a Canton "Red Flag" group[22] made 15 accusations against General Yü Li-chin, political commissar of China's air force, who was well-known for his discipline and personal asceticism. He had allegedly carved out for himself an "independent kingdom" in the Nanking military district's air force before his transfer to Peking in mid-1965. Yü is alleged to have condoned the use of air force units in Wuhsi, near Shanghai, to support one civilian group's attack against another. In fact no military intervention took place because Yao Wen-yüan, a young Shanghai ideologue who rode his sharp pen to power during this period, telephoned the local Wuhsi commander from Peking in the name of the Central Cultural Revolution Group and ordered the officer not to commit his forces. Chiang Ch'ing launched a public attack against Yü on March 18, 1968.[23] Yü eventually survived the Cultural Revolution; but for a while he had contravened, albeit ineffectively, the somewhat laissez-faire attitude toward civilians that was explicitly identified with the Nanking District Military Control Commission and with General Hsü Shih-yu, a land soldier. Yü was charged with having attempted a coup against the Nanking military district,[24] whose commander was Hsü and whose first political commissar was Chang Ch'un-ch'iao, Shanghai's head—and very much a civilian politician, not a soldier. In order to retain the confidence of urban workers, the army had to enforce a policy of restraint in many disputes among civilians.

"The Situation and Tasks of the Current Great Cultural Revolution in Shanghai," a draft document adopted by the revolutionary committee and sent to all lower units, gave the first extended statement of Shanghai's "postrevolutionary" constitution.[25] The militia and army were distinguished from one another and called "strong pillars of the provisional power organs at various levels." It was quite clear, however, that the newly formed groups which had enabled this "revolution" now plagued it. The draft document warned that the Shanghai Revolutionary Committee itself would have to approve the formation of any "power organs" at or above the level of "vital" departments of hsien, ch'ü, or city government. It also admonished that the new militias could not be dispatched at will by anyone. Leaders who ordered militia into action for unapproved purposes would be prosecuted as counterrevolutionaries. The need for the warning says even more than its contents about the distribution of coercive power after the January struggle.

A tradition separate from the army's was assumed from the beginning by this new "civil offense, armed defense" force. The *Wen hui pao,* that champion of civilians, publicized the opposition of professional soldiers P'eng Te-huai and Lo Jui-ch'ing to earlier militias.[26] Lo was associated with the old public security system's OGPU nature noted above. The militia were indeed to take the PLA "as their example," but organizationally they were not commanded by it, as in theory even the public security apparatus had been. Precisely because of the urban militia's separate tradition and independence, the army did *not* abolish the public security system, even after cadres running it had been attacked. The bureau's most conspicuous role during the Cultural Revolution was the crass one of executioner, which it had earlier played in various other political campaigns. Shanghai's leaders personally officiated at trials with mass juries on several occasions from mid-1967 to mid-1968. The death sentences of ordinary criminals, carried out immediately after verdict to shouts of "Long Live Chairman Mao," were televised throughout the city to arouse people.[27] But the best continuing reason for the public security system's existence was as a means to control new groups that had emerged at lower levels in the city.

*Shanghai's Residential Institutions*

The traditional unit in the villages of east China is the *hsiang lin,* or "neighborhood." People living within this unit had some ceremonial, social, and economic obligations toward one another,* but the concept changed drastically when it was brought to the city. Japanese-occupation, Nationalist, and Communist governments all tried to organize "neighborhoods" for the political purposes of information gathering, mass loyalty campaigns, low-level dispute mediation, and later production. To serve these purposes, the "neighborhood" was expanded. The original *p'ai,* the lowest unit of the *pao chia* control system, was about equal in size to the hsiang lin.[28] But as the functions of residential organizations expanded by stages under the Communists, the size of these organizations expanded similarly.

The history of these stages will not be rehearsed here.[29] The most conspicuous continuing function of residential organizations was the

---

* Fei Hsiao-t'ung, *Peasant Life in China: A Field Study of Country Life in the Yangtze Valley* (London: Routledge & Kegan Paul, 1939), p. 98. William Geddes, who returned to Fei's village under the Communists, reports the continuing existence of hsiang lin, consisting often of five households on either side of a given house. They are the source of labor for big projects and are associated with rural street committees. See *Peasant Life in Communist China* (Ithaca, N.Y.: Society for Applied Anthropology, 1963), p. 31. (Fei wrote *"shanlin"*; see his note on transcriptions, Fei 1939, p. 8.)

control of ruffians and street gangs. These were often considered undesirable by residents, and could be controlled with the help of higher-level government. It was a joint task of public security offices and civilian street offices to handle these *"ah fei"*; in fact the intensity of the effort at various times was an index of the desire or pressure among residents and police to cooperate. In the mid-1950's, this sort of effort conscripted large numbers of "unemployed tramps" who after some training were dispatched to Shanghai city government-managed farms in places like southern Anhwei, and to projects like the Huai River water conservancy scheme.[30] This sort of population control was the main traditional function of government-recognized residential units. When under Communism these units acquired more economic functions, they changed in nature. For example, ah fei were often indistinguishable from *she hui ch'ing nien,* "social youth," a beautifully ambivalent expression referring to the whole gamut of youths who are unemployed. These youths are unwilling to accept manual labor, which is the only sort open to them. Often they have failed to finish middle schools, sometimes for political or other nonacademic reasons. Residents' committees were involved in the campaigns to send many of these youths out of Shanghai. This was a logical development of the committees' main pre-Communist function —but in performing it now, the residents' organs became involved also in recruiting labor for large economic projects.

The traditional neighborhood polity could be used for new and old purposes together: to control "social youth" was also to generate manpower. The old network of neighborhood relations (especially among women) could also generate enthusiasm and information—which are usable even to challenge the insularity of traditional groups. By the end of 1951, 80 per cent of Shanghai's residents were in "small groups,"[31] which were formed only after ch'ü-level governments had been strengthened to "lead" them. The Communists found new functions for old low-level urban activities, and so wove city, district, street, lane, and residence into a somewhat closer texture than before.

This does not mean that the levels were coordinated perfectly from above. The procedure for selecting intermediaries to staff street committees indicates that middle leaders were subject to norms assigned both from higher political levels and from the groups they led.[32] At the lowest levels, candidate lists for these organs were not determined by the Communist party, whose problem was to persuade "real" lane leaders to sit on the basic committees. Above this level, there were two criteria for nomination: the street committeemen had to be both ideologically orthodox in state terms, and representative of their district in local terms. After 1956 the amalgamation of urban ch'ü was paralleled by increasing initiative and independence at the street level.[33] For example, street residential organizations reasserted control over their traditional function of dispute settlement. The full-time judicial personnel of Shanghai at all levels were reduced by half during the mid-1958 attack on professionalism in the anti-rightist movement.[34] Street-level mediation committees, which took over their work, emphasized substantive and informal justice rather than formal laws. Further to please the urban residents, who traditionally distrusted bureaucrats as non-productive, the judges were ordered into factories to work part-time.[35] Shanghai did not set up urban communes during this period: high-level officials were not willing to grant so much autonomy to the strong groups below the ch'ü level. The tasks assigned to residential organizations changed slowly over time as China's development demanded; and they also changed as the need to control these low levels increased.

Many government functions that directly affect the daily lives of residents in Shanghai have very little to do with high-level politics. The opening hours of stores is an important political issue at the street level in Shanghai; for example, the Huang-p'u District Commercial Department once proudly announced it had founded ten new stores that would remain open for long and unusual hours. We may point out the specific importance of this issue to residents and may quote the department about "serving the people."[36] But present political theories are so inadequate that such concrete data are hard to aggregate.

Some local issues can be grouped around the old ideas "traditional" and "modern." The Shanghai government often did not oppose traditions imported from the countryside. It found some of them positively useful: to fund investment, "mutual help savings societies" (*hu chü ch'u chin hui*), strongly resembling rural village loan associations,[37] were established in great numbers in poorer areas of the city.[38] These and other traditional institutions flourished in Shanghai before 1949. When they were useful, the new government encouraged them. Although *simple* adaptive issues and *simple* value-choice issues cannot be ignored in discussing Shanghai's pre–Cultural Revolution problems, they will not take us nearly as far as the ideas of changing uses and mixed meanings toward explaining the political events after mid-1966. Before then, there had been a certain prosperity, and plenty of ideological cocksureness.

Part of the gap between Shanghai's governors and residents, which isolated the former and enabled a "cultural revolution," was due to resentment by followers of old norms against bureaucrats who wanted to regularize new ones. As late as May 1, 1963, for example, the local office of the New China News Agency issued a glowing report—not about International Labor Day, but about the seven-day festival to celebrate Buddha's birthday held at Yü Fo Temple in Shanghai. "Large crowds of people" came to the religious ceremonies and to the traditional fair, held on streets near the temple. Over two thousand booths sold food and handicrafts. This sort of religious tradition was *strong* despite frequent celebrations of the opposite sort sponsored by bureaucrats. For example, in 1964 Huang-p'u ch'ü's Scientific Technology Association held a "discard superstition" exhibit lasting more than six months.[39] Even better examples of norm-ambiguity can be found in Shanghai's suburban rural areas, where the two-edged political effects of value conflict are very evident: a *Wen hui pao* correspondent visiting the Sung-chiang hsien town of Feng-ching, which is one of the farthest villages from Shanghai city still under its jurisdiction, was shocked to find in 1965 that the local teahouse was still a main source of news, that village politics of the old variety still flourished, and that traditional stories and singing were popular. To improve all this, the local party committee fired the teahouse manager and established a course to train fifteen narrators in revolutionary tales. Spittoons were emplaced to preserve the hygenity of the floor.[40] But one may doubt that these lessons in progress were deep enough to prepare for the advances of the Cultural Revolution, or that they brought the party committee much mass support in Feng-ching, to help sustain it later.

The policy that most powerfully alienated many Shanghai residents from their local intermediary leaders was without doubt the campaign to send youths, technicians, and professionals to the countryside. This mobilization seems to have been of at least two different types in Shanghai, which vary in their modes of recruitment, in the type of agencies organizing them, in the places to which people were rusticated, in the age of the recruits, in the economic purposes of their going, and apparently in the proposed length-of-stay there and the career rewards promised. The first, which might be called *residential mobilization*, was organized jointly or separately by street committees and middle schools, usually to persuade graduating students to volunteer for assignment to very distant places (from Shanghai, particularly to Sinkiang) so that they could participate in agriculture and quasi-military colonization in the style developed by several of China's expansionist dynasties. These volunteers were often expected to remain for life in remote locales. In return for this, they would be given honors and political power in their new lands, particularly if they had been originally sent out of Shanghai because they were altruistic, rather than unemployable. The second form, *technical mobilization*, was generally organized by factories, offices, and universities. Staff members would volunteer or be assigned to less developed cities like Sian, or to populous rural areas. Usually they remained in the Yangtze Basin provinces. They would manage enterprises and frequently train replacements against the day they could return to Shanghai. Sometimes a Shanghai firm would be assiged to provide technical personnel for particular inland jobs; so it could just rotate its own staff there, with each member serving equal time. Tours of duty outside the metropolis could sometimes be quite short—regular stints in regular careers—and honors like Communist party membership were less likely to follow than for "residential" rusticates. Professionals employed more independently, such as doctors or artists, were often more bitter about the experience because they received fewer honors, their replacements were less often available, and they were usually assigned to less urban inland sites.

Training for residential mobilization begins at an early age. It is the joint responsibility of the municipal Education Department and of street-organization leaders, who are under the guidance of the ch'ü-level government, to accustom youth to country life. For example, the office of P'ing-liang Street, Yang-p'u ch'ü, organized a "youth education group" to arrange the summer vacations of middle-school students. The P'ing-liang Street authorities coordinated lane committees, party branch secretaries, women's league branches, education-and-culture cadres, people's police, and school principals to cooperate in this effort.[41] At a lower level in Shanghai, there is evidence that very traditional family organizations were used to recruit youths and that volunteer campaigns were geared to specific destinations. On the morning of May 6, 1964, youths named Ch'in, sent by the Ch'in Family Committee of Chiang-p'u Street, went as a group to the local registration office to volunteer for Sinkiang. Chiang-p'u Street, like P'ing-liang Street, is located mostly in a workers' residential area behind the riverside factories in Yang-p'u district. This is a fairly poor part of town. The Yeh Family Committee of Chiang-p'u Street also persuaded some of its youth to register.[42]

It is not surprising that parents were the objects of special pressure in campaigns to send their children to the boondocks; their resistance is understandable. It is more surprising that the municipal government could concoct for them such a calculus of interests and ideals that they would cooperate—however reluctantly or corporately—in plans to ship their offspring to China's farthest frontiers. Extended-family organizations were used for this campaign and clearly justified their continued existence on the basis of such activities. Bonds of this form—*holding intermediate leaders between high and low constituencies, representing each to the other*—are common enough at higher administrative levels. As we shall see later, Shanghai's mayor relates to China's Central Committee very largely as these Ch'in and Yeh family heads relate to the People's Committee of Chiang-p'u Street. There are conflict and cooperation in each case. It is surprising that the relations between public and private have remained so constant in structure, both for high-level intermediaries and for the very low-level leaders active in mobilization.

Gala farewell parties were held for the pre-1966 mobilizations at which all the levels involved in this politics were represented: consenting parents came and were duly praised; local lane, street, and women's federation committeewomen took credit for the registrations on behalf of their units, as did education bureau cadres for their schools.[43] Sometimes very high officials attended, like Municipal Council Secretary Shih Hsi-min, or deputy mayors Sung Jih-ch'ang and Chao Tsu-k'ang (a talented ex-Kuomintang notable, good for ceremonial occasions), and "commanders" from the quasi-military organization that the volunteers were about to join.[44] On one occasion, Chou En-lai himself met a "Shanghai youth company" which was part of an "army group" working as a unit to plant winter wheat and build a road in Sinkiang.[45] There are many farms in Sinkiang where everyone can speak Shanghai dialect. The Sinkiang Production and Construction Army Group (*Hsin-chiang sheng ch'an chien she ping t'uan*) is apparently attached to the Sinkiang military district.[46] Its relation to Shanghai is unclear, except that its officials visit the city to escort new wards to Sinkiang. The "army group" has administered way-stations in Sian and Urumchi for this purpose at least since 1964.[47] These facilities portended the later logistics system used for Red Guards' travels. The low and high levels were partially linked together by mobilization.

Mobilization is related very directly to the beginning of the Cultural Revolution among Shanghai residents. In the critical month of June 1966 there was a sharp increase in the rate at which youth were asked to volunteer for Sinkiang. After a complete suspension of these activities for six months, street committees—and now increasingly Shanghai's rural hsien boards—decided to send large groups of youth every three days on the train to Urumchi; and the first group of almost one thousand left on June 23.[48] June 1966 also saw the beginning of another trend in which newspapers suggested, ever so gently, that some people thought there might be some irregularities in administration of the mobilization draft: the Overseas Chinese father of a Shanghai middle-school graduate was reported to have written a party department to prevent his daughter from going to Sinkiang, on the grounds that she had had tuberculosis; his plan did not work, because she reportedly insisted on going anyway.[49] Later when the Cultural Revolution was in full swing, these accusations became more blunt. A party member in a Shanghai steel plant "sabotaged the state plan for unified allotment" of volunteers, and tried to bring his daughter back from Shantung after she had been assigned there upon receipt of her M.D. degree in 1961.[50]

There is evidence from several periods that lane committeemen were challenged to practice as they preached and to volunteer themselves or their children for Sinkiang. A report from 1964 tells of one street committeeman who visited a "six-good" barbershop worker for instruction before boarding the Urumchi train. Another tells about a street-level women's federation representative who presided at a well-publicized family meeting, no less, to honor her eldest daughter who was about to depart.[51] An item from the crucial summer of 1966 lists by name three street committeemen who pledged in big-character posters to go to Sinkiang—and another seven (apparently older) who volunteered publicly, on blackboard newspapers, to send their own children.[52] These events were due in part to revenge against the draft committees, and in part to idealism for China's growth. Their phenomenology was ambiguous in that way. The position of residential group leaders was especially difficult when the powers above and below them prescribed the same unpleasant action on the basis of different, conflicting values.

It is difficult to write objectively about the bitterness generated in some Shanghai residents by mobilization. The official press can speak for itself: the Wen hui pao reported in 1968 that a "bad element" in Hsü-hui district had distributed handbills claiming residents' committee cadres received 800 to 1,000 yüan in cash for each youth they sent to Sinkiang. The rumor is probably without basis, but its very existence reveals disenchantment with the ideal of mobilization. This bad element also told the parents of a volunteer that their son had been nailed to death on a wooden plank in Sinkiang. The Wen hui pao admits that the possibility was so credible to the parents that they were benumbed and could not work. (The imagery of this torture is obviously Christian; Catholics originally settled Hsü-hui, or Ziccawei, which contains the Roman Cathedral.) The news article went on to say that this bad element incited families to telegraph their children in Sinkiang to return, and it concedes that many did in fact come back to Shanghai. The struggle meeting against this counterrevolutionary was used as a forum at which youths could pledge again to live in the countryside.[53] The intense conflicts of the mobilization campaign go far to explain why Shanghai politics polarized during the Cultural Revolution.

Lane cadres were sometimes physically attacked in the January revolution and shortly afterward.[54] But revolutionary committee policy indicated that some of these intermediaries could not be replaced by reliable hands quickly; so a general movement against them was discouraged. The immediate problem was to find any street leadership at all—old or new—that would be bold enough and popular enough to maintain order after the public security system's demise. The formation of local revolutionary committees at the ch'ü and street levels was generally quiet.[55] The later review of residential committee memberships, to "purge class ranks," was usually not violent even when the pugilistic verbiage of some newspaper reports made it seem so. The reason is simply that residential intermediaries themselves did not resist. Mobilization had denied them the respect of their subordinates, and their superiors had made the duties of local leadership greater than the rewards. Extractive campaigns to build China had broken the syndrome in which intermediaries could flourish. Many were only too happy to be rid of their vulnerable posts between two constituencies.

There was therefore a vacuum of leadership at the street level of Shanghai politics after January 1967. Higher authorities saw the need to reinstall or repair the political conveyor-belts that had been torn out. They wanted local organizations to build spontaneously, and they also wanted to control the process somewhat. Democracy was clearly the right remedy: open *elections* at the lane level might bring forth some group leaders; and *debate* might even find reliable ones, because it would usually be conducted in the old grammar and vocabulary. These reforms were adopted in fact. The governing committees of street offices were also enlarged, possibly to expand the sources of local leadership initiative.[56]

The most urgent task in neighborhoods was to send returned youths back to the country. The reasons for this urgency were numerous: the youth who had overthrown the old ch'ü and street committees might try their hands at the new ones, which were therefore eager to see them depart. And to some extent the Communist government in Shanghai may have staked its credibility at low levels on enforcement of this method of national development. The commitment was too deep to pull out of, even after such a massive attack on party cadres. That attack had been launched in the name of an ideology requiring mobilization. Now the new ch'ü revolutionary committees, with their "civil offense, armed defense" corps, were in a position to challenge the youth to put their feet where their mouths had been.

Population control of this sort is not easy, especially in a city like Shanghai, which was still the greatest urban hiding place in China.

The municipal government made strong efforts in 1968 to improve the registration of persons and to restaff the public security apparatus. During this 1968 campaign the independence of ch'ü- and sometimes street-level governments may have decreased, even while independence was increasing at the lane level, because municipal authorities could more easily overcome resistance to the campaign at higher levels. It is possible that the enlargement of street *committees* from mid-1967 coincided with an amalgamation and reduction in number of street *wards*, in order to improve control over this increasingly powerful administrative level both immediately (because of the personnel shuffle) and in the long run (because of their larger, diluted jurisdictions).

These renovated agencies could control the returned "social youth" in part by launching campaigns against quarreling and card games[57] and in part by renewing mobilization. The first part of this task was easier than the second. There is plenty of evidence that new lane residents' committees were unwilling to take the path that had made their predecessors vulnerable to criticism. The *Wen hui pao* complained that "some cadres of residents' committees and other units also think it difficult to mobilize revolutionary youths to go to rural and mountain areas. They cherish 'fear.'"[58] Fear was not such an unnatural reaction, given the precedents. Several articles even suggest that the newly more independent lane leaders resumed an avuncular function that was traditional in their posts: the approval of marriages for reasons of specifically local politics. As the *Wen hui pao* ruefully pointed out, cadres who could find mates for their local young rebels might avoid censure from them. Many committeemen refused to counsel youths against pregnancies and childbirths (which made trips to Sinkiang less likely) and were afraid of "saying the wrong things" when talking to youth.[59]

The ch'ü-level governments were not without resources to help enforce mobilization directives. On the morning of June 6, 1968, "civil offense, armed defense" troops rounded up Shanghai residents who had organized into conflict groups to oppose remobilization and who had attacked piers, railroad stations, and loyalist committeemen in an effort to halt the campaign.[60] More important battles for consolidating the new high authority were less spectacular and slower; they were fought in the street committees throughout 1968. Editorials averred that some of the street-level revolutionary committees did not have popular confidence when they were founded, and that the committees needed to have new memberships.[61] A "model revolutionized street committee" was set up in Huang-p'u district, in the center of town, to edify cadres from other streets who visited it. Even public security cadres could now expect representation on these committees. Shanghai's residential control system was being restored.

### Shanghai's Educational Institutions

It is not pressing a point too far to say that the main short-run political function of schools in Shanghai was also mobilization. Schools were involved as much as residents' committees, though their role was less coercive and more propagandistic because their constituency was somewhat different. They did not have to deal with drop-outs or so directly with parents. Education's role in this movement began on a large scale in 1956, when Shanghai schools ran a domestic peace corps to supply Kansu with teachers.[62] The launching of this early, relatively happy, campaign coincided with the addition of about 25,000 new members to the Shanghai Communist Youth League[63] and with a new law conscripting some youth into prestigious army careers. (It also coincided with a much harder residential mobilization for less well-educated people, sending them also to the northwest to construct the Lanchow–Urumchi and Paoki–Chengtu railways and the Yü-men oilfield.[64]

The mobilization of Shanghai university students sometimes exhibited "technical" and sometimes "residential" characteristics, depending largely on whether or not the current economic policy emphasized self-sufficiency. The Great Leap Forward involved very large numbers of university students in these campaigns for the first time—which was lucky for those who did not want to go far, since the Leap was a self-sufficiency campaign. Shanghai, at that time apparently under less direct national guidance, allowed mobilization of a more technical type to less distant places. For example, Futan University's Philosophy Department (one of the best in China) was able to establish relations in 1958 with a commune at Hai-ning hsien in nearby Chekiang province, to which it sent teachers and students for periods of only eight months.[65] Other Futan people worked at the "East Is Red" People's Commune in Pao-shan hsien in Shanghai itself, just north of the city and a short bus ride away. They took up sinecures as work-point recorders and the like. Half of them attained the rank of platoon chief (*p'ai chang*). They sometimes complained,[66] but with less cause than the residents who were sent to build railroads in the northwest.

Mobilization in most of its forms is defensible on grounds of rural China's economic development. But there can be no pretense that it helped Shanghai's economic growth, or was generally popular there. In this early period, mobilization was for most students a temporary experience. When the policy was later enforced more stringently, defection seems to have risen apace. China's polity has many intentions, and they are not all defined in Peking.

After the Great Leap Forward, nationwide manpower planning again became modish; and Shanghai middle schools held meetings of their senior classes regularly each year urging the graduates to accept party assignments to Sinkiang. These pledge meetings now had another function, too. Party officials explained that Shanghai itself was a major, sophisticated economic base in China, that some graduates would now have to continue their studies in order to run it—and that this was a perfectly rational and normal situation.[67] It was not, however, a classless situation. By 1963, the rhetoric at these meetings had changed importantly. There was immense emphasis on the debt that the working class owed the party, and on the idea that volunteering for rustication was the way a worker's child could repay it.[68] Many of the less successful students were from educationally deprived poor families. They would now be urged to leave Shanghai and would not be admitted to universities. There was certainly no discrimination against workers or peasants as such; on the contrary, they had some advantage in obtaining admissions. But the Leap's legacy of greater municipal independence (and the increased ability to capitalize heavy industry within the city) had manpower implications with social content. A humanistic elite was not needed, but skilled technicians of high quality were. (As we shall see later, technicians with fewer skills were also needed, but in Shanghai the supply of them far outran the demand.) Files had to be kept on each student, to assure that the machine's inputs could be properly supplied.

The ambiguous criteria for admission to higher education were used flexibly: for promotion one had to be both smart and red, but it was moot how that idea might be put into practice. The Ministry of Education established "unified leadership" throughout the nation to standardize admissions, but even this was ambiguous, not unified, in structure. Local party committees and local academic "enrollment organs" jointly chose students for universities. This dual structure reflected a commitment to the two values of political loyalty and academic excellence.[69] School administrators represented the value of expertise in this dualism. They placed themselves in a position vulnerable to later attack from socially poor students who did not receive admission, because the norms for the choice were ambiguous and pragmatic.

League and Education Department officials gave equally fuzzy reasons when encouraging students to work in the countryside after graduation. Previously they had said mobilization was needed for national development, but in the 1964–66 period they also quite openly used career promises as incentives. They implied that even mediocre middle-school graduates would have wide scope to use talents in the country-side, and they suggested that fortunes would be better there than in the city.[70] In mid-1964, a large exhibition on "youth in Sinkiang" was held in Shanghai, and Shih Hsi-min made speeches calling for volun-teers and depicting the glory of their commitment.[71] In 1966 it was re-ported that more than seven hundred Shanghai youth living in Sinkiang had joined the Communist party, and nearly five thousand had joined the youth league in the "past two or three years."[72] The New China News Agency's Shanghai office proudly reported on May 8, 1966, that "in the past few years" more than seventy thousand youths had gone to Sin-kiang from the city and that almost half of them had received special honorary titles for their work there. In Sinkiang, there were not the long-time Communist peasant leaders typical of Yangtze Basin rural areas, who might resent the political power of urban visitors; so it is probable that young intellectuals who went to the northwest were given some real power, in addition to the awards and titles. But this mixture of ideal and incentive was proven unstable by later events.

Economic development is slow, and individual lives are short. The official phenomenology—that the significance of individual lives is en-tirely comprehended in the significance of the nation's life—was not believed in practice by many who went, because in practice many of the rusticates later returned to Shanghai. This does not mean that com-mitment for the flexibility of norms, and against their fixity, can be re-jected by youth, just because Sinkiang turns out to be hard work. Youth establish careers. They are interested in succession—and therefore in the host of issues Weber put under the notion "charisma" or Etzioni under "normative compliance." The graduates came back to Shanghai not only to reject the reasons they had left, but also to restate them.

June 1966 saw the first major public expression of the Cultural Revo-lution in Shanghai, when all kinds of units and individuals put up post-ers "supporting Peking University" (*Pei ta*).[73] Schools and factories in Shanghai were clearly expected to approve the attack on three admin-istrators in Peking University, Sung Shuo, Lu P'ing, and P'eng P'ei-yün. This attack had been posted on May 25 by members of the Philosophy Department at Pei ta. Just a few days later it was announced that the school admissions system in all of China would be reformed drastically and that the use of examinations would be reconsidered. The anti-democratic aspects of the exam system were decried for having created an elite of cultivated men divorced from China's masses. Shanghai's papers printed support for this syllabus review from school teachers, street cadres, and graduating students. Groups defined in many different ways (by department, schools' staffs, teachers' groups, academic classes, social classes) coalesced quickly and stayed up all night writing big-character posters.[74] The first actual change in Shanghai's educational policy was that the 1966 middle-school graduates were more heavily propagandized to go to the country, but less coerced to go, than in previous years. That year many stayed in Shanghai to carry out the Cultural Revolution instead. Youths were more independent and better organized into groups than before. Pledge meetings concerning careers were no fewer; in fact they were extended to cover still younger people. A consortium of various government units in 1966 called an all-city conference of junior-middle-school graduates, at which they were urged to politicize themselves.[75] But few of them went to Sinkiang.

One report of events at the Shanghai Foreign Languages Institute has been written by Sophia Knight, an English girl who taught there in 1966. The school's party secretary in early June called a general meeting and made a flexible, vague speech urging his students to be active in the Cultural Revolution, to preserve unity among the majority, and to distinguish between enemies and friends. Five teachers in the Russian Department shortly put up a poster criticizing him. This led to further attacks against him and the youth league secretary, and to arguments. An open letter was received on July 5 from the Peking Foreign Languages Institute, after which the party secretary wrote a poster welcoming criticism. That came quickly enough, owing to national publication of the "sixteen points" of August 8. By August 12, two rival Red Guard groups had organized at the Institute. Some radicals held a meeting of their own to "criticize ogres and monsters"; but the English Department's moderate party secretary organized another important meeting in such a way as to offend the radical students, who were a minority. By September, most of the institute's students were traveling, without cost, all over China on these expeditions.[76]

No attempt will be made to describe comprehensively the student activities in Shanghai after August 1966, when the Red Guards became very active in public.[77] Student groups of one stripe or another took part in every major power struggle and strike-breaking action; they spent considerable effort fighting one another; and they earned temporary seats on some of the new organs of power. There is no simple way to conceive their larger coalitions in Shanghai. Even the chaotic seesaw between "east winds" and "red flags" in Canton seems quite orderly (if only because those two names persisted) in comparison to the Shang-hai melee. The Shanghai Revolutionary Committee itself had trouble obtaining information about student factions. No less an organ than the *Jen min jih pao* saw fit to praise one 12-member Shanghai group, composed exclusively of athletes aged sixteen and seventeen, which had "opened the door" to give outsiders some idea of their internal debates—and external plans.[78]

The student groups were initially formed in mid-1966. Well into 1968, Shanghai municipal and ch'ü-level governments were still expending considerable effort to dissolve them. The attempt to have students "resume classes, raise revolution" in February and March 1967 did not have much success. An instructor at East China Teachers' College, for example, says his students came to the campus only occasionally in those months—to read what was posted on the walls.[79] Later, local government made greater efforts to end this political truancy. In April 1967, for instance, New China News Agency reported that the Shang-hai No. 6 Girls' Middle School had been split for a year between two rival groups. The girls were divided in this case by the "reactionary theory of class origins" (alias the "blood doctrine") into children of poor parents and children of rich parents. This division split every classroom. Each group claimed its half of each room and refused to communicate with each other. This report does not mention what brought them together; it merely says they saw fit to form a united "Red Guard army corps," which may be suggestive. Each class became a subcorps of this organization, and considerable time was spent attacking China's Khrushchev, a cause for which all could unite.[80] This school, in downtown Huang-p'u district, then became a model for forming revolutionary grand alliances among students throughout the city. But the imperfections in its own coalition were not kept secret. Radical groups openly called this alliance "a big hodgepodge" and disliked the model. They in turn were accused of "closed doorism" (*kuan men chu i*) for their secretiveness and refusal to associate with the majority of students. This model was said to have inspired eleven Shanghai secondary schools to create such alliances—although each one of these schools had other nonalliance student groups too! The model also inspired "more than twenty" other secondary schools to set up "preparatory groups" for such alliances.[81] Progress toward uniting students in schools was therefore only partial by mid-1967.

In November the ch'ü governments, which have great authority in secondary education, changed their emphasis and tried to form Red Guard alliances on a ch'ü-wide basis.[82] The effort within schools had not been abandoned, but ch'ü officials apparently hoped it might be more feasible to deal with group members indirectly, through leaders brought together in larger forums. "Factionalism" was both praised and condemned by various norms dispensed at that time. The *Wen hui pao* entitled one of its editorials "Factionalism Must Be Subjected to Class Analysis," and showed dialectically that "proletarian" factionalism was good, whereas "bourgeois" factionalism was evil.[83] This begged the question with gorgeous abstractions, because each group in Shanghai used those two words as it pleased, and there was no consensus on proper definitions.

"Moderate," evolutionist student groups were scarcely less divisive than "radical," interventionist ones. At New Normal University in Shanghai, the leader of a moderate faction, who had apparently been excluded from the school's revolutionary committee, recruited defectors because he opposed "totally negating the past 17 years." He warned that the radicals would be "rehabilitated" when in future he obtained power.[84] During the party rectification of 1968, some radicals who were willing to cooperate with higher authorities received committee and party memberships. This made some moderates, and the radicals who were unwilling to cooperate, very bitter. The *Wen hui pao* said these radicals "took advantage of the situation" by alleging that the new basic-level party organization was "rotten" and that many members were "impure."[85]

Almost all student groups joined in broadside attacks against the admission and rusticate selection systems. There was common fear of what the official files might contain. Interventionists and gradualists alike could detest Yang Hsi-kuang, a major speaker in earlier mobilization campaigns, but government efforts to make them organize permanently on this basis were not successful. Yang had been head of the municipal education bureau, and he apparently held considerable power over party-admissions organs in Shanghai between 1961 and 1966. The all-city Red Guard Congress, the associated institutes of higher learning in Shanghai, and the Shanghai City Middle-School Red Guard Congress joined together to sponsor a televised struggle against him. Yang was accused of crimes since 1940, but especially of having placed many "representatives of the bourgeoisie" on faculties, in the party, and on "administrative committees," including presumably those that admit students and advise graduates. It was said that under him these committees sometimes became 80 per cent bourgeois.[86]

The student groups must be given credit for assessing their capabilities quite accurately. They quoted Mao to the effect that destruction comes before construction. They insisted that "making mistakes" in criticism was a lesser sin than allowing "nonproletarians" to be free.[87] This world view did not prepare them to organize a policy or to establish new authorities in Shanghai after they had toppled the old ones.

Rebels during the January revolution in 1967 set up group headquarters in schools, restaurants, official buildings, and often in mansions of the old French Concession in the Western part of Shanghai. As early as February the city's revolutionary committee ordered them to move out of any room in excess of their "reasonable needs." This was probably the first effort of the new local regime to regulate all student groups directly, no matter what their politics.[88]

These efforts to unify groups caused one major change in the structure of Shanghai education. In pre–Cultural Revolution times, it had not been necessary to keep young junior-middle-school students from forming political groups; but in 1966 they followed their elders' example when no legitimate control could be exercised over any such activity. After 1966 they had to be controlled more intensively than before. Junior-middle-school graduating classes now held meetings similar to those of older students, though there seems to have been no movement to send them as far as Sinkiang.[89]

In 1968, the mobilization of youth toward rural areas began again— but with differences related to the normative ambiguity of the Cultural Revolution itself. The moral value of mobilization now took clear precedence over its economic value. The deserters were told to go back to Sinkiang, but now there was much more emphasis on sending educated youth to places closer to Shanghai, and for much shorter periods. Two hundred thousand students, teachers, soldiers, and revolutionary cadres, largely from cities but not all Shanghainese, helped with the spring plowing in Kiangsi in 1968. They stayed there for "a number of weeks" only. Educated people were put into contact with nearly ten million peasants in this one province during a short period.[90] The purpose of this interaction between peasants and city dwellers was to develop modern, unselfish, ideal personalities in both, more than to yield rice. Residential campaigns had certainly not been abandoned, particularly in rhetoric; but some interpretations of 1968 have underestimated both the strength of student veto power over new rustication and the reluctance of residential organs to enforce the policy.

In part because of such power, cooperative youth leaders in Shanghai could not be excluded from low positions in the new party. Hsü Ching-hsien, a leading speechmaker on the revolutionary committee, understated the case in May 1968 when he said, "The youth problem is very important to the party and is rather outstanding at present." On several occasions he spoke, and the *Wen hui pao* wrote editorials, calling for "reinvigoration" of the party at its basic level by the admission of "successors" even into the "leadership core." He reported that many of the new members then were only eighteen to twenty years old.[91]

Beginning in the middle of 1968, there was more pressure against political independence of students. The *Chieh fang jih pao* on August 7 strongly condemned the "reactionary" theory of "many centers," which undermined the "proletarian headquarters."

There are some people now in our ranks who have become infected with a very bad style of study. The way they study Marxism runs directly counter to Marxism. They are great talkers, quoting the classics by the yard, not to guide their revolutionary practice but to serve as a red veneer protecting their bourgeois individualism from criticism. . . . They yell for "firm compliance" with an instruction that benefits their grouping. Otherwise, they ignore or resist it, or even quote it out of context and twist it.[92]

These people were further accused of forging documents and speeches and of printing and distributing their fakes. The editorial boasted that "the unprecedented Great Proletarian Cultural Revolution has brought into being a high degree of democracy on an unparalleled scale." But one can detect a note of rue in that!

"Alliances" in Shanghai's Cultural Revolution originally had two concurrent purposes: 1) to include both group leaders and higher-level representatives (often soldiers) on committees and thus to establish communications between groups and government; and 2) to create forums in which leaders of rival groups might talk with one another. After the middle of 1968, the first of these purposes became relatively more important and the second relatively less so. But these groups' experience of Cultural Revolution will probably have a permanent effect. At least among Shanghai's students, the taste of factional "democracy" will not soon be forgotten.

### Shanghai's Labor-Recruitment Institutions

The municipal education bureau administers Shanghai's regular system of schools, but during the Great Leap Forward a second and much larger educational system was established by industries to train skilled labor. The graduates of this system were called "technicians," and they hoped for jobs of high status to match the title. In the sudden flush of municipal independence that the Leap represented for Shanghai, factories and unions were leased authority and money to set up technical schools to reward their workers and to increase productivity. Most, but not all, of these technical schools were operated on a part-time basis. The most famous of these institutions, the Shanghai Municipal Part-Work Part-Study Industrial University, was founded jointly in 1960 by over one thousand firms. Smaller technical schools had operated in large numbers since 1958. The level of training was usually elementary. By 1961, three thousand such schools were open in Shanghai. Over one million workers, at least one quarter of the city's total urban labor force, enrolled in them. But the distribution was far from even; one metals plant was said to have over 90 per cent of its workers enrolled. Many of these schools were staffed by factory foremen, although outside teachers were also hired.[93] Veterans who "taught new workers selflessly" and "work and teach simultaneously"[94] received high praise. For young workers, this education promised promotions and was in any case a change of pace from ordinary humdrum labor. The political advantages of this new system accrued particularly to the low levels at which it was established, not to higher levels.

The Great Leap's optimism about capital formation extended to what some economists call "investment in human capital" as much as to machines. With immense confidence, the Shanghai government in 1959 claimed to have found full-time university positions (either on old campuses or in the eight new technical universities) for 95 per cent of the city's regular-system middle-school graduates![95] From one girls' school where statistics were reported, 90 per cent of the graduates were admitted to higher education in science, mostly applied science. Many of the beneficiaries of this municipal policy were not workers' or peasants' children: one 1959 survey of Shanghai's secondary technical schools boasted that 60 per cent of the students were proletarian in that sense[96]—but 60 per cent is not high, considering the constant efforts of badly classed people to move "down" in the world. In addition, the Great Leap was not a period of extensive mobilization to northwest China, as were the periods before and after. Many graduates of secondary schools, who might aspire to "technical" jobs, now stayed in or near the city. Many Shanghai people went to rural parts of east China to work, but during the Great Leap the city apparently did not meet a high quota in any national plan to send youth to far frontiers.

Early in 1961, a conference on spare-time education was called in Shanghai to bring control over the newly established technical schools. A policy of "dealing with different students in different ways" was now encouraged. A "state of imbalance" was declared in Shanghai spare-time education: it was alleged that factory-run schools had not carried out enough ideological training, had not instructed "according to available teaching materials," and had not "emphasized current production." The attendance rate at spare-time lessons was admitted to be low. Above all, the "target of training" had been left "too vague."[97]

It was not until the Cultural Revolution that information surfaced about the clamp-down on careers which these changes had implied. One analysis of the Shanghai Municipality Sea Transport Bureau noted that in 1958 Mayor K'o Ch'ing-shih had helped to establish a training course for ships' engineers and officers. Sailor-apprentices and workers in this merchant marine bureau could enroll as they wished. There is no information about the number of ships that were available for staffing by the graduates these courses created, but in 1962 Deputy Mayor Ts'ao Ti-ch'iu and the East China Bureau chief, Ch'en P'ei-hsien, endorsed an order by which "over two hundred apprentice steerers and engineers of sailor and stroker origin were driven out of their posts."[98] The boat-people were not happy.

Labor training certainly did not end after 1961, but it was less generously financed by municipal authorities. A local newspaper reported that fifty new vocational schools had been established in the first half of 1964 to offer two- and three-year industrial courses—but these new schools received no government funds whatsoever. Students had to pay their own tuition, fees, board, and book costs, as the local paper states very carefully![99] It is unclear how many of the enrollees were Sinkiang nonvolunteers waiting for a different political season. It is very clear that part of Shanghai's population felt a need for these schools, and was willing to pay for them if the government wouldn't.

Government-sponsored training did continue, but it was much more carefully controlled than before the 1961 conference. Official career norms both discouraged and encouraged workers, who were constantly reminded by the reigning ideology that they were the salt of the earth: workers were indeed to be promoted through education—but only some, only to certain levels. Deputy Mayor Ts'ao himself pointed out that there had been a 70 per cent increase in the number of technicians between the first and second five-year plans in Shanghai (even at the end of 1963 only 38 per cent of them were ex-workers).[100] But another source said that between 1957 and 1963, there had been a 700 per cent increase in the number of workers and technical-school graduates promoted to "technicianship."[101] Some of this excess low-level talent went to fill inland posts; but even if these statistics are quite inaccurate, it is evident that Shanghai's ambition to obtain *low-skill* technical training far outstripped its ability to create technical jobs of the status that graduates wanted.

The "veteran workers" who had these posts, and could teach skills, comprehended this situation quite well. If Ts'ao and Ch'en were restricting this education, it was because they had a constituency. Both apprentices and veterans had to be trained ideologically to reduce mutual friction. Veteran workers in a Shanghai shoe factory were reluctant to impart their knowledge; they were "backward" and had "not acquired a deep understanding of certain problems"—because they understood quite well the threat to their jobs.[102] The apprentices, most of them at least junior-middle-school graduates, complained that their talents were being wasted in lowly work. This problem was particularly great at pre-Liberation "red forts" like the Yang-shu-p'u Power Plant, where a few workers, apparently with long revolutionary histories, filled up the department directorships and shop foremanships. Newer employees were left without much chance of promotion.[103] In a few other plants, workers were more mobile. The Shanghai Machine Tool Plant, a model in the Cultural Revolution, was by 1963 already creating foremanships to which young, semi-educated workers could be promoted, particularly as a reward for technical innovations.[104] But this plant was a model exception; and even its 1961–66 management came under attack later, just as did the managements in other factories, and for similar reasons.

Part-time universities after 1961 were still a means by which management could reward workers—but the level of that management was now higher, and the rewarded workers were fewer than before. In 1963, the course at the Shanghai Municipal Part-Work Part-Study Industrial University was increased from three to five years. In 1964, that university had only 4,300 students, working for sixteen hours a week and studying for eight hours.[105] By 1966, it had been reduced to 3,500 students, even though its sponsoring companies numbered 1,419. The students were few in number, but half of them became "technical cadres" upon graduation.[106] The case of the Shanghai Television University is even more striking. Even in 1961, when it was founded, teachers who were transferred from other full-time colleges complained about its low academic standards. The party organs put politics in command. By 1966, 56,000 students were enrolled in this university—but in its five-year existence only 12,000 graduated from it.[107]

The perquisites of the few workers favored under this system were considerable. One hundred "five-good" workers of the Shanghai Railway Bureau were every year treated to a summer vacation at the famous resort of Lu-shan in Kiangsi.[108] One article reported that the Shanghai Teachers' Union in the hot season of 1964 sent some of its members to Hangchow and Tsingtao to rest. Others went to spots like the Yang-shu-p'u Power Plant, the Shanghai Machine Tool Plant, and the rolled-steel factory for moral betterment that same summer;[109] and the hills of Hangchow differ from the coal-dumps of Yang-shu-p'u. Vacations were not the only labor benefit to be distributed unevenly among workers. The Shanghai Federation of Trade Unions enrolled only 130,000 pensioners in early 1966,* and it is probable that most retired workers followed tradition and depended on their families for sustenance. In June 1966 the differentials between favored and unfavored workers came to a head: in that month, 20,000 Shanghai workers were admitted to the Communist party;[110] but a major, apparently abortive, rustication campaign was launched at the same time. Workers were now asked to go in large numbers to Sinkiang—for "residence" mobilization of the sort youths do.[111] The explosiveness of this policy is obvious. It may have reminded some proletarians of the pre-1949 labor-compensation systems that allowed a few foremen to have immense power over many workers.[112]

In May 1966 the *Jen min jih pao* reprinted an article by a locomotive conductor in the Shanghai Railway Traffic Station that called for workers to join the Cultural Revolution. They should "not merely take care of their work," but also struggle and "fight with guns and pens" against the "class enemy."[113] This inflammatory, clannish language must still have been safe in mid-1966. At least it did not find much immediate response then. Students—in Shanghai largely from bourgeois families—made cultural revolution at least in part to prove their own political legitimacy. But most workers had no such problem. How could this ideology hurt them? If China has any real proletariat at all, it is certainly in Shanghai. The cultural emphasis of this revolution must at first have seemed remote from working-class issues—until the municipal leaders who had made decisions affecting workers were seriously threatened by students. With that, and the decline of party and public security in factories, the workers themselves could and did form groups to defend or attack these leaders. The process took place gradually in Shanghai, from August to December 1966.

By the end of the year, many of Shanghai's worker groups were affiliated with two loose coalitions. The Shanghai Workers' Scarlet Guards General Headquarters (*Shang-hai kung jen ch'ih wei tui tsung ssu ling pu*) was at first much the larger of the two. It was an agglomera-

* *New China News Agency*, Shanghai, Mar. 12, 1966. Joyce Kallgren is engaged in research on this problem, which is vitally important to explanations of the Cultural Revolution. Statistics on labor perquisites in Shanghai are difficult to interpret because many separate schemes exist, but clearly the number of beneficiaries in the 1960's was not large relative to the total labor force.

tion of previously existing, worker-led organizations in factories, hostile toward bourgeois students and sometimes defensive of low-level party authorities. The other coalition had a similar name, the Shanghai Workers' Revolutionary Rebel General Headquarters (*Shang-hai kung jen ko ming tsao fan tsung ssu ling pu*). It opposed Ts'ao Ti-ch'iu and was also worker-led for the most part. We shall not attempt to give a play-by-play account of the events of December 1966 and January 1967, but the Scarlet Guards are extremely important in this period because they formed the best-organized nonradical unit in Shanghai after the local party had been neutralized. This coalition was closely associated with the militia in factories, which was not yet under the new authority's control. It clearly represented the majority of Shanghai's workers at least during the first half of January. The General Strike, which it sponsored, was extremely widespread—even according to hostile accounts put out by the new government at that time. The Scarlet Guards advocated a policy of "three-stop" (*san t'ing*)—stoppage of water, electricity, and work. The *Wen hui pao* on January 5 published the "Message to All Shanghai People," which said that "large numbers of members of the workers' red militia detachments" had been incited to "undermine production," and "to sabotage transport and communications under the pretext of going north to 'lodge complaints.'" The message reported that "lately, in many factories and plants, it has occurred that some or even the majority of the members of the red militia detachments have suspended production and deserted their posts in production."[114] This message, and the "Urgent Appeal" of January 9, did not call for punishment of strikers but called for their return to work.

In the second half of January events were even more complicated. Neither the radical nor the striking coalition was really unified; each was split into groups. A defector from the Scarlet Guards gave information that suggests why that movement and its successor organizations lost momentum: many moderate groups did not realize or could not believe the extent to which radicals would obtain central support, and they wanted to apply pressure on Peking to stop radical activities.[115] Chang Ch'un-ch'iao was the representative sent from Peking, but only in late January was the significance of this fact perceived by most Shanghaiese. When strikers could no longer imagine that in opposing him they were engaging in a loyalist revolt that later might be legitimized by the Chairman, then the movement began to decline, slowly group by group.[116]

On January 20, a *Wen hui pao* editorial entitled "Welcome to Scarlet Guards Who Rectify Their Errors" suggested it was more important to co-opt the workers than to suppress them. The real culprits were said to be a "small handful." But "middle-level" leaders should be "welcomed"—and presumably it was also feasible to negotiate with them.[117] Since the Scarlet Guards had significant armed organizations (essentially the old militias) organized by ch'ü in at least nine out of Shanghai's ten urban districts (plus some in rural hsien, and more in Wu-sung city),[118] they probably could not have been suppressed except by major army action, which the Nanking Military District was definitely not willing to take. Scarlet Guards did lose specific engagements to radicals and to small army units in late January and mid-February, but their overall organization remained very large. At least one member of the guards' city-wide committee, Li Shih-yin, was praised rather than punished when he defected. The whole organization seems to have been eminently a middle-level affair. We may infer that the relevant "handful" was tiny indeed.

Although most workers' groups were willing to cease active resistance to Chang Ch'un-ch'iao's new government, they were less willing simply to dissolve. In February and March, Shanghai newspapers attacked the "guild mentality" under which workers set up low-level organizations "according to their occupation and branch of work" rather than according to "class." Any special interpretation of this term "class" would have been inevitably arcane in a context so solidly proletarian; but nothing daunted, the *Chieh fang jih pao* deduced that workers should now be organized into "different factories, different systems, different departments," which in practice meant: into units larger than the units then existing.[119] The government was clearly hoping that ex-Scarlet Guard workers' groups might simply disappear, or at least might be shaken into some other, more manageable form.

This kind of advice was taken very slowly, and often not until soldiers arrived to help persuade the workers, usually by peaceful means. For complex reasons (related to events in Wuhan, Canton, and Peking), the Shanghai labor-pacification movement took place in irregular waves, of which the three troughs in 1967 were January, March-April, and July-August. The army was extremely important in this pacification. For example, on June 13 the New China News Agency finally announced that "with the help of army men from the Shanghai Garrison Command of the PLA, the proletarian revolutionaries at the Yang-shu-p'u Power Plant have succeeded in correctly handling the contradictions among themselves." The events in this strategic thermal plant, which supplies a very high percentage of Shanghai's electricity, can exemplify what happened elsewhere too. After "power seizure" and the formation of a unified "fighting headquarters," the plant's rebels split between moderates (probably some of them "veteran workers" who recalled strikes against the pre-1949 American owners) and a minority of radicals, centered in the steam-turbine workshop. The radicals "smashed" the moderate headquarters' office. Some moderate group leaders, apparently representing a majority of the workers, then ordered the radical coalition to dissolve. The radicals refused. Troops came to mediate; but even in this extremely vital plant, where production was admittedly affected by internal disputes and by coal shortages, soldiers used words, not guns. The moderate majority then called a meeting. The radicals came, but demanded that the opposite coalition withdraw immediately, since it had been "insincere" about making revolution. Later, everyone read Mao about how to handle contradictions among the people, and the army convened self-criticism meetings for both groups, at which China's distant Khrushchev was also attacked.[120]

Most Shanghai factories generally had younger staffs than did the Yang-shu-p'u plant. Most plants, particularly in new heavy industries built after 1958, did not have so many veteran workers who had established their positions and labor benefits over many years. But there was an overriding similarity between old and new plants: workers' armed militia strength (and the unwillingness of the army to intervene violently) allowed as much "democracy" and as many communal groups in more established staffs as in more dissatisfied ones. The Cultural Revolution therefore had results to different degrees in different factories, but some generalizations about the direction of change are possible.

The widest change is phenomenological: the historic tradition of "arcadian nativism" in the urban mass, which Frederic Wakeman pointed out, is now reactivated in terms of a quasi-racist communal notion of a "proletariat." Shanghai's post–Cultural Revolution workers now credit themselves with marvelous special characteristics that impartial examination might not always warrant. Nativism has all sorts of modern uses. The innovations made by "technicians of worker origin" are said to "develop more quickly and make greater contributions" than those of bourgeois experts—and not just for any technical reason, but because the workers have "profound proletarian feelings" and love Chairman Mao better.[121] The use of foreign production methods no doubt harms Chinese economic progress in many specific cases; but for Shanghai's proletariat this became an article of faith beyond the reach of empirical refutation or proof. In the Shanghai No. 2 Camera Factory, collective leadership replaced one-man responsibility; all workshop directorships were summarily abolished, and workers' elected representatives took charge of production. The advantage claimed for the new structure was technical through morals: it was said to *inspire* output.[122] In the Shanghai No. 3 Iron and Steel Plant, workers of ten factional groups united to seize power. They reduced the temperature in the heat-treatment furnaces by 60 degrees centigrade, and open-hearth smelting time by more than one-fifth. They claimed that the products from both processes had improved physical qualities, a claim that is much more credible for the heat treatment than for the smelting.[123] In fact, the cruder steel these workers made was quite probably much more appropriate for China's needs. Bourgeois experts may well have wasted inputs by religiously insisting on unneeded quality. But the workers did not say that, and the religious nature of their own commitment was exhibited in the claims of the progress they had made. Their revolution is not to be condemned, though this is its nature.

The most persistent aspect of Shanghai workers' new self-confidence, however, was their open criticism of the bourgeois students who had largely made "proletarian cultural revolution" in Shanghai. The army, whose job in schools was apparently even harder than in factories, was not about to disagree with workers in this criticism. As early as the revolutionary committee bill on Shanghai's "situation and tasks," of February 27, 1967, there was already criticism of having students in labor unions; contact with bourgeois people was to be avoided.[124]

On December 3–5, 1967, an extremely important meeting of workers' representatives took place under the direction of Chang Ch'un-ch'iao and Shanghai's most active labor-organizer, Wang Hung-wen. Soldiers also participated. The conference should not obscure two facts: workers' leaders still retained some independence, and the garrison's restraint from attacking workers' militia had generally avoided bad blood between them. Workers' resentment against bourgeois students emerged very clearly from the conference. Wang himself mentioned that nonproletarian people had entered factories and that their influence was poisonous because they inevitably brought with them nonproletarian ideas.[125] Wang said this at a time when the students' own representatives were still sitting on the revolutionary committee, although they were later purged from it.[126]

Young Shanghai workers' attitudes toward some labor problems coincided with Peking's attitudes late in 1967. The *Jen min jih pao* used a full page to reprint items from several Shanghai "rebel" papers, all associated with the general headquarters. Some ideas in them escaped the censor.[127] The concept of "welfare trade unions" was brought to task —by Peking because welfare unions cost money, and by the young workers because such unions had discriminated against them in welfare before 1966. Unions, the papers said, should not try to arrange holidays, distribute housing, take care of funerals, send condolences, or even pay for long convalescences. Factory managements should not sponsor competitions or offer prizes or honors, even for good goals like industrial safety, product quality, input economy, quota fulfillment, and innovation proposals. These competitions had put pressure on workers before the Cultural Revolution, and the honors had been used to justify discriminatory rewards. Opposition to technical reform is hidden in these papers under the veil of opposition to rewards for innovation; it nonetheless seems more Luddite than Marxist. The ideas expressed in the papers came amazingly close to doubting the motive force of Marxist history. In a developing country, such attitudes could affect policy. These workers' rebel papers also said that trade union membership (which in China as in other countries is sometimes connected with hiring policy) should be granted even to ideologically backward people, as long as they are true workers. Liu Shao-ch'i was associated with the idea that landlords, rich peasants, and counterrevolutionaries might join trade unions after changing their thoughts. According to these rebel papers, elite positions in unions should be reserved for true workers only; members of "third parties" (mostly bourgeois) must certainly not be allowed to hold such offices.

These events suggest that the proletariat of Shanghai did not want to be exploited any more, or to be mechanized out of their jobs, or to be flattered by an ideology from which they could derive no pride as a group. In the Cultural Revolution they formed factions to press these desires, which may be as dear to them as the grandeur of China and the correctness of Communism. If China's central leaders in future find more real proletarian dictatorship in the local politics of Shanghai, they may discover that the city is harder to control and to tax.

### Dilemma One: The Actors in a Local Chinese Polity

From here on, this essay presumes an independent interest in social theory. A narrative of four Shanghai institutions has been presented above; and no less courtesy will be afforded some social ideas now, which can throw light on Shanghai and to which the Shanghai data can contribute.

The most obvious actors in Shanghai's Cultural Revolution were political groups of students and workers. These groups were not equivalent to the four institutions examined above; they were smaller and were formed within those institutions. For all their independence during the more spectacular moments of "rebellion," the new political groups emerged from previously tame, subordinated agencies (often from students' social clubs or workers' militias). Our concept to comprehend them in these phases must be flexible enough to describe both conflict groups at war and interest groups in a bureaucracy. To repeat language used at the beginning of this essay, we need to develop a system of *political* levels. With systems and levels, there is an operational difficulty—as with rubbing one's belly and patting one's head. The trick is not to achieve either one, the trick is to achieve them both at the same time. The unit of analysis must allow, but not require, a coordinated nesting of smaller groups within larger. It must allow, but not require, the possibility of conflict (coordination's opposite) among those same units in a different phase. We will try first to approximate such a unit; later we will refine the idea to make our end notion better than the concept of "group."

To say there are "groups" in a space is to point to the existence of certain broad qualities there, which together make a definition.[128] (1) Groups do not come singly; they perceive themselves to be separate from similar related groups. Any space must contain two of them "immanently" (i.e. in the perceived purposes of action if not in unintended effects, phenomenologically if not institutionally), or it will contain none. There must be at least the immanent possibility of conflict between these groups. (2) Immanent or obvious, the conflict is general; it stems from diverse issues and is carried out in many ways. The group's jurisdiction over a member is not restricted by the group's norms. (3) Groups are not corporate; their existence is tied to a particular leader or to a leading clique modeled to resemble a family. The leader assumes some responsibility for the economic provision and physical protection of the members. (4) The existence of groups at one time in a space will help justify the use of this term to describe a later time. Groupism is typical of the slow-changing constitution of a polity, and is not an ephemeral condition.* Particular groups can recur even after long periods of latency.

---

* The fourth characteristic is an idea, not an empirical observation. In those terms there is no objection to it. I doubt the concept of logic that maintains there is some uncreated bond which must marry together the parts of any ideal type or definition. In fact, human intermediaries constantly relate empirical tests and logical operations. The only question here is whether "group," as defined in terms of these four ideal characteristics, has any examples.

A more modish objection would be that "group" is a thin veil for "faction," and represents some original sin with which a malicious Westerner would yoke the Chinese polity. But two reprises are in order. (1) The common use of "faction" is much less inclusive than our use of "group" here. Unlike factions, groups can be merely immanent and so can "nest" in a coordinated system. The present concept is a cri-

Either the long-term presence of any groups, or the recurrence of particular groups, can be offered as evidence that the total definition applies.

Groups, having these four characteristics, may differ in other respects. They vary in the extent of their internal discipline, in the kinds and amounts of power resources available to them, and in whether they have a particular territorial base, or a base in some office or level of a bureaucracy. The most obvious variable along which two groups can differ is the extent of equal or unequal political relations with other groups. Objective relations among groups may cover many or few issues; they may be long- or short-lived.

There is an ambiguity built by intention into the phenomenological idea "group." It can refer either to *situations of indirect rule*, as in a hierarchy or a colony, or to *situations of conflict* among factions between which there is definitely no relationship of dominance or subordination. We have seen that "conflict groups" form among Shanghai's youth to oppose rustication, and in factories to oppose the bureaucrats who accorded leisure and honor only to some workers. We have seen "subordinate groups" operate in Shanghai's democratic parties, at the family and residence levels, and indeed in most of the city's organizations prior to the Cultural Revolution.

This idea of group, with these limits and freedoms, applies in history too. Sun Yat-sen once described China as a "heap of sand" because he found its people so well organized in small groups that he could not unify them into a national group. His description is a hypothesis, and others could be made about China in later years. It is beyond the scope of this paper (and perhaps of any discussion of Mainland China) to develop exact quantitative methods by which groups and levels might

---

tique of the older one. It claims that "faction" was not broad enough to describe the constitution which has been endemic in China for some time. There is no space in this paper to contrast this "group," as a draft unit of analysis, with units suggested by others. This unit, when it is later refined to incorporate the idea of "levels," will bear even less resemblance to alternatives. (2) Some people think it wrong to discuss any long-lasting characteristics of a polity, lest they blind themselves to its political will by condemning their subject to a particular enduring classification. "Group" is based on Shanghai political data, and the concept does subsume many of them. The term "group" says nothing about permanent "national character"; it will not explain everything about China or constrain anything. But to look for categories which may hold true tomorrow is not the same as to sustain a condition which might be shown bad by communicable ethics. The thrust of these objections may be lessened when groups are later placed in levels of polity, to form a compound unit of analysis.

"Institution," as used above, is not identical with either "group" or "level." The procedure here is scientific because an analysis based on one set of instruments ("groups" and "levels") may explain large parts of a narrative organized by a very different tool (functional "institutions").

be defined more operationally. Methods to survey the texture of conflict relations and coordinated relations have not yet been invented even
for countries in which they might be used. Such methods would show
what data are relevant for China. Statisticians and phenomenologists—
quantitative and qualitative scientists—have not yet discovered that
they are natural allies, because conflict and coordination as regular
habits are both organized by mental sets, and they are both matters of
degree.

There is a relationship between groups and ideology. China at low
levels apparently has a strong spontaneous organization ethic. This resulted in small, autonomous guerrilla bands to fight Japan; in the Great
Leap it wrecked food distribution when its level of organization was
superseded; it structured the responses of Shanghai's workers and students when the Cultural Revolution neutralized police that previously
had kept their groups in check. We must think about the origins of this
local behavior ethic because of its obvious importance to our topic.
Weber would look at religion; so let us only be somewhat abashed and
do so briefly. The Chinese family's religion, for example, is in many
ways a worship of organization. The ordered phalanxes of generations—
the young standing respectfully behind the old, who stand respectfully
before the tablets, each in his place at a ceremony—can serve as symbol
of the social content of this ethic. City dwellers were not ideal patri-
archalists indeed, but migrants to the cities brought with them some of
the social values of this religion. Wakeman has described groups which
these immigrants formed in Canton in the last century.[129] Their belief
in secret societies was "nativist" in a social rather than a biological sense,
as is the particularism of Shanghai's proletariat today. They remembered
the Ming as a regime that protected them as Hans against the Mongols
and Manchus. Only after the influence of specifically Western ideas was
this ideology directed against the large Han upper classes—against the
image of a consuming, nonproductive, foreign-associated bureaucrat.
These groups did not unify the urban community; they split it precisely
while galvanizing its members with social ideals. We have seen a similar pattern in Shanghai in 1966–67.

There are many ways of looking at this pattern. A dynamic theory
of groups can be translated into the terms of "circulating elites," though
admittedly some of the other defining characteristics are lost in translation. For example, Shanghai after January 1967 retained "leading
cadres" in many units. These men were called "revolutionary" because
they had not opposed attacks on some of their fellow functionaries.
"Revolutionary leading cadres" underwent examination and criticism
by mass organizations—i.e., by their previous subordinates, now organ-

ized into new, nonsubordinate groups with new group leaders. Between the "leaders of mass revolutionary organizations" and the "revolutionary leading cadres" there was a mid-level conflict of elites, widely perceived and written about in editorials at that time. The Shanghai Revolutionary Committee usually worked to dampen this conflict, to ensure its own power by keeping a balance between the lower-level forces involved.[130] Each group was held together under its leader; so conflicts between leaders were nearly indistinguishable from conflicts between groups.

G. William Skinner has shown that in Southeast Asia, Chinese leaders are simultaneously agents of their non-Chinese local governments, often with high bureaucratic rank, and leaders in their own communities. They are respected in each constituency largely because of their position in the other.[131] These communities can lose the characteristics of "groups" when their self-perceived identity is weakened by assimilation and when their leaders lose Chineseness by joining the native Establishments. But as long as these groups remain phenomenological units, without conflicting openly, their captains can continue to interact profitably both with group members and with superordinate powers, so that the conflict will remain latent until perceptions change.

Because perceptions take a long time to change, the last part of the definition of "group," which insists that groups are not ephemeral, is related to the other three parts. Not only do groups recur as an endemic, constitutional, slowly changing characteristic of their polities; particular groups also recur after long periods of dormancy or suppression. Even in Shanghai's Cultural Revolution, when the unspecific sort of groupism was more prominent, the specific sort was not absent. Some months after units of the Shanghai Workers' Revolutionary Rebel General Headquarters were disbanded, local newspapers began to complain that these units were springing back to life and were reorganizing in places where government control was weak.[132]

Phenomenological groups, having the characteristics and variations shown above, are the dynamic, will-expressing units of the Chinese polity. To the extent that the national polity has been unified, it has mirrored their characteristics. Because the national polity is somewhat divided, a theory of regional political levels that really engage in politics can be constructed. The concept of "polity" mutually relates personal meanings, regional projects, and national policies. That philosopher's word is not a rejection of science; it is accurate because it suggests for many levels that the perceived semantic of political behavior is as necessary to scientific understanding as are the social functions of political behavior.

We are mired deep in problems of relating the unit of analysis and the dynamic of this theory. "Group" without "level" is an insufficient unit for Shanghai's drama. Moreover there is a relation between players and plot. Members' actions and perceptions define a unit's existence; but the unit is a platform for further actions and can constrain the substance of further perceptions. Unit and action help define one another. Explanation of either will often depend on refinement of the other. Later we will try to combine them.

## Dilemma Two: Motivations for a Cultural Revolution

An attempt to explain the motives of Shanghai's Cultural Revolution is hindered mostly by the difficulty of obtaining categories strong enough to comprehend the political goals that arise and quickly change there. Cities like Shanghai are not Western—but they are "modernizing," and we cannot ignore what their inhabitants consider to be modern in the West. They are not villages—but they are full of *dépaysées*, immigrants whose consciousness bears some resemblance to the consciousness of peasants, and whose family and neighborhood organizations are somewhat similar to rural types.* Western urbanism does not suffice as a goal or "final cause" to explain politics in these cities, and village cultures do not supply "original causes" for many events.

Some early analysts split the difference, saying that we should imagine a mixture, a little bit of old with a little bit of new. For example, the typical Asian city was said to have two parts, the "Western-type area" and the "indigenous-type area consisting of an agglomeration of villages."[133] Two points were located, the line connecting them was bisected, and vectors were measured in various ways to assess the effects. This analysis works for many purposes. But the logics governing politics are less simple than the logics governing human interaction with physical things or even with stable institutions; and China's identity will not allow the "Western part" to be perceived as only Western now; and the transition between old and new is quicker and less smooth in cities than in the countryside. To study politics in Chinese cities, this

---

* Joseph Levenson was going to write a history of cosmopolitan consciousness in China, but because of his death we have lost much more than the possibility of reading that in its full form. An essay on the subject by him is "The Province, the Nation and the World: the Problem of Chinese Identity," in Albert Feuerwerker, Rhoads Murphy, and Mary C. Wright, eds., *Approaches to Modern Chinese History* (Berkeley and Los Angeles: University of California Press, 1967), pp. 268–88.

In 1937 Olga Lang compared the functions and forms of families in Shanghai, Peking, Tientsin, and certain rural areas. She found that urbanization had only limited effects on family structure, although Shanghai showed the greatest departure from traditional models. See her *Chinese Family and Society* (New Haven: Yale University Press, 1946).

two-model analysis will not work. Even abstractly, we do not just select, discard, or mix models as the fancy strikes us. Our procedure of building models is not to achieve general statements at the expense of interesting exceptions; it is based on a psychological relation, in scientists, between large surveyable numbers of cases and the likelihood of convinced understanding. That relation is real, but irregularities may also help us understand. When all the data may be exceptions (models in fact, but exemplary ones not made by us!), then our problem is to remain convinced. With the old logics of Eastern origin and Western goal dead, we hope for present surveys—and find that our present information on Shanghai is too much affected by practical attitudes toward truth. There is no need here to prove that this is a common issue in many countries; but the categories of serious analysis are either way not government policies—Chinese or American. In other disciplines, at other times than now in American history, for other subjects than Chinese cities, it has been possible to analyze non-Western countries with a simple dynamic of first and final causes, or by behavioral observation. Now there is scientific confusion for China, because we cannot conventionally do any of these things. The primary reaction has been to accept, as science, the categories of understanding of the people whose behavior we study.[134] The best trick will be to eliminate neither Western observation nor Chinese meaning from our analysis.

The processes that generate those two are both mental, and a relation can be established between them. We will first state what they are abstractly, and then we will illustrate each of the two with Shanghai examples. Talcott Parsons distinguishes the "situational referent" (here, directly perceived data and "Western observation") from the "normative referent" (phenomenological data, "Chinese meaning"). The surest way of making this distinction is also most practical: There are *two different sets of logical operations* which describe our mental interaction ( 1 ) with physical and quasi-physical objects and ( 2 ) with remembered ideas. Processes of either type occur in actors' minds, and the student of action can reproduce them in his own mind. For our purpose here, it will be enough to speak simply of situations and intentions.* Sociologists and

---

* The abstract ideas in this paper have more concern for methods useful in dealing with the title's subject than with "systems"; but it will nevertheless be useful to follow a fashion and outline the system implied here, because its terms may simplify what is found elsewhere. This system would have two major sets of variables: the stages between intentions and situations, and the stages between individual and collective. These are the two "dilemmas" that arose out of Shanghai data above. The four sectors of Parsons's social system are the quadrants generated by these axes. Political events (decisions, policies, movements) might be classified by their variations in these two ways. Many would be definable only within wide limits

political scientists have best explored the logics by which we calculate
in the former realm, and intellectual historians have done the same for
the latter. Each group in practice has used the simple transforms developed by the other—even when they have felt camouflage to be necessary, and when they have most adamantly denied the professional legitimacy of the opposite group's method. Both approaches see the levels of
society as places of interchange between outer situation and inner intention, places where men constantly cause these to modify one another.
The two different logics are compatible for their purposes. When talking
about Shanghai, we have used them both.

Two paragraphs of examples can show concretely how each of these
modes of analysis is necessary to explain our subject. China, and particularly its large coastal cities, suffers immense problems first on the
"situational referent." Objectively, China's population is now in the
midst of "demographic lag" between slow-declining birth rates and
quicker-declining death rates; and in cities this problem is aggravated
by migration. In Shanghai immigrants have been disproportionately
fertile and young; the marriage rate of Shanghai in the mid-1950's was
1.6 per cent to 2 per cent per year—about double the figure for most
countries.[135] Demographers debate whether to blame urban immigration or natural increase more, and proponents of the concept "overrural-
ization"[136] point out that low labor productivity may be the essential
problem in both factories and fields. Lax migration control has coincided with declining food surpluses, and also with self-sufficiency movements like the Great Leap Forward during which the number of counties placed under Shanghai's jurisdiction has gone up quickly.[137] The
province-level government had almost half again as many people to
cope with in 1964 as it had at the end of 1957.[138] During the Cultural
Revolution large numbers of peasants came into the city demanding
more benefits and year-end bonuses;[139] there is no doubt that the large
rural population then inside Shanghai's boundaries held the municipal
government responsible for providing concrete welfare and protection.

These situational difficulties would not have been politically so dangerous had there not also been normative conflicts and perceived social
gaps in Shanghai's polity. Local public security agents too often remained the only government representatives with whom urban residents came in contact, and frequent mass movements failed to close
the historic gap between people and mid-level government.[140] Mass

---

because of what this paper calls "ambiguity." The whole intent anyhow would not
be to bound the political system but to exhibit the lively relations and interchanges
that it represents.

movements, contrary to their purpose, sometimes gave rise to personal antisocial, escapist activities (which certainly could be represented by suicide rates if survey data were available). Normative ambiguities can have good status in a logic for intention, even when they are patently absurd in situational logics that were never built to apply to them. In these terms we have tried to explain how Shanghai's workers kept alive an independent historic militia tradition, whose freedom the Shanghai Public Security Bureau could not deny precisely by the lights of the "proletarian dictatorship" that had justified its own power. We have seen how "social youth," sent to Sinkiang for collective purposes, could later attack the sending agencies for insufficient public interest. We have seen how Shanghai students could form the most unified groups exactly when they had the least well-defined goals to serve together. And we have seen how Shanghai workers could justify their technical reforms virtually on the ground that they lacked the preconceptions instilled by technical education.

Even the state, as well as groups and individuals, has not let its ideas be much restricted by situations. The frequent ambiguousness of Chinese Communist ideology is a prime symptom of the need for pragmatic flexibility in dealing with a myriad of concrete problems. Examples of this pliable "metaphysic of organization," this "practical sociology of action,"[141] are not hard to locate: "walking on two legs"; "agriculture is base, industry is leader"; "concentrate the basic authority, diffuse the smaller authority"; "both red and expert"; and many more, especially the notorious near-contradictions "mass line" and "democratic centralism." Even single words like "class" or "commune" are carefully defined between contradictory poles. These ambiguities can be interpreted infinitely—but that has information-gathering, experimental uses, as much as tyranical ones. For example, the idea "commune" arose twice in Shanghai: first "urban" commune (an ideal that China proposed and Shanghai rejected);* then "Paris" commune (an ideal that Shanghai proposed and China rejected).[142] "Commune" was a word that could

---

* A suggestive treatment of ambiguities in the notion "urban commune" is by J. Salaff in "The Urban Communes and Anti-City Experiment in Communist China," *China Quarterly*, 29 (Jan.–Mar. 1967), 83–84. On the question of whether Shanghai ever had such communes, even nominally, I shall not try to cite all the sources, but only the types of them: Henry Lethbridge, *China's Urban Communes* (Hong Kong: Dragonfly Books, 1961), pp. 71–72, says they did exist; but his footnote— a report of the Shanghai's Women's Federation reprinted in *Peking Review*, 1 (Jan. 6, 1961), 5—actually implies the opposite, that there were only rural communes in the suburbs. The *Ching hu ti ch'ü tzu liao mu lu* (Catalogue of materials on the Nanking-Shanghai region) (Taipei: Kuo chia an ch'uan chü [State Security Bureau], 1967), p. 169, agrees there were none, as does Frederick Nossal, *Dateline*

justify many things; it was a facade of some meaning behind which various actions with additional meanings could be tried.

Ambiguity is at the heart of half the motives in Shanghai's Cultural Revolution. Students, who can look forward to the longest and best future careers, formed the initial backbone of an anti-careerist movement. Thousands of city-dwellers who had been sent by local party committees to work in the country now came back to overthrow those committees—in a movement whose ideology would have sent them out again. But again, the most flexible words of all were single, like "left" and "proletariat." The party's claim to these titles was weakened; so new leaders conferred them on anyone who would join their groups—in Shanghai, often on radical persons of bourgeois family background. The *Wen hui pao*'s editorial of February 15, 1967, made clear that people should be condemned not because of their family origins but only because of their bad acts or attitudes. Later, in the summer of 1967 and after, some factions thought Shanghai's largely bourgeois "little generals" should be brought under control; so "ultra-left" became "right"; and "proletarian" was familial.

Normative ambiguity affects behavior. For example, ill-definition often prevailed regarding which groups were leftist. If Chairman Mao sent into this context some "latest instruction" ordering "true leftists" to unite against the class enemy, then various groups would indeed strengthen their organizations—and would be the readier to fight one another. The experience of battle would make such groups even harder to reconcile than before, more prepared for the next "latest instruction" to initiate the cycle again, so that the syndrome reinforced itself.[143] Urban groups often coalesced at first on the basis of tenuous bonds during the Cultural Revolution's early authority vacuum (for example, many schoolchildren first formed "five-red" groups, although that basis for unity was not often cited later). Such groups were consolidated quickly enough if they fell into a syndrome of battles and loyalty to vague goals.

---

*Peking* (London: MacDonald, 1962), pp. 189–97, who like many travelers around 1960, saw Chang Family Alley, an "embryo urban commune" mobilizing 96 per cent of the area's able housewives to sew, wire telephone receivers, and save staples from old magazines. Nossal's information suggests that the canteen was subsidized, but residential customs caused many to eat at home even when they bought food there—which was hardly the Government's intent. He says Shanghai's slowness embarrassed Ts'ao Ti-ch'iu, who had publicly pledged quicker communization. But Audrey Donnithorne, in *China's Economic System* (London: George Allen & Unwin, 1967), pp. 227–28, points out that these street organizations did not differ from other cities' full "communes" except in name. Residential Shanghai did reject the basically rural *idea* of "commune," and the city government was not willing to resist that opinion finally.

At the prestigious Shanghai Chemical Engineering Institute, the struggles between groups came to resemble an old-fashioned clan war. The first pitched battle was fought on July 26, 1967; but a year later the constant efforts of army instructors had still failed to persuade the two major groups to stop sporadic, self-reinforcing violence—or even to dismantle defense works around the buildings they occupied.[144] The editors of the *Jen min jih pao* hardly got the point, or helped this kind of situation, in their leader of September 18, 1967. They first discoursed on the current "latest instruction" and urged that it be firmly executed by all those who understood it. They then added, for safe measure, that it should also be firmly executed by all those who did not yet understand it.

If a government is interested in having specified, well-defined norms, then that interest betrays a purpose—to make sure that instructions are executed accurately by subordinates. But vague rules are not to be condemned; they display another possible interest. Normative ambiguity allows each level of politics to work with its own full energy so that the aims which are partially prescribed might be fulfilled more quickly. Of course one can object that normative ambiguity has other results too, which can vitiate the intent to mobilize social energy. Some ambiguity is not just a result of current official intention; it can arise from historical residues also. As we saw above in rough terms, the combination of modern and traditional values creates a dishomogeneous mixture, a new beast whose characteristics need not be present in either of the value sets from which the new thing is nurtured. In spite of such objections, it is still true that different degrees of norm specification can fulfill different intended functions; for example, norms can be structured either to control energy or to maximize it. Men at various political levels are conscious of these alternatives. They can make decisions about whether or not norms should be specific.[145]

This analysis of action under ambiguous norms can be expressed in terms of a post-positivist decision theory. The traits of an organization or system were usually thought to be determined by its mutually consistent goals. If those goals went unfulfilled, the organization might engage in "search behavior" to seek an optimal, or at least satisfactory, method of fulfilling them.[146] But the analysis of our present topic must be different in two ways: (1) In the hierarchy of a political "system," each level is willful. The old fudge-factor distinction for bureaucracies—between "formal" organization to speak of sovereignty and "informal" organization to allow real politics in the levels—will not do for a serious political science of regions, because it does not clarify the relationship between those two. (2) Even more important, the structure-generating goals and values are now ambiguous. Their characteristics are indeterminate, or at least inconsistent. Decision-makers actually take into account not just the situational options open to them, but also the array of ultimate goals and intentions "open to them" at all levels. We can talk about the patterns that relate such goals; they are organized in the logics explored by intellectual historians (whose exemplar in Chinese studies was Joseph Levenson). But a purely positivist science cannot admit these—even when it can observe the decisional behavior they affect.

"Decision" is not the only event in a decision theory for ambiguous norms; equally important are the births and deaths of plausible options in either the normative or situational referents. These changes may occur simultaneously with decisions, or also at other times. For example, a situational decision may by intention leave norm-options inconsistent with it still alive, for use later if the original decision proves to have been bad. Or again, the *degree* of norm ambiguity at any level (inversely, the degree to which any positivist concept of "system" applies there) may itself be subject to conscious decisions, to the extent that various inconsistent goals cannot be specialized over time or space. This is the kind of theory that applies to local politics in Shanghai's Cultural Revolution. Decision theory, behavioralism, and functionalism need only admit some concepts to account for these politics, but need not eliminate any methods. Organizations, once founded, may search for new ultimate goals in a logical field, just as easily as they search their concrete environs for new resources.

This formulation allows us to reconsider our unit-of-analysis in the light of dynamics. The original attractiveness of the notion "group" was that it could apply in situations either of conflict or of coordination. Although groups are perceived as competitive, they can be organized into hierarchies. "Group" in this sense is an eminently political idea; it can help us refine the originally administrative concepts of "level" and "nested" units, to make them really political terms. The following definitions apply only in systems of groups. A *"political level" is a space of groups that perceive themselves to be in conflict.* Political levels may overlap administrative ones. There is a complex relationship between those two, as the following ideas suggest. Lines of different darkness are to be drawn between political levels; their very existence is a matter of degree (for which quantitative measures should be developed). Imagine three conditions: (1) If there is extremely high perceived coordination or unity between sets of persons, then there will be little conflict; so the idea "political level" will not be of much use. (2) When there is a medium degree of perceived subordination and conflict, then the idea "political level" is usable, because only then can *two* levels be distinguished *and* related. (3) General conflict does not occur at all *between* "political levels"; the concept is pointless on any single level, and no two different levels can be distinguished between groups in general conflict. These three conditions show the applicability of the notion that political units at lower levels might nest inside units at higher ones. Political nesting means nothing unless it is applied to less-than-general politics—jurisdictional and bargaining politics—which takes place between self-perceived groups. One can speak of political interaction between levels only in mixed cases, where there is neither total conflict nor total subordination. Shanghai provides many examples: small businessmen in the early 1960's outfoxed the ch'ü auditors, while also paying considerable taxes; ex–Scarlet Guards in 1967 would always "support Mao," but they retained independence from Chang Ch'un-ch'iao much longer; residents would migrate to Sinkiang for economic purposes, but by rule of their own family leaders, only so many, only so far, and often for a short time. The political words "level" and "nesting" will apply only when norms are partially specified, only when there is both some coordination and some conflict, only when leaders are attempting both to control and to maximize social energy in response to different problems, and only when goals are part set and part uncertain. This can all change in degree over time or by location. "Groups in levels" can have dynamic intentions and are a unit of analysis for recent Shanghai politics.

This scheme may throw some light on the main controversy dividing students of American regional politics, for it suggests that there are substantively different kinds of local politics for which different methods are appropriate. Many American scholars have tended to phrase their debate as if method were primary over substance, and they have neglected the extent to which scientists might use a variety of methods.[147] Robert Dahl studied decision-making behavior with regard to particular issues in New Haven, and he showed how a city government mediated conflict between sets of people with different interests in these issues. Dahl's method and conclusion are appropriate to a situation where low specification of norms allows social energy to be maximized (the case with less coordination, as described above). Floyd Hunter studied perceptions about leaders' power over the general jurisdiction in Atlanta, and he showed how politics helped maintain a stable social and economic structure there. Hunter's method and conclusion coincide with our case in which norms are specified to coordinate social efforts (the case with more imperative control). New Haven and Atlanta may have some substantive differences, to which the different approaches were appropriate. Dahl's decision theory and Hunter's reputation theory may each be valid for variant phases of politics.[148]

In China, also, these variants can specialize geographically as well as over time. They determine the types of agency used for control. There is no need to spell out Franz Schurmann's multifacet historical distinction between "exploitation" and "control" systems,[149] or his discussion of "dualisms" in commune organization;[150] but they exemplify this specialization. In Shanghai, the norm split is administered most obviously at street levels by two separate offices: the public security *p'ai ch'u so* system for "control," and the district residence office *pan shih ch'u* system for "exploitation."

### Conclusion: Search Behaviors for Urban Values

Our model is still static. It shows tension between two aspects of ambiguous norms. It clearly implies how a leader, preoccupied with ensuring the accurate efficiency of his organization, could come under attack from would-be leaders for stifling the members' energy. In fact, this was a common theme of 1966 attacks on Ch'en P'ei-hsien and Ts'ao Ti-ch'iu. The model, however, does not yet transform this mere tension into rebellious group politics. It notes that political goals may be specified or not—but why does any particular degree of specification become policy in real decisions? "Cycle" has been mentioned—but what impels a cycle to start? Answers have already been implied, even though they have not been stated. The "normative referent" requires that meaning be attached to behavior in the behaver's mind. A "level" needs identity to act, just as much as it needs any other resource. Policy choices, including the choice of which aspect of a two-faced norm to emphasize, must at any time be cogent to the policy-maker at any level. His experience determines what seems cogent; and if the experience itself is ambivalent, the policy will follow suit.

Shanghai's Communist leaders know cities well, though their party gained power in the countryside. They are aware of the pleasure and peace of life inside walls, but guerrilla warfare is not urbane. This dilemma is not new for them. They want a consistency in work style and in thought style, but their problems are more complex than any policy they could concoct even if their own ideas were perfectly definite. A discrepancy arises between the norm-choice they in fact make at any time and what would be required by an abstract calculus of control and enthusiasm over all levels. Their phenomenology is a bit off-phase with their situation, and the former is not mere dream; not only is it unavoidable, it is connected with why men make policy at all.

*Notes*

# Notes

## Introduction: Order and Modernization in the Chinese City

1. For a discussion of Mao's long-range policy toward the cities from 1920 to 1959 see John W. Lewis, "Political Aspects of Mobility in China's Urban Development," *American Political Science Review*, LX: 4 (Dec. 1966), 899–912. A comprehensive study of the takeover and subsequent periods in Canton is Ezra F. Vogel, *Canton under Communism: Programs and Politics in a Provincial Capital, 1949–1968* (Cambridge, Mass.: Harvard University Press, 1969). See also Lai Chih-yen, ed., *Chieh kuan ch'eng shih ti kung tso ching yen* (Experiences in the takeover work of the cities) (Canton: Jen min ch'u pan she, 1949).

2. "Appendix: Resolution on Certain Questions in the History of Our Party" [Apr. 20, 1945], in Mao Tse-tung, *Selected Works* (Peking: Foreign Languages Press, 1961–65), III, 177–225.

3. *Ibid.*, p. 200. Later in this resolution (p. 202) Mao explicitly praised Liu Shao-ch'i's "ideas on tactics for work in the White areas . . . and particularly in the cities." The awkwardness caused by Mao's praise of the now-purged Liu helps account for the elimination of this resolution from recent editions of Mao's *Selected Works*.

4. For a sampling of Mao's views on the city between 1945 and 1949, see Mao 1961–65, IV, 81, 85, 187–88, 203, 215, 221, 247–49, 273–74, 337–39, 363–65, 373–74, and 394.

5. The most spectacular denunciations of Liu Shao-ch'i in this respect relate to his alleged policies toward Tientsin and his personal ties with family members in that city. For a sample of these denunciations, see *Jen min jih pao* (People's daily) [hereafter JMJP], Apr. 15, 1967; *Chieh fang chün pao* (Liberation army daily), Apr. 15, 1967; *Pa erh wu chan pao* (Aug. 25 battle news), Feb. 14, 1967 in *Selections from China Mainland Magazines* [hereafter SCMM], No. 574, pp. 1–3; a Red Guard leaflet of Apr. 20, 1967 in SCMM, No. 584, pp. 27–35; and a Red Guard pamphlet of June 1967 in SCMM, No. 619.                                                                    \

6. Though much of this discussion concerns politics and ideology, Mao placed heavy emphasis on the economic power of the city, which was often measured in fiscal terms. As early as June 1950, Yang Pei-hsin, in reporting on "How China Conquered Inflation," noted that "urban taxes ... already surpass rural taxes in total volume." *People's China*, I: 12 (June 16, 1950), 8. For a comprehensive study of Chinese taxation, see George N. Ecklund, *Financing the Chinese Government Budget: Mainland China, 1950–1959* (Chicago: Aldine, 1966), esp. pp. 20, 58–71, 77–85, and 98–99.

7. This report to the Second Plenum was republished with fanfare in 1968 in JMJP and *Hung ch'i* (Red flag). For a discussion of its relationship to the general political system Mao was fashioning in the Cultural Revolution, see my Introduction to John W. Lewis, ed., *Party Leadership and Revolutionary Power in China* (Cambridge, Eng.: Cambridge University Press, 1970).

8. The essential Communist policy toward the cities is found in *Kuan yü ch'eng shih cheng ts'e ti chi ko wen hsien* (Several documents concerning policies in cities) (Hantan: Hua pei hsin Hua shu tien, 1949); and Liu Shao-ch'i *et al.*, *Hsin min chu chu i ch'eng shih cheng ts'e* (The new democratic urban policy) (Hong Kong: Hsin min chu ch'u pan she, 1949). For an early discussion, see H. A. Steiner, "Chinese Communist Urban Policy," *American Political Science Review*, XLIV: 1 (Mar. 1950), 47–63.

9. The interdependence of urban systems, of course, is characterized by the flow of commodities, money, and information, as well as the movement of commuters and immigrants and the extension of political institutions and influence. Nevertheless, in China the fundamental prerequisite for such interdependence was bureaucratization. A theoretical discussion of these problems is in Philip E. Jacob and James V. Toscano, eds., *The Integration of Political Communities* (Philadelphia and New York: Lippincott, 1964), chap. 5; and Olof Wärneryd, *Interdependence in Urban Systems* (Göteborg: Regionkonsult Aktiebolag, 1968). As Wärneryd suggests, a tendency toward urban interdependency commonly arises during urbanization, and in China this tendency is most pronounced in the areas of the north and northeast where urbanization is well advanced.

10. Point 13 of the Central Committee's "Decision ... Concerning the Great Proletarian Cultural Revolution" (adopted Aug. 8, 1966) stated in part: "The cultural and educational units and leading organs of the Party and government in the large and medium cities are the points of concentration of the present proletarian cultural revolution." *Peking Review*, 33 (Aug. 12, 1966), 11.

11. Compare Georg Simmel, "The Metropolis and Mental Life," in Kurt Wolff, trans., *The Sociology of Georg Simmel* (New York: Free Press, 1950), pp. 409–24.

12. See Dwight H. Perkins, *Market Control and Planning in Communist China* (Cambridge, Mass.: Harvard University Press, 1966), chap. 2; and *New China's Economic Achievements, 1949–1952* (Peking: Foreign Languages Press, 1952).

13. See the essay by Richard H. Solomon, "Mao's Effort to Reintegrate the Chinese Polity: Problems of Authority and Conflict in Chinese Social Processes," in A. Doak Barnett, ed., *Chinese Communist Politics in Action* (Seattle: University of Washington Press, 1969), pp. 271–351.

14. In "On the People's Democratic Dictatorship" (June 30, 1949), Mao said: "Our present task is to strengthen the people's state apparatus—mainly the people's army, the people's police, and the people's courts." Mao 1961–65, IV, 418.

15. Hsieh Fu-chih has accused P'eng Chen and others of copying the legal system of the Kuomintang and the Soviet Union. See *Fan P'eng Lo hei hsien* (Oppose the black line of P'eng and Lo), 2 (July 1968), in SCMM, No. 625, p. 16. According to Huhetot Radio, Dec. 5, 1969: "P'eng Chen argued that those laws of the KMT government and Napoleonic codification that suit this country should be included in our legal code. . . . He repeatedly instructed his henchmen to base themselves on the feudal, capitalist, and revisionist laws."

16. Thus, for example, former public security chief Lo Jui-ch'ing was de-nounced during the Cultural Revolution for his alleged sponsorship of "ten-no" campaigns whose purpose was to transform cities into models of tidiness. See the untitled Red Guard pamphlet of July 1967 translated in SCMM, No. 641, pp. 13–15.

17. Charles Tilly, "A travers le chaos des vivantes cités," in Paul Meadows and Ephraim H. Mizruchi, eds., *Urbanism, Urbanization, and Change: Comparative Perspectives* (Reading, Mass.: Addison-Wesley, 1969), pp. 379–94.

18. See *Ching-kang shan* (Ching-kang mountains), Apr. 18, 1967, in *Survey of China Mainland Press* [hereafter SCMP], No. 3946, p. 9; and Red Guard leaflet of Apr. 20, 1967, in SCMM, No. 584, pp. 32–33.

19. For discussion of this slogan, see "Sixty Work Methods (Draft)," in *Current Background*, No. 892, p. 9, and the Central Committee resolution of Sept. 27, 1962, "On the Further Strengthening of the Collective Economy of the People's Communes and Expanding Agricultural Production," which says "The Party Central Committee has consistently maintained the principle of unifying the supreme authority in the Central Committee and of delegating lesser authority suitably. On this principle we are implementing a system of unified leadership and delegated management." In C. S. Chen, ed., and Charles P. Ridley, trans., *Rural People's Communes in Lien-Chiang* (Stanford: Hoover Institution Press, 1969), pp. 87–88.

20. Franz Schurmann, *Ideology and Organization in Communist China*, rev. ed. (Berkeley and Los Angeles: University of California Press, 1968), p. 402.

21. Edward C. Banfield, *Political Influence: A New Theory of Urban Politics* (New York: Free Press, 1961), pp. 326–41.

22. Uncertainty about the cadre's proper role was also a common prob-lem in the countryside, where cadres who formed too close ties with the masses were considered "tailist" and those who were too aloof "commandists." See Thomas P. Bernstein, "Keeping the Revolution Going: Problems of Village Leadership after Land Reform," in Lewis 1970, chap. 7. The best study of the cadre's world is A. Doak Barnett, *Cadres, Bureaucracy, and Political Power in Communist China* (New York: Columbia University Press, 1967).

23. For a note on typical accusations of cadre elitism, see Leonard Schapiro and John W. Lewis, "The Roles of the Monolithic Party under the Totalitarian Leader," in Lewis 1970, pp. 134–35.

24. The "three-anti" campaign was begun by Kao Kang in China's north-east during 1951. Its target was party and government cadres. This campaign

coincided with the rectification movement in the party planned by the first national conference on organization work in March 1951. For a discussion see An Tze[Tzu]-wen, "The Consolidation of Party Organisations," *People's China*, 13 (July 1, 1953), 5–10.

25. This urban campaign was launched in 1952 against industrialists and businessmen who allegedly were guilty of bribery, tax evasion, theft of state property and economic information, and cheating on government contracts. For a discussion, see A. Doak Barnett, *Communist China: The Early Years, 1949–55* (New York: Praeger, 1964), chap. 12; and John Gardner, "The *Wu-fan* Campaign in Shanghai: A Study in the Consolidation of Urban Control," in Barnett 1969, pp. 477–539.

26. See Lewis Dec. 1966.

27. The best study of urban bureaucratic development is found in Ying-mao Kau, *Bureaucratic Development and Politics in Communist China* (Stanford: Stanford University Press, forthcoming). For comprehensive studies of similar struggles in Soviet urban policy, see B. Michael Frolic, "Soviet Urban Politics," unpub. diss., Cornell University, 1970; David T. Cattell, *Leningrad: A Case Study of Soviet Urban Government* (New York: Praeger: 1968); and Robert J. Osborn, *Soviet Social Policies: Welfare, Equality, and Community* (Homewood, Ill.: Dorsey Press, 1970).

28. See Schurmann 1968, pp. 368–71.

29. In December 1954, the Standing Committee of the National People's Congress passed the regime's three most important urban organization laws; these concerned the organization of public security stations, city street offices, and city residents' committees. For the text of these laws, see Jerome Alan Cohen, *The Criminal Process in the People's Republic of China, 1949–1963: An Introduction* (Cambridge, Mass.: Harvard University Press, 1968), pp. 106–7, 109–12. See also the "Organic Law of the Local People's Congresses and Local People's Councils of the People's Republic of China" [Sept. 21, 1954], *Documents of the First Session of the First National People's Congress of the People's Republic of China* (Peking: Foreign Languages Press, 1955), pp. 213–31.

30. For a typical article on letter writing and visits, see *Cheng fa yen chiu* (Political-legal research), 2 (May 5, 1962), 27–30.

31. Chang Jui-nien, "A District Government," *People's China*, 20 (Oct. 16, 1955), 17.

32. A typical denunciation of this sort is in Peking Radio, June 19, 1970.

33. I have followed particularly here the discussion in Banfield 1961. One can also infer what is going on in the cities from articles that attack factionalism or stress the importance of following approved work methods. One of the most important such articles since the Cultural Revolution is in JMJP, Nov. 5, 1969.

34. Norton Long, "The Local Community as an Ecology of Games," in *The Polity* (Chicago: Rand McNally, 1962), esp. pp. 146–48.

35. See, for example, the report on Shuang-ya-shan city in *Hung ch'i*, 6–7 (July 1, 1969), 60–67.

36. See JMJP, Aug. 24, 1969, for an editorial on mass criticism. The classic statement on the relationship of democratic participation and centralism is Mao's *On the Correct Handling of Contradictions among the People* (Peking:

Foreign Languages Press, 1957), pp. 13–15. A typical recent article on the public interest is JMJP, Aug. 9, 1969.

37. JMJP, July 24, 1969, carries a detailed report on the upgrading of workers in Shanghai.

38. Quoted in Jerome Ch'en, ed., *Mao* (Englewood Cliffs, N.J.: Prentice-Hall, 1969), p. 75.

39. I have discussed this more fully in "Revolutionary Struggle and the Second Generation in Communist China," *China Quarterly*, 21 (Jan.–Mar. 1965), 126–47, and in "The Social Limits of Politically Induced Change," in Chandler Morse *et al.*, *Modernization by Design* (Ithaca, N.Y.: Cornell University Press, 1969), pp. 1–33.

40. A "balanced" relationship between urban and rural areas was advocated in the immediate takeover period. For representative articles on the subject, see *Lun ch'eng hsiang kuan hsi* (On the urban-rural relationship) (Tientsin: Tsung hsüeh hsi wei yüan hui, 1949). This theme was picked up with communization and the subsequent Maoist socialist education campaign. See, for example, Kao Cheng-sheng, "New-Type Urban-Rural Relations in China," *Peking Review*, 13 (Mar. 29, 1963), 19–22.

41. Kau's forthcoming book, chap. 4, discusses the series of directives from 1957 to 1958 dealing with the "blind drift" into cities. The problem that worried the government is discussed by Franz Schurmann (1968, pp. 381–82), citing a Communist source of 1958: "The report . . . notes that the government had carried out a survey on population growth in fifteen cities. The 'basic population' of these cities had increased by one million or 28 percent from 1953 to 1958. 'Service population' had increased by only 5 percent. The 'dependent population,' however, had increased by almost two and a half million or 70 percent. The report notes that 60 percent of the total population of these cities consisted of dependents. Of these, 1,200,000 immigrated from the rural areas. This meant an immensely greater burden on housing, welfare, city engineering, and public services. The report ends by stating that every additional inhabitant required an outlay of from 558 yuan to 695 yuan for welfare construction and urban engineering."

42. This theme has been treated more fully in Morse *et al.* 1969.

43. See Michel Oksenberg, "Getting Ahead and Along in Communist China: The Ladder of Success on the Eve of the Cultural Revolution," in Lewis 1970, chap. 9.

44. For a discussion of urban expansion in the fifties, see Morris B. Ullman, "Cities of Mainland China: 1953–1959," in Gerald Breese, ed., *The City in Newly Developing Countries: Readings on Urbanism and Urbanization* (Englewood Cliffs, N.J.: Prentice-Hall, 1969), chap. 8; and Kau, chap. 4. Kau shows how Peking expanded from 706 square kilometers in 1949 to 17,100 in 1959. Comparable figures are 617 and 5,800 for Shanghai, 252 and 700 for Canton, and 185 and 2,300 (1958) for Tientsin. Boundary shifting (changing the size of the political unit) has been a major form of political manipulation in the Communist period.

45. On the general problems involved in the study of urban economies, see especially Wilbur R. Thompson, *A Preface to Urban Economics* (Baltimore: Johns Hopkins Press, 1965), esp. chap. 10.

46. See Yu-min Chou, "Wholesaling in Communist China," in Robert Bar-

tels, ed., *Comparative Marketing: Wholesaling in Fifteen Countries* (Homewood, Ill.: Irwin, 1963), pp. 253–70; Ralph W. Huenemann, "Urban Rationing in Communist China," *China Quarterly*, 26 (Apr.–June 1966), 44–57; and Perkins 1966, chap. 9.

47. Compare Edward C. Banfield, *The Case of the Blighted City* (Chicago: American Foundation for Continuing Education, 1959).

48. A preliminary review of urban planning in China is found in Chung-chin Ch'en, "Urban Policies, Planning, and Housing in Communist China," unpub. ms., Dept. of City and Regional Planning, University of California, Berkeley, 1965. The two main journals dealing with urban planning are *Ch'eng shih chien she* (Urban construction) and *Chien chu hsüeh pao* (Journal of architecture).

49. *First Five-Year Plan for Development of the National Economy of the People's Republic of China in 1953–1957* (Peking: Foreign Languages Press, 1956), pp. 223–24.

50. Edgar Snow, *The Other Side of the River: Red China Today* (New York: Random House, 1961), p. 29.

51. Quoted in *Current Background*, No. 892, p. 24. See also Li Fu-ch'un's remarks in *New China Advances to Socialism* (Peking: Foreign Languages Press, 1956), pp. 91–97.

52. Kuei-sheng Chang, "The Changing Railroad Pattern in Mainland China," *Geographical Review*, LI: 4 (Dec. 1961), 547–48; C. Ch'en 1965, pp. 26, 29–30; and Herold J. Wiens, "The Historical and Geographical Role of Urumchi, Capital of Chinese Central Asia," *Annals of the Association of American Geographers*, LII: 4 (Dec. 1963), 441–64. Other new cities are listed in Theodore Shabad, "The Population of China's Cities," *Geographical Review*, XLIX: 1 (Jan. 1959), 38–41.

53. For a review of known information on China's urban growth, see, in addition to the Emerson chapter in this volume, the Ullman article in Breese 1969; John S. Aird, *The Size, Composition, and Growth of the Population of Mainland China* (Washington, D.C.: U.S. Government Printing Office, 1961); Leo A. Orleans, "The Recent Growth of China's Urban Population," *Geographical Review*, XLIX: 1 (Jan. 1959), 43–57; and Shabad 1959.

54. See Mao's undated instructions to metallurgical organizations in *Joint Publications Research Service* [hereafter JPRS], No. 49826 (Feb. 12, 1970), p. 25.

55. Kang Chao, "Industrialization and Urban Housing in Communist China," *Journal of Asian Studies*, XXV: 3 (May 1966), 381–96; C. Ch'en 1965, chaps. 10–14; and Christopher Howe, "The Supply and Administration of Urban Housing in China: The Case of Shanghai," *China Quarterly*, 33 (Jan.–Mar. 1968), 73–97.

56. Joyce K. Kallgren, "Social Welfare and China's Industrial Workers," in Barnett 1969, p. 567.

57. For a typical manual on urban public health programs, see *Chieh tao li nung chü min sheng huo shou ts'e* (Street and lane residents' health manual) (Shanghai: Hsin wen jih pao kuan, 1951).

58. Mao's "Instructions on Public Health Work" [June 25, 1965], in JPRS, No. 49826 (Feb. 12, 1970), p. 24.

59. Nai-ruenn Chen and Walter Galenson, "Urban Living Standards, 1952–1956," *The Chinese Economy under Communism* (Chicago: Aldine, 1969), pp. 171–81.

60. See Lewis Dec. 1966; and Snow 1961, pp. 194–95.

61. On interest payments, see Barry M. Richman, *Industrial Society in Communist China* (New York: Random House, 1969), chap. 12; and Snow 1961, chap. 26. In a speech of Jan. 29, 1965 (quoted in JPRS, No. 49826 [Feb. 12, 1970], p. 23), Mao noted that highly paid managerial personnel were in constant danger of becoming bourgeois elements and thus class enemies.

62. The urban people's communes are studied by Henry J. Lethbridge, *China's Urban Communes* (Hong Kong: Dragonfly Books, 1961); Janet Salaff, "The Urban Communes and Anti-City Experiment in Communist China," *China Quarterly*, 29 (Jan.–Mar. 1967), 82–110; Schurmann 1968, pp. 380–99; and Shih Ch'eng-chih, *Urban Commune Experiments in Communist China* (Hong Kong: Union Research Institute, 1962).

63. These figures are found in *Chung-kuo ch'ing nien* (China youth), 17 (Sept. 1, 1960),10.

64. Liu's handling of the urban communes is discussed in a Red Guard leaflet of Apr. 20, 1967, in SCMM, No. 584, p. 34. On the broader issues, see John W. Lewis, "The Study of Chinese Political Culture," *World Politics*, XVIII: 3 (Apr. 1966), 518–20.

65. See Merle Goldman, "Party Policies Toward the Intellectuals: The Unique Blooming and Contending of 1961–2," in Lewis 1970, chap. 8.

66. In any attempt to gauge the extent of discontent in Chinese cities, it is important to keep in mind the basic conservatism of cities noted by Banfield in the United States. See Edward C. Banfield, *Big City Politics* (New York: Random House, 1965), p. 12.

67. Vogel 1969, p. 352.

68. Compare R. P. Dore, *City Life in Japan: A Study of a Tokyo Ward* (Berkeley and Los Angeles: University of California Press, 1967), pp. 387–93; and Jane Jacobs, *The Death and Life of Great American Cities* (New York: Random House, 1961), *passim*.

69. Richard Baum, "The Cultural Revolution in the Countryside: Anatomy of a Limited Rebellion," to be published by the University of California Press in a volume entitled *The Cultural Revolution in China*. I am grateful to Professor Baum for letting me read his essay in manuscript.

70. Long 1962; and Jacobs 1961.

71. This theme is discussed more fully in my Introduction to Lewis 1970.

72. In this regard, see the important article on Tientsin in JMJP, Aug. 28, 1969.

73. See Tsingtao Radio, June 18, 1970.

74. The constant exhortation of these veteran workers could mean, however, that with the ending of the Cultural Revolution their position has become precarious. See *Hung ch'i*, 1 (Jan. 1, 1970), 65.

75. I have gained substantial insight into this problem from Annmarie Hauck Walsh, *The Urban Challenge to Government: An International Comparison of Thirteen Cities* (New York: Praeger, 1968), esp. chaps. 2, 3, and 5;

and the essays by Robert T. Daland and Frank P. Sherwood in Daland, ed., *Comparative Urban Research: The Administration and Politics of Cities* (Beverly Hills, Calif.: Sage Publications, 1969).

76. JMJP, Sept. 8, 1969, gives an excellent case study of Ch'eng-kuan *chen*, a city of over 7,000 inhabitants, 1,789 of whom were sent to live in villages thirty kilometers or less from the city.

77. G. William Skinner, "The City in Chinese Society," in Skinner, ed., *The City in Late Imperial China* (Stanford: Stanford University Press, forthcoming).

78. *Hung ch'i*, 6–7 (July 1, 1969), 64.

79. For a discussion of the 2–5 system of this period, see John W. Lewis, *Leadership in Communist China* (Ithaca, N.Y.: Cornell University Press, 1963), pp. 230–32.

80. See Richard Lowenthal, "Development vs. Utopia in Communist Policy," in Chalmers Johnson, ed., *Change in Communist Systems* (Stanford: Stanford University Press, 1970), pp. 33–116.

81. JMJP, Oct. 14, 1969. Mao's regional ideal has much in common with the geographer's diffusion models. The best study of such models is Torsten Hägerstrand, *Innovation Diffusion as a Spatial Process*, trans. by Allan Pred (Chicago and London: University of Chicago Press, 1967). For an application of geographical models to China a fine work is Joseph B. R. Whitney, *China: Area, Administration, and Nation Building* (Chicago: Department of Geography, University of Chicago, 1970), esp. chap. 2.

82. See the important article on science and engineering in *Hung ch'i*, 8 (July 21, 1970), 5–19.

83. Whitney 1970, pp. 70–72, 160–65; and Jacob and Toscano 1964, chaps. 4 and 5. For examples of the many reports on the opening up of small-scale factories, mines, and repair facilities, see Peking Radio, Dec. 12, 23, 27, and 31, 1969. For typical examples of industrial cooperation, see JMJP, Aug. 22, 1970, and *Hung ch'i*, 1 (Jan. 1, 1970), 16–23.

## Drafting People's Mediation Rules

1. Jerome Alan Cohen, "Chinese Mediation on the Eve of Modernization," *California Law Review*, LIV: 3 (Aug. 1966), 1201.

2. See "Regulation on the Commercial Arbitration Bureau" (promulgated Jan. 28, 1913, as amended July 28, 1913, and Nov. 19, 1914) in *Fa ling ta ch'üan* (Complete laws and decrees [of the Republic of China]) (Shanghai: Shang wu yin shu kuan, 1924), p. 1173; and "Detailed Rules on the Operation of the Commercial Arbitration Bureau" (promulgated Sept. 18, 1914), *ibid.*, p. 1174.

3. See "Revised Brief Regulations on the Anti-Litigation Associations" (promulgated Aug. 18, 1927) in Ts'un cheng chü (Bureau of Village Administration), *Shan-hsi ts'un cheng hui pien* (Complete collection on the village administration of Shansi [province]) (1928), ch. I, 7a–8a. The text of the original Brief Regulation (promulgation date unknown) has not been available to me. See *ibid.*, ch. I, 2a.

4. The first Nationalist legislation referring to mediation appeared in the "Law for the Enforcement of the Autonomy of Administrative Villages and

Towns" (promulgated Sept. 18, 1929, as amended July 7, 1930) in Hsü Pai-ch'i, ed., *Chung-hua min kuo fa kuei ta ch'üan* (Great collection of laws and regulations of the Republic of China) (Shanghai: Shang wu yin shu kuan, 1937), II, 641. Similar provisions regarding mediation were enacted shortly thereafter in the "Law for the Enforcement of the Autonomy of Districts" (promulgated Oct. 2, 1929, as amended July 7, 1930), *ibid.*, II, 638; and in the "Law for the Organization of the Cities" (promulgated May 20, 1930), *ibid.*, II, 519. The experience of the mediation committees established by this body of legislation promptly demonstrated the need for more detailed guidance of their work and initiated a process of revision that has continued to the present.

5. For discussion of the difficulties of conducting research on the Chinese legal system, see Jerome Alan Cohen, "Interviewing Chinese Refugees: Indispensable Aid to Legal Research on China," *Journal of Legal Education*, XX: 1 (1967), 33.

6. For a glimpse of the post-1954 history of China's experimentation with mediation institutions, see Jerome Alan Cohen, *The Criminal Process in the People's Republic of China, 1949–1963: An Introduction* (Cambridge, Mass.: Harvard University Press, 1968), pp. 123–24, 179–88; and Stanley Lubman, "Mao and Mediation: Politics and Dispute Resolution in Communist China," *California Law Review*, LV: 5 (Nov. 1967), 1319–20. See also note 31, below.

7. Promulgated Mar. 22, 1954, in *Chung yang jen min cheng fu fa ling hui pien* [hereafter FLHP] (Collection of laws and decrees of the Central People's Government), 1954 (Peking: Fa lü ch'u pan she, 1955), pp. 47–48.

8. Ma Hsi-wu, "People's Judicial Work in the Shensi-Kansu-Ningsia Border District During the State of the New Democratic Revolution," *Cheng fa yen chiu* (Political-legal research), 1 (1955), 7, 13.

9. See, e.g., *T'ai-hang ch'ü ssu fa kung tso kai k'uang* (Report on the general situation in judicial work in T'ai-hang district) (1946), pp. 2–13.

10. These were among the reasons why in mid-1950 the Peking People's Court reported that the accumulation of cases constituted a serious situation. "Peking People's Court Raises the Rate of Resolving Cases, etc.," *Nan fang jih pao* (Southern daily), June 23, 1950. The next few months witnessed a gradual decline in its case load, in part because of the strengthening of mediation work in city districts. See Secretariat of the People's Court of Peking, ed., *Jen min ssu fa kung tso chü yü* (Examples of people's judicial work) (Peking: Hsin Hua shu chü, 1950), p. 3. However, nationwide statistics made it clear that local government agencies and the courts were being burdened by increasingly heavy case loads. See "Instruction Concerning the Speedy Clearing Up of Accumulated Cases by the People's Judicial Organs" (promulgated by the State Council and the Supreme People's Court, Oct. 13, 1950), FLHP, 1949–50 (Peking: Jen min ch'u pan she, 1952), p. 177.

11. See Lubman 1967, pp. 1314–15.

12. For illustrations of how these persons engage in mediation, see Cohen 1968, pp. 141–53.

13. See editorial, "Do People's Mediation Work Well, Strengthen the Unity of the People, Impel Production and Construction" [hereafter editorial] *Jen min jih pao* (People's daily), Mar. 23, 1954 (English translation

in Cohen 1968, pp. 125f). An early 1949 decision that was promulgated as the Communists advanced over northern China authorized village governments to establish people's mediation committees and stated at the end that "the above decision is also applicable to the cities." "Decision of the North China People's Government Concerning the Mediation of Disputes Among the People" (promulgated Feb. 25, 1949), Art. 3, in *Jen min jih pao*, Mar. 5, 1949, p. 2.

14. See Lubman 1967, pp. 1315–16.

15. See "Instruction Concerning the Speedy Clearing Up," FLHP, 1949–50, p. 178.

16. See Lubman 1967, pp. 1315–17.

17. See "Second All-China Judiciary Conference Convened in Peking," *New China News Agency*, May 12, 1953, in *Survey of China Mainland Press*, No. 573, p. 15.

18. See editorial, pp. 127–28.

19. *Ibid.*, pp. 128–29.

20. *Ibid.*, p. 128.

21. *Ibid.*, p. 127.

22. Provisional Rules, Art. 1. For the Chinese text of the rules, see FLHP, 1954, pp. 47–48. For English translation, see Cohen 1968, pp. 124–25, which will be the source of subsequent references to the rules.

23. Editorial, pp. 125–26.

24. See Article 57(7) of the "Act for the Provisional Organization of County, District and Village Governments in the Chin-Ch'a-Chi Border Area" (promulgated June 1940) in *K'ang Jih ken chü ti cheng ts'e t'iao li hui chi, Chin Ch'a Chi chih pu* (Collection of policies and acts for the anti-Japanese bases, Chin-Ch'a-Chi section) (1946?), pp. 37, 46.

25. Articles 3 and 9, "Regulation on Mediation Work in Administrative Villages of the Chin-Ch'a-Chi Border Area" [hereafter CCC Regulation] (promulgated Apr. 1, 1942), in Chin Ch'a Chi pien ch'ü hsing cheng wei yüan hui (Chin-Ch'a-Chi Border Area Administration Committee), ed., *Hsien hsing fa ling hui chi* (Collection of current laws and decrees) [hereafter *CCC Laws*], I (1946), 319.

26. "Instruction Concerning the Strengthening of Village Mediation Work and the Establishment of District Adjustment Work," June 1, 1944, in *CCC Laws*, I, 326.

27. "Regulation for the Mediation of Civil and Criminal Cases in the Shen-Kan-Ning Border Area" [hereafter SKN Regulation] (promulgated June 11, 1943), Arts. 4 and 5 in *Shen Kan Ning pien ch'ü cheng ts'e t'iao li hui chi* (Collection of policies and acts for the Shen-Kan-Ning Border Area) (1944), p. 266.

28. Art. 7 in "Regulation for the Organization of Mediation Committees in Administrative Villages and Towns" [hereafter 1943 Nationalist Regulation], promulgated Oct. 9, 1943, by the Ministry of Interior and the Ministry of Judicial Administration and contained in *Ssu fa fa ling hui pien* (Collection of laws and decrees pertaining to judicial administration) (Shanghai: Fa hsüeh pien i she, 1946). Because this regulation was still in effect in Nationalist China when the Communists drafted their 1954 rules, the Nationalist mediation law referred to in this article is the 1943 regulation.

29. Compare *ibid.* with Provisional Rules, Art. 5. That Nationalist law associated the qualities it sought in mediators with their educational level, family background, and property holding was suggested by Article 10 of the 1943 Nationalist Regulation, which required the local government office that organized mediation committees to report this information about each mediator to the county government and the competent court.

30. 1943 Nationalist Regulation, Arts. 17 and 21. Article 22 provided that when mediation committees found it necessary to call on local government personnel to help them settle disputes, expenses of those personnel were to be paid by the local government.

31. "Act of the People's Republic of China (PRC) for the Organization of City Residents' Committees" (promulgated Dec. 31, 1954), Art. 9, in *Chung-hua jen min kung ho kuo fa kuei hui pien* (Collection of laws and regulations of the PRC) [hereafter FKHP], 13 vols. (Peking: Fa lü ch'u pan she, 1956–64), I (1956), 173–75. Promulgation of this act required some minor organizational adjustments in cities in order to integrate mediation into the residents' committee structure. A residents' committee either could have one or more of its members take charge of mediation work or could organize its own mediation committee. In the former situation, the persons charged by the residents' committee with responsibility for mediation work usually served as members of a higher-level mediation committee whose jurisdiction is the entire area covered by the public security station and the street office. For the formal establishment of the latter, see "Act of the People's Republic of China for the Organization of City Street Offices" (promulgated Dec. 31, 1954), in FKHP, I, 171–72. Following the promulgation of the legislation that formalized their existence, the street office and the residents' committee appear to have taken over the role of directly leading mediation work that Article 2 of the Provisional Rules had assigned to the basic-level government.

32. *Ibid.*, Arts. 9 and 10.

33. Compare SKN Regulation, Art. 2, with 1943 Nationalist Regulation, Art. 3. The latter provided that there could be no out-of-court mediation of a dispute at the same time that it is being mediated under court auspices.

34. CCC Regulation, Art. 4.

35. This interpretation is confirmed by an explanatory handbook published by the Ministry of Justice shortly after the promulgation of the Provisional Rules. It identified a variety of family, property, landlord-tenant, inheritance, and debt cases of an interpersonal nature as "ordinary civil disputes among the people." In addition to stating that relatively complex, important, or sensitive cases should go directly to court, it excluded from mediation disputes involving public against private interests, labor-capital disputes, and disputes involving overseas Chinese or questions of religion. Chung yang jen min cheng fu ssu fa pu (Ministry of Justice of the Central People's Government), ed., *Jen min t'iao chieh kung tso shou ts'e* (Handbook for people's mediation work) [hereafter *Handbook*] (Peking, 1954), pp. 8, 32. Yet reports on actual practice after "socialist transformation" of the economy in the mid-1950's have indicated that the category, "ordinary civil disputes among the people," was subsequently construed to include such disputes as those over "work points," which normally arise between an in-

dividual and a collective, and those over timberland, which normally arise between collectives. See, e.g., Yeh Ku-lin, "Fully Developing the Role of People's Mediation Work to Serve the Construction of Socialism," *Cheng fa yen chiu*, 4 (1964), 12, 14. Reports on practice also suggest that unimportant civil disputes involving disfavored elements have also been handled by mediation committees. *Ibid.*

36. See Wada Sei, ed., *Shina chihō jichi hattatsu shi* (Historical development of China's local autonomy) (Tokyo: Chūka minkoku hōsei kenkyūkai, 1939), pp. 77, 80, 236, 239–48; also Cohen 1966, p. 1209.

37. Revised Brief Regulations, note 3, art. 4. This provision reflected actual social practice during the latter part of the Manchu dynasty much more closely than did Manchu legislation itself. See Cohen 1966, p. 1221.

38. 1943 Nationalist Regulation, Art. 4.

39. See Ma 1955, pp. 12–13.

40. "Decision of the North China People's Government Concerning the Mediation of Disputes Among the People" (promulgated Feb. 25, 1949), Art. 3, in *Jen min jih pao*, Mar. 5, 1949, p. 2.

41. Nevertheless, as in the case of civil disputes, since the Provisional Rules failed to provide specific guidance, explanations of the rules had to provide it. The *Handbook* issued by the Ministry of Justice stated that "minor criminal cases" generally included minor instances of misappropriation, fighting, infliction of bodily injury, destruction of property, theft, fraud, and damage to reputation or credit. It also provided a long list of serious offenses that could not be mediated. *Handbook*, pp. 8, 33.

42. See Wada Sei 1939, pp. 239–48; and Cohen 1966, p. 1209.

43. This prohibition was implicit in Yen Hsi-shan's regulation but explicit in the Nationalist regulation. Compare Revised Brief Regulation, note 3, Arts. 4, 6, with 1943 Nationalist Regulation, Art. 19.

44. See, e.g., *Chih chin cheng wu ch'üan shu ch'u pien* (Complete collection on the government of Shansi) (First series, 1928), IV, 303; A. Doak Barnett, *China on the Eve of Communist Takeover* (New York: Praeger, 1963), pp. 131–32.

45. Promulgated Feb. 1942, Art. 16, in *Collection of Policies and Acts for the SKN Border Area*, note 27, pp. 107f.

46. Ma 1955, p. 13.

47. See "Rent, Debt and Interest Act of the Chin-Ch'a-Chi Border Area" (promulgated Feb. 4, 1943), Arts. 33, 39, in *CCC Laws*, I, 164, 171, 173; "(Draft) Decision Relating to the Adjustment of Cases by the District Government Office, June 1, 1944," Art. 1, in *ibid.*, p. 323; "Instruction Concerning the Strengthening of Village Mediation Work," note 26, in *ibid.*, p. 326.

48. See p. 33.

49. The Handbook issued by the Ministry of Justice provided some concrete guidance concerning techniques for mediating various kinds of disputes, but failed to discuss a surprising number of aspects of mediation that had been dealt with in earlier regulations; see generally *Handbook*, esp. pp. 37–40.

50. See Cohen 1966, p. 1219; and Sybille van der Sprenkel, *Legal Institutions in Manchu China* (London: Athlone Press, 1962), pp. 120–21.

51. 1943 Nationalist Regulation, Art. 13. This represented a change from

the 1931 "Regulation on the Powers of the Mediation Committees in Districts, Administrative Villages, Towns, and City Wards," Art. 7, in *Chung-hua min kuo fa kuei ta ch'üan*, II, 665, which imposed time limits for the termination rather than the commencement of mediation.

52. Editorial, p. 128.

53. The *Handbook* issued by the Ministry of Justice stated that whenever a difficult problem was encountered in the course of mediation the mediation committee should ask instructions from the basic-level government and court. *Handbook*, pp. 11, 41. In addition, the committee was periodically to report summaries of its work to both the government and the court, and representatives of these agencies, especially judicial cadres, were to pay visits to and hold meetings with mediators to instruct them. *Ibid.*, pp. 25–26, 40.

54. The *Handbook* appeared to contemplate only judicial review of reconciliations brought to the court's attention by a party or the mediation committee. It stated that if the terms of the reconciliation were not carried out and neither party took the matter to court, the committee itself should do so. *Ibid.*, pp. 9–10.

55. The *Handbook* shed light only on the easiest of these questions. It stated that, generally, successful mediations should be registered in a simple (but unspecified) way and that in disputes relating to property, mediation certificates were to be issued if the parties requested. *Ibid.*, p. 40.

56. SKN Regulation, Art. 16.

57. CCC Regulation, Art. 14 provided that such agreements were void *ab initio*.

58. *Ibid.*, Art. 13. Although this was stated specifically with respect to disputes in which litigation had not yet begun, it implicitly embraced other disputes as well.

59. *Ibid.*, Art. 11. The village administration was expected to devote equally serious attention to reviewing unsuccessful mediation. Article 12 required it to write out a statement explaining the reasons why mediation failed and to authenticate this statement with the village's official seal.

60. See note 31, above.

61. See, e.g., Chou En-lai, "Report on the Work of the Government," FKHP, VI (1957), 93–94; Liu Shao-ch'i, "The Political Report of the Central Committee of the Communist Party of China to the Eighth National Congress of the Party," in *Eighth National Congress of the Communist Party of China* (Peking: Foreign Languages Press, 1956), I, 13, 81–82; Tung Pi-wu, "Speech by Comrade Tung Pi-wu," *ibid.*, II, 79, 84–89, 94–95; and P'eng Chen, "Report Relating to Circumstances of Political Work and Current Tasks," May 1951, as quoted in Teaching and Research Office for Criminal Law of the Central Political-Legal Cadre's School, ed., *Chung-hua jen min kung ho kuo hsing fa tsung tse chiang i* (Lectures on the general principles of criminal law of the People's Republic of China) [hereafter *Lectures*] (Peking: Fa lü ch'u pan she, 1957), pp. 24–25.

62. *Ibid.*

63. *Lectures*, p. 32. This description closely followed that given by Tung Pi-wu at the Eighth Party Congress. See Tung Pi-wu 1956, p. 86.

64. John W. Lewis has written that during the 1950's there "was an increasingly acute disharmony between Mao's preference for a loosely defined

educative law based on inner moral conviction and the bureaucrats' belief in a rigid and efficient system of social control." See his book review, *China Quarterly*, 33 (Jan.–Mar. 1968), 123.

65. See note 6, above.

66. The *Handbook* issued by the Ministry of Justice, itself an attempt to fill gaps in the Provisional Rules, reprinted the *Jen min jih pao* editorial announcing their promulgation, note 13, and referred to the other techniques of providing guidance.

## *The Public Security Bureau and Political-Legal Work in Hui-yang, 1952–64*

1. Hui-yang was selected for my study because data concerning this area are relatively easy to obtain. The Library of Congress holds an almost complete run of the *Hui-yang pao* (Hui-yang news) from Oct. 7, 1956, to Apr. 13, 1958. During this period, this newspaper was published every third day, and usually consisted of four pages. In addition, the Union Research Institute files contain numerous articles on Hui-yang from Canton and Hong Kong newspapers and a few clippings from other sources.

Much of the information about government and party operations, and thus much of this chapter, is based on refugee interviews conducted in Hong Kong and Macao in 1965 and again in 1968. Most of the refugees from Hui-yang were ordinary residents and were helpful mainly in describing the work of the neighborhood apparatus. Descriptions of public security work were obtained mainly from one informant who had been a public security cadre in Hui-yang for nearly ten years and had reached the rank of acting chief of a public security station. Over two hundred hours of interviews were conducted with him.

For a more thorough discussion of refugee interviewing, see Victor H. Li, "The Use of Survey Interviewing in Research on Communist Chinese Law," and Jerome A. Cohen, "Interviewing Chinese Refugees: Indispensable Aid to Legal Research on China," in Jerome A. Cohen, ed., *Contemporary Chinese Law: Research Problems and Perspectives* (Cambridge, Mass.: Harvard University Press, 1970). See also A. Doak Barnett (with a contribution by Ezra Vogel), *Cadres, Bureaucracy, and Political Power in Communist China* (New York: Columbia University Press, 1967), pp. xi–xx.

2. Hui-yang has gone through many administrative changes. At Liberation, Hui-chou was a shih under the Canton Suburbs District, and Hui-yang was one of 15 hsien under the East River Special District. In 1950, Hui-chou was reduced to a chen, and placed under Hui-yang. In 1954, the East River Special District was abolished, and Hui-yang became a part of the East Kwangtung Administrative Office. This continued until 1956 when the Hui-yang Special District was formed out of nine hsien, including Hui-yang. During the winter of 1957, Hui-chou was converted back into a shih, a part of Hui-yang was given to Pao-an hsien, and another part was cut off to form Hui-tung hsien. Two years later, both Hui-chou and Hui-tung were returned to Hui-yang. The 1964 changes appear to have returned Hui-yang to the 1957–59 situation.

3. See generally, Jerome A. Cohen, *The Criminal Process in the People's*

*Republic of China, 1949–1963: An Introduction* (Cambridge, Mass.: Harvard University Press, 1968), pp. 4–53; Shao-chuan Leng, *Justice in Communist China: A Survey of the Judicial System of the Chinese People's Republic* (Dobbs Ferry, N.Y.: Oceana Publications, 1967), pp. 77–178; and Tao-tai Hsia, *Guide to Selected Legal Sources of Mainland China* (Washington, D.C.: Library of Congress, 1967), pp. 1–64. See also Stanley Lubman, "Form and Function in the Chinese Criminal Process," *Columbia Law Review*, LXIX: 4 (Apr. 1969), 537–75; and Victor H. Li, review of Cohen, *The Criminal Process* in *Michigan Law Review*, LXVII (Nov. 1968), 179–212.

4. A good study of the public security system is Kuo Shou-hua, ed., *Kung fei kung an chu chi yü jen min ching ch'a chih yen chiu* (Studies on the public security organization and the people's police of the Communist bandits) (Taipei: Yang-ming shan Publishing Co., 1957). See also Barnett (with Vogel) 1967, pp. 218–35.

5. For descriptions of the work of the procuracy, see three articles by George Ginsburgs and Arthur Stahnke, "The Genesis of the People's Procuratorate in Communist China: The Institution in the Ascendant 1954–1957," *China Quarterly*, 34 (July–Sept. 1968), 82; and Leng 1967, pp. 102–20.

6. Arts. 4(1), 4(3), and 4(4), "Organic Law of the People's Procuratorates of the People's Republic of China," in Albert Blaustein, ed., *Fundamental Legal Documents of Communist China* (South Hackensack, N.J.: Rothman, 1962), p. 145.

7. On the work of the courts, see Jerome A. Cohen, "The Chinese Communist Party and 'Judicial Independence': 1949–1959," *Harvard Law Review*, LXXXII: 5 (Mar. 1969), 967.

8. For a more thorough discussion of the divergence between theory and practice in the Chinese legal system, see Victor H. Li, "The Evolution and Development of the Chinese Legal System," in John Lindbeck, ed., *China: Management of a Revolutionary Society* (Seattle: University of Washington Press, 1971). I do not mean to suggest that the divergence between theory and practice is a uniquely Chinese failing. Indeed, I do not think that the legal system in the United States fares much better in narrowing this divergence.

9. Before 1955, the work of filing complaints with the court and acting as "prosecutor" during criminal trials was handled by the secretariat section of the Public Security Bureau. The *Kung shang jih pao* (Industrial and commercial daily), a right-wing newspaper in Hong Kong, twice mentions a "chief procurator" participating in trials in the early 1950's, but this probably is erroneous. See *Kung shang jih pao*, Dec. 11, 1951, and Mar. 25, 1952.

10. See Cohen 1968, pp. 238–95.

11. See, e.g., "Old judicial personnel are accused by the masses of corruption, violations of law, and aiding the enemy," *Nan fang jih pao* (Southern daily), Sept. 12, 1952; see also "There are serious improprieties in the organization and thinking of the people's courts of the East River *hsien*," *Sing tao jih pao* (Star Island [Singapore] daily, Hong Kong), June 2, 1951.

12. For a criticism of the lenient treatment of landlords by the courts, see "The East River judicial conference decides and handles accumulated cases," *Sing tao jih pao*, June 2, 1951.

13. The results of the election were publicized widely. See, e.g., "Mei and

Hui-yang *hsien* elect *hsien* chiefs," *Ta kung pao* (Impartial, Hong Kong), June 30, 1955.

14. For a detailed discussion of the work of the sector offices, see pp. 59, 62, 69–70.

15. Cohen 1968, 200–237.

16. The collection camp holds suspects in attempted escape cases pending the final disposition of their cases. For a description of the work of this camp, see "Concentration camp in Hui-yang," *Sing tao jih pao*, Mar. 12, 1956.

17. Before 1954, the party divided Hui-yang into three sectors for administrative purposes, but the government did not. In 1954, the government, including the public security system, formed three sectors at Hui-chou, Tan-shui, and P'ing-shan. Two more were added in 1957 at To-chu and Nien-shan.

18. There were 17 stations at one time, but when a part of Hui-yang was transferred to Pao-an in 1957 three stations were eliminated. Besides the four stations in Hui-chou, there are others located at Tan-shui, Au-t'ou, San-men, Ta-chou, Nien-shan, P'ing-hai, Kang-k'ou, P'ing-shan, To-chu, and P'ing-t'an.

19. On the work of the household patrolman and the neighborhood apparatus, see Cohen 1968, pp. 104–70; Stanley Lubman, "Mao and Mediation: Politics and Dispute Resolution in Communist China," *California Law Review*, LV: 5 (Nov. 1967), 1284; Franz Schurmann, *Ideology and Organization in Communist China* (Berkeley and Los Angeles: University of California Press, 1966), pp. 371–99; and the papers by Ezra Vogel and Janet Salaff in this volume.

20. In the early years, these cadres were called *chu li yüan* and *kan shih*, respectively.

21. There were several other organs that were involved in public security work, although they were not part of the public security system. The most important of these is the people's armed police (*jen min wu chuang ching ch'a*).

22. Art. 17, "Security Administration Punishment Act," in Cohen 1968, p. 221.

23. See also pp. 69–70.

24. In 1955, for example, there were seven chiefs or deputy chiefs in the public order section. Of these, only three were engaged in public order work; the others helped out wherever necessary in the bureau.

25. The bureau chief appears to act on his own authority even though the approval of the local people's council supposedly is necessary for the imposition of the sanction of rehabilitation through labor ("Decision of the State Council Relating to Problems of Rehabilitation Through Labor," Art. 3, in Cohen 1968, p. 250) and for the analogical application of the "Security Administration Punishment Act" (Art. 31, Cohen 1968, p. 220).

26. Sometimes there was more than one bureau chief. In June 1957, Chang Yung-lu became bureau chief, but Hsü Yu-t'ang was not transferred away until early 1958. In late 1959 and 1960, there were three bureau chiefs; Teng Hua-chang handled public security work, and the other two participated in the work of "reforming the backward areas."

27. See Ezra Vogel, "Land Reform in Kwangtung 1951–1953: Central Control and Localism," *China Quarterly*, 38 (Apr.–June 1969), 27.

28. For more detailed descriptions of the su fan campaign in Hui-yang, see "Good results in rectification of party branches in rural areas," *Nan fang jih pao*, Dec. 9, 1955; and "All the old cadres of Yeh Chien-ying are purged," *Shih Pao* (Times, Hong Kong), Nov. 8, 1955.

29. Such transfers often were not demotions, but merely the changing of a person's place of employment. For example, Wang Chiu-ming was deputy bureau chief until the winter of 1957, then was transferred to another hsien. He returned in late 1960 as deputy bureau chief, and was promoted in 1962 to bureau chief.

30. See Michel Oksenberg, "Local Leaders in Rural China, 1962–65," in A. Doak Barnett, ed., *Chinese Communist Politics in Action* (Seattle: University of Washington Press, 1969), pp. 173–85, where most of the county- and district-level cadres were old cadres and land reform cadres, and very few were recruited out of the PLA and the middle schools.

31. These offenses appear to be much more serious than the offenses committed by the cadres of Lien-chiang hsien. C. S. Chen, ed., and Charles P. Ridley, trans., *Rural People's Communes in Lien-Chiang* (Stanford: Hoover Institution Press, 1969), pp. 44–49.

32. See also Barnett (with Vogel) 1967, pp. 194–97; and Cohen 1968, pp. 493–506.

33. After some initial reluctance, there appear to have been many complaints in Hui-yang during the Hundred Flowers. In some districts, 90 per cent of the masses had "opinions." See "The experience and lesson of the great debates carried out by two cooperatives in Hui-yang," *Nan fang jih pao*, Oct. 9, 1957; see also "The work styles of the cadres have changed and most of the 'opinions' have been taken care of," *ibid.*, Dec. 7, 1957; and two summaries of internal contradictions made by the first secretary, Ch'ang Sheng, in *Hui-yang pao*, May 19, 1957, and June 19, 1957.

I have found only three published criticisms of the court, the procuracy, or the public security system. A member of the Hui-yang People's Consultative Congress criticized the court for being too slow in deciding cases and also said that a particular public security cadre, apparently a household patrolman, acted "like an emperor." Another member of the same congress criticized the public security for placing under supervision a former defector from the Nationalist army and preventing him from finding suitable employment. "A few good words," *Hui-yang pao*, June 19, 1957. In addition, an article appeared during the anti-rightist campaign citing the Tan-shui tribunal of the Hui-yang court for coddling those who improperly attacked the regime. "Hui-yang special district deeply criticize the rightist tendency thinking of cadres," *Nan fang jih pao*, Aug. 14, 1957.

34. On simplification of procedures and reduction of personnel generally, see a speech by the second party secretary, "Simplify procedures, reduce personnel, mobilize cadres to the labor front," *Hui-yang pao*, Jan. 1, 1958.

35. The court and procuracy were not moved near the public security bureau until the summer of 1959. The hsien party committee was moved to the same area in the winter of 1960.

36. Cohen 1968, pp. 360–63.

37. *Ibid.*, pp. 107–8, 205–37, and 249–50.

## Preserving Order in the Cities

1. For an analysis of the conflicting demands of law and order, see Jerome H. Skelnick, *Justice Without Trial* (New York: Wiley, 1966); James Q. Wilson, *Varieties of Police Behavior* (Cambridge, Mass.: Harvard University Press, 1968).

2. For an account of Chinese Communist legal efforts see Jerome Alan Cohen, *The Criminal Process in the People's Republic of China, 1949–1963: An Introduction* (Cambridge, Mass.: Harvard University Press, 1968).

3. See Sybille van der Sprenkel, *Legal Institutions in Manchu China* (London: Athlone Press, 1962).

4. For a summary of regulations and the information on neighborhood organizations see Stanley Lubman, "Mao and Mediation: Politics and Dispute Resolution in Communist China," *California Law Review*, LV: 5 (Nov. 1967), 1284–1359.

5. Sources: *Nan fang jih pao* (Southern daily), Dec. 4, 6, and 30, 1955.

## Patterns of Recruitment and Mobility of Urban Cadres

1. Mao Tse-tung, *Selected Works* (Peking: Foreign Languages Press, 1961–65), IV, 337, 364.

2. *Ibid.*, p. 374.

3. I have elaborated on this and other aspects of development in my *Bureaucratic Development and Politics in Communist China* (Stanford: Stanford University Press, forthcoming). Important scholarly analyses of various aspects of Communist China's bureaucratic behavior may be found in John W. Lewis, *Leadership in Communist China* (Ithaca, N.Y.: Cornell University Press, 1963), and "Political Aspects of Mobility in China's Urban Development," *American Political Science Review*, LX: 4 (Dec. 1966), 899–912; A. Doak Barnett, *Cadres, Bureaucracy, and Political Power in Communist China* (New York: Columbia University Press, 1967); and Ezra Vogel, "From Revolutionary to Semi-Bureaucrats: The 'Regularization' of Cadres," *China Quarterly*, 29 (Jan.–Mar. 1967), 36–60.

4. Excellent discussions of the conflicts between the political leaders and the bureaucratic force may be found in John W. Lewis, "Leader, Commissar and Bureaucrat: The Chinese Political System in the Last Days of the Revolution," in Ping-ti Ho and Tang Tsou, eds., *China in Crisis* (Chicago: University of Chicago Press, 1968), I, Book A, 449–81; and A. Doak Barnett, *China After Mao* (Princeton: Princeton University Press, 1967), pp. 69–117.

5. *Ibid.*

6. Elsewhere I have analyzed aspects of conflicts in social roles and perceptions. See Kau (forthcoming); and his "The Urban Bureaucratic Elite in Communist China: A Case Study of Wuhan, 1949–1965," in A. Doak Barnett, ed., *Chinese Communist Politics in Action* (Seattle: University of Washington Press, 1969), pp. 216–67.

7. "State cadres" refers generally to officials who are on the state payroll and work in organs at the *hsiang* level or higher. The estimate is based on data provided in *Chung-hua min kuo t'ung chi nien chien* (The statistical

yearbook of the Republic of China for 1948) (Nanking: Chung-kuo wen hua shih yeh kung ssu, 1948), pp. 38–45.

8. An Tzu-wen, "Chung-hua jen min kung ho kuo san nien lai ti kan pu kung tso" (Cadre work of the People's Republic of China in the past three years), *Jen min jih pao* (People's daily), Sept. 30, 1952. An English version of the article may be found in "Training the People's Civil Servants," *People's China*, 1 (Jan. 1, 1953), 8–11. It should be noted that there were some differences in figures between the two versions.

9. In comparison with, say, the ratio of one cadre for every eighty people for 1958, the 1949 ratio was certainly small.

10. For Liu's report, see Liu Po-ch'eng, "Hsi nan ch'ü ti kung tso jen wu" (Work tasks in the southwest region), *Hsin Hua yüeh pao* (New China monthly), II: 5 (Sept. 15, 1950), 996–99.

11. "Kuan yü chia ch'iang tsai chih kan pu li lun hsüeh hsi ti chih shih" (Directive on strengthening the theoretical study of the on-the-job cadres), *Hsin Hua yüeh pao*, I: 5 (Mar. 15, 1950), 1234.

12. Mao 1961–65, IV, 337–40.

13. For a succinct discussion of the criteria for party membership, see Lewis 1963, pp. 101–7.

14. Lewis Dec. 1966, p. 902.

15. For example, see Mao's criticism of the party's reluctance to admit urban intellectuals, in Mao 1961–65, II, 301.

16. The membership for 1949 was 4,488,080; and the population for the same year was 541,670,000. The significance of these ratios can be seen when compared with those of the later periods.

17. Data on the Wuhan bureaucrats are drawn from the author's Wuhan biographic file, collected from *Ch'ang-chiang jih pao* (Yangtze daily), *Hupei jih pao* (Hupeh daily), and other local newspapers published in the Wuhan area. See particularly *Ch'ang-chiang jih pao*, Feb. 20, 1952, for a report on the number of middle-level cadres.

18. In fact, this may reflect more than anything else the desire of the party to monopolize power and the competition for leadership posts among the Communists at the top level.

19. *Ch'ang-chiang jih pao*, Nov. 11, Dec. 15, 1951, Jan. 13 and Apr. 16, 1952. For example, Liu Ching, an illiterate until the age of thirty-six, was appointed director of the Production Training Institute. For more discussion of the Wuhan bureaucracy, see Kau 1969.

20. For P'an's report, see *Hsin wen jih pao* (News daily, Shanghai), Nov. 17, 1952.

21. *Chieh fang jih pao* (Liberation daily), Mar. 16, 1956.

22. *Ch'ang-chiang jih pao*, Dec. 14, 1950.

23. Data for this portion of the discussion may be found in *Ho-pei jih pao* (Hopei daily), Oct. 16, 1950.

24. *T'ang-shan lao tung jih pao* (Tangshan labor daily), Mar. 9, 1951.

25. Mao 1961–65, IV, 337. See also an editorial in *Jen min jih pao*, Sept. 18, 1949, in which the problem of the shortage of cadres was analyzed.

26. *Jen min jih pao*, Sept. 18, 1949.

27. For the texts of the directive, see Lai Chih-yen, ed., *Chieh kuan ch'eng*

*shih ti kung tso ching yen* (Experiences in the takeover work of the cities) (Canton: Jen min ch'u pan she, 1949), pp. 47–52.

28. *Ibid.*

29. Ch'en Po-ta, "Pu yao ta luan yüan lai ti ch'i yeh chi kou" (Do not disrupt the original organization of enterprises), in Chieh fang she, comp., *Lun, kung shang yeh cheng ts'e* (On the policy toward industry and commerce) (Peking: Hsin Hua shu tien, 1949), pp. 97–113.

30. Ch'en I's report may be found in Lai Chih-yen 1949, pp. 4–17.

31. *Hsin wen jih pao,* Nov. 17, 1952.

32. For Li Wei-han's report, see *Jen min jih pao,* June 10, 1951. Another typical appeal for cooperation may be found in *Hsin Hua yüeh pao,* III: 1 (Nov. 25, 1950), 33–34.

33. This portion of the discussion is based mainly on An Tzu-wen 1952, but figures and percentages are from *Jen min jih pao,* Sept. 30, 1952, and *People's China,* 1 (Jan. 1, 1953), 8–11. Franz Schurmann also discussed An Tzu-wen's report in his book, *Ideology and Organization in Communist China* (Berkeley and Los Angeles: University of California Press, 1966), pp. 167–72.

34. *Ibid.*

35. *T'ien-chin jih pao* (Tientsin daily), Nov. 5, 1952.

36. *Jen min jih pao,* Apr. 2, 1954.

37. *Chieh fang jih pao,* June 27, 1952.

38. An Tzu-wen 1952.

39. "Hua pei mu ch'ien hsing shih yü i chiu ssu chiu nien ti jen wu" (The current situation in north China and the task for 1949) in *Lun ch'eng hsiang kuan hsi* (On the urban-rural relationship) (Tientsin: Tsung hsüeh hsi wei yüan hui, 1949), pp. 1–4.

40. An Tzu-wen 1952.

41. *Ibid.*

42. This portion of the discussion is based on An Tzu-wen 1952.

43. This was mentioned in an editorial of *Jen min jih pao,* Apr. 17, 1955, entitled "Jen chen chih hsing cheng tun pien chih ching chien chi kou ti kung tso" (Seriously proceed with the work of readjustment of structure and the simplification of organization).

44. *Ibid.*

45. *Ibid.*

46. Ts'ai Ch'ang, chairman of the All-China Democratic Women's Federation, mentioned the 1955 figure indirectly. According to her, there were 764,000 female state cadres in 1955, and they constituted 14.5% of the total cadre forces. *Hsin pao* (New news, Djakarta), Sept. 25, 1956. A rough estimate of the number of cadres based on data provided by the official source below was about 5,600,000 for Sept. 1955. T'ung chi kung tso t'ung hsün tzu liao shih (Office for Correspondence and Materials of Statistical Work), "I chiu wu wu nien ch'üan kuo chih kung jen shu kou ch'eng yü fen pu kai k'uang" (General patterns of size, structure, and distribution of the nation's functionaries and workers in 1955), *Hsin Hua pan yüeh k'an* (New China semimonthly), 2 (Jan. 25, 1957), 87–89.

47. *Jen min jih pao,* June 11, 1956.

48. *Shen-yang jih pao* (Mukden daily), Dec. 14, 1957.

49. The figure was derived from a report that 32,900 cadres, roughly one-third of the cadre force, were to be involved in the hsia fang transfers.

50. This figure is estimated on the basis of the findings presented in Tables 4 and 5. The ratios of state cadres and street cadres in 1957 were conservatively estimated at 3% and 2%, respectively.

51. For a discussion of the shifting priorities of party recruitment, see Lewis 1963, pp. 101–20. The most important shift took place in June 1950, at the Third Plenum of the Seventh Central Committee, at which the decision was made that recruitment in the rural sector should be suspended in favor of the urban sector.

52. See, for example, Merle Fainsod, "Bureaucracy and Modernization: The Russian and Soviet Case," and Carl Beck, "Bureaucracy and Political Development in Eastern Europe," in Joseph LaPalombara, ed., *Bureaucracy and Political Development* (Princeton: Princeton University Press, 1963), pp. 233–67, 268–300.

53. *Jen min jih pao*, Apr. 17, 1955.

54. *Ibid.*

55. Wu Yüan-li, *The Economy of Communist China* (New York: Praeger, 1965), p. 91. See also Ta-chung Liu and Kung-chia Yeh, *The Economy of the Chinese Mainland: National Income and Economic Development, 1933–1959* (Princeton: Princeton University Press, 1965), pp. 221–24.

56. For a general discussion of the traditional aspiration after a bureaucratic career, see, for example, Chang Chung-li, *The Chinese Gentry* (Seattle: University of Washington Press, 1955).

57. Peter Schran, "The Structure of Income in Communist China," unpub. diss., University of California, Berkeley, 1961, p. 350.

58. The question of bureaucratic mobility has been considered in Kau 1969.

59. For a typical criticism of this inclination among cadres, see Fu Yung, "T'i kao wo men ti kung ch'an chu i feng ko" (Raise our Communist personality), *Cheng chih hsüeh hsi* (Political studies), 6 (June 13, 1958), 27–33.

60. For a discussion of this reorganization movement, see Roy Hofheinz, "Rural Administration in Communist China," *China Quarterly*, 11 (July–Sept. 1962), 140–60.

61. *Jen min jih pao*, Jan. 24, 1957. The statement was made in connection with a criticism of the poor personnel situation in Ting hsien.

62. *Ibid.*, June 24, 1955.

63. The survey data used for this portion of the discussion may be found in Ch'en Shu, "Ching chien shang ts'eng ch'ung shih hsia ts'eng" (Simplify the upper levels to strengthen the lower levels), *Jen min jih pao*, June 24, 1955.

64. For example, see *Nan fang jih pao* (Southern daily), May 22, 1955, for a report on Kwangtung; and *Jen min jih pao*, Jan. 24, 1957, for a report on Hopei. It is important to examine, for instance, how officials at various levels view such flows and contractions of cadres in terms of their power and financial burden. Unfortunately, relevant information is still wanting.

65. "Wen ting kan pu ti chih wu t'i kao kan pu ti neng li" (Stabilize cadres' functions and raise cadres' ability), *Hsin Hu-nan pao* (New Hunan daily), edit., Apr. 15, 1957.

66. Teng Hsiao-p'ing, *Report on the Rectification Campaign* (Peking: Foreign Languages Press, 1957), pp. 55–56.

67. For detailed information on overstaffing at various levels, see *T'ung chi kung tso t'ung hsün* (Statistical work bulletin), Jan. 1957, pp. 87–89.

68. *Jen min jih pao*, Apr. 17, 1955. See also "Yen ko chieh yüeh chi kuan ti hsing cheng ching fei" (Strictly economize the administrative budgets of the organs), *Jen min jih pao*, edit., July 19, 1955.

69. Yü Ya, "Tsai i ko jen fu yü shih ti chi kuan li" (In an organ where men outnumber jobs), *Chieh fang jih pao*, July 5, 1955.

70. Other revealing stories may be found in *Jen min jih pao*, May 11, 1955, Dec. 31, 1956, Jan. 24, 1957; *Kuang ming jih pao* (Bright daily), May 18, 1958; *Ch'ang-chiang jih pao*, Jan. 5, 1957; *Chung-kuo ch'ing nien pao* (China youth daily), Dec. 16, 1956; *Nan fang jih pao*, June 13, 1957.

71. Mao 1961–65, IV, p. 374.

72. Ho Kan-chih, *Chung-kuo hsien tai ko ming shih* (A history of the modern Chinese revolution) (Hong Kong: San lien shu tien, 1958), pp. 366–67. According to An Tzu-wen, roughly 10% (nearly 600,000) of the total membership was purged from the party in this campaign; see *Ta kung pao* (Impartial, Tientsin), Feb. 10, 1953.

73. "Jen chen chin hsing cheng tun pien chih ching chien chi kou ti kung tso" (Seriously conduct the work of readjusting organizations and retrenching structures), *Jen min jih pao*, edit., Apr. 17, 1955; reprinted in *Hsin Hua yüeh pao*, 5 (May 28, 1955), 67–68.

74. This was stated in *Jin min jih pao*, May 11, 1955. The adoption of this policy may be connected with the revision of the First Five-Year Plan, which was also discussed at the Conference. See *Documents of the National Conference of the Communist Party of China, March 1955* (Peking: Foreign Languages Press, 1955), p. 11.

75. See, for example, major reports and editorials in *Jen min jih pao*, Apr. 17, May 11, June 24 and 29, July 13, Sept. 3, 1955; *Chung-kuo ch'ing nien pao*, edit., June 9, 1955; *Chieh fang jih pao*, July 5, 1955; *Hsin Hu-nan pao*, edit., May 8, 1955; *Nan fang jih pao*, June 5, 1955.

76. *Jen min jih pao*, Apr. 17, 1955.

77. Chang Yu-yü, "Pei-ching shih ti cheng pien kung tso" (The reorganization work in Peking), *Jen min jih pao*, July 13, 1955.

78. For the text, see *ibid.*, Jan. 7, 1956.

79. See, for instance, reports and criticism of organizational matters in *ibid.*, Feb. 29, Oct. 22, Dec. 26 and 31, 1956.

80. "Ta tan ti cheng ch'üeh ti hsüan pa yu hsiu kan pu" (Boldly and correctly select and promote able cadres), *Kuang-chou jih pao* (Canton daily), edit., Sept. 4, 1956.

81. "Ta tan ti cheng ch'üeh ti t'iao hsüan ho t'i pa yu hsiu kan pu" (Boldly and correctly select and promote able cadres), *Jen min jih pao*, edit., June 11, 1956. How this editorial could appear at the time of the retrenchment movement is a mystery. Lack of coordination between the paper and the central leadership, or a deliberate maneuvering by Peking bureaucrats are among the possible explanations.

82. For the text of the notice, see *Chung-kuo ch'ing nien pao*, Nov. 17, 1956.

83. In addition to the newspaper reports listed in the source note for Table 7, see *Jen min jih pao*, Jan. 22, Apr. 2 and 4, Aug. 23, Sept. 11, Oct. 29, Nov. 17 and 29; *Ha-erh-pin jih pao* (Harbin daily), Jan. 17; *Nan fang jih pao*, Jan. 22; *Kuang-chou jih pao*, Feb. 25; *Chieh fang jih pao*, Mar. 3; *Hsin Hu-nan pao*, Apr. 15; all for 1957.

84. *Kuang-chou jih pao*, Dec. 7, 1956, and *Nan fang jih pao*, Jan. 22, 1957.

85. *Ibid.*, Feb. 25, 1957.

86. *Jen min jih pao*, Nov. 17, 1957.

87. *Ibid.*, Oct. 29, 1957.

88. The Personnel Bureau of the Mukden People's Council was also re- ported to have cut out over 70% of its cadres. See *Jen min jih pao*, Nov. 29, 1957. In fact, during Sept.–Dec. 1957, the local newspapers were filled with reports on retrenchment and simplification. See sources in note 83 above.

89. *Pei-ching jih pao* (Peking daily), Mar. 30, 1958.

90. This assumes that there were about 6.5 million state cadres in 1957 (see Table 2, p. 106) and that roughly 40% of them were sent downward.

91. The directive issued on Dec. 29, 1955, appeared in *Jen min jih pao*, Jan. 7, 1956. Another major directive, which was issued on Nov. 16, 1956, stressed the same principle: see *Chung-kuo ch'ing nien pao*, Nov. 17, 1956.

92. *Ch'ang-chiang jih pao*, Dec. 24, 1957.

93. See, for example, "Kuo chia chi kuan ch'ing nien tsen yang tui tai cheng pien kung tso" (How the youth in the state organs should treat the reorganization work), *Chung-kuo ch'ing nien pao*, edit., June 9, 1955; also Ying Ling, "An hsin tsai chi ts'eng kung tso" (Work at the basic levels with peace in heart), *Jen min jih pao*, Mar. 30, 1957.

94. Teng Hsiao-p'ing 1957, pp. 55–56.

95. Some statistical summaries of the achievements of the hsia fang move- ments in its early stage may be found in *Kuang ming jih pao*, Dec. 15, 1957; *Chung-kuo ch'ing nien pao*, Feb. 17, 1958; *Wen hui pao* (Cultural exchange news), Mar. 18, 1957; and *Pei-ching jih pao*, Mar. 30, 1958.

96. Although two types of hsia fang, long-term and short-term, had worked simultaneously from 1958 on (Lewis 1963, pp. 220–25), the pre-1958 ching chien movement stressed organizational matters, whereas the post-1958 hsia fang movements were concerned with the cadres' ideological outlook and production.

97. Many reports appeared in *Jen min jih pao*, May–June 1958.

98. *Ibid.*, Sept. 30, 1958.

99. *Ibid.*, Jan. 18, 1960.

100. *Ibid.*, Mar. 22, 1959.

101. For a succinct explanation of the tun tien movement, see "Dundian: Key to Successful Leadership," *Peking Review*, 33 (Aug. 14, 1964), 37.

102. A major article on the subject is by Yüeh Chao: "T'an tun tien kung tso chung ti chi ko wen t'i" (On a number of problems regarding tun tien work), *Ta kung pao* (Peking), Oct. 30, 1964. Several major reports on the movement may be found in *Jen min jih pao*, July 19, Aug. 26, 1964; Sept. 7, 1965; and *Kuang ming jih pao*, Sept. 10, 1965.

103. This pattern of the pendulum-like swing of bureaucratic expansion and contraction in the cities corresponds in many ways to the cyclical pattern of compliance in rural China observed by G. William Skinner and Edwin A.

Winckler. However, it should be noted that the rural phenomenon of the phases of mobilization being periods of organizational expansion and cadre increase appears to be quite different from that seen in the urban bureaucracy. During the typical phases of mobilization in the countryside, such as the socialist upsurge (1956), the people's commune movement (1958–59), and the socialist education campaign (1963–65), it was true that formal organizations at the basic level swelled as a result of the heavy involvement of the masses and cadres in such campaigns. But for the bureaucratic organizations in the cities, those phases generally provided the leadership with opportunities to retrench personnel and streamline organizations and represented periods of hsia fang and ching chien movements. See Skinner and Winckler, "Compliance Succession in Rural Communist China: A Cyclical Theory," in Amitai Etzioni, ed., *Complex Organizations: A Sociological Reader,* 2d ed. (New York: Holt, Rinehart, and Winston, 1969), pp. 410–38.

104. For a detailed discussion of the large-scale replacement of local leadership by cadres sent down from the cities in this period and its impact on local and national politics, see Kau (forthcoming).

105. In fact, speculation of this type was frequently expressed by Chinese writers in the press and journals. See, for example, Liu Shou-p'eng *et al.,* "Hsia fang kan pu pi hsü fu ts'ung tang ti tang wei ti t'ung i ling tao" (The hsia fang cadres must obey the unified leadership of the local party committees), *Hsüeh hsi* (Study), 6 (Mar. 18, 1958), 22–23; Liu Tzu-cheng, "Hsia fang lao tung tuan lien shih kai chao ssu hsiang ti hao pan fa" (To go down to the basic level to labor and temper is a good method for thought reform), *Kuang ming jih pao,* Sept. 30, 1959.

106. See, for example, "Proletarian Revolutionaries, Form a Great Alliance to Seize Power from Those in Authority Who Are Taking the Capitalist Road," *Jen min jih pao,* edit., Jan. 22, 1967; reprinted in *Peking Review,* 5 (Jan. 27, 1967), 7–9.

107. For a lucid analysis of the first two years of development, see Chalmers Johnson, "China: The Cultural Revolution in Structural Perspective," *Asian Survey,* VIII: 1 (Jan. 1968), 1–15.

108. For major reports on Mao's new instruction on ching chien and progress of its implementation, see *Jen min jih pao,* July 11, 13, 20–22, 27–28, Aug. 25, 31, Sept. 21–22, and Oct. 5, 8–10, 1968.

109. "Hsiang-ch'eng hsien ko ming wei yüan hui ching ping chien cheng ti ching yen" (Experience of the revolutionary committee of Hsiang-ch'eng hsien in better troops and simpler administration), *Hung ch'i* (Red flag), 4 (Oct. 14, 1968), 32–37.

110. See note 108, above.

111. The printing plant of the Chinese Academy of Science in Peking, for instance, was reported to have reduced its nine sections (*k'o*) and four offices (*shih*) to two groups (*tsu,* one for political work and one for production), and also transferred 69.4% of cadres downward. At the First Automobile Plant of Changchun, the hsia fang rate was reported to have reached 77%. See "Chung-kuo k'o hsüeh yüan yin shua ch'ang chien chüeh tsou ching ping chien cheng ti tao lu" (The printing plant of the Chinese Academy of Science firmly follows the road of better army and simpler administration), *Hung ch'i,* 4 (Oct. 14, 1968), 37–38; and *Jen min jih pao,* Sept. 22, 1968.

*Trade Union Cultivation of Workers for Leadership*

1. Bruce H. Millen, *The Political Role of Labor in Developing Countries* (Washington: The Brookings Institution, 1963); and Sidney C. Sufrin, *Unions in Emerging Societies: Frustration and Politics* (Syracuse, N.Y.: Syracuse University Press, 1964).

2. S. N. Eisenstadt, *Modernization: Protest and Change* (Englewood Cliffs, N.J.: Prentice-Hall, 1966), pp. 10–11.

3. Wilbert E. Moore and Arnold S. Feldman, eds., *Labor Commitment and Social Change in Developing Areas* (New York: Social Science Research Council, 1960), p. 1.

4. Manning Nash, "Kinship and Voluntary Association," in *ibid.*, pp. 313–25; and Morris David Morris, "The Labor Market in India," in *ibid.*, pp. 178–200.

5. See Morris 1960, pp. 187–91; see also Richard D. Lambert, *Workers, Factories and Social Change in India* (Princeton: Princeton University Press, 1963).

6. William H. Knowles, "Industrial Conflict and Unions," in Moore and Feldman 1960, p. 307.

7. Eisenstadt 1966, p. 11.

8. For a discussion of the eras of CCP-union relations since 1949, see my "The Party and the Unions in Communist China," *China Quarterly*, 37 (Jan.–Mar. 1969), 84–119.

9. "Resolution of the Central Committee of the Chinese Communist Party, Northeast Bureau, on party leadership in state enterprises," May 1951, *Chieh fang jih pao* (Liberation daily), Sept. 12, 1951. This resolution, drawn up at an Urban Work Conference in the northeast region in May 1951, details the division of labor between the primary trade union organization, the party branch, and the administration in the enterprise. The tasks of the unions outlined here have not basically changed over the years, but the tasks of administration and party committee have altered significantly. See Franz Schurmann, *Ideology and Organization in Communist China* (Berkeley and Los Angeles: University of California Press, 1966), for a discussion of the shifting responsibilities of party committees and the administrators since 1949.

10. The Preamble to the Constitution, in *Chung-kuo kung hui ti pa tz'u ch'üan kuo tai piao ta hui chu yao wen chien* (Important documents of the Eighth All-China Congress of Trade Unions) (Peking: Kung jen ch'u pan she, 1957), p. 81.

11. For a discussion of the Chinese Communist view of "democracy" as mobilizing the masses to participate in making or, more realistically, discussing and ratifying decisions made from above, see James R. Townsend, *Political Participation in Communist China* (Berkeley and Los Angeles: University of California Press, 1967), especially chap. 5.

12. See David Tornquist, *Look East, Look West: The Socialist Adventure in Yugoslavia* (New York: Macmillan, 1966); also Jiri Kolaja, *Workers Councils: The Yugoslav Experience* (London: Tavistock Publications, 1965).

13. See *Lao tzu hsieh shang hui i* (The labor-capital consultative confer-

ence) (Peking: Kung jen ch'u pan she, 1950), esp. pp. 1–5, for an outline of the duties and powers of these conferences in management decisions.

14. Text of the rules, provisionally drafted at the national level, may be found in *The Trade Union Law of the People's Republic of China* (Peking: Foreign Languages Press, 1952), pp. 27–32.

15. *Eighth National Congress of the Communist Party of China* (Peking: Foreign Languages Press, 1956), II, 242–43.

16. *Jen min jih pao* (People's daily) [hereafter JMJP], May 29, 1957, in *Survey of China Mainland Press* [hereafter SCMP], No. 1547, pp. 10–12.

17. See, for example, "Metallurgical Works of Shenyang Improves System of Workers Congress," *Kung jen jih pao* (Daily worker) [hereafter KJJP], Oct. 13, 1965, in SCMP, No. 3576, pp. 11–13.

18. For a more detailed discussion of the industrial education system, see my *Spare-Time Education for Workers in Communist China* (Washington, D.C.: Office of Education, 1964), and "Closing the Education Gap," *Current Scene*, III: 15 (Mar. 15, 1965).

19. Mao Tse-tung, *Selected Works* (Peking: Foreign Languages Press, 1961–65), IV, 364–65. This 1949 speech of Mao's has become an important and often cited document since late 1968, with the renewed emphasis on the role of the working class.

20. Lai Jo-yü, "The Permanent Development of the Movement for Advanced Workers," *New China News Agency* [hereafter NCNA], May 2, 1956, in *Current Background* [hereafter CB], No. 389, p. 11.

21. Text in *Labour Laws and Regulations of the People's Republic of China* (Peking: Foreign Languages Press, 1956), pp. 81–88.

22. Lai Jo-yü, "Strengthen Trade Union Construction and Improve Connections Between Trade Unions and the Masses" (Report to the Third Plenum of the ACFTU Executive Committee), NCNA, Aug. 30, 1955, in CB, No. 363, pp. 14–15. See also *Chinese Workers March Towards Socialism* (Peking: Foreign Languages Press, 1956), pp. 69–70.

23. *Ten Great Years* (Peking: Foreign Languages Press, 1960), pp. 180, 183.

24. For a brief discussion of labor conditions in China in the late 1940's and at the time of Communist takeover, see A. Doak Barnett, *China on the Eve of Communist Takeover* (New York: Praeger, 1963), pp. 71–82, 347–48.

25. "Technical Studies for Young Workers," *Chung-kuo kung jen* (Chinese workers), 3 (Apr. 15, 1950), 73–74.

26. *Ibid.*, p. 74.

27. *Ten Great Years*, p. 180.

28. "The Development Made in the Chinese Labor Movement in 1954," KJJP, Apr. 29, 1955, in CB, No. 363, p. 62; and *Chinese Workers March Towards Socialism*, p. 72.

29. "Educational Facilities for Coal Miners," NCNA, Nov. 23, 1955, in SCMP, No. 1177, p. 12.

30. "Overcome the Rightist Conservative Way of Thinking, Vigorously Develop Regular Spare-Time Education for Workers," *Kuang ming jih pao* (Bright daily), edit., Jan. 20, 1956, in SCMP, No. 1221, p. 18.

31. "National Work Conference on Spare-Time Education of Workers and Employees Opens," NCNA, Dec. 19, 1955, in SCMP, No. 1202, p. 14.

32. "The Current Important Task of Spare-Time Education," JMJP, edit., Aug. 3, 1960, in SCMP, No. 2318, p. 7.

33. For a discussion of the problems, see "Exert Active Efforts Aimfully in Conducting Workers' Spare-Time Education with Better Results," KJJP, edit., Jan. 20, 1962, in SCMP, No. 2673.

34. "Conference on Developments in Workers' Education," NCNA, Nov. 1, 1958, in SCMP, No. 1889, p. 13.

35. "Tientsin Workers Advance Through Spare-Time Education," NCNA, Aug. 10, 1960, in SCMP, No. 2318, p. 17.

36. "130,000 Workers in Tientsin Join in Spare-Time Studies," JMJP, May 15, 1963, in SCMP, No. 2992, p. 14; and "Workers' Education Develops in North China City," NCNA, Apr. 25, 1963, in SCMP, No. 2969, p. 3.

37. KJJP, Feb. 4, 1965.

38. NCNA, Dec. 5, 1965, in SCMP, No. 3598, pp. 13–17.

39. In SCMP, No. 3601, pp. 8–11.

40. KJJP, edit., Jan. 26, 1964, in SCMP, No. 3161, pp. 4–7. On the same day, a JMJP editorial directed the party to pay attention to workers' spare-time education in order to expand the scientific and technical force; also in SCMP, No. 3161, pp. 1–3.

41. *Ibid.*, p. 5.

42. See *The Chinese Trade Unions*, 8 (1965), 16.

43. "Premier Chou En-lai's Report on the Work of the Government," *Main Documents of the First Session of the Third National People's Congress of the People's Republic of China* (Peking: Foreign Languages Press, 1965), pp. 11, 18, 31–32.

44. NCNA, Sept. 2, 1964.

45. Hu Chao-heng, "The Superiority of Part-Work Part-Study Schools Operated by Tientsin's Factories," KJJP, Jan. 6, 1965.

46. For further discussion of the new thrust in education for the industrial working force from 1964 until the Cultural Revolution, see the papers in this book by John W. Lewis and John Philip Emerson.

47. Liu Ning-i, "The Working Class Leads the Chinese People," *For A Lasting Peace, For A People's Democracy*, 15 (Aug. 1, 1949), 3.

48. NCNA, May 24, 1951, in SCMP, No. 107, p. 20.

49. Chu Hsüeh-fan, "Chinese Workers March Forward," *People's China*, 1 (Jan. 1, 1952), 5.

50. NCNA, May 19, 1951, in SCMP, No. 106, p. 45.

51. Liu Ning-i 1949, p. 3.

52. *Chinese Workers March Towards Socialism*, p. 72.

53. *Ibid.*

54. "Over 13 Million Chinese Workers Enrolled at Spare-Time Schools," NCNA, Dec. 25, 1959, in SCMP, No. 2167, p. 17.

55. "The Popular Movement for Spare-Time Education," JMJP, edit., Mar. 23, 1960, in SCMP, No. 2228, p. 23.

56. "Chinese Workers' Material and Cultural Lives Improved Constantly," *The Chinese Trade Unions*, 5 (1964), 22.

57. KJJP, edit., Jan. 26, 1964, in SCMP, No. 3161, p. 4.

58. JMJP, Jan. 26, 1964, in SCMP, No. 3161, p. 8. By 1965, the number

of worker graduates of spare-time universities was 20,000; see *The Chinese Trade Unions*, 7 (1965), 11.

59. See "The Popular Movement for Spare-Time Education."

60. *Chinese Workers March Towards Socialism*, p. 67.

61. On labor emulation, its key role and features, see: *Kung hui hsiao tsu chang kung tso* (Work of the trade union small group leader) (Peking: Kung jen ch'u pan she, 1955), pp. 4–9; *The Seventh All-China Congress of Trade Unions* (Peking: Foreign Languages Press, 1953), pp. 55–62; and *Eighth All-China Congress of the Trade Unions* (Peking: Foreign Languages Press, 1958), pp. 36–42.

62. For an elaborate system of handling individual or unit recognition, see the First Engineering Ministry's "Temporary Regulations for Socialist Emulation Awards," *Ti i chi chieh kung yün* (First engineering workers movement), 22 (Nov. 1959), 9–16; "advanced factories" in this and the Ministry of Electrical Machinery are listed in *ibid.*, pp. 4–5.

63. Yüan's story is told in *Chieh fang jih pao*, July 15, 1951, in SCMP, No. 140, pp. 14–16.

64. "All-China Federation of Labor Report on the Work of the Past Year," *Chung-kuo kung jen*, May 15, 1950, in CB, No. 24, p. 2.

65. See the ACFTU release, "Basic Experience of Wusan Factory Trade Union Work," NCNA, Jan. 3, 1953, in SCMP, No. 488, pp. 10–16.

66. Hankow: Hsin Hua shu tien, 1950. For other examples of trade union cadre manuals dealing with political education and its content, see *Kung hui ti tso yung yü jen wu* (The functions and duties of the trade unions) (Peking: Kung jen ch'u pan she, 1954), esp. pp. 5–9, 21–26; and *Kung hui hsiao tsu chang kung tso*, pp. 10–13.

67. Liu Shao-ch'i, "Message of Greetings on Behalf of the Central Committee of the Communist Party of China," in *Eighth All-China Congress of the Trade Unions*, p. 18.

68. The number of industrial workers almost trebled in 1958, rising from 7.9 to 23.4 million persons. See John Philip Emerson, "Manpower Absorption in the Non-Agricultural Branches of the Economy of Communist China, 1953–58," *China Quarterly*, 7 (July–Sept. 1961), 74.

69. See, for example, Ch'i Ko, "Nurture New Workers into Loyal Fighters in Building Up the Border Country of the Fatherland," KJJP, Aug. 7, 1959, in SCMP, No. 2097, pp. 44–46; and "Political and Technical Education for Newly Recruited Workers Strengthened in Anhwei, Kansu and Other Areas," KJJP, May 19, 1959, in SCMP, No. 2025, pp. 1–2.

70. The following figures are from Nym Wales (Helen Snow), *The Chinese Labor Movement* (New York: John Day, 1945), cited from official CCP statistics on pp. 60–61.

71. Robert North, in *Kuomintang and Chinese Communist Elites* (Stanford: Stanford University Press, 1952), p. 32, cites a Comintern publication that stated "at least 66 per cent of the Chinese Communist Party membership could be classed as proletarian" at the end of 1926.

72. See John W. Lewis, "Political Aspects of Mobility in China's Urban Development," *American Political Science Review*, LX: 4 (Dec. 1966), 899–912.

73. Quoted in: *For A Lasting Peace, For A People's Democracy*, 24 (June 15, 1950), 2. See also P'eng Chen's May Day article in *ibid.*, 17 (Apr. 27, 1951), 2.

74. See Joyce K. Kallgren, "Social Welfare and China's Industrial Workers," in A. Doak Barnett, ed., *Chinese Communist Politics in Action* (Seattle: University of Washington Press, 1969), pp. 540–73, for a study of the welfare programs run by the unions.

75. ACFTU membership figures are from: *Chung-kuo kung jen*, 4 (Feb. 1958), 7; *The Chinese Trade Unions*, 3 (Sept. 1959), 8; Bruno Di Pol, "Position of Trade Unions in Communist China," *Avanti*, Dec. 3, 1960, in *Joint Publications Research Service*, No. 6631, p. 14; and "Trade Unions in China," *The Society for Anglo-Chinese Understanding News*, Jan. 1966, p. 1.

76. *Hsin Hua yüeh pao* (New China monthly), I: 4 (Feb. 1950).

77. *Chinese Workers March Towards Socialism*, p. 14.

78. There were 3,495,000 activists out of 17,400,000 union members in 1958; see Liu Ch'ang-sheng, "Growth of the Chinese Working Class," *The Chinese Trade Unions*, 3 (Sept. 1959), 7.

79. John Gardner, "The *Wu-fan* Campaign in Shanghai: A Study in the Consolidation of Urban Control," in Barnett 1969, pp. 530–31.

80. *Chieh fang jih pao*, Mar. 28, 1952.

81. See the Tientsin NCNA release in *Nan fang jih pao* (Southern daily), May 24, 1952.

82. NCNA, May 21, 1952. For some other examples of reorganization of union leadership, see *Ch'ang-chiang jih pao* (Yangtze daily), Apr. 6, 1952, and *Ch'ung-ch'ing hsin Hua jih pao* (Chungking new China daily), May 23, 1952.

83. See John W. Lewis, *Leadership in Communist China* (Ithaca, N.Y.: Cornell University Press, 1963), pp. 108–20, and Schurmann 1966, pp. 128–39, for discussions of recruitment policies.

84. "Communique of the Enlarged Twelfth Plenary Session of the Eighth Central Committee of the Communist Party of China," supplement to *Peking Review*, 44 (Nov. 1, 1968). See also the *Hung ch'i* (Red flag) edit., "Absorb Fresh Blood from the Proletariat," reprinted in *Peking Review*, 43 (Oct. 25, 1968), 4–7.

85. Lin Piao, "Report to the Ninth National Congress of the Communist Party of China," *Peking Review*, special issue, Apr. 28, 1969, p. 23.

86. Teng Hsiao-p'ing, *Kuan yü cheng feng yün tung ti pao kao* (Report on the rectification campaign) (Peking: Jen min jih pao ch'u pan she, 1957), p. 27.

87. *The Chinese Trade Unions*, 3 (Sept. 1959), 8.

88. JMJP, Apr. 25, 1953.

89. *Ibid.*

90. *Ibid.*

91. This was the case in Tangshan, for example; see Lewis 1966.

92. See Gardner 1969.

93. JMJP, May 1, 1950.

94. See Lewis 1963, pp. 118–19, for a discussion of how party recruitment drives concentrate on bringing production team leaders and "advanced pro-

ducers" into the ranks of the activists so that they may then be selected for induction into the CCP.

95. In *Eighth National Congress of the Communist Party of China*, II, 315.

## Commerce, Education, and Political Development in Tangshan, 1956–69

1. For the figures on urban places in China, see Morris B. Ullman, *Cities of Mainland China: 1953 and 1958* (Washington, D.C.: Bureau of the Census, 1961). The population of Tangshan changed as follows: 146,000 (1938), 137,000 (1948), 693,000 (1953), and 812,000 (1958).

2. The best study of Tangshan's development in print is Wei Hsin-chen and Chu Yün-ch'eng, *T'ang-shan ching chi ti li* (The economic geography of Tangshan) (Peking: Shang wu yin shu kuan, 1960).

3. See, for example, Max Weber, *The City* (New York: Free Press, 1958), pp. 181–92. For a discussion of the question with respect to medieval Muslim cities, see Ira Marvin Lapidus, *Muslim Cities in the Middle Ages* (Cambridge, Mass.: Harvard University Press, 1967), pp. 185–91.

4. Franz Schurmann, "Cities," *Ideology and Organization in Communist China* (Berkeley and Los Angeles: University of California Press, 1966), pp. 365–403.

5. See Lewis, "Political Aspects of Mobility in China's Urban Development," *American Political Science Review*, LX: 4 (Dec. 1966), 901–10.

6. Lewis, "The Social Limits of Politically Induced Change," in Chandler Morse *et al.*, *Modernization by Design* (Ithaca, N.Y.: Cornell University Press, 1969), pp. 1–33.

7. This is *T'ang-shan lao tung jih pao*, for which copies are available from late 1950 through 1958, with many missing issues for 1954–55 and 1958. This has been supplemented by a reading of *Ho-pei jih pao* (Hopei daily), which covers the years 1950 to 1965 and has substantial news coverage of Tangshan.

8. For a detailed study of one such group in Tangshan, see Huang Chieh-shan, "Political Influences on the Ch'i-hsin Cement Company," unpub. M.A. thesis, Cornell University, 1968, chap. 5.

9. On this point, see Lewis, "Party Cadres in Communist China," in James S. Coleman, ed., *Education and Political Development* (Princeton: Princeton University Press, 1965), pp. 408–36.

10. This is based on *Shang yeh shih yung fa kuei shou ts'e* (Handbook of applied commercial law) (Peking: Fa lü ch'u pan she, 1958), pp. 154–77. The number of units in Tangshan special district changed from 1957 to 1960. The district seat in 1957 was Ch'ang-li and at the time there were only ten hsien with all municipalities coming under the jurisdiction of the province. The figures for each year can be found in *Jen min shou ts'e* (People's handbook), published annually by Ta kung pao she.

11. *Kuan yü shang yeh kung tso wen t'i chüeh ting*. These decisions have never been publicly referred to even in the Cultural Revolution, presumably because Mao claims to have been in charge at the Tenth Plenum. Another possible reason is given by *Sing tao jih pao* (Star Island [Singapore] daily, Hong Kong), Jan. 24 and 25, 1968, which states that Ch'en Po-ta and Li

Hsien-nien, both on the Politburo at the time, clashed over these decisions. It seems clear, however, that de facto they have been repudiated. At the time of their approval they inspired a number of articles on the subject of "the rational simplifying of links in commodity circulation." See, for example, *Ta kung pao* (Impartial) [hereafter TKP], Feb. 1 and 24, and Mar. 13, 1963. For a 1965 article on the same subject, see Chiang Huai, "On Simplification of Links in Commodity Circulation," *Ching chi yen chiu* (Economic research), 11 (Nov. 20, 1965), in *Selections from China Mainland Magazines* [hereafter SCMM], No. 508, pp. 19–26.

12. This is based in part on my earlier article, "The Study of Chinese Political Culture," *World Politics*, XVIII: 3 (Apr. 1966), esp. 520–23.

13. TKP, Apr. 8, 1965.

14. *Ibid.*, May 15, 1964; see also *Jen min jih pao* (People's daily) [hereafter JMJP], June 6, 1964.

15. I have discussed this in Lewis 1966.

16. See Chu T'ien-shun's article on the rational organization of transportation in *Hung ch'i* (Red flag) 23–24 (Dec. 5, 1962), 35–39.

17. TKP, Apr. 8 and May 13, 1965.

18. See the article written on supply and marketing cooperatives at the time of the Tenth Plenum in *Kuang ming jih pao* (Bright daily), Aug. 27, 1962.

19. In 1965 it was made clear that these co-ops nationally corresponded to the existing standard marketing areas. See TKP, Sept. 23, 1965, which reported on the existence of 80,000 co-ops. On standard marketing areas, see G. William Skinner, "Marketing and Social Structure in Rural China: Parts I, II, and III," *Journal of Asian Studies*, XXIV: 1–3 (Nov. 1964, Feb. 1965, May 1965), 3–43, 195–228, 363–99.

20. JMJP, May 19, 1965. The government had also decided that "in general, processing factories should not be set up in hsien cities." See Chang Ho-wei, "The Worker-Peasant System in Finance and Trade Departments," *Hsin chien she* (New construction), 1–2 (Feb. 20, 1966), in SCMM, No. 534, p. 26.

21. TKP, Aug. 12, 1965. This was part of a campaign to simplify operations generally at the hsien level. See JMJP, July 26, 1965.

22. TKP, Apr. 8, 1965.

23. For a discussion of nested systems see G. William Skinner, "The City in Chinese Society," in Skinner, ed., *The City in Late Imperial China* (Stanford: Stanford University Press, forthcoming).

24. TKP, Apr. 8, 1965.

25. JMJP, Aug. 12, 1965.

26. *Ibid.*, July 26, 1965; and TKP, Aug. 12, 1965.

27. JMJP, Aug. 12, 1965.

28. TKP, May 13, 1965, Aug. 23 and 31, and Sept. 10, 1965; JMJP, Apr. 3, 1965.

29. TKP, Apr. 8, 1965.

30. See Chang Ho-wei 1966, pp. 24–38; "Sources of Labor Discontent in China: The Worker-Peasant System," *Current Scene*, VI: 5 (Mar. 15, 1968); and "Information about Liu Shao-ch'i in the System of Temporary Labor and

Contract Work," and "Liu Shao-ch'i Is the Arch Culprit Initiating the Reactionary System of Contract Labor," in SCMM, No. 616, pp. 21–28.

31. According to "Information about Liu Shao-ch'i," pp. 21–22, regulations on temporary workers date back to 1951. The language of the worker-peasant system in this source is traced back to 1958. For this period and earlier it is equated with the contract system of labor. By 1958, there were more than 12 million "contract" workers in China.

32. This surplus had already begun to be built up in the early 1960's because of the economic crisis following the collapse of the Great Leap Forward. See JMJP, Oct. 22, 1964; on concentration in hsien towns see *New China News Agency* [hereafter NCNA], Dec. 27, 1965, in *Survey of China Mainland Press* [hereafter SCMP], No. 3615, p. 16.

33. See, for example, NCNA, Dec. 27, 1965, in SCMP, No. 3615, pp. 16–20.

34. *Ibid.*

35. *Chung-kuo fang chih* (China textiles), 1 (Jan. 10, 1965), in SCMM, No. 458, p. 32. For articles explicitly relating the commercial arrangements of the economic regions to the worker-peasant system, see Kuan Ta-t'ung, "Commerce to Serve the Countryside: Its Revolutionary Significance," *Ching chi yen chiu*, 12 (Dec. 20, 1965), in SCMM, No. 536, pp. 19–27, and TKP, Aug. 31, 1965, and Oct. 8, 1965. The August article refers specifically to the arrangements in Hopei.

36. On the two-track labor system, see the Peking poster of Jan. 11, 1967, in *Joint Publications Research Service* [hereafter JPRS] Special, "Samples of Red Guards Publications," Aug. 1, 1967, pp. 53–54; and "Information about Liu Shao-ch'i" and "Liu Shao-ch'i Is the Arch Culprit."

37. *Shou tu hung wei ping pao* (Capital Red Guards newspaper), 21 (Jan. 10, 1967), states: "It is also the cheapest system in that the average wages . . . are far below the average wages of the normal factory workers." See also NCNA, Nov. 1, 1964, in SCMP, No. 3337, p. 17.

38. Peking poster, Jan. 25, 1967, in *China Topics*, No. YB 415, p. 14.

39. *Shou tu hung wei ping pao*, 21 (Jan. 10, 1967).

40. The sending of dependents to the cities began as early as 1964. See JMJP, July 27, 1964. Later the trade unions allegedly would not give these dependents any benefits. See *China Topics*, No. YB 415, p. 14, for reprint of a Peking poster on this subject.

41. As various sources have made clear, the labels for the worker-peasant system changed. In the Cultural Revolution it was described in the most pejorative language possible. On the contract system in the 1920's, see Jean Chesneaux, *The Chinese Labor Movement 1919–1927* (Stanford: Stanford University Press, 1968), pp. 54–64.

42. See JMJP, Sept. 22, 1964; *Pei-ching jih pao* (Peking daily), Aug. 19, 1964.

43. On the general political evolution of unions in China, see Paul F. Harper, "The Party and the Unions in Communist China," *China Quarterly*, 37 (Jan.–Mar. 1969), 84–119. The most comprehensive denunciation of the trade unions in this period is in JMJP, May 27, 1968. There is some evidence that hsien-level trade unions attempted to fight back for their workers in this period. See *Kung jen jih pao* (Daily worker), Nov. 25, 1964.

44. JMJP, May 27, 1968.

45. Most of this is based on later revelations and accusations found in the documents of the Cultural Revolution. For the major directives of the Cultural Revolution on this subject, see *Current Background*, No. 852, p. 83; *Shou tu hung wei ping pao*, 21, and SCMP, No. 4129, pp. 1–2. The source cited in footnotes 38 deals with the role of the trade unions.

46. On the formation of workers' clubs, for example, see *Kung jen jih pao*, Nov. 17, 1964.

47. NCNA, Dec. 27, 1965, in SCMP, No. 3615, p. 18.

48. According to a Peking poster of Jan. 11, 1967, the two kinds of labor systems "and two kinds of educational systems" were put forward by Liu Shao-ch'i at a conference in Hopei on Aug. 7, 1964. See JPRS Special, "Samples of Red Guard Publications," Aug. 1, 1967, pp. 53–54. See the article on the "small pyramid" system of education with "ordinary" schools for less able students and "key" schools for the brightest students in *Wen hui pao* (Cultural exchange news), May 11, 1968, in SCMP, No. 4199, pp. 1–5.

49. "Premier Chou En-lai Reports on the Work of the Government," *Peking Review*, 1 (Jan. 1, 1965), 14. On other aspects of his half-work half-study system, see Donald J. Munro, "Maxims and Realities in China's Educational Policy: The Half-Work, Half-Study Model," *Asian Survey*, VII: 4 (Apr. 1967), 254–72.

50. JMJP, Dec. 9, 1965. For evidence that a disproportionate number of these were coming from hsien towns, see *Kuang ming jih pao*, May 10, 1964.

51. For a discussion of these problems, see *Ko ming ch'ing nien* (Revolutionary youth, Canton), Nov. 10, 1967, in *China Topics*, No. YB 465, p. 10. On general aspects of mistreatment, see *China Topics*, No. YB 465 and YB 483; and "Translations on Communist China: Political and Sociological," No. 436, in JPRS, No. 44052, Jan. 17, 1968.

52. Many youth apparently went through this ordeal because cadres promised them that this would be temporary and it would be good for their careers. This was later denounced as a part of the Liuist strategy. See *Wen hui pao*, May 25 and June 3, 1968.

53. See the sources cited in note 51.

54. On the crucial importance of the socialist education campaign at this time see Charles Neuhauser, "The Chinese Communist Party in the 1960's: Prelude to the Cultural Revolution," *China Quarterly*, 32 (Oct.–Dec. 1967), 3–36; and Richard Baum and Frederick C. Teiwes, *Ssu-Ch'ing: The Socialist Education Movement of 1962–1966* (Berkeley, Calif.: Center for Chinese Studies, 1968).

55. On recruitment into the party of these youths, see NCNA, June 30, 1966, which emphasizes the percentage of youths in the 95,000 recruits from Hopei between mid-1964 and mid-1965.

56. Shanghai poster, Jan. 14, 1967, one translation of which is found in *China Topics*, No. YB 415, p. 5. Sometimes this was expressed more generally as follows: "There are no good people in the countryside, because good people do not come to the countryside." *China Topics*, No. YB 483, Appendix, p. 4.

57. On the relationship of job placement to education and the worker-peasant system see "Translations on Communist China: Political and Sociological," No. 436, in JPRS, No. 44052, Jan. 17, 1968.

58. *Ibid.*, p. 2. Another directive stressed the importance of this system

for handling surplus labor on a permanent basis: see *Chih nung hung ch'i* (Aid agriculture red flag), Jan. 1968, p. 2.

59. On cadre schools, see *Ch'un lei* (Spring thunder), 4 (Apr. 13, 1967), in SCMP, No. 3940, pp. 6–15.

60. *Kuang ming jih pao,* July 19, 1964.

61. The notion of "many centers" was not, of course, introduced until much later and was applied to a number of different kinds of political arrangements. For evidence that it applied to the kind of bureaucratic independence as defined here, see JMJP, Aug. 13, 1968; *Wen hui pao,* Aug. 6, 8, and 15, 1968.

62. TKP, Apr. 8, 1965.

63. *Ibid.*

64. *Ibid.*

65. JMJP, May 19, 1965.

66. *Ibid.* This was put as follows: "Partial interests must submit to the interests of the integral whole because convenience for the integral whole is the greatest convenience." At this time the interests of the "integral whole" were defined by the urban leadership in Tangshan.

67. *Ibid.*

68. "Decision of the Central Committee of the Chinese Communist Party Concerning the Great Proletarian Cultural Revolution" (adopted Aug. 8, 1966), *Peking Review,* 33 (Aug. 12, 1966), 11. This quote is part of the 13th point of this famous "16-point decision."

69. At this time *Shou tu hung wei ping pao,* 21 (Jan. 10, 1967), denounced the system of temporary and contract workers.

70. NCNA, Jan. 21, 1967, in *Current Background,* No. 818, p. 13.

71. On Wang Kuo-fan and the "paupers' co-op," see Lewis, *Leadership in Communist China* (Ithaca, N.Y.: Cornell University Press, 1963), pp. 204–11.

72. See Mao's comments in *Chinese Law and Government,* I: 4 (Winter 1968–69), 66.

73. For an article by Wang on the eve of the Cultural Revolution, see *China Reconstructs,* Nov. 1966.

74. For material on Wang in the Cultural Revolution, see Richard Baum, "A Parting of Paupers," *Far Eastern Economic Review,* LIX: 1 Jan. 4, 1968), 17–19; NCNA, Sept. 28, 1967, Dec. 12, 1967, Feb. 7, 1968, and May 1, 1968.

75. NCNA, May 15, 1968, and Aug. 17, 1968. For evidence on similar developments among the railway workers in the Tangshan area, see NCNA, May 26, 1968.

76. See the order for the dissolution of "a great number of so-called national organizations" in *CCP Documents of the Great Proletarian Cultural Revolution 1966–67* [hereafter cited as *CCP Documents*] (Hong Kong: Union Research Institute, 1968), pp. 278–79.

77. JMJP, Feb. 6, 1967.

78. "Notice of the CCP Central Committee and the State Council," Feb. 17, 1967, in *CCP Documents,* pp. 305–6.

79. "Sources of Labor Discontent in China," p. 10.

80. For text see *CCP Documents,* pp. 372–75.

81. Text of undated directive in *Kuang t'ieh tsung ssu* (Canton railways general headquarters), 28 (Feb. 1968), in SCMP, No. 4129, p. 2.

82. *Kuang ming jih pao*, Mar. 11, 1967.

83. *Ibid.* See also the directive cited in note 78, which states: "Those temporary workers, contract workers, workers by rotation and piece workers who have been branded 'counterrevolutionary' because they criticized their leadership in the initial period of the great proletarian cultural revolution should be acquitted ... [and] allowed to return to their former posts of production and work according to their former contracts." *CCP Documents*, pp. 305–6.

84. NCNA, Dec. 12, 1967.

85. See the Nov. 1966 directive in *CCP Documents*, p. 118, which shows how early publicity was given to the leadership of "experienced and politically reliable old workers as the bulwarks, and with the participation of technicians."

86. NCNA, Mar. 3, 1968, in SCMP, No. 4133, pp. 18–19.

87. A measure of localism has long met with Mao's approval. In 1956 Mao stated: "For the development of regional enthusiasm, each region must have its individuality congenial to its local conditions, which is at the same time conducive to the interests of the totality and to the strengthening of the unity of the country.... To summarize, the region must have adequate power and this is helpful to building a strong socialist country." "On the Ten Great Relationships," in Jerome Ch'en, ed., *Mao* (Englewood Cliffs, N.J.: Prentice-Hall, 1969), pp. 75–76. A recent expression of this same idea is found in the article on "The Road to Socialist Industrialization," in JMJP, Oct. 14, 1969.

88. Reported in JMJP, Mar. 15, 1967.

89. See speech by K'ang Sheng of May 30, 1968, in SCMM, No. 625, p. 9.

90. Tientsin Radio, Jan. 11, 1968. The creation of this committee was celebrated by a rally of 200,000 people in Tangshan.

91. NCNA, May 15, 1968.

92. Tientsin Radio, Jan. 11, 1968. For Wang's triumphant article assessing his experiences over the past decade, see JMJP, Aug. 20, 1968.

93. Wang earlier had become a member of the Hopei Provincial Revolutionary Committee. In April 1969, at the Ninth Party Congress, he was elected to the Central Committee.

94. As in 1956–57, there is once again a widespread discussion in China on "changing the superstructure." See, for example, the article "The Working Class Must Take Over All Positions in the Superstructure," Nanchang Radio, Aug. 27, 1968; and *Wen hui pao*, Aug. 19, 1968, in SCMP, No. 4255, pp. 5–7.

95. NCNA, July 25, 1968, in SCMP, No. 4229, p. 7.

96. For a typical article on this plant, see NCNA, July 22, 1968, and Sept. 1, 1968; *Wen hui pao*, July 22, 1968; and JMJP, July 30, 1968. For an article on the general education of intellectuals, see *Hung ch'i*, 3 (Sept. 10, 1968), 2–4.

97. NCNA, July 22, 1968. See also NCNA, July 27, 1968.

98. In Hopei, 6,000 college graduates of the class of 1967 were working in rural areas, factories, and lower-level units at the end of 1968 (NCNA, Nov. 13, 1968). See the directive of the CCP Central Committee on the "allotment of work to school leavers" (June 15, 1968), in SCMP, No. 4221, p. 14. For evidence on Hopei, see Peking Radio, July 18, 1968; NCNA, Aug.

18, 20, 1968; and JMJP, July 19 and Aug. 21, 1968. Because of bitterness on the part of students, Chou En-lai was led to tell them in January 1968 that the decision to send students to the countryside on a permanent basis "is an idea of Mao Tse-tung." Text in SCMP, No. 4134, p. 5.

99. NCNA, Oct. 31, 1968. On the national movement to put workers in charge of Red Guards and education, see JMJP, Aug. 18, 1968; *Hung ch'i,* 2 (Aug. 25, 1968); NCNA, July 26, 27, Aug. 16, 18, 21, 27, and 28, 1968.

100. NCNA, Mar. 3, 1968, in JPRS, No. 44937, Apr. 4, 1968, p. 22.

101. On the Kailan mines in this respect, see NCNA, Jan. 5, 1968, in SCMP, No. 4095, pp. 20–21.

102. For one article that suggests that veteran village leaders such as Wang Kuo-fan control the actions of the hsien committees in the Tangshan area, see NCNA, Feb. 7, 1968, in SCMP, No. 4115, p. 24.

103. JMJP, May 16, 1968. For Peking's authorization of the takeover of commercial systems by workers and other "revolutionaries," see JMJP, Jan. 22, 1967. At the Ninth Party Congress in April 1969, Kailan miner Fan Te-ling was elected an alternate to the Central Committee. Throughout 1969 the Kailan Revolutionary Committee was a model for the rest of the country.

104. The present leadership reconciles a bias toward regional-sized units with an emphasis on the urban committees by stressing the components of the various units. The stress is not then on the city as such but on its parts. Nanchang Radio, July 4, 1968, put it this way: "We must establish in a big way the policy of facing the four areas of countryside, frontier regions, factories and mines, and basic units." A Red Guard publication of Mar. 27, 1967, quoted Ch'en Po-ta in this same vein: "It is not good for the school to be too big. From now on we should reduce . . . the 'three big' (*san ta*): big cities, big universities, big factories. If things are too big they are not easy to control." *China Topics*, No. YB 427, Appendix E, p. 4.

105. A drive for "better troops and simpler administration" began in the late spring of 1968. Administrative staffs at the provincial level and below reportedly were cut as much as 85%, and many factories lost 10% of their workers to propaganda teams assigned to schools and universities. By September 1968 some Maoists appeared to recognize that the cutback in administration in the middle levels was cutting off information from below and called for "strengthening the system of asking for instructions and making reports." *Wen hui pao*, Sept. 25, 1968. Nevertheless, the revolutionary committees continued to deal with problems in the broadest possible terms and with little reference to sources of potential conflict.

106. For a typical article on the Tangshan Revolutionary Committee, see JMJP, July 19, 1969.

107. This in part is based on Theodore J. Lowi, "American Business, Public Policy, Case-Studies, and Political Theory," *World Politics*, XVI: 4 (July 1964), 677–715; Theodore Caplow, *Two Against One: Coalitions in Triads* (Englewood Cliffs, N.J.: Prentice-Hall, 1968), esp. chap. 9; and Lewis Coser, *The Functions of Social Conflict* (New York: Free Press, 1956), esp. pp. 121–49.

*Manpower Training and Utilization of Specialized Cadres, 1949–68*

1. In the author's opinion, the chief data collection agency of the regime, the State Statistical Bureau (hereafter SSB) from its inception in 1952 made sustained efforts to develop economic statistics for Mainland China as a whole with varying degrees of success. Defects in the data produced were the result of faulty methods, inadequate training of statistical personnel, and unsolved problems in statistical management and not of deliberate falsification, except during the brief period of the Great Leap Forward (1958–60) when party officials who had taken charge of data collection work from professionals greatly exaggerated economic production figures. Evaluations of SSB statistics are given in Choh-ming Li, *The Statistical System of Communist China* (Berkeley and Los Angeles: University of California Press, 1962); Helen W. H. C. Yin, "The Industrial Statistics Reporting System of Communist China: 1949–1958," unpub. diss., Columbia University, 1966; John Philip Emerson, *Nonagricultural Employment in Mainland China: 1949–1958* (Washington, D.C.: U.S. Government Printing Office, 1965), pp. 11–39, 63–76.

It seems clear that the most important use of SSB statistics by the regime was as the basis for economic planning and evaluation of plan results. These were given as the chief reasons for data collection work in Li Fu-ch'un, "Chung yang jen min cheng fu cheng wu yüan ts'ai cheng ching chi wei yüan hui Li Fu-ch'un fu chu jen tsai ch'üan kuo ts'ai ching t'ung chi hui i shang ti chih shih (i chiu wu i nien ch'i yüeh)" (Directive of Vice Chairman Li Fu-ch'un of the Finance and Economics Committee of the Central People's Government, Government Administrative Council to the All-China Conference on Financial and Economic Statistics [July 1951]), in SSB, *T'ung chi kung tso chung yao wen chien hui pien* (A compilation of important documents on statistical work) (Peking: T'ung chi ch'u pan she, 1955), p. 3. Six years later in 1957 near the end of the First Five-Year Plan period, the same views on the role of statistics were given by Hsüeh Mu-ch'iao in his "Ti i ko wu nien chi hua ch'i chien wo kuo t'ung chi kung tso ti ch'u pu ching yen ho chin hou jen wu" (Initial experiences in Chinese statistical work during the First Five-Year Plan period and future tasks), *T'ung chi kung tso* (Statistical work [hereafter TCKT]), 21 (Nov. 14, 1957), 1. Other uses of statistics, for example as propaganda tools by the party and the New China News Agency, were of secondary importance.

2. Emerson 1965, pp. 70–73, 77–78, and 128.

3. Victims of this campaign said that it was far more arbitrary and brutal than any of its predecessors. For an official evaluation, see Lo Jui-ch'ing, "The Struggle against Counterrevolutionaries," *New China News Agency* [hereafter NCNA], Sept. 14, 1956, in *Current Background* [hereafter CB], No. 420, pp. 10–18.

4. The plight of primary education in rural areas in the latter part of the First Five-Year Plan period is candidly discussed in Wu Yen-yin, "We Should Pay Enough Attention to Middle and Primary School Education and Teachers," *Kuang ming jih pao* (Bright daily) [hereafter KMJP], Aug. 16, 1956,

in *Survey of China Mainland Press* [hereafter SCMP], No. 1380, pp. 12–15. Less was spent per rural middle school than per urban middle school, according to Yeh Feng, "Ju ho pien hao 1958 nien tu wen chiao wei sheng shih yeh chi hua" (How to do a good job of compiling 1958 plans for cultural, educational, and public health undertakings), *Chi hua ching chi* (Planned economy) [hereafter CHCC], 9 (1957), 18.

5. State Council, "Kuo wu yüan kuan yü ch'eng hsiang hua fen piao chun ti kuei ting" (State Council resolution on the criteria for demarcation of urban and rural areas), TCKT, 12 (Dec. 17, 1955), 4. For additional details on the classification of urban places as municipalities (*shih*) or as towns (*chen*), see Morris B. Ullman, *Cities of Mainland China: 1953 and 1958* (Washington, D.C.: Bureau of the Census, 1961), pp. 2, 4, 6. This report has been reprinted with deletions in Gerald Breese, ed., *The City in Newly Developing Countries* (Englewood Cliffs, N.J.: Prentice-Hall, 1969), pp. 81–103.

6. SSB, "Kuan yü ch'eng hsiang hua fen piao chun jo kan chu yao wen t'i ti shuo ming" (Explanations of several important problems in the criteria established for the demarcation of urban and rural areas), TCKT, 12 (Dec. 17, 1955), 5.

7. A careful reading of the notes and text that accompany the most important series of urban and rural population statistics published by the SSB suggests that the bureau did not have much confidence in the accuracy of these figures but published them for their utility as indicators of population change. See Data Section, "1949–56 nien wo kuo jen k'ou t'ung chi tzu liao" (Statistical data on China's population, 1949–56), TCKT, 11 (June 14, 1957), 24–25.

8. The system is discussed in John S. Aird, *The Size, Composition, and Growth of the Population of Mainland China* (Washington, D.C.: U.S. Government Printing Office, 1961), pp. 31–40.

9. See the sources for Table 1, p. 188.

10. The same figure was later quoted in Anna Louise Strong, "Interview with Po I-po on Economic Readjustment," *Ta kung pao* (Impartial, Hong Kong), Jan. 15, 1964, in SCMP, No. 3152, p. 7.

11. The 1964 investigation is briefly discussed in Hsüeh Feng, "Chung kung ti i chiu liu ssu nien jen k'ou p'u ch'a" (Communist China's 1964 population census), *Tsu kuo* (China monthly), 56 (Nov. 1968), 17–18 and back cover; and H. T. Wang, "Analysis of Mainland China's 1964 Census," *Free China and Asia*, 2 (Sept. 1964), 7–9.

12. Some persons took advantage of chaotic conditions during the Cultural Revolution to return to urban areas from the rural villages to which they had been sent. See, for example, "Rural Shantung Youths Defeat Class Enemies," NCNA, June 6, 1968.

13. These figures are given in Roland Pressat, "La Population de la Chine et son Economie," *Population*, XIII: 4 (Oct.–Dec. 1958), 572–73. The exception is Hofei, the very low birth and death rates for which suggest acute underregistration.

14. Official figures on the rate of natural increase of the total population during the First Five-Year Plan period given to the Indian demographer, Sripati Chandrasekhar, in 1958 vary between 20 and 24 per thousand popu-

lation. See Chandrasekhar, *China's Population Census and Vital Statistics* (Hong Kong: Hong Kong University Press, 1959), p. 50.

15. For the urban population in 1952, see Table 1, p. 188. Estimates of eight million rural-to-urban migrants and an urban population of 92 million in 1957 are given in Wang Kuang-wei (State Planning Commission, Vice-Chairman), "How to Organize Agricultural Labor Power," CHCC, 8 (Aug. 9, 1957), in *Extracts from China Mainland Magazines* [hereafter ECMM], No. 100, p. 11.

16. Literate persons in Mainland China are more likely to migrate than illiterates, according to H. Y. Tien, "The Stabilization of Urban Population in Communist China," paper presented at the Fifteenth Annual Meeting of the Association for Asian Studies, Philadelphia, Mar. 25, 1963, p. 9.

17. Sung P'ing, "T'an lao tung chiu yeh wen t'i" (Let's discuss problems of labor and employment), *Hsüeh hsi* (Study), 12 (June 18, 1957), 26. For the worker and employee increase, see Emerson 1965, p. 129.

18. "Ranks of Our Working Class Have Grown to Unprecedented Size," NCNA, Jan. 18, 1957, in SCMP, No. 1460, p. 2.

19. Emerson 1965, p. 129.

20. *Ibid.*

21. Li Chih-han, "Nu li t'i kao lao tung sheng ch'an lü" (Struggle to raise the rate of labor productivity), *Chi hua yü t'ung chi* (Plans and statistics), 7 (Apr. 23, 1959), 18.

22. Some of the ad hoc measures adopted by the regime to stem the flow of rural-to-urban migration from 1952 through 1957 are described in the following: "Notice of Central-South Military Administrative Committee on Prevention of Flow of Rural Labor Power to Cities," *Ch'ang-chiang jih pao* (Yangtze daily), Oct. 21, 1952, in SCMP, No. 444, pp. 30–31; "We Should Dissuade Peasants from Blindly Moving Towards Cities, Declares Social Affairs Department, Ministry of Interior," *Jen min jih pao* (People's daily) [hereafter JMJP], Nov. 26, 1952, in SCMP, No. 468, pp. 11–12; "Government Administration Council Directive on Dissuasion of Peasants from Blind Influx into Cities," NCNA, Apr. 17, 1953, in SCMP, No. 554, pp. 24–25; "Central People's Government Ministry of Interior and Ministry of Labor Issue Joint Directive Concerning Continued Implementation of Directive Advising Against Blind Influx of Peasants into Cities" (dated Mar. 12, 1954), JMJP, Mar. 15, 1954, in SCMP, No. 774, pp. 8–9; "Mobilize the Nonproductive Population in Cities to Return to Rural Areas for Production," KMJP, Dec. 29, 1955, in SCMP, No. 1203, pp. 8–9; "Nonproductive Populations in Cities Too Large and Growing Too Fast," NCNA, July 25, 1957, in SCMP, No. 1582, pp. 1–2; "The State Council's Provisional Regulations Governing Recruitment of Temporary Workers in Rural Areas by Various Units," and Ma Wen-jui, "Explanations of State Council's Provisional Regulations Governing Recruitment of Temporary Workers in Rural Areas by Various Units," NCNA, Dec. 13, 1957, in SCMP, No. 1699, pp. 22–26.

23. "Labor Reserve Universally Built up by Agricultural Cooperatives in Shansi"; Wang Po, "Important Reform for Labor System," and "Labor Contract System Pushed in Chungking," in JMJP, June 7, 1958, in SCMP, No. 1795, pp. 25–29.

24. Li Yüeh, "T'an t'an ho t'ung kung chih tu ti chi ko wen t'i" (Let's talk about several problems in the contract labor system), *Chi hua yü t'ung chi,* 9 (June 23, 1959), 20.

25. JMJP, Dec. 28, 1965. The contract system as it was used during the Cultural Revolution is described in "Sources of Labor Discontent in China: The Worker-Peasant System," *Current Scene,* VI: 5 (Mar. 15, 1968), 1–28, and in Colina MacDougall, "Second-Class Workers," *Far Eastern Economic Review,* LX: 19 (May 9, 1968), 306–8.

26. Wang Kuang-wei 1957, pp. 11–12, and Sung P'ing 1957.

27. Yü Sheng-fang, "Cheng ch'üeh chang wo hsin chien ho k'uo chien ch'eng shih jen k'ou ti fa chan" (Correctly regulate the population development of newly built or expanding cities), *Chien she yüeh k'an* (Construction monthly), 11 (Nov. 3, 1957), 29–30.

28. Liao Lu-yen, "Participate in the Large-Scale Development of Agriculture by the Whole Party and the Whole People," *Hung ch'i* (Red flag), 17 (Sept. 1, 1960), in *Selections from China Mainland Magazines* [hereafter SCMM], No. 228, p. 1.

29. Ma Yin-ch'u, the prestigious president of Peking University, who was not a party member, in one controversial article did refer to the political repercussions that could follow excessive rural (not urban) population growth. Ma Yin-ch'u, "A New Theory of Population," in CB, No. 469, p. 8. Although Ma stated the idea, there is no reason to think that he originated it.

30. The SPC estimate of eight million rural-to-urban migrants during the years 1953–57 would mean an average of 1.6 million per year (Wang Kuang-wei 1957). It was assumed that at least half of this number were of working age.

31. Workers and employees comprise the largest statistical employment aggregate in Communist China. They work in nonagricultural branches of the economy (with the exception of state farms and forestry). About 83 per cent were urban in 1957, according to Hsü Min, "K'ao lu sheng huo wen t'i yao yu ch'üan chü" (Consider the problem of livelihood in terms of the whole), *Kung jen jih pao* (Daily worker) [hereafter KJJP], Dec. 20, 1957, p. 3.

32. Some aspects of this subject are treated in more detail in John S. Aird, "Population Growth and Distribution in Mainland China," in U.S. Congress, Joint Economic Committee, *An Economic Profile of Mainland China* (Washington, D.C.: U.S. Government Printing Office, 1967), II, 383–91.

33. Data Section, "1949–1956 nien wo kuo jen k'ou t'ung chi tzu liao" (Statistical data on China's population, 1949–1956), TCKT, 11 (June 14, 1957), 24.

34. "New Progress Reported in China's Cadre Work: Number of Transferred Cadres Reaches 1,300,000," NCNA, Feb. 23, 1958, in SCMP, No. 1724, pp. 5–6.

35. "Tang ch'ien nung ts'un hsing shih ta hao" (Present rural conditions greatly improved), *Kung tso t'ung hsün* (Work bulletin), 16 (Apr. 19, 1961), 24. This periodical was irregularly published by the People's Liberation Army, General Political Department, and was restricted to circulation among various grades of officers depending on the security classification of a given issue.

36. Vasil Magdeski, dispatch in *Vjesnik* (The herald, Zagreb), May 26,

1962, in "The Chinese Puzzle," *East Europe*, II: 10 (Oct. 1962), 25, and Vasil Magdeski, "Great Migration from Chinese Cities," *Politika* (Belgrade), July 25, 1962.

37. "Press Communique of the Third Session of the Second National People's Congress of China," NCNA, Apr. 16, 1962, in CB, No. 681, p. 2.

38. Strong 1964.

39. "A Million Educated Young People from Cities Work in China's Countryside," NCNA, Sept. 25, 1965, in SCMP, No. 3548, p. 24.

40. Feng Chi-hsi, "The Growth of the National Economy as Viewed from the State Budget," TCKT, 12 (June 29, 1957), in ECMM, No. 96, p. 30.

41. SSB, *Wei ta ti shih nien—Chung-hua jen min kung ho kuo ching chi ho wen hua chien she ch'eng chiu ti t'ung chi* (The great ten years—statistics on economic and cultural achievements in the People's Republic of China) (Peking: Jen min ch'u pan she, 1959), p. 178.

42. Workers and peasants are said to have made up 80 per cent of the total population of Mainland China, in Chang Chien, "Why the Door of Institutes of Higher Education Must Be Open to Workers and Peasants," *Chung-kuo ch'ing nien* (China youth), 9 (May 1, 1958), in ECMM, No. 133, p. 10. The proportion was probably somewhat higher in rural areas and lower in urban areas.

43. In 1955, assuming an average of four persons per urban household, there were 21 million urban households. The number of peasant households in 1955 was computed as 119 million from data in SSB 1959, pp. 29–30. It was assumed that the number of households in rural areas totaled about 130 million.

44. During the years 1953–56 scholarships totaling 605 million yüan were made available, according to Data Section, "Kuan yü chih kung sheng huo kai shan ch'ing k'uang ti t'ung chi tzu liao" (Statistical data relating to the rising standards of living of workers and employees), TCKT, 14 (July 29, 1957), 13.

45. Chang Chien, "Wo kuo ti kao teng chiao yü shih yüeh pan yüeh hao le" (Higher education in our country is getting better all the time), *Jen min chiao yü* (People's education), 10 (Oct. 9, 1957a), 6.

46. In 1961, there were 819,000 students in higher education, according to Chou P'ei-yuan, "Higher Education in China," *China Reconstructs*, 2 (Feb. 1963), 9. For the number enrolled in 1955, see Table 2, p. 200.

47. "Thirteen Years of Education in New China," NCNA, Sept. 24, 1962, in SCMP, No. 2828, p. 13.

48. These aims are given in *First Five-Year Plan for Development of the National Economy of the People's Republic of China in 1953–1957* (Peking: Foreign Languages Press, 1956), p. 176.

49. National Economic Commission, Cultural Affairs, Education, and Public Health Bureau, "Kuan yü ti i tz'u ch'üan kuo wen chiao wei sheng chi hua tso t'an hui so yen chiu ti chi ko wen t'i" (Several problems studied by the first all-China cultural affairs, education, and public health symposium), CHCC, 3 (Mar. 9, 1958), 30.

50. At the end of the plan period, education planning was described by two Chinese Communist critics as "full of defects and without accomplishments." Ko Chü-po and Liu Ts'un, "Kuan yü wo kuo chung hsiao hsüeh

chiao yü shih yeh fa chan chi hua wen t'i" (Planning problems in the development of middle- and primary-school educational undertakings in our country), CHCC, 10 (Oct. 9, 1957), 20.

51. Huang Chih-yin, "Ti shih ssu chiang: wen chiao wei sheng shih yeh chi hua piao ko" (Lecture 14: cultural affairs, education, and public health planning forms), CHCC, 2 (Feb. 9, 1958), 39–40.

52. Abolition of the Ministry of Higher Education was announced in "NPC Closing Session on February 11," NCNA, Feb. 11, 1958, in SCMP, No. 1713, p. 1. A statement on abandonment of central control over higher and specialized secondary education is given in "Ministry of Education and Business Establishments of the Central Government Place a Number of Institutions of Higher Education and Secondary Vocational Schools under the Administration of a Lower Level," NCNA, Aug. 16, 1958, in SCMP, No. 1841, pp. 11–13.

53. The Ministry of Higher Education would hardly have been reestablished, as it was in 1964, if a decision had not been reached to return a sizeable number of higher educational institutions to central administrative control. For the reappointment of a minister of higher education, see "Chairman Liu Shao-ch'i Appoints Four Government Ministers," NCNA, July 22, 1964, in SCMP, No. 3266, p. 1.

54. The figures on which these percentages are based are given in Emerson, "Employment in Mainland China, Problems and Prospects," in *An Economic Profile of Mainland China*, II, 424–25.

55. Quotas were set by planners to provide enough graduating students to meet estimated future needs for personnel with specific kinds of specialized training. For the use of entrance examinations, see National Economic Commission, Cultural Affairs, Education, and Public Health Bureau 1958.

56. In 1949, 41 per cent of higher educational institutions, 54 per cent of technical middle schools, 56 per cent of general middle schools, and 10 per cent of primary schools were privately run, accounting for 27 per cent, 39 per cent, 39 per cent, and 11 per cent of student enrollments, respectively, according to Data Section, "Chi nien lai wo kuo chiao yü shih yeh ti fa chan kai k'uang" (Development of education in our country in the last few years), TCKT, 20 (Oct. 29, 1956), 6.

57. Tseng Chao-lun, "Improvements in Higher Education During the Past Three Years," *Jen min chiao yü*, 1 (Jan. 5, 1953), in CB, No. 238, p. 2.

58. For the Soviet system, see Nicholas DeWitt, *Education and Professional Employment in the U.S.S.R.* (Washington, D.C.: U.S. Government Printing Office, 1961), pp. 225–26 and 657–77.

59. "Kao teng chiao yü pu i chiu wu ssu nien ti kung tso tsung chieh ho i chiu wu wu nien ti kung tso yao tien (che yao)" (A summary of Ministry of Higher Education work in 1954 and important points in work in 1955 [excerpts]), *Jen min shou ts'e* (People's handbook) [hereafter JMST] (1956), p. 557.

60. Chang Chien, "360,000 College Graduates in Eight Years," *People's China*, 16 (Aug. 16, 1957b), 25. See also Data Section, "Hsin Chung-kuo chiao yü shih yeh ti fa chan kai k'uang" (Developments in the educational program of new China), TCKT, 22 (Nov. 29, 1957), 30.

61. Dewitt 1961, p. 659.

62. Huang Tsu-yu, "Kuan yü chung teng chuan yeh kan pu ti p'ei yang ho fen p'ei wen t'i" (Problems in the training and allocation of specialized secondary-level cadres), CHCC, 4 (Apr. 9, 1957), 19.

63. Joint speech by Fang Chih-wu, Kuang Sheng, and Shih Lei-ping at the Third Session of the Anhwei Committee of the First Chinese People's Political Consultative Conference, *An-hui jih pao* (Anhwei daily), May 3, 1957.

64. For enrollments in higher educational institutions, see Table 2, p. 200; for those in specialized secondary schools, see Emerson 1967, p. 424.

65. The plan targets of 434,000 students enrolled in higher educational institutions and 671,800 in specialized secondary schools in 1957 are given in *Chung-hua jen min kung ho kuo fa chan kuo min ching chi ti ti i ko wu nien chi hua, 1953–1957* (First Five-Year Plan for the development of the national economy of the People's Republic of China in 1953–1957) (Peking: Jen min ch'u pan she, 1955) [hereafter FFYP], pp. 120 and 123 respectively.

66. Chang Chien 1957b, pp. 18–19.

67. Data Section, "Chi nien lai wo kuo chiao yü shih yeh ti fa chan kai k'uang (Development of education in our country in the last few years), TCKT, 20 (Oct. 29, 1956), 6.

68. Chou En-lai, "Report on the Second Five-Year Plan" (dated Sept. 16, 1956), NCNA, Sept. 20, 1956, in CB, No. 413 (Oct. 5, 1956), p. 26.

69. Data given in SSB 1959, p. 170.

70. FFYP, pp. 136–37.

71. National Economic Commission, Cultural Affairs, Education, and Public Health Planning Bureau, Education Planning Office, "Kuan yü k'ou ch'u hsüeh sheng liu tung shu wen t'i ti shuo ming" (Explanation of problems related to making deductions for changes in the numbers of students), CHCC, 12 (Dec. 23, 1956), 19.

72. A ratio of four senior middle-school students to one college student was considered adequate to produce a desirable number of applicants for admission to higher educational institutions among senior-middle-school graduates, according to Ko Chü-po and Liu Ts'un 1957, p. 22, but this ratio did not reach two to one until the school year 1955–56.

73. Yang Hsiu-feng, "Higher Education in China," NCNA, June 20, 1956, in CB, No. 400, p. 21.

74. Enrollments in higher educational institutions totaled 441,000 students in the school year of 1957–58 (Emerson 1967, p. 424), of whom 72,000 graduated (Table 4), leaving 369,000. The difference between this figure and the reported enrollment of 660,000 in the school year of 1958–59, 291,000, does not include dropouts. The dropout rate was probably at least 5 per cent, which would have meant that there were more than 300,000 new entrants.

75. Senior-middle-school graduates averaged 92,500 per year during the years 1953–56, according to Chang Chien 1957b, p. 18, and probably did not number more than 150,000 by 1958.

76. Higher education enrollment in 1962 was five times the pre-Liberation peak, according to "Thirteen Years of Education in New China," NCNA, Sept. 24, 1962, in SCMP, No. 2828, p. 13. The pre-Liberation peak of 155,000 students (Emerson 1967, p. 424) would have meant 775,000 students in 1962.

77. "In 1962 the total enrollment in universities and colleges is expected to reach approximately 850,000 . . ." from "Proposals on the Second Five-Year Plan for Development of the National Economy," NCNA, Sept. 28, 1956, in CB, No. 413, p. 44.

78. The burden of teacher training on the educational system was much heavier in Communist China than it was in the Soviet Union at comparable periods of development, according to Chang Chien, "Wei p'ei yang i chih hung ta ti hung hsiu chuan shen ti k'o hsüeh chi shu tui wu erh nu li" (Strive to train a mighty army of "red and expert" scientists and technologists), CHCC, 5 (May 9, 1958), 5–6.

79. A total of 271,000 is given in Chang Chien 1957a, p. 6.

80. Even by the end of 1956, little had been done to take dropout rates into account in educational planning, as is evident from National Economic Commission, Cultural Affairs, Educational, and Public Health Planning Bureau, Educational Planning Office 1958, pp. 19–20.

81. Numbers of graduates of higher educational institutions by field of study for the Second Five-Year Plan period (1958–62) were derived by first subtracting data for 1949–57, reported in SSB 1959, p. 172, from figures for 1949–63, given in "College Graduates in Post-Liberation China Top Million Mark," NCNA, Aug. 14, 1963, in SCMP, No. 3042, p. 15, to obtain data for 1958–63, and by next subtracting from the latter data 1963 figures, reported in "200,000 Graduates from Institutes of Higher Learning Throughout the Country in 1963 Are To Take Up Posts of Reconstruction of the Motherland," NCNA, Aug. 11, 1963, in SCMP, No. 3040, p. 7.

82. Specialty group (*grupovaya spetsial'nost'*) is a Soviet term used to designate the first level of aggregation of academic specialties above the individual specialty. In 1959 there were 22 specialty groups covering 346 specialties in higher education. For this, see DeWitt 1961, p. 226.

83. FFYP, pp. 23–24.

84. Only a small proportion of the 25,100 students shown under the subheading of building construction and city planning would have been in city planning.

85. The 13 departments included nuclear physics and engineering, technical physics, applied geophysics, chemical physics, radio electronics, radio and radiative chemistry, thermodynamics, high polymer chemistry and physics, applied mathematics and computer technology, dynamics, biophysics, automation, and geochemistry and rare metals, according to "Chung-kuo k'o hsüeh chi shu ta hsüeh k'ai hsüeh" (The China Science and Technology University opens), *Chin jih hsin wen* (Today's news), Sept. 21, 1958, reprinted in *Hsin Hua pan yüeh k'an* (New China semimonthly) [hereafter HHPYK], 19 (Oct. 10, 1958), 137.

86. These numbers were unusually small because of the lengthening of courses from four to five years in some universities and colleges in 1955. See Yeh Feng, "Wei ming nien kung yeh ti ta yüeh chin chi chi chun pei chi shu li liang" (Actively prepare a technical force for next year's Great Leap Forward in industry), CHCC, 12 (Dec. 9, 1958), 35–36.

87. SPC, National Economic Summary Planning Bureau, Methods Office, "Kuan yü i chiu wu liu nien tu kuo min ching chi chi hua piao ko pien tung ch'ing k'uang ti shuo ming" (Explanations of changes in 1956 national economic plan forms), CHCC, 9 (Sept. 27, 1955), 13.

88. Cheng K'ang-ning, "Tsung chieh 1956 nien ti ching yen kao chin lao tung kung tzu chi hua kung tso" (Summarize 1956 experience and improve labor and wage-planning work), CHCC, 8 (Aug. 9, 1957), 9.

89. A year-end 1956 total of 24.23 million workers and employees is reported in SSB 1959, p. 159.

90. Sung P'ing, "Lao tung kung tzu chi hua shih kuo min ching chi chi hua ti i ko chung yao tsu ch'eng pu fen" (The labor and wage plan is an important constituent part of the national economic plan), CHCC, 1 (Jan. 27, 1955), 8.

91. SPC, National Economic Summary Planning Bureau, Methods Office 1955. The categories were wage workers directly concerned with production, apprentices, engineers and technicians, salaried managerial and administrative personnel, minor service personnel, and guards and firemen.

92. Sung P'ing 1955.

93. SPC, National Economic Summary Planning Bureau, Methods Office 1955.

94. Ch'en Chi-ch'en and Ch'en Chih-chang, "Ti shih i chiang: kan pu chi hua piao ko" (Lecture 11: cadre planning forms), CHCC, 11 (Nov. 9, 1957), 35–37.

95. SPC, National Economic Summary Planning Bureau, Methods Office 1955.

96. CHCC Editorial Board, Data Unit, "1956 nien lao tung kung tzu ti ch'ing k'uang" (1956 labor and wage conditions), CHCC, 3 (Mar. 9, 1957), 13–14.

97. For example, the inadequacy for planning purposes of data on engineers and technicians available in 1955 was said to have been one of the chief reasons for taking a census of state-sector workers and employees in the latter part of the year. See "Chia ch'iang tsu chih ling tao, k'o fu k'un nan, an shih wan ch'eng ch'üan kuo chih kung tiao ch'a kung tso" (Strengthen organization and leadership, overcome difficulties, and complete on schedule the nationwide census of workers and employees), edit., TCKT, 9 (Sept. 17, 1955), 2.

98. This point was recognized by Chinese Communist planners at least as early as the end of 1955. See Li Yü-hang, "Ti shih chiang: lao tung chi hua" (Lecture 10: the labor plan), CHCC, 11 (Nov. 27, 1955), 31.

99. Wang Kuang-wei, "Kuo min chi hua wei yüan hui ti kung tso jen wu" (Work tasks of the State Planning Commission), CHCC, 2 (Feb. 23, 1956), 13.

100. Wang Ssu-hua, "Fully Bring Out the Role of Statistical Work in Socialist Construction," *Hung ch'i*, 18 (Sept. 16, 1962), in SCMM, No. 335, pp. 14–20.

101. Emerson 1967, p. 455.

102. The 1957 total of 175,000 industrial engineers and technicians is reported in Chou En-lai, "Report on Government Work," NCNA, Apr. 18, 1959, in CB, No. 559, p. 2, and the 1958 total in SSB 1959, p. 75.

103. Ratios of building and installation engineers and technicians to workers are given in Data Section, "Ssu nien lai wo kuo chien chu ch'i yeh sheng ch'an huo tung ti chi pen ch'ing k'uang" (Basic conditions of production activities in the building enterprises of our country in the last four years), TCKT, 18 (Sept. 29, 1957), 32.

104. That these were standard practices is clear from Hsü Heng-mao and Sung Yung, "Wei shen ma yao an kung tso kang wei lai t'ung chi kung ch'eng chi shu jen yüan" (Why engineering and technical personnel must be classified statistically according to positions held), TCKT, 18 (Sept. 29, 1956), 22; and Statistical Work Handbook Editorial Committee, *Lao tung t'ung chi kung tso shou ts'e* (Labor statistical work handbook) (Peking: T'ung chi ch'u pan she, 1958), pp. 17, 100.

105. For a discussion of practicals in the Soviet Union, see DeWitt 1961, pp. 437, 482, 488, 501, and 502.

106. Data Section, "China's Workers in 1955: Their Number, Composition, and Distribution," TCKT, 23 (Dec. 14, 1956), in ECMM, No. 68, p. 30.

107. There were to be 802,000 persons in engineering and technical positions at the end of 1957, according to Chang Hsing-fu, "Wo kuo kung yeh hua ti tao lu ho fang fa" (The road and methods of the industrialization of our country), KJJP, May 23, 1957, reprinted in JMST, 1958, p. 447. Of these, 370,000 were to be graduates of higher educational institutions or specialized secondary schools, according to Yang Ying-chieh, "Pao wei chi hua chih tu, t'i kao chi hua kung tso shui p'ing" (Protect the system of planned economy, raise the level of planning work), CHCC, 1 (Jan. 9, 1958), 5.

108. Emerson 1967, p. 454.

109. Chao I-wen, *Hsin Chung-kuo ti kung yeh* (The industry of new China) (Peking: T'ung chi ch'u pan she, 1956), p. 30.

110. For 1950, 41,000, and for 1955, 70,000 doctors of Western medicine are reported in SSB, "Kuo min ching chi t'ung chi t'i yao" (Statistical abstract of the national economy), HHPYK, 17 (Sept. 6, 1956), 50.

111. Data Section, "China's Workers in 1955," pp. 30–31.

112. Data Section, "Chi nien lai wo kuo chiao yü," p. 6.

113. Ko Chu-po and Liu Ts'un 1957, p. 21.

114. Data given in Emerson 1967, p. 451.

115. A detailed statement on this question is given in Chou En-lai, "On the Question of the Intellectuals" (Jan. 29, 1956), in CB, No. 376, pp. 3–23.

116. This division of authority is outlined in "Some Fundamental Provisions Governing Distribution of Work to Graduates from Institutions of Higher Education This Summer," NCNA, July 19, 1957, in SCMP, No. 1580, pp. 4–6; Wang Po-kung, "Study Urged in Assignment of Graduates," NCNA, June 1, 1957, in SCMP, No. 1555, p. 15; and T'ao Kung-chih, "We Cannot Distribute and Use College Graduates Like That," JMJP, Mar. 18, 1955, in SCMP, No. 1015, pp. 11–13.

117. T'ao Kung-chih 1955, pp. 11–12.

118. Between 1953 and 1956 only one-tenth of the graduates in mining engineering of the Peking Mining College were assigned to mining engineering jobs, according to "Students Discuss Future Assignments," NCNA, May 19, 1957, in SCMP, No. 1546, p. 10.

119. Wang Po-kung 1957, p. 13.

120. Ma Wen-jui, "Kuan yü lao tung kung tzu kung tso" (On labor and wage work), NCNA, June 29, 1956, in HHPYK, 15 (Aug. 6, 1956), 116–17.

121. Li Mu-chieh and Kuo Hui, "Chih wu kung tzu chih" (The professional duties salary system), *Chung-kuo ch'ing kung yeh* (Chinese light industry), 17 (Sept. 13, 1957), 18.

122. Chou En-lai 1956, p. 7.
123. The number of technicians was derived from Data Section, "China's Workers in 1955," pp. 30–31.
124. Yang Ying-chieh, *Kuo min ching chi chi hua chung ti pi li kuan hsi wen t'i* (Problems related to ratios in national economic planning) (Peking: Jen min ch'u pan she, 1957), p. 53.
125. Data Section, "China's Workers in 1955," p. 32.

## The Level and Structure of Employment and the Sources of Labor Supply in Shanghai, 1949–57

1. In this paper we are primarily concerned with Emerson's estimates of the utilization of the nonagricultural labor force. See John Philip Emerson, *Nonagricultural Employment in Mainland China 1949–1958* (Washington, D.C.: U.S. Government Printing Office, 1965). Further analysis of this material by Emerson appears in U.S. Congress, Joint Economic Committee, *An Economic Profile of Mainland China* (Washington, D.C.: U.S. Government Printing Office, 1967), II, pt. 3.
2. Liu and Yeh estimate that the rural component of the nonagricultural labor force was 67%. See Ta-chung Liu and Kung-chia Yeh, *The Economy of the Chinese Mainland: National Income and Economic Development, 1933–1959* (Princeton: Princeton University Press, 1965), pp. 102–3.
3. See particularly the discussion in Emerson 1967.
4. The best general account of this is Choh-ming Li, *The Statistical System of Communist China* (Berkeley and Los Angeles: University of California Press, 1962), pt. 1. See also Emerson 1967, p. 419. Although comprehensive statistics are poor throughout the period, from 1953 onward a number of important specific surveys were undertaken. Those on private industry (1954), handicrafts (1954), and private trade (1955) contained information about employment in these sectors. In 1955 there was also a major survey of employment of workers and staff in the public sector.
5. The category of "workers and staff" (*chih kung*) includes all persons who are basically wage earners. Such persons may work in the public or private sectors, in industry, trade, or administration. It excludes persons whose income is variable, such as capitalists, persons engaged in small-scale production, in trade or transport (whether private or cooperative), temporary construction workers, etc. A succinct account of this classification may be found in "Problems in defining the scope of the numbers of our workers and staff at the present time," *T'ung chi kung tso* (Statistical work) [hereafter TCKT], 1 (Jan. 14, 1957), 19–20. In Shanghai in 1956, approximately 70% of those in employment were workers and staff. Data on total employment are found in Table 1. The number of total workers and staff is reported in Wang Ko, "The livelihood of the city's workers and staff has markedly improved," *Hsin wen pao* (Daily news) [hereafter HWP], Sept. 2, 1957. (Wang Ko was the chief of the Shanghai Labor Bureau at the time.)
6. Liu and Yeh 1965, pp. 102–3.
7. Sung P'ing, "Let us discuss problems of labor and employment," *Hsüeh hsi* (Study), 12 (June 18, 1957), 25–28.
8. *Labour Insurance Regulations of the People's Republic of China* (Pe-

king: Foreign Languages Press, 1961). The 1955 regulations for employees
in the public sector are in *Chung-hua jen min kung ho kuo fa kuei hui pien*
(Collection of laws and regulations of the People's Republic of China) (Peking: Fa lü ch'u pan she, 1956), II.

9. P'an Hsüeh-min, "The Development of Shanghai Industry," *Ti li chih
shih* (Geographical knowledge), 7 (July 6, 1959), 302–5.

10. *New China News Agency* [hereafter NCNA], Aug. 17, 1957.

11. See Chang Jui, "Some views on Shanghai's population and area," *Wen
hui pao* (Cultural exchange news) [hereafter WHP], Feb. 11, 1957.

12. Data in "Total output doubled in five years," HWP, Dec. 28, 1957;
"The ranks of the Shanghai workers and intellectuals grow strong," WHP,
Jan. 10, 1958; *1954 ch'üan kuo ko t'i shou kung yeh tiao ch'a tzu liao* (Ma-
terials from the 1954 national survey of the individual handicraft industry)
(Peking: Hsin Hua shu tien, 1957), pp. 11–22.

13. *Ibid.*, pp. 11–23.

14. Data in "Shanghai thoroughly cleans up and reorganizes autonomous
enterprises," *Ta kung pao* (Impartial) [hereafter TKP], Aug. 19, 1957;
"Shanghai eliminates the phenomenon of unemployment," *Jen min jih pao*
(People's daily) [hereafter JMJP], July 16, 1958; "The Labor Bureau reforms its work," HWP, Aug. 3, 1957.

15. Data in "Summary report concerning the problems of unemployment
relief and production," TKP (Hong Kong), May 4, 1950. The figure in this
article is almost exactly confirmed in *Shang-hai chieh fang i nien* (A year of
Shanghai's liberation) (Shanghai: Shang-hai chieh fang jih pao she, 1950),
p. 80; "Shanghai industry helps national construction," WHP, Aug. 27, 1954;
"700 construction sites busy," HWP, Sept. 28, 1957.

16. Data in "National [survey] of the numbers, structure, and distribution
of workers and staff in 1955," TCKT, 23 (Dec. 14, 1956), 28–30; "40,000
pedicab men participate in rectification," *Chieh fang jih pao* (Liberation
daily) [hereafter CFJP], Apr. 8, 1958; "How should we view the difference
in living standards between workers and peasants?" WHP, Oct. 29, 1957;
"Thank you comrade," *Kung jen jih pao* (Daily worker) [hereafter KJJP],
Aug. 6, 1957; Fang Fu An, "Rickshaws in China," *The Chinese Economic
Journal*, July 1930, pp. 796–808.

17. See *A Year of Shanghai's Liberation*, p. 80; Sun Ching-chih and others,
*Hua tung ch'ü ching chi ti li* (An economic geography of east China) (Peking: K'o hsüeh ch'u pan she, 1959), chap. 5; "Fully use [Shanghai's] existing
dock facilities," CFJP, Aug. 11, 1956.

18. Data in "National [survey] of the numbers, structure, and distribution
of workers and staff in 1955," TCKT, 23 (Dec. 14, 1956), 28–30; "Concerning the reform of private commerce and supply work," CFJP, Aug. 17, 1956,
and HWP, Jan. 18, 1957.

19. "500,000 Shanghai women participate in construction," WHP, Mar. 8,
1957. A 1955 survey reported 42,000 in the public sector of education (of
these 10,000 were in higher education). Since a source for 1950 reports that
30,000 were employed in private-sector education in that year, it seems that
employment in this sector remained constant until the socialization of 1956.
See *A Year of Shanghai's Liberation*, p. 80; "National [survey] of the num-

bers, structure, and distribution of workers and staff in 1955," TCKT, 23 (Dec. 14, 1956), 28–30.

20. See *A Year of Shanghai's Liberation*, p. 80, and Emerson 1965, Table 1.

21. Population data from Rhoads Murphey, *Shanghai: Key to Modern China* (Cambridge, Mass.: Harvard University Press, 1953), p. 22, and WHP, June 6, 1958.

22. The estimate for 1930 is based on detailed age-structure data for Greater Shanghai in 1930. The 1949 estimate is based on the same data adjusted slightly in the light of an important fragment of information on the age structure of the Shanghai population in 1947. See *Statistics of Shanghai* (Shanghai: The Shanghai Civic Association, 1933), Table 4, p. 3. Wang Shan-pao, "Research into Shanghai city's grain consumption," *She hui yüeh k'an* (The monthly journal of the Bureau of Social Affairs), Series 3, 5 (May 5, 1948), 36. Data for 1957 are based on population and migration data presented in this paper and data on the components of the natural increase of population in "Reduce Shanghai's natural population growth rate to 2 per cent," WHP, Jan. 23, 1958; examples of age-structure data for the suburbs are in *Chien chu hsüeh pao* (Journal of architecture), 10 (Oct. 30, 1958), 7, 19.

23. For details of the sex and age structure we have preferred the 1931 survey of the labor force in Chinese-owned factories to any other. D. K. Lieu, *The Growth and Industrialization of Shanghai* (Shanghai: China Institute of Pacific Relations, 1936), pp. 224, 228. For more detailed information on the structure of the textile labor force see H. D. Fong, *Cotton Industry and Trade in China* (Tientsin: Chihli Press, Inc., 1932), p. 116.

24. See Li Li-san's speech on the establishment of the Labor Ministry and its subsidiary bureaus in *Hua tung ch'ü ts'ai cheng ching chi fa ling hui pien* (Compendium of financial and economic regulations and laws for the east China [military] region) (Shanghai: Hua tung jen min ch'u pan she, 1951), pp. 1678–89.

25. "National [survey] of the numbers, structure, and distribution of workers and staff in 1955," TCKT, 23 (Dec. 14, 1956), 28–30.

26. Lieu 1936, p. 228; and "Childbirth must be planned," HWP, Jan. 1, 1957.

27. The relevant sections of the educational system are strictly only the upper-middle schools, universities, and other institutions of higher learning. However, some allowance has to be made for over-age children in junior-middle schools. See data in *Ten Great Years* (Peking: Foreign Languages Press, 1960), p. 192; "Problems of the development plan for our country's junior and middle schools," *Chi hua ching chi* (Planned economy), 10 (Oct. 9, 1957), 20–27, and "The development of our country's educational activity in recent years," TCKT, 20 (Oct. 29, 1956), 5–6.

28. WHP, June 6, 1958.

29. Total population minus temporary and illicit residents (800,000) and agricultural population (400,000), HWP, Nov. 17, 1957.

30. Derived from data cited in note 22.

31. We have assumed that 55 per cent of the resident population over 16 was male. This is probably conservative in view of our knowledge of the sex

structure of China's urban population before 1949. See, for example, Yang Hsi-meng, *Shang-hai kung jen sheng huo ch'eng tu ti i ko yen chiu* (Research into the standard of living of workers in Shanghai) (Peking: She hui tiao ch'a so, 1930).

32. "500,000 Shanghai women participate in construction," WHP, Mar. 8, 1957.

33. The middle-school figure of 72,000 for those retained in the system has been estimated from data in WHP, Apr. 4, 13, and 16, 1957; and HWP, Aug. 9, 1956. Figures for those retained at university level are taken from data in Chu-yuan Cheng, *Scientific and Engineering Manpower in Communist China, 1949–1963* (Washington, D.C.: U.S. Government Printing Office, 1965), pp. 74, 85.

34. Evidence for this is the very rapid increase in female employment in urban areas during the Great Leap Forward of 1958.

35. National data quoted in Emerson 1967, pp. 418, 427.

36. 1929 data as Table 7. 1949 data estimated from "The development of Shanghai's textile industry," *Ching chi chou pao* (The economic weekly), Series 10, 23 (June 8, 1950), 5. 1957 as Table 1. The prewar data are often extremely difficult to handle as they rarely define "factory" consistently or include both Chinese- and foreign-owned establishments. The 1929 survey covers both types of establishment and excluded workshops. The figures from this survey are probably fairly comparable to the 1957 figures.

37. 1931 data from Lieu 1936, p. 296; 1957 data estimated from CFJP, Aug. 13, 1956, and WHP, Mar. 8, 1957.

38. Data for 1950 are in *A Year of Shanghai's Liberation*, p. 80.

39. Data on the age structure of the population of Greater Shanghai in *Statistics of Shanghai*, Table 4, p. 3. The age groups in this table do not coincide exactly with our requirements. Thus we have assumed an even distribution of population within each age group, and reconstructed the table to yield the information required. Data for 1947 are in Wang Shan-pao, "Research into Shanghai city's grain consumption," *She hui yüeh k'an*, 1948.

40. This figure is suggested by data in Chang Ching-wen, "Why the urban population must be reduced," KJJP, Jan. 4, 1958. "We must persuade peasants who have infiltrated into the city to return voluntarily to the countryside," CFJP, July 31, 1955. See the article by Hsü Chien-kuo, WHP, Jan. 7, 1958.

41. See Hsü Chien-kuo 1958.

42. See "The number in employment rises by 630,000," CFJP, Aug. 16, 1957.

## Educated Youth and Urban-Rural Inequalities, 1958–66

1. For an analysis of the trade unions' role as an "interest group" see Paul Harper, "The Party and the Unions in Communist China," *China Quarterly*, 37 (Jan.–Mar. 1969), 84–119; for an analysis of the privileges available, see Joyce K. Kallgren, "Social Welfare and China's Industrial Workers," in A. Doak Barnett, ed., *Chinese Communist Politics in Action* (Seattle: University of Washington Press, 1969), pp. 540–73.

2. Excerpts of Chou's speech reprinted in *K'o chi chan pao* (Scientific and

technological combat news), June 2, 1967, in *Survey of China Mainland Press* [hereafter SCMP], No. 4011, p. 5.

3. For general overviews of Chinese education since 1949, see Chang-tu Hu, *Chinese Education Under Communism* (New York: Teachers' College, Columbia University, 1962); Fang Chen, "Chung kung ti chiao yü ko ming" (The educational revolution of the Chinese Communists), *Tsu kuo* (China monthly), 45 (Dec. 1967).

4. "Chronology of Seventeen Years of Two-Road Struggle in Education" [hereafter "Chronology"], *Chiao yü ko ming* (Education revolution), 4 (1967), in *Joint Publications Research Service* [hereafter JPRS], No. 43204, p. 176.

5. *Ibid.*, p. 177.

6. *Jen min jih pao* (People's daily) [hereafter JMJP], Sept. 20, 1958.

7. Lu Ting-i, *Education Must Be Combined With Productive Labour* (Peking: Foreign Languages Press, 1958).

8. *Ten Great Years* (Peking: Foreign Languages Press, 1960), p. 192.

9. Yang Hsiu-feng, "Actively Carry Out the Reform of the School System to Bring About Greater, Faster, Better, and More Economical Results in the Development of Education," Apr. 1960, reprinted in Chang-tu Hu 1962, p. 99.

10. Robert D. Barendsen, *Half-Work, Half-Study Schools in Communist China* (Washington, D.C.: Office of Education, 1964), p. 24. This monograph is the most detailed study of half-work half-study schools, as they developed up to 1964.

11. *Ibid.*, pp. 28–29.

12. *Ibid.*, pp. 30–31.

13. *Ibid.*, p. 29.

14. Chengtu Radio, Jan. 13, 1968.

15. *Ibid.*

16. "Down with the Chief Backer of the Revisionist Educational Line," JMJP, July 18, 1967, in *Current Background* [hereafter CB], No. 836, p. 15; Han Suyin, *China in the Year 2001* (London: New Thinkers' Library, 1967), p. 195.

17. "Chronology," p. 181.

18. *Ibid.*, p. 182.

19. "Repudiating the Revisionist Educational Line of China's Khrushchev and Lu Ting-yi," *Peking Review*, 2 (Jan. 12, 1968), 32.

20. "Down with the Chief Backer," p. 17.

21. *Ibid.*

22. "The Wrong Approach to the Full-Day System," *Shan-tung chiao yü* (Shantung education), 2 (1965), in JPRS, No. 30222, p. 49.

23. "Effects of Work-Study Schools on Full-Time Schools," *Shan-tung chiao yü*, 2 (1965), in JPRS, No. 30222, pp. 42–47.

24. "Peasants Consulted in School Operation in Commune," *Nan fang jih pao* (Southern daily), Mar. 27, 1965, in JPRS, No. 30168, p. 57.

25. *Ibid.*, p. 56.

26. "The New Part-Study, Part-Work School System: Some Readers' Views," *Kung jen jih pao* (Daily worker), Apr. 22, 1965, in JPRS, No. 30069, p. 32.

424 Notes to Pages 250–61

27. "Penetrating Expansion of Educational Revolution," *Hei-lung-chiang chiao yü* (Heilungkiang education), 2 (1965), in JPRS, No. 30168, p. 4.

28. "How We Built the Communist Labor College," JMJP, Apr. 17, 1965, in JPRS, No. 29989, pp. 27–39.

29. *Ibid.*, p. 29.

30. *Sing tao jih pao* (Star Island [Singapore] daily, Hong Kong), Nov. 11, 1965.

31. Barendsen 1964, p. 56.

32. Yang Hsiu-feng 1960; Lu Ting-i, "Our School System Must Be Reformed," reprinted in Chang-tu Hu 1962, pp. 130–45.

33. "Demolish the 'Little Pagoda' System of Revisionist Education," JMJP, Dec. 17, 1967, in SCMP, No. 4100.

34. *Ibid.*

35. "Cut Off the Sinister Hand Extended into No. 22 Middle School by the Old Municipal Committee," *Chiao yü feng pao* (Education wind and storm), 1 (1967), in JPRS, No. 42070, pp. 22–23.

36. "Thoroughly Smash the 'Ten Year System Experiment,'" *ibid.*, in JPRS, No. 42070, p. 24.

37. "Liu Shao-ch'i and Experimental Elementary School No. 2," *Chiao yü ko ming*, 5 (1967), in JPRS, No. 42070, pp. 3–6.

38. "Tsai kan pu tzu nü hsüeh hsiao wen t'i shang liang ko ssu ming pu ti tou cheng" (The struggle between the two headquarters over the question of schools for cadres' children), *Pa i feng pao* (Aug. 1 wind and storm, Canton), Jan. 1968, as reprinted in *Sing tao jih pao*, Apr. 5, 1968.

39. *Ibid.*

40. "Demolish the 'Little Pagoda.'"

41. *Ibid.*

42. "Ideological Guidance of Our Graduating Students," *Che-chiang chiao yü* (Chekiang education), 4 (1965), in JPRS, No. 33142, pp. 1–5.

43. "School Work Not Measured by Students Taking Up Higher Studies," *Shan-tung chiao yü*, 2 (1965), in JPRS, No. 30222, p. 54.

44. "Chronology," p. 178.

45. "Liu Shao-ch'i's 'Sixty Points on Higher Education,'" *Ching-kang shan* (Ching-kang mountains), 47 (1967), in JPRS, No. 42887, pp. 19–25.

46. *Ibid.*

47. For an analysis of Liu's views on this, see Stuart R. Schram, "The Party in Chinese Communist Ideology," *China Quarterly*, 38 (Apr.–June 1969), 1–25.

48. Ch'en I, "Tui Pei-ching shih kao teng hsüeh hsiao ying chieh pi yeh ti chiang hua" (Speech to the graduating students of Peking's institutions of higher learning), reprinted in Ting Wang, ed., *Chung kung wen hua ta ko ming tzu liao hui pien* (Compendium of material on China's Cultural Revolution) (Hong Kong: Ming pao, 1967), I, 650–57.

49. *Ibid.*, p. 651.

50. Ch'en I, "Wo ti chien ch'a" (My self-confession) (June 24, 1967), *Hung wei pao* (Red Guard news), Feb. 28, 1967.

51. "Teng Hsiao-p'ing ti shih tsui chuang" (Teng Hsiao-p'ing's ten crimes), *Pa erh wu chan pao* (Aug. 25 battle news), Feb. 24, 1967.

52. "Thoroughly Criticize and Repudiate the Eight-Year Course Promoted

by China's Khrushchev," JMJP, Dec. 17, 1967, in SCMP, No. 4100, pp. 5–8.

53. "China's Khrushchev Resurrects Peking Union Medical College to Advance Revisionist Line in Education," *New China News Agency* [hereafter NCNA], Feb. 29, 1968, in SCMP, No. 4130, pp. 26–28.

54. *Ibid.*

55. *Ibid.*

56. "Thoroughly Criticize."

57. "Down with the Executioners Who Strangled the 1958 Educational Revolution," "The Exposure of the Anti-Party and Anti-Socialist Dark Gang in Wuhan University," "Smash the Counterrevolutionary Attack of the Great Educational Revolution," in *Chiang-han hsüeh pao* (Chiang-han journal), 12 (June 1966), in JPRS, No. 37514, pp. 6–14.

58. *Hsin Pei ta wen hua ko ming chan lan hui* (New Peking University Cultural Revolution exhibit), undated monograph, in JPRS, No. 43416, p. 4.

59. "The Black Program for Fostering Intellectual Aristocrats," *Hsin Hua kung pao* (New South China Engineering College journal), Jan. 13, 1968, in SCMP, No. 4128, pp. 8–12.

60. *Ibid.*

61. *Ibid.*

62. "Let the Storm of Educational Revolution Become More Tempestuous," *Ching-kang shan*, 47 (June 14, 1967), in JPRS, No. 42887, pp. 6–8; "Ask the Worker-Peasant Masses for Advice, Take the Road of Thoroughgoing Revolution," JMJP, Nov. 21, 1967, in CB, No. 846, p. 32.

63. "Reckon with the Crimes of China's Khrushchev of Promoting the Old School System at Tsinghua University," JMJP, Jan. 9, 1968, in SCMP, No. 4109, pp. 11–13.

64. *Ibid.*

65. C. G. H. Oldham, "Science and Education," *Bulletin of the Atomic Scientists*, XXII: 6 (June 1966), 47.

66. *Hsin Pei ta*, pp. 5–6.

67. "Horrible Figures—Towering Crimes of the Liu-Teng Counterrevolutionary Line in Education," *Steel August 1, Combat Flag* and *Educational Reform Bugle Combined Issue* (Peking, early Dec. 1967), in *Union Research Service* [hereafter URS], L: 4 (Jan. 1968), 55–56.

68. "Ts'ung Shang-hai chi chi hsüeh yuan liang t'iao lü hsien ti tou cheng kan li kung k'o ta hsüeh ti chiao yu ko ming" (Look at the educational revolution in engineering and science colleges in the light of the struggle between the two lines in the Shanghai Institute of Mechanical Engineering), *Hung ch'i* (Red flag), 3 (Sept. 10, 1968), 7–13.

69. Han Suyin 1967, p. 183.

70. *Ibid.*

71. "Horrible Figures."

72. *Sing tao jih pao*, Dec. 23, 1965.

73. For the importance of differentials in China, see A. Doak Barnett (with a contribution by Ezra F. Vogel), *Cadres, Bureaucracy, and Political Power in Communist China* (New York: Columbia University Press, 1967), esp. pp. 41–43.

74. Michel Oksenberg, "The Institutionalization of the Chinese Commu-

nist Revolution: the Ladder of Success on the Eve of the Cultural Revolution," *China Quarterly*, 36 (Oct.–Dec. 1966), 69.

75. "Shorten the Period of Schooling and Revolutionize Education," JMJP, Jan. 9, 1968, in SCMP, No. 4109, pp. 6–8.

76. *Ibid.*

77. JMJP, Dec. 12, 1965.

78. "A Letter from Ch'a-ling," *Ko ming ch'ing nien* (Revolutionary youth, Changsha), 2 (Nov. 10, 1967), in URS, XLIX: 20 (Dec. 1967, 271.

79. "Letter to Educated Youth All Over the Country Who Go to Mountain and Rural Areas" (issued on Dec. 22, 1966, by Red Guards in Lü ta [Port Arthur]), in JPRS Special, "Samples of Red Guard Publications" (Aug. 1, 1967), p. 4.

80. "K'an, Liu Shao-ch'i ti ch'ou erh tsui lien" (Look at the evil mask of Liu Shao-ch'i), *Ching-kang shan*, undated, reprinted in Ting Wang 1967, p. 291; "Educated Youths Going to the Countryside Must Integrate Themselves with Workers and Peasants Making Revolution," *Nung ts'un ch'ing nien* (Rural youth), 20 (Oct. 25, 1967), in *Selections From China Mainland Magazines*, No. 612, p. 8.

81. "Three Years of Blood and Tears," *Chih nung hung ch'i* (Aid agriculture red flag), 7 (Jan. 1968), in SCMP, No. 4125, p. 8.

82. *Ibid.*, p. 9.

83. *Ibid.*

84. *Ibid.*, p. 8.

85. "A Letter," p. 272.

86. "Intellectual Youth From Canton Praise Life in Rural Villages," *Yang-ch'eng wan pao* (Canton evening news), Feb. 17, 1965, in JPRS, No. 30039, pp. 6–9.

87. "Comfort Visits Paid to Educated Youths Building a New Countryside," NCNA, Feb. 11, 1964, in SCMP, No. 3170, p. 12.

88. For example, in Nan-kang commune in Ho-p'u hsien, Kwangtung, 95% of the teachers in the half-work half-study schools were "educated youths" in 1965, *Nan fang jih pao*, Mar. 27, 1965.

89. See, for example, "Reply to Readers' Questions on Youths Who Have Returned from Frontier Regions to Shanghai," *Wen hui pao* (Cultural exchange news), Feb. 25, 1968, in SCMP, No. 4146, pp. 15–16; "Go Back to Fight in Sinkiang," *ibid.*, Mar. 2, 1968, in SCMP, No. 4146, pp. 13–14. These articles reveal that as late as March 1968 the leadership was extremely concerned about the "returned youths" who were using every possible means to resist being sent back to the rural areas, including the plaintive cry: "You have no class affection for me if you urge me to return to Sinkiang." Among specific objections raised by these youths was the fear of discrimination and retaliation. Apart from putting various social pressures on them and their parents, it was necessary for the Central Committee to issue a directive stipulating that such youths were "not to be given resident status in cities where they are insistently staying."

90. *Chung-kuo ch'ing nien pao* (China youth daily), Apr. 17, 1962, as quoted in L. F. Goodstadt, "Prospects and Frustrations of Young People," in E. Stuart Kirby, ed., *Youth in China* (Hong Kong: Dragonfly Books, 1965), p. 220.

91. "A Letter," p. 268.

92. "Three Years of Blood," p. 10.
93. *Ibid.*
94. "A Letter," p. 272; "Three Years of Blood," p. 10.
95. "A Letter," p. 269.
96. As quoted in L. F. Goodstadt 1965, p. 220.
97. "Three Years of Blood," p. 12.
98. "A Letter," pp. 275–76.
99. "Three Years of Blood," p. 13.
100. NCNA, May 27, 1957.
101. "Three Years of Blood," p. 12.
102. Until 1957 the youth organization was known as the New Democratic Youth League," but its functions were the same.
103. James R. Townsend, "Revolutionizing Chinese Youth: A Study of *Chung-kuo Ch'ing-nien*," in Barnett 1969, p. 463.
104. *Ibid.*, p. 475.
105. *Chieh fang jih pao* (Liberation daily), Jan. 8, 1952.
106. JMJP, May 3, 1959. Since that date no total figure has been published, but in view of the massive influx of 8,500,000 new members in 1965, league membership probably totaled about 35,000,000 on the eve of the Cultural Revolution, making it a far less "exclusive" organization than the CCP itself.
107. *Chung-kuo ch'ing nien pao*, Apr. 2, 1964, as quoted in A. S. Chang and Wen Shih, "The Political Role of Youth," in Kirby 1965, p. 128.
108. It is indeed possible that between 1959 and 1964 there was a slight decline in the percentage of the rural youth population in the league.
109. The urban population also had greater opportunity to join the CCP, although the discrepancy was not nearly so marked as in the league. See, for example, the figures quoted in Franz Schurmann, *Ideology and Organization in Communist China* (Berkeley and Los Angeles: University of California Press, 1966), pp. 137–38.
110. John Israel, "The Red Guards in Historical Perspective," *China Quarterly*, 30 (Apr.–June 1967), 5. In August 1959, it was reported that at Peking Normal University 85% of the students were league members. *Kuang ming jih pao* (Bright daily), Aug. 27. 1959 .
111. "Training Successors—A Long-Term Plan for the Revolutionary Cause," *Hung ch'i*, 14 (1964), in *Training Successors for the Revolution is the Party's Strategic Task* (Peking: Foreign Languages Press, 1965), pp. 46–47.
112. *Chung-kuo ch'ing nien pao*, Apr. 2, 1964.
113. JMJP, Mar. 17, 1964.
114. The preamble to the 1964 constitution stated that the league would be "guided by Marxism-Leninism *and* the thought of Mao Tse-tung" (my emphasis).
115. The five requirements for revolutionary successors, as laid down by Mao, were: (1) they must be genuine Marxist-Leninists; (2) they must be revolutionaries who whole-heartedly serve the overwhelming majority of the people of China and the whole world; (3) they must be proletarian statesmen capable of uniting and working together with the overwhelming majority; (4) they must be models in applying the party's democratic centralism, must master the method of leadership based on the principle of "from

the masses to the masses," and must cultivate a democratic style and be good at listening to the masses; (5) they must be modest and prudent and guard against arrogance and impetuosity and must be imbued with the spirit of self-criticism and have the courage to correct mistakes and shortcomings in their work. An Tzu-wen, "Training Successors for the Revolution is Party's Strategic Task," *Hung ch'i*, 17–18 (1964), in *Training Successors*, pp. 12–13.

116. JMJP, Mar. 17, 1964.

117. *Ibid.*

118. *Chung-kuo ch'ing nien pao*, Nov. 18, 1965.

119. *Ta kung pao* (Hong Kong), Feb. 11, 1966.

120. Oksenberg 1966, pp. 67–68.

121. *Chung-kuo ch'ing nien pao*, Feb. 19, 1966.

122. "Primary, Secondary Schools Begin New School Year and Carry on Revolution," NCNA, Nov. 5, 1967, in CB, No. 846, p. 30.

123. Hans Granqvist, *The Red Guard* (London: Pall Mall Press, 1967), p. 70.

124. "The Great Lesson of the Former Peking Municipal Committee of the Communist Youth League," *Chung-kuo ch'ing nien* (China youth), 13 (1966), in JPRS, No. 37914, pp. 1–5.

125. *Ibid.*, p. 3.

126. *Ibid.*, p. 4. According to an account written by Red Guards of this particular school, it was one of ten "keypoints" in Peking chosen by Lu Ting-i and his supporters for the implementation of "revisionist" policies. The school helped widen the "three major differences" by functioning as an institution training students for the "key universities"; since little attention was paid to political activities, students who did no productive labor became "political idiots." Students were also encouraged to study for political gain. "Five Major Charges against the Old Educational System," JMJP, Dec. 17, 1967, in SCMP, No. 4100, pp. 9–11.

127. "Be Forever Loyal to Chairman Mao and Be Successors to the Cause of the Proletarian Revolution," JMJP, Apr. 25, 1968, in SCMP, No. 4173, pp. 11–18.

128. Townsend 1969, p. 465.

129. *Ta kung pao* (Hong Kong), Feb. 19, 1966.

130. "Do Not Be Afraid of Being Too Close," *Chung-kuo ch'ing nien pao*, Apr. 22, 1965, in JPRS, No. 29974, pp. 42–44.

131. Townsend 1969, p. 465.

132. "Be Forever Loyal," p. 13.

133. Israel 1967, p. 4.

134. Michel Oksenberg, "Communist China: A Quiet Crisis in Revolution," in Franz Schurmann and Orville Schell, eds., *The China Reader* (New York: Vintage Books, 1967), II, 392.

## Urban Residential Communities in the Wake of the Cultural Revolution

1. Three basic pieces of People's Republic of China [hereafter PRC] legislation on urban administration were all promulgated on Dec. 31, 1954. Chinese texts appear in *Chung-hua jen min kung ho kuo fa kuei hui pien* (Col-

lection of laws and regulations of the People's Republic of China), 13 vols. [hereafter FKHP] (Peking: Fa lü ch'u pan she, 1956–64). I have used the English translations in Jerome A. Cohen, *The Criminal Process in the People's Republic of China, 1949–1963: An Introduction* (Cambridge, Mass.: Harvard University Press, 1968).

(a) "Act of the PRC for the Organization of Public Security Stations," FKHP, I, 243–44; Cohen 1968, pp. 106–7.

(b) "Act of the PRC for the Organization of Street Offices," FKHP, I, 171–72; Cohen 1968, pp. 109–10.

(c) "Act of the PRC for the Organization of City Residents' Committees," FKHP, I, 173–75; Cohen 1968, pp. 110–12.

2. Robert Tung, "People's Policemen," *Far Eastern Economic Review*, LIII: 7 (Aug. 18, 1966), 319–21. Also see "Public Security Organs to Hold a 'Love the People' Month Campaign during the Spring Festival," *Jen min jih pao* (People's daily) [hereafter JMJP], Dec. 25, 1963, in *Survey of China Mainland Press* [hereafter SCMP], No. 3134, pp. 7–8.

3. Cohen 1968, pp. 18–20; Stanley Lubman, "Mao and Mediation: Politics and Dispute Resolution in Communist China," *California Law Review*, LV: 5 (Nov. 1967), 1284–1359.

4. See the general discussion on urban administration in *1967 fei ch'ing nien pao* (1967 yearbook of Chinese Communist affairs) (Taipei: Institute for the Study of Chinese Communist Affairs, 1967), pp. 412–44, esp. pp. 433–34. Also Li Meng-ch'uan, "Chung kung ch'eng shih shih hsia ch'ü cheng ch'üan" (District administration in urban municipalities), *Tsu kuo* (China monthly), 12 (Dec. 1965), 10–16; and Kao Yun-shan, "Ch'eng shih chü min wei yüan hui" (Urban residents street committees), *Tsu kuo*, 12 (Dec. 1965), 17–20.

5. "Let the Red Banner of Mao Tse-tung's Thought Fly over Every Street and Every Neighborhood" (Special article by "Commentator"), *Wen hui pao* (Cultural exchange news) [hereafter WHP], Jan. 5, 1968, as reported in Shanghai Radio, Jan. 4, 1968.

6. JMJP, Jan. 15, 1968.

7. Janet Salaff, "The Urban Communes and Anti-City Experiment in Communist China," *China Quarterly*, 29 (Jan.–Mar. 1967), 82–109.

8. William H. Starbuck, "Organizational Growth and Development," in James G. March, ed., *The Handbook of Organizations* (Chicago: Rand McNally and Co., 1965), pp. 474–76.

9. An estimate given, probably by informants, in "Sources of Labor Discontent in China: The Worker-Peasant System," *Current Scene*, VI: 5 (Mar. 15, 1968), 18.

10. An estimate given to me by an ex-secondary school teacher from Canton. Interview with South China refugee, Hong Kong, May 1968, interview number 68-A1.

11. *Current Scene*, VI: 5 (Mar. 15, 1968).

12. WHP, Jan. 25, 1967.

13. WHP, Feb. 16, 1967.

14. WHP, Jan. 25, 1967.

15. WHP, Feb. 11, 1967.

16. "CCP Central Committee's Notifications on Question of Wages—the

Target of Criticism, Repudiation or Struggle," in "Collection of Material on Reversal of Verdicts," *Selections from China Mainland Magazines* [hereafter SCMM], No. 617, p. 5.

17. Gordon A. Bennett, "Political Labels and Popular Tension," *Current Scene*, VII: 4 (Feb. 28, 1969).

18. "Collection of Material on Reversal of Verdicts," SCMM, No. 617, p. 5.

19. WHP, Feb. 14, 1967.

20. WHP, Feb. 11, 1967.

21. WHP, Feb. 12, 1967.

22. Changchun Radio, May 25, 1967.

23. WHP, Feb. 11, 1967.

24. Shanghai Radio, May 3, 1968.

25. Canton Radio, June 7, 1968.

26. Hangchow Radio, Oct. 13, 1968.

27. Harbin Radio, May 6, 1968.

28. Changchun Radio, May 26, 1967.

29. Dick Anderson, "Street Committees in China—1968," *Eastern Horizons*, VII: 6 (Nov.–Dec. 1968), 27–30.

30. Shanghai Radio, May 3, 1968.

31. "Three-in-One Residents' Revolutionary Committee Fortifies Red Political Power," WHP, May 5, 1968, in SCMP, No. 4187, p. 8.

32. *Ibid.*

33. "Eight Merits of Revolutionary Committees—In Praise of Residents' Revolutionary Committee of Hsin-hua Road, Ch'ang-ning Ch'ü, Shanghai Municipality," WHP, May 4, 1968, in SCMP, No. 4187, p. 11.

34. *Ibid.*

35. *Ibid.*

36. WHP, Feb. 16, 1967.

37. Shanghai Radio, Jan. 4, 1968.

38. *New China News Agency* [hereafter NCNA], Jan. 14, 1968.

39. WHP, June 22, 1967, in Shanghai Radio, June 21, 1967.

40. "Let the Red Banner of Mao Tse-tung's Thought Fly over Every Street and Every Neighborhood," in Shanghai Radio, Jan. 4, 1968.

41. Anderson 1968.

42. Peking Radio, June 8, 1967.

43. JMJP, Sept. 19, 1968, p. 3, reports excerpts of a heart-to-heart talk between three workers and a student Red Guard leader at Futan University, Shanghai. The workers convince the leader he is wrong in resisting their team, and the leader then convinces his followers.

44. WHP, Sept. 3, 1968, in SCMP, No. 4276, pp. 12–13.

45. *Ming pao* (Hong Kong), Aug. 4, 21, and 23, 1967.

46. Genevieve Morel, "What It's Like to Live in Peking Today," *Réalités*, Mar. 14 and July 2, 1968, pp. 30–34.

47. Lu Yung-shu, "Peiping's Conscription and Retirement Program," *Issues and Studies*, V: 2 (Nov. 1968), 7.

48. According to Jean Vincent, correspondent for Agence France Presse, Peking wall posters commented that public sale of Red Guard papers was forbidden as of Jan. 1968.

49. Kwangtung Radio, May 8, 1968.

50. See Nanchang Radio, Sept. 4, 1967; Shanghai Radio, Mar. 25, 1968;

Shanghai Radio, Jan. 19, 1968, for reports of various types of worker participation in residential security work.

51. Shanghai Radio, May 3, 1968.

52. Jerome A. Cohen, "The Criminal Process in China," in Donald W. Treadgold, ed., *Soviet and Chinese Communism, Similarities and Differences* (Seattle: University of Washington Press, 1967), pp. 118–19.

53. Investigation Report, "Dictatorship by the Masses is the Fundamental Method to Protect the People and Suppress the Enemy," *Chieh fang jih pao* (Liberation daily), n.d., in Shanghai Radio, Oct. 30, 1968.

54. *Ibid.*

55. *Ibid.*

56. I thank Stanley Lubman for calling this parallel security form to my attention.

57. Shanghai Radio, Oct. 30, 1968.

58. "Extensive Mass Dictatorship in Shanghai Encloses Class Enemy," WHP, May 19, 1968, in SCMP, No. 4198, p. 4.

59. Bennett 1969.

60. Charles Hoffman, *Work Incentive Practices and Policies in the People's Republic of China, 1953–1965* (Albany: State University of New York Press, 1967), p. 22.

61. "Why Can't High Salaries Be Lowered?," SCMM, No. 616, pp. 16–20.

62. "Opinions Concerning Cleaning up of Teachers' Ranks," Educational Workers Revolutionary Rebel Joint Committee of Middle Schools, Shanghai Municipality, *Tung fang hung tien hsün* (East is red telegram), 2 (July 1968), in SCMP, No. 4227, pp. 4–5.

63. Bennett 1969.

64. "Primary and Middle-School Operation in Urban Areas" (Collection of material from JMJP, Nov. 15 to Dec. 27, 1968), in *Current Background*, No. 870.

65. Peking Radio, Feb. 10, 1969.

66. "The Orientation of the Revolution in Medical Education as Seen from the Growth in Numbers of Barefoot Doctors," WHP, Sept. 4, 1968, in Shanghai Radio, Sept. 23, 1968.

67. "Many New Things Emerge in Kiangsi Struggle," NCNA, Jan. 12, 1969.

68. Yang Ta-wen and Liu Su-ping, "T'an wo kuo chieh hun chia t'ing chih tu ti kai ko" (On reform of China's marriage and family system), JMJP, Dec. 13, 1963.

69. Ai-li S. Chin, *Modern Chinese Fiction and Family Relations* (Cambridge, Mass.: MIT, Center for International Studies, Dec. 1966).

70. Anderson 1968.

71. NCNA, Jan. 14, 1968.

72. Ezra Vogel, "Voluntarism and Social Control," in Treadgold 1967, pp. 168–84.

73. "Let the Red Banner of Mao Tse-tung's Thought Fly over Every Street and Every Neighborhood," WHP, Jan. 5, 1968, in Shanghai Radio, Jan. 4, 1968.

74. "Family Criticism and Repudiation is Fine," WHP, Dec. 15, 1967, in Shanghai Radio, Dec. 14, 1967.

75. *Ibid.*

76. *Hsiao ping* (Publication of Canton's Red Guard General Headquarters, Canton Area Middle-School Revolutionary Committee), Dec. 24, 1967, in *Joint Publications Research Service* [hereafter JPRS], No. 45194, pp. 52–55.

77. *Nueva Unita*, July 1, 8, 15, 27 and 29, and Aug. 5, 1967, in JPRS, No. 42525, describes in an interview with a factory rebel committee in Peking, the difficulties rebels faced when coping with the economic and welfare decision making and planning formerly done by management and cadres and unions. See guidelines on rehabilitation and temporary support for those suffering wrongfully under the Cultural Revolution, "Kwangtung Provincial Military Control Commission Instructions Concerning the Active Implementation of Rehabilitation Work, 1967," Kwangtung Military Control Series, No. 38, Hsin-hsing County, Kwangtung, by *Hsin-hsing hung ssu* (Hsin-hsing red headquarters), Dec. 30, 1967, in JPRS, No. 45589, pp. 99–100.

## Shanghai's Polity in Cultural Revolution

1. For a clear description of the control structure of the People's Liberation Army, see John Gittings, *The Role of the Chinese Army* (London: Oxford University Press, 1967), pp. 106f. For a comment on the strength of civilian control in urban garrisons, including Shanghai's, see Ellis Joffe, *Party and Army: Professionalism and Political Control in the Chinese Officer Corps, 1949–1964* (Cambridge, Mass.: Harvard East Asian Institute, 1965), pp. 132f. My information on divisions within the public security system comes from interviews conducted in Hong Kong.

2. Frederic Wakeman, Jr., *Strangers at the Gate: Social Disorder in South China 1839–1861* (Berkeley and Los Angeles: University of California Press, 1966), pp. 95–96.

3. *Hsin wen jih pao* (News daily, Shanghai) [hereafter HWJP], Sept. 5, 1955.

4. For example, see *Wen hui pao* (Cultural exchange news) [hereafter WHP], July 10, 1959.

5. See *Hsin min wan pao* (New people's evening news) [hereafter HMWP], July 9, 1964.

6. At least the Huang-p'u ch'ü militia functioned as a unit for some activities. See *ibid.*, May 24, 1964.

7. *Ibid.*, May 25, 1964.

8. In Shanghai, this campaign naturally emphasized the Nanking Road Good Eighth Company. See *Kung jen jih pao* (Daily worker) [hereafter KJJP], May 9, 1963.

9. Franz Schurmann, *Ideology and Organization in Communist China*, rev. ed. (Berkeley and Los Angeles: University of California Press, 1968), p. 374, cites an official Communist historian that the su fan campaign was important in this.

10. WHP, June 5, 1968, in *Survey of China Mainland Press* [hereafter SCMP], No. 4210, p. 1.

11. *New China News Agency* [hereafter NCNA], Jan. 11, 1967.

12. *Ibid.*, Feb. 9, 1967.

13. This account is an interpretation of "Shih hsien ko ming ti ta lien ho pi hsü ta tao ssu tzu" (To realize great revolutionary alliance it is necessary

to destroy the private), reprinted from *Hai kang chan pao* (The harbor warrior), in *Hung ch'i* (Red flag), 10 (Aug. 9, 1967), 36–40.

14. WHP, Mar. 17, 1967.

15. Another example in the field of education: the author interviewed in Hong Kong an elderly Russian (not Soviet) who had taught language at East China Teachers' University for many years until May 1967. He vividly described disruption there up to that time. NCNA, Nov. 28, 1967, reports that PLA soldiers later entered his department to teach courses in the thoughts of Chairman Mao.

16. Shanghai Radio, Mar. 25, 1968.

17. NCNA, Sept. 18, 1967.

18. Shanghai Radio, Mar. 25, 1968, said that such actions had begun about six months before.

19. NCNA, Oct. 23, 1967.

20. WHP, Apr. 22, 1968, in SCMP, No. 4178, p. 3.

21. NCNA, June 25, 1968.

22. *Ts'an k'ao tzu liao* (Reference materials), 1 (July 1968), in SCMP, No. 4222, p. 1. It is important to the interpretation of this article that the Cantonese anti-gradualist "red flags" very definitely had their own bloody run-ins with local military authorities whom they considered too interventionist.

23. *China News Summary*, No. 217 (Apr. 25, 1968), 2.

24. Tu Fang-p'ing is accused by another Canton Red Flag faction of having attempted the same thing. SCMP, No. 4234, p. 16.

25. NCNA, Feb. 27, 1967.

26. WHP, Mar. 26, 1968.

27. For details on one series of such trials, see *China Topics*, No. YB 481 (May 20, 1968), 1–3, and WHP articles of Apr. 11 and 28, 1968. Comparisons and gloomy contrasts with the mass political-religious devotions of the northern Wei and early T'ang (and later copies in Chinese history) might be attempted. This is, after all, a metropolitan function.

28. Compare William Geddes, *Peasant Life in Communist China* (Ithaca, N.Y.: Society for Applied Anthropology, 1963), with Schurmann 1968, p. 369.

29. One such history may be found in Schurmann 1968, pp. 371–99.

30. *Kuang ming jih pao* (Bright daily) [hereafter KMJP], Mar. 29, 1956.

31. James R. Townsend, *Political Participation in Communist China* (Berkeley and Los Angeles: University of California Press, 1967), pp. 158–59.

32. Compare G. William Skinner, "Overseas Chinese Leadership: Paradigm for a Paradox," in Gehan Wijeyewardene, ed., *Leadership and Authority* (Singapore: University of Malaya Press, 1968), pp. 192–94.

33. See the excellent descriptions in Townsend 1967, pp. 164–65, 122–26, 106–10, and 160–61.

34. *Chieh fang jih pao* (Liberation daily) [hereafter CFJP], Nov. 9, 1958.

35. Compare Wakeman 1966, chap. 11.

36. HMWP, June 24, 1966.

37. Sidney D. Gamble, *Ting Hsien: A North China Rural Community* (Stanford: Stanford University Press, 1968), pp. 260–71.

38. HMWP, June 29 and July 13, 1964.

39. *Ibid.*, July 2, 1964.

40. WHP, Aug. 14, 1965.

41. HMWP, July 4, 1964.

42. *Ibid.*, May 8, 1964. It is no accident that articles about residential mobilization fall in the early summer of various years; these are the months of graduations. In 1966 some students found an alternative: preparation for an intensified Cultural Revolution and Red Guardhood. It is typical of normative ambiguity that this alternative should also support rustication as an idea.

43. One of these celebrations, from Hung-k'ou ch'ü, is described in HMWP, May 17, 1964.

44. HMWP, May 21, 1964. The volunteers in this article are from only three districts, Ching-an, Yung-p'u, and Nan-shih. *Ibid.*, May 28, carries a sequel story on the reception of this same group apparently in Urumchi by Liu I-ts'un, Deputy Political Director of the Sinkiang Production and Construction Army Group. An enthusiast named Shen Hung-chüan (loosely translated, Miss Redbeauty Shen) gave a speech on behalf of the Shanghai youth.

45. HMWP, June 3, 1966.

46. A letter from Sinkiang suggested this in *ibid.*, June 22, 1966.

47. *Ibid.*, May 15, 1964.

48. *Ibid.*, June 23, 1966.

49. *Ibid.*, June 3, 1966.

50. WHP, May 25, 1968, in SCMP, No. 4207, p. 15.

51. HMWP, May 17, 1964.

52. *Ibid.*, June 27, 1966.

53. WHP, May 26, 1968, in SCMP, No. 4207, p. 16.

54. *China News Summary*, No. 161 (Mar. 15, 1967), 3, is the best condensation of many Shanghai Radio reports on this from Feb. and Mar. 1967.

55. A partial list of the order of formation of Shanghai's ch'ü, hsien, and municipal-department revolutionary committees may be found in *1968 fei ch'ing nien pao* (1968 yearbook of Chinese Communist affairs) (Taipei: Institute for the Study of Chinese Communist Affairs, 1968), p. 294.

56. An excellent description of such reforms, in Canton especially, is Janet Salaff's "Revolution in the Streets," *Far Eastern Economic Review*, LXI: 35 (Aug. 29, 1968), 433f.

57. See WHP, May 19, 1968, in SCMP, No. 4198, p. 1.

58. *Ibid.*, June 17, 1968, in SCMP, No. 4231, p. 15.

59. *Ibid.*, Apr. 23, 1968, in SCMP, No. 4181, p. 17.

60. *Ibid.*, June 7, 1968, in SCMP, No. 4216, p. 3.

61. *Ibid.*, May 4, 1968, in SCMP, No. 4187, p. 8.

62. *Ibid.*, Feb. 22, 1956.

63. *Chung-kuo ch'ing nien pao* (China youth daily), Mar. 28, 1956.

64. NCNA, Apr. 1, 1956.

65. *Hsüeh shu yüeh k'an* (Technical monthly), Sept. 1958, p. 37.

66. *Fu-tan* (Futan), 2 (Feb. 1959), 14.

67. KMJP, Aug. 8, 1961.

68. NCNA, June 11, 1963. Dozens of further sources could be cited for 1964–66, too.

69. See the Education Ministry's directive on admissions published by NCNA, May 12, 1961.

70. *Chung-kuo ch'ing nien pao*, Sept. 8, 1964.
71. HMWP, June 24 and July 1, 1964.
72. NCNA, Mar. 17, 1966.
73. HMWP, June 3 and 4, 1966.
74. *Ibid.*, June 19 and 20, 1966, contain articles of support from many different groups concerning the anti-examination policy.
75. *Ibid.*, July 18, 1966.
76. Sophia Knight, *Window on Shanghai: Letters from China, 1965–67* (London: Andre Deutsch, 1967), pp. 228–29. This paper was written before the publication of Neale Hunter, *Shanghai Journal: An Eyewitness Account of the Cultural Revolution* (New York: Praeger, 1969), which contains a much more precise account of the Foreign Language Institute's "struggle." Hunter's book is based mostly on Red Guard tabloids, and its considerable detail for 1966 and early 1967 makes it required reading for anyone interested in Shanghai's Cultural Revolution. Miss Knight and Mr. Hunter both taught at the institute during this period.
77. Some description of student activities in the autumn of 1966 is in Hans Granqvist, *The Red Guard* (New York: Praeger, 1967), which relies heavily on the better but less available series of "Shanghai Letters" written for the Hong Kong *South China Morning Post* by a non-Soviet Russian, now presumed still in a Shanghai jail. See also Evelyn Anderson, "Shanghai: The Masses Unleashed," *Problems of Communism*, XVII: 1 (Jan.–Feb. 1968) and Hunter 1969.
78. *Jen min jih pao* (People's daily) [hereafter JMJP], Feb. 26, 1967, carries both the public poster that these athletes wrote, and the editor's praise for their having done it.
79. Interview with an ex-faculty member from there, now in Hong Kong.
80. NCNA, Apr. 13, 1967.
81. JMJP, July 4, 1967, in SCMP, No. 3985, p. 1.
82. NCNA, Nov. 13, 1967.
83. WHP, Apr. 21, 1968, in SCMP, No. 4180, p. 4.
84. *Ibid.*, Apr. 11, 1968, in SCMP, No. 4178, p. 5.
85. *Ibid.*, Mar. 22, 1968, in SCMP, No. 4170, p. 13.
86. *Ibid.*, May 20, 1968, in SCMP, No. 4197, p. 1.
87. *Ibid.*, daily, mid-1967 through mid-1968.
88. NCNA, Feb. 27, 1967.
89. WHP, May 26, 1968, in SCMP, No. 4207, p. 5.
90. NCNA, June 19, 1968.
91. See *Wen ko t'ung hsün* (Cultural Revolution bulletin), 16 (July 1968), in SCMP, No. 4237, p. 1.
92. CFJP, edit., Aug. 7, 1968, released NCNA, Aug. 13, 1968.
93. NCNA, Apr. 28, 1961.
94. *Ibid.*, Nov. 2, 1959.
95. *Ibid.*, July 4, 1959.
96. *Ibid.*, Aug. 7, 1959.
97. KJJP, May 14, 1961.
98. NCNA, Aug. 10, 1968.
99. HMWP, July 3, 1964.
100. *Peking Review*, 41 (Oct. 9, 1965).

101. NCNA, June 21, 1963.
102. *Chung-kuo ch'ing nien* (China youth), 2 (Sept. 16, 1964).
103. NCNA, June 19, 1963. Also KJJP, Apr. 4, 1963.
104. NCNA, July 18, 1963, and Dec. 1, 1963.
105. KJJP, Aug. 16, 1964.
106. KMJP, Jan. 26, 1966.
107. *Ibid.*, Mar. 1, 1966.
108. HMWP, July 4, 1964.
109. *Ibid.*, July 11, 1964.
110. NCNA, June 30, 1966.
111. HMWP, June 12, 1966.
112. These systems are superbly described for the 1920's in Jean Chesneaux's epic now translated as *The Chinese Labor Movement 1919–1927*, Hope M. Wright, trans. (Stanford: Stanford University Press, 1968), esp. pp. 54–57, 64, and 89–94.
113. JMJP, May 8, 1966, in SCMP, No. 3700, p. 4.
114. NCNA, Jan. 9, 1967.
115. KMJP, Jan. 25, 1967.
116. Compare Gerald Tannebaum, "The 1967 Shanghai January Revolution Recounted," *Eastern Horizon*, VII: 3 (May–June 1968).
117. WHP, Jan. 20, 1967, and CFJP, n.d., in SCMP No. 3876, p. 11.
118. KMJP, Jan. 25, 1967.
119. CFJP edit., Mar. 15, 1967, in SCMP, No. 3904, p. 14.
120. NCNA, June 13, 1967.
121. *Take the Road of the Shanghai Machine Tools Plant in Training Technicians Among the Workers* (Peking: Foreign Languages Press, 1968), p. 15.
122. NCNA, Feb. 17, 1967.
123. *Ibid.*, Aug. 24, 1967. I thank Mr. Ian Davies for pointing out the difference between smelting and heat-treatment, which affects the interpretation of this item.
124. *Ibid.*, Feb. 27, 1967.
125. *Ibid.*, Dec. 6, 1967.
126. This December conference coincides with the first main wave of purges on the revolutionary committee itself. Members Chu Ken-fu, Min K'ao-ssu, and Hu Chih-hung, apparently workers leading a mysterious group named the *Kung hsiang tung*, were "dragged out" that same month. The academics seem to have survived half a year longer. Two members of the revolutionary committee's standing committee were purged in mid-1968—Chu Hsi-ch'i, for his alleged conspiracy to topple Chang Ch'un-ch'iao, and Lu Wen-ts'ai, a party second secretary in the Shanghai College of Social Science. See the Canton *Tung fang hung tien hsün* (East is red telegram), 3 (July 1968), in SCMP, No. 4234, p. 15; and also the Canton *Chiu i liu t'ung hsün* (Sept. 16 bulletin), Aug. 1968, in SCMP, No. 4240, p. 10.
127. JMJP, Dec. 1, 1967, p. 4, is entirely devoted to articles from a variety of Shanghai "rebel" workers' newspapers, whose ideas are combined in the text's interpretation.
128. For another list, see Ralph Nicholas in *Political Systems and the Dis-*

*tribution of Power* (London: ASA Monograph 2, 1965), pp. 27f. The list given in this text is adapted beyond recognition from Mr. Nicholas's, which was generated from a superb study of factionalism. The concept here is substantively different from his, by intention.

129. Wakeman 1966, p. 121.

130. One of many examples of this is NCNA, Shanghai, Apr. 2, 1967. In this period, part of the city government made an attempt to save some "leading cadres" and to halt the indiscriminate attacks on them by former subordinates. The anti-top-leader (anti-Liu) campaigns could be cited as an effort to divert attention from the conflict of more immediate, lower-level elites.

131. Skinner 1968, pp. 191–207. Throughout this essay I have used and no doubt often distorted Prof. Skinner's ideas so that there is no single place to put the superscript.

132. An example of such complaint is in an editorial note of CFJP, Dec. 20, 1967.

133. UNESCO report on Asia and the Far East, quoted by Gerald Breese, *Urbanization in Newly Developing Countries* (Englewood Cliffs, N.J.: Prentice-Hall, 1966), p. 98.

134. See the best book yet on modern China, Schurmann 1968, where there was phenomenological analysis. The best interest often lay in comparing Chinese Communist and Western sociological categories, to test each against the other.

135. See Kang Chao, "Industrialization and Urban Housing in Communist China," *Journal of Asian Studies*, XXV: 3 (May 1966), esp. 385–86.

136. See Breese 1966, p. 135.

137. A preliminary, though not entirely accurate, list of hsien jurisdiction changes is found in *Ching hu ti ch'ü tzu liao mu lu* (Catalogue of materials on the Nanking-Shanghai region) (Taipei: Kuo chia an ch'uan chü [State Security Bureau], 1967), esp. pp. 31f.

138. Calculated from figures in *1968 fei ch'ing nien pao*, p. 46.

139. Shanghai WHP edit., Jan. 20, 1967.

140. See the use of this Eric Hoffer concept in Salaff 1967, pp. 83–84.

141. The terms are Schurmann's. Weber's constant insistence on the efficacy of clear norms is mistaken, because clear rules can be applied most easily even in situations where they are inappropriate. To use another of Weber's own distinctions: there must be a more substantive, less formal approach to the idea of efficiency.

142. This paper avoids reproducing any of the fine play-by-play accounts of the events in the January revolution and the "Paris" commune. The most detailed, which was published after its viewpoints could benefit this paper, is Hunter 1969. See also Anderson 1968. For an official Communist interpretation, see Tannebaum 1968, pp. 7f. The Paris commune ideal has an interesting history in China, which goes back long before the Cultural Revolution, but is cited with increasing frequency in the 1960's. About its application, Jack Gray and Patrick Cavendish, *Chinese Communism in Crisis: Maoism and the Cultural Revolution* (London: Pall Mall, 1968), p. 135, note a Kyodo News Agency report of Feb. 6, 1967: Red Guard posters in Shanghai, seen

by a Japanese correspondent, indicated that the committee to prepare for Paris-style elections was divided functionally; it consisted of five workers, two peasants, two soldiers, one party member, and one student.

143. The ideas of an ex-Red Guard, interviewed in Hong Kong, suggested this analysis of a self-reinforcing syndrome—therefore the theory came from participation and is to be trusted better than if it were just mine. I must thank Ronald Montaperto for pointing out that his interviewee, with whom I also spoke, had these ideas.

144. WHP, July 31, 1968.

145. Some of the ideas in this paragraph were suggested in Fred Riggs, *Administration in Developing Countries* (Boston: Little, Brown, 1964), pp. 341–46, and in Schurmann 1968, pp. 188–94.

146. Amitai Etzioni, *Modern Organizations* (Englewood Cliffs, N.J.: Prentice-Hall, 1964), pp. 30–31, explains the term "search behavior" with fine clarity.

147. A two-sided theory, similar to the one here in that it avoids this dubious kind of professionalism, is to be found in J. P. Nettl's distinction between "elitist" and "constitutional" political cultures in *Political Mobilization: A Sociological Analysis of Methods and Concepts* (London: Faber, 1967), pp. 72f.

148. The studies mentioned here are by Robert Dahl, *Who Governs? Democracy and Power in an American City* (New Haven: Yale University Press, 1961), and by Floyd Hunter, *Community Power Structure* (Chapel Hill, N.C.: University of North Carolina Press, 1953).

149. Schurmann 1968, pp. 410f.

150. *Ibid.*, p. 389.

# Index

Abortion, 194

Agriculture: crisis in, 3, 191; agricultural producers' cooperatives, 111f, 189–90; study of, 133n, 200–204 *passim*, 244ff; collective farms, 154; in Shanghai, 221, 224, 226

All-China Federation of Labor, 142

All-China Federation of Trade Unions, 125, 134, 139, 144

Amoy, 272

An Tzu-wen, 99, 103, 105, 116–17

Anhwei, 199, 296

Anshan Iron and Steel Works, 136

Anti-rightist campaigns, 19, 67–74 *passim*, 127, 186, 318, 334. *See also* "Bourgeois" attitudes

Apprentices, 129, 207

Army, *see* People's Liberation Army

Banfield, Edward C., 7

Banks and banking, 162, 220, 223

"Barefoot doctors," 18, 286

Bargaining, 10f, 165

Birth control, 194, 292

Birth rates, 194, 364, 410n13

Black market, 78, 83

Boarding schools, 256

"Bourgeois" attitudes, 19, 80, 87–88, 113, 242, 266, 304, 346, 356; attacked by the Red Guards, 235, 285; among teachers, 255, 257, 285; in Communist Youth League, 278, 282, 284. *See also* Anti-rightist campaigns

"Brainwashing," 89

Bureaucracy, 1, 6–13, 20, 23–24, 59, 105–20 *passim*, 245, 256, 292; Mao on, 11, 97ff, 113; in Tangshan, 12, 156, 162, 167, 169–70, 176–79. *See also* Cadres; Trade unions

Businessmen, *see* Commerce

Cadres, 2–3, 6–9, 20, 23, 89, 91, 97–121 *passim*, 150; "liberated," 13, 300; in Hui-yang, 51–74 *passim*; quality of, 68, 102; shortage of, 98–105, 391n9; state cadres (*kuo chia kan pu*), 99, 106, 114, 116, 390–95 *passim*; in Shanghai, 101–9 *passim*, 118, 125, 223, 299, 303n, 340–41, 351, 360; women as, 104, 392n46; overrecruitment of, 105–13, 116, 120–21; street cadres (*chieh tao kan pu*), 107f, 299f, 393n50; *ching chien* (retrenchment) movement, 112, 115, 116–21, 395–96 *passim*, 408n105; *hsia fang* movement, 112, 117–21, 223f, 393–96 *passim*; and unions, 124–25, 127, 134f, 140–41, 145, 165; children of, 135, 255ff, 278, 312; in Tangshan, 156f, 164, 166f; specialized, 183–214; and education, 183–206, 247–48, 270, 281–82; and neighborhoods, 294–316 *passim*

Campaigns, 3, 17–18, 22, 66, 145, 168, 187, 279ff, 291f; anti-bureaucratic, 8–9, 106, 114; anti-rightist, 19, 67–74 *passim*, 91, 127, 186, 189, 318, 334, 409n3; rectification, 60, 66–67, 83–84, 98, 100, 186, 346, 376n24; and public order, 79, 81–84, 90ff; so-

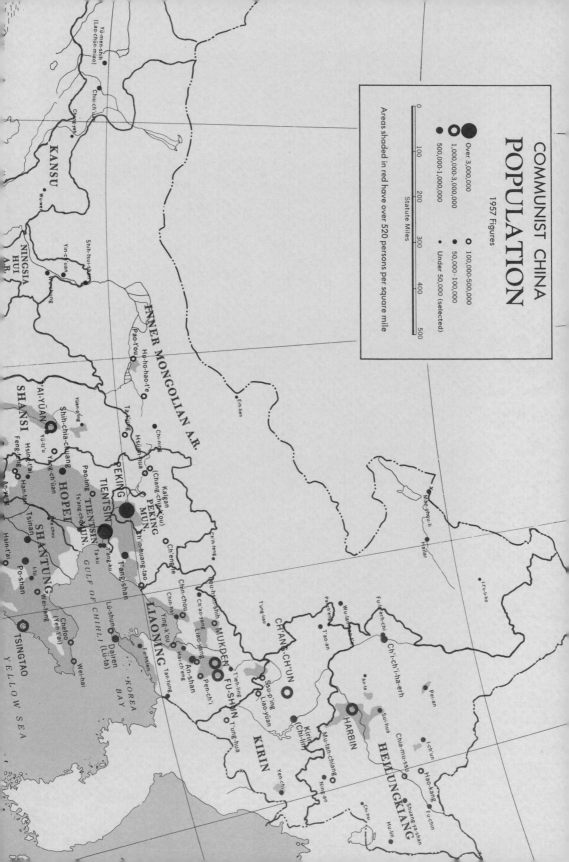

COMMUNIST CHINA
POPULATION

1957 Figures

○ Over 3,000,000
○ 1,000,000-3,000,000
● 500,000-1,000,000
● 100,000-500,000
● 50,000-100,000
● Under 50,000 (selected)

Areas shaded in red have over 520 persons per square mile

Statute Miles
0    100    200    300    400    500

KANSU

Yü-men-shih
(Lao-chün-miao)

Chu-ch'üan

Ch'ing-yen

Wu-wei

NINGSIA
HUI
A.R.

Shih-tsui-shan

Yin-ch'uan

Chung-ning

INNER MONGOLIAN A.R.

Pao-t'ou

Hu-ho-hao-t'e

Ta-t'ung

Chi-ning

E-lien

SHANSI

T'AI-YÜAN

Yüan-p'ing

Shih-chia-chuang

Yü-tz'u
Yang-ch'üan

Hsüan-hua
Kalgan
(Chang-chia-k'ou)

Chang-pei

Fen-yang

Hsin-t'ai

Han-tan

An-yang

HOPEI

Pao-ting

PEKING

PEKING
MUN.

TIENTSIN

TIENTSIN
MUN.

Tsang-chou

Ho-chou

Shih-chia-chuang

Shih-chia-chuang

Ta-ku

Shih-huang-tao

Tsinan

Chi-ning

Feng-jun
Tang-shan

Tangku

Ch'eng-te

Ch'ih-feng

Lin-hsi

Chin-chou

SHANTUNG

Hsin-t'ai

Po-shan

Hu-tu

Wei-fang

Tsingtao

Weihai

Chefoo
(Yen-t'ai)

Wei-hai

Lü-shun

Dairen
(Lü-ta)

GULF OF CHIHLI

KOREA
BAY

YELLOW SEA

LIAONING

Chin-hsi

Ch'ao-yang

Pei-p'iao

Liao-yang

Hai-ch'eng

MUKDEN

An-shan

Pen-ch'i

FU-SHUN

T'ieh-ling

Ssu-p'ing

Liao-yüan

Fu-shan

Tan-tung

Ying-k'ou

Tung-hua

T'ung-hua

KIRIN

Yen-chi

Hai-lung

Chiao-ho

CH'ANG-CH'UN

Kirin
(Chi-lin)

Tung-liao

Tao-an

Wu-lan-hao-t'e

T'ao-an

Pai-ch'eng

An-ta

Su-hua

HARBIN

A-ch'eng

Chia-mu-ssu

Mu-tan-chiang

Ning-an

HEILUNGKIANG

Pei-an

Pei-an

Fu-yü-erh-chi

Ch'i-ch'i-ha-erh

I-ch'un

Hao-kang

Shuang-ya-shan

Fu-chin

Hu-lin

Chi-hsi

Mu-chu-li

Hailar

I-t'u-ho

Ning-nan